FOR THE LAN

How To Get Ready For God

Fire

Earth

Water

Air

HINONO

Grateful acknowledgement is made to the Foundation For Inner Peace for:

A COURSE IN MIRACLES

©1975, 1985

P.O. Box 598

Mill Valley, CA 94942

FOR THE LAND OF THE LOST
How To Get Ready For God
Fire, Earth, Water, Air

Seven Eagles Publishing

751 Riverside St.

Ventura, CA 93001

Ph/Fax(805) 643-6625

carolyn@hinono.com

805
302
3371

Library of Congress Catalog number: 96-72650

Hinono.
  For The Land Of The Lost: How To Get Ready For God. Fire, Earth, Water, Air.
  Seven Eagles Publishing.- 1st. ed., p.504

ISBN 0-9656795-4-3   24.95

FOR THE LAND OF THE LOST
How To Get Ready For God

Fire
Contents

FOR THE LAND OF THE LOST
How To Get Ready For God

Earth

Contents

FOR THE LAND OF THE LOST
How To Get Ready For God

Water

Contents

FOR THE LAND OF THE LOST
How To Get Ready For God

AIR
Contents

Fire

Book One

Hinono's Preface

About channeling: Channeling is a subtle and consistent voice that desires to be communicated through the mind of the living, whether the person allows only the "silent" connection, writes down what is said, paints, speaks, sings, plays, or performs. The two that heard, wrote. When appropriate, they also spoke, so others would remember the same kind of hearing for themselves.

My words are gifts and not possessions. You may quote me but do not hold me or bind me to your English words by putting me inside your quote marks.

Scribes' Notes

True to his wishes, we have kept Hinono's informal style of speaking as near as possible to what was originally given. We did not want to impose so much of our rigid rules of English grammar that we lost the texture and feeling of his intent. We did not quote-mark his speaking at all, as he requested, but we did mark others for whom he spoke. We hope your adjustment is as easy as if you were listening to the storyteller yourself. Our suggestion is that you read as if you were entering the house of a stranger, with the intent of discovering a relative. Were you to discover that your relationship with this new relative were real, then judgment would only come, if at all, after celebration.

Introduction

Before this, there was a very pregnant Nothing. You see, life always was... somewhere. All things of substance were brought about by thought. You see, mind is all there is. Why were bodies thought up? Why is it not enough for us to be a tree, a rock? Because thought desires movement, expression, discovery, challenges.

Life should not be so easy that it is taken for granted and nothing learned. There should be difficulties to overcome. The biggest difficulty physical life had to overcome was inertia, just the sheer weight of itself. It had to develop energy on its own, with a self-sustaining momentum. Life had to be independent and yet able to connect to everything at any time for assistance. You see, Love would not abandon you, ever.

Thoughts without love have no substance in reality. They can but appear to play out in this place. Yet, this bubble, this planet is the limit of thoughts without love. Beyond this place, you cannot go without the True Fire of Love.

The material mind wrapped in a body cloth must be fed and kept warm... it thinks. Surely, it will freeze and be no more. But which fire is the Fire that truly nourishes and keeps you warm, the fire of the body that needs feeding perpetually or the Fire of the Spirit which when discovered thaws the frozen tundra?

Mankind's search for the truth has been intense. There were even times when man believed he could make it up and it would be true. But even the most persistent intellectuals finally come to realize that they did not create themselves, and that they know not how the universe was made. The truth is awe inspiring and must be experienced directly by each aspirant, each seeker, each troubled soul that walks this planet and asks "why" of anything.

I have no body now, so I will not speak of its limitations to you. I will speak beyond those limitations because they are truly self-imposed. You may go beyond limitation any time you truly desire it. The body is not a prison but merely a temporary teaching device.

In the last decade, *A Course in Miracles* was finally prepared for the world and distributed. The Voice that speaks as its Author is a familiar one to the western world and, by now, familiar to all the world in some form. Much confusion abounds about this personage called Jesus. Much has been made of his teachings. Jesus taught nothing more than what the old people taught. He taught love and forgiveness. Yet, he did one other important thing for the world, for those who would hear it. He created a way back to the truth from illusion.

Throughout these books, I have attempted to create a bridge between the concepts taught in *A Course in Miracles* and native teachings. *A Course in Miracles* and native practices are a direct path to experiences of Love, Truth and Spirit.

To step on this path, you must ask truly and desire wholeheartedly. You must put nothing before your desire for the truth and the desire for correction of all the errors in your thinking that have prevented you from knowing love.

I will endeavor to tell stories of times past, with relevance to present time. To aid you with your difficulty in attention, I will try to entertain you. I found my life very rewarding, very entertaining and very challenging, as I'm sure you do yours. I cannot ask you to tell me your story in these books, but I can tell you mine. Your life writes a story, and as you join this story, your life will join Spirit. You see, we are all part of the same story. We are all Spirit.

Fire - The First Elemental

Fire was the first thing man sought for his comfort. Even before food was this thought of warmth. Always there was the sun, the fire in the sky. There were no people under this sun that were not indigenous. All people were native to their spot.

Natural curiosity widened territories, exchanged languages and promoted the trading of goods. In this trading, the secrets of fire, both of substance and Spirit were shared. Always there were conflicts between peoples, and always those conflicts were resolved. "How" was the question.

The first prayers were sung. Why? Because the early peoples knew that without feeling their words, they would have no effect. Even the guttural cries of children got more attention than the unfeeling complaints of grown-ups. There was something about true intent that delivered the message.

So fire is from where? How did it arrive? Lightning? Where did lightning come from? Nature, you say. What is nature? The friction of warm and cold winds on the earth produces static electricity, and pretty soon there's a discharge... lightning. That explains it?

To native peoples all over the world, all events were significant. The big problem was, who knew how to interpret them? Who could decipher the meaning in unusual events? Who could understand them and communicate their meaning?

Thus, the path of shamanism was born. Some took that place and learned. Sure... many better than others and some worse than many. There will always be a fool standing at a high place. The ones that come down from that high place live much longer than the ones that don't.

The *Fire* book is about the first of the four elementals–fire, earth, water, and air. It describes early native spirit to anyone who cares to listen. I will tell you of my journey and show you how to begin yours. Two people have been picked to record my journey because they picked the journey. They volunteered. They have gone to "high places" and come down. And now I think they will live long lives and be helpful. Our journey is told, so that you may see your journey in it.

Barbara and John were given the task of writing these stories down because of their true intent, through the strength of the desire of their asking for their own journey. And within their asking was the only Real Question that must be answered and must

10

be asked by each person on this journey called life.

To get down this path, we must, along the way, redefine words that are commonly used without meaning in the English language. (See the Glossary in the *Water* book, Chapter 14.) We will, hereto, give meaning to each word in question that we use, so that we may accomplish our journey together, for what is lacking in this world today is a reason to be here... meaning. Even native peoples who still carry on their ceremonies have begun to feel an emptiness within some of their traditions because the Old People are no longer available to demonstrate the meaning.

It is time this book be written for those who desire help with meaning in their lives. I will act as the Old Person for all the Old Ones who have walked on, the ones who have taught good lessons to all their children for so many generations past.

To go on this journey, you must slow down, for what truly empties life of meaning in this world is speed... busyness... distractions. Fears, all of them, weaken the soul and separate it from truth. I will take you on a journey that only the old people remember, but that the young people are crying out to have back in their lives. Patience is required. Meaning comes from steady attention.

Perhaps you will read these books in four days. If you do, I suggest you put them away and read them again later. *Fire, Earth, Water,* and *Air* are the first four books.

A fifth book may be written later in which all the stops will be pulled out of all the conversations that all the old ones have ever had with all the young ones. The gentleness will be gone. The forthrightness will be present. Love always comes with a stern warning. It is this: "Don't stop loving! Don't even think about it! If you do, Love is lost to you, and you too will be lost in It somewhere, searching for an anchor point."

The Ocean of Love is so huge that you are sure to get lost without Guides. The Old Ones before you are your Guides, the Ones that know. How do you find One... ask everyone, everywhere, and listen endless hours to stories told? Few old ones remember why the stories were told. Even fewer remember how to tell them. Their lives have become too fragmented in this modern world. Their certainty is gone. Their bitterness is too apparent. So I will act for the Old Ones long gone, without bitterness, with good attention, and with true intent. I will tell you all I know. Ah ho.

Hinono

Chapter 1
First Walk

So we begin. Yes?

My first memory of being alive was the warmth of my mother's belly against my face. I must have been very small, and I must have been held very closely for a very long time. They told me I was born in the winter. I remember the smell of berries and meat and wood fires... always some noises–other children, probably. Rarely was there ever any excitement in the camp, except when a great hunt was on.

Daily life consisted of endless hours of gathering wood, hunting for berries and roots and other foods. The older men hunted and they would be gone for days. And if hunting was too poor, the camp would be moved. Always there was the thought of winter... storage baskets to be filled with dried food. We thought of spring and summer as the time of plenty, yet half of what we gathered, we dried and put away. Perhaps there was only an appearance of plenty, for when winter came and stores got low, there was a general quietness and fright among all in the camp.

The accepted rule was that old ones too sick to walk would give up their food first for the young ones. Then, since the young ones could not bear children, they would give up half their rations for the hunters who would go out in the cold and seek food for the camp. Many died all the time. Death was a frequent companion of our hearts and minds. In the taking of large game, death was ever present. There was great risk in hunting antelope and in hunting buffalo on foot, especially in hunting the great elk. All these creatures provided food, shelter, clothing, tools, and even glue.

As a child, I always watched ceremonies performed by older people, some ceremonies very old, some very personal, but I never knew what they were about, really. I was told some general idea about them, but the feeling truly was that I was too young to understand, so little was said. Always though, there was reverence. The naming of a baby, rites of puberty, marriage, more births, hunting honors, and the introduction to spiritual matters... all were very interesting, but the last one held the most interest for me. I was possessed to know these things.

I once saw a man standing for seventy hours speaking in different languages... tongues. He was held up by two ropes woven of raw hide and elk hair. The drumming and chanting nearly made me fall over with dizziness. This was the first ceremony I witnessed where someone was talking to Spirit. I think, perhaps you would say, I was six or seven years old then.

The passing of time for people close to the earth was marked by the movement of the animals responding to the changes in the weather. It was known to us that the animals knew these changes before man. The buffalo always knew when and where it was going to rain, and they would walk that direction because their wallows were the only respite from the heat and the insects, the ticks especially. We had remedies for ticks, but the buffalo did not, except the mud wallows... smother them with thick mud.

Our sense of time was not measured in minutes or even hours. It was measured in cycles of the moon and, less importantly, cycles of the sun. Sun cycles were too fast. Moon cycles were a bit slow. So we lived in between them, and we talked to Spirit often.

I didn't marry until I was twelve... late by most people's standards at that time, for we matured early and were independent quickly. I didn't marry because I couldn't choose. Too much fright. But eventually, I was chosen. It was easier that way. I was a bit odd, even at the age of twelve, so I was surprised to have been courted. I was more interested in standing on the hill and talking to Spirit... trying to, at any rate. I certainly did a lot of talking.

Spirit was kind to me, though. One day, standing on a nearby hill, I actually heard something. Scared me to death. A part of me had never really thought Spirit was real anyway. I stayed off that hill for a month. I wouldn't even tell the old people, but I think they knew anyway. They would look at me funny and turn their eyes to the ground and smile. That aggravated me. I could never know what they were thinking... I thought.

Most of the old people thought I was crazy anyway because I would miss meals when ceremonies were going on. Other people who were not attending would go on about their business, especially the business of gathering and eating. But food, for me, wasn't so important. I had never really suffered, you see. Fasts were a common practice and I was very strong. But the old ones could never figure out why I would attend everyone's ceremony, every time.

I was hungry. What for, I wasn't sure. Perhaps it was the feelings that were being shared. Perhaps it was the honesty and the depth of the old ones who spoke. Reverence was present, respect, honor, and trust. There were a few old ones who were fools, but they were fools when they were young. Everyone knew this. They had their place.

When I was thirteen, I set out on a walk with my wife. This walk changed me into a man and my companion into a woman. At thirteen we were children, more like brother and sister, but with serious thoughts on our minds and challenges ahead.

I told my wife I wanted to learn about medicines and become a healer, like the old people. For a time, there was silence and true concern. Why she knew more than me, I didn't understand, but I could tell she did. Perhaps while I was at some ceremony, she had been watching the other women whose husbands were always at one medicine ceremony or another, and she saw the loneliness they felt. I don't know. She never said. But when she decided she would go with me on this walk, then I knew the goal would be accomplished. I finally had agreement from someone about something. And the path with four shoes is warmer than that with two.

The journey began like this. A child with a dream and another child in support of that dream set out on foot to the south. The old ones had told us of a place to go, a mountain far away. They said that mountain would be a good place to talk to Spirit. I didn't trust the old ones much, but what else was I to do? I was serious. Secretly, they thought we would be back in two days, hungry and tired, too young to withstand the rigors of a quest. If for no other reason than to show them they were wrong, I would go. But truly, after several days of walking, the resolve must be much stronger than to prove old ones wrong.

Grasses cut. The dry wind chapped. The hot sun burned. We

questioned our motives continually to ourselves. But always between us was this silent nod of agreement to continue.

You measure distances in city blocks or acres or miles. We saw only the goal ahead and were duly warned it might take many moons to arrive at this place... if we were able. You see, there were no maps and the stars moved. We had only the point of sun in the morning and at setting to guide us. True desire was the beacon light, the homing device to that mountain.

Does anyone remember what true desire is? I'll define words for you, like I said I would. True desire is a magnet that has attraction to a goal. Even though the possessor of this magnet knows not what the goal is in truth, the pull is felt and followed. True desire does not give up but continues until its answer is found. It knows nothing of time and does not weaken. It knows nothing of comfort and only strengthens. It does not seek demise and is ever alert. Above all, it waits patiently when there is nothing to be done. It comes with certainty, and therefore is a gift from Spirit. Some days, it may seem like a curse. But in my mind, I see others at camp with no purpose, and I wonder how they feel about their lives. Would I want nothing, passively, or the unknown, actively? I would not choose for them, for my way this day seems hard, and sleep comes easy this night, as I am weary and questioning in my dreams.

In the night I am awake in my dreams, imagining the goal achieved, and I am strengthened again. I am a healer, a shaman. I am wondering, does my friend and wife and companion feel the same? And so, I ask. Some grumbles come. Impressive. It is obvious that her dreams are hers and mine are mine.

But on awakening that morning, she says, "Yes, we have the same dreams. It's just that your timing is different from mine."

I asked, Why would you want me to be such a healer in the tribe?

"Because you would be very important, and people would bring you food, and you wouldn't have to hunt, and I would keep you longer. Hunters die often," she said.

Oh, are you sure we dream the same dreams?

"Yes, my dear husband. Your dreams are certainly more colorful than mine, but they are the same."

That day, together, we walked a great distance. We did that for a hundred days to come, digging roots along the way, carrying water in a bladder. In this hundred days, I remembered every person I'd ever seen who had gotten sick. Some of the animals who had taken sick had been killed for meat, and we wondered about their sicknesses too. Almost no one lived past the age of forty. The winters were too harsh. And yet, to the south there was no game and much less water, so less grew. Less to eat... that is why our tribe stayed north.

The fiercer the conditions became on this journey, the more I noticed a transformation in us. We were both walking out of our skins. The children we were, were at our feet, beaten down by the hard terrain. A new mind was standing above the weakened us–children, whom we had to leave behind. We died as we walked and were reborn, all our complaints left in a bag, like trash you leave on your curb, things not wanted, left behind.

You say, did we truly die? No. The idea of childhood died. The carefreeness and innocence died. All this, walking to the south.

I could see the old ones with their wry smiles, eyes to the ground. I saw what they saw–me, a child full of dreams and desires, with no awareness of how to accomplish these things, frightened and excited.

Their smiles were very kind, indeed. I had thought them cruel, but their smiles were remembering their own childhood. Like a butterfly, their minds are light and float on the wind. The slower their bones got, the lighter their minds got. Thank you, old ones, for those good thoughts you gave me this day. I caught them when the winds blew my way. It's nourishment to me.

My skin is taut and dry, and my eyes burn like fire from the heat of the sun. But now there is a fire burning in my heart for the people we left behind on this quest. What was it for, anyway? I forgot. Oh yes... to talk to Spirit, truly, and to learn some things to help my people.

So, I'm thinking this day that this woman by my side, this child, sister, person I've known since I can remember... what does she think? I see her limping. I see the sores on her feet. I see the burned face. She suffers like me. For what? And I ask her, Why did you come, really?

"Because you asked me, really."

Just like that?

"Well, I had to ask you to marry me. This was the first thing you ever asked. I couldn't turn you down."

So it was with us, lots of laughter in hard times. It was a good thing she married me. I would have been far too serious. I probably would have perished early. And I wish I could carry her to help her feet.

I save some grease and rub it on her feet daily to keep the cracks from bleeding. And we are tougher now. Our hide is thickening. We don't lose so much water through our skin anymore. We've had to learn new foods here and they are sparse. But I've gotten good with a throwing stick, and we catch rabbits and squirrels. It's not the same as elk and buffalo, but we are alive and we still have a goal ahead of us.

The old ones said we would know the mountain because it was the only one with snow on top in the summer. "When you go past a large desert, there will soon be trees and animals and water. If you get that far," they said, "you are a man. If you get to the top of that mountain and are not struck by lightning, you will be a healer and a shaman, like your uncles. Remember this one thing," they said. "Ask the Creator to give you signs to tell you when to go up and when to come down. The signs must be clear or you haven't heard. If you deceive yourself, your life will be a life of deception and foolery. So, do not be tempted. Take someone, one who can speak truly. Have them tell your story as they witnessed it, or it will be no good to tell anyone at all. We will know if you are there. We will know if you turn back. We will know when you succeed. We have done this for ourselves a long time ago. All your questions will soon be answered, perhaps not the way you imagined them, for the Creator is still a mystery, but what is said is always clear. So, good journey," they said. And they were pleased to know my wife would accompany me.

Looking back at our feet this day, I see the many miles behind us and the many miles ahead, and my eyes go to the ground and I smile. How do they know these things? I asked. They always knew them. Someone old always knew these things. I will have many questions for them when I return. But return is far away, and I lift my eyes and scan the sky for a white-topped mountain, once again.

I know we have been gone a long time because the rains are coming, and the heat at night is not so bad. We have walked a long time. I think we have missed it. Somehow a mountain isn't large enough to see? I've never seen one, you know, not with snow on top. Just hills. "This mountain is rock nearly up to the moon," they had said. This is some mountain... I have to see!

My wife is pregnant, I think, and eats little. Still, she gets sick... not all day, not to frighten me, just enough to let me know. So we walk less, rest more, try to have more to eat. I have not been gentle in my obsession, so now I think I better be. I see my mother having more children after me. She died in childbirth. I think I didn't want to marry because of that. But everyone died sometime. My father was a great hunter and a good spokesman, and he liked to dance. He died too, in the cold while hunting. So did three others that day.

I think modern people don't experience death directly, much. They are so isolated from each other. Because we were all relatives of some sort, we attended every dead one's rite of passage into Spirit. We cried easily because we cared freely. We were not weak. We were accepting. A dead person's belongings were given away immediately, so those left behind would have no reminders of their physical life with that one. Unhelpful attachments to a dead one were released through song and ceremony.

All this was meant to ease the dead from this world to the next. If these attachments were not quickly broken, then the past could become an addiction, and any addiction in our risk-filled lives was a dangerous distraction. It is good the dead don't hang around and trouble our lives, because if we're distracted by an unreleased ghost from our past while hunting, we could make a mistake and easily die too. Dying was not a good solution to hardship. During these hard times of death, renewal of our spirits was based upon Creator's gift of new life. Children were what we lived for, not the dead.

Beyond all else, the children were loved and nurtured and fed and cared for in every way. For without them, I now see, there would be no us. Thank you again, dear old ones, for all your kindnesses. We will have this baby, and it will be healthy and strong. And we will care for it like you cared for us... and please, don't let childbirth hurt my wife.

Finally, after four moons, we see a mountain far away... maybe two or three days walk, or if it's a really big mountain, maybe four days walk.

We keep up a pretty steady pace of walking, and the closer we get, the more awestruck I become at the size of this thing rising straight up out of the dirt.

It took six days to get there after I first saw it, so it was much bigger than I thought. I'd never seen anything like this. Even Shuhinono was surprised. And truly, she's never surprised by much, except perhaps the little critters that crawl on the ground. They fascinate her, especially the ones that fly and hop. She said, "If I were one of those, I would just fly to the top."

I wish we could too, but I know from what the old ones said, this was no small journey. And it had just begun.

Chapter 2
Great Mountain

The shock of seeing this mountain close up was almost too much to bear. I couldn't believe that anyone could get to the top of this mountain. It was cinder cone with rubble all around, and every step you took forward, it seemed you went backward two. And then I remembered what the old ones had told me... *to ask.* I forgot so easily. We were excited. We thought by arriving, our journey would be half over. We would take the prize and return and be done. But imagination is never as satisfying as the Truth. The truth was, we felt like we were going to fail.

We camped seven days at the base of that mountain. And I prayed from sunup to sundown for help and understanding on how to get to the top. "How" was my question. I forgot to ask when. It's funny how you must listen carefully to what the old ones have to say. They did not make mistakes, not in these matters. Finally, together, my wife and I asked "when." We did not think it could not be done any longer. We chose to think it was possible, if we only knew when.

There are levels of giving up... quite a lot of them. There is only one level of giving up that is not good, and that's giving up the goal. Trying to figure out how and where and why... these things are good to give up.

Where does trust come from? What is it? And what in life is there to trust anyway? I think after these seven days, we found the reasons for our being here, the truth of it. We trust Creator this day. We give up all our questioning of how and where and why. Our tears of failure were replaced by our tears of gratitude, gratitude for all the people before us who have stood in this place, for they are here with me now. I even see them. Are we hot with fever or sick in our heads? But they're here and I feel their touch.

I look for my wife and she is two feet off the ground in their arms, and Spirit is walking her to the top of the mountain. Soon, under my arms, I feel hands, not warm or cold, just friendly hands, helping. And I, too, rise up and drift up that mountain.

This time I was not afraid when Spirit spoke. My mind questioned... Who are they? Do I recognize them? I can see them, and yet I cannot. I certainly know they are here because I am floating up this mountain... impossible thing. Am I dreaming? Dreams do this. I actually pinched myself and yelled. That was foolish, I said. And an Old One looked me in the eyes and smiled that wry smile again. So I asked, Who are you?

And those eyes asked me, "Who are *you?* All will be answered. Be patient."

What is the difference between vision and dreaming? I asked. Am I alive or am I dead? I don't feel anything, yet I am happy.

"A vision is a gift. You did not make it up or take it. You just received it. That is all. Dreaming is a wish for vision," I was told.

I don't know how long that journey took up that mountain. I don't think I was really conscious for much of it. I seemed to float in my mind, like my body rising up that hill. A floating mind is hard to keep hold of, and I'm sure I went out in sleep-like stupor a few times before we reached the top. It was frozen all around, but it wasn't cold. It was so bright... it was whitest white.

I saw my woman standing with me and our child was grown, to my surprise. How long have we been gone? I asked.

She said, "This is our son, his spirit self. He is strong and healthy, yes? You see, Spirit answers all your questions here." My eyes filled with tears. I knew what she said was true.

No questions formed in my mind. Frankly, I didn't even know I had one. The peace I felt was so far beyond anything I had ever experienced that I was satisfied with just bathing in it, in the purity of it. I still remember the colors vividly, and you are talking to a man long dead to your world, so my memory span extends a long way through time. The Love in that Light was powerful enough to clean you of all sorrows, to clean you of all sicknesses, and to restore you to the Truth.

What was that... the Truth? Of this experience, all of it is true. Why do the words fail to describe it or to speak the feelings directly? What is the quality of love that makes it so difficult to express?

I know. It's because it contains all thought that is real, from everyone, for all times. All living things come together here, atop this sacred mountain, so it must be that this Love is the Fountain of Truth.

Slowly, gently, as each idea passes through my head, as each temporary solution to my confusion leaves my mind, another answer with more questions come. I see sickness as a fear or an anger or a carelessness... each one of them, hundreds, one by one. Oh yes, I thought. I forgot. I wanted to be a healer. Something didn't forget... something is remembering for me.

I see all the animals as relatives, each with their own families and their own concerns, and yet conscious of being in a larger family. I see the puzzle of life before me, everything intertwined, interwoven, interconnected, everything the same, all love. Everything volunteered, I said, even me. Now, that's the Great Mystery.

I turned to my wife to ask her if she volunteered, and I saw the most radiant being before me I'd ever seen in my life. I could not even imagine such a woman. Her heart was golden and shot rays of light, blue and yellow and pink and green... all through me. It stung my eyes. It was so bright. And I knew it was her. I fell down on my knees, and I touched her robe and kissed her feet and thanked her for her help and her companionship.

I again looked up. This time I could not see her. She was too tall. She was like the mountain, very tall, all light on top, and I lost her in this Light. I didn't feel loss, but I couldn't find her either. I turned to look, and all I saw around me was... standing-up water, what you call "glass." And I saw my face was looking for something... looking at me as I was looking at it. My whole mind collapsed with the thought that I could see myself and yet not know me. It was shock, I think I felt. What do you do with shock?

A Voice said, "It gets stuck if you do not ask for help."

Ah ha! Then I ask you for help with this shock I feel. What am I?

And the Voice said, "You are the love that sent you."

Like my wife?

"Yes, like your wife."

Are we really alive?

"From this day forth, yes."

I was perplexed and satisfied. I was full to the brim and overflowing. Later, I would think, why didn't I ask this or that? But

They seemed to know what was in your mind, and They seemed to answer you before you asked. Ahh... I remember our old ones. Their faces are very clear. Now I know. They *have* been here before.

While I'm lost in my reverie, my wife takes my hand and says, "It's time to go." I'm glad somebody knows something because I think I would have stayed there forever. I think you do stay in that Love forever, if you ever experience It while you're in a body. Some part of you never leaves again. There is a hole filled where emptiness was. There is a fullness where searching to have, turns into having.

We awoke the next morning... I think it was the next morning. I really don't know how long we were on that mountain. All I knew was that it was morning, and I felt that I'd had a powerful dream that couldn't be true. But I felt so good. I turned to my wife who was still sleeping, and I put my hand on her back. She said nothing and I became frightened, but she was warm.

So I said, Good morning... very good morning. You tell me what happened and I'll tell you. Do you remember?

Two fuzzy heads remembering slowly. Were we done? Is it time to leave? We must ask. Ah, I do not forget so easily now what the old ones said about asking. There is truth in their words.

We sleep more that day, and we bathe in the streams below the mountain, and there is plenty of game... deer. We feel the chill of the evenings now, so we're happy to have a deer skin for rain shelter. I notice everything now. *Everything.* My obsession is fulfilled. There is nothing blocking my sight, my vision. Spirit gives me pictures to follow and wordless words in my mind. I even hear my wife thinking her thoughts, which are the same as mine. She was right. We do dream the same dream. And I am grateful... again and again and again.

We both hear, "Good journey," so we depart that same hour. We ask Spirit to point the way, to keep us out of harm, and They do. The magnet, you see, is stronger now.

Each tree we pass says, "This way" or "That way." Each gentle breeze that blows repoints us anew, for the winds now blow from the south in the day. The walk home is much easier. There is no death. It has been defeated. It was not defeated by us. It was defeated by our true desire. Only fear stands in the way of achievement. Today, we have no fear and will offer none to anyone we meet.

The game stands and waits for us now. It offers itself and we thank it for the generosity of its life, and we bless it with all our hearts as we take it to eat, to dress, for tools, and for warmth. Even this gift saddens us because we know we are no more important than they. We are all equal. We all have the same life to live. I find we eat more roots and berries, though they are diminishing quickly with the cooler weather. I think we do so because we do not want to impose ourselves on our brother creatures too much.

Why did not anyone else come and do this thing... go to this mountain? The answer I got was, they were afraid. They did not desire it like we did. Perhaps it was not their part to play, as it was mine and my wife's. You see, most people don't seem to practice good feelings to any great depth. They are satisfied with a shallow life, I suppose. They seem happy. I wonder what they dream.

That night, I was shown. They are fearful, indeed. Their dreams are of death–all kinds–starvation, injury, war. They seek the company of others quickly and marry early to keep the bad dreams away. I never had bad dreams, so I can't say.

Did you have bad dreams before we were together? I asked my wife. And she looks at me, steps back two paces and looks at me again.

Finally, we walk on and she says, "Why would you ask what my dreams are after I have already told you, we have the same dreams?"

Oh! I forgot.

"You get so wrapped up in your own thinking, don't you?"

Yes, I guess I do.

"What is it with this questioning? Don't you see? The mountain gave you everything. Will you worry about nothing and make things up and have bad dreams too? I don't want any."

No, I will not have bad dreams. Thank you. Thank you for showing me how easy it is to invite another's troubles into your mind and into your life.

When we went to the top of Great Mountain, that energy of Love was all there was. We were not different. We were the same. We *joined* It. It did not join us in our ignorance. We joined It in all Its glory. So why would I want back what I put aside like trash on the road?

Rabbits dash by and I know I just called my fears. Wow! That must be what it's like for the fearful... scared like a rabbit, humping in the dark, always searching for food to eat, for surely there will not be enough. Worries and concerns and fears strangle the life out of life. The walking dead worry. So thank you again, wife, for helping me to realize my mistake, I thought silently.

"Don't mention it," she said out loud.

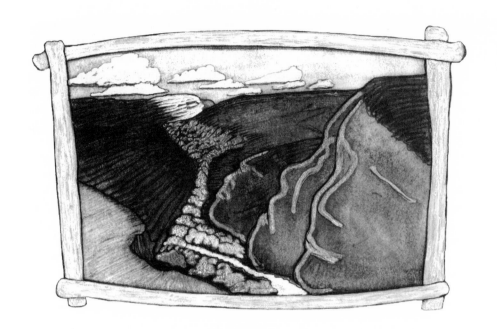

Chapter 3
First Return

The weather worsened as we traveled, and my wife's pregnancy began to show on her strength. We walked slower, rested often, and built shelter for the evening. Always we gathered roots and berries and seeds. I'm not sure how long it was before she gave birth. I remember it was only a short while before we arrived back at camp. You see, we were gone much longer on the return trip.

All during this time, there were visions and revelations. There were the faces of our people and other tribes and the tribes of animals. There was learning all the way. The most disturbing vision came to my wife. She saw that we would perish in a great storm. The whole tribe, very nearly, would perish in this great storm, but she did not think it was soon. It was a matter-of-fact picture that unfolded before her eyes one night while tending fire.

It is hard to know how to deal with these visions. They come and speak of distant things and sometimes very immediate things, but to interpret them takes great discipline and more experience than I had. I trusted her feelings about the timing and meaning of these visions more than my own. There is something within woman that makes her feet deeper in the earth than man's.

Modern woman has lost instincts and intuitions and feelings, even for her children. There are too many distractions for the modern person. They forget what is real. They busy themselves with worrying over a fence line or the color of a house paint. To us, any form of house, even the most basic lean-to of trees and leaves and shrubs and bark was a luxury, and something to be thought out. We did not want to denude the land entirely, based upon our own want or desire for fresh leaves on our roof.

Cleanliness was not so much a concern of our smell sense as it was our health sense. Women, here again, instinctively knew more than man. Perhaps she observed more closely the behavior of flies than men did. She noticed there must be some connection between those flies and this runny nose. So we burned sage and we smoked our clothes, as this simple method of preserving our tanned hides deepened their good color, lengthened their life, and kept the damn bugs out.

Yes, I'm sure they have a part to play–bugs... to pester us eternally. And that is good because an untested soul is weak. And, believe me, the flies of summer can test you greatly. Hunters used to smear their bodies with mud for two reasons. The first was to keep the sun from burning them. The second was to keep the insects from biting them. There was a third which everyone imagined, and that was to keep the human body odor away from the nostrils of the hunted deer.

But, truly, deer are smarter than that. They hear so much better than man that they could often tell we were coming two miles away. So we planned feats of trickery. We stayed in one spot so long, they didn't see us as human because humans move. We could lay in the grass until a deer stepped next to our hand, and we literally grabbed it down. This was meditation and concentration. This was patience and alertness. Not even a breath could be audibly breathed.

So you try it... control your breath. See how long you can be silent and still. Our men were called warriors because of this feat, not because they were brash and foolhardy. And because they had tremendous discipline, strength of will and the character to withstand great hardships, they could achieve the goal of the hunter for *all* the people. They always shared everything.

Modern people have many fears about abundance. The reason why is that they haven't figured out where it all comes from. Do you know what abundance is? Is it too many socks? Or is it something larger?

Shuhinono and I named our son, but he was not well. My

prayer was answered, for the birth was easy. All young women were trained early how to deliver. Physically, he was very strong, but there was torment in his eyes... anguish. Something was lost on his journey to birth. He cried and cried, not deeply, just sorrowfully. We did not fear for his life. We feared for his soul. He would nurse hungrily but stop to cry occasionally. I've never seen a child like this.

So we headed for the old camp but didn't know whether it would still be there or not. Spirit was kind, though. They guided us the whole way, then turned us slightly from the old path that led to the old place. We see from a distance that camp has moved a little, a half mile or so. We are excited, and yet very uneasy about our return. We don't remember for a time that the old ones had said they would know if we made it to the top of that mountain or not. When we remembered this, we sank into a kind of peace that we visited only in memories of our childhood. We relaxed completely.

There was a small group of people waiting for us at the edge of camp when we arrived. It was not until we were several hundred feet away that they realized who we were. A runner was sent to the old ones' camp nearby. Word got out among the tribe very quickly, and soon everyone was there to gather us in, to offer us food and shelter and warmth, as the evenings now were very cold. We noticed frost on the ground in the mornings. God, it's wonderful to have a large family that knows how to love.

I think at first I couldn't smile because I was still in an altered state, you might say. Spirit never left us from atop that mountain. They guided our every thought and our every movement. They guided our direction and our feelings. We allowed this because we trusted Them. It was easy for me to see now, why one should never trust one's own decisions made alone. It is better to have a friend, a Guide that shares your mind and can see the concern from another place, within your own mind. This way, you climb ladders to the truth, slowly and with humor. Because, truly, most of my thoughts still tasted of fear.

These fear thoughts concerned my son and nothing else. I couldn't stop the worry, and no matter how much I asked Spirit to disclose this difficulty to me and show me how to help him, They either would not or could not. This perplexed me, since I had known nothing but perfect companionship from Them and perfect communication. I could see the same question on Shuhinono's face. She was happy to be home and to see her friends and family, but behind those cheerful eyes there was a questioning, waiting to be answered.

Now, believe me, this child was not a pest or colicky. I cannot explain how we knew that it was sorrow for something lost, but we did. The question in my mind now was to the old people who would know the answer to this problem. There were a few children in the camp who had sorrow in their eyes. They did not flourish and they often did fail. For those children, only a few, the reason for their problem was clear. In their mind, they thought they were not loved enough or love was not enough. This, I'm sure, was not a fault of the parents because all children were loved. Was there some error in my own child's mind about love, perhaps? Why was love not enough?

It is hard to say what puts a hole in a human's heart. But if a sorrowful child lived long enough, the old ones would work with them, and soon the child would see the error of gardening a hole in their heart. Trials and tests would develop the child's will to live, if they lived. The old ones knew what will was for. So we will ask them tonight, I think, if that is not too far away. These celebrations can go on too long with such concerns behind our eyes.

I noticed this one thing. When I left, my friends and relatives would jump all over me and hug me and say rude things and wish me well. When we arrived, they greeted us with... *circumspection*. Much like a deer revisiting her fawn, she smells it to see if it is hers, even though she was only a few paces away a few moments ago. We were different and yet the same, so I smiled painfully long, but my excitement did not lift my feet off the ground as it would have before.

Toward evening, I saw one of the old ones looking at us, pensively, deeply. It even made me nervous to feel it... such penetration of thought. I was not afraid but I was aware, and I soon got a glance of recognition and a nod of approval. So, I will be able to see them tonight. That is good.

I told Shuhinono of this silent dialogue and she said, "Will you take him with you? I will stay with the others."

I said, Yes–no–I want you to go.

She said, "I already know what they will say. You go. It is for your mind these questions must be answered."

How does she know these things? I'm pretty good at seeing fish in the river, even when it's a little muddy sometimes, but how do you practice such knowingness? I pleaded with her, Teach me how to do that. Let me practice. I'll become better at it.

She said, "Not on my life."

I will tell you this one thing now, just to clear it up before I get into trouble. Women in our tribe have always carried the medicine of prophesy. I think they can make things happen, especially when they get together and decide on one thing... all of them. That's how chiefs are chosen, by the way. Them women all get together and talk for days, and when they decide, it's done, even though the person elected has no idea what's going on. It just happens. One day that chosen person steps forward and says, "I know where to go to get food and skins. I saw it in a dream." And everyone would follow, and it would be true. This happened enough times where this good person would be elected without his knowing it. My father told me all this. In matters of the heart, the women had medicine far greater than any man I've known, except perhaps Jesus. I think he truly learned something wonderful.

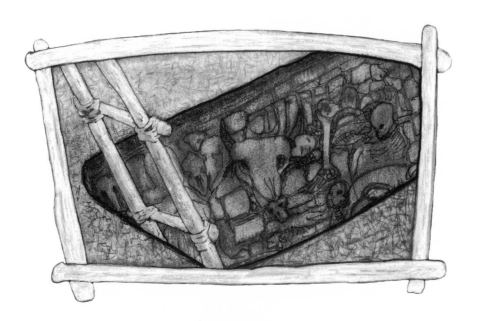

Chapter 4
The Trap Door

I broke away from the reunion when the hunters started their stories and the women retired to another fire. I carried my son in a blanket made of woven rabbit skins, for this night seemed especially cold. My ears stung when the breeze would blow, and the saliva would get stuck in my cheeks and would not flow until warmed by a fire. I think I'm a bit nervous to hear what the old ones may have to say, but I quiet myself and just walk the sixty yards or so across the camp to the quieter side. It's funny how many levels life has, even in such a small village as this. The old ones were farther from the water, farther from the wood, farther from the big fires. They gave up many comforts for silence.

As I approached this lodge made of large skins, a person stepped out and invited me in. They had known I was coming. This person, I noticed, was not so old as the rest, perhaps in his twenties or thirties. I didn't recognize him because he was much older than me. Rarely did the older men take on much responsibility for the younger ones, unless they showed some strong interest in being taught about spiritual matters. There was a great distance between tag-a-long and expertise. So far, I had been a tag-a-long. Today is different.

I will let the old ones speak for themselves. Just as John and Barbara are doing for me, I will do for them.

"Sit. Be quiet. I will tell you your question. You have born a sorrowful one and want to help. We are aware of your journey to Great Mountain. We are aware that you got to the top the way we did. We are aware of the way that you walked back to this camp. We do not need to hear your story, unless you think we missed something.

"Hinono, this child that you and Shuhinono received is not happy here without his other half inside himself. So, to fulfill a prophecy that some of the women have remembered to me while you were gone, you will give this child back to Creator. I cannot tell you how to do this. You must discover it with your asking. There has been no mistake. It does not matter when. I will tell you what these women have told us, as I know you will pester me for this prophesy anyway. The great, great-grandmothers before our time have handed this story down to us. This is the story they told.

"'There will be two children born to our tribe very many years from now. We will be gone, but this is what we saw. These two will marry and they will strike out for Great Mountain after their first year of sharing a blanket. They will return successful, but they will be carrying a sorrowful child. This child will not live among the camp for very long because of his agreement with Spirit that was broken. We are not sure what this agreement was, but this child must be returned to Creator. Later, there will be another child born to this couple that will possess many powers of observation that we ourselves do not have. Between these two children that are to be born, there is a missing one not born. All three have been asked to return to help reawaken the spirit of our culture in a new age, far beyond us. They will hold memories for our people. If we were to guess when this would be, we would say more than twelve cycles of seven generations. There are great changes coming, and our people will be spread far and wide, and our culture will be diminished. Many will perish in a big cold to come, and all of the ways to Spirit will very nearly be forgotten. These three children will help carry the memories of our old, simple ways into this new age. To be sure, it will be hard to know who these three are. There will be signs, the earliest of which will be the two young ones to marry and seek Great Mountain. If these first two succeed, they are your Guardians for the future. Train them well. Listen to their children. Let this family help guide you.'

"So Hinono, we have told you what was told to us. And now, when you are ready to take your place in this lodge, we will show you everything that was shown to us. Then, perhaps, you can help our people when the big storm comes. We know your wife walks with feet deep in the earth. Learn from her too, as you have done already. Go."

So there it was... whatever it was. The air was acrid with some smoke of something. I was having trouble focusing at all. There was no light in that lodge, except from a few glowing embers, and it was packed with elders. I was stunned at the certainty of that voice without a face. This is no thirty-year old in here speaking to me. Come to think of it, I don't even know how old some of them are. I'm so young, how could I notice? Besides, hardly anyone sees them anymore.

I don't remember leaving that lodge. I'm only aware that my mind goes on like that for a solid hour after I leave the elders, until Mohinono cries, and I have to go back to the new lodge our relatives built for our return.

What do they mean... "this child must be returned to Creator?" Shuhinono is quietly crying in the corner. She won't look at me. She *does* know already. But what does that mean exactly? I asked her, So what does this mean exactly?

Silence. A small sob.

Your son is crying, I said. Will you take him and comfort him?

"It will do no good for me to comfort him. It is another he seeks for comfort," she said.

How do you know these things? I asked. I saw no vision, heard no answers, and came back with a hundred more questions. You sit there like the old ones. I think I'm going crazy. Am I the only one here that doesn't know anything?

"My mother doesn't know anything," Shuhinono said.

That doesn't help. Your mother never did know anything.

"Shush. Give me him," she said.

So what does this mean exactly... giving back to Creator? And then it dawns on me what they meant and I'm horrified! I think I better ask them some more questions. What do you think? This worries me. I can't set my child out in the cold to die. It's not right. I won't do it.

Slowly, she got up, looked me in the eyes and said, "Go to sleep. Stop worrying yourself. If you don't know what to do, then do nothing. Yes?"

Good idea. We slept, barely, if at all. Exhaustion came when the sun came up. I think we slept then, until the noise of children running by awoke us. The sun was higher... midmorning. Not too many people were out, as the cold was becoming significant.

If it weren't for the buffalo and the elk, there would be no shelter and clothing for this cold. We would have to migrate like we used to, until we found this place. Big game... they come in the spring and they go in the fall. This is the place they do that.

31

Without them, we would perish. I give thanks today to those creatures of the Creator's who follow this path, so that we may live also and care for them as they care for us. They are wise creatures and very hard to fool. Sometimes, I think we are the fools, and they allow our games to come too close, so the weakened creatures will not have to make the hard journey to the south or to the north. It is better, I think, to go quickly than to waste away from sickness and injury.

Caught in my own thoughts, I realize I am talking about my son. How do they do that? They have my thoughts, the old ones, and are helping me to see correctly in this matter. But I will not do it, no matter what they say or think inside my head. I don't like it!

I kick things aside and curse and swear, make a mess all over the place. Shuhinono looks up at me and says, "Good morning?" with a big question mark in it.

No–yes–I don't know.

"I see you haven't stopped thinking yet," she said.

No-o-o... ye-s-s... well, no... I can't stop. There's an old one in my head showing me things, making me think certain thoughts. I know it's not me because it's too gentle, too subtle. I don't like it, none of it! I'm going for a walk. I'll be back in two days.

So away I went with one robe for comfort against the cold and a throwing stick. That was the longest two days of my life. I didn't know I had such strong emotions about such a wide variety of things. All, of course, centered on our tribe's feelings for children. Finally, I prayed to see how it is in the mind of this child, having learned by now that it doesn't take language to have vision. What was this sadness in my son? And is there any other way to deal with it?

The second night out, I had dreams. I saw many places unfamiliar to me. I heard a soft calling. I could not see who it was that called. The voice was female and she called, "Mohinono." I thought... How can a child possess the memory of a woman? That doesn't make sense.

I heard in one of the ceremonies a long time ago–I think I was eight–an old person saying, "You think this life is all there is? You think that man comes to turn to ashes and never comes again?"

I remember saying out loud, I don't know, and having to excuse myself out of embarrassment. I tried to answer the question. I stand here in the same embarrassment tonight, pondering the same thought that old one gave us.

Well, I know I had a grandfather and a grandmother and older ones yet we call ancestors, but I've never seen them twice. I know some of the women say they see their husbands who have died. I, myself, once sensed my father and felt his loving touch after his death. But will I see him again? It's a good question. Does love die with the person, or do you hold it close to you when you remember your ancestors? Do they live again from this love you carry forward? I don't know. Perhaps not just here with us they live, but somewhere, nearby. Some, I think, far away.

The old ones... they're doing it again... thinking thoughts in my head... Mohinono would never be lost to us. I don't like it though, **and I won't do it!**

The dreams helped, though. I think I understand... barely–something, perhaps. I'm not as angry. I'm sad now, sad because my mind desires proof that only experience can bring. I have had so little, and yet so much.

I walk home in the dark. Sunrise comes and I'm not even aware I am sleeping as I walk. But stumbling awakens me, and in front of me stands a very large tree, just there before I injure myself. The surprise causes my heart to beat very fast. But my mind is so slow to catch up to what's happening that I totter backwards and end up sitting in the grass looking at this huge tree. And in the branches, I notice a bird sitting, watching me. This is no ordinary bird, I think, for it doesn't move, really. It's eyes move, but it doesn't. I can't explain it. Those eyes sucked me in hard and my heart beat faster, and there was a flash of light. I felt like I had been struck and killed. Yet, I felt nothing, really.

There was that quiet again, no insects, no wind in the grass, no tree leaves fluttering, not even the sound of my own voice, not even my heart beating. Nothing. Perfect quiet. But I can't see a thing. I'm blind, I think, like snowblindness. Such brightness, the eyes see nothing in it.

A Voice said, "Do as you are asked. All will be explained. Give the child back to his true Father, so he may be healed."

Okay, I said, I'll do it, but only in my mind and in my heart, for I truly will not take the life of my child.

"You need do nothing. Go. Be at peace. Give us your willingness and we will show you the truth. We mean you no harm, but you must do your part."

You know, it was days later that I realized I could have asked questions, like, what is my part? But there's something about those events that leave you wondering if you will ever hear yourself breathe again or taste a nutty root.

That tree really was there, I swear, but I don't see it now. I really am going crazy, I think. You tell me what happened. I don't

33

know. My small mind can't even conceive of it, and yet there it was. Something happened.

I think you should have one of these experiences. Ask for it. It's really quite interesting and fills many hours with thought. I haven't been bored since the top of that mountain, I'll tell you that.

When I saw Shuhinono again, I asked, What does all this mean, really? And damn! She knew exactly what I was talking about.

This is really getting frustrating. She said, "I'm really happy you had a vision. Maybe I need one too."

Woman, I said, you are a vision. I'm out of my mind.

"If you keep on that way, you will be out of your mind. Relax. Have you forgotten the top of the mountain already?"

No. What do you mean?

"Was that Love up there or not?"

Yes, as far as I know what that means. That's what it felt like. But would Love take back a first child?

She said, "Would you rather try to figure this out on your own and try to make a decision by yourself again, or will you trust Spirit one more time? We must trust. Yes?"

The rest of the day was spent in silence. I tried to sleep. I couldn't. I think there will be no more rest for me until I know the meaning of all this. And I see understanding only comes after the experience. But you cannot hurry up to have an experience, and you certainly cannot figure it out before it happens.

Does it take greater courage to put trust in front of your life and live it in front? Or would you consider it foolishness not to prepare yourself for these things that surely will come unannounced? It's hard to let go of pain, especially when you haven't experienced it yet.

So this day, I vow to walk behind my trust and stop toying with pain before I know the truth. To reserve judgment is wise, I think. I see the old ones do that often. Eyes wide open, they stand there and just watch, expressionless, fearless, without wonder, no thought perceptible in their mind. Everyone else has something to say and some way to express it... continually, without break, no rest. Their lives are very different, I see. I think Shuhinono knows more of this than I do. I am grateful for her companionship and for her words which help me decide how I want my life to be. So in this quiet space, I choose peace. This time, I am conscious of my choice. I think it will stick. I say, thank you.

It stuck. It's now been almost a year since I've even thought about the problem with Mohinono. We sat around many fires and ate the winter stores, and spring flew by. We were carefree and we enjoyed the time playing with Mohinono. Summer came. It was hot quickly. And all this time, I did not think.

One afternoon on a walk in late summer, I noticed an old woman standing by a gravesite, softly muttering something and burning something sweet. As soon as she noticed my approach, my peace was shattered. I started muttering to myself, quickly walking around in circles, feeling agitated for the first time in nearly a year. That old woman sent thoughts to awaken my fears again. I knew she was inviting me to the old ones' lodge.

I fussed around all evening, almost, muttering to myself. I think I was working up courage too. When I finally did go to that lodge, there was no one there. I mumbled rude things and spit on the ground. Nearly at that instant, I was struck in the back of the head with a log, and I reeled to see this old woman standing over me, screaming and shouting, eyes flashing with fire. And I realized I had been coming to this place puffed up like a prairie chicken to look bigger, full of arrogance and anger and disrespect. While stumbling to get out of her reach, I asked for her forgiveness. She quickly quieted and invited me inside. She said, "How dare you spit on this place?" And I nodded and entered.

We sat in silence for nearly two hours. Something told me I shouldn't speak. When she began talking, it was from a place of knowingness, and I knew I was right for not speaking. She said, "It is time now that you come here and learn something. For a whole year, you have controlled your mind. You have shown discipline and patience." And after a long pause, she asked, "Have you had any visions this year?"

I said, No, I don't think so. Dreams, perhaps. Not visions.

She asked, "Why?"

I said, I don't know.

She said, "Of course, you do. Don't be foolish. Look."

I closed my eyes and immediately saw a trap door, with me standing on top. Wherever I walked, this trap door was beneath my feet, closed. I opened my eyes and the old woman said, "So what does this closed trap door keeping you out mean to you?" I close my eyes and look once again. She said, "You wear your energy at the top of your head and not below your feet."

The trap door opens slowly, and there are steps going down. I peer inside and see an underground house, with bones sticking out of the walls. I can't tell if they are human or animal... just bones. I become afraid and quickly open my eyes. The old woman asks, "What is this fear? What are you afraid of?"

I think without speaking... it is a graveyard, a sacred place, and no one is to enter. She speaks with her words, without opening her eyes and says, "You heard that when you were a child. Are you a child now?"

I said, No.

She said, "Since you are a man now, we will change the rules for you, so that you may see inside. So, close your eyes. Go back. Look."

After some minutes, I am again at the bottom of those steps, looking at the bones in the walls. This time I can see there are all kinds, human and animal. I begin to look at skulls, and their eyes open and look at me. My heart races and I again open my eyes.

The old woman said, "Breathe, big and deep... slowly. Go back. Look again."

Without knowledge of my breath, I look, and this time I'm in the corridor. The bones have hands and they're touching me on my arms and legs, friendly-like, like a greeting. I relax. The old woman is behind me saying, "Go forward." So I do. I bump into a shiny wall that I cannot see, like light would appear on water if it was not wet. I notice if I press forward, this wall resists. If I slowly move into it, it resists much less. My hands, I feel, are rock and dirt. They aren't dead. They're just rock and dirt. A faint voice says, "Go forward," so I do. Within this envelope, I am rock. I do not feel like staying. It's too different. I look around and see pitchers, like to hold water, except bigger. I peer inside and see something like your paper, as if the leaves have fallen from a tree and layered. On each one of them was pictured some negative human emotion or thought, stored there like that in the pitchers. I begin to feel those negative emotions and I want to leave.

I try to go and I hear, "Thanks for coming this far." I realize the rocks are alive. They are conscious. I turn to look at someone, but it's all rock and dirt.

I remember in a ceremony once, the old ones saying that everything is alive and that there is no death, but I did not know what they meant, for I saw death often.

Now I know what they meant. The things your mind sees with your eyes are either dead or alive to you. And if they are alive, then they are conscious. But to actually know this thing is a feat.

The next thing I realize is that I'm sitting in the lodge with tears running down my face, and the old woman starts singing softly the sweetest song I have ever heard. With each phrase, she wrings out of me all the tears I have ever felt for the loss of anything or anyone. Death is not real anymore.

I don't remember a thing after that, except awakening later that night covered with robes, seeing Shuhinono by the fire with the baby. I slept, I think, for two days. I don't remember.

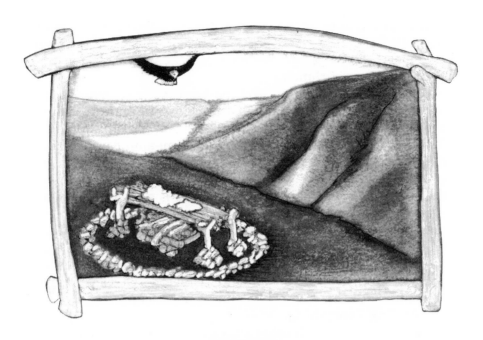

Chapter 5
The Little Deaths

The next two years, I spent pretty much all that time, either with the old ones or thinking about what they were telling me and showing me. I'll try not to bore you with too many details, but I'll tell you the things I learned, and I'll try once again to put a definition around the word shaman, without boxing it in.

You see, shaman is outside the box, really. So any definition attempted would surely be thrown away soon for a new one, to include more. I'll say this, though. I found out that shamen were people who could talk to Spirit and did that daily for themselves and for others. I was fortunate in that my teachers were not bogus. They knew how to share and to join. They knew that two human beings joined in the same purpose see farther and greater things than one alone.

I will start with fire, for that is where they started me, once I died to death again in that earthen tunnel. The shock of dying and awakening and hearing my own breathing took me many moons to work out in my mind. What died, I saw, was fear of death. As with our walk to Great Mountain, we were to experience many times the little deaths that are a part of our awakening. And the old woman was right, because my energy is now below my feet. It includes the earth and all its experiences.

With the old ones, I visited many places, talked to many people, learned the lives of the trees and the grasses, learned the lives of the animals. We began to decipher, for me, what hierarchy there was in the sense of things.

Deep in the earth, we visited the hot fires that keep the earth alive and warm in the Mother's heart. This is where land is formed and pushed up. There are many thoughts down there. Some say it is like hell, whatever that is. The word is meaningless to me, but there is a lot of experience down there where I first saw the rock people storing negative energy. The deeper you go, the farther from light you get, yet there is a fire, there is a heart, and there is love there too.

I saw the Mother's fire is the female aspect of God. It is the brightest red light. I saw the Father's fire is the male aspect of God. It is the brightest blue light. Beyond the two combined aspects of God, male and female, is Creator. Of all imaginable gods combined, Creator is First and final. **There is One... only One... All One Everything.**

This fire within the Mother's core is the basis for all life in the body. The body would not exist without the physical laws that govern the material universe from which life evolves. Spiritual life, however, can and does exist beyond these physical laws. The body self, alone, is foreign to our Spiritual Self. The Father's core is the Spark or Reason for life. Acting together, the physical laws of the Mother, the Love to do it, and the Spiritual laws of the Father, the Reason to do it, combine here on earth to create an experience for us of a physical and spiritual life.

We are all pulled between a feminine self and a male self in a single body, being expressed both physically and spiritually. There is a longing, it seems, for the Spiritual Father by the female self and a longing for the Spiritual Mother by the male self. The closest thing to this longing for the Spiritual Mother is to say, it is Her love men seek in their women. Such is true of the female longing for the Father. It is His love women seek in their men. This is not to say that a female would not desire her Spiritual Mother, nor a male desire his Spiritual Father. The combinations of pulls and desires within a single human entering the spiritual realm for the first time seem to be endless, as we are truly both male and female, regardless of which physical body we may be in at the moment.

To satisfy this longing in a child, the love you give your children needs to be like the true Mother or Father's love that They give you. The question is, are you able to receive this love yourself? Truly, we are all children to Them. They gave and give still... endlessly.

38

We saw other places where other spirit people lived... here and yet not here. In the sky, we visited the cloud people who were carried by the winds... the Mother's breath. Powerful memories were in that wind and in that sky. The memories went back to Creator Itself and the decision to have earth.

I saw that Love split Itself in half, so It could see Itself and honor Itself and give gratitude for Its creations. One life by itself doesn't even know it's alive. Even the rude jostlings are better than no stimulation at all, wouldn't you think? I saw there are two kinds of love with the same beginning; a hot fire with a heart and body, and the cold fire of pure mind. That cold fire pierces even the dullest of minds. I'm living proof.

Shuhinono recognizes my increasing depth and awareness of her thoughts and of the thoughts of the camp as a whole. This act of recognition by her shook me into another level of awareness. And so it went for two years.

Mohinono died that winter, his lungs filling with fluid until he drowned. None of the herbs that had always worked were helpful. I saw the look in his eyes, no fear, a kind of certainty. He made no effort to recover. None. Didn't even cry, and I know he hurt. Even with this loss, we both knew it was decided and that's that. We tried to mourn, but in the middle of our efforts, we kept getting visions and hearing, "Everything's fine. Thank you."

Now, how can you be sad when you've been thanked? It doesn't fit. They sure know how to stop your thoughts, those old ones. The odd thing was, no one in camp even acknowledged Mohinono's death. This was very strange. Usually, what you call funerals, to us were rites of passage into Spirit and were well attended. Some attended because it was the sharing of sorrow that brought them closer together.

This one thing happened. An old woman, wrapped in a large robe, walked into our lodge, sat herself down, and offered these words to us. "What you give once comes back twice–what's to eat?" You know, I think I must have thought she was crazy because I never asked what that meant... "What you give once comes back twice." Another one of those wise old sayings at a rotten time, I suppose. But she ate good. Funny thing, she left without even saying thank you.

I started to ask Shuhinono what that was all about and caught myself. I knew the retort would be sharp. She looked at me and said, "I wonder what that means?–'coming back twice.'"

For weeks to come, people passed at a distance from us with eyes downturned. Why do they not come and be sorrowful with us? I don't understand. But it was better this way because I didn't have sorrow like I thought I would. I missed the little guy.

Well, shoot, I said, I guess I'll have to go in the tunnel and look for his bones, so I can see his eyes again.

Shuhinono threw something at me. "Stop it," she said.

I waited a long time to go back to the old people's lodge. I wasn't sure I wanted to know anymore. I slept fitfully... not real sleep. I noticed that consciousness sometimes takes a break, but the thinking goes on. Mind is very large. It was awhile before I realized that it didn't matter whether I slept at night or daytime, lying down or standing... consciousness takes a break. Like if you were to stick your head out the lodge in freezing, windy weather, you'd have to take a break. So I think it's like that... too much is too much.

I heard these words once when I was very young... "harmony" and "grace." And now, thinking about Mohinono, I wonder what they mean. I think harmony is when you're unconscious and comfortable, and grace is when you're conscious and comfortable. I don't think I've made it to grace yet.

Look here, reader. Am I boring you? Am I going too slow? Well, a biography, by its very nature, is self-absorptive. "Innerlooking," they call it... going over the past. But I say this. **There is no past.** Look again, I say. Go deeper. There is no past, I tell you.

You think, well, then there is no future, so we'll all just lay down here and die. Hear this: If there is a future, it is you living in the now and hopefully not in the past. There is a forward and a behind as well, but it has nothing to do with time, really. Space has to do with the physical place. Time has to do with the non-physical plane. Forward and behind applies to mind, as well as past and future, but mind is bigger than time or space. Mind applies to all events and the intent of the source of those events. So who or what is intending us?

In these two years, I have found out that though we all live our individual lives, singly and in pairs, there are very few people who are joined to all the minds that were or will ever be. With this joining, there comes a bigger sense from our expansion, within the realm of intent, within the realm of knowledge. What the old ones did was open the doors and windows on our perception, so that we could become aware of the intent running all events. They threw off the covers on everything that we made assumptions about, so that we would not stay locked in time and space or in forward and behind. Their minds were piercing. Their intent was clear. They did not push holes in illusions to get to power. They did it to keep love present. They did it in the Now that transcends human perception, so we could see that what intends love is what heals all wounds and all confusions.

40

Shuhinono shared in all the elders information and never went to that lodge once. How did she do that? I asked her one day, Do you have strange dreams? What do you dream?

She said, "I have a life. Get your own."

I seemed to like being hit over the head with a log. But oddly, I knew what she meant too. Still I said, No, really, what do you dream? Tell me something.

She sat down and got serious and said, "I'll tell you this one thing. I saw Mohinono and his mate together in a dream. They're twins, the same mind and spirit, except Mohinono is male only inside and his mate is female only inside. They are unlike us and other people who are both male and female inside. Why they split, I don't know. They were happy, though. That was it."

I asked her, When did you see this? Why didn't you tell me?

"Oh, I don't know," she said. "Better not to bother you with things that take you to the past."

Well, but that was helpful. I like to know he's happy and with his mate. Twins, you say. Interesting. I wonder, were they to be born together to us as twins or as a single being? Something happened?

"I don't know," she said. "Now don't pester me anymore. That's all I know."

So you do dream, I said. Good!

Her dream of 628 B.C. spans the time beyond 1994 A.D. when these two began helping this book to be written. And these two helping this book to be written are our twins. Now, you explain that. Probably you'll forget it was even said because it will not make sense to you or your linear thinking about time. Because you see a straight line between then and now, you miss the fact that I'm telling you this story outside time and space. I'm not here with you in flesh and my twins are. Only one was there in the flesh with us then, but the dream was present. Even the great-great-grandmother's prophecy was first given well before our time in the flesh. So then was not now, and now was not then. But the dream persists. So intent drives the dream and the flesh. Yes?

You may disregard the dream as fantasy. You may even disregard me, the storyteller. You may even disregard Barbara and John putting this story to paper, which could never be remembered without me. You might even assume they are making the whole thing up. Okay fine. But I'll continue loving them all the same, if it's all the same to you.

Later that year, Shuhinono and I decided to give the unborn female twin a name. It was funny how that was done. We were fixing the hides that covered our lodge, and I poked her with a bone awl, right in the soft parts. She reeled and swung at me hard from the shock of it, and I lunged back, laughing. I said, Shuhinono, you are the largest person I've ever met.

She said, "You noticed!" And she wasn't fat. That wasn't what I meant. She was becoming so expanded in her mind that I couldn't even touch her with my understanding sometimes. Once in awhile, I would bump into her mind, and I would notice her flying with the hawks that were catching game on the ground. Her flights of vision were not daydreams, I'm telling you. This is not imagination, now. She *joined* those creatures, their *consciousness.* I think she started with the bugs, the flying and hopping ones.

She said to me then, "It worries me some, how big creation is. I don't know if I can stand too much more, but I want to know it all... all of it, everything. The Mother comes to me and shows me things, takes me places, helps me join the difficult things to join, shows me the north and south and east and west of it, the above, and the below, and even my own within. Sometimes, I think I will burst."

You know, I saw then that pregnancy is a kind of bursting. Something grows until it pops out, just like my poking her in the rump with the awl made things burst out. But I'll tell you, it was enlightening to see her that way... very human and very expanded at the same time.

Well, it's a good thing we got together. Two crazy people tolerate each other better than one crazy person and one sane one. Nowadays, two sane people would drive each other totally insane, though. They're trying too hard to be sane in a perplexing world. I see most everyone trying to keep things simple... keep the shutters on the windows, so to speak. But you can tell, something slips in. They won't speak about it much, but you can see it in their eyes. It's hard to be alone in an expanded universe without something of it slipping in. Just the stars give me a jolt. So, I think we're not alone.

Shuhinono and I are just more obvious. I'm still that same child in ceremony, trying to answer that old person's questions and only coming out with, I don't know, and embarrassing myself. I'm still that child, an ancient child. Shuhinono is more like an ancient Mother. She never played like children played, even when I played. She saw deeper into things. I think her feet were below the ground long before mine.

Now, I warn you, readers, from here on you might not like what you hear all times. So if you're squeamish or if you don't like your ideas challenged, I suggest you go read someone else. From here on, our lives become very complex and interwoven with many events. It's as if the observer got thrown into the game. Yes? What I will endeavor to do is to give you tips to shorten your journey, to ease your discomfort and give you encouragement, for you're about to embark on the hardest journey of your life. Tomorrow, I will tell you why.

Chapter 6
The Weaving of Mind

I know that was a very dramatic ending last night, but "why" is really very easy to explain. **You cannot remain asleep within love forever.** It is fear of the unknown that keeps you asleep. Trusting in events in the world and in sleepy people is not a good idea. This world was meant to challenge us and to relax us beyond our deepest concerns. For truly, the agreed upon events in our lives to help awaken us cannot be slowed by our resistance, defiance or torpor. These events will occur, no matter how hard we try to keep them away, and it is up to us to catch up after they have passed.

I see now that what a shaman does is enter those spaces willingly, before the events. The best of the shamen have already endured their own physical death in vision, and some have even returned to body after an actual death experience. That makes them more peaceful and clearer when someone comes to them for help and brings their terror.

Now, I'm sure modern medicine has many remedies for fear and sickness, just as we had many remedies. But I'll say this. For a mind in pain and conflict that witnesses strange visions and has no support in the world, sedation only makes it worse. You say, well, maybe worse is a remedy too. Sure, worse works. But it is not very compassionate or understanding.

So if you want to be a healer or a shaman, there is one funda-mental understanding that you must grasp. Because what a healer does often looks crazy to a mind stuck in perception, it is very important that everyone in your tribe is well aware of the fact that you're "crazy," and that you are willing to do anything in love to help them. Or surely, in your society where you judge everyone and everything all the time, it is better to have compassion and proceed slowly, for I know you don't live in tribal families anymore, and love's true intent is not always understood. You don't even live with your own families anymore. None of you know each other at all anymore. Your sicknesses aren't even recognized as a malady of your spirit anymore. And it is easy to recognize that you do not even know the Creator's true intent of love for you... any-more.

So why this will be the hardest journey of your life is simply this. You are unprepared. You believe your fears and you spend your entire existence defending yourself, pretending you already know, trying to prove your perceptions are right.

We had a few pretenders in our camp too, but they seemed to work these things out much quicker than in your times, today. You call your corrective measures "tough love." We called them "obvi-ous necessity." That is, make too many people angry and you will have no place to sleep, and you'll be eating food you catch and cook yourself, and you'll become more like a wild dog than a hu-man. In your cities, because of fear and separation among you, your uncorrected are wild dogs you keep at bay. It is you as well as them who go uncorrected. Yes?

Well, in our camp, it doesn't get that far because, you see, we start very young. At three, when words are formed in the mind of young ones, we put ideas in to help them. Above all, they are loved. Just below that all consuming love for the young ones is the desire for them to grow and be independent in their physical needs. So we tell 'em, "You pee in the lodge one more time and you're outa' here." And believe me, indian boys spent lots of nights out-side, especially in the spring and fall... spring because you want them to connect to the Mother, and fall because you want to warn them about winter. It is not a good time to wait 'til winter to learn discipline. Indian girls don't pee, of course. Just joking. Truth is, they learn where not to, much quicker than the boys.

So when were you thrown out of the house last? What hard-ships do you endure? Carrying a load of laundry? Changing a tire? Washing a floor? Good thing about dirt floors. Don't need washing.

Smells? Now, there's another one. Sure, everybody gets a chance to smell. Some smell pretty good–others, pretty bad. But I don't know anyone in our tribe that has a job to keep everything clean and smelling good. Have you ever smelled a buffalo? It doesn't smell good. The only thing we truly do wash hard is a new hide.

Do you get upset when your house is dirty? Do you bitch when you have to take the garbage out or change a tire? Your many conveniences make your mind unruly and undisciplined. Try doing without those conveniences. Will you still be grumpy?

I think lack of mental discipline is the cause of grumpiness, not old age. It looks like impatience, yes? My father was never grumpy. He liked to dance and laugh. But my uncles who were working to be shamen were very grumpy people. No tolerance for questions. You know, I don't think they really knew anything because they never shared anything. Must be they haven't learned anything. What do you think? Shuhinono shares her whole being all the time. The only time I don't notice it is when I'm stuck in my own thinking. But she has her ways to pull me out of it... and I still miss the little guy.

I spent two years with the old ones, and for all the doors and windows they opened in my mind, I still feel in the dark, not because their thoughts are dark or because the underworld is dark, but because every idea brings so many thoughts and questions.

You know how you make baskets? You start with a little knob of grass, and you work your way out in a sunwise circle, putting in new grasses as you go, wrapping and wrapping and wrapping. I think I'm making a basket in my mind. Maybe, when I'm done, it will actually hold something. For now, it seems like a great sieve, and whatever I put in seems to drain away and disappear. You try it. Hold onto one thought all day long. These snippets of all my thoughts and those that follow here are the wrapping grasses of a basket weave. Be patient and you will see what the basket will hold.

A Course in Miracles teaches you that this discipline of holding one thought all day is difficult... takes practice. It's a wonderful book. The ideas are helpful because they stimulate the part of your mind that is concerned with reality. Reality is not the private mind that you made up which frightens you in your dreams. Reality is the One Mind that belongs to all living things, equally.

In our tribe, artists were very important people because they could give substance to a person's visions. And this substance was an anchor point from which to grow beyond one's small mind to a larger mind. Without the artists' pictures to remind us of these visions, we forget too easily. Our mind slips into meaning-lessness, and we forget everything is alive and has a voice and is here to help us.

Now, when we're two days away on a hunt and our companions die of cold or injury, and we have nothing to eat and must melt snow for moisture, returning to camp is not our first goal. For a modern person, the goal would be getting home, going somewhere safe, getting warm. But you forgot your true goal. Why did you go out in the first place? In our time, the hunter never forgets his goal is to feed his people. It's an honor thing to stay out, even if we die trying to get game for our people. Now, that's love. Besides, Creator seems to like us to put something at stake. With you, hey, store will be open tomorrow, so what's the big deal?

In European past, you speak of martyrs for a cause. I think love is the only cause there is. So how big do you love? Are you tested? That last hunter standing in the cold prays not to get home but to find game for his people. He tries to stay warm, not to save his life but to get meat for his people, so they will not starve to death... the women and children, especially, and the elders.

So I ask you, what are the priorities in your life? What do you put at stake each day? Do you even know what true stress is until you put something at stake... like your life? In your modern day, hunting for food causes you no stress. What stresses you, you think, is living with so many different people spread all over, all with different views and values. So war is your stress, not food.

We were not a warring people, it was true. We would rather move than fight. But what we would not tolerate was the stealing of our women and children for slaves. And for this, all of our wariness, all of our cunningness, all of our deepest and worst kind of thinking came out. But we would get our women and children back, even if they were dead, even if it killed us. So, even peaceful people set limits on what they will tolerate.

Family was what we valued, not war. And of these warring tribes that stole women, our old ones said they were doomed anyway because any people that did not have the voluntary agreement of their women would perish. Bad feelings would kill them.

To us, it was cowardly to go into another tribe's camp without an invitation. Arrogance is a bit like war, isn't it? Does it take courage to make war, or does it take courage to keep peace? If we wanted to parlay with another tribe, we would go near the perimeter of their camp and sit with our bows in the air and our arrows on the ground. Sometimes we would sit for days until someone would come. And when they came, they always brought food and

47

water and invited us into their camp, even if they were the bitterest of enemies, because it took courage to walk to their camp and wait defenselessly. These were tests. Each time we put our life at stake, we achieved our goal, and peace was made and trade begun, especially with medicines, for everyone loved their people and wanted to end their sicknesses and sufferings.

But I tell you, a modern person creates suffering wherever he goes because he has not put his life at stake nor found meaning in anything. What he values is meaningless. I wish to help you with this meaning in your lives because I do not like to see my relatives suffer needlessly. So as hard as this journey may seem to you, it is truly the only worthwhile journey you will ever make.

I will begin with the end of the story, then perhaps work you back to the beginning, so you will understand consciousness knows not of time. Because you cannot see my face, you are not distracted from my words, I hope. Because you cannot see John and Barbara and question them about their beliefs, you will have to read this story and take what you take and leave what you leave. But what about the truth? Because I know my mind, I know yours is tricky. I know you may leave behind what is most important and take the odd, strange things to play with in your mind... to try to justify or describe or define. But what about the truth?

Try and determine truth by yourself? Well, you can see the folly of that, can't you? Did you make truth because you spoke something that you believed? And those who speak freely about what they experience, like me, does that make our words only beliefs and not the truth? The strident voices who preach their philosophies loudly to anyone who listens on any street corner, I think they're trying to convince themselves, because they sure get worked up. Maybe safety to them is being a leader. But, to me, anyone who wishes to lead should never be safe. We died to save our people, and we were not professed leaders, nor did we ever stand on any soap box.

These stories I tell, though changed for the modern ear and the English language, are handed down to you to help you decide where truth lies. Truth lies? English is very interesting. It just said truth lies, at the same time it's trying to tell you it's right here in front of you... lying right here in front of you, truth is. There it goes again. Truth lies? Doesn't truth tell the truth? No wonder you're confused. Your language says truth lies. Interesting.

Now, I don't know if you ever thought about this, but I wish you would sit down right now with a pencil and paper, and write down as many things as you absolutely, without a doubt, can get agreement on with anyone that is the truth about anything, any-where, anytime. If you get *one,* you're doing well. I think that one would be love. What do you think? Problem is, define love. Prob-ably won't get much agreement on that either.

Wonder what it is about love that is indefinable, indescribable and all encompassing? Perhaps it is the fact that it is all encom-passing that we use up all our words in the meager effort to recre-ate it. Surely, love goes well beyond words. Yes? I will not at-tempt, therefore, to recreate love in English. I will do my best, however, to return to the events in which love was present and speak from there within my experience, within love.

The older I get, the more I understand how little risk there is in being inside love. The risk anyone takes is being on the outside. Like fiery young warriors, perhaps you like entertainment and feel love is boring and is for women and children. Well, perhaps those young warriors just miss the carefreeness of their own childhood and are trying to force their way into adulthood. It matters not but that all these people on the outside of love will eventually become tired of war and will see through their own thinking and return to love again... if they live long enough and the world does not col-lapse from the burden of their errors.

So tell me, can you love someone you haven't met yet? I know I loved the twin mate of my son before we ever met. And I know I told you before that Barbara and John are the twins, but I never told you quite how the daughter we had not yet held got her name.

When I poked Shuhinono with the awl in the soft parts and saw that she was very large, expanded in mind, more like the Eternal Mother, I failed to tell you that at that point, we both saw the daughter's face. The odd thing was, Shuhinono saw her as the daughter's own face, and I saw her as Shuhinono's face, but the voice was truly of the daughter's own self.

Days later, this vision would not leave our mind. When we closed our eyes, it was there, the face of Shuhinono's and the daughter's voice, her own. We couldn't tell what the voice was saying, but the tone and inflection were clear. Perhaps it was singing. With every living thing that I saw or felt, she was heard.

Now, many civilizations have their theories about what chil-dren are. The typical idea that runs throughout almost every cul-ture, in some form or another, is that the son is the creation of the father, the daughter is the creation of the mother, and that children are the extension of the parents into the future.

Well, I say this. You don't need bodies for that. Love does that anyway. My father is here in my mind, while he is not here for my hands to touch. Mohinono is here too, but I do not see him as a child anymore. I see him as the grown son, like he was shown to me by Spirit on top of Great Mountain.

This daughter we have not touched was named after Shuhinono because, like the mother she was not born to, she seemed to want it all, to be connected to everything in love, to have perfect relationship with the world and all the creatures and all the life forms. And, like her mother, this child understood about the fire within and what it was for. Shuhinono gave this unborn daughter her name, so that she would not feel hemmed in by the world.

This young daughter was bound to us in a sense because, if an image of a person is in your mind, to some degree they must abide by the laws of the earth. And yet, Shuhinono set her free again with her name. In your language, Shuhinono means, "The love that binds all, one, everything." It was the openness, the wide prairie openness of her mother's name that pointed the young daughter's mind and heart toward this freedom of truth. This is the legacy Shuhinono passed to her.

The open heart is willingness. The heart cannot open unless the mind is fluid and willing to change and learn. A closed mind will surely close the heart. It is easy to stand in the prairie and see the coming storms, the lightning kissing the earth, and not feel defensive.

In your towns, the straight-up walls are a defense, and they make everyone feel defensive. Square things are prisons. So if you want to relax, get on your roof, breathe deep, let go of your defenses. Maybe, finally, being on top will help. There, perhaps, you will learn what's true. Ask. Receive.

I thought about wanting to see the twins together in the flesh, just one time. But I knew Spirit's laws regarding flesh were very strict. So I asked an old one how this could be done or if it should be done at all. It took three days for her to invite me back for an answer. I figured it would be a tough one. You see, I already know you can call the dead back to life, if only for an instant, because it is an illusion that life is only in bodies. But I think it is an imposition too, calling the dead back. What do you think? What would we learn? Is love not enough?

When I sat in the lodge with the old ones, they were in counsel. Usually, only one would be with me in my questioning. But they were seven, sitting around a small fire. Again, acrid smoke in the air made me close my eyes. I think they do that on purpose, so you don't waste your thinking on your eyes. Again, I do not speak, for I know they know the question already. And I certainly, by now,

50

know they are not stupid or forgetful. Their whole lives taught consciousness. It is I who am asking for help, and I say so in my mind and in my heart, silently.

I know they hear me because two of them begin to look for something, act busy, even seem a little irritated. I'm not so young now to think that everything is my fault, so when they find what they're looking for, they open a bag and drop more acrid-making smoke stuff on the fire. It is some kind of root, I see. It could be from a pepper tree, the way it feels to my eyes.

Quickly, my mentor asked, "Why exactly do you want this thing you ask for? It is not good to disturb those in other worlds. Crossing worlds is tricky, at best."

In my mind I said, I don't know. Then, in my heart I said, I don't want to bother them.

She said, "I see you are confused, but you must decide what you are before we can help you. Does your mind run your heart, or does your heart run your mind? You tell me."

I see what you're saying, I said. I'm divided on this. I'm split. And because I am not seeing my True Self, I come to you to answer the question.

"Well, I would not answer it for you until you decide who you are."

Now? I asked.

"Yes. I think it is better not to put this thing off, for you can sicken and die with this conflict."

Well, in that thirty minutes, sitting there in silence, I went through every scenario I have ever imagined–what if, but why. And still, at the bottom of all that thinking was the feeling that I didn't want to disturb them or cause them difficulties.

I said to the old woman, My heart has won over my thinking. My thinking showed me nothing but problems. My heart gave me solutions. So I'll just love them from here and ask no more.

The old woman said, "Good. This agreement you made with Creator regarding your son Mohinono and his agreement with his mate will go on for centuries before it is completed. They are to resolve their split between male and female in a world yet to come, far more lost than we. We have seen this world of pale people, colorless. We have seen these pale people come to this land, and love is dead in many of their hearts, even for their own kind. They see no larger family, and they use everything until it is gone. They are like the grasshoppers that came two years ago in a big, black cloud and ate all the grasses. Not one living thing was left behind. Everything fled, except us. We sat and watched, absolutely amazed, and wondered what we had done wrong to deserve this treatment. The answer we got then from Spirit was this.

"'Prepare yourselves for this great hardship to come and be strong in Spirit or you will perish.'"

The old woman continued, "We don't know when this world of pale people is to be exactly, because when you pass through the barrier of time it is hard to tell the future exactly to the moment. But Spirit left us this one mechanism for knowing. They told us this:

"'You will feel it when it comes, and those of you most sensitive will feel it first.'

"So we will watch the birds and the rabbits," the old woman continued. "They always know when something big is going to happen. The birds flutter everywhere, nervously. Rabbits run zigzag and forget where their hole is, then they stop and listen. I think they all hear what we hear, but better."

Do you know more, I asked the old ones, or is it foolish of me to ask anymore?

"We understand your desire to know more, so I will tell you this one thing. The twins will talk to you directly, sometime. You will be able to hear each other clearly. You will have a relationship, but it does cross great spans of time."

Ah, that is good. Thank you. To lose one child at three years was bad enough, but to lose two, never having seen one, was a bit too much, I think. So I will save my fatherly pride for a later date when we can all talk to each other.

Then I bid them farewell, the elders and the twins, and crawled out of the lodge on hands and knees. I bent down and kissed the earth, and I thanked everything that was alive. I thanked the dead too because, still, they are alive.

Shuhinono was actually excited, I think, when I told her what the old ones had to say about the twins. Well, she smiled anyway. I could tell she was pleased, but she said nothing. We had been together nearly four years in this same lodge. And, by now, you'd think I would know if her silence was indifference, and I do. She just looks deeper and deeper. She knows that to say anything prematurely is a waste of time.

Nearly three weeks later, I guess she worked it all through because she said, "I think we will hear from these two later, but I'll not trouble about it anymore. Are we going to have another baby?" she asked. "I hardly got to know the last one."

You know, that one stumped me. Here we are preparing ourselves for a future of hard times and thinking of having a baby. I don't know, I said.

"Well, I don't know about you," Shuhinono said, "but I can learn with a baby on my hip."

By the way, I said, where do you go to learn? Do you see anyone, the old ones?

"No," she said. "Since the top of Great Mountain, it seems I have a constant companion, over here on the right side of my mind. It's not that it's a personality, as much as it is a preview. I can't hear any words, but I do see pictures. I don't know anyone in camp that can truly help me because I don't know what it is that this Guide is doing for me."

Why don't you ask the old ones? Perhaps they know.

"What good would it do to hear what others think about something that concerns only me? I think it more important that I find out what is within me, myself. And then, I really will know."

In my case, I said, they showed me many things I was not aware that existed. I didn't even have the questions when I first began talking with them. I guess they were my guides.

"Well, I think you need an external teacher until you have an internal one," she said.

Humm, I wonder if I ever will.

"Oh, I think you do already, but because you are a man you need stronger clues and louder notes to get your attention. As a man, you push your energy higher up, feeling more responsible for everything, while I as a woman walk deeper in the earth and claim responsibility for nothing but my own thoughts."

That's odd. I thought you cared for the camp, I said.

"Oh, I care. But I can do nothing for them except learn within myself first. When I enter this learning place within myself, I sink and rise at the same time, and there's a pop in my ears and my eyes go blank for a second. Then I see visions. Here in this camp, in our world, there's always one thing pulling against another or one thing pushing against another. But within me, there are no opposites anymore. There is no push or pull."

Well, I said, I don't think I've ever experienced that exactly. But in spite of a few camp conflicts, I think I'm happy. I know I'm not sad.

Now, my father, he was happy. When he danced, everyone got happy. I've never tried to dance. Perhaps I should go to a big dance and see how happy I am. I think I'm far too serious, however. My mind is occupied with large questions, with no answers in sight.

"Why do you want to remain here?" Shuhinono asked. "Why not strike out on our own?"

Sure. And have so many babies, we have a new tribe to look after. The pride tribe, yes?

"Oh, you're being silly now. Go get into trouble somewhere else."

Weeks went by with normal activity. Even in the busiest of times, we weren't that busy, especially in spring and summer. We got pretty darn lazy and it felt good. I think our life was really quite perfect, even with the daily quarrels of husbands and wives and daughters and sons. Even those fights didn't disturb the peace we felt as a whole.

The only times I ever got worried was when there was a great sickness passing through the people. I guess you call it flu, but to us any loss of body heat was cause for great concern. I'd rather see children sweat than go dry and clammy and cold. Somehow, hotter is better and colder is deader. That worries us some. So there is a flurry of activity in camp to gather herbs and try this or that, to talk to the old ones to see if there's some spiritual reason why a child is sick, and why the sickness is spreading throughout the community.

Of greatest interest to me was when the old ones said, "We have to go talk to Spirit to find out what the sickness in this one is all about. It is not obvious." And they would retire for days in that lodge. They wouldn't eat and they wouldn't drink. Sometimes they went five days. For an old one, that's dangerous. You stop salivating. You stop peeing. Your bones get stiff. Your fingers stop working. Sometimes the old ones go blind, temporarily. Sometimes they make a great deal of noise. They certainly are wailing and talking to something. Sometimes there are songs.

I'll tell you this. It looks harder to get information out of Spirit than it is for me to think about going back to the top of Great Mountain. But maybe they are one and the same. The old ones just concentrated their suffering in four or five days instead of a year. And maybe they did go back to that mountain each time they talked to Spirit.

Now, when you get sick, what do you do? I'll bet you ask yourself why, decide you can't figure it out, and certainly don't ask Spirit. You go to the drug store and buy something to cover it all up, so you don't have to deal with it. And mostly, this seems to work because you have medicines that are very powerful... antibiotics. Our antibiotics came from bee pollen and a few other herbs. But mostly, pushing something out that is foreign requires an act of will. And we know that children do not have much will yet, so that is why we are afraid for them.

Now, I think, maybe you must be children too, because the comforts that you have gathered around you have made you weak, and you depend upon your antibiotics more than on Spirit. So in your life, taking medicine and pushing ahead to gain greater comfort becomes your idea of wellness... "getting on with it," you say. Why not go to the top of your mountain and ask Spirit about your sickness? It will save you lots of time. But then, I guess asking Spirit is an act of will too. And not everyone in our tribe makes that effort either.

Well, for me it was clear. I had an easy life. I knew I wanted to learn these things. It amazes me that Shuhinono makes no apparent effort directly and gets everything anyway, while I make obvious effort in a hundred directions and go very quickly... nowhere. But I think I would not trade my experiences, nor would I expect you to become me in your experiences. My life has been enriched by the many voices that try to help me in my search. They are included inside me.

I think you only have your drug store. Am I wrong? The medicine people you seek, do they speak to Spirit and ask what is wrong? Do they ask in each moment how to help each individual? Or do they use science and guess... probabilities? Your medicine people say, "You will probably this or that, will you not? The book says so. Since it was this way yesterday, it will probably be this way today." Now, that's stuck to reliving the past!

If you take anything with you out of this, remember this one thing. **You get what you want.** Right here, my daughter expects that you will confuse this point because it is human nature to ask for the impossible or the improbable or the generally just no damn good for you. So I'll try to put some words in between the statement and your understanding of it.

First of all, the purpose in coming to the planet is for you to awaken to the truth of what you are. Second, when you awaken to this truth, you are to accomplish something you agreed to before you came. To that end, Creator gives you what you want because you can only have what God wills for you anyway. In so far as you ask for what is good for you, you get it. In so far as you ask for what is not good for you, if Spirit can turn what is bad for you into a good lesson, you get it anyway. So be careful what you ask for. You will get it. God loves you and gives to you because you ask.

So ask yourself, what is it that I truly want? How do I want my life to be? What do I love? And when will I stop taking and start giving? This is your journey, dear ones. This is everyone's journey. But most will not look deep enough to see. They are asleep, trying

to awaken. Perhaps most would rather ask for material possessions than spiritual wealth.

Shuhinono and I will strike out soon, I think. Her idea was not
such a bad one. I think I am stuck here asking the old ones for
answers, instead of living within my own. I think the old ones
have become convenient. Besides, I have itchy feet. Walking helps.
I'm not sure I want another baby, though. I think I'm getting too
old. I must be eighteen now. But we don't count time the way you
do, so it's hard to know.

Well, while we're talking about time, I'll slip another good one
in on you and see how your mind deals with this. When I was very
small, I remember a funny ceremony that we went to, my father
and I. There was dancing and singing and a lot of fun-making.
And at the very end of it, everyone brought out huge baskets with
grains and roots and dried things in them... all kinds of things.
They put it all in a big circle around this fire. An old one, who is
now long gone, spoke very quietly. In this large crowd, I had to
run to the front and push through all those legs to get to where I
could hear something. Sitting in front of all the people, looking at
this old person, I heard this:

"This is the time we call harvest. We repeat this yearly all our
lives, and we give thanks each time we harvest food to fill our
bellies. We grow new souls and send them forward as we weaken
and die here. This way, time is not an end but a beginning to be
continually renewed. But what does Creator harvest from this? I
ask you to think about that. I ask you to discuss it among yourselves and decide. Next harvest, I will ask you again what it is
that Creator harvests from us. What do the rabbits get for their
being eaten by the coyote and by us? What does the grain get
when it gives its life to us? What does the air get that we breathe
in and out? Where does the water go when it passes through us
and changes color? I ask you to use your minds, together, to answer this question. What do you get from all this taking, and what
do you give back to Creator? Are you inconvenienced or are you
truly grateful and understand? I think that without this understanding, there is no tribe or community. And if we forget this, we
will perish with meaningless lives, deposited along the prairie in
holes. You have one year. Don't be tardy."

You know, everybody walked away, and they were laughing
and chattering. "Oh, that foolish old man. What does he know?"
But I sat there and sat there and sat there. My mother had to
come get me. I really wanted to know the answers. I thought
those were good questions. You know, I thank my mother a hun-

dredfold, for she never said, oh, don't be stupid. You'll never figure it out. She never said that. She said, "Well, maybe you will. You seem to want to badly enough."

As I grew older, I noticed the old ones were the only ones that could see through the illusion of time. They made it look a little scary, however, a little dramatic, with fasts and hollering and singing and stinky smoke and all kinds of things. But that just fascinated me all the more. I thought it was all those things they did that made it happen... seeing through time. But I soon realized that their minds were going somewhere, traveling on the *intent* they had within those songs and that chanting and that smoke. I noticed what they had, more than the average person, was *tenacity*. When they made a decision to do something, they didn't stop until it was done, and they risked everything to do it. They gave it all.

Most people will get hungry or thirsty or sleepy. It was the stickiness of time in the daily life, seeing time as only in the present and bound to the past, which made the people forget their long-term goals. And only when the water was low or the meat was gone or the field mice had stolen all the last berries or grain would they even think about hunting, because it took effort and there was a risk. But because we were a community, there was always someone to stand forward and say, "I'll do it," especially among the young men and boys, for they were looking for mates... some young girls to impress, perhaps.

This year, I saw Shuhinono look through time. She called her parents to her who were long dead. And I even saw them, just for an instant. What I question, she *does*. I question so much. I go back and forth to the old ones and ask them if this is the right thing to do, and this and that and the other, while she's in there doing it. And I noticed the heavens didn't crack open and spill things out because she put a hole in time.

So, I guess it's okay sometimes... calling the dead back. You see, creation is so much bigger than what your eyes or even your mind can encompass, for our individual minds are small. It takes the minds of seven old ones sitting in council doing their work, just to keep daily life here together and to keep us all from making too many mistakes. A community that doesn't care what it does to anyone or anything will soon perish of its own disharmony.

I remember a man walking across the prairie, approaching the camp, just recently. I couldn't see his face, but I could *feel* him. I think he was the craziest person I have ever bumped into with my mind. It was like six people inside, arguing, all with different ways of looking at it. He was split in so many directions. Who knows which one was real? He was like a maelstrom, kicking dust as he went. Now, we all knew he was crazy, and simple beans would not satisfy him. This man's hunger was for something else.

So there was a rush to the old ones' camp. And they said, "Oh yes, we saw him coming yesterday. Give him what he wants. Treat him well. Do not let him harm anyone or take too much, but do not hurt him. And let him go where he wills."

I asked from the back, Is there any way we can help him?

An old woman turned, looked to the ground and shook her head. "No, I don't think so. This one has taken on a big journey for many people. There are two kinds of sickness of the human spirit. One is because you don't want to enter the spiritual realm and would do anything other than transform. The other is a person who comes here to absorb the world's difficulties. They get lost in all the peoples' lives. This we do not understand completely, but we do honor their attempt. So we will take care of this one who passes our way. Perhaps he will take some of our troubles with him. Don't stare! Study from a distance but, trust me, you do not want to get in this one's face!"

So everyone did what was asked. It was amazing. It was like everyone knew he was coming and here he came. And everybody did what they were supposed to do and it was done, and he was gone and that's that.

But Shuhinono saw something deeper. She saw him suck the anger out of a child. Standing twenty feet away, he drew in a breath that sounded like water going over a waterfall. And out it came. And the little one fell, sitting on the ground, and started crying. And off he goes, muttering and kicking the dust... everyone handing him something as he went. Some things he'd toss in the air. Some things he'd stuff away in his shirt.

Shuhinono told me what she'd seen a week after he left. She was still trying to figure it out, I think. But she saw his intent was to help. She saw his mind was not with us here but somewhere high above us... talking to Spirit, I suppose. That little child, who had been a total misery to her parents, changed that day completely. She was sweet and was kind and was not selfish anymore.

The child's mother asked the little one what happened, as she knew there was a connection between that man and her child. But she didn't *see* what happened, like Shuhinono did. The child said to her mother, "I don't know what happened. He took something awful from me. It's gone now. I'm sorry."

The good thing about this incident is that we did not judge this man or dishonor him before he arrived at our camp. We had guidance, so we could see his role and allow him to do it. Now what could be more important than that?

The truth is, none of us had anywhere to hide anyway, so we had to deal with these things. You have doors on your houses where you hide from madness, even your own. I'm not sure whether you're the prisoner or the guard, but you seem to feel safe in them houses. But all the madnesses that we come here with have a solution, if we allow one to come... if we ask. Your doors, in this case, are part of sickness. Hide something and it will fester and grow. Speak your worst fears and allow the light to come into that darkness, behind your doors. Not speaking allows the darkness to deepen and take on form.

So, back to time. I was later told by one of the old ones that this strange fellow who came to our camp didn't live in our time, but that he had taken on this job. I asked this old one, Who gives these jobs? They're very strange.

He said, "I don't know, but I do know it's by agreement."

So what time was he from? I asked.

"Hard to say. The past was harder and we knew less, but the future is more complex and much more stressful. Perhaps this one knew both the past and the future. My grandfather called those who come in that way "Fixers" or "Adjusters" because that's what it looks like they do. I remember asking him if he ever talked to one of those "Adjusters." And my grandfather said, 'Can't talk to them. Not a good idea. Their mind is not in the present, except for one flash, and it is done and they are gone. Usually, anyone who tries to stop or influence that one in any way will soon perish of madness. The average human can't stand that much time inside a small brain.'"

So I recommend this for all you seekers who want to know what the truth is, the Big Truth, all of it. Take it a little at a time. Judge nothing and do not ask for more than your mind can expand to in a given lifetime. Being in a hurry and wanting to influence things from where your little speck of a perspective is, is not a good idea.

I don't mean to discourage you or frighten you, because those who will push forward will do so anyway. They will be frightened, but they will get over it. And they will expand and grow and adapt. That is their nature. That is their desire. That is their intent. Most people just want to be happy, safe, comfortable, and warm. And within all that, they want love, to have it and to give it, to share it, some equally, some not, but that is the game. But seekers want to see how big love is, where it came from, what it wants, and where it's going.

That next year, after many months of genuine debate amongst family members and especially between Shuhinono and me, we decided to set out on a journey. We didn't know why exactly. We had a thousand reasons. The truth is, none of them fit perfectly. One day we looked at each other and said simultaneously, "It's time to go." Now, you tell me why it happened like that.

When the same two people have the same single thought and act, it must be true, yes? Now, you might think, when two people get up from the table and go to the bathroom at the same time, that's truth. But there's not really much at stake, waiting two more minutes for someone else to pee first.

I think toilets are a good idea, though. Don't get me wrong. But I also think, modern people stopped accepting their humanness when they stopped peeing in front of each other. The women of our tribe just squatted and never pulled their dress above their hips. That wasn't necessary. But the act of peeing was enough for us to realize that we were the same.

When two minds join, there is agreement. There can even be harmony around them. But unless they are joined with the many, there will not be love, except perhaps in a very small, personal sense. Two joined minds don't necessarily mean truth or love or even grace.

You see, two sick people can go rob a store and hurt someone, in complete agreement. But I don't think what they decided was truth, unless they choose to learn love, regardless of their behavior. On the other hand, if two people's intent is to be helpful and to learn to love those around them, then what they decide together with Spirit will most likely be helpful.

Deciding to buy a house here or a car there, or to eat here or there, or to work this place or that... two people may decide it, but it usually has nothing to do with love or helpfulness. Personal desires belong to the body life and have nothing to do with Spirit. In fact, two people cannot truly join in their minds about anything except love. It's the only thing they share totally in common, equally. The rest is distractions, avoidance, and unwillingness to learn. And a person's growth is truly stunted, I see, if they do not partake fully of their own journey.

So what is this mind-joining or "telepathy," as my daughter calls it? Well, it depends, I say. The only thing that moves through time, truly, is energy. So I think it is with telepathy. What is communicated depends on the energy behind it, the thoughts behind it. And it is either a deterrent or an attractant. Devious people, I see, put up many deterrents. I think they do not want to be seen inside for what they decided they were. So, deterrents are fear.

Deterrents can be of two types: to keep out noise and psychic investigations or to stop joining from happening at all.

So it is with attractants. The mind can attract with truth, or it can delay joining by using the body as bait. You see, the only thing that truly joins is a bodiless love. Although minds can appear to join at a bodily level, that joining is not true joining because it does not include Spirit.

All the discussions and conversations a person has with another are designed to get to this point of joining, so that they won't need all of those words anymore. They just *know* what each other is thinking. The old ones were like that. They hardly spoke to each other, but they acted as if they were one person, one mind.

This chapter, with its many snippets of my thoughts, have told you what is hidden within the art of basket weaving. The wrapping grasses of this basket were about focus, mental discipline, giving substance to a vision, setting a goal, choosing love as the only cause, putting yourself at risk, setting limits of tolerance, letting love determine value, being courageous, and allowing true meaning to emerge. Love is the beginning weave of all baskets, and truth is what is woven by your experiences.

The basket weave of my mind now begins to hold, so my mind is no longer a sieve. Shuhinono, I think, started with knowledge and had to come back to earth some. And this trek, for us, was to be a new opening to greater knowledge yet of what we were and what we were to do here on earth. Camp life got way too easy.

Chapter 7
The Fire Above, The Fire Below

So, in the spring, we left. We chose the spring because the game was plentiful, the water was abundant, there were plenty of roots to pick, and we knew we had to make some distance before winter. To where, we had no idea.

Shuhinono said, "I hear there are more trees to the east where the sun comes up. I'd like to see really large trees sometime. And someone else said that to the east, there is this place where the rock is red, and people dig up this rock to make things. I'd like to see that someday too. Wouldn't you?"

I said, Well, I heard that to the south, somewhere east of Great Mountain, there's a raging river and a huge chasm, and that there are many Spirit Helpers there with lots of answers.

"Who did you hear this thing from?" Shuhinono asked.

I can't remember. Maybe the old ones. No, I don't think so. Maybe my father spoke of it. I can't remember.

"You expect me to go southeast with a guide who can't remember? I have directions. What do you have, lunatic?"

Well, I guess all I have is my willingness.

"That's enough. We can go then, but we're going east first. And if the trees are too short, we'll go see your chasm... if it's there."

For being so sharp, you're very reasonable.

"Well, I just didn't want to die before I got to see the big trees," she said. And we laughed.

Packing doesn't take long in our culture. Just decide how much you can stand carrying around forever, and say "Help yourselves" to everyone else. I think we packed lots of jerky, a little water (you see, water's very heavy, if you haven't noticed), a couple of buckskins, and one robe for night warmth. And, of course, the throwing stick.

By now, some of us have made arrows and bows, but we really haven't learned how to use them yet. The throwing stick was natural. The bow was given to us by another tribe and somehow feels foreign. I think my throwing stick goes farther, and it doesn't break as often as does the sinew we tie our bows with. Besides, I think the bows made from the limbs of the trees around here aren't so tough either.

The first night out, we had a big fright. A comet–I think that's what you call it–struck the earth a long way away, not on our side, but you could see its blue tail streak around the sky. And for days after that, the sky grew darker and darker, becoming redder and redder. It stayed that way for several days. Then, at sunset one night, we noticed the red colors becoming fainter. Each night they became fainter until the red was gone.

We wondered who that was coming from the spiritual fire above, back to the red fire of body so quick like that, for in our eyes the stars are our ancestors. You see, we believed that the spiritual fire that awakens in you when you become a true adult can be seen in the eyes as a blue light and felt in the mind as a lightness.

This blue fire of Spirit that you can sometimes see in the eyes, evolves from the red fire in the below. This is what we thought that comet was... a Spiritual Helper from above, returning to this place backwards for some good reason. That comet struck somewhere in the east, we thought. It took nearly a day to tell that it actually hit. The earth did not shake, so it must not be so huge after all, but it sure was bright. But if you've never seen a comet like Halley's, you wouldn't know my description because, I think, none of you or almost none have ever seen Halley's anyway, especially when it was bigger. The tail was longer and it was brighter.

Well, for us it was quite something, and it occupied our thoughts for many days. It got us talking, Shuhinono and me. Not often, but once in a while one of us would say something about the fire in the sky. We are like that fire, we say, and must all leave these bodies someday. Although most of us can't see Spirit leave the body when someone passes away, we think it is so.

We talked about the way that fire rises from below our hips someplace, and how if we take it inside and live it in the front of our body, there are countless experiences to be had, almost endless in complexity, and how if that fire is allowed to move to the back, with the help of Spirit it will rise up the spine instead. And though the acceleration sometimes makes you feel like you are going mad, you are truly becoming spirit. This forward journey is one of fear, and the rearward journey is one of allowing Spirit to lead you and to release those fears. What we both agreed upon fully was that in this journey, the problem is fear–what to do with it, how to deal with it, how to reduce its effects and pressures, how to release all that energy coming up to your head.

Running was one way we released that energy. And we had some great runners. Not many women were runners, but once in a while there was one or two. But the men seemed to have endless energy to burn, especially after courting or after a big hunt where they scared themselves.

In your culture, many of your young ones release this energy through sex. But in our culture, rules about the fire in the below were clear and obvious. Rules about sex before marriage were very strict, for the old ones saw that mismanagement of this fire at a very young age would very nearly ruin your mind.

Rules concerning sex between parent and child were even more strict. For instance, if a father was discovered using his daughters, he could be banished, left out to starve, and die of loneliness. But first, any father who was having difficulty with his wife or with his daughters was encouraged to live on the side of the camp with the old ones for awhile, and an old one would go counsel the women while the father was getting his treatment.

You call your treatment "reality therapy." We didn't have jails, you see, because we knew the true jail is in your mind. To be more accurate, the true jail is the mind not knowing what it is, stuck within the brain. So the treatment our old ones gave those stuck in deviant thoughts and behaviors was simple: four days fast, one day break with water and berries, and if that wasn't enough... two more days fast, alone, on top of the mountain overlooking camp. This reality check would be imposed on you if necessary.

Our Vision Quests, however, were voluntary things, a way of voluntarily learning that your body was not meant to run your mind. All fasts, imposed or voluntary, slowed the sexual fires and calmed the over-energetic. You see, obsession and addiction were not much of a problem in our time. But we knew that it didn't take more than one or two incidents to unleash an uncontrollable fire, if not dealt with as a spiritual issue.

Most other sexual offenses are dealt with either by fights among the men, humor among the general population, or fights among the women. We have plenty fiery ones stuck in the below. They come in all ages. There are even grandmothers who are still mad at dead husbands for something they did when they were children. What I see, though, is that those who have not made the effort to learn they are spirit are doomed to the lower realms of bothers, worries and concerns, of anger and judgment, of guilt and vengeance, and other generally senseless acts that make your mind useless to you.

And I see the only test of usefulness is, has anything good come of all this? What did you learn? If the older ones still have learned nothing and there was no good come of it for anyone around them, then those old ones, those weak, old ones would go and camp near the strong, old ones. And somehow, those elders would work their love back into that weakened person's life. Somehow, some solution came, and those weak, old ones were stronger and were tolerated better by everyone else.

Deliberate cruelness, however, was dealt with by the deliberate cruel act of expulsion, to show that person that what they did would not be tolerated. Whereas in your modern societies, you put people in jail, feed them better than the general population, keep the heat on to keep them from getting cold, and make sure, by all means, that you're not cruel to them. And you teach them nothing real at all.

Your old way was, offenders were put to work, and if they were not worth what they ate, they were shot. I think you call that the "Protestant work ethic." Nowadays, even our method of expulsion wouldn't work for you because there's no punishment in being banished. You aren't dependent upon nature and family for survival. So you have capital punishment to put you at risk, though your death penalty is rarely imposed. Even when it is, what has the offender learned? What have you taught?

It is appropriate, I think, to give a mistaken one time to learn. However, I'm not sure you know what correction is. In our time, striking out on our own without Spiritual guidance was virtually a death penalty. But as far as I know, no one left because we knew what correction was and how to teach it.

All this training of mind, this discipline, started for us about age three when language began. Silently, you teach from the moment your child is born anyway. But at three, corrections can be made and the old ones knew how. They knew how because they counseled with Spirit. They didn't make something up and try it to see if it worked, then try it on everyone else. They asked what was truly helpful for each person. They spent days going into that person's life and seeing all the facets that led up to the present behavior. Then Spirit gave them the true cause and cure in one simple phrase, and they waited to hear *when* to say it. And then, like little Billy Tippet, they really "fixed his wagon." And generally, his ass rolled around pretty good from then on.

Sometimes they scared the poop right out of kids. No joke! They were good at it. And though it was never our teachers' intention to teach the children to fear, it was their intention to teach about it and have the children learn to master their reaction to it, because on the prairie, you have to learn that your physical mortality is a fact, whether you think so or not. You need to know this quickly. If you are pampered, you are weakened. It is not the laws of nature that rend us asunder. It is the simple fact that we are born stupidly happy and hardly ever observe anything at all. We're too busy.

To nail your shoes to the ground, as you would say, is to stand in one place long enough for all that chatter and noise to stop, so reality can dawn on you of its own. Our Vision Quests were for those who understood this process or were attracted to this process, so they were voluntary. Reality checks as a form of discipline were involuntary. The result was the same.

When I was with the tribe, we didn't expunge anyone that I can remember. But then, I wasn't privy to all the activities of everyone. I do remember two young fellows who got into a fight and one was killed. Usually, fights were supervised and no weapons were allowed. But this time the fight came too soon, and a young one was impaled on a throwing stick. You know, I remember this so well, because what the old ones did was to leave that young person there dead, in the center of the camp, for three days. The parents were not allowed to fetch him and prepare him for burial until those three days were up. I think it drove home to everyone why we don't fight amongst ourselves. You know, having a friend laying in the dust was a hard thing to see. Three days was plenty of time to get the lesson, but the old ones did not want anyone to mistake this teaching.

So we did not war amongst ourselves, for there were only two-hundred of us, ever, at any one time. If there was war among us, maybe there would be one-hundred on each side and half of us would die. What good is that?

We did, however, have many who bid for power, but because we had agreement amongst tribal members that the council was to resolve conflicts, we were able to remain unified as the over-enthusiastic young ones were educated in our way of peace. We also, you see, did not have a chief that ruled by force. Those who led us did so with open hearts and true meaning in their lives, so it was easy to follow. Those who bid for power always called for war on someone, somewhere, but we believed we were the someone, everywhere, so why war on ourselves?

I try and show you that we used sharp words, because I do not want you to think of us as living in a time of Eden or paradise. We were just people doing people kinds of things. We made mistakes. But in our time, surviving without love, even if you thought it fun for a time, was not a sustainable way of life.

We are still walking east, and the days get longer and longer and more humid. There are rainstorms with lots of lightning, but they pass quickly. However, we don't dry, nor do our clothes and robe. And the discomfort we felt, we projected onto each other for a time, until we caught what we were doing. We would start... bitching.

The mosquitoes came in groves, flocks, hoards. And between my wife and I, there came a split, and I saw that I blamed her for the insects and the humidity.

I said, You're the Mother. Fix it.

She said, "You're the man. You take care of it."

What's being a man got to do with it?

"What's being a woman got to do with it?"

And in the insanity of it, we started laughing and saw that we had become very small, very quickly. We sat there laughing, re-membering our childhood where everything was too hot or too cold, too slow or too fast, too big or too little, not enough or too much... bitching, going on forever, it seemed. We laughed and laughed and laughed. And you know, those damn mosquitoes left. Must be they serve a purpose too, maybe an even greater purpose than just to pester us. So we said, "Thank you," and scratched our way on.

You see how easy war is? Just try to be right in spite of all odds, and you'll either be standing there alone, or somebody may split your scalp because you're too stupid to stop fighting. You'll still be standing there wanting to be right... dead right.

The struggle over power between two minds... that's that fire rising in front, trying to be God for a minute, trying to be right without God.

"If only I were king," the song goes. Well, I think there's plenty fantasies going 'round. Good thing God's in charge. Somehow seems more fair than having millions of little gods running around doing stinking things. Maybe it wasn't a good idea you moved your toilets inside. But then, one bad smell deserves another. These stinking ideas can be given up, though in the physical world there will always be opposites to deal with.

So how can you get rid of warring dualities in your own mind? Well, by not living them at all. Why be in opposition to anything, especially insanity, because it will not get well with opposition. Stay in the eye of the hurricane, and you will see the winds of insanity blow fiercely around you. But if you stay in the eye of the calm, there is a chance that the one who is lost will return to the peaceful center again. Remember, love is a magnet. So is love your center or is war?

In our day, we didn't even spank our children, because to hit someone you love didn't make sense, though at the moment you felt you could kill 'em. Take a break. The answer you seek is not in overpowering but is in empowering with love. And don't get so worked up that you have to live out insanity yourself before you see what sanity is.

If you indulge yourself in anger, you only add unhelpful energy to the storm. You will have a longer and more difficult journey struggling to return to love, to the center. And you will confuse all those around you, especially your children. But if you are accepting and see lessons in everything and see helpfulness everywhere, then you can see that those who are insane believe they cannot help it. Then maybe you will remember to ask Spirit what's helpful for everyone. Then maybe the insane will be given what they lack in their own minds. And finally, with their will they will be able to produce the thoughts necessary for peace and harmony within themselves.

Now, I know there are some people who just can't stand peace, but they don't really know what it is. They believe that a lack of strong opinions is to be weak-minded, and that without judgments they have no center from which to intelligently view the world. This creates an illusion of safety, an imaginary anchor to hold onto. They fail to see that in the act of demonstrating their beliefs, true or false, they demonstrate one of the laws of mind. This law says that personal perception is totally fluid and is determined by each person's personal experiences and beliefs, regardless of the Spiritual reality of those beliefs.

So if you want your personal reality to stabilize within Spiritual truth, or another way to say it is, if you are tired of changing lodges and now prefer peace to conflict, then surely you will give up the ideas in your head that make war on your own mind and on your family. Ultimately, this way you can expand your healing to include the whole world.

Those opposites are there in your mind so you can choose what you want, what you prefer. What is hard to get a hold of is how easy it is to slip from sanity into madness, from peace into conflict.

The hardest thing a young person has to learn is to discern what is reality within what is not. Learning discernment needs to start with the fearful dreams you have when you're real little. It starts with the idea of mortality and acceptance of the fact that the body is mortal, and that the body doesn't get to stay with you forever. It's borrowed. All the physical materials come from the Mother, while your genetic traits are borrowed from your two bodily parents. The real you is Spirit, eternal, but only in the Truth.

I never had bad dreams much. I never cared for them. I was always more fascinated with the external world and all its wonderful, magical details. But for others, I see their life is inside. I think inside is bigger than outside. What do you think? My thought, even when I was very little was... If creation is this wonderful outside, there must be some good reason for it to happen at all. But I wasn't to discover inside until Shuhinono and the old ones guided me there.

I now see this woman walking beside me, scratching her bites, is large inside, larger than me because she already knows something of the inside. And what I was awakening to by walking with her was... I, too, could begin to open that inside to the present, to the now, to the here. Each time my mind opened for a fraction of a second, something would slip in and perplex me. Shuhinono would look over at that moment and smile. I noticed there was an uneasy me and a wow-that's-interesting me. It took me a long time to figure out this male thing... being male. Seems to be some kind of obstacle, because women don't have it. At least mine doesn't. And I see myself becoming slightly frightened each time I'm introduced to a bigger inside, like... Uhh, something's-going-to-die-I-know-it-is-I-don't-know-what-it-is-but-I-can-feel-it-dying, kind of feeling.

It was a good thing we had a long walk that summer. I think I needed the time just to relax. Sometimes, walking at seven or eight miles an hour for hours at a time relaxed me. Now, you figure it out. Shuhinono usually had to bring to my attention that we were damn near running, and what for? But I swear, something was chasing me. It wasn't outside. It was inside. Something was trying to catch up to my mind that was trying to go faster, so as not to see it. And I'm pretty sure that when I did sleep, it was out of pure exhaustion. There were no dreams... on purpose.

I think I know why you people have bars and smoke cigarettes and take pain killers and sedatives. You're running from your own mind, like I did. You're too scared to slow down and look inside... going faster and faster, buying more and wasting more.

I'll tell you this. Just brace yourself and get on with it. Stop delaying the inevitable. Face your fears. Do it now. Your delay only wastes your children's inheritance and makes them frightened and weak like you. For if their inheritance is poverty stricken because there is no truth in it, it is because you are stealing from their future now.

If you care for anything at all besides yourself, take a good look. What do you give that's real and true and worthy to be passed on through seven generations? And what is this place for, anyway? And is love enough?

For me, the truth dawned slowly because that's as fast as I could stand it. But everything changed one day when I sat with Shuhinono and stopped being male. I had already known that Shuhinono was both male and female inside. She cared for them equally. She joined them easily... no distinctions or differences. Young or old, it didn't matter.

I said, She's a better man than me. I don't think I knew I was talking the truth, though. But I sit here being female, or rather being male-less, and I see that the forms we come in are obstacles to us, to true peace, to true understanding.

I was always mystified by woman, and in this place in my mind, I now see it was because I saw only differences when I looked at women. I did not see past their physical role unless they were old. And I believed that, somehow, Spirit only came to the old.

All these obstacles I had within me, I now see, melted away like spring snow. It took a little getting used to, but Spirit was kind and kept this state within me for four days. There were times I cried because I saw the injustices that men impose upon their women with their judgments. I think I am woman inside now too, for I feel all their pain and suffering and abuse, and I love them completely.

Shuhinono said to me one afternoon with a heart bigger than the sky, "I love you, Hinono, for what you have been able to open to, and I'm grateful. I don't feel alone anymore. Thank you."

I think we both wept. Or maybe it was raining. I think the whole sky and ground got wet. I think it rained everywhere, all over the earth that day. It sure felt like it. And you know, it was the next day, we began to see tall trees in the distance.

How long has it been since we left? Let's see. Two months, maybe. Maybe a little more. I don't know. I know this thing, though. The humidity continued to get worse, but boy did things grow! We never once lacked something to eat. But remember, we weren't too picky either. I think the worst is still insects. The crunch is terrible. But some grasshoppers get pretty big, and it doesn't take too much to fill you either, I'll tell you that. Look, I'm telling you all the bad things too, but I'll only go so far.

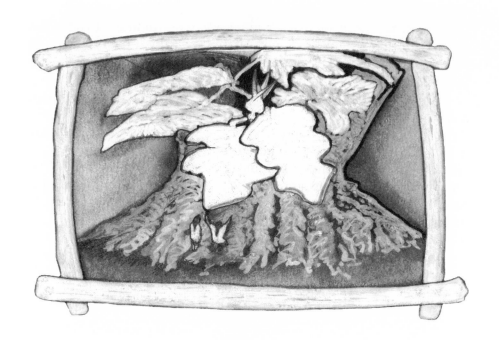

Chapter 8
Taking and Receiving

Our journey continues in wonderment at the new scenery. There is more water, and therefore fish. There is more foliage, and therefore creatures. Because. Because. Because.

Because I've promised you definitions, I urge you to look above and *be* your *cause.* It will save you plenty time.

I know you do not think I am indian because I use big white words in a good white way. Trust me, if it were not for Mohinono and his mate, Shuhinono, I would never have known such a thing as English could be possible for me to use. Because your words are assemblages of everything taken to pieces and never quite grasped in their wholeness, my task of speaking the truth to you is no less difficult than your part of trying to catch it as the words fly by, like millions of insects. I'll say this one more time. Mohinono is John, and Shuhinono, the daughter never held, is Barbara. If you ever see through this crack in the illusion of time, your whole thought processes that keep everything separate will collapse. Because. Be cause. Be Cause.

Now, if you want to be an effect, it's okay with me. But you will not have such joy and fine surprises if you do this in your mind, for it will only be half your mind you have accepted and enjoyed. Don't

72

get me wrong. I don't want to push you into seeing it my way. I've proven this by not making you learn my language, my phonetics, my pictures, or my visions. I have translated all I've learned or experienced or questioned into your language and your sounds and your pictures, to encourage your visions and your own experiences.

My goal is not to scare you into awareness of God, for truly God is not scary. But the separation you experience in your mind does frighten you and prevent you from knowing God. I have heard foolish words all my life and throughout the span of my consciousness, but never have I encountered such a resistant language to true meaning as English. It is a language built upon a conglomeration of individual perceptions, all pointing at the same thing from so many different places in the bubble called mind... each bubble, each different person separate from the whole, speaking from outside the mind of the listener.

Now, if you will allow me, I will try to connect the dots in your mind to join you to all the other listeners and, above all, to bring your fragmented perception into a wholeness that will make you sane and unafraid. I will try to play our way back to a unified perception of the world, acceptable with the grace of God to everyone.

*

The big trees got bigger and bigger, and our eyes got bigger and bigger. Like little children chasing the myriad wonders of awakening in a fascinating, complex world, we would run from old tree growth to new tree growth and marvel at the mysteries of those trees with their huge leaves.

See, you think the sycamore trees that you have in your west have big leaves. But I tell you, back then there were some trees whose leaves you could wear for clothes. Those ancient trees, I don't think, lived through the big changes that came, the big colds. Some of those trees, I think, towered nearly two-hundred feet tall. We laughed and played and ran around them, wondering, will I see him tomorrow? Because the trunks of the trees were so big and round, it seemed like it took a full ten or fifteen seconds, both of you running opposite directions, to see each other again. Now, that's big!

Shuhinono played like a baby, lost all of her concerns, lost all of her seriousness and was truly happy, fulfilled. The nice thing about those big trees... there were lots of game, and always later in the season, lots of nuts to taste and try to figure out how to eat. Some

73

of them were pretty tough, like rocks. Some of them were pretty mealy or bitter and needed washing. Some of them were pretty resinous and needed roasting. But it was a good challenge and life was pretty easy.

We watched for larger animals, especially bears, when those nuts and berries were out. I guess you'd say bears were our biggest competitors because they ate anything, including you. And they climbed much better than you did, and they could smell and hear much better than you. To them, your throwing stick was like a sting of a mosquito. They were tough.

So we were like the deer. We had our ears up and our eyes flashing from side to side and front to back all the time, especially in the spring and fall. In those thickets and in those woods, we were watching extra carefully.

You don't have those worries. You just look left and right before you cross the street. I wouldn't say that our watching caused anxiety. I would say our watching was integrated into our life, like you breathe.

Of course, we didn't smoke. And I think, even in that way you test yourselves by inhaling all kinds of funny things, just to see what will happen. Well, being in the old ones' lodge with that acrid smoke was a test too, but it was voluntary, although sometimes I thought I wanted to get out of there pretty bad. But leaving, I felt was not voluntary. Once you stepped in, you were theirs.

So during these easy days of late spring and summer, I wished a little bit for some of those tests that the lodge brought me. And on days like that, my dreams would be especially alive that night. Shuhinono and I made love often these days, these easy times, and I was sure that we were going to have another baby... because she wanted to! But it was wonderful, the freedom. It was wonderful, the playfulness. It was wonderful, the togetherness of it all.

I'm sure I wouldn't like working on Wall Street. Too many rules. Too many eyes watching you. Too much expectation. Too much pressure to produce something. I don't even think this tree here has that much pressure to produce its seeds. We were natural people doing natural people things, like the trees doing natural tree kinds of things. Whatever pressure we had was just to stay alert and listen.

Our minds were never split in two directions, unless there was great conflict and turmoil. The only thing that could do that would be other warring tribes or our own warring minds cut in half by conflict. Good thing all our conflicts were simple. They were easy to fix. You think... this is implausible because here's this man in

what sounds like paradise, telling me all these things about conflict, and how I got to do this and that to fix my life. Well, I told
you, this planet is not exactly paradise or Eden yet. If a person is
split and in conflict, it doesn't matter how many things are pulling
this way or that. In my day, the fact that there was a split at all
was life-threatening.

In your time, you have a judge and a jury; a judge to keep order
and a jury to decide a right and a wrong. They pass judgment, and
someone wins and someone loses. That isn't the kind of conflict
that we had in our minds. Ours was a conflict about meaning.
And it was only together that this conflict could be resolved. In
agreement, we all had to choose the meaning we would have to
guide our lives, all of us together, no matter what problem was
brought to the so-called court. There was no jury to be guilty of
deciding for everyone else what meaning their lives held. Even
the "judge" who kept order was part of this decision-making group
called tribe.

I'll give you a good example. Let's say someone stole something from someone else. It happens all the time. You bet. You
see a pretty thing you like, and you pick it up and walk off.

Now, in your camps, everything has lines and borders. You
have fences. You have sidewalks. You have rooms. You have
drawers and doors. Everything is subdivided into many small pieces.
And among all these things something belongs, you think. You
say, "This here is my grass, my tree, my underwear, my apricots,
my raisins, my coat, my wife, and my kid. And over there stands
my kid who stole something from this yard over here, they say.
Yes, he's my kid, even though he's in your yard. I know because I
can smell him." (So could you, if you tried. You know your own.)

So here comes all these people in our camp, all upset, sayin',
"Hey, this one did this, that, thus, and so on and so forth." And
they go, "Okay, we go see this guy." And this guy says, "Oh, problem too big. Got to go see all the old ones. We'll do it together,
tonight. Big fire. Bring food."

So all of a sudden, you got this huge thing called "court." And,
you know, sometimes I think it was just for entertainment. Everybody was kind of in a rut, and they just wanted to see what would
happen if they did this or that. They just liked to stir it up. So hey,
we got a big party. Okay fine. So nighttime, big fires, lots of food,
big party, like a movie you go to, like a stage, like a sym-pho-nee.
Big drama! Big solution needed!

So all seven grandmothers and grandfathers sittin' around with
these robes on looking pretty darn good sayin', "I'm this old. I've

been here this long. I've done this this long, and this is my place and that's your place, and don't you forget it!" And everybody is acknowledging everybody else for what everybody else is supposed to be. Yes, yes, yes. Now, all of a sudden, there's differences and distinctions, instead of sameness and oneness. Okay fine.

Long nights and long days cause trouble. Hot summers are tough and cold winters are tough. Spring and fall are joyous, wonderful times. Creator made it that way to stir our pots.

So the stolen thing is thrown out front, and the two parties who are arguing state their case, and the young ones sit there looking all droopy and funky, and there's this big wind come up. You know, superstition didn't come before the wind. The wind brought it. Don't you forget it. I'll explain later.

Everyone froze, and the leader took his cue from the Great Mother's breath and started to speak. He said this, "It's good to see you all here being good people together, solving your problems like this." And the thing that was taken was given to him. And he held it for a minute, and he looked up into the sky. He looked up into the eyes of the Mother and he prayed inside, "What can I say to these people, so these boys in conflict won't stir up too much trouble from now on?"

You see, we all knew a little trouble was okay. To find out what's important, you either ask someone or you push against all the barriers to find out how come they're there.

Then that leader's head dropped, and you could hear him hum and sing inside. Once in awhile, a little sound would come out. Frankly, I don't think he sang too good out loud. But we were patient because that wind wouldn't stop yet. He had us in that powerful wind, stuck there frozen, wondering... Where is power and what is it and who has it, and how come it is this way for us and for him?

Then that wind stopped and he looked at the people, one by one. We're talkin' almost two-hundred people here, so it takes a little while for him to grab an eye out of every head in the crowd. And when he had an eye in the head of every person in that crowd, he spoke. "All that you have is borrowed. It is given to you freely out of love, so that you may have these things for a good life, that these children may live and play together and learn to love and give to each other freely what is given to them freely. What belongs to you, truly, is only one thing... love for each other.

"So be parent and child to each other. If another lacks something, you give it freely, like the Mother gives it to you. Now, you say, "But I have to go get it to make it." Well, sure. The Mother would not make you weak. Maybe a young one says, "My stick's too short." You point to the bush and say, "There's plenty sticks. We'll help you get a longer one." Or another young one says, "My robe's too small." "Fine," you say, "you give it to this other young one, and we'll make you a bigger one, but first you give it away."

We didn't store more than we needed, so that our animals and our plant people didn't feel we were stealing what we didn't really need. Love is trust.

"So I trust amongst you now, you will solve this problem with these two young ones," the old one said.

Boy, did the food come out then. I always did like court. And you know, I think I did because my father danced a lot when court came. He liked to celebrate love and the renewal of our commitment to give love to each other, freely.

Now, he didn't say, oh, this man wants this woman and this one and this one, so give yourselves to each other freely, like that. That was tried, believe me. You have nothing new in "free love." I say, good, you give love freely. But what is love and what is freedom?

When a woman gave herself to a man, we knew it was a joining that took place in all the minds of all the conscious beings on the entire planet. It was an agreement, and therefore permanent. We didn't enter agreements lightly, you see, because we knew what it meant... "agreement." Do you?

Now, you can go to Webster and look it up. There's more of those funny English words all separated. You try to stick them together, so you got a picture to look at. To paint you a picture, I have to use twenty-five of your words, rather than seven of mine, because in your language your words don't contain experience. They describe appearances. And what is civilization but all its collective experiences? What is consciousness but all the experiences of all the ears and eyes and noses and mouths and skins and bones and hearts and minds of all living things awakening to itself as alive, here at this moment? So there's no such thing as dead ones, because the experience doesn't die with the body, does it?

You have history books, don't you? Although there are lies in them, the minds that wrote them tried to collect the experiences and put them together for you to understand the past. Their fatal mistake was that they tried to summarize, to make palatable, and to sanitize men's deeds. The publishers didn't want any bad smells or painful noises, so the reader could read on without any real challenges to the accepted perceptions. They wanted easy reading, so the reader could swallow history like a pill and get well according to local convention. Because you thought you were stupid and didn't know what the past was, you swallowed this pill without asking for the truth. Most of what you swallowed was bad medicine, because you cannot summarize or sanitize human experience. It is as important to tell how a thing was done, as it is to tell what was accomplished. Yes? To get well of historical stupidity, all the bad smells and bad noises must be included. Only the truth, in all its explicit humanness, is good medicine. Only in the truth can you never be deceived by history or any experiences, whether past or present.

This was the experience of those two boys and the truth within it. That young one whose stick was stolen had to give that stick to the one who stole it. That one who stole it had to go make that other one a new stick, a better one. Now, what was learned? You tell me. What was the experience in it that was taught? Is it valuable for an old indian like me to bring it forward and give it to you in this old way of telling stories? What will it mean in your life? Is it a sweet or bitter pill to swallow? Are you those boys... the older one or the younger one? Are you the old man? Are you the crowd and each eye in it? How big is your life?

You don't have to go where I went and step in the holes I stepped in to grow and to become a magnificent human being. But I would add my experience to yours, if you would have it, for could we be magnificent without each other, each one of us, everywhere, for all times? Perhaps it will make you think.

I want to find out what that means... "think." I see myself doing it. I have a thought today, and I see tomorrow it either came true or it did not. I thought maybe tomorrow it might rain because it feels like it today, unbuilding the pressure I feel, sinking, sinking. And tomorrow, oh well, it rains or it doesn't. Mostly, I'm a no-good weatherman, so it doesn't. So thinking is what, exactly? I think, guessing? I think-guessing? How can you think, guessing?

In my language I would say, Hrrooroot-goot-dasl-deept-da-lau-choot-cha-neet-tal-toe-ya-chutt. Now, I know there is some poor fool who might spend the rest of his life trying to find out what language those words came from and who these people are I call mine. He'll go get a Ph.D. trying to figure it out, who I am from these words. Don't do it. There's an easier way to find out about other people's language. It's much quicker *this* way... love joins all things and all experiences, for all times.

It took me two months and more, to learn something of English with its forty-thousand rules. My own language changed every day because it was based upon what we learned. Everyone was a student, so new ways of describing the meaning of things were shared. That's how language grows. This lost language of mine isn't lost, nor is its experience. You just don't see it or hear it. So if you really want to learn it, just ask. Some "dead" person will answer you. But don't try to learn it by yourself because it's not an alone language.

Now, back to the weather. Hrrooroot-goot-dasl-deept-da-lau-choot-cha-neet-tal-toe-ya-chutt means... "Sinking air feels like wet tomorrow." I see that as an observation, but you say that is thinking. So I say, actually, we were the first scientists, and it took you guys a long time to catch up. How can an indian know that the air sinks when it's going to rain? 'Cause it does. Your ears pop, don't they? Your rotten teeth hurt and the stuff stuck in your nose makes your face ache. If it's a bad storm, sometimes you pass gas and your bones hurt bad. So what's the big mystery, high-and-low-pressure weatherman?

I'm going to stick science up the butt for a minute. All that thinking! Maybe you only think you think. I think humans do good to think at all. All that thinking and you still don't know whether it's going to rain in Los Angeles today or not. Seems to me that making things to measure stuff is for modern man to stay busy and look good. But I tell you, you're not in charge, and you're missing something truly wonderful, and that is a relationship with your planet. You live on top. You do not even sense its feelings for you. You would know you were loved if you could *feel* it. Stop thinking so much, pitiful ones. You kill your children's spirit and eat their food.

"Wow," he says. "That's too tough. I can't read this! This guy, Hinono, is making me uncomfortable, poking at me. Attacking already." The first person to read the first few pages of this book said that.

To you, I'll say this, you arrogant little fart. If you even ever knew what attack was, you'd be ashamed because you do it in your mind to everyone, every second. You have no self-discipline. You care for nothing but your own thinking. You think you, alone, own your thinking. If you were mine, I would put you out to sleep in the snow in winter... out of love. I would not want you to be this way and suffer such and pass it on to anyone I know or anything I feel for.

Now, did I throw you out because I wanted you to be outside of love and to feel badly? No. And yes. Out of love for you as myself, I threw you out, so you would see love is bigger than your thinking.

Do you want to know what the devil is? Have a good look. I think you made mirrors to tell you all this. I even think you know it. So the question is, is all that thinking really you, or is it just a mechanism? Look deeply. Don't give up until you have the truth.

I cannot apologize for the truth and I will not. And if you would crucify me like Christ for speaking the truth, I would say, thank you for that, for I would not want to be amongst you anymore. And if love is our judge of truth, would you correct yourself or wait to be corrected by Spirit? I ask you, would the whole tribe voluntarily throw itself out for correction into the snow, leaving only one person inside in the warmth and the love? Would that person inside be Christ? I tell you, you are never outside love, whether in correction or waiting for correction. What are you waiting for? Waiting to be thrown outside?

Why do you think so much? Why do you try to twist and reverse everything you see? Has the gift of truth got some reason except love behind it? I think you have to find out, for you're bored with love giving you everything you need or want. I think you are all in the lodge, all fat and cozy, and Christ is outside in the snow.

I told you this journey would be a bit rough at times, but if there is any truth left in anything, anywhere, for any reason, it is this. **Love does know why It Loves**. And if you don't see this, it is that you must learn from Love what love is. There is but one place to learn it, so why go looking all over everywhere for what you do not see right in front of you? Why not sit down and receive it from the Source that gives it truly? Stop talking! Start listening! Close your eyes. Ask but one question, and do not stop listening until the answer is given and received and understood.

You only sit for a moment, then say to yourself, "Oh, excuse me. Time's up. I've got to go now. I have an appointment to get my hair done. I've got to paint my fingernails red. What the hell for, I have no idea, but it looks good... to *me.*" Did you forget your question already?

The phone rings. "Oh, excuse me, I got to answer it, God. Maybe it's my boyfriend. May *be* my boy *friend*." Is not God the Source of all boyfriends, young girls? Is it not love you seek, to have and to give? And when you two make love and a baby results, is that not love given to you? When you two have a baby, is that not love from God given to you as you have asked, whether you ask consciously or not? Is not that child receiving a mother and father as it has asked? Are the parents not God to that little child?

There is nothing that is separate from this idea God, and yet you say, "What's God?" Stop thinking. Sit down. Listen. Look. Show some discipline. You asked, so wait to receive, unless you think, of course, nobody's there listening. I'll say this over and over. Everything listens to you and gives you what you ask. You do not hear or receive. You take.

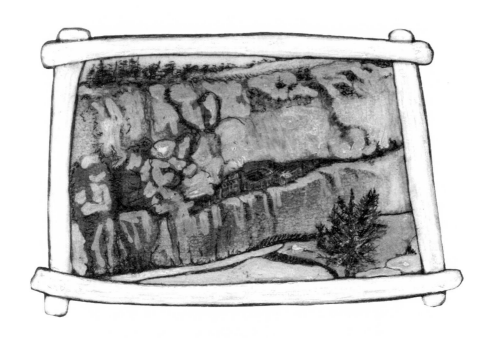

Chapter 9
South and North

Suddenly, in the middle of everything, which is always the way it is for us, Shuhinono says, "Let's go see that big chasm. I think I could die now and be happy. Besides, we have another baby on the way, and a walk would do me good."

Well, I did the flop again. My butt hit the ground so hard, I thought my teeth would fall out, but inside I knew we were going to have another baby too. We laughed and we were happy, and we were really healthy, even though the humidity was very high. There was so much to eat here–good things. There were fruits of all kinds, berries and nuts. There were animals, creatures–weird, flying things of all colors. It was really pretty neat, as you would say. I think it was like your zoo, without cages. That's how close animals were to each other in that forest.

So we struck out. You know how you know when it's south? We know it's south because it gets drier as we go, a little bit at a time. The other thing is, it gets hotter. We follow the rivers down too. Anything that runs down is south, unless the mountains play tricks and make the waters run right and left.

My children writing down these words live in a place where the river runs south for a hundred miles, almost, then hits rock and runs west a little bit. And then, believe it or not, it runs northwest almost two-hundred miles. It's a funny place they live in. All the land goes down until it hits this one place where the rock underneath is so hard, it won't let the water go by. The only way it can get back to the south is to go northwest, cutting a little gorge two-hundred miles long. Way up north and a little west, that little river hits a big, south-flowing river you call the Colorado. That river runs fast and deep through soft, red rock, cutting a huge gorge. That's where we're going, to that big chasm.

My father told me about this river that runs backwards and then goes to the big chasm. So, on this trip, I want to find it. My father camped for nearly a year where this little river begins to run backwards. He said the game was plentiful, the fish large, the weather perfect. And he said the Spirits lived in that place and liked it. He said the Spirits protect this place, and that my children would live there someday.

We walked two-hundred days to get there. In some places, the mountains were very high. But mostly, we stayed to the edges of them, west. Here, at the edge, there were buffalo, big as a Mack truck, like you say, and when they started moving, you could hear it with your feet. You didn't even need ears. Your feet could hear it... thunder. That's what it felt like... thunder.

Needless to say, the two of us did not hunt buffalo. Not a good idea, just two people trying such a big thing. But when we got to high places, we looked down and marveled at the abundant buffalo and said, "I pray it is this way forever, that abundance can bless us and fill our hearts and eyes with confidence, that love will live forever here."

Now, how many people walk down the streets and can see so far out around those big, square buildings you planted, and see the abundance we saw, and say what we said about love living here forever? My native descendents sit in hovels and don't even care to hear the stories of how it was for the old ones about abundance.

Nowadays, instead of buffalo, you've got cows... sweet, slow creatures, lots of heart, slow spirits, kinda' dull... not too risky to catch. Walk right up, hit 'em in the head. No wonder you don't feel good when you eat one. Took a lot of years to breed the fight out of them, like your house cats and dogs.

If you want a chicken, go right up to the shelf. Grab a bird. Squeeze its head off. Feel good. Try it. There they are in the cage—one, two three, four. Okay, ring its neck. Have one. Eat it. Not me! It's not like it's a bean. It's got wings. It can fly. Let it go, then try to catch it. Then eat it... if you can catch it. Then that chicken says, "Hah! I gave it my best! And my spirit's good! And when you catch me, you can have me. And I will love you like you will love me because we're even, equal! Thank you for not killing my spirit before you kill my body! I give you my body! I keep my spirit! *That's love.*

Now, I don't mean to spoil your trip to Moo-Burger or Kleen Plucky Chicken or any of what you call... "fast food." But I'll say this. You're not too fast to see your food's too slow to give you any fight. And so, you're dead before it is.

Now you say, "Only savages hunt." Yeah, I seen 'em. Thirty-aut-six-rifles with high-power scopes, wide-angle too, hunters sittin' high up, lookin' down, stayin' warm with battery-powered socks, drinkin' whiskey or beer... waitin', hidin', braggin'.

I seen them savages elsewhere too. They're all in the stock exchange. But they're all dead already... nickels and dimes looking for dollars.

I saw that shiny, yellow metal lots of times in the river. I'd pick it up and bite it and say, Wow, that's soft. I never seen a rock that's soft like that and doesn't go all scruffy. And we carried it around until we got tired of carrying it around. We'd give it to somebody, and it goes to the chief and he says, "That's a perfect rock 'cause it's bright like the sun. It doesn't scruff, and we can hit it and hit it and hit it, and it's still the same color. Pretty stuff. I think we'll give it to Creator. It's perfect. Must be Creator's."

But long time later, somebody built a church and put a face in it with gold all around, like somehow that face isn't you and me. And no, we don't go collecting gold up into big piles like you do, 'cause we don't like to carry things that are really heavy. If I put something around my neck and walk a hundred miles, it'll be my own kid. *That's love.* You want to wear a necklace that weighs five pounds, looks beautiful, okay fine. Your kids are starving for love, while you're lookin' good... to yourself.

So, shop around. Find God. Find love. Go ahead. Keep shopping 'till you drop. Maybe dropping down will help you see your mistake. Maybe then the buffalo will come back and the cows will go away. Better yet, maybe those cows will breed with those buffalo and remember who they are too.

You know, I talk like this because my brothers all over, my native brothers, their hearts are split and they're bleeding to death with longing for Big Love to return to this place. They had a promise from Spirit that it would happen. They did. And they're waiting. But they're pretty miserable waiters 'cause they're still pissed off.

83

My brothers, I think love waits with a good heart. I know this test has been very long in your eyes. When the old ones die and the young ones come, and the young ones have young ones, and their young ones have young ones, the old ones still wait... and wait... and say, "When, Creator, when?"

But I tell you, if your heart is closed, so will your mind close, and you will forget to tell anyone what you're waiting for. So the young ones never get to be old like the old ones, and their children never grow up to be like the old ones either. There is no one to tell the stories anymore. All are children. All are at the mall... lookin' good.

Now, I think it's this way. Try it on and see if it fits. You're waiting for the white man to go away. He won't. You should be helping the white man to become native in his heart. You are all waiting for the same God to return, so that all you natives from all those different places–white, red, yellow and black, in the north, west, east and south can love each other back to abundance again and turn the buffalo loose in open land.

So what you waitin' for? Get tellin' them old stories, folks. Share yourselves. Share your lives. Share your families. Laugh about what we have done to this place because it's only temporary... unless you want it permanent. If you cannot laugh at foolishness, it will not go away. If you fight and are angry and withhold your love, you keep foolishness prisoner to fight and be angry with. If you died with the buffalo, be reborn for the buffalo. If you drink too much, dream more. Clean up, so Spirit can help you dream those buffalo back again. Don't flop down and die. Flop down and forgive. Your dreams of love will create anew and will heal the wounds lying deep in your bones that we are waiting to help you see. And when you see, you will cry for sure. And in the midst of that crying, if you do not get angry, you will see through the illusion of death and loss, and your dreams will turn powerful and will call the truth back to you. And it will come to pass. Abundance will be here again. So don't give up. Don't make yourselves sick, while proving that body is weaker than mind. Give your minds back to Spirit to cleanse, and you will see your healed mind is all there is for love to see itself with.

*

So we kept following the water down. And when we got to the red rocks–and boy, that was some walk, I'll tell you–I was encouraged and I thought, well, the chasm can't be too far. But I'll tell you, it was another hundred days before we got there, not because the water ran up or down but because it wiggled all over. It went this way and that way.

You know, if you drew a straight line and walked from this place to that, you'd get there pretty quickly. But I didn't see straight lines for a hundred days. I did see a place where there was a big table rock, what you call a mesa. And I was gonna' go walk to that mesa and get up top and look around. But my eyes played tricks on me, just like when we walked up to the base of Great Mountain that first time, and it took six days instead of three or four. That darn mesa was so far away, you couldn't even imagine how long it would take to get to it. And Shuhinono said, "No side trips, bud!"

I said, If I could get up on top, I could see where that chasm was, maybe.

And she said, "There you go thinkin' again. How did we get to the top of Great Mountain?" So I sat and I remembered.

Now, when you are on your journeys to your goals, I want you to remember once in a while what leads you there. I ask you this, truly. Recount the successes you've had in your life, and don't look at what you think you did to succeed. Look at what guidance you got. Be honest with yourself. Is it you telling you where to go and what to do and how to see a thing correctly and what to say? Do you sit at home and practice and write it down and then go do it? No. It's fluid. It happens in the moment, does it not? And some things you speak, you don't even know before you say it. All of a sudden, pop, out come the words. And the other person's eyes get big and they say, "You're an interesting person. That's what I was thinking–what you said just then." So help is spontaneous, yes? But because Spirit is so subtle, you think you're pretty clever... all by yourself.

Now, most women, they know about intuition pretty good. They're more flexible, less likely to imagine themselves as being their best guide. Men? Nah, they like to think they are the best God to guide themselves. Let's face it, ego wasn't meant to be God at all. Most women are ahead of the men about accepting guidance, don't you think? They ask more questions too.

I want to tell you about this chasm. You would not believe it. Somebody could look down from the top of the Empire State Building and pretend to understand what that chasm looked like, the one you call the Grand Canyon, but to a pitiful, old indian who darn near fell in because it came up so sudden-like—all of a sudden it was there, and it was two miles across and one to one-and-a-half miles deep. I'm tellin' you, that was something! It was as if the world got bigger, right now, in my head. I think a wren could have set up house in my mouth. That's how long my mouth stayed open. I only had one experience that even remotely compared to it, and that was with Spirit on top of Great Mountain. If this place is that big, then surely love is bigger yet... that's what I thought. And I smiled, I think. Now, I'm sure. I'm still smiling. I passed on smiling.

How you folks can be disappointed, I'll never know. Look around you. Someone's gone to a lot of trouble around here to entertain you folks. Colors, highs and lows, wides and fars–everything in it always moving, always changing. Barely do you sleep, even, for the fullness of it. How can you be sad? All us Old Ones on the other side singing songs to you of sweetness and love, poking you sometimes when you get too indulgent... but, *all that love.* Please wake up to it. Don't delay too much. You spoil a good time.

*

Before we could make it around that gorge–and truly, we never did cross it, we just sort of followed it down some more–a baby was born to us in that magnificent place. It was in this place Shuhinono became a mother again.

We met people who lived there all the time and never felt there was another place for them but this. I can say to them with my heart and mind, I see why you never left. They were good to us, them Hopi. Their language was very different, but those eyes knew what ours did, so we were safe here.

Shuhinono found women friends who took her into deep holes in the ground. They sang ceremonial songs in there and showed her great things.

I went to ceremonies with the men too, but I didn't understand their symbols. I had good dreams and great visions. I knew I was guided in this place and to this place. It was paradise here. This was Eden here. I've never seen harmony among any people quite like this. Everyone knew what they were doing. There wasn't any confusion here.

These people whose language was like singing, constantly paid respect to each aspect of their life through symbols and dance, all very old practices. These people had structure in their stories, songs and dances. And that structure was in everything they did.

It was good to see them gather their creatures and farm their lands and hunt and run. When big celebrations were going to happen, they had runners run to all their different places, so all of their people could celebrate on the same day, simultaneously. In that way, they were all joined in their minds and in their ceremonies and singing. They *would* join too. I know because I joined them, and I didn't understand a word they spoke. But I was them and I felt what they felt. And I'll tell you this. Those human beings loved big.

Our new baby didn't look a thing like Mohinono had looked. First of all, it was a girl. Second, she didn't even have hair same color as mine. Now that was different. In our tribe, everybody's same. All black hair, that's that! All brown skin, that's that! All big thumbs, fat fingers, that's that! All big butts, that's that! All short legs, that's that!

Now folks are always trying to figure out some reason why things are as they are, like why our legs were short. Folks, there ain't no other reason for our short legs except it was cold, and you got your ass too far off the ground and it froze.

Now some big anthropologist comes along and says something like, "All indians got black hair unless their blood is mixed, and that's the way it is for everybody in every root culture... there's just one gene for one trait or the race is mixed." He claims that's true, and that idea rules a people's thinking for centuries. But here we got a blond indian with no mixed blood. You figure it.

Now I'm gonna' give you another example of an idea running people's thinking. This guy, what's his name?–the one that said sucking nipples is bad for babies, so use a bottle–Dr. Spock, he apologized. Now there's a good man. But how do you undo the damage, fool? How do you take back the years of confusion between mothers and babies? Sometimes apologies don't do any good. I don't say this to cause him a heart attack 'cause he's guilty. But I do want to say this. **Don't say shit you don't know anything about!** If you don't know something, say, "I don't know." More better. Less damage. Everybody's looking for help because everything is so mixed up. But what's helpful? Do you know?

You want to be helpful, be a big leader, have lots of people listen to your words, have them follow you everywhere, have them ask you sixty-four-billion questions a hundred-and-fifty times a day and never listen? You better think about it. And remember, Dr. Spock apologized. I'll bet he's been on the run for half a century, 'cause being an authority, being the author, being the one that thinks he *knows,* is a damn big job. Want it?

I think it's better and more honest to be a children's story writer, and say, "I authored this little book, this story," than it is to be a big leader and make generalized deductions based upon changing beliefs. But even writing children's stories is a little tricky because you ain't the first human being to ever open your eyes on this place and tell a story to little children.

See, you still think the past is dead. God said the past is gone. God didn't say it was dead. God just didn't want you to relive it again and again. So if you see everything we ever learned as dead, then you're cut off from what we learned. You're supposed to be learning something from us, getting smarter from our mistakes. But if you see no value in what we learned, then you never learned nothin' and you sure got to be dumb, because you will continue making the same mistakes, over and over and over. Now, correct me if you think my reasoning is faulty.

You ask me, who can you learn from, and how can you tell when somebody's lying to you, like in school, in the textbooks, in the histories? How can you find a true storyteller who tells true stories? Child of wonder, I don't know but one way. Pray and pray until you hear Spirit inside your own heart and your own mind, until you hear it almost out loud and it frightens you, until you are convinced Spirit is real and life doesn't die, until there's nothing in you but the love the Creator sent you. I'm here to tell you and to try to demonstrate to you that this is true. So are my children. So are all the children of all the fathers and mothers who ever found love too. So there's lots of help out here, sweet folks. Don't give up.

Tomorrow, we will begin again at the bottom with fire and talk about Spirit some more. You have a view from where you are inside that form, as we have a view from where we are outside that form. I wish to turn your eyes around and have you see inside what we see. It will be tedious. It will be difficult. It will be enlightening. And, above all, it will burn out your fears of awakening.

Chapter 10
The Kiva - The Center of Below

So reader, let's jump into a hole. Let's go to ceremony with those Hopi, the long time ago ones, not the new Hopi. These are the Hopi that were so close to their stories that their whole life lived inside of them.

From the dark unseen to the seen in the light... everything emerges. Way before I was born, people always were. What was not seen became one, then two and more. So it was with the first people living at the emergence place.

These first people of the Grand Canyon were originally one tribe but later spread out around the surrounding area to become twenty-one tribes. They took on different names, derived from their new places. One group came to be known as "the people of the blue-green water," the Havasupai. Another group... "the people of the tall pines," the Hualapi. And another... "the people of the blue corn," the Hopi. So when I casually use the modern name "Hopi," I am including all of the twenty-one tribes of the Grand Canyon.

Today's Hopi, only the really old ones can truly remember. The new Hopi, well, they have school to distract them. They have cars and they have TV and they have music. And they even have drugs that make them think that they can go farther back than the old ones, faster, and understand more, more quickly. But that isn't how it's done. Unless they learn which drugs can be used as medicines and use those medicines with the Guides of their elders, unless they choose guidance within the structure of Hopi stories, they won't learn much of the truth within those old stories. They'll skip so much, they'll emerge a bit lost. And, dear ones, a return to truth can take much longer than just walking a straight path.

You see, once you "think" you know something, it's harder to be convinced that you don't, and then to relearn from a place of humility. But if you start out not knowing, there's no convincing necessary. Not knowing is not nearly as deep a hole as thinking you already know. The ones that start convinced they don't know, just need assurances that they can know. It is then that true learning begins.

Well, there's all kinds of holes, some helpful, some not. So let's just jump into this helpful hole, this kiva, and have a look. What do you say?

Here I am walking toward this kiva, thinking, the old ones didn't tell me about this. I'm not so sure I want to do this. I'm a bit nervous. I don't like this, maybe, sitting in the dark and doing this. Maybe their smoke stinks worse than ours. Reminds me of that trap door and going down to them dead ones. I'm just flat scared is what it is. I think it's because I can feel these people's energy drop way below their feet.

I, too, feel the energy drain out of me and into the earth, and it frightens me... and down we go. I think of my wife and say, I'll either come out okay, or they'll bury me in this place, and I won't get to know my daughter. So you know I'm kinda' scared.

That's how it is when you dive deep into the human psyche, and I don't care whether you're in an underground hole or not. You see, it was the agreement these people had between them to do this, to go seek the truth, to see into the future by asking for their Guides. And I'll tell you, if it wasn't for the kindness and the humor and the sweetness of these people with whom I didn't understand one spoken word, I would never have gotten in that hole.

Now, if you're Christian, you might even think, "That's devil worship stuff and, boy, you should be afraid!" But when Love leads you in there, which voice are you going to listen to, the voice of fear that tells you to decide against the Love that led you there, or the Voice that tells you to just focus on the Love that brought you and not let the voice of fear run you off?

The ladder was steep. You know, I never saw a ladder before, so I was pretty amazed. Worked good too. Took me a few minutes when I first got to this place to figure out how they stuck them logs together like that. Smart folks. And then to pile up all those rocks? Wow! They're some workin' fools. We're pretty lazy compared to them, I think. I'm not sure we wanted things to last as long as they did.

Anyway, their smoke was just as acrid as ours, I can tell you that. My eyes burned just for a little while, then they stopped. After that, I saw darn good in that dark. Them folks never made a fire that put much light into that room. There were only hot coals. I think, maybe they had made those hot coals already and just brought them down to that pit, 'cause I didn't see bright flames leaping anywhere. There was only a dull, red glow that would be bright for awhile, then ashes would cover it over with gray. Looking at that glow, gone gray, would very nearly put you to sleep, and you would slip deeper into that darkness. One of the old ones would begin to chant very gently, and coals would be put in that pit again. Those coals would begin to glow pretty good, and it would brighten up the room, then the old man would speak again. He would tell stories. Those stories introduced you into another realm, another reality, and you would go journeying as those coals got grayer and quieter, and that room got darker and darker. I don't know exactly what those stories were, but I'll tell you, they had intent in them. And it was the power of the intent of all their minds joined together that took me journeying with them.

At certain times during those stories, one of the young people dressed up as one of their spiritual characters would make a brief appearance by those glowing embers. On cue, that person would jump out and say something. Because I didn't understand their language, I didn't really understand their characters either. But, boy, the people in that room would really swoon. It meant a lot to them, I could tell, but it just scared me some. Whatever they did worked, though. That's all I know.

It all started like this. After a bath of water or corn pollen, a bath of dust or ashes, we went each time into this hole. Then we'd sit and follow the wisdom of these old people. When I say we went below our feet, that's exactly where we're going to start right now. I won't tell you how the story went as much as to tell you what I saw and what I learned. I'll recommend you read the Hopi world view, if you wish. I might get it wrong anyway. I don't speak Hopi. But I'll tell you what I experienced.

Before there was anything at all, there was Nothing... a big one. I told you that when you first opened these pages... the Void that wasn't empty, the pregnant Void. You will have to visit this place someday because it's where life began, where you began. It's where everything began. And unless you go back to The Beginning, you won't be able to get love right because you won't have a foundation that's true and whole. So the Hopi go into this hole to get whole.

It's quiet. I can hear the chanting in the distance, but for some reason it sounds farther and farther and farther away, like walking down a long hallway and somebody's mumbling at one end, and you walk farther and farther and farther away, 'til you can't hear it anymore. I think all chanting is supposed to do this, 'cause when you can't hear anything anymore, you also can't feel anything anymore. This was such a completely peaceful experience that I wasn't even aware that I couldn't feel anything anymore... no sensation, no awareness of any sensation.

There's a hole beneath your feet you fall through, but your body stays above. Your mind just drops through. I told you about the trap door and the old one who first guided me. This experience occurs in your mind, so you can go to other places with Guides. But if you try to go by yourself and do not ask for help, you will just wander aimlessly and learn little.

When I am afraid, I ask for those Guides on top of Great Mountain to help me, or I ask for the Old Ones who guided me when I was a bit younger. And They come. Sometimes I see Their faces, but mostly I do not. I can sense Their presence and our minds join as one. I am told, without words, what to do and where to go. They suggest these things to me. They do not push me or pull me, as a friend does not do these things to you. A friend is someone who has been there, then encourages your own journey in good, kind ways. He does not hurry you or make you feel foolish for feeling weak and frightened. He just puts out his hand and says, "When you're ready, I'm here."

That old Hopi man separated me from my body real easy-like, real kind-like, and I saw animals go by very fast, all kinds, some I'd never seen before. Many were familiar. My interest would sometimes stick on one animal, then it would change form, perhaps from a flying one to a standing one, and it would tell me things. Sometimes it would change into another guide animal that I recognized from home, like a beaver. Mostly, the guides would just be behind me and point this way or that as I journeyed.

"Look at this," one said. "This is your mother." And I would see my blood mother and my Spiritual Mother at the same time. Then I would see my wife, Shuhinono, and I would see the daughter,

Shuhinono. Then I would see my own child-daughter and see the Mother in her. Even as an infant, the Mother was there in her, strong as life itself. And I would weep for thankfulness at this glimpse of a way to honor my own child, so I would not treat her with disrespect... ever.

Then that guide animal would point another direction and say, "This is your father," and I would see my father. And in his laughter and in his joy and in the sparkle of his eyes, I would see the Light of God come from him and envelop everything that was, and I would very nearly collapse from the exquisiteness of it, from the awesome beauty of it. Then I would see myself, and I would see Mohinono, and I would again see his partner, his spiritual twin in that Light. And I would see my new child-daughter in It, and I would see all these people in It and all the people I'd ever met. Then the door would open further, and I would see all the people on the earth, where they came from, from the One Seed, and why they went in four directions, and what the Plan of Creation was. And I saw that to truly find yourself, you must first lose yourself in the Everything. I see my wife, Shuhinono, as Everything already. I see that she lost herself as a child in the All, One, Everything, and came back a greater human being, walking with little, bitty feet in the sand. So that's how come she seems so huge. She is. And now, I am too.

Now, you tell me how long this reverie lasted. I surely don't know. I visited so many places. I even saw on the planet, there was ice in the south and ice in the north. I saw how the fire in the sky created the weather. I saw there was a fire in earth's center as well. And I saw as the ego sees the world... looking down on everything from above. Bad perspective. I think maybe you need to bring your energy down from your head to your knees, then fall down on them and ask forgiveness for the things that you think. I see wickedness and fear start with misunderstanding and get stronger with indulgence. The fight to return our energy to our root fire, from the truly dead ideas we have about life, is a hard one. The only thing that keeps a person's energy stuck is that they must still prefer their personal ideas more than the truth.

You could always tell who the truly wicked were. What was more difficult was to determine who was not conscious but still using people with their own ideas. Truly wicked people are few. Most of us fall into the much larger category of the marginally insane. Would you not say that to not know the outcome of your own behavior is insane? Yet, most who believe a certain way or behave a certain way do not understand the consequences of what they do or believe. I say, most people are being used more by their own ideas, rather than their ideas using other people.

Even the Hopi had users, but they were pretty darn tolerant of them. They had ways of dealing with them. Different clans would take on this user. Each clan had a medicine or a way of teaching that was healing, even for crazy ones or sick ones or angry ones or mean ones, even for the psychic ones who saw too much and used it as a weapon. You see, there is the key. It is okay to see this psychic world and its power, but what use is it?

Use anything without Spirit's guidance and it will use you!

The psychic world has this single spiritual usefulness... experience leads to understanding which leads to knowledge. Knowledge keeps you from getting stuck from behind with a thought that can kill, slowly or quickly, depending upon your level of fear and ignorance.

I'll say this. Thoughts have power. Cause has effect. Yes? For such a thought of hatred, the only safety is consciousness in love and the truth within it. This state of consciousness is the realm of knowledge. Unconsciousness cannot know anything. You may have all the love in the world for a hateful person and want to help them out of their deep, dark hole, but without being conscious and knowing the truth about what that hole is, good luck! That's like cuddling a porcupine or trying to change a wolverine into a koala bear. Better to know how the human heart and mind got to be a porcupine or a wolverine. You need a Guide, I think. I did. I see others do too.

The unique thing about ego is, it's very "creative" in an unreal sense. It is insane and can easily trick you, 'cause it's making the whole thing up as it goes along. If you believe its antics, you give it power with your attention. And as it runs from your advance, you chase its tail. And because you're chasing its tail, you give it your power and its got you. So better to get guidance from someone who can see this game from outside the ego's thought system and can see how to stop an injurious thought this crazy one sent you. You can't see because you're chasing the tail. You're behind, not in front.

So, you want to fix a crazy one just with love? Good luck! They may not want to be fixed. Maybe they're trying to hold onto power by wanting to hurt. And you are feeding your power to them, unconsciously, by being hurt. If you love somebody and you're not conscious in it, you've got a hole in you that's leaking energy, and it's going to the crazy one who's using you. Even the crazy one may not be conscious, but craziness running ahead of love outside the truth is not a good idea. Love must wait for craziness to cross the line into sanity by asking for help. Why should truth chase illusion and feed it energy for its unreality?

In this kiva, we sit and we pray, and we see through the illusions of life, one by one by one by one, so we all become conscious. And because we do this thing together, we love and trust each other, and trust and love the Guides that guide us. And we are strong in our hearts and secure and not fearful. And no bad medicine, no hateful thoughts thrown at us can tear us apart because we are together in our strength. We are a rock, a wall, a fortress but not a force, a fortress of peace, a fortress of truth, a fortress of consciousness, a rock of love. It is our agreement to do this that forges these bonds between us.

The Hopi accept strangers from outside because their medicine is so powerful that the insane will either perish or get well in it. How long can a crazy person maintain a crazy idea against all odds? Well, some are pretty good at it... "until death do us part." The truth, however, never changed one instant.

So all you dark ones having dark thoughts, you frighten yourselves. Stop it! You climb so high in your tree that you scare yourselves. You try to get above everyone else climbing in their tree. And the ground gets so far away that your feet don't even remember what it was like to stand on the earth. You frighten yourselves and look foolish, all of you together who agree you have nothing to agree upon that's real.

Come down from them trees. There's nourishment here. See through the thing that drove you up that tree. Take your power back from fear and anger and judgment. We are not telling you, you have made an error. You are. Your Guides only want to show you how to have peace again. You are not going to be punished in this hole, this kiva. In this hole is a "television" (telepathic vision) that shows you what illusion is and what truth is, and how you can tell the difference, if you ask.

Now, you bring your awareness down that hole, I guarantee you, you're going to see some pretty awful stuff, but fear is just in your mind. Your mind did it to you. All your brothers and sisters are doing it to each other in their minds too. And when you're tired of being afraid of fear, you'll see love again, I promise you. Where the dark hole of fear was, the Light of Love will be. You see, it is illusion that made fear, not truth.

All of us in this hole, we didn't make up what love was, but we got sick of fear and found out. We asked. So don't be afraid of letting your energy down from that tree. Don't even be afraid of letting your energy go past your feet, deep into the core of the earth, because there's love there too. That's where the Mother's cleansing fire turns you into love again. That's where Her eternal giving comes from... feeds your body and soul, fills your mind and heart. All life is born through Mother. Yes? How can you know the Father without knowing the Mother first?

If you don't remember this Mother loves you, of course you'll be afraid. All you'll see is that everything eats everything else, and the place doesn't look friendly. Well, look deeper and ask what the truth is. Keep looking and don't give up until you get to the truth of it. And, I guarantee you, at the core of life is agreement and love. If you don't like the game of life, then you are only seeing the play of the illusion of it. You're seeing how the game got all screwed up from fear and judgment... not enough food... don't like this... not enough water... don't like that... not enough love....

Well, we'll stop there because there's the hitch. If there's not enough love in the world, it's because you're not giving it. Somehow it got stuck, and the circle didn't get completed. God sure gave you love. God the Father and the Mother split Itself, the idea God, and gave you love twice. Then, because you wanted a body to prove to yourself you're alive, They gave you the world and everything in it. And everything here gives itself to you in love to prove that you are loved. And yet you say, "Love is not enough... I'm still scared."

Creator then gave you the Holy Spirit to come back here and help you, to prove to you that death is not real and that your asked for experience of the body, even though temporary, does not change the lesson of love that you are supposed to learn here.

The physical world has its laws, and the Mother operates all Her love within those laws. She calls Spirit here to give a Voice to everything for you, through the plants and creatures and rocks and wind and water. Spirit stands beyond all those physical laws to remind you, you are spirit first and body last.

That kiva was the symbolic womb of the Mother, and that fire pit was Her symbolic heart that took your mind on a journey of love to discover all that was not seen before, to discover the meaning beyond the surface of illusion. And in this dark place where your eyes do not work, vision is born, so that you may go on this journey in the true Light. And because no sound other than the chanting voice of that old one could be heard in that place, your ears went with your vision, and Spirit could tell you what was happening and why.

But to get to this place, you must ask truth continually and not listen to what your mind says about how come you shouldn't be here doing this thing. That's fear speaking to you. That's your body, who thinks it's going to die, speaking to you. And if you would rather hear what death has to say about life, than what Life has to say about death, then I suggest you change your mind, for you truly will not learn anything about life by fearing and worshiping death.

I found that minds are split in half on this issue. Half agrees that love is all there is. The other half wants to know what death is and looks for it in everything. Now, which half you listen to is for you to say. For me to know, I would have to sit with you and ask you how you see this world. What do you value? What do you look upon that pleases you? What do you want? What do you do? Tell me of yourself and of your life and where you've been and what you've learned. What do you love?

There is a journey to the left in your mind that tries to understand everything, based upon its physical appearance and a description of the behavior of everything. It's a big library full of books, has lots of ideas, lots of questions, lots of assumptions, corollaries, theorems, and postulates. And at its worst, it has beliefs. And when a belief becomes more cherished than the truth, it becomes an obsessive conviction. And I say to you, what becomes a convict is not free. It is an error. You become the convict in the prison of that thinking, and you too are not free. And you will seek to imprison everything around you in your crazy beliefs.

So, okay fine, journey down that road, but be conscious in it and learn what it is. Then please hurry back, for there is joy to be had on this other side. There is freedom over here. There is light. There is play. There is warmth. That left-out-of-love mind over there is damn cold... just wants to know stuff for power, for gain. That left-brain mind just wants to increase the size of the ego of the person who believes in it. It just wants to strangle everything around it for the truth it thinks is inside of itself. But if you kill something, will you be able to see the life come out, and therefore prove what life is? I think not, but it is attempted millions of times a day all over this planet... people killing people... life not knowing what itself is, taking life, trying to find out what it is and even believing it has found out.

So, back up. Go ahead and look, but back up. Back up looking. Back up all the way to The Beginning, to the Light, looking. I say back up 'cause I suggest you don't turn your back for a minute on this evil thought man formed in his mind called power. Love doesn't live in man's idea of power, because true power belongs to God

Who loves, Who made love, Who gives love eternally without looking left.

It is amazing that you can shoot a rocket to the moon but not know what for. Maybe so you don't feel like you're trapped here on this earth with all these issues to work out. Well, go where you wish. Your issues go with you, crazy people. You're very inventive, very willful, very enterprising, very blind. You'd rather ignore your babies crying and go to the moon. You'd rather tell doctors to figure out your illnesses, than to spend the time with yourself, healing yourself by giving up your bad thoughts.

I know most of you folks are too busy trying to make a living, rather than trying to heal yourselves of all your bad thoughts. Take a stand against those bad thoughts. I know you'd rather take a pill or pay some guy a hundred bucks an hour to listen to your shit. But that guy is probably sicker than you 'cause he'll listen to it. Even though everybody's trying to do something good, they better look deeper, deeper even than Freud, deeper even than Jung. Get down to your feet, below them, even to the heart of the earth. Look at all the crap that's in the mind of a human being. You've got one. Stop denying it. It's just like everyone else's. So start looking at your own first. Just because you came from a fine family, with a big home and lots of money, doesn't make you any poorer or any richer than the first person that ever stepped foot on this planet, barefooted.

Now, I will not ask for your forgiveness for telling you this truth because, truly, if I left you in the state you're in, I would have to ask Creator for forgiveness. My silence would mean I didn't care enough about you to speak it, or maybe I was too selfish to stop and help or to ask why and how to help or to be humble enough to ask God for help to even ask you these questions.

So, dear ones, humility begins at your breast. It goes down your knees to your feet and below those feet to the core of the earth. And that core of the earth is linked to the core of the sun and to the stars and to everything that has light in it.

Even the rocks are humble. They are spirit. You think them dense. Well, maybe you think dense means stupid. Maybe human thinking is stupid and dense means heavy. A rock is heavy because of all the horrible thoughts it's had to carry for mankind. That's its job. All the horrible deeds any living thing has done or thought are stored as energy in the rocks. The Mother, in her friends the rocks, stores all these negative things, all these lower emotions, all these horrible thoughts of murder and mayhem and of rape.

And down here in this kiva, by us sitting here going through all our stuff to get to the core, we see the Mother's heart is only love. Seeing this truth takes all that negative emotion out of those rocks and gives that energy back to Her fire to purify. That purified energy from Her core goes to our feet and back up our spines, out the top of our heads and back to Creator as joy. It is conscious love and joy the Creator gave to you, and that is what you need to return to Creator. So, truth is known once again, and your mind is free of fear, once again.

So I tell you, that spiritual fire in us, that willingness to learn, that purity of desire and that love of truth, renews us in our form and shows us why there is male and female, and why a child is born through sexual coupling. That spiritual fire shows us there must be balance between two of us asking Creator for consciousness... that it must take two voices in agreement to ask for this fire to rise above our hips and give us reason for children, for this fire to rise into our belly and give us reason to gather among us food, clothes and shelter. It shows us how to take our will back from fear of lack, from greed, from jealousy, and from all the horrible emotions a human is subject to. That spiritual fire shows us how we may love one another, support one another and give these things to one another. Our will may then be used to get our hearts and minds to open to God, to give gratitude and give love in return for what we've all received here, to experience a life of being fully alive in joy.

It's when your heart opens that the Fire of Love goes still higher yet, into your throat where the Holy Spirit can speak with your voice to help your brothers. You've returned your mind to God this way and you will be helpful, for your words will heal other people on their journey. And in gratitude, God gives you the energy to bring your mind from your eyes, to give your mind spiritual eyes inside, to see in vision what Spirit would give to guide you. Then love's reward gives gratitude again, for in joy and truth you will see where power lies and why it is given to you to help.

That fire rises through all the energy centers, through all their colors, through all the emotions, to burn out all the fears and join you with the Creator, the Mother and the Father and the children, all of them. And in that state, you understand why Creator cannot come down to show you love. You must come up to see it... out of the battleground. And you see why Spirit will do anything to teach you this lesson, because until this is done, a human being is not yet truly alive... only halfway.

So look around you. Are you alive or are you just judging other people, saying they are not alive but you are? Or are you alive, saying that if they are not alive, then you must be part dead too because you are them, and love is not complete without all of us awake in it? Would God abandon anyone? I think not. I think that Love would not abandon life or it would not be Love. What do you think?

So when you choose fear, you slow your growth down, as well as everyone else's. It's okay to slow down sometimes. It's not okay to stop making progress at all. The Mother was given a budget, a time frame, as there are limitations to insanity, thank God! There is a definite point at which patience becomes indulgence. And, dear ones, you've reached it and gone past.

I urge you all to look deep. Take two months off. Put yourself in the closet with a bucket and toilet paper and fresh water to drink. Don't come out until that bucket's full or that water's gone. Then go back in all cleaned up, fresh, more water. Keep it up until you get to the point where you're willing to ask what love is, where you truly know you did not make it up, where you truly know you don't know what it is, and you truly know you did not create yourself or create love. The True Fire will then rise within you. You will know love. If you set a goal beyond the body, then the mind will go beyond the body's limitations.

Now, you say you make fire rubbing two sticks together. Fine. Stick your hand in it. Do you know what it is? Breathe it in. Do you understand what fire is for? No, I think not. You're afraid of it. The body is afraid of it and only needs it on cold days. You don't even understand the chemistry of the fire in your body that keeps you warm. You take it all for granted.

So, sit there in the dark and wonder about this form you're stuck in, and wonder what it's for. And wonder about this mind you have stuck in a brain, wondering what it is. Make a lodge or kiva in a dark closet, and go in there and ask for help. Then look at all the crazy ideas you have about devils coming to get you, and still ask for help from God, from Spirit, from the Holy Spirit. Ask for the good folks. Don't ask for more crazy folks to come in your head, 'cause they're out there, stuck in between worlds, not wanting to leave.

So before you go into your closet, I'll help you out with this one thing. God did not *create* a devil. Love would not do such a thing. Fear *made* it. Fear is not creative. It ain't real, folks. So dive deep and ask to learn with a clear mind. Say this:

Help me, God. I forgot You. I want to remember. I know You made me. I didn't make myself up. I'm not that smart. I give up my already knowing. I want to know what true love is. I've pretended so long. My beliefs have made me weak and separate from everything. I want to give pretense up and be shown what the truth is. I do not want to be separate anymore from the Mother here, Who nurtures us on this planet, and from my mother who gave of herself and nurtured me, this body, on this planet, in my time called now. I want to feel gratitude, instead of feeling regret or nothing at all. I do not want to waste my life, and I especially do not want to waste the lives of my children's children and their children's children for seven generations. I cannot think past my own pitiful concerns for yesterday, today or tomorrow. My mind has grown small. I want now to have a mind that can understand the world and the people in it, for the truth of it. And I'll trade all the sadness I've made for joy that comes from knowing death is not real and love is eternal.

Do this thing for yourself and for your children and for all the generations to come, for if you do not, there will soon be no more generations because you have stolen the life from the future by not giving love now. For, you see, love spoils inside fear and becomes useless. There is no nourishment from fear, I tell you.

I told you it'd be tough, listening to me in this way, in this hole. But you know, I haven't given you so many details as to spoil your journey of discovery yourself. We have been in that hole, haven't we? It's been me talking to you in there. You can go into that hole any time you want to talk to me. And, by God, I'll be there for you, and I'll love you all the way back to the Light, just like I'm doing for Barbara and John. Take a chance.

Now, to just reinforce the things that I've told you, I'll give you some details. I'm gonna' use many people's lives because I've been blessed with the ability to touch many people. I'll start with where we go wrong in interpreting our own energy. And I'll tell you when it begins, because I've seen it so.

The first mistake a parent makes is to try to make a child theirs. That child comes from God and goes back to God, so damn it people, give them some space. You get a baby and it needs all your tenderness, all your closeness, and all the security of a fearless teacher. From your mind and eyes and voice and heart, you show that baby that love is not fear. And that's your job. But don't try to tell them that you know anything more because you truly do not. Be honest. Be humble. And don't be too proud because life will come and snatch the good things away from you to teach you what is real.

If you've got a dog and you make it stay in the house and hold its pee water until it damn near pops because you're too busy to pay attention to it as a living thing, then, by God, that thing's gonna' leave you, whether it dies or walks off. And you will never really know what love is, will you?

So it is with children. You can kill 'em or set 'em free, and the sooner you set 'em free, the better off they are. And I don't mean free to be spoiled brats, tearing the place up, being rude, and showing no gratitude for their life and the life around them. I mean, set them free to learn that what you give is what you get. What you put out into the world is what is returned to you. If you are selfish, you will breed selfish people all around you, and you will have war all the time. And life to you will be merely a possession, devoid of meaning, with no love in it.

If you see that your child is from God, with God's lessons for you and God's lessons for that child, and you take a step back to ask Spirit what would be helpful for the growth of this child and for yourself, then you will not be so apt to indulge that child or spank that child or abuse that child or starve that child of love.

And when that child asks a question of you like, "Why is the sky blue?" you can tell that little one there are two ways to see an answer to this big question. You can say, "I don't really know, but science says the sky is blue because the light is trapped between the water in the ocean and the water in the stratosphere, and it reflects the color. Or you can say this, "I don't really know, but the old ones told me it was because the smile in God's heart for His children here is blue. That's the color of the truth of creation and the love surrounding it."

Now, which one you think will satisfy your child? Which one keeps a child's dreamtime from being terrible? Which one points to love and not to fear? It's better the scientists say, "I don't know. This is what the books say. This is what I was taught. But the truth is, child, the answers of our science only create more questions. We just made it all up because that's the way it appears to us with our instruments that measure things, with our telescopes and our satellites. We're having a good time finding out, just like you. Maybe when you're older, you'll be an astronaut and go see for yourself and tell us what you think. The universe is a big mystery to us too." Now, that's honest.

The second big mistake a parent makes is in misusing their own sexual energy, then communicating to their children these same errors about sex. And, boy, do you guys lie about that! Some poor little thing looks at itself and says, "Look, I got this innie or outtie. I see I can pee out it, so I guess that's what it's for." And you say, "Yah, that's what it's for, for now. But don't let anybody see yours 'cause they'll do bad things to you, take advantage of you, make your mind crazy."

Well, that's a pretty rough start on love, isn't it?–guilt and fear. You tell 'em, "Don't ask questions." And when those little ones do ask, nobody will tell them anything useful anyway, 'cause I don't think anyone knows anything useful, except "That's where babies come from."

I know a young 'un that still thinks dogs come from his mother's vagina because "That's where babies come from." Nobody said whose or what kind. So be careful what you say, folks. Little ones' minds are a literal sponge. What you say, literally gets sponged in there and stuck. And, I'll tell you, most of the stuff we speak to each other doesn't make any sense at all to a young one. Sciences' explanations are too dry and never talk about sexual energy at all... what you call "the chemistry between people." Lengthy discussion isn't helpful for a child's mind at the moment, so you don't say anything out loud, though all your thoughts are communicated instantly, whether you're confused or not. You demonstrate with your energy all that you believe anyway. Sex, then becomes a big mystery with much conflict in it, within the child's energy body. All sexual conflicts get stuck and eventually become an obsession because the energy isn't moving. Whether you are conscious or not, life moves on, and you and your children are left to play out your obsessions.

Now, you want to know how come pre-teenagers don't seem sick to the parents, then suddenly when they're in their mid-teens, they're really sick, doing weird things, being angry, hurting themselves, hurting others, even? What's that all about? Stuck stuff, I tell you. Things you said and demonstrated upside down and backwards. No one to unwind this stuck stuff with old stories. Grandparents don't live with you anymore. You don't like 'em 'cause maybe those grandparents never grew up either... too bossy, too petty, too slow, no wisdom, no stories... you name it. So, everything's stuck and confused.

Sex, if it wasn't natural, you'd have to buy it. "Excuse me, I'll take one long penis and two vaginas to go. I'm gonna' have sex." Doesn't work that way. You got one of those, and she's got one of those, and sex is a fact. But what about love? You see animals doing it and you say, "I don't see love. That just looks like sex to me–dogs and rabbits, you name it."

Well, I'll tell you what. You get out there in front of other humans lookin' at you, and I think your mind would be on them humans lookin', wouldn't you? Now when you're not lookin', and that horse and that dog and that rabbit are being natural, I guarantee there's love there. Because, you see, they don't have the same mind you do. Their mind is natural, unconflicted... innocent.

The only time I ever see an animal worry is when it's standing around a human. I don't see animals worry a lot elsewhere. Worriers don't live long. They think too much. They're not paying attention anymore. That animal worries because he gets what humans think.

You don't have the same survival pressures as animals, but maybe you hide in your room and think a lot. And what you think projects out of your mind and hits the mind of any living thing you're thinking about. But is what you're thinking what you want for yourself? Because minds are all the same, everything gets what you think, and their mind gives it back to you just as you sent it, like the reflection on the water. And, by God, you think your judgment is right 'cause you sent it and got it back as you sent it. Send your thoughts to love, and maybe you will get the truth back, if you ask. Send worry or judgment and that's what you get back.

Now, you look into a newborn's eyes and see what it's sending you. Before your mind can screw it up, that child sends what the Creator gave it to send. And if it wasn't for this, you would all be gone and dead from this place, long time ago. That's why you have children... to look at your innocence again, to look at the Love that sent you again, and to remember what you can of It.

So, when our young ones asked, "What's this part for?" we said, "That part you got there? It's to confuse you about what love is. Those girls, they've got the same part... looks different for growing babies. But makin' babies is only one way to find out what love is. I say, love is in your eyes, my young one who is now asking me what love is. Love is learning. I'm learning with my life while you're learning with yours. We'll all talk more, together, with your mother about marriage soon enough, young 'un. Let's go play."

If you don't demonstrate love to that young one, it must be because you don't know what love is yourself. True? If sex embarrasses you or obsesses you, then it's because you don't know what sex is for either. True? If you only want to take what you want from the world and give that selfish view to your child, then you don't demonstrate what love is, do you? And trying to steal love is a form of vengeance, is it not? They have it. You want it. So you try to take it because you're mad. You're mad 'cause you think you don't have it. But a heartless mind or a mindless heart attached to a penis or vagina is not love.

104

So maybe that child will need another teacher from somewhere else. But even the act of saying, "I'm not your best teacher–I screwed up–go ask someone else" is an act of love. You're halfway home already because that's the truth, and truth is your only way home. So if you find yourself in the questioning of the young ones and tell the truth, they will take you Home on their questioning. Let them. That's what they're here for, to help you too.

But if you are so bitter and angry that you'd rather squash the children like bugs, than to get down on your humble knees and look into their eyes, then God help you. Please see love somewhere in something, I beg you, not just for me or for them, but for all of us who want to go Home and will not go without you. We're all here waiting with you... still. And we will not leave you here by yourself to perish in ignorance and bitterness.

The third error parents make with their energy in communicating to their children really stems from the second and the second from the first. If it is your sensations that guide you, then you are asking the body to be God. If you are most sensitive in one place, then your god is obvious to you. If in this obviousness, you do not ask for help from Spirit, you may very nearly go into oblivion following this sensation. You could die from it. Others may die by your hand.

It's like this. If you press one spot hard on your arm and don't let up, two things die... the tip of your finger and the point you press on. That's a no-win situation. Both die. An overused organ either eventually fails or gets cancer from the excess energy channeled to that area. This is whether you exhibit some external behavior or not. Simply repressing behavior does not remove the conflict or energy. Still no-win, yes?

You have a thing in your culture called a win-win situation. That is where the giver gives and is happy, and the receiver receives and is happy. Only equality has value, so the giver gives and receives, and the receiver receives and gives, equally. Since giving and receiving are the same, there is no conflict. So remember, you only have conflict when there are two unequal or opposing forces, push and pull or push and push. So, you see, there is no compromise between conflict and agreement, between fear and love. There's just clearly one or the other, is there not?

My point to you is that love and fear are two totally opposite ways of being, and that there is no bridge between them except Spirit. If you are looking for healing in the world and you are not asking Spirit for help, then you will wander and wander and wander. And you will be uncomfortable until you do ask, for the world itself does not contain the answers you seek for your healing.

Now, conflict can come from different places. It doesn't necessarily have to be made up by you. You could be at peace, walk into a room, and two minutes later walk out of that room in total conflict and not know why or what it was about. If you ask Spirit for help to clear up the conflict, the feeling of being dis-eased will go away because we will take it and change it for you. And you may never know what was in that room.

But if you want to be conscious, we will even show you where that conflict came from, who originated it, and some idea of why. But until you want to be conscious, we will not bother you with those details because we love you, and you're not ready for them until you ask.

So please don't feel like I'm trying to shove down your throat the curriculum of becoming telepathic or psychic or becoming a medicine person or a guru or anything that doesn't suit you at the moment. We only wish to help you with your discomfort. But I'll say this, if you do not become conscious, you will again feel discomfort and still not know why. This world is complex, full of many peoples, all at different levels of their understanding, growth and healing. And you will soon bump into one another and have interactions that will cause you confusion, conflict, pain or grief, because love and truth pressure you to grow up whether you want to or not. You made an agreement.

So, you can drag out your lessons as long as you wish, until there is no place to work on them anymore. And there you are, procrastination in hand, wondering when your mind will change again, when you will have a chance to grow again, for truly you have not practiced growing, so you have stopped. And so it is until you wholly desire growth again. Yet, if we destroy this place where the Mother makes our bodies ready for us, where the laws of the world support God's wishes that we understand what love and truth are, this place will be gone because of our delay, our wastefulness, our lack of gratitude, and our unwillingness to learn what we have asked to come here to learn.

You give words to your energy without remembering that it is the energy of your thoughts that make the emotions. It's like this. Envy lies somewhere around the ankles, I think... about that level. Desire for power begins somewhere above the navel and goes down. And all the lower emotions of greed, jealousy, covetousness, anger, lust, and fears of all kinds live in the organs and intestines. I don't even know some of the words your language has because, frankly, we didn't let it get that far to catalogue all the ugly possibilities that a human could experience. We just said, "They're negative energies, bad ideas," lumped them into one pile and said, "Go have a look. Don't stay long. We'll wait for you here. Get your fill. When you're done, I hope you'll return to us with your mind blessed and clean. Because, as you descend into the lower worlds, you must ask for help from Spirit, and you must have a Guide, for you will surely get lost there to wander for years or centuries or eons, until you finally ask for help from the truth, from Those Who know it, from Those Who speak it from God, from Those Who saved the memory of what you are for you. When you have relearned what you are, you will return to us, a real human being."

You see, the truth by its very nature is automatically shared among all people, instantaneously. Everyone knows what the truth is, except the ego. The ego tries to persuade everyone else it knows the truth and pretends it is powerful. Because it has to spend so much time posturing and defending and convincing, you can be sure it knows nothing, because with the truth comes peace. An ego knows nothing of peace.

The young ones nowadays, they have egos for sure, but they're harmless... you think. Well, they're harmless until they give personal power to some belief, then act it out on the world. This idea of trying to be God gets started pretty young. They see their parents' egos pretending they created themselves, and the children imitate them.

In our society, we had structure for everyone, with certain goals that were not easy to accomplish. These goals took patience. They took courage. They took endurance. They took alertness. There were feats of character that introduced us into what being a true adult is.

In your society, you're an adult when you get a license to drive a car, can drink beer and have sex. That's your rite of passage... sex, beer and cars. Most recently, the subculture has added murder to the list of juvenile accomplishments required to be an adult. I think you cheat your young ones of knowledge of what they are.

It was a good thing to send your young ones to the military, I think, at least for basic training. They got their egos smashed a little bit. Only problem is, at the same time, they were brainwashed into believing the highest honor you can give to your country is your life. I think a higher honor is to give your life to truth and not die foolishly. To live for truth, for the love of it... now there's great honor in that, and it helps folks because you demonstrate for them while you're here. To run off and die for some small truth somewhere is not, I think, what God asks you to do with your life. What do you think?

How many people can name three martyrs out of about 5.8 billion people now alive? You can go way back in your history books, and maybe you can find three, maybe more. But add up all those ancestors that loved you, from the untold billions born, and you'll see that all the mothers and fathers for all times are martyrs for love. We had many chiefs and good people that died for love and truth as well. But I tell you, there aren't a lot of martyrs that stood for something that lasted forever, like love of the truth. There's one you know. That's your Jesus. Now, I think he stood for the truth because his heart was open. He loved. He gave. Can't say much for most everyone that followed. But what that one demonstrated was clear, don't you think?

Now, here you are in a wicked world trying to be good. None of you want to try to be Jesus because you don't want to be a martyr. But here you are, living between what Jesus taught with his life and what this world teaches today. You are trying to balance these forces of fear and vengeance with peace and love. And you try to balance your expression of love between powerful and weak. You experience difficulty because you don't choose between them. You just walk the tightrope between powerful and weak, between love and fear, between hot and cold... not choosing. You are still afraid of what will happen to you if you choose. Is *not* choosing any better than choosing in error?

I say this. Those who choose in error are at least learning. Those who never choose and protect themselves with walls of lukewarm indifference keep the world stuck in judgment and fear. Better not to be frozen by fear. Better to leap into the fire to find out what you are. Being willing is the first act of true will you must learn. Learning to learn is why you're here. The ego would teach you to learn only what it wants you to learn, but it is your will you lose. What it teaches will leave you in the cold, hungry, tired, and guilty... always you are left. What love teaches you, sets you free of the ego and all its contradictions. All love asks is that you trade your indifference for true neutrality, stop succumbing to fear as your teacher, and ask that Love once again be your Guide.

So, down the hole to the bottom we go, once again proving you needn't hold your breath, for even though there's fire in the below, Spirit will breathe for you and you will not burn. Though you take a great fall from up in your tree, your bones will not break. Spirit is your Guide and you are spirit too. Illusion is weak and cannot harm you. Fear is not real.

Chapter 11
Love's Will

The first energy center–and I'll borrow the word chakra from the east because you've all heard it by now–is that root fire that corresponds to the core of the earth, the Mother's heart. Be sure you do not understand what this is about, so that you may relearn it firsthand.

Picture yourself as never having seen a vehicle before. You jump in and try to operate it. Chances are you're going to get hurt if you've never read the manual for that vehicle or had a teacher. You either learn or destroy the thing you're trying to drive, or it destroys you because of your inexperience. That is what you are doing with your root fire.

Why everyone is so afraid to ask Spirit about sex, I'll never know. Why so much shame about this sexual root fire and so much confusion about coupling for love? Do not the Mother and the Father aspects of God do this? One spinning through the other, air moving, tension building, and there's lightning and thunder. Now, you may think it poetic, but I'll tell you, it's also literal.

Enclosed within this bubble of air around the earth, the fire from within the Mother's core heats, and the light from Father sun heats. And to keep things from cooking too bad, our Earth Mother spins and travels in an elliptical orbit which changes tilt season to season. All this causes friction of the air on the spinning surface. And all the dust blown up collects all the moisture that evaporated, then becomes heavy and descends as rain with the colder air. And the complex union of the light on the surface and the heat from within creates wind, lightning and thunder.

Now, you rub each other and have orgasm. And I say, They do too, our Mother and Father. Your mind wants to say, "Oh, this guy Hinono is a sun worshiper, an animist or a pagan, and there's no higher philosophy here with this. It's just loving the sun or objects or animals."

Well, you're part animal too. What you've done, however, is just worship yourselves as the highest creatures on the planet, and you imagine the One God as only male. Jesus tried to tell you that you're not so hot. Don't climb so high in that tree. Come down. Pick up the pitiful ones and help them, because they are you too. As for the One God, the Great Mystery, the Creator, all is included... the Mother aspects of creation, as well as the Father.

Well, kings and queens, walk-ins and walkouts... the starships, I don't think they're coming so soon. Relax. Be human again. Then maybe they'll come. I don't think they want you like you are. Just think of the chaos you'd bring with you in your mind. Why would perfection care to have you out there causing all kinds of trouble?

So, now you know why you're here... to get well. You are meant to laugh and love and dance together, and to have respect and gratitude for the things that you receive. And yet, you are to be willing to give all that away in an instant to one who thinks they have nothing. Spirit will tell you when to give. Your heart will know. Ask it.

So no one goes without. They walk in your within. Then I think a ship will come and take you home where you belong, for in this hospital you've gotten well from the inside out. Now, they might even overlook the plastic tits and the thousand nose jobs because you did that when your mind wasn't right. And all is forgiven, of course. But what have you taught those behind you who haven't made it to health yet?

Well, go back. This is your purpose... go back, confess your errors, help them forward. You get humble and show them how. You speak the truth and show them how. You forgive yourselves and show them how. You give thanks for all you've received and show them how. You give love back to the Creator, and show them how to do that too.

Start with one thing and expand. It's easy. Find one thing that you're grateful for. Find one person who has given you love, and expand to see the whole universe is here to give you love. All you need to do is stop chasing shadows... all those–what if but whys. Sit down. Pray that you can see truth. It's simple. It's not hard. It's not complex. Only the ego is complex because it is contradiction. Ego sees nothing but opposing forces... chess games, checker games. But there is no game to lose in love. There's only peace.

*

During the two years we were in Hopiland, that little one grew strong and wild like a bobcat. Her hair! Boy, was it–it was–it wasn't black–it wasn't brown–it was almost white. Now, you figure it. Boy, them Hopi looked at us funny too. That was the wildest creature-child I've ever met in my life. Even at two, she would run around and very nearly bite everybody's leg. She was a crazy one. She had the wildest sense of humor. You know what I think it was? I think it was because she spoke mostly Hopi. I think she was raised by them Hopi with Hopi language, and here she was living with us who spoke this other one, this northern plains language, this Athabaskan-like language.

Now, you want to find one root human being? Good luck! Won't happen. You are right, though. We all do have the same Mother. She bore quadruplet races, all different colors–red, yellow, white, and black. (Brown is a mix of any of these.) There's four races of us all. And we were put in four places. And then, we moved all over. Some of us were very adventuresome, very hardy souls, willing to risk everything just to know something more, to see something more.

Hopiland was magnificent. If I could sit at the Grand Canyon and play wren house with my mouth, awestruck at the beauty, those first people must have been stunned into silence, and that's why language didn't develop for so long. You see, Creator's very generous. Went to a lot of trouble here to make us alert and challenge us, so we don't get weak and fat and lazy.

Now, if you want to live life in Disneyland, you go ahead. But spinning around in a cup and saucer isn't what I would call a challenge. You see, I mix it up with you here on these pages. I give you a little entertainment, and then I whack your pants off. Well, that's good. See, a little challenge is good for you. You want to read a mystery? Well, how deep you want that mystery to be? You want a who-done-it that'll go to the end and still you don't learn anything? That's kind of the way life is. There's a who-done-it in this story too. But who is not so important as is, the Isness of it. It is still being done, the who-done-it. And you can see it firsthand yourself. Don't get stuck in cheap paperback thrillers, though. It ain't in there. The Big Mystery ain't in them books.

I suggest you turn around and look in the mirror, and see if your life is a cheap thriller or if it's a deep mystery. And then, honestly ask yourself what you prefer. All you have to give up is your fear of finding out the truth. Step out. Put yourself at risk. Find some folks who'll put you on the hill for a Vision Quest, then go without food and water for three or four days and nights. Put something at risk. And instead of bitchin', try praying. You might get guidance for your life, and Spirit may become more important than a house and a new car or social security or welfare or veterans' benefits. Quit playing pitiful to the system that's killing you with kindness.

This will sound silly to you, but we called that child Feice. Feice was a name that we had for a little animal that lived in the ground. This critter was wider than he was long, and he had stripes on his face. And he'd come out and grab something and pull it down the hole with him. And if you walked by that hole, he'd growl like crazy at you. You call him badger. They're just about the fiercest little things I ever saw. Now, if there had to be a demon on earth, it'd have to be that one.

That one had some good traits, though–fierce will and tenacity. Never gave up... ever! You could stand behind that thing and poke it with a stick, and it had its idea it was going to dig a hole and, by God, it'd get the hole dug. It don't care how many sticks are stuck in its butt. You get too close and it'll eat your ankles right off. Better be a long stick and you a good runner too. They're tough buggers... tenacious... dig fast too. They get to the bottom of things pretty quick. They make a decision and, boy, they do it! Them things were born with fire in their hearts.

So, you want to learn what a warrior is, go check out the badger. And be sure and notice that even the male badgers run from the female badgers when they got an idea going. There is a peckin' order, folks. Wake up. The earth belongs to female, and all you little egos running around the surface trying to look good and powerful, watch your ass! Screw up too much and you'll be brought down quick. If the badger women don't do it, the Mother will. It's Her job to discipline Her children when they get way out of line.

Now, if you're clever in the below, you can probably avoid correction for a long time 'cause you can feel it comin', and you straighten up a bit. But for those who trip past the barriers into true insanity, living in that underworld by lying and cheating and stealing and overpowering the normal people who fear you, you better watch out! There's a place for you where it all comes back tenfold. Maybe you're living it in the moment, but to relive it ten lifetimes.... I think I'd think about that if I were you. If you care to go that far away from love or peace or life, then it's your hell you make doing this.

The hell anyone makes has descending levels. What you think is one level. What you say is another level. What you do is another yet. What you do with full intention is deeper yet. What you do intentionally with vindictiveness, with true spite and defiance, with a complete split from any feeling whatsoever, that's another level yet. There are seven more levels after that. I care not to mention them, and I suggest you don't ask either. I hope the first three or four will suffice you to know that the end is physical death. At the bottom of these levels is total insanity, eternal hell, no return to God at all... in their minds. But even at the end of this corridor, God leaves a door open because God loves even the craziest of minds. At least that mind had the tenacity to get to the bottom of it. Always there will be a hand outstretched and Someone saying, "Are you ready to go back Home yet? Have you not had enough pain?" Dear ones, love has the same levels, ascending.

That thin membrane of honesty–whether you know the truth or not, to be able to say, I don't know what this means, what this is for, why this is happening–is the key. To say that and then inquire of the Holy Spirit, some source beyond yourself that is in touch with the Greater Plan for your life and for life itself, will deliver you from death. Then learning, true learning begins and you realize you don't have to be God. You can just be human. And as your mind matures and as your discipline over your emotions and your feelings increases, you'll be given more information, and you'll be tested to see if you still lust for power. And as you shed the encumbrances of the lower realms of emotions and sensations, your faculties of perception will change into vision because you'll have given those faculties back to Spirit to show you what they're for. You will learn faster and faster. You'll begin to see through time and see that life was not made to be terminal. And your fears will be replaced with wonder, once again.

Even an infant can walk this road. Especially infants walk this road. You see it in their eyes and in their smiles. They don't even know ego or what it thinks. They forgive it already. They see only God. They see only love 'cause that's what they've been given.

That's what they give. That's what they are. Do you not long for your innocence again?

This wild one, Feice, was a special gift to those Hopi, I think. They took to her pretty good. But the time came as spring arrived when we knew we had to travel back northwest to home. And during that year, Shuhinono and I were to recount, both of us, what we had learned.

We calculated it would take nearly a year to make this journey back. So one bright day, we struck out, one robe and a throwing stick amongst us, for now the child's things took prevalence in our minds. It's pretty hard to keep a banshee at peace, so we had lots of things to dangle and entertain her with, I'll tell you. You know what two people look like trying to carry a hot rock without it hittin' the ground? That's what we looked like carrying that baby. Tossed her back and forth we did, pretty often. Never seen anything like it. I even asked the Creator one time, what's this torture all about we got here? Didn't hear nothin', so I suppose maybe Creator is a little guilty up there about it, like we didn't deserve it, but somehow a mistake was made and here we are. Good luck!

But I loved that child. I looked into that baby's eyes, and there was just fire and play in there. That's all there was, fire and play. And I'm not sure which one was running which. I'd shake my head and say, Boy, this is going to be interesting when this one grows up. I think we'll have to live away from camp just to keep from having it torn up every day. If she's as smart as her eyes tell me she is, boy, is she going to create havoc in people's minds in our camp! Wow! I'm going to ask the old ones to start preparing themselves now to help us. I think we're in for a good ride. Never tried to ride a buffalo, but that's the kind of ride I think it might be. Fast. Full of dust. Lots of broken bones. Certainly, lots of bruises. Grab some hair and hang on for dear life!

This time walking, we decided not to go back to the tall trees. We went a bit west. It was a big mistake. It was the roughest spring and summer I've ever spent walking. The heat was intense and the thunderstorms that came up were fierce, dangerous ones, hail stones hitting the ground sometimes, torrents of rain. It was dangerous to stand on high ground, and it was just as dangerous in a storm to stand on low ground 'cause the water would come at you like a wall, rolling you over and over and over, 'till you thought you would surely die from it, then finding everything gone, including your clothes and half your skin. Took us nearly two hours to see clearly with our eyes again from all the silt and mud.

But way before we can see, there's the horrible realization that we didn't know where that baby went. When panic stopped, we realized she had to have gone downstream farther than us 'cause she's lighter than we are. So, away we went downstream still cleaning crap out of our eyes. Three-hundred yards, maybe, there she was, sittin' on a rock, pickin' at ants. Damndest thing! I've already buried her and given thanks that we had time with her, what little we did. Sure, she was dead. Had to be. I'm dead myself. No skin on my knees or elbows. Fingernails ripped off. But there she sat, pretty as a picture. All wet, but still got her clothes on, I see. Who is this woman in this child's skin? Shuhinono just looks at the ground and laughs. She says to me, "I've sure never seen anything like that. No, I haven't. Wonder who that woman is in that child's skin."

Feice can almost talk. I swear she talks Hopi. She talks to herself some. Doesn't sound like anything I know. So we gather her up, to her disappointment, since she was busy doing something else at the time. And off we went, Feice muttering... something.

Needless to say, our load was a lot lighter. This time we were careful to watch for those crazy storms building. Sometimes they'd roll through, three and four at a time. You get ten minutes off in between, lightning for fifteen hours. I thought we were goners for sure.

But Shuhinono, she'd sit beside some scruffy little bush and watch it all. And that baby would watch it all too. Heck, I'm 'bout ready to dig a hole. I guess it'd be like if you went to war, and you had a pee shooter, and the enemy had lightning bolts to throw at you... endless ones. Shell shocked, I think I was. How do you fight back against power like that? Go ahead. Turn all your lights on in all your cities all over the world. One storm like that releases more power than all of you consume in twenty days all over the planet.

Got to see something interesting, though. We happened upon a place where lightning had struck a tree. I think it sort of half missed, because it hit the ground right next to that tree. There was smoke coming out that hole when we walked up. So I dug down there to see what was still burning, 'cause I've never seen rock burn. I got down in that sand, and what I found would amaze even you. In your gas stations, you give away cups if you buy so much gasoline. And here it was, a whole set of cups stuck in the ground, six of 'em... glasses, sand turned to glass.

Now, it took me awhile to figure out how to get them unstuck from each other, but it was real simple. Just drop them. Yup, the klutz dropped 'em! And apart they came. One wouldn't hold water, but the rest of 'em would. Now this was a treat. I bet none of our old folks ever seen this. So we packed 'em in and carried 'em.

We left that one with the hole in the bottom though, since we couldn't figure out what we could use that one for.

Now, they were rough and knobby and scratchy all over, but they held water. Some of 'em had pretty colors all in 'em. Most of 'em were brown or black, though. We thought, this *had* to be medicine business, so we'll tote 'em back to the old ones. You know, I thought for a minute that maybe that lightning would find us carrying those things and get us, 'cause we didn't really ask for them. Usually, we ask for things and they come. This time, bang! And there they were. So, after about five minutes talking, we decided it was a gift and said thank you, picked 'em up again and walked on.

Feice got one. Wouldn't let go. So... guess that's hers. Except I hate to see her chewing on it. I don't know what it is, really. Never seen one before. I know now that it's glass, fused from all that 'lectricity comin' out of them lightning bolts. I tried to get that glass out of Feice's hand once. I'll tell you what. She was well named. Now, I could go to war with this young one and prove to her that I'm stronger, but I'll tell you one thing. Her will was stronger than mine... 'cause I wouldn't go to war with her over a glass.

Now, in our society, we pretty much let kids do what they wanted, as long as they didn't hurt each other, which they often did. But we tolerated that a little bit 'cause there's good lessons in bullying and getting bullied. Might call it grade school for what comes up in adulthood. But I don't think if a child wanted something that the parent wouldn't try to give it, not to spoil them but to help them learn with. We encouraged curiosity and learning. We encouraged questions. We encouraged their involvement in tribal matters and even family matters and even somebody else's family matters because it all mattered to us. True, sometimes we were short and didn't have time for good answers, but because we lived close together, everyone could hear what was said. And if what we said wasn't good enough, somebody would offer more to that young one. Never did we discourage that bright mind from participation in anyone's life, because we were all the same, you see. We had no secrets, no need for secrets, no need for lies because we didn't punish.

To ignore another human being in their questioning and in their sufferings is to kill half of yourself. It makes you sick, conflict like that. So we all watched for it in each other and tried to bring it all back to a place where we could have that mistake undone. It was simple. We communicated with each other. We forgave each other for mistakes. And we didn't punish, either in our thoughts or in our deeds.

116

And if a young one was to make a serious infraction, like the one who killed the other in a fight, well, that action itself was punishment. We needed do nothing more. Either that young one repented, as you would say in Christian religion, or he did not and got worse. The old ones would come and try to see into his mind and heart, to see if anything could be done. If there was any willingness on this child's part, they would help until they dropped. Usually, a young one that far gone would have to undergo his own visionary death experience, in order to be spiritually reborn, free of deep conflict. In a specific ceremony, the medicine people would induce him to have an experience of the death of the young one he killed. In that lodge, he would see himself as the other and die from his own hand. He, then, would shift into each one of the mourning family members and experience their suffering. Then, again, he would shift into the whole tribe and mourn for that young one. And if he emotionally lived through that, he would then mourn for the death of his own innocence and the innocence of all mankind.

Jesus did this and killed no one. Such a return to innocence by this path is guaranteed. We respected this rare person who made this hard journey back from death. It took immense will. We knew that if that young one did not run away, he would finish this process, and his will would be right-side up again. And we would all become whole again. Spirit promised it to us this way, long time ago.

The medicine people point one way, and if you go, you find out what's there. They point another way and warn you and say, "Only go so far, and please come back." And we do. And in that way, our minds stay whole. We see all the confusion a person can collect in their life, and we see there's really only one problem and one solution.

So, I suggest to you, simplify your lives. Use your wills not against one another but to bring yourselves to your knees and ask Spirit to help you. Give your will back to Creator to show you what it's for, truly. And you will find you are a healer and a medicine person too, because your own healing demonstrates to others that Spirit is real, that love is real. Your will apart from God is not real.

Now, I ask you, is it better to encourage your child to make a good living by being smart and learning the ways of the world, or is it better to encourage your child, while learning the ways of the world, to look upon it without judgment or fear in his or her mind? I think, if you want to be rich or famous, it is better not to let ego lead your life, or you will be rich and famous for a bad cause, and no one will truly be happy.

Fall came and we were still heading a bit west as we went north. The terrain was very rough and dry. There wasn't much game either, so we subsisted on mostly roots and seeds. The thunder storms were fewer, and the air at night was colder.

This little one, I think, is like her mother, yet stronger even. She sure likes the bugs. Eats 'em too. Fact is, she eats everything in sight, little rocks and big rocks, little bugs and big bugs. But I see those teeth are driving her crazy, so we let her do it. Keeps her regular, all them little rocks.

The longer we walk, the more mellowed out Feice becomes. She can't walk all that far by herself, but she's got a right-left grip on our little fingers and just sort of skips across the stones. That one has the strongest hands I ever saw. Doesn't like to walk much, but her hands are strong. Keeps her feet off the ground. And when we go to digging, she's right there, boy. She's got her stick too. Gonna' find something to eat. And she does. Everything!

I keep tellin' her in our language, You got to be a little more discriminating about what you eat. You're not going to have teeth and be an old one. And she looks at me with those fiery little eyes, her will stuck out there in her hand, holdin' on to something I'm trying to get away from her. And I go, Okay, have it your way. I warned you. And she mutters something in Hopi. I swear she does. What a funny kid.

I asked Shuhinono, Hey, is she speaking Hopi? What is this?

Shuhinono says, "I have no idea what she's saying. She's in her own world. Best we just observe, and wait and see how it turns out."

Never known anybody to have a will as fierce as that. Best not to fight it. Only creates hatred and spite and defiance, don't you think? Now, if that little one walked up and tried to take the eyeballs outa' my head, I probably would strike a fight, but it's got to get just that clear, believe me. There are limits for everyone. But without first communicating what those limits are, and without some warning to the perpetrator, those limitations can be misunderstood.

So it is with will. Two minds can do battle with each other for power, even two opposing thoughts in the same mind. But how does truth fit in? Is truth an item to be possessed by one person and not another... one side or another? No. I think truth does not belong to perception. I think truth has to be learned... how to sit in

118

it and see it and speak from it and speak with it and to be guided by it and stay in it. I think perception does not have time to wait for truth. What do you think?

You see, to possess a thing in the ego's world is to have a physical sensation of it. If the body cannot sense it with the five senses, then it does not belong to ego. The corollary, then, is that everything the ego can sense, it thinks belongs to it. This is a dangerous paradox. For truly, God would not have given you truth without the ability to sense it, to feel it, and to know it's true. Yet, truth cannot be possessed by the ego, so here we have a conflict. Do you evoke feeling within yourself, or would you have Spirit give you the truth that evokes a feeling?

I'll give you an example. Are you feeling hungry? I'll assume you'll say yes. Then I'll say, are you sure that's what you're feeling? And on second look, you'll say, "Well, my stomach's growling." Then I'll say, Yes, well, how did you interpret that as hunger? Does your stomach or intestines know what hunger is? What's hungry? If you sit Vision Quest or voluntarily fast for three days, you will find that there are many, many levels to this concept of hunger.

Now, a truly comfortable people would really never know what true hunger was, would they? Eat one bowl of white rice a day for six months, and you tell me what hunger is. It will keep you alive, but it will not nourish you. Ask an anorexic if they're hungry. They'll tell you they're not. So what is this mechanism?–hunger. I think it's a decision. What do you think? Tell me, based upon the urges your body sends to your brain or the sensations that it has when it has nothing to do but digest itself, is the body in charge of the mind or the mind in charge of the body? You can disregard the messages the body sends to you saying it's hungry, to the point that the messages are no longer heard at all, and you become anorexic and starve to death.

So, you can take charge and dispose of the body if you want. But why? Is will to be used against the form because you do not love it? What was given to you was given to you by Love. Yes?

I suggest you go deeper and deeper into the meanings of the sensations you feel. I will tell you that emotions are not the body's sensations. Emotions are sensations produced by the brain when a decision has been made. So, would you rather be run by your emotions or sensations based on erroneous decisions, or would you rather know what the truth is? If you do not choose truth, you will be unconscious. And I'll say once again, if you are unconscious in love, then everything will come your way to help bring you out of this state of stupor or resistance.

Remember always, beyond all these considerations, beyond all this learning, and beyond even me, the peace of God waits for your return. You try to give peace to yourself in little snatches and intervals. You cheat yourself. You could have peace as the foundation to all your thoughts and actions in this world. I don't mean weak peace, either.

Imagine this, love and will combined. I don't think you have imagined that before. Somehow you think will is power and love is weak. So you don't exercise your will to try to balance out this weak love, so love will come forward and be seen. But I say to you, this is an error. What good is aimless love? What good is a good aim without love?

The choice is clear. Wander this earth murdering to eat, scrambling for position and space and possessions, or let Love turn you to the right place, at the right time, to say the right things to the right person. Let your will be Love's Will, not aimless but purposeful. And everything you receive will be a gift. You will not have to steal love or steal food or steal time. If you would but receive the gifts that you are given and acknowledge them and be grateful, then you truly would be free.

I tell you this only because I look at my child, Feice, and I think, I'm not sure she knows what love is yet. But then, I'm not sure I do either. It's big! But I'll say one thing. She's got will down pretty good. This one will not be a child to have her treats stolen from under her eyes. This one participates in her life and does not shirk any approach of anything. I even think the real badger would back off some, taking one look into her eyes.

Now, I'm not suggesting that you go out and overpower everything or everyone. I am suggesting, however, that if you see love as weak or if you are afraid of the world, that you step out into your own yards and start looking around at what's there to help you. All those creatures are there for you. The wind is there, the earth, the water, the fires. They're there for you. And if you have not looked deeply into their meanings, then you are missing yourself. So, step out. Be a child again. Grab at life and seize it, and drink its depths and learn it.

Feice does not cry unless she falls and darn near knocks herself out. Little falls don't bother her a bit. Big ones, well, I think she spends about sixty seconds crying, then she's got no more time for it and goes looking for something better. So when Spirit gives you something tough to look at, some grieving thing, if you want to stick with it and cry for years, you can. You can get into it... sorrow. You bet. Lots of other good lessons will go by while you're stuck in sorrow. So the sorrow isn't really for a person or thing lost. It's for the fact that you never fully had it.

If a person dies and you miss the body, then you are forgetting the truth of what they are. Loving someone in truth is a permanent state, regardless of the presence of the physical form. Love completely one thing and, I swear to you, the whole of creation is yours, never to be lost. Don't worship sorrow as God. Give it sixty seconds and move on. Vow to yourself that love is greater than possession, and see that there is no loss in love. If you love totally, you know it cannot be lost. Those gone, love you still. If you miss someone because of love, you have made missing them separate you. If you love them still, then missing them becomes a bridge, and the energy between you flows, still. If you trust in love, then you trust that love can deliver your message. You trust then, also, that love will return a message to you. That's what Spirit's for. But you think Spirit's dead... ghosts... gone. Truth is, you're scared to invite "dead" people to talk to you. But Jesus said to talk to the Holy Spirit. He didn't say Spirit's dead. He proved Spirit lives beyond the body.

So try loving more than fearing. Try it. Holy Spirit is here in all languages and for all cultures. I learned English, and yet I talk to you with the thoughts of my culture, and I am what you call "dead," "ghost," "gone."

I want to put at rest all this fussing about how come I call myself an indian and use a little i. First of all, none of us came from the West Indies or from India, so we're not place bound and see no reason to use the capital. Second, if I didn't call myself something that didn't offend anyone in their belief systems, then I probably wouldn't be able to communicate at all in English. So I'll settle for you thinking I'm an indian but not so important as to want to be "Capital." The Hopi are just called, the people. The Navaho kinda' get some pride going and call themselves, the First People or the Real People. My tribe just settled for being good people.

Down under in the outback, my black friends have proof they were there thirty-thousand years ago. Their oral tradition has been maintained for nearly twenty-thousand years, and they still walk this earth for a time, though some of them have chosen not to have children anymore. Their understanding makes them the first people to stay in the same place that long and the first people to willingly leave this good earth. God bless them. This world will miss an ancestor. But it is up to you to remember them and to speak to them and to ask them what they learned. That way, their legacy will go on to help those remaining, as long as the earth shall support us in the lands that we all live. Their land has become too hot and dry to provide them what they need. And surely you see, the cities, though comfortable for the white person, don't sing the same song for the black native.

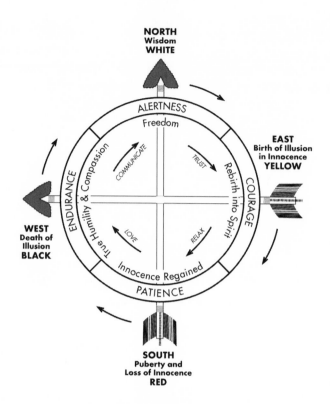

NORTH
Wisdom
WHITE

ALERTNESS
Freedom

EAST
Birth of Illusion
in Innocence
YELLOW

COMMUNICATE

COMPASSION

TRUST

Rebirth into Spirit

COURAGE

ENDURANCE

True Humility & Compassion

WEST
Death of
Illusion
BLACK

LOVE

RELAX

Innocence Regained

PATIENCE

SOUTH
Puberty and
Loss of Innocence
RED

Chapter 12
Circle of Love

There's a belief that our love for someone who is dead or no longer present, holds us to the past. This belief also says, since they are no longer present, they are lost to us. Certainly, they are missed in the physical present, if they are loved ones. But what is lost? The person or the love? There is a shift in perception that is necessary in order to escape grief or sorrow of any kind. The shift must be from missing something or someone, to gratitude for their having been a part of our experience.

What is helpful is that we feel love in the present in our thoughts about that one whose physical presence belongs to the physical past, whether they are alive or not. What is important is that we love them now, and although we miss them, we do not bind them here but thank them for having been a part of our lives. This love and gratitude links the past to the present. It is the thread which your heart calls God with. It is what you call the ancestors with. It is what you call a Holy Spirit or Guide with.

Seeing that heart thread is essential because you are used to using your minds to drive your life. It is important to learn to let your heart guide you and put your mind second. Believe me, you can still hear the mind chattering away, but make it the background to the heart. Don't make a decision in this world without checking your heart, first. You know what the truth is... in your heart. And if you don't think you do, you can ask Spirit, and you will be told as you ask. A gentle Voice, quiet, will remind you of what you truly want. This is enough for the average person's life, I think.

I'm not sure most people ever really desire to know God personally. Shuhinono and I did. Still do. Think about it every day. You bet. Feice, on the other hand, I think she already knows, and she's just going to go around playing tricks on everyone, just to keep them from getting stuck. There's something about a bright-eyed child that crawls up in your lap, grabs your food, crawls right back down, and never asks or says thank you that makes you check your thoughts, doesn't it?

Now, every one of us would have given freely what that young one grabbed freely, and yet it was the fact that it was taken from us that we objected to. So there she is checking everybody's thoughts, seeing how they're all doing. She'll take that thing and ten minutes later when your thoughts about it are all boiled over and dried up, she'll come back and give you a little kiss or a little pinch or a little kick in the foot or whatever is appropriate for your thoughts. I watch her do it. She'll catch you out. Good to have little teachers around you can't fight with 'cause they're too small. Keeps things clear. Creator's pretty witty.

Shuhinono does the same. She is more subtle, more quiet. But her piercing view of it all gives her the perspective to pop in one word or two and change your mind... let you know that you were wandering off into useless thinking based on errors, assumptions, misconceptions, hypothetical problems, and probable nonsense all the way. And I say, thank you, dear wife, you saved me some time. I haven't gotten to say that to Feice yet. She doesn't stick around anyway. I don't think she even needs to hear thank you yet.

Besides, how does ego get started? Tricky. One way is, somebody gets thanked so much, they think that that's the way to go to get to be God. All of that approval! Well, maybe so. Maybe not. Depends upon how high up the tree you climb. I think your own height off the ground is about all you should go, because if your ego gets outside the top of your head, you won't be able to get it back unless something traumatic happens to you. So keep all them thoughts in your head, so you can see what's happening. And pay attention. And when you get high, so high that you feel so good by yourself and there ain't nobody home on the ground, you better stop it or you're in for a big fall!

There are two ways to fall: one, you find yourself totally self-absorbed with how wonderful you are because you figure you're a finished piece of work, or two, you totally scrutinize other people by judging their weaknesses, so as not to observe your own. This second one is what I call an upside-down tree. Either high tree space creates the same hard fall. The higher the tree, the harder the fall. Remember, you made the tree and created the fall. Perhaps you should choose a small tree, though the lesson is the same, tall or small, rightside up or upside down.

Now, I'm not saying once in a while you can't have ice cream and cake and have a good time and feel high. I know you do it lots of other ways too–drinking coffee, smoking joints, bettin' horses, drinking alcohol, snortin' stuff, peeking in windows.... I won't go on. There's any number of aberrations you can collect along the way of that kind of thinkin'.

Yet, with God and the guidance of the Holy Spirit, all situations and substances can be turned into something helpful. If you decide alone what the meaning or use of anything is, you are aberrant. If an aberrant mind uses mind-altering substances of any kind without Spirit, including sugar, air or water... no good will come of it, except perhaps a lesson that can be learned in reverse. Yes?

So, don't get too separated from love, or you're gonna' have a hard ride back. Start lying to yourself about these things, these attractions, these addictions, and that ride's going to get double tough. Start pretending you never had these thoughts at all, and I wouldn't give you two nickels as a bet you'd get back by yourself.

Mind is not a joke, folks. It's got lots of rules. If it didn't, there never would be a paradise. There would be nothing but chaos and confusion. Kinda' like now. Lots of little gods pretending around. What do you think?

So stop lying to yourselves about all these things I bring up. I don't mean you got to own them all by yourself. I'm saying, the ones you do own you better be willing to look at. Truth is, there's only one mind and everything that is human you do own, ultimately.

In the next book, the *Earth* book, I will tell you more about this collective unconsciousness of which all must eventually be responsible for their share in ownership of it and end their unconscious part in it. But time is short, folks. The game's about up. You believe the truth can be kept below consciousness and not looked at, and therefore avoided. Although the truth is never altered in any way, your altered perceptions call to you all the lessons necessary to return you to truth. You cannot change reality, but you can believe because of your altered perception that reality is not real. So, what is in your mind will soon be played out in your life, whether you like it or not.

It has been said that with your perceptions, you create your own reality. I agree. However, to me, the One Reality is all there is. And that could never be created by you or anyone else with such a small mind. There will be a separation made between truth and illusion. I wish you not to be separated any longer from the truth. All illusion will return to the nothingness from which it came... all made up of fearful imaginings.

So, I tell you, there's a shake-up comin'. It's called clean-up time. People all over this planet have been asking for the Holy Spirit to come back and help. And we have. We've been here. Never left. Just waiting for you to ask... anything! And the time is now that this help is being received by those who want it and ask for it. Spirit can't do anything against your will, folks, except follow the path of truth.

Now, if you want to divert from that path, you can do it on earth time. But when earth time is up and you're called Home, you get what you get and you reap what you've sown. And the horrible thing is, the Creator reaps that too. That's what you'll return to Love for all the love and support you've been given here... whether you've taken it or not, whether you've received it or not. You see, receipt is an act of opening of the hands and mind and heart. It's not just stickin' your stinkin' hand out and takin'. Good thing God remembers you for what you truly are, rather than what you think you are.

You can teach your children to say please and thank you, but do you demonstrate gratitude so they know what it feels like in truth? Do you truly know what gratitude feels like? Without an open heart, how could you know? Are you grateful to man's world for the comforts you've won, or are you grateful to the Mother for the nourishment you've received as you are growing to maturity? Give lip service and pretend you know what gratitude is, and, oh boy, there's that tree again!

You know, porcupines, they climb trees to sleep, but damn, they don't live there all the time. No. They get down. They go from place to place. They find things to eat. They live their little porcupine lives, and nobody messes with them because others know from experience what the borders and limits are. Porcupines don't bother anyone. You've never seen a porcupine come up and sniff in a dog's face, but a dog will always go sniff in a porcupine's face and get whacked, don't you think? So, is that dog conscious or not? Well, he is after he gets whacked. I guarantee you, he won't go to another porcupine and sniff him up.

So how do you get conscious, folks? You make mistakes. The Source of Love left you here in good hands to handle those mistakes with Spirit. That's what this place is for, folks, to become conscious in love, not to see how much you can consume in one year. What good does making three-and-a-half-million dollars in one year do you, if you don't know what for? If you don't know what to use it for, it's just selfishness. And well, you're stealing, folks. You're stealing from the future if you don't give to it now.

How do you make money? Well, you buy this piece of land, cheap. You go over here and cut all the trees down, and you sell all the lumber off. Then, you wait fifteen years after that's been re-planted, and you turn around and sell it for ten times what it was worth, yes? That's how it's done. You bet. Where'd that money go and what's it for? "Investment in your future," you say. "Retirement," you say. Well, you ain't done nothin' yet. Why retire? Who have you helped? "You had jobs," you say, "lots of jobs." For what? What helps the people? Sure, you need to work in your world where plenty means lack. My people were thankful for everything, whether they had it in their possession or not. That's gratitude.

Sure, in your society, there's lots of things. You're very ingenious... lots of things made from trees, from oil, from milk, etc. Everything comes from the land, folks. The Mother knows that. Do you? Even the genius doing organic chemistry, making polymers, plastics, and hundreds of things, knows this. Where'd he get that base material from, them carbon chains? Something lived before us. That's what.

*

Only the heart can complete the Circle of Love and give back what it has received. The mind can't make this jump by itself. It can think it does, but there it is thinkin' all by itself again. I'll tell you, one mind by itself is damn near the most useless thing I could ever imagine. You could even write down every word you thought, every concept you ever had all by yourself. And I'll tell you, it wouldn't give a soul a thing because there is no soul by itself. Perhaps you could distill some meaning out of all that blabbering and lips flapping, for truly the mind is trying to find soul in all that thinking and searching. But I'll tell you once again, God gives meaning, not you. And you will not find it searching in an empty mind. So please stop trying to fill such a good vessel with meaningless babble. Open and be filled.

Stop cataloguing your world and start living in it. Participate. Don't slam your front door and think truth is not there all night. Dream some about the truth. Ask some in your dreams what the truth is. Ask how to see this world in a better way, so as to be helpful and to return some love that you've received. And if you think your life is so miserable you haven't received any, then maybe you should look again with the Holy Spirit's help and see all those folks, all this Motherland, all this Father Spirit that's poured into you to enliven you here. Perhaps your agreement to come here and be alive is not about what you came to get, but what you came to give.

So, here we are at the fourth chakra. I went through the first one pretty quick. I didn't mention the second much 'cause that's all your society's about anyway. Stuff! Socks, shoes, shirts, skirts, pants, hats, ties.... Damn! I've never seen so many things stuck on a human being in all my life. You're like a Christmas tree.

Diamonds, stuck on your fingers, saying you love each other. So who gets the diamonds when you split, when your lessons together are over? Where'd the love go... with the diamonds or with the person? If you fight to possess a thing, be it your perception of love or the diamond, I guarantee you, there's no real love in it. Remember, those negative emotions are stored in rocks. Diamonds are rocks too, folks.

Earrings stuck in your ears saying... something. Colored lips, colored fingernails, colored toes, tattoos all over the place... some in funny places. Little, tiny rings stuck in the nipples. I've seen some funny stuff while hanging around these two, Barbara and John. Now, I'm not saying all this stuff is hangin' off either of them, but I do ask them to go places and see folks with strange ways. It's a test for them to see if they still judge anything or if they can just be there and be helpful.

I'll tell you, the world's a strange place, and there's some strange minds hangin' around in it, thinkin' some strange thoughts. But you know what? I think you're all bored with your own minds and don't know what to do with your lives. The plain ol' love you see in your own society, you don't like. It stinks! And I agree. It's pretty shallow stuff. But what have you risked to deepen your love?

Put something at stake, bud... not just your nipples. The fact that you pierce them and torture your body is proof that you think it's a prison. And yet, you cling to it for so-called safety, like it was going to save your life. Take a chance.

If you're bored, it's because your own mind bores you, and you judge the world for your own mind's emptiness and shallowness... because you'd rather project onto the world what *you* really own. If you look at your own mind, you'd have to do something about it, wouldn't you? Can't do a damn thing about anybody else's, can you? Pretty safe, I'd say. Take a chance. Look inside and do what Spirit suggests. Ask for help. Give up the idea of yourself as body, then you won't have to die to prove you aren't it.

Now, I'm not saying you have to give up skimpy briefs and performance bras in order to get to God. You can stick all that shit all over you if you want. But forget it's there while we're talking, 'cause if you're paying attention to how you look or how you sound or how you feel, you'll never get to the part of your mind that talks to us.

Now, you're sayin', "This guy's pretty feisty. I'm not sure I want to talk to him." Well, there are other people, you know. I'm not the only Holy Spirit in the crowd. Christianity says, "The Holy Spirit." Well, that's true. There is One Holy Spirit, but it's like a vast room. How many Holy Spirits in the universe can you fit in this room? Well, everyone who knows what God is, everyone who knows what they are, and anyone who asks to do this job and is asked by Creator to do it... that's the Holy Spirit. Anyone who can do God's will and say God's words and love like God, that makes them Holy, doesn't it? The key is that they know they are Spirit and not the body. And yet, they must have had experience of the body. How else could they know what you're going through?

Sure, you got bishops, you got cardinals, you got priests, you got ministers, you got seers, you got prophets, you got shamen, and you got medicine people. And somebody in your crowd, they're gonna' try and pick one out and say, "Hey, he's a holy man" or "She's a holy woman." Just like in our tribe. We got serious ones... old ones, some of 'em pretty darn wise, some of 'em fools... born that way, can't stop, won't ever, never thought they could, never tried. Sweet as raisins, but being shriveled and sweet don't make you smart or a Holy Spirit. Takes work.

So there is one guaranteed fact. To be Holy in Spirit, you got to go through death. You got to go through that final illusion to know what you are. Now, I'm not saying you have to wait 'till you die to do that. Spirit can show you that right now. It's not hard. Do it in your dreams... easy. No sweat. The experiences Spirit gives you can change your feelings and thoughts and emotions about the fear of death... easy. Just let 'em. Ask 'em. They'll give you visions and dreams. They'll give you experiences that you don't have to go out into the world to get and probably couldn't anyway. There's not enough people out there conscious enough to really help you.

So, right now, let 'em pour it out, just like promised... Holy Spirit all over the damn place. What you gonna' do now? Here it is. Offer yourself up. Are you going to grab at it, or are you going to receive it? You can pretend you got it, but do you?

Now, there are those that truly do channel a Holy Spirit. The Holy Spirit does speak through them. And there are those who "think" they channel... something. Because of this more recent phenomena, there are those that think their life is somehow special because they channel, but wanting to be special does not make it so.

So who is fooled? Are your thoughts and desires for specialness using you? This foolishness is apparent to anyone who is no longer a fool. Always a fooler is the last to give up foolishness. If you have a role to play with Spirit, it is because you have earned responsibility and are humble in it. Joy is not remotely similar to an exalted ego. Fulfilling your purpose will bring you joy. Pretending to have a purpose other than to let Spirit lead you to the truth is ego.

I tell you, you don't have to pretend. You can receive the Holy Spirit and it's yours forever. Everyone will see it in your eyes and in your mind and in your heart, and they will hear it in your voice, because all your energy centers will be joined, and people will joyfully join you too. And when you speak Spirit's words, Love's power will fill the room to overflowing and will go to those for whom it was meant.

Now, you'll be tested for your desire to use this power for personal gain and edification. But as long as your attraction to ego is weaker than your love for God, you will not seek weak power. Love and truth will just flow through you unimpeded, and you will learn and learn and learn, and you will help and help and help. And you know, feels better than stealing, I bet. Feels better than taking, I bet... giving.

A Course in Miracles says that Spirit's purpose is to reverse all the laws of man's world and make them align with the laws of God, transforming this planet into heaven again. No big deal. Easy. Starts with you. Any volunteers? Anyone willing? Doesn't take too much, just a little willingness to get started. Once you get started, takes a little bit of courage, a little bit of patience, a little bit of endurance, a little bit of alertness to keep on learning. Creator gave you these things already, but you must relearn their true meanings and use.

There's lots of plateaus. Just like hell, there are twelve levels of heaven. But by the time this book is written, somebody may have thought up a thirteenth heaven or a thirteenth hell. Any volunteers? Lots of thinkers out there. I volunteer for heaven, but the rest of that thinkin' can go to hell. If you make it up to the fourth level, the heart level, you're doing better than almost anyone ever thought of. If you make it through the first seven levels, you're doing as good as Jesus did when the blood ran through his veins, and his feet walked this good earth. What do you think about that? Sound too tough? Just don't look down on anything, for although you are ascending out of hell, you will miss the good parts, the release, as you ascend into heaven. You will miss seeing the face of the Helper Who was sent to you. Keep looking up.

The one thing about the truth is, there's certainty with it, and it will not waver or falter or compromise. So if that's tough, then, yes sir, the truth is tough. And the love behind it is not weak either, is it?

So, you can walk this way or that. No big deal for you. But I'll say this. Every mind is joined. The strong ones will lead and the weak ones will follow. So what do you want to teach? Love or fear? Abundance or lack? Peace or conflict? As a leader, would your strength come from ego or the Source of Truth? Would you pretend knowing to appear strong and then lead your people to disappointment? Go first to truth and return with certainty, and the people will know you are a leader, and there will be no disappointment. See how sad the world is? Do not disappoint.

From here, I'm sure it's easy for you to see that it is good to light the Fire of Love within one's heart. But first, you must get through base desires in the below... a hot, fiery place, full of sensations, temptations, dreams of the body and of death.

I'll say this, if death was real in any place, it would be at the bottom. But you see, the ego is upside down and worships the bottom. So, if your consciousness is obsessed with all these bottom parts and ideas, at least you know where you're starting. I know other folks climb so high in their tree that they don't even know their bottoms exist or that there is a bottom. I'll say this too. Everybody gets a turn. Nobody that gets a body escapes the learning that it has for them. You can't skip anything.

So if you'd rather be high and mighty and live in a museum... spotless, than to come down and wipe the dirty noses of little children or the backsides of old people, then it's fear driving you

130

up in that tree, in that museum... fear of living your life in your body. You'd rather live it in your mind and not be touched by anything dirty or unclean.

I'll say this, you are worshiping what is unclean by putting perfection in such a dead place. Leave perfection down here on the ground. Get down here and wash the dirt off for someone. And give love through your heart, so that they know that they are not their dirty nose or their backsides. Lend a hand. Don't strand yourself or abandon yourself in a high place. Give it all away. Give it and it will be returned ten-thousand times. Keep it stored, protected, locked away, and you're its prisoner and it owns you. You have nothing.

Our people gave everything away when someone close died, like right now, so the grieving one left behind in that camp would take their eyes from those things and put their eyes to the people around them for help in their sorrow. All personal things of the departed one were burned or buried, so that the loved one left behind would not hold to this place the one that had dropped their robe and walked on. They must continue their journey to Creator, knowing they are loved by you, and that your love will set them free on their journey Home.

Usually, the one left behind would give away even their own clothes, to show that they are both free and willing to start a new journey. All the other people around them would help them gather *only* the new things that were needed for the living of one's new journey. For one year, the one left behind could recount their experiences with that good one just parted. By doing that, the one left behind worked through any remaining grievances or attachments, so the one gone could walk free, with no ties to this world except love and gratitude.

How many of you have unfinished business with your mothers or fathers? Wow, save everything for the last. I say, it's too hard to work all these things out without that person present. So do all you can now, for you have no elders to help you relive the past in your visions. You have no visions. You've blocked them out. You don't want to see what the truth is. You're hiding from it. You think you have to give something up to get love. I tell you, love gives everything. Take a chance. Risk something.

Don't be afraid of nothin' because the ego talking to you about what might happen is still nothin'. Never was something. Never will be anything. But if you stop and listen to it, it will guide you... nowhere. If you hear it, say, "Thanks for sharing, but buzz off." Then, maybe you will pray some that day and ask for guidance

131

from Love. Then, maybe you'll get somewhere.

Belief in death has no possibilities. And love does not need your belief, for it is the only thing that is possible. There would only be death if there was not life. Yes? You think it's genetics and copulating that makes life continue. I tell you, it's love that continues life. Perhaps, when you find out your genetics can change as your mind changes to the sweet singing of true love, then you'll see what guides what.

You still think that it's survival of the fittest, perhaps. Well, I'll tell you this. The buffalo was the fittest creature I've ever met, and man had ways of killing it, didn't he? And if there's still some buffalo left, boy, you'll be sure to take their spirit so they can't roam free and get strong again. Set a beefalo free and it will perish or become buffalo again.

So, be careful. Turn back to what love is. Don't sacrifice one thing for another. Love makes no sacrifices. I'll say it again. You can wear your leather shoes and eat your fried chicken, but honor the thing that gave itself to you of love, through love, and by love's direction. It is not that you take. It is that you take without receiving. It is that this Sacred Circle of Love, this one of giving and receiving, is not completed. Are your cows happy to die for you? It is your recognition of the completed circle that is necessary. It is that you become conscious in love that is required.

The Void is about what is unconscious. It is love in there, unformed, ready to try again. I wonder if you would rather go to the Void, unconscious, and wait to be reborn again to learn these lessons or if you would rather have them learned within you now and remembered and given, so that the future may have brighter eyes and stronger will.

I think Feice is a good teacher. I'll tell you why. She is not self-conscious in her perfection, so there is no interference. When she gets older, maybe she will become self-conscious of her body-self and will begin to interfere, to make objections, to have doubts about herself, to lose her will at various times, to play with her mind and her feelings, to examine what she thinks she is... without Spirit. Then her gifts will diminish for a time, until she has conflict with her ego and takes her will back from it. When her will is her own again, it is God's again too. That is the Will of God, is it not? Why would God give you a will and not have it be your own? God wants your agreement that your life is for love, for joy, for learning, for teaching, and for sharing.

So in her perfection, she's not aware she's Feice at all. Even the name Feice, I assume, will soon irritate her, and she'll choose one of her own. She might even grow out of this extreme willfulness and have it be balanced with purposeful will, helpful will. Her will, right now, is like a waterfall. Not much use you can make out of a waterfall. Look at Niagara. Go ahead, put it to use. Good luck! Go downstream, since things are a little tough at the waterfall, then you can harness a little energy from that water, then you can bathe and wash and you can drink. But at the base of that waterfall, there's so much happening, there's so much power hitting those rocks or hitting that water, you do good to see or think or hear.

Our will is like that. At the point of service, will is too strong for us and causes us great confusion. We think we're it, and there goes power. Wow! We think we're powerful now. I tell you, if you seek power, you seek death, because power in the world... that's all it is. Don't do it. Whenever it is offered to you, you can be sure it's the dark one speaking. Wants to drag you down the hole for awhile, suck the good energy out of you and use it for nothing good. So beware. Be aware.

Do not lose consciousness if you have it, even a little. Hang on to what you got. Don't be ashamed to say it's not enough and doesn't look good. Say, "This is what I got. I'm working on it. What do you think?" And the other person's saying, "I think you're doing a darn good job. Keep it up. How can I help you? Got any questions? I'm not the brightest light in the universe, but I see I've been down this road and you haven't. So I'll tell you what I did, how I got into trouble, and how I got out. Maybe it'll save you a trip. But far be it from me to tell you not to take this trip, if you want it. Plenty lessons."

So folks, it's not what you choose to learn or choose not to learn, for in this you truly have no choice whatsoever. You must eventually learn the lessons put before you. Unwillingness to learn is what creates distortion in your perception. Therefore, every decision you make has a consequence, a road to travel. And you will learn something. You might not like the lesson you are learning, or you might like it lots. That's your choice. That is the nature of perception, though all God's lessons go beyond perception. There can be no distortions with the truth. Yes?

You can go traveling with the gophers, livin' on roots in the dark, scratchin' around under the ground, diggin' forever, never findin' nothin'. Can't see anyway. It's dark. Find gold... bite it... oh, it's soft... spit it out... not root... bye. I never seen one of them gophers that's got pockets, but they claim they do. Never saw one carry anything out of a hole, except a dead brother.

So, you want to mine for riches underground in the dark? That's first, second, and maybe even third chakra stuff. You see, joy comes out the top of your head, seventh chakra. If there is another hole, it's got to be in your rear end. And lookin' out your rear end at the world is upside-down thinking. What you find looking upside down at everything may look like reality to you because, yes-siree, everybody's got one, but it doesn't mean they're lookin' out of it. Nymphomania... lookin' out your vagina. Anal sexuality... lookin' out your rear end. Wherever you focus your attention, that's where sensation will be... first chakra front or backsides, male or female. First chakra is root fire.

Now, I'm gonna' add this because I'm sure all this chakra talk is confusing. Upside-down thinking is drawing conclusions and acting from your head without your heart, while looking down through the first chakra or any lower chakra. Backwards thinking is when you are in an emotion while you're upside down, and instead of directly feeling that emotion, you have a fear of it and project its effects on others.

I'll give you an example that covers all others. True love is a total experience. In this world, most experience love upside down and backwards. It's like this. Upside-down love is experienced merely as sensation of the body. Let's say, sex. Backwards sex is then experienced fearfully, and all kinds of mechanisms are invented to project guilt on others for the lack of performance in sexuality to prove the impossible. The impossible, of course, is to prove that the body can love at all. Love comes from the Source, and unless you join with that Source and become rightside up, you will not face the truth frontwards and become love and become able to give it. Anything less than this is a distortion.

Second chakra. Wherever you focus your attention, that's where you'll be. Upside down... lack, greed, jealousy, envy. Backwards... fear of lack, fear of greed, fear of jealousy. You can reverse everything. There's always an opposite. But these lower emotions don't serve mankind too good, do they? Even frontwards and rightside up, this chakra is only about basic physical survival.

Third chakra... will. Upside-down will is will to power over everything and everyone. It is force, constant battle and conflict, whether within yourself or projected outward. It doesn't matter.

Fourth chakra... upside-down heart. Wow! What do you think that would look like? Giving is taking. Giving to get. Taking everything. Never enough. An emptiness bigger than the universe. God's not there. Can't see God anywhere. Sure you can't. Your head's on upside down. You're bringing darkness up to the light, but darkness still fills your eyes. You haven't let it go yet.

134

Backwards... you're mad as hell and won't take it anymore off anyone... especially God!

Try an experiment. Go outside with a candle or flashlight. Point it into the darkness and see how far it goes. See how much candle power is required to brighten. Now, tell me, to make it daylight in your town, how much candle power would it take to light up the place for everybody? I don't think you got that kind of power. What do you think? And that's just physical light.

But if you add your little candle power of your consciousness to Spirit's candle power from God, you will get enlightenment as quick as you want it, as quick as you can stand it. And you will find out what you cling to is what you prefer more than God, I assure you. These temporary preferences will come up, and you will be surprised. Is it your "thinking" you prefer more than God?

Don't get too personal with all your thinking because it's really the ego's thinking and the fears of the world. Give it up. Say, "I don't want that. I didn't want to do that. I didn't know I thought that, so that must not be truly me. Good-bye." That easy. To do it, to actually give ego thoughts up is what's important, not thinking about doing it or thinking you've already done it. If you think you've already done it, believe me, it will come by again just to see if you've really done it or not. You will be tested. Only the truth is true, folks. Ain't no wobbles in it It's certainty.

Trick is, maybe you think you originated all the thoughts in your head and nobody else had 'em, huh? **The truth is, you never originated one thought that hasn't been thought before.** But you do have the problem of sorting it all out, what's true and what's not. I suggest, to make your life easier, that you watch your mind like a picture show and be dispassionate. Don't add your belief or will to any of its suggestions or judgments, until you ask Spirit what the truth is. Then reality will dawn on you of its own. It is God's Will you know the truth. Your will was meant to be joined to God in certainty. In that joining is the effortlessness that love would have you experience. Without that joining, extreme effort will be required, but still you will be alone and will never be able to transfer your learning to anyone.

If ever there was a certain person of certainty in the whole world, it's certainly got to be Feice. So I'm hoping she doesn't lose herself when she awakens to the fact that she is in a body and gets all those sensations and emotions that women get when they mature.

In our tribe, maturity happens about eight to eleven, with the majority at nine. And most are married by twelve. Some are married at ten. Those that lived past the age of two, if they didn't sicken or were not killed by accident, lived pretty long... for us. I think the oldest person I met in our tribe was, in your years, about sixty-two.

We heard tell once of one woman living to her eighties, but that was before my time. And for us, it wasn't how long you could live, but what you learned that was useful and were able to communicate to your storytellers, to be preserved for the next generation coming up. In this way, we gave to our children our entire lives, so they would not have to start all over again and repeat all our mistakes. It was this that gave our lives meaning.

If you were thirty-nine and debilitated with chronic pneumonia or gangrene, then what good life was it? We gave it up easy 'cause we knew we could get another one. And if you were sixty and senile and couldn't see or walk, couldn't hold your water, couldn't chew your food, what good was it to live longer? No quality. We'd give it up, so we'd get a new one. We'd be happy about that, you see, because then those here didn't have to drag us around and waste their lives wiping our butts. What good was that? Sure, people take care of you past your time 'cause they love you, but who is it up to?–leaving. Are you going to let it be up to everyone around you to tell you when to go? And are they going to let you go when you want? Would God take you before your time, or are you eased up to the time so you can choose to go, rather than being pushed out of a rotten form? Come on, folks. Take responsibility. Learn what you are.

If you love something, like your children, why burden them with your pitiful life? Why have a pitiful life? Have something more. Drop your fear. Talk to Spirit. Ask, Hey, where's the door, man? I'm tired. This body's worn out. Gimme' another one. I want to come back and help... do this love thing with my people, but I can't do it without my eyes and my ears, without my hands and feet, without my heart, and without my mind. And if these things don't work in harmony, then get me a new one. You're the Creator. You love me, yes? I ask. I'm asking now. Pass me on. Teach me what I need to know to let me go. Give me a new body. Have me come back and be with these good folks, in good time. You do it. You plan it. You fix it. I know You know how, 'cause I'm here now.

Your people's time is a little different. In your time, you got to look at why you got something like pneumonia... 'cause you got time. In our time, we got no time. If we got pneumonia, we either lived or died, and that's that. Problem is, hangin' on because you're afraid to go is like saying there ain't no God and love ain't real. Well, look it here. We worked that out quick. We asked. And, by God, Spirit talked back.

So, we talked to God that way, real personal. Even when we were mad, we'd cuss and say all these crummy things, but you know, Love only hears love. It gets only what It gives. If you don't give it, It don't get it. That's that.

Now, I think I'm the only philosopher in my tribe. They said, "Oh well, you're a shaman, you know, 'cause you've been through this training." And I said, Oh yah, okay sure, fine. But I knew that I wanted to see something... deeper. And I wanted to have it, so I could give it away. So instead of practicing my trade, so to speak, I recognized I didn't know enough to practice anything, except learning.

If you give up learning for anything, you are dead and don't know it. If you are discouraged in your world and choose to stop learning, you burden your children and their children and the children after them. If you do not communicate what you have learned to those following you, you cripple your children and their children and the children after them. You need to ask Creator to help you have a better heart and mind now, whether you choose to live or die. If you leave, you must start over. If you stay, you must start over. Either way, you must awaken into Conscious Love, because if you don't, you're eating your great-grandchildren's food right now because you're too afraid to do anything and too arrogant to admit you couldn't ever have created yourself.

Everyone's counting on you... even Creator. Because you got this chance to learn like this, everyone's counting on you. So how 'bout it? Now, love doesn't have a bank or investments that go bust or empty. Love just is. You only *seem* to lose if you don't return what is given you, because you never *received* it. You can't have it until you give it because you'll never see you have it until you desire to give it. Truly, it cannot be given to you until you have a need to give it. When you need to give it, it will be there. God promises it. That's the Circle of Love.

So relax. Receive what's given when you need it, and in giving it away, you will feel gratitude for its receipt... for having it... for giving it.

It's like this. Carrying water is very heavy. No one would leave camp for anywhere if they didn't have faith they would find water. Yet there are people all over the planet, so water shows up when you need it. If it doesn't show up, then your passing on was arranged... agreed upon. Trust and Love are conscious. Fear is not conscious. When we went walking, we went walking with Spirit, so Love gave water and food when we were thirsty and hungry. And we gave that to our child, and we all sang songs of gratitude for what was given us. That's what we gave back for the love given us... gratitude. Creator didn't run out of love, and we never ran out of gratitude.

Love is not like a dry-cell battery, either, that you just keep using until it runs out and it's dead and that's that. Love is like one of those batteries that have seemingly endless recharges. You, too, get recharged endlessly, if you just expend some energy in giving gratitude. If you don't discharge, you will never receive more energy than you already have. And if your batteries aren't discharged to the fullest, you will not receive a full recharge.

I hope I explained that. That was a tough one for an old indian. Never seen a battery in my life. They say these new nickel cadmiums, they can recharge 'em a hundred times. Good idea. The new alkalines you can recharge, maybe, a thousand times. I'd like to know how they get that energy in there in the first place. Tell me that. I can learn something too. How'd they stuff all that 'lectricity in there anyway?

Now, I know how you get sugar out of sugar cane and sugar beets, and how you dry it all up and stick it in a candy. Good idea. Lot easier to carry than a whole bunch of sugar cane. See, you're just like us. Don't like to carry too much. And I see how you refine all that oil to make all that gasoline and diesel fuel and kerosine and all that. I understand all that... how you take one thing obvious and cook it up into lots of little unobvious things. That I got. But when you take a little carbon and you stuff it into a little container, I'd like to know how you can keep those electrons from runnin' wild in there, how you can keep 'em inside that thing. That I don't know. Even electric thunder bolts don't keep their charge. They've got to give it. How you keep it all stuffed up in there like that, I'll never know.

God gave you love too. How come you keep it all stuffed up inside like that and never give it? Don't make no sense. What you saving it for? Think you won't get more?

God is life. God is love. Life is love. There's always more. Never was *none*. Never will not be any, either. It's your mind joined to the ego that tricks you into thinking there is not enough love. So work on your own mind. Don't judge the world outside for what it thinks. You're it. It only thinks it because you don't demonstrate anything different. Think different. Ask the Holy Spirit to show you the truth. Now, that'd be different.

Give love... free. Now all you young ones go giggles and say, "Oh, got to screw everyone whenever we want... give it to everyone, free." Spirit never said screwing until your head falls off has anything to do with love. I know all these people that do lots of boppin'. Don't know anything about love. More like a new kind of fad exercise. I'll tell you, you play on the brink of madness. This earthly world has checks and balances for foolish behavior. Makes you put something at risk. Makes you pay attention, yes? You think about it.

Playing your way back to God unconsciously has a playback that's just as intense as the forward play you ran out. If you go fast-forward through your life, the abrupt halt at fast speeds is sometimes more than a body can stand. There's a comedown from that high tree. There's a halt from that fast speed. In stillness, the truth remains firmly on the ground for you to see.

Take your mind and treat it like a seed. Find a good spot on the earth that feels good to you. Put a shelter over it. Build a fire outside. Put rocks in the middle of your shelter, hot ones. Take 'em in that covered lodge, and pour water over them hot rocks. In that Sweat Lodge, you learn to pray by planting your mind like a seed in that fire. You give that prayer to that fire, and that steamy water turned to air will carry your prayer to God. Stop pretending your life and ask for truth to come in. And in that lodge, that womb of the Earth Mother's, you too can be reborn into truth. Honor all living things in that place. Spirit will talk to you in there, but tell the ego to stay outside because it's dead, and you don't want dead things to enter the Mother's womb with you. Treat those around you with deepest respect. Honor their lives and your life will be respected and honored too.

Give gratitude for what you receive, and all that you receive will be alive... not dead. The air you breathe will enliven you. The water you drink will cleanse you. The food you eat will sing good songs to your form and make your body healthy. Your will... *will* come back. And you will see that the truth can make you strong. And you will see that Love is the only Power there ever was or ever will be. And in this sight, your physical eyes will give up their preferences, and your mind will see the whole picture... the One Picture God would have you see.

All at once, your mind will be returned to you, and it will help you, for there will be no more war in your mind, no opposites, no dark corners to frighten you. Then, finally, you will know that ego was never real, just as the idea of death never was either. And you will know that you are not this body you inhabit for a time. You will see the innocent child you thought you were is still there, and is you. You will see the illusions of birth, growth and decline are nothing more than brief moments in time on your walk around this beautiful and Holy Circle of Love.

Chapter 13
Feeling Your Song

Feice's been talkin' for awhile. But honest to God, although I knew what she meant, I couldn't understand a word she said. Nowadays though, she's around us more on this walk than the Hopi. And frankly, she's beginning to make a little more sense with her words. I noticed at first that she would just kind of point and grunt, "Uhhhh"–There it is–that's what I want–give it to me.

That was good. That was fine. We could deal with that. Shuhinono knew instantly anyway. It's like their minds were one. Me, I kinda' knew. And because she was such a curious child, I paid close attention. Other kids go play and you don't even bother with what they're saying or what they're doing. You're not interested in their fantasy life much. They just go play, and they come and try to get you in it. And you go, "Oh, too hard a switch for my mind. Check me later." And then you never do, so you don't know what's going on inside your child's mind.

Well, there's just the three of us walkin', you know. Not too many distractions. And it was good to watch her. I got to see the interaction between her mom and her, and I got to see that these two didn't think that they were not capable of understanding each other. They didn't give up 'till they did.

Now, with Feice, I'll say this, she had much less patience than Shuhinono did. If you didn't get it right **now**... heck, she was gone, outa' there. Had something else in mind. Too busy. Didn't want to explain it to you, you know... like you're the one that's fallin' behind here. So I paid close attention to that one. She was fun.

Language is an interesting thing. To be able to say this or that has meaning for you is an accomplishment. It is a human accomplishment. And I can't say humans accomplish much in their lives, frankly, except trying to stay dry or fed or snuggled somewhere to keep comfortable.

But they can accomplish this one feat. It is that when you have something in mind, you translate that into words, and you express it to another person so well that they experience what you experienced when you first had that experience. Got that? They join the experience you communicate. Now, that's communication. Most people spend all their lives talking about their experiences from a distance.

You remember what it's like to have felt something very strong... good or bad? Now, look at your language. Maybe you don't want to make the effort to feel that feeling again, so you stand way back in your mind and describe it to someone, and there's no feeling in it, and there's no experience in it for the other person. So there is no joining in humanness with you in that experience. You separate yourself from it and communicate that separation to one another with your words.

Now, what if you were to take that experience and relive it for them in a story, so they could be there with you? Ahhh, what joining there would be, what humanness... no longer alone in any of our experiences... all family.

I tell you, there's a language of the heart that goes beyond words, that any living thing can share with you. That's what I want to talk about. That's what Feice showed me.

Like always on our walks, we pick up everything and look. We look at a plant. We dig a root and taste it. We see what effects it has with us, see if it would be a strong medicine or a weak one or just a nothing at all. There's lots of nothings at all. It takes Spirit to point you this way or that to find something truly useful.

So we're always walking and praying and talking and remembering our songs and stories. We tell our stories to each other to practice them. We sing songs to practice them.

And here's this little Feice, almost old enough to walk for more than an hour at a time. Now, there's a blessing because my arms truly have just about fallen off from carrying this one. Shuhinono's too. She'll pick something up, this young 'un, and look at it, and she'll say something to Shuhinono, and it will be in old, funny Hopi language, all full of pictures. See, Hopi, they talk pictures. They have few words, but the sounds... to them, that's what's important. And they'll sing them to you, and you'll see these pictures. That's their language.

Shuhinono never lost a beat. She knew what that child was sayin' and would turn and respond perfectly. And that child kept talkin' Hopi after that, in total agreement with Shuhinono. And you know what they were talking? Bugs! Them two knew bugs. Them two liked them bugs. Them two had more enlightening conversations over bugs than anybody I ever heard tell about anything. Bugs! But seein' as how there were plenty of 'em, it gave them lots of opportunity to talk to each other in different languages and practice understanding the meaning behind the song. The sounds that come from the chest of a person who is in their heart is unmistakable.

They were loving each other with sounds. It didn't matter whether the mind knew what pictures you were lookin' at or talkin' about. It was agreement. And it was love. Now, if you wanted proof that this one understood that one and that one understood this one and they were in perfect understanding, well, go looking. You can tear it all apart and diagram a sentence and find out whether this is this and that is that. But I'll tell you, it was the love between those two that was communicated to me clearly... the sounds they made.

You think about your language. It's made up of sounds. Some of them are smooth and joined, and some of them are sharp and separate. You look at all this. This is what you're communicating. Someone who had never heard your language before, if they sat and heard the two of you talking together, if that new one was astute, they could tell what was being said and whether you two loved each other or not, yes? I think you know that. So, here in this book, I'm redefining words for you... maybe just giving them their correct emphasis and use.

The heart and throat chakras, together, were what invented language, not the mind by itself. Sounds put together in a string have a feeling like music. It is this feeling that is transmitted and received. That's communication.

Now, a child doesn't know whether killing is good or bad until you give it feeling, yes? You can teach a child to be a soldier or a priest, yes? They don't know what the words really mean. They have no experience, so they just repeat them after you or do as you do. It is the feeling behind the words with which you communicate everything. If you are angry, then whatever you teach them in that mood will have that flavor, yes? If you are sad, depressed, even suicidal, you will frighten them, yes? What you say will not teach them encouraging things with such discouraging feelings.

So it is about energy. Sounds are energy. Voice is, then, a tool for the energy behind the sounds, yes? Words simply follow.

The fifth chakra is about communication. Now, I know people who never had ears, but their eyes saw what you meant. They could see by reading your eyes what your voice intended, though they couldn't hear your voice. I even knew some people who could feel what's what. They had no ears or eyes. They would put their hand on something hollow and let it reverberate with your sounds, and they would interpret the feeling of those sounds for meaning by the energy in them. Pretty good, huh?

There's another level yet beyond the physical sound of a voice. A person can read the energy that sent the sound... the *intent*. That's next. I'll explain more later. For now, your heart is a drum. If your voice is in cinque with your heart, the drum beat will carry to every living thing. They will feel your meaning.

You say, "Oh well, the hummingbird heart has too high a beat." I say, the drum knows how to beat that high. You don't have to think how to communicate with a hummingbird. The heart knows already. Because it is a tiny heart and beats very fast, does not make it not a drum. All drums are drums, yes? Big or little, any color, made any way you like... still a drum. Hearts and people... just like that. All living things... just like that.

Now, you say, "Oh well, bacteria don't have hearts." Oh, I beg your pardon. Because you don't see a thing there muscled out like a heart, human like, you think there's no heart there. Oh, I beg your pardon. Look again. If they didn't have the heart to do the job, believe me, they'd die. Life is for those that have heart. Now, I ain't sayin' bacteria are particularly smart, but for what they do, they do it better than you. So give 'em a break. They got value.

Now, you got poisons to keep them bacteria from giving you pneumonia. You call them antibiotics. "Oh well, then, maybe that's good," you say, "because people live longer." And I say, it doesn't take long to get the final lesson if you want to... or it will take forever, if you procrastinate. You need to live longer because you delay so much. You invent devices to keep you alive, but for what? You don't know.

My daughter met a man once who said he was a good hunter. He would just call the deer with his love, and that deer would come and he would shoot it. Well, we come to find out that this man who does this sort of thing and thinks these sorts of thoughts is a trickster, a magician, interested in illusions. You see, the worst trick you can play on yourself is to think that love is an illusion. Sure, you can call things to you... anything. God loves you, gave you this will and this heart to call with. This man, a professed hypnotist, thought himself clever and saw this ability as a possession of power. Truth is, love is a gift from the Source that you may receive guiltlessly. The difference here is, this man thought himself powerful by taking what was offered in love, rather than receiving what was offered in love. Here, you see, the loser is not the deer but the fool who steals love when it has already been given freely. Pitiful, huh? That's the ego trying to make up some reason to be bigger than love. Queer thinking!

All us Spirit folks have these stories to give to you, what we learned from our lives and what we have assembled from all those before and after us. We have this to offer you, these stories. Now, you can't hear my voice, but I know you can feel the heart in my words because that is where they come from. You cannot hear my voice directly yet, because your voice is not awakened yet.

My son here had a monotone voice all his life, until recently. Only one feeling he had. I'll tell you what it was. It was called desperate waiting... discouraged, desperate waiting. Well, I say to all of you, waiting time is up! Time to put fire in your voice. Give it heart and clarity of mind, looking at what is at stake and seeing the choices to make.

Now, pretending that fire can become a habit, and once that habit is established, it will seem like getting beyond pretense is like getting over the Wall of China with the hoards before you. It will look impossible, because in all your pretending you had to believe you didn't know how or couldn't learn or would not learn.

*

We're nearly home. We've been walking for, oh, over a year, I think, but having a good time. Storms were over. Winter was a little tough. We stayed in one spot for a long time. It was a cold one for two months, so we burrowed into the earth like a cave bear, and we stayed there and only went out just to melt spring snow to drink. Occasionally, I went out to hunt, and we would eat one bite a day for two months between both of us. We lost a little weight, but we kept snug and warm. And you know, that little one, whom I would have never thought could stay still for two months, found lots of things to do in that little cave. Entertained herself real good. Still breast feeding, so we weren't worried about her food.

Today, Feice sang a song, a complete one, from beginning to end. Now remember, this kid is only a little over three years old. I wish you could have heard it. I'd sing it to you now, but truly I could not communicate it because my voice for you as yet has no ears. When you give up these pages and talk to me directly, then you will hear my voice, and I will sing that song to you. For now, suffice it to say, this sweet little creature communicated in vision, through the intent and the sound of her words, her love for the little, bitty bugs and creatures that walk on the ground and fly... like insects, not like birds. She ain't looked up high enough to see no birds yet.

It was a Sweat Lodge, thank-you song for the entertainment of the bugs and the wonder at their variety and strange looks. She called them, "Them whose bones are outside." Now, I know you got scientists and they call them, ectomorphs. They wear their skeletons on the outside. Well, look it here, here's a three-year-old kid who looks and says, "They're hard on the outside," feels herself and says, "I'm hard on the inside, so must be they're wearin' their bones on the outside." Pretty good, huh? But she thanked them bones-on-the-outside people for all their enterprising tricks and devices for moving and flying and crawling and doing this and that... funny little green ones with crawly legs, about thirty of 'em. And there's a centipede over there with about a hundred of 'em, and there's a millipede with what looks like a thousand of 'em. That really got her when she saw that thing. That just about blew her mind, to use your current phrase.

In fact, it did blow her mind. It blew her mind up so it wasn't so damn small anymore. I saw it happen and out came that song. And there was all that singing, with her lookin' up into the top of this little cave we're in. It was dark in there, and I knew she couldn't see a darn thing, but I joined her in my mind, and I saw all them things that she'd seen over the past three years. All those little bugs were in her head, all the little grains of sand they crawled over, all the little grasses and everything was right there in vision, and she just re-looked at the whole thing and was just singin' her little heart out.

She's alive, yes-siree, this one's alive. Not wastin' no time either. Not worryin' about whether there's milk on the table or an extra blanket or whether or not I'm too close to her mom when she'd rather be in between us. She don't think like that. She likes

145

in between, not to separate her mom and me, but because she likes to be in that energy between us. She likes to hear our words when we talk together close like that. She likes the love we feel for each other.

It's like when the dog barks or yelps. In those sounds, the difference in feeling is communicated. You know happy from sad, scared from glad. When you walk towards two people on the street, whether you overhear the conversation or not, you can hear by their tone whether a person's up or down. And if you listen with your whole being, you can even tell about what, even though they aren't speaking their feelings in the least.

How about those stuck in the middle who don't have any feelings at all? Whew! How come? Scared? Don't want 'em? Too much trouble? I tell you, they're a communication device... all them feelings. They're to tell you what other people are sending you or what you're sending yourself. They're to tell you what your thoughts are doing to your form, whether you feel good or bad. They can even be so specific as to tell you what thought corresponds to what physical place in your body. As you think it, it heals or sickens... as you wish.

But the most damage ever done in this world is done with words without a heart. If you can't hear the heart's inflection, you don't know what's meant. No true feelings are communicated and the intent is unknown.

Now, English language tried to nail this all down, right? It is very objective, and it has adjectives and adverbs which try to tell you the feeling in those words, passively or aggressively. So you have substituted a mechanical way of expressing feeling by using words for which you may not really have any experience. You're taught language as a device for communicating but without the reason for communicating.

How can you get passionate over a scarf or a new car unless you're taught it by someone who deceives you and says, "This is love." Is a salesman's enthusiasm for his product a substitute for true love? Do not be deceived by the song without heart. Thank you, Feice. Thank you, Shuhinono. I guess I'm not too old to learn after all, huh?

There is a way to reach God through this energy center, the throat, that has to do only with its connection to your heart. Now, if you want to sing to your mind to get high, you can do that too, but it won't get you to God without your heart. If you don't care about any of it, then all you're doing is trying to escape before anybody else does. Chicken shit! You don't want to feel what everyone before you felt or after you will feel, yes? Running and hiding, whether it's in a tall tree or in a deep hole will not prevent you from having to experience your life and feel it. But it will prevent you from reaping any rewards from these feelings, however. You can even defy the fact that they have any meaning at all. However, these "death defying" acts don't defy death. They defy love. They call death to them with their defiance. And okay, you can learn that way too, because Creator will still be there waiting for you with a hand outstretched, just milliseconds away from your asking for help.

So, would song be possible without silence? Impossible! Language, also, would be impossible without silence. There would be no break in the sounds, would there? It would be like a continuous tone that wouldn't end, each note *not* dropping off into nothingness, and not to be played at a different octave later.

Minds are simultaneous sounds. Conscious minds are like a symphony... not prearranged, but certainly preordained. All of them teach something, and there is either a balance or an imbalance in it for the earth because it is energy you use to create those sounds. It is your energy you communicate to the earth and to each other. It is your collective energies to which the earth responds. So if all our voices in totality were to have a sound, would it be harmonious or cacophonous? This is what you are giving back to Creator and what you are giving back to the Earth Mother as female God.

She, the Mother is here, you think, and He, the Father is not. So creation is split into male God and female God, just as your relationships are split between male and female. If you want to check for harmony, look at your relationships. What sounds do you make between you? If creation is truly split into male and female, then what sounds do each of them make separately? Are they separate or not? If you perceive separation, then you perceive the two aspects of God as warring, yes? What sound is war? Who started the war? Who divided creation in half?

Is it the male side of mind that asked for female and split the mind that was whole into halves? Something had to intend to split and ask for it to happen. I ask you this, why would female ask to split from male? She had the seed of the memory of love. She had the ability to ask Creator for union and to have children. Men run around with a pocket full of seeds often pretending to be God. It is said that Jesus was born to a woman by God, so get it straight, men! You aren't the first choice! God was. And when man gets this straight and makes God his first choice too, then he will begin to learn something that is true.

So men, don't jump ahead and think you deserve Godhead before woman. If you do, only wars will ensue your path. If you see you are also female, that the experience that females have are available to you too, then you can be joined. Then Creator can acknowledge you. If you think you are not female in the least and take pride in your maleness, then I assure you, you will not see the truth. It takes the sacred asking of the combined energies of male and female within you to get to the truth. Creation is harmonically whole. In relationships, the resolution of misunderstandings between male and female energies can bring you to the truth very quickly if guided by Spirit. It is the purpose of your relationships to mirror these energies for each other. It is the purpose of Spirit to guide you to the truth. You must, of course, prefer the truth, rather than your own personal perceptions. You must step beyond conflict in any form to join energies, whether within you or with a partner.

So stop fussing about worthless, meaningless shit, and pray together for truth to be shown to you and your lives will change. You might even get a little one like Feice who teaches you, quickly, what's important and what's not. And instead of trying to teach your children what you do not know, they will teach you and you will know. That's their gift to you before they're touched with self-consciousness of body, before they're embarrassed by their experience of themselves. While they are innocent, they will remind you that you too are innocent, since you have forgotten it.

So in this tiny child's voice was sent a song to God, which I know got there because our joined hearts were immediately filled with the love that was poured into this child. She and the love that filled her, kept that song going for ten or fifteen minutes. And in that time, we were filled a hundred times by the Creator's love for this child. And we passed it on to her, and she sang it back to Creator, and the circle was complete once again.

This is what we do around our campfires... tell stories like these, sing songs like hers, praise creation, and ask for forgiveness for all our foolishness, all our silly side trips into fear. And we thank God for there being love and the truth that is born within it. So, harmony we have with the earth. Yes, we do, because we sing our thanks to it, and it gives us everything.

I want to continue for awhile with the importance of connecting your heart and mind together before you speak. You know, us natives as a group don't talk much. It's not just because you're a stranger. It's because we're aware of a different form of communication that goes beyond ever-changing words and sounds. But if

148

you were going to make a sound, wouldn't you rather it not be such a foolish one? Or is that too much work, to think before you speak? For some people, it is. It's a lot of work. For all of you who want to walk a spiritual path, I suggest you stop and take a look at all the things you think and all the assumptions that you make... *before you speak.* Try some discipline and see if you can, for a whole week, just watch your thoughts. Don't say a word. Get the agreement of the people around you that it's not their fault, that they agree you can do this thing as an experiment. I guarantee you that after that week, your words will have more meaning to you, and you'll begin to understand how busy the mind is and how quick we are to speak our judgments. We don't like this, we don't like that, too hot, too cold, too noisy, too quiet... constant judgment.

Well, I'll tell you. Communication is beyond your judgment, so if you're not aware of what your mind's doing, you're not communicating with anyone. You may be talking a lot, but I guarantee you, you're not *hearing* anything. You know the old saying, "Walk a mile in my moccasins and you'll know my life." Well, that's a difficult metaphor to accomplish in terms of physical sense. But in a psychic sense, it's very easy to step into someone else's life. I know most women join very easily. Men, well, mostly they're in competition, more or less, all trying to be the perfect man. Of course, this all goes on in their own head, but when one man looks at another man, you'll see that both are doing the same thing, just like the women, though they are pretending they are not. It is the nature of minds to join, so that's where you get it from, from each other. All of a sudden, here you are all standing around doing the same thing. Of course, everyone has ego, but men more than women seem to want to do everything differently so as to appear different.

Until you get a grip on your mind, you will not be able to hear your heart speak to you. It speaks in perfect silence, undisturbed by the chatter of the world. Remember, it is your mind that produces fear for you. The heart knows nothing of it.

So when you gain discipline over the wild horses in your mind, then you will hear your heart. I know you hear it in the early morning hours before you get out of bed. After you have awakened from a dream, your heart speaks to you. You see pictures. Depending on how your life goes, that's how you experience your dreams. Some days are good and some days are not. Some lessons are hard and some are easy. And until you see all those lessons as the same, you will think that there is progress to be made and that you are somewhere at the beginning or at the middle or near the end of this linear journey. But there you go thinking again. Eternity does not have any of those things... beginnings, middles and ends. **It just is.** It is this Isness, this Eternal Now, that your heart can bring your mind into alignment to experience... the Isness of life and the Oneness of everything in it.

I'll bet each of you has had an example in your life of one person that you've known that could communicate love to you with their voice. You could feel it and hear it, whether it was a teacher, an aunt or uncle, a grandfather or grandmother. And you remember them because of the quality of the sound of their voice and the intent in their mind and heart, because these two centers were joined.

So that is harmony, when everything is in agreement, yes? Like Feice who could sing a song from nowhere, full of meaning and love, full of vision, full of enthusiasm, everything was in perfect harmony in that moment.

Now, that is the true meaning of magic, and that's what you want for your lives... a little magic, a little harmony, a little experience beyond ordinary life.

You see, when we lived, the earth was in this kind of harmony already, and it was easy for us to join it. Now that you have put black ribbons across the land and made the water run into pipes instead of into the dirt, you have changed the balance of the energy between the sky and the ground. You have created great heat to be dissipated. It has caused an imbalance, this heat... the heat of the cities, the burning of fuels, the pollution of the air. There are some places on the earth that are too hot to live in now, and they weren't fifty years ago. Climate has changed. Weather patterns are shifting. This imbalance will continue and worsen.

Most importantly, you must learn to balance yourselves, for without that you cannot lead anyone else into balance by example. And I tell you, it is the example you set that others follow, not what you say. The mind and heart have to be in agreement before the voice can speak the truth. If you do something different from what you say, I'll tell you, your heart and mind are not in agreement. Usually, this lack of agreement is not a major difficulty. It probably occurs because you are afraid, afraid you won't be loved. So you say one thing and do something different. You pretend agreement and then dance the way you wish. Mostly, you get caught because lies are not true and you don't remember them. To be a good liar, you have to practice and remember them, but most lies are based upon illusion and don't remain very long in your memory, so you

150

forget and get caught. That's why it's so easy to catch the young ones in their deceits. They forget. They're too busy getting on to the next thing to remember their last lie.

So, what do you do if you catch one lying? Do you voice your disgust or dismay or create guilt in them? Well, where does that come from in your heart, that guilt? Sounds like your mind is in conflict with your heart, yes? You want to teach that? I think, by example, you can demonstrate to them that the truth is much easier, even if it temporarily makes one feel smaller than one wishes to feel.

Now, I hear people say "I love you" to each other, and I know they want to. But you know, what love feels like is total harmony. And usually when people say "I love you," it is to make up after a fight. Now, women, in good, tender moments might say "I love you" to their husbands. And their husbands turn around and say, "Oh yah, I love you too." It's the woman who in that tender moment felt that feeling of love. I'll tell you how. She dropped her energy. She no longer carried it in her head but allowed herself to feel something. She dropped that energy beyond her feet and asked sometime in her life to be shown what love was. And so, wham-o, all of a sudden, in her mind is this image, this feeling in her heart, and her voice spoke it. And it takes that man by surprise. Because he doesn't walk in love all the time, he can't quite manage to get right down there to the bottom of it at that moment, so he says, "Oh yah, I love you too."

Well, in his mind he loves her, and I'm sure in his heart, if he'd ever look closely, he would say, "Yes, I love her." But how many people spend the time turning off the thinking and sink into their heart and ask their heart what the truth is? Do I love this person, this place? Do I know what love is? Have I given a moment to the feeling of love? Do I know the Source of Love? Good questions. Try 'em out.

When Feice is being a brat, I question these things. Since we are not in camp with a hundred other people, it's easy to watch my mind and my reactions to this young one. And I see that everything that she does or says rests on two simple ideas. The first is, I am loved or I am not. The second is, I am comfortable or I am not.

So all I have to do is to decide whether she's asking for something in the way of assurances that she is loved, or if I'm angry with her behavior, whether she is trying to find some way to know when she will be loved again. She never gets stuck in the error. She just knows that somehow love was withdrawn for a moment.

151

I think she looks at me like there was some kind of sickness I have, just for a few minutes while I'm being weird and angry. So she crawls up in my lap and looks in my eyes, and I say, Okay fine, I still love you. That's all she wants. Bang! Outa' here, things to do, but everything's all right now. Daddy's not crazy anymore. So, that's how it is.

We indian folks have a lot of tolerance for physical discomfort and we're fairly strong. So with Feice, physical discomfort isn't such a big deal either. But nowadays, for some people, if you've got pain, well, that's the only time you ask for God to help you, 'cause you don't want that pain no more. I tell you, all you folks walkin' around on them streets without your heart open, you got a pain. And you learn to live with it, and it's not a good thing. It'll get you. I suggest you sit and do what the Easterners call "meditate." That means, sink into that pain and find out its source.

Now, if you trip and fall and hit your hip and it hurts, you already know the source. If it's one of those pains that just came up sudden-like and you don't know why, then if you sit and you sink into it, and you give that pain a voice, you give that heart and mind and voice to that pain, that pain will take you right to where that conflict is. It will tell you and show you what's wrong and how come and what to do. But you have to ask Spirit to guide you to that place, then give Them your voice and your mind and your heart. It is then you will know the answer to your question.

You have only one responsibility on this planet, just one, and that is to find your own inner voice and deliver it back to the Creator, to give your voice, your heart and your mind back to Creator. Then Creator can guide you and show you what the truth is. Until then, good luck!

*

Well, here we were, five or six days from camp. The terrain was looking familiar again. Winter was over. Spring was finally bursting forth with all its colors. And, of course, more bugs than ever. So we walked slower 'cause Feice's got to see every darn one of 'em. Every flower has a bug. There must be bazillions of flowers, bazillions of bugs. So we sort of wander back to camp. But that's fine. We weren't in a big hurry anyway. It's not like we had an appointment.

Even at this distance, I can feel the old ones coming into my head. Their minds reach a long way, I find. Here we are walking along and Feice pops up, looks at me and looks at mom, then looks up at me again, and in our language says, "Home." Now, where did she get that word?–"home." I know we talk about home once in awhile, but how'd she know that we were nearly home? Got to be them old people, beamin' out like a radio tower, friendly conversation to us as we walk home singin' our songs.

So now I find Feice speaks Hopi in Hopiland, but speaks our language as we're nearing our homeland. It's funny, I can feel all you anthropologists about to ask, "What's the name of your tribe?" Well, we didn't name our tribe. We never thought we were anything special or different. We were just people, people who stuck together because they agreed. It's easy to stay together when you agree. Don't you agree?

Nice thing was, the old people could show you the wisdom of agreeing, even when you didn't. And then you would and everything was fine. Only rarely was there a real rebel who had to go see the world for himself and needed no agreement from anyone. Well, that one wandered and was lonely, and maybe that's how new tribes got started or how blood got changed from one place to the next. Mostly, we never heard from them again, so we don't know what happened to them, but they just had to go. Usually theirs was the loudest voice in camp. It's kinda' how they got rid of us. The louder that you blame someone else for your troubles, the sooner that you will probably leave. And it wasn't about this place or these people. It was that you had a calling elsewhere and needed to hear, but you loved this place and the people here. So you tried to spoil it, so you would look the other way and hear this calling. That's what we think. What do you think?

It's easy to try to wash over things that people do. "Oh, he did this because of that. Oh, she did that because of this." Then you feel like you really understand or know the reasons for things. I tell you, you don't.

The simple mind that deals with the physical world spends most of its time conjecturing, making great assumptions about things. But if you want to know the truth, check your heart. Give it voice. Join your mind to it. Give it all to God. Ask that way. Then don't lose the grip on the wild horses in your mind. Keep them quiet and let that answer bubble up from inside you. You'll know. Your life will change because you'll see everyone different, because you'll now *know,* rather than being involved in all the conjecture. And you will see how insane all the conjecture is. What a waste of time. What a waste of energy. What a waste! What a waste! Sure, it's a waste. Stop doing it. Makes you crazy.

If Feice knew where home was, I guarantee you, you can too. She was only a little over three. Some of you are in your forties and fifties. Still don't know where home is. Don't have one. Wander all over. Do all kinds of crazy things all over the planet... sell guns to Iran, sell guns to Turkey, go poking around for minerals and oil everywhere, ripping off the local folks for their energy 'cause they don't know what it's for yet. You do. You know its true value... you think. So you go buy it there and sell it here. Big business. Exploitation.

Stop and think before you voice anything. Better yet, stop thinking, then let the heart voice it. You'd be surprised how your life would change if you'd just say what you are feeling, if you'd just stop and see what you are feeling. Don't even have to say anything. Just feel the truth and the room will change, and everyone in it will change.

I know that you want to be connected, or you would not be reading these words. There is no easy way. The Buddhists have described the ways, and the American Indians have described the ways to the truth. Truth is, there is One Source, so all paths lead to the One. Let's say, from a single point, the paths radiate out into seven things, seven ideas, seven directions. Now, anyone can break those seven up into a million more little pieces, radiating out in all directions. I know that some native descendents think that there are four-hundred-and-ten ways. And other foreign traditions think, maybe, four-thousand ways.

But for the sake of simplicity, let's say you've got seven energy centers. If you enter any one of them in totality, you will eventually get to the truth if you don't stop learning, because they are all connected. Stop at any point and you are lost. So it is best not to have attachments along the way. It is best to just observe and learn. When you are dealing with your own energy, there are tricks that the ego will play on you. All of them are but the same thing. They are all fear: fear of death, fear of God, fear of self, fear of loss of self, fear of loss of love... and on and on. To become dispassionate about fear and to use your will to go beyond it by going through it... that's courage. There is no other form of courage that is important in this world. Jumping off high buildings, well, it takes a certain fearlessness, yes-siree. Takes will to do that. That's one way, but that's the world's way. That involves risk of your body only. I say, sit in a Sweat Lodge and face your fears in your mind. And then, face death within those fears. And then, be reborn as a spiritual human being. That's courage.

Insanity is jumping off a tall building without a parachute. Insanity in spiritual life is not facing your fears, not standing up to your own ego because it claims it will kill you if you abandon it. It

154

may try, and that's where you decide what you are. Are you spirit or are you ego? Are you the body that dies, or are you the energy within it that lives? Are you the battery that gets discharged by life and then thrown in the trash as useless, or are you recharged by some Source outside the world and outside the laws of this physical planet?

There is an experience that you can have so you can know. And it will be only your experience that will prove to you that you are spirit. And because it proves to you that the truth is true, it also allows you to join every other living thing. I think it is this you fear... this joining. I know it is this joining that the ego fears. Ego would rather be separate forever and right to the death. Just remember, it's your death it wants to be right about... that you are dead and it is alive.

But I tell you, no matter how many people martyr themselves for the ego's cause, the ego is still not alive and never was and never can be. And its will is not stronger than yours, because it is yours that you mistakenly gave to it to guide you. If you have given into it for a long time, you will seem to be the weak one, and it would seem to be the strong one. But like a dike with too much water on one side and no water on the other, dig a little hole and it will even out. Don't indulge in thinking that the ego is impregnable. It isn't. If it built the dike to separate the waters between you and it, then you can build a tunnel to get that water back too. It's not that smart. Only live things are truly smart because they have Creator's help.

Exercise your will each moment in denial that the ego can run your life. You do this by not living the thoughts it thinks. Step back. Take a look. Observe the thoughts. Decide which ones you would have and which ones you would reject. Step back. Take a look. See all the emotions you have with those thoughts, and decide which ones you would rather feel and which ones you would not.

I tell you, there is no pain in love. If you think there is, it's because the ego is trying to tell you what love is. It does this by telling you that it is God and God is pain and love is pain and life is pain. And with eyes full of pain looking out upon the world, it proclaims God is dead... God does not love the world because there is so much pain. But I tell you, God is not the source of pain. The ego is. So I don't want to spend too much time on this pain business because it is the problem, not the solution. I prefer spending time on the solution. What do you think? Good idea?

As you learn to choose a return to love, you will soon find that all the decisions you made by yourself were in error. It is then that perception begins to turn around. Without the heart and the voice and the mind in alignment, without the first chakra being the fire for the furnace to produce the energy necessary to transform these centers into light, without those three things acting in harmony, there will be no vision. Just as the burning fuel of the fire lights all the faces around it, and your awareness turns from the darkness around you to the loving stories the faces are telling you, so will your inner fire light the darkness within you. And you will see the faces of your Guides and Ancestors, Who in the Light tell you stories to guide you Home.

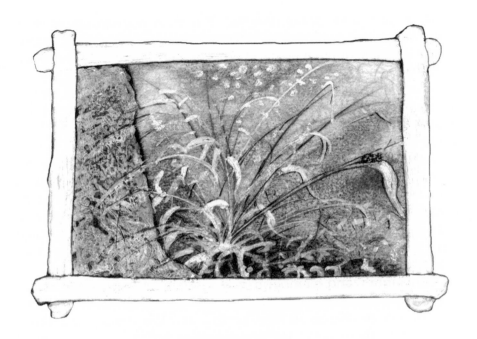

Chapter 14
Smaller's Bigger and Bigger's Smaller

Returning, for us, this time is great fun, full of excitement because we don't have to come home. We just want to. So when we get there, we won't be thinking about all the disadvantages of being around a-hundred-and-some folks, maybe more than two-hundred by now. Who knows what's happened since we've been gone? Every woman could have had a baby, and there's the double.

Right now, we have our own little child, Feice, to be thinkin' about, dancing around beside us, trepsin' off in the tall grass. Once, I even had Shuhinono get on my shoulders, just to see if she could find her. We had napped and Feice had wandered off. And we thought, well, you know, take a look. We were good trackers, so we knew we could follow her trail. But somehow, standing on my shoulders was an adventure in itself.

Now remember, we're butt heavy and got short legs. And the sight of Shuhinono clamberin' up my back trying to stand on my shoulders while I hold her calves has got to be one of the funniest things that any human being could ever watch. We were laughing so hard at ourselves that we just couldn't quite make it. We'd get up there and something would slip and give. And boom, down we went!

Now, you think, crazy parents! Not even worried about their kid! Well, in this wild prairie in the daytime, the only thing to fear would be fallin' down a hole that was bigger than you. Then there might be some trouble getting you unstuck. But knowing Feice, she'd crawl down in a hole face first, meet the badger, tell him to get out of the way, and he'd clamber backwards up the back hole. And then she'd get out, and she'd probably eat his food in the hole while she was there.

So we didn't worry about that one too much. We did finally get a look, and we saw which direction the grass was pushed down. And, mind you, she's just over three, so there ain't a lot of grass being pushed down. But where that buffalo grass was thick and darn near four feet tall, maybe when she walked through it, she'd push some down and we'd see that once in a while. So her trail won't be so hard to follow.

So, laughin' and clamberin' and brushin' ourselves off, we go trepsin' after the little one. And all we were thinkin' of was, it'll be nice to see so and so or that person and that family and those folks. Then there was that tender feeling for the old ones who'd helped us out so much, made us free. We could wander the earth freely, fearless... damn alert, but fearless. In other words, fear was not guiding us. Love was. That's a bubble, a safety bubble, love is. You build it around you by giving it to those around you. And the more you give, the bigger it gets.

So tribe was nice because love got darn big with them. Everybody passed it around and pinched and touched and said how much weight this one was gaining and how big those feet were getting and how your lips were getting lower to your chin and how your color in your eyes... everything. Everybody talked about everything. And really what they were doing was pokin' around in there to see if you were still the same person who'd left. It's like we're all just really children, just all want to be loved and know what we're loving. So we poke around a little bit just to see if somebody loves us.

So yah, we were looking forward to being poked and prodded and questioned and examined, and all in good fun and all in love. And everybody wants to know what you learned. See, 'cause they were too scared to go out and learn it themselves, so it's up to you to come back and share it. And since they didn't want to admit they were scared, they would just call you the crazy one for doing it. And we said, "Yah, that's true. We're crazy for doin' it, but I'll tell you what happened, and let me tell you this story, and there went this, and this is what I learned, and look at this new one—

158

watch her, she's crazy, she's crazier than we are." And everybody laughs and has a good time.

Turns out Feice started walkin' home and never looked back. We didn't catch on to her being gone until she was nearly an hour down her trail home. Well, we didn't think we slept that long, maybe twenty, thirty minutes. And how fast could a kid go? And wouldn't they get tired and slow down and maybe lay down and rest... find a bug and get distracted and forget the whole thing? Not Feice! She got it in her mind that we were wastin' time and she was headin' home. She wanted to find out what all this love was about... family, home, people, bliss. Off she went. Bye-bye. Have a good life, parents!

You know, there was something in me that was just dumbstruck, feeling the perfect confidence this child had. Not that she could get home, but that she never once thought about where home was or how she was going to live until she got there. Little person, big confidence. Now, even I don't even have perfect confidence. I fuss around–well, I guess we better stop soon 'cause it's gonna' be dark. But not Feice. No way. Dark? So what? Tired? If you fall down tired, sleep and get up again, that's the plan. Anything in between is a waste of time. I've never seen drive and will like that from anyone in all my life.

And so, we catch up. It's two-and-a-half hours later and we catch up. And she's just striddin' right along. And we go, "Feice, what are you doing? Where are you going?"

"Home. Bye."

"Don't you want company?" we asked.

"You sleeping. Me not sleep."

"Well, how do you know where home is?"

"I hear 'em talking."

And we go, "You do? What do they say?"

"Some words I don't know, but they're talking about you. They're singing songs for you."

Now come on, she's only a little over three. How could she get "singing songs for you?" Where did that come from? Who thought that thought? The three-year old? No, I tell you again. There's somebody inside that baby acting like a woman. I don't know who that is.

Now, not all children were like that. Many were, you know, pretty willful. And many knew what they wanted... like, they want to be a great hunter. And off they go with all the great hunters, and that's that! Boys, you know, you expect that from them. But you don't expect a female child at age three to take off across the

159

prairie without their parents or without knowing exactly where home is, never having been there. That's a little unusual.

But I'll tell you this. We never frightened our children. We never frightened this child with our words. We never said—it can't be done—don't do it—don't run off—a bear will eat you. We never said that. If she met a bear... huh! No tellin' who'd lose! Out here in the tall grass, we don't see much of bears. Only up north, north of our old camp, in the mountains are where the bears live.

I call 'em mountains. They're really kind of squat-lookin' things compared to that cinder cone that went straight up into the sky. But not even Great Mountain compared to that canyon that went straight down for a mile. Now, that was somethin'! Our mountains at home were just fuzzy bumps that tended to get snow first, ten minutes before you got it on the flats. But if you went to walk up there, it would take you awhile 'cause they've smoothed out. Takes a long time to walk up a little way.

Does it take any longer to walk a ladder laying down than it does to walk it going straight up? Well, it depends on how heavy you are. If your legs gotta' push you straight up, I bet you'd get tired before we got tired walkin' up our mountain, 'cause it's more like a ladder layin' down. Took longer, I think, like more ladders end to end, but didn't wear you out as fast.

So Feice hears inside already. Okay fine. We wonder how this could be, other than the fact that maybe she got a head start because of us. Who knows? I am aware that we weren't trying to slow her down in any way on the trip. First part of the trip back, we were trying to get her to walk by herself. Now, we can't pick her up. Lot has happened in three years.

You think about it. You look at your life and you say, "Oh, these years have gone by so fast. What have I learned? What have I accomplished?" And you think, well, time drags out pretty slow. Sure, remember when you were young? Time didn't even exist, except when someone said, "Bedtime," and you didn't want to be-cause you weren't tired. Now, as an adult, you who are pooped, sit up half the night watching your young ones play in the dirt or by the fire 'cause they're not tired. And then, you walk around all day carrying a sleeping baby. But you can't tell 'em that's not the way to do it and force them into a pattern that slows down time for them. They get grumpy. They get sick.

You used to go that fast when you were two and three and four. You didn't weigh as much, so it wasn't as much effort to carry yourself from place to place following your fancies, following your imagination, following the Voice of Spirit... the Spirit Mother showing you all the wonderful things to look at.

You're old now and maybe you don't see wonderful things to look at anymore. Maybe you're not encouraged by your travel, and time drags. And yet, when you stop and look back as a child would, looking over the years, you say, "Why does time go so fast? Where did it go? What happened?"

Well, I'll tell you. You lapsed into a fantasy where nothing mattered. Nothing had meaning. And yet, the only thing that changed was your mind in relationship to time. Time remained the same and sped by, just like when you were that little child lookin' at each new rock and each new bug and each new flower. You just missed it all.

Now, I'm not so dang quick, but around Feice I got quicker. And in that quickness, I started seeing as she saw. And you know what? I even started to appreciate bugs... just a little bit.

I know my son did too, because one time he was tellin' a lady bug how it was so tiny and little bitty, had a little, bitty brain and couldn't really enjoy what life was about because its brain was so little. Then that lady bug crawled up to the top of a blade of grass, and he said, "Oh, lady bug, you're gonna' have to turn around and go back down. There's that tiny, little brain, you know. Can't figure out that the tip of that plant is the end of the road, so you're just going to have to turn around and go back down."

And you know what? That little bug popped open her wings and flew right off, right in front of his face, laughin'. And she was laughin' and she was laughin'. She was laughin' at this tiny-brained human with no wings, sittin' here tellin' her that she was tinier. Well, she may have been tinier in size, but God gave her wings to get out of his arrogant face and all that noise he was makin' about how tiny something's brain was. So, smaller's bigger and bigger's smaller. Joke's on you, folks. Nothing Creator makes is in small regard. And if there is a fool, it is someone that judges anything.

So I learned somethin' from a bug, once. And I know my son did too. And when my son learned what he learned, I relearned what I had learned. And that is... don't judge anything. Even the smallest creature has something huge about it. It has a life and it's unique, and it's the same as yours. And Love is so big that It can contain all those lives all at once, inside Itself.

So now my three-year old is teaching me to be bigger inside. And I have to accommodate the idea that what I work so hard to achieve, she's got naturally. Like, I still have difficulty hearing the old people sometimes. It's all like mumbling to me, but I know their voices. And here my little one is striking off in the direction of those voices. And you know, when I check, she couldn't be off more than two degrees. You figure it. I can't.

It's that magnet, you see. She's got that magnet and it's real strong, that love magnet. And it don't matter what you think about it, it pulls at you in the right direction and you go. And if you get sleepy, you sleep. You wake up, you go again. You get hungry, you stop. You find something to eat because love's leading you. It's there, otherwise you wouldn't be on this journey.

Now, go on a journey for wrong reasons, and you'll struggle to find things. You might not even live that long, if it's a big journey. Crummy things might happen to you. But I tell you, we let Feice lead this journey home, just about. And she did better than if we were to do all that scoutin' out ourselves. She had all that trust in love's magnet. Our trust was very general, in the sense that we knew we were going approximately where camp was. Feice's trust was very specific. We had more practice and stamina, but she was right on.

So after about ten minutes of walking behind her, we asked her, "Would you like to rest a minute? We're getting tired."

She said, "No."

So we asked her again, "But Mama's getting tired. Rest with us for a minute."

"I don't want to."

Mama said, "Well, how about some chi-chi?"

And that little rascal said, "Don't need chi-chi no more."

We said, "Oh yah? What you going to drink?"

"Like you... water."

We asked, "Out here, in this place? We've got to wait for it to rain."

"I know."

Nothing shook her. Craziest thing I ever saw. Finally I said, I'm tired. Mom's tired. We're stoppin'... see you later... have a good time–'cause we figured we could track her in the grass anyway. We did need a few minutes rest.

So we stopped and we looked at each other, and sure she goes, right off into the distance. And we just laughed together and Shuhinono said, "Have you ever seen anything like it in your life? You know, we can't leave her go too far ahead again. She might fall in a hole or something." My thoughts earlier.

But we didn't worry about all that too much, I tell you. We just had to get our little tired butts off the ground and get walkin'. That girl's gonna' be home before dark, whether it's a thousand miles away or not. Humm!

I don't know how long it was, but it was getting toward evening. And finally, that little one's feet gave out. Good thing I saved grease. I seemed to have remembered doing this once myself... but she's only three!

Finally, I convinced her to have a rest. I made her a little grass shelter like a rabbit would make for himself to keep the dew off its face, so it don't get cold in the morning. I tucked that grass in all around her and said, I'm going huntin'. Be back shortly. And for some strange reason, she left me to go by myself. Feice, I think, didn't want to, but those little, tiny feet had just about had it. Too much stompin' around without paying attention to 'em.

So here I was, tall enough to see out, lookin' for a little draw of water, with an idea that by sunset we'd have a meal. Oh, it must have been about a half-a-mile or so and I saw some trees. Had to be water nearby. Figured there'd be game there. Walked up real careful, so as not to make a big mess, found some plants to rub all over me so I wouldn't smell so much like myself, and up that cottonwood tree I went. Not too high because I got short legs and a big butt, and if I hit the ground hard, that'd be the end of that chase.

So I laid down on that limb, like a cat would stretch out, so that I'm not too obvious lookin' up there. Takin' note of where the ladies were, I settled down for a little snooze until the sun started to go down. Hard to say how long I was there, maybe two hours, maybe three. And when my eyes popped open, the sun was headin' for the dirt.

Up there, I got a glimpse of what it's like to be a cat in a tree, waiting for a kill. These things come to you. They're not recollections exactly. They're gifts. They are not normal reality, because your eyes stop seeing and your ears stop hearing, outside. They turn inside. Your eyes roll back in your head and turn your ears off. And your vision center takes over and shows you something, with all the smells and sounds and feelings that your whole being can give you, except you are not doing it. It's a gift.

I saw myself as a spotted cat, waiting, pretty patient too... better than me. That cat knew dinner was usually here. So it waited until dinner either showed up or it didn't, and it got so hungry it had to go looking. Meanwhile, here it is resting with fierce alertness. Now, I'm not saying it had its claws dug into the tree ready to pounce, but I'm saying it was alert and awake with an attention that had no rival, even Feice's. This cat could turn its eyes off and turn its ears up and wait while it appeared to sleep. 'Course, it's not Manhattan with honks and beeps and sirens and yells and traffic to distract it. It had just the sound of the wind up in the tree and the sound of anything else moving on the ground. Even the heat made noise to this cat. And when evening came, it would turn its eyes back on because the air would cool and the wind would change direction, signaling dusk. You sit outside and notice it. One hour before dusk, the wind changes, almost imperceptibly, but it changes. This the cat feels and senses, and its eyes open.

When my eyes opened, I was a cat. I didn't even see the landscape with human eyes. There were fewer colors. The distinction between light and dark was very great. And as a matter of fact, the dark was gray, not black. And in that grayness were innumerable shades, distinguishable. Whereas with human eyes, you can only really see light and dark, even when the moon is out. This vision persisted and the moon wasn't out. The cat saw in between grey and dark. So it was better to hunt in the dark the cat felt... I felt. Funny how that works.

Now, I'm used to these altered states somewhat, so I didn't panic when I didn't immediately come out of the vision of being a cat. I figured, wow, this cat's here to help me out. Okay fine. Hope we both get enough to eat. I don't want to fight the cat for something to take to my family to eat. And I'm sure the cat doesn't want to either.

Thus, having agreement, the hunt was on. Now, mind you, I don't know whether I'm still up in the tree or I've fallen down and cracked my head. This is all a faith walk, this vision. But only having heard about cats and not having seen any myself, I felt it was a great honor to have this animal help me hunt. So, I trusted.

The moment I trusted, I felt deep within my chest, a purr that filled my whole being with softness. The mind sharpened because the heart was fulfilled in its task of being cat. It was content with itself. It gave itself love through sound, through vibration. And so, within its mind was calmness and love and great appreciation for all the creatures and things around, gratitude for its life and gratitude for the lives of the creatures that it was dependent on. Now, who would have ever thought that a creature would have this so down pat that he could teach it to a human... how to purr, how to be content and grateful?

We all ate that night. A small antelope came to drink water, a little male, probably not much bigger than me, but certainly larger than the cat. The absolute certainty and power of that cat as it leapt out of the tree onto the back of that animal and with one bite broke its neck... the absolute certainty of that follow through had to do with the prayer that cat purred before it hunted. It was in

164

agreement with the antelope that it was donating itself to keep that cat's family alive. Except, you know what, folks? It was me that jumped out of that tree onto that antelope. The surprise of having caught an antelope by hand was so great that I darned near lost it, but being as I had a fat butt and short legs, I broke its neck when we fell to the ground. It scrambled for a moment and fell over dead. In that moment of scrambling around, I felt like a silly human again, surprised at my vision and the guidance of the cat. I was completely dumfounded. I'd never caught anything by hand in my life. Can't even catch Feice anymore. She's too fast. And here a bowlegged indian jumps out of a tree and conks an antelope. I was surprised I didn't get skewered on its horns.

Well, a good thing it was only an antelope, 'cause I had a little walk to get back. I think that little antelope must have weighed seventy pounds, wringin' wet. But I'll tell you, fifty pounds of dried meat at this time of year would carry us for two months in winter, the three of us.

So it was a good catch, one we don't usually get when we hunt alone. Usually, two or three of us try to run a critter into a little gorge, one the critter can't get up quickly before someone shoots it with a stick or a bow. Usually we just try to out smart them. Sure can't out run 'em.

The drawback with a hunting party is the noise, so we all became experts at silent walking, silent talking, silent breathing. And only when the hunting was good and we had plenty meat would we take someone new with us, for if someone new broke a stick at a critical moment, it was all a waste, the whole day or two days or three days. And we didn't want to discourage a new hunter with such pressure.

Now, that cat up in that tree was the champion of quietness. I saw that the silence that the cat lived in was what it trusted, and anything that came within that silence was guided to it. It had knowingness... didn't have the clutter of language, just had piercing knowingness. The nice thing about that knowingness is that even though something doesn't always show up at the water hole today, it knows it will sometime. So there it sits, peaceful.

In a natural way of life, there is always another animal, another something to walk into the water hole. In unnatural places where everything is cut into little squares or circles and farmed like crazy, where water is reused until it's too polluted to support life, the animals don't always show up at the water hole anymore. Have you noticed? Have you noticed anything about the system you have made for yourself, except that you get bored with it but don't think you can do anything else... because everybody else is doing the same thing?

The best examples of an insane people's vision of life are them boxes you got all them bugs in at the Smithsonian, pins stuck in 'em, all dead, with names by 'em... natural history museums with stuffed animals and painted plants, stuffed cavemen and women... zoos, where you can actually see with your own eyes how insane an animal gets when it's contained. If you feel nothing in these zoos while you're looking at these animals, then God help you. If you see their sadness or dullness or insanity, then you're also looking at your own society whose ideas constricted it into a box. If you laugh at the monkey throwing shit at you, remember, you are the monkey throwing shit at you, as well. You're also the one with shit all over your face. It's a clue, folks. Take a good look. If you see a wolf pacing until its toenails fall off, it's you there pacing like that, folks. If you see a spotted leopard used to running seventy-miles-an-hour in the wild, now stuck in a small cage under a little tree, getting its daily shots of Valium, it is you under that tree, restrained from your true spirit... getting your doses to stay calm.

My vision told me I'm cat too. Now, up in arms go all the people who think that animals are a lower order and man is a higher order. I tell you, the only order there is, is love. And in love, we are all equal. Otherwise, there is nothing but chaos. You may think it's too painful to view life the way I see it, so you go back to your old way of thinking to protect yourself from the truth, but once the heart opens, once the mind inquires, there will be an answer in truth. And, in truth, your vision center can show you what you truly are.

Now, you may think God held out man as something special. The only thing I know of that is different about man, compared to the cat, is that man doesn't know what he is. He looks out with empty eyes on the world and uses his eyes like a vacuum device, sucking up everything around him. This is fine, but what he gives in return is pitiful judgment. It is best, until you know the true meaning of a thing, not to judge it. The less judgment you accumulate, the more you are able to become what creation is, until the idea of God becomes a reality.

Now, if you were to be born again, it would only be because you had things that had to die away in order for you to awaken further. I tell you, the only thing that can die is illusion, and in vision you will see that this is true.

So I got to be a hero today for my family. I showed up with meat and a beautiful hide to keep us warm or to make clothes or to make shoes. I saved the brain, boiled it in the skull, and rubbed that hide for three hours while my wife and the little one cut the meat up. I made Feice a pair of little shoes and put grease in the bottoms, so that her feet would soften and her little fire peds could cool. I think it cooled her temperament a little too. She seemed grateful.

The next morning, we had the rest of the hide to pack the meat in. And along the way that day, we all took turns gathering little herbs, little flowers, checking for deep sand, so we could dry some of this meat as we rested. And we slowed down. Feice agreed we didn't have to be in such a big hurry after all. She was just excited. We asked, "Excited about what?"

She says, "I hear 'em talkin'. They're talkin' about us."

And we said, "What are they sayin'?"

"They're sayin', 'Here they come. They're comin' back.'"

So they're all gettin' ready. They're going to have a celebration is what Shuhinono thought.

The little one just said, "Dancing, dancing." That's all she could say. I didn't even know she knew the word for dancing. Oh, I must have talked about my father on the trail, perhaps... dancing. Remember, I think she knows more Hopi than our own words, but somewhere "dancing" got in there, I guess. She also said there was some shrunked-up folks, waitin', all sittin' around, bunch of 'em, smokin' somethin', like them Hopi did.

I said, Oh, it must be the old ones... shrunked-up folks.

She says, "Like wrinkles, everywhere." But she didn't know the word wrinkles. She just made her face wrinkle like she thought they looked. She pushed her lips up under her nose and squished her eyebrows down over her cheeks and pushed her ears forward 'til they reached for her nose, almost. She's funny, that one. She's so funny, she even makes herself crack up. She's sure she's funny.

Now if I were that old and funky lookin', I probably wouldn't laugh, but I laughed. And, boy, she's *really* sure she's funny now. She pops over backwards with her toes in her hands and just cracks one up, makin' all those faces. And we start makin' faces and crackin' up too. She may be three, but she's the most self-confident three I've ever known. Even knows how to crack herself up. Heck, I'm still learnin' how to do that. I'm too serious. Everyone says so. Her laughter wasn't at wrinkles. Her laughter was joy at being so close to love. We're going home.

This is the last chapter. I won't be talking about joy, the crown chakra, the seventh seal, until we get to the *Water* book because there's no sense in it. It would just be my lips flappin'. I want you

167

to go with me through all these energy centers, so this book, *Fire,* will end here with this chapter on vision, the sixth seal or chakra.

When the heart fills and overflows, and the mind can no longer entertain itself with its own thoughts, those with love greater than yours will pour their thoughts into your mind to light this blue flame of vision. You need help here lighting this sixth energy center. You need all the fires that went before you to light your fire. No one ever goes on alone from here.

I prayed and asked Spirit to show me how to catch game in this country by myself. I was led to that tree, and I was made to lie down like a cat. I didn't complain about the discomfort of laying on a limb all stretched out. I dropped my energy, and I stopped my thoughts and asked for help. I didn't forget my question, but I did not question further either. So when the answer came, I was accepting of Spirit's method of answering my question. I was sure I didn't know how to answer it myself. The trap door in my mind opened, and I dropped through with my energy into my heart. Then the light came on in the center of my mind, above my eyes. I did nothing that the vision did not direct me to do. I did not object to this visionary experience, as I had been having other glimpses since the top of Great Mountain. I was not afraid I was losing my mind, because this cat was inside me, living and breathing like me. He had a family, a mind and a heart like mine. His language was different. His abilities were strange, but he was alive, conscious. And we were one in that consciousness.

So when we shared consciousness, we shared knowledge. That was its gift to me... knowledge, ability, gratitude. And it could even purr and make itself feel good any time it wanted. Every time I made a noise like that, I'd get hit on the head. "Stop snoring," they'd say. "You're drivin' us crazy." Well, maybe snoring is a human way of purring. Who knows?

Perhaps your comfort zone is too small, if you don't care to learn what knowledge has to offer you. Only Spirit can transfer your direct experience into knowledge for you. No one else can.

The visions continued. Before we stepped back into that camp, we could see them folks gathering at the edge. As the old ones welcomed us, we saw they knew many of our experiences already, and they were waiting to tell us about our travels, not us tellin' them our stories. That would come later for the young ones who didn't believe the old ones were telling the truth. We'd tell the youngsters stories or parables or metaphors to simplify what we learned and how we learned it. We were to be surprised over and over and over again by these old ones who could get the gist of a thing from a thousand miles away. They may not see the exact faces or exact places, but what we learned, they got. They got it because, being connected to you, you couldn't help but give it. That's the way love works. And what we saw on our trip, they got in vision. Their Spirit Guides looked after us and passed on to them what we learned. Why, you ask? Well, because that was their job, these Ancient Ones, to learn through our experience and collect knowledge and pass it on.

You see, once we went to the top of Great Mountain, we were joined with everyone who had ever been to the top of the mountain and was still here on this side. Well, I hadn't quite grown up to that until this moment when I could see that our old ones were gonna' tell us our story.

Shuhinono confirmed she had the same vision and was honored to stay silent. That our old ones would care so much to follow us everywhere we went with their Guides was a great honor. We were just young, crazy people to most everyone in the tribe. But to the old ones, we were knowledge seekers. We were experiencers. We were the stuff stories were made of.

So they poured all of their energy and effort into praying us to where we were going and into praying us home. So I ask you, who had the harder job–we who went walking, saw and slept and ate and suffered in the cold and heat, or these old people who stayed connected to us the whole journey and never went anywhere?

I think there are two ways to live your life. Maybe everything in between is being afraid of having a life. We were actively seeking knowledge, and the old ones were actively seeking knowledge. And everybody else was waiting for the story. Where do you fit in? Check and see. It's important that you know where you're at.

Awareness of this blue flame of vision that burns in the center of your mind is a result of risk and effort. Now, everybody has a flame, but whether or not they're aware of it or work against it or just give it all to serendipity, who knows? I see around me on these walks and in my short life, there is no such thing as chance.

Just as Feice was not drowned in that flash flood and was left high and dry with everything intact was not an accident. Just as we were bowled over and just about obliterated by that same water was also not an accident. That you have will centers and don't know anything about them, that too is not an accident. It is because your will is being used against itself that you do not learn what will is or what it's for. Try to take it back, and you will find out what's got it.

This light in your mind can be lit through true desire. And true desire is a function of your willingness to be shown by Spirit. After you are shown and have some experience, then you can learn what will is for. If you take it by yourself and run with it, good luck! Your life will be full of so-called "accidents" if they're hard lessons, and so-called "coincidences" if they're curious lessons. But remember, you call to you the lessons you need to learn... always.

If this fire is lit and an upside-down will takes it, ego will project onto the world, pictures that are truly horrible. If a heartless mind does as ego projects, the horror is unimaginable. One saving grace is that those who are very sensitive, opened and awakened know that the dreams, the sick dreams of a mind barely awake, are not real. But the pictures do frighten the children because they bump into them in their dreamtime. This is the collective mind the unawakened are afraid of, be it a child or an adult. This collective dreamtime is what you fear. Sorting out what is truth and what is illusion is its purpose. Sorting out what you would have be real is your purpose in it.

One true visionary can send pictures with their mind to all they touch, to any mind willing to accept the vision, giving hope and strength to all the people. When tragedy strikes, the people will take this vision of love, tap into the energy that sent it and be healed of sorrow and pain. It is the ultimate medicine... love.

People are still tapping into Christ's vision and being healed of all their sorrows. They are trading their fearful mind in for a mind guided by Love. That's what was on top of that mountain, the power to heal that only Love has. That's what our walk was for... to bring healing visions back to our people.

So, what is your part and what vision of the world have you to give to your people? What do you dream? It is good to look at these things. I am happy you are on this walk with me, and I am grateful to you for your company. Ah ho.

Earth

Book Two

Chapter 1
Second Return

We arrived at camp... oh, I think it was early evening. Naturally, Feice was about fifty paces ahead of us. There was quite a crowd there. This time it was a joyous celebration. You know, I don't know why exactly. Nothing special happened, I thought, that I could bring back to our people to save them from the coming great storm or any such catastrophe, but everyone was happy.

Feice? Wow! What a strange kid. The first person to stand in front of her, she climbed right up her legs and was just talkin' a mile a minute. And, you know, half of it was Hopi, and half of it was our language. Feice and that old person–well, wasn't that old really... middle-aged like me 'cause by the time you're twenty, you're middle-aged–they were just yakin' away at each other like they both perfectly understood one another. I wasn't close enough to catch all the conversation, but they were lookin' like they were havin' a good time. So was everyone... smiles all around, jumping up and down, happy people. God, it's good to have a large family that knows how to love.

I tell you, this spring will probably be the most abundant one we've ever had. You know, with all these open hearts around here, I think that's what makes everything flower. I think abundance is bigger than what you can stuff in your pockets. What do you think?

There was plenty love going around, I'll say that. Nobody really asked any questions except, "How was your trip?" And then they'd start some talkin' that goes beyond that 'cause they knew your trip was fine, but they just had to ask. It was like a courtesy thing, but they really were more interested in–well, now you're back, let me tell you what happened around this place while you were gone.

So it was. It seemed as if they had absorbed everything that we did on our walk already, and we were the ones that were missing and had to catch up. That's fine. I like that. I was curious. Shuhinono disappeared for, I'd say, four or five hours, and that was unusual. What was that about? But I figured, oh, it was family and catchin' up. But no, she really disappeared. I have to ask her when I see her... if I ever see her again.

Feice, well, she's been in six or seven laps in an hour. Told her story six or seven times already, especially 'bout the bugs and all. She even mentioned to one person–it was an older person–about that big water that came and rushed her away. Now that was the first time she'd ever spoken about that to anyone. She's a funny one.

The skies were spectacular in the evenings. All the grasses were blooming. All the birds were singing everywhere. All the people had smiles in their eyes, and their feet were firmly on the ground. It was a good place to be just now. But I think it will take me some time before the walking empties out of my shoes.

It's like you people get after you go on a big trip on the highway. When you crawl into your bed, all night that bright yellow stripe goes by, and everything seems like it's moving.

Well, walking is no different. It's the movement. It's addictive... the movement. I find myself sitting by fires, having meals, talkin' stories and having to stand up, step outside the lodge and walk around, and after I've taken some fresh air, step back inside for more. That walkin'... it's addictive. To slow down now and not need that walkin', well, that's a challenge for me. When I did see Shuhinono, I asked her, Where you been?

She says, "Couldn't get the walkin' outa' my shoes. Couldn't stand still. Besides, there were so many minds probing. I'm not used to this kind of excitement. I was used to sweet solitude and the Creator's Voice. Now, all of a sudden, we're thrust into all this people business again. Dearly I love them, but they tire me. So I had to go connect with the Mother and get my feet grounded in one place... get that walkin' out. I had to ground to this land right here in this place, with these people. Took a while. I liked my walking. Got used to it. Did anyone ask after me?"

I said, No, I don't think so. Your mother, she asked... without words. She just stood there and looked at me like–I'm here, and so where's Shuhinono? And I looked at her with my funny eyes and I winked, and she stomped her foot and walked away.

You see, there's this respect thing, children to elders. And it's, like, pretty formal. And we're, like, pretty informal people now. On this walk, we kinda' forgot a lot, so things that are expectations here, we let slip by. So her mother got her feelings hurt because Shuhinono didn't come right to her and say hello and have her get the story firsthand, first.

So I said to Shuhinono, I think you better fix it.

And she says, "Okay, I remember. I'll fix it. Besides, I haven't been to tell anyone my story yet anyway."

So off she goes. Now, I don't see her again for another five hours. That's the way that is... family. Big family, you know, takes time to get through them all. Don't want anybody to get their feelings hurt, by God, or you'll pay for it. Aunts and uncles and sisters and brothers... boy, they'll get you. Treat you kinda' funny for a little while if you miss any of the finer points. Never mind you been gone for years and may have forgotten everything. But generally, it's all good humor. They're happy to see us.

I've talked a little bit about home, and I've talked a little bit about the earth as the Mother. How do you feel about going back to your mother's home? Does it bring you joy and peace? Is there love in it? Well, I tell you, if there's love in it, it's because you bring it with you and give it.

I know people who are unhappy being indians because it's a hard life, harsh sometimes. They think nature is cruel at times. They kinda' resent physical laws and earth laws, so they don't give love to the Mother. So their homes are hard places to sit. Same dirt, but it sure seems harder. Same robes, but in their homes the wind seems colder. Same food, but in their house it has a bitter taste.

Some people been dealt pretty hard blows... losing family members, marital problems and just general discord between male and female... blame, suspicion, guilt. But if there is to be a spring and there are to be flowers in abundance again, the heart must open for spring to happen. Oh sure, you look around and spring's happening without you. Well true... *without you.* Let it happen... *within you.* That's renewal. That makes the ground soft, the food tasty and the robes warm. The gratitude for what is given from the Mother makes your life worthwhile. But if you cannot receive the love in the form in which it's given, you have not received the love at all.

So, to return to this homeland, to this large family, to feel the gratitude that we felt for their warm reception, made the ground soft, the robes warm and the food tasty. We were grateful to them. And we were grateful for the abundance that the Mother provided for us all. This gratitude filled everyone's hearts over and over, and sent us into song and dance, sent us into stories of what we'd learned, stories of our experiences. And those who could not go on a long walk experienced our experiences through the pictures we'd saved for them in our minds.

Now, you take Polaroids and show them around. That's good. That's fine. But what happened to communication? It's left up to the person looking at the Polaroid to discover what you took it for. And I don't think people are too conscious when they take those Polaroids. Artists, maybe, are trying to communicate depth with pictures, but when the average person takes Polaroids, it's hard to get the meaning out of them. The pictures you want to share are in your minds... the feelings and meaning of having gone somewhere and taken those pictures in the first place.

I see Feice's off in the corner of my brother's lodge, going through his belongings, and I think I had better step in at this point. So I go over to her and I say, Little one, these are your uncle's things.

"I know."

Don't you think you should respect them and leave them be, and maybe ask your uncle to show these things to you?

"I asked already."

I said, You did?

"Sure."

I said, How did you ask?

"In Hopi. He said, 'Sure, help yourself.'"

I said, That was a good one. Don't you think he might now be upset that you're going through his things?

"Maybe."

What you lookin' for anyway?

"I'm lookin' for a rattle. I heard one over there, and I want one to play with."

I said, Oh, I'll go ask uncle.

"Okay."

So, over I go. This is one of my brothers that I didn't really get along with too much. And I say to him, Hey, my young one's over there in your stuff wantin' a rattle to play with. You got one over there that's not too important to you?

He looks up into my eyes. Now, this brother was never generous with me. He looks into my eyes, and he looks real hard and long, then he says, "You find something in there you like, you take it."

175

I was stunned. This was not the brother I'd left behind. And then his eyes twinkled, and he smiled real big and gave me a big hug. And I just sank into him. There was gratitude in my heart, and I just sank into him. He was a big guy too, bigger than me. He turned away and didn't look back and walked on. Feice looks over at me and smiles... a big, long smile, holdin' a rattle in her hand. I go, okay, okay.

You know, I think we're in for a real surprise here. Something's cookin' with this little one. She's a funny kid. I bet, three years ago, my brother would have thrown me out of his lodge for messin' in his stuff or any of my people messin' in his stuff. He was a big shaman studier, you know... like me, but older. Something big's changed since we been gone.

This *Earth* book is gonna' be about relationships because, truly, that is what the earth is about... total interrelatedness of everything, total interdependency of everything, total union and Oneness of everything.

When the Europeans came to this land, they were told by their white leaders that this was their land and they could own it. Well, they went on good faith and tried to make it their homes. But I'll tell you, very few of you have made it your homes. You still feel guilty that your leaders lied and that there were people here before you. This made for bad communication. Now, trust me, we would have shared everything we had, and we did... with the earliest of you. We did not expect dominance, however, so we were easy prey. Even now, we want nothing except equality.

So relationships, I think they're about equality. That means I could be equally as dull as anybody else, and I could be equally as brilliant as anyone else. Everything in its time... turn taking.

Everybody gets a turn.

Now, you can ignore what lessons are before you for a time, but whenever you allow meaning to come into your life again, those lessons will bring you back to equality. And the interesting thing about meaning is that you can't have it by yourself and have it be the truth. It must be shared equally among all living things to be the whole truth.

I think we partied three days, three nights. All I know is that we were all pretty pooped out. They had prepared a lodge for us. It was a grand one, and I didn't know why we were getting such special treatment. Usually, we would lodge with someone else until we gathered the things necessary to build our own. But this was all done in advance, even stocked with some foods. So I was anxious to talk to Shuhinono when we got time to ourselves.

Finally, with little Feice over in the corner, playing with rocks and bugs and sticks and flowers, the fire made, crackling, competing for lighting the lodge with the evening sunset, Shuhinono said, "This is interesting, don't you think? It's like we're actually important or something."

I nodded and said, If we are, I think the novelty will wear off. What I'd like to know is, what have we done?

She said, "Well... walked a lot."

Feice says, "Yeah," from the corner, "walked a lot."

Maybe they all did want to go some place and look around. Maybe they were happy someone else had the guts to go do it, so they'd come back and tell fresh stories. Maybe they're gettin' tired of the same old stories.

Shuhinono said, "I've never done so much talkin' in my life. If I tell one more story, I'm going to burst. I think I need a rest."

And just then, in walks an old one. Now, this one I remembered. This was that crazy, old lady who talked about that "comes back twice" stuff. I expected her immediately to ask, What's for dinner? But she didn't. She says, "I've been trying to get you to come to our lodge, but you seem to be too important now to hear us. So when you're ready, we'd like to see you both... and bring Feice."

I stuttered a bit and said, Oh-well-okay-like what-tonight?

She says, "You been away and alone in your thoughts way too long, son. Welcome back. Yes, tonight." And out she goes.

Shuhinono made funny little faces, like... Oh, isn't she kind of uppity! Feice, holding her head down, never even looked over at that old one.

So I asked, What's with you, little one?

She says, "I don't like her."

Oh, I said, be careful. That one hit me over the head with a big stick once.

And she said, "Not me!"

Boy, I can tell, we're in for an interesting journey this summer. I don't know what that old one's got in mind for us, but she seems kinda' all worked up. Shuhinono's stayin' out of it, and Feice's in the middle of it. Uhm-humm.

Shuhinono looks over and asks, "Why on earth would they want us to bring Feice? Interesting. Now this perplexes even me. She's only three and some."

Well, we forgot all about it and went about making a little meal... lazyin' around, takin' our sweet time. The sun's going down. It's gettin' dark... sun's beyond the hills already... kinda' orange out, just before it gets purple-gray. I'm thinkin' about going to that lodge. Shuhinono's busy doing something else, and Feice says, "Time to go."

Oh, I said, Okay.

Shuhinono says, "I'm not ready."

I said, I'm not ready either, but we gotta' go. Feice said so.

"You and Feice go. I'll be along."

I said, I'm not sure that's a good idea.

Feice says, "Fine," grabs my hand and out we go.

Whew! Now, I expected to be married to one strong woman, but I never really expected two. And as I look back at our lodge, Shuhinono's using her hand to say, "Go."

So okay, we go. Besides, that little Feice's got such a grip on my little finger, I think maybe I'm gonna' have to rub it some when she lets go. Now she's draggin' me. She's runnin' almost.

So here we are at the lodge, real quick-like, and I'm not ready. I'm kinda' all flustered and surprised that this little one has this much energy... "fearlessness" is the word, I think. She's a stand-up little kid, I'll say. She doesn't hardly wait for anyone to come out and get us. She's ready to walk right in that lodge, and I have to hold her back some until somebody sticks their head out, at least. They wave us in and in we come.

I said, Shuhinono will be here shortly.

"No matter," an old one said. "She hears just fine where she's at."

Now, mind you, I've never been in ceremony with Feice, so I have no idea how she's gonna' act in a closed space full of acrid smoke. Most three-year olds, they just fidget and cry and fuss. Can't stand adult business. They're bored, you know... not enough bugs on the floor, or something's wrong. So I fully expected there to be nothing but disturbances.

We sat there for a full three minutes in total quiet as the old ones prepared for ceremony, but Feice was respectful. I saw that. She watched everything they did.

There was a hole dug in the middle of the lodge floor. One glowing stone was brought in and placed in the middle of the hole, then some herbs, sweet ones, were put on top of the hot rock. Sweet, warm air went all through the lodge. This time the door flap went down. Most times we sat there with it open, but this time the door flap went down. We sat in total darkness, except for that glowing-red stone. I reached over for Feice, but I couldn't find her. I got a little nervous, but I didn't hear anybody complain, so I forgot about it.

An old one said, "You been a long way. You went as far south as any of us have ever gone. You met some people there, old as us, maybe older. And you learned some things in those pit houses. We want you to tell us your story at this time because we were not able to go into those pit houses with you. Their medicines kept us out. So we want to know what you learned. And what were the powers of these people you call Hopi?"

There was a pause and I said, Their powers are like yours. They guide in vision. They have song. They use animals as guides, like you do... different ones... some I've never seen.

"Yes, but I want to know what you learned."

You know, I paused as I realized for the first time that because our old ones couldn't see what went on in the kivas of the Hopi, they were a bit scared of us... coming back with powers they didn't possess.

Now, here I had to be careful. I couldn't smile because my smile could be read as possessing knowledge, rather than smiling at how silly it was for them to worry. So I did nothing. But I did say, You need not worry. It was good. They didn't take from us. They only gave.

It was at that moment I heard a little squeal. And it wasn't Feice. It was one of the old women in there. My heart went out and I felt it was Feice... somewhere, doing something. And I went... Oh, my God... here we go. But I didn't say a word.

An old one said, "This child you brought back with you is not of us. She is part Hopi."

I said, Well, she learned Hopi language some because she listened to them when she was very young.

I was interrupted and it was told to me this child was not welcome as a spirit of our people but was part Hopi sent here to pester us and trouble us. They as much called her an infection from another culture.

Well, I was having trouble understanding this. I was trying to be kind and all, but to be honest with you, I was more interested in how come the old woman squealed and what that was about, rather than the fears of this other old one.

So I said, Feice, you come over here. Sit with Daddy. Sit with Papa. But I didn't hear a word out of her. Now I was nervous. I told the old one, I'll consider what you say, but I think you are worrying unnecessarily. And I would like to see my child, so would you open the flap?

The flap came up but, frankly, it was darker outside than it was in that lodge, so it wasn't much help. But the fire man brought in a stick that had flame on it, and I could see Feice in the back of the lodge, behind an old woman. She had one finger stuck in that woman's back and was holding that old one there, still as a ghost, with that one finger.

I said, What ya' doin', Feice?

Feice says, "She got to get out."

I asked, How come? Why you being so angry?

She says, "I don't like her. Thinking, no good."

I was all embarrassed and looked around at the others, and they were all astonished, except for an old one who was sitting there with a kind of knowingness in his eyes. I looked at him and I said, Look it here, you. You tell me what's going on.

Feice's still got her finger stuck in this old woman's back, and that old woman's eyes are terrorized, lookin' like she won't breathe again for another hundred years.

That old man's eyes went to the ground and he said, "Since you've been gone, we've had a disagreement, an argument. There's been no vote, so I don't know who thinks what, but the voice for dissension is this one here, the one with Feice's finger in her back." And I think, it's sad how minds fallin' out of love can't read each other anymore.

I said, Feice, stop it! Let the woman talk!

Feice took her finger off that old woman's back, and the old woman gasped for air. You come over here with Daddy, I said. So she did. But she still had a defiant look on her face.

I asked this old one, So tell me, what is this about?

The old woman would not speak, so the old man said, "She believes that you bring back with you demons from the under-world that would destroy us in this place, and that they ride on the Hopi's goodwill and good intentions, unknowingly to them.

I said, Well, what is this demon? I see only one demon here tonight and it's fear... fear of the unknown. That's what our walk was to dispel, and here we are bringing it back to you. So you tell me, what demon is it?

The old woman spoke up, shrill, angry, "This crazy child you bring back here. She'll be the death of us all."

I said, Wait a minute. You and I all have the same visions. We know about this big storm to come. Feice wasn't even born when we all saw this, so what are you bothering me with this for? What is this fear you have about the Hopi's underground lodge?

So she starts in... Ah well, they teach this, they teach that, everything looks different, they use this different, they use that different... and on and on. And her complaints are all about what things *look* like.

The old man looks down at the ground and he says, "We've been trying to work this out a long time, about ceremony and meaning. Because of our feelings that our tribe is doomed to per-ish in a great storm, we're trying to find meaning in it. Some cling to ritual to try to escape this vision, and others try to throw away the old ways. So we have a split. There are those who believe we can escape this doom, and there are those who believe that we must find meaning in our trials. So, I think, maybe we are going to have a new leader or maybe even two tribes if the council is split in half. This is what was going on while you were gone. And I see your child at three has powers beyond perception that we, in many ways, do not possess and it worries us."

Just then the old woman screeched at Feice, "I will fight you to my last breath" and stormed out of the lodge.

Now, imagine me, the father of this child trying to imagine that little Feice was conscious enough to tell me what this was all about. She's only three! So I asked her, Do you know what's going on? Do you know why this woman's angry with you? Can you tell me why?

Feice says, "Some big problem, huh?" And the old ones laugh at her.

I said, No really, Feice, can you help us out with this?

She says, "I not Hopi." The old ones look astonished that she could even grasp the problem. She says, "I like Hopi, but I not Hopi."

So it is in the world with people, being aboriginal, Asian, African, European, North or South American, or whatever. Fear separates. Love joins.

Then Feice said, "Feice too little to know." And I knew she said that because that's what we all were thinking. The old ones look at the ground, and they shake their heads. And all of them in unison in their minds go... Boy, we're in for a real ride. This one's too smart, too quick, too powerful.

So I scoop her up and I say good night. Feice wiggles out of my arms, runs back into that lodge, looks up into that old man's eyes, and she says, "Don't worry, Feice loves you." And that old man just looks at the ground and shakes his head again.

All the way home, I kept lookin' back at that lodge to see if anybody got out of it. I didn't see one soul get out of that lodge. We're talkin' fifteen minutes they were in there, at least, after we left. I bet they brought in more hot rocks and just went to sweat. I was impressed. What the hell is this all about? I said to myself.

Shuhinono pops her head out of our lodge before we even got there and said, "Well, how was it?"

I said, I wish you were there.

She said, "I was. I could see. So how was it?"

What do you mean? I asked. If you were there, you saw it. You tell me how it was.

And she said, "No, I mean how was it for *you*?"

Well, I'm confused, I said.

She said, "No, you're not. They are. Don't join their confusion. Look and see how it was."

The firmness of her voice kinda' stunned me. And, by God, I got a good look at it. I see that there's some kind of power struggle going on in there with those old ones. I'm not sure about what. But for some reason, for the first time since I've ever known any of them, they've disagreed about something. And this doesn't make sense to me because the camp is so wonderfully loving and happy. When did this discontent begin, I wonder? Since it hasn't boiled down to the tribe yet, I have to assume it's pretty recent.

I look at Shuhinono. She nods and says, "Is it Feice that's causing the trouble?"

Well, from the looks of that old woman it was, I said, but from the firmness and certainty of Feice, it wasn't. It was that old woman.

Shuhinono says, "Don't be so sure yet."

What do you mean? I asked.

She said, "That old woman may have been feeling pretty upset and pretty against Feice for callin' her out, but maybe there's something more going on in that lodge worth findin' out about. Maybe that sly old man over in the corner's got something to do with it."

Well, you know, I've been away for three years, and all this intrigue is too much for me. With all the peace and love that I've enjoyed for the last three years, now I'm thinkin' all of a sudden, it ain't so good to be back.

Shuhinono says, "Oh, stop indulging yourself. You're here. We're here. It's what's up."

Okay, I said. I think I'll get some rest. You figure it.

Well, this is where, for me, religion and politics separate. If it's a power struggle between these two old people, fine, let 'em have at it. Give 'em big sticks and send 'em out into the prairie.

But my thinking was a little simplistic for Shuhinono, even for Feice. What they saw, I wasn't privy to yet. So I'll assume you're like me. Since you're not in on what the issue is, I'll bring you along with me, askin' all my silly questions. Together, we'll find out, okay?

To me, it was inconceivable that spiritual people and Spirit could ever have a conflict about anything, except the untruth. Even the untruth is irrelevant, since it's not true. Anybody could speak garbage if they wanted, but speaking untruth doesn't make it true, so we didn't worry about its consequences too much. Only when it spilled over and seriously affected another person, only when there was serious conflict between two people, did anyone else get involved at all. And they only got involved if somebody was asking for help or if there was violence. Then we all got involved.

It's hard to have a spiritual community when people are beating each other. In the past, it was easy to know what to do because we all had decided that we were going to be a spiritual community based upon love, rather than a warring one based upon chaos, confusion, individual perceptions, fears, and aggressions.

That night, I sat until I slept. I pondered over all the agreements ever made in our community that had been taught to us in story form. And I remembered all the lessons that we'd learned together about why we don't kill each other, for any reason. It would be like you going back and reviewing all the reasons why your society is the way it is, based upon your Constitution, your Bill of Rights, and your individual states' agreements with the national government. All the way down to the local level, you elect people to represent you. It would be like you sitting there and seeing exactly why each person was ever elected, for every reason, and why your government exists at all.

Well, that's what I did, as best I could, considering I'd been gone three years and didn't know much about the council members. But I did see that our method of self-government wasn't very much different from the Hopi's method. Ours was a bit more linear, and theirs was a bit more abstract. But their reasons for having clans and clan medicines were the same reasons we had a council of seven members or more. Our council members were mixed, female and male, and each council member represented different aspects and needs of the community and the needs of the individuals, just as did the Hopi's clan system.

So now, okay fine. I know some questions to ask that I'd never asked before because I was busy with my own life and my own journeys. Who was this fearful woman and what did she represent? What was her role in council? And what was everyone else's role in the council? These are questions I'd never asked. So fine, I'll get some sleep. Tomorrow, I will ask these good questions.

Shuhinono, under the robes with Feice, rolls her head over, looks at me and says, "Ready?"

I said, I love you, Shuhinono. I'm ready.

Then I crawl under those good, warm robes, and I snuggle those two ladies, and I'm a happy man. Politics can wait!

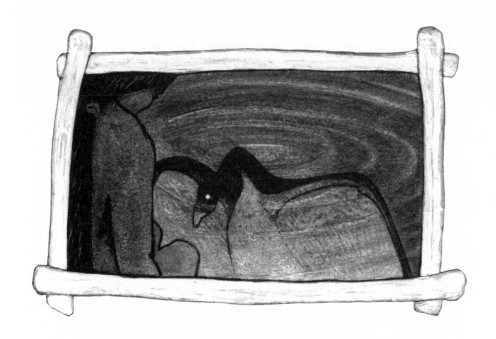

Chapter 2
Gifts of Vision

I won't say bright and early 'cause it was still dark when I got up, but early it was when I went to my brother's house. I don't know why my brother's house, but I went to my older brother's house. Probably 'cause now I know he loves me. Then I shuffled around outside until I could hear his voice say, "Come in out of the cold, whoever you are."

So I scooted into that lodge. It was still dark inside, as no fire was yet lit. Couldn't see nothin'. He says, "Over here," so I scoot around to the left. We always went to the left of a fireplace, lit or not. And he said, "Sit here, brother." So he knew me. He knew it was me. So I sat.

I said, I need you to tell me about the council members, one by one.

He says, "Oh, this early? Must be serious." So he began. "The oldest one is Three Feathers. He was a duly appointed chief. You know how that goes. Father told you the story."

I said, Yes.

"He's a good man. He looks after the harmony of the council, because whatever is decided affects everyone. He listens to all sides when there is trouble and dissension. He seems to be able to work out solutions. That's not to say there aren't strong feelings, but usually when everyone walks out, there is agreement about the solution. There are seven others besides Three Feathers.

"The next one we call Yak-Yak. He's like the bluejays, always talking. Seems like Yak-Yak has all the words for people when they don't have them themselves. This man's got memories for stories long forgotten, so he's the principal storykeeper.

"The next one in line is Whistling Woman. You remember her from our youth. She taught you how to whistle."

Oh yes, I know who you mean now, I said.

"Whistling Woman represents the medicine women, the keepers of all the medicines. She is the one that looks deep. She's the one that took you down that hole the first time, just like me.

"Next one is called Wishing Far. He's always hopeful or happy. This is the one that can see long distances. This is the one that knows about all the hopes and aspirations of our people. Wishing Far has medicine of breadth. It is to this one that we turn when our visions cannot easily be explained. Between Wishing Far and Whistling Woman, there is always a story that comes out and Yak-Yak remembers it.

"The next one is a woman, no longer young. Her name looks like the pink blossoms in the spring. She's called Flowering Tree. Flowering Tree is concerned about the mind and feelings of the whole tribe. She is aware of all the difficulties in the camp between everyone... men, women, children... anyone. If there is any disturbance in camp, in any family, she is aware of it. This is the one that was angry last night, the one that Feice poked in her back. We heard about that already. That went around the camp pretty quick. Some kid you got there."

Yah, I said, wish I knew what it was all about.

He said, "Well, you keep an open mind when it comes to Flowering Tree." I nodded a yes.

"The fifth member was a great hunter when he was young. He represents the men and their pursuits and concerns. He is the keeper of ceremonies for hunting... keeps us in balance with nature, so our egos don't get too outrageous and cause us harm. We call him Twin Secrets. And I'll tell you, he got his good name because of a big argument that erupted one time in camp between two hunters. They darn near killed each other, those two men did. And, you know, he took them out into the prairie, and some big thing happened out there which nobody will talk about, but it solved that big fight. Those two men were changed. Those two men won't tell to this day what happened and neither will he. So he got this name, Twin Secrets. It was big magic he pulled off, 'cause that was such a big fight, it could have torn the tribe in half.

Maybe someday, he'll tell us his story, or those two men will tell us their story.

"The sixth member is one of the youngest members. Her name is Smiling White Hair. She got her name because her hair went white when she was only twenty. There are big stories about that too, what that means for us. She sits council and she's only twenty-six. She is the camp mother, and she represents all the children. She also represents the feelings that the Earth Mother has for us, so we all look to her for balance in our activities and in our thoughts and in our songs and in our ceremonies. She is aware of the children and their need for participation in all these things. She is a great teacher as well.

"The seventh member is kinda' new. He got his calling to this council because of his abilities to talk with other tribes. He can communicate with people whose languages are not our own. He's our peace-talker. We call him Six Trees. I'll tell you just briefly about that name 'cause it's an odd one.

"As you know, to have council, you need at least seven people, seven trees. You see, a grove of trees stands in one place. They are standing people. Around that grove of trees is open possibilities. When there is agreement, the grove of trees flourish, make fruit and expand into the open meadow. So it is with us, a small tribe in agreement, flourishing here in the prairie. When Six Trees is negotiating or talking to other people, he's six of those seven trees, and he makes that person he's talking to the seventh tree. He can have council with one person for all of us. No one else does this.

"So we have a good council, but we have a problem. Flowering Tree sees a problem with this vision about the big snow. Right now, no one agrees on anything, and it has thrown the council into chaos. What I'm curious about, dear brother, is Feice. What is your child's part in all this, and why did she single out Flowering Tree to not like?"

We sat there for some time pondering these things. Then I said, I guess I'm not going to find the answer here in the dark with you so early in the morning, but thank you for giving me good pictures. I never paid enough attention to these council matters when I was younger. You have answered what I've come for.

It was then his wife stirred, and she turned and said, "It is good you are studying this problem, but I trust when you learn what it really is, you will tell us and we all will shift our attention to the solution."

I said, Thank you for those good words, and I turned to leave. She reached up and touched me on the arm and said, "Shuhinono knows what this is about. You ask her." I was rather stunned for two reasons. The first is, the wife of another doesn't touch any other male, even the brother, so I was shocked. And yet, my brother's eyes looked at me with the same intent as hers... piercing. It was okay. The second reason was, how could Shuhinono know anything about this since we've been gone for three years?

My brother said, "You ask her. We saw it this way ourselves. You ask her." I nod and leave.

Genuinely perplexed, I walk around the camp for an hour at least. People were beginning to stir. Fires were being started. Children were crying. Some little boys left to sleep out at night were coming into the lodge. There was a mist on the ground. Everything was damp. The grass had an electric, loamy smell... fresh like. The earth had a flavor... rich, smooth, potent. I could feel this trouble of ours was about growth too, so I stopped worrying about the big cold and saw this issue more as one of growing pains for our council and our people. But I had never experienced this kind of dissension before. Sure, there were arguments, but this was a gulf, like the chasm where the Hopi lived... almost seemed impossible to cross. What could cause such division, I couldn't fathom. I certainly knew it wasn't Feice. And yet, she sure seemed to play a role.

Back to my lodge I went, fully expecting to crawl under the robes again to two sleeping ladies. I lift up the robes, but there's no one there. I wonder... So early, where could they be? I crawl back out and stand up and look around, and there in the distance is little Feice and Shuhinono walking in the grass, carrying a little basket. Must be digging roots, I thought. So I went off to walk with them and say good morning.

As my thoughts drifted to the Hopi, my wife and daughter disappeared to my eyesight. I shook my head and looked again, and they were there. I walked on to greet them. Ten more paces and my thoughts are pulled to what the Hopi may have to do with this issue. I look up and again I don't see Shuhinono or Feice. Now, the grass isn't tall yet, and even if they stooped down, I could see them. I look back at camp, and I see all the little huts, some smoke rising here and there, and as I turn around and look ahead again, there's Shuhinono and Feice. Now I wonder, what the heck is going on? I plop down on my rump in the grass, and I let my thoughts go to them Hopi again, this time not looking to scare myself by not seeing Shuhinono and Feice. And I ask, What are you trying to tell me?

I sink into full vision and a voice says to me, "We gave your child what we knew would help you in the hard times to come.

She will point out your difficulties. But be sure, though she is young, she will show you the solutions too. So pay close attention. We did this to help you, not to harm you."

I find myself staring at my toes in the grass. And I say, Thank you for that. I know your hearts are good.

I look over to see Feice and Shuhinono waving at me, coming toward me. Shuhinono stops ten feet away, looks real hard at me and says, "So, them Hopi visited you too."

I say, Yup. Good thing too. It helped.

She said, "Yup. Me too." Then we both look over at Feice, and she's standing there just as quiet as can be with a funny lookin' smile on her face. Suddenly she shifts back into being just a little kid again, jumps up, runs to me, and gives me a big hug. I think without the tenderness I feel for this young one, the trials of life wouldn't be worth it. But today, because we love each other, whatever is going to happen, whatever comes of this trial is okay.

Now, I know you folks in your families have the same feelings for your children. They help you out when you're in need, and you help them out as best you can when they're in need. But I tell you, the young were given to us to guide us into the future. Because our young one was never taught fear, Feice never doubted what her heart and her mind told her. She was never made to feel small, even though in stature she was short. She was never made to feel like her contribution of herself was incomplete in any way, even though her years were not long. So she was not split by doubt and confusion or fear. What she said and what she did arose from within her and from within those guiding her. Her heart and mind were joined in wholeness, and we honored her role, whatever it was to be, instead of judging it.

Shuhinono wasn't the least bit nervous about Feice's role, I could tell you that. It was I who was nervous. Mind you, I'm not a great politician. I'm not an ambassador being Six Trees. I'm not the camp psychologist, and I'm not that old man who could remember everyone's stories. I'm not the great hunter or problem solver. And, surely, by my telling you this story, you can see that I don't keep secrets well. So if there was nervousness, it was mine because I didn't know what my part was. I think it's to ask questions. I think I'm the only one who doesn't know their role here, and the only way I'm going to find out is to ask questions.

Later that day, I walk off by myself with a little ember in a clay cup. I put sweet grass on that ember, and I look up to the heavens. I pray that I be shown what my part is and that I do it without fail. I feel like something is going to happen, and it's up to me to have it come out okay. So I ask for guidance and strength to do my part, for clarity of mind to know *when*... rather than how. It is better, I think, to be ready and willing to do what's needed in the moment, rather than to know how to do it and miss the moment it is to be done.

As I walk on, I see that all the animals have a gift to give us. They are a vehicle of Spirit. They are here to teach us that we, too, are spirit and are never alone in any part of creation. They hear the Creator's Voice and try to guide us through life, whether we are aware of it or not. Their wisdom is their gift.

Feice, I see, has badger medicine... tenacity, powerful will, fearlessness. Within Shuhinono, I see, is every one of the creatures. So by joining Shuhinono's mind, I fill this day learning from her about each animal's medicine, each animal's teaching. As Shuhinono and the creatures share with me, I will share with you.

Call upon eagle as I do, to give its gift of clear perception, keen eyesight, perfect concentration, perfect willingness to complete whatever its task is. Today, I ask eagle to help me to complete my task, whatever it is.

First, I am shown that the little squirrels that run on the ground have keen noses and find what they are looking for. They save it for when they will need it. They save, they gather, they put things away until their proper time, as I am being asked to do. To be truly helpful, one must gather understanding, gather the tools of application and save the energy of action for the perfect moment... Spirit's moment.

I see the little ants take the big mountain apart from underneath, one grain at a time, and rebuild it on top. They go deep inside that mountain, grab one stone at a time, bring it out and build a new mountain on top. They unbuild the mountain from the inside out.

Now, to take a mountain apart takes significant, collective commitment, but to take a mountain apart from inside out takes a combination of characteristics of the whole community. That means when a single individual apart from the whole cannot see how it can be done, the rest of the community still does it because it works.

So when we're speaking in council, we call on ant to help us to see from the inside out. Then, if something is wrong, fix it from the inside out, never acting upon it from the outside. To unbuild from the inside, this is ant.

Now, you think, because an ant carries one rock at a time, that each ant acts all alone. But I tell you, they have the same mind and they're acting together. They can move that mountain because they have agreement. Ant showed me that we will find our solution from the inside... together.

189

So all day goes like this, Shuhinono's mind showing me each creature and its value to us in this struggle, in this conflict that's in our tribe, in our council.

Next, I am shown that the hawk is the messenger for action, the start and finish of it. A hawk carries the message without first reading it. I see Feice, little badger baby, being hawk. She has other medicines, other tools to complete her task, yet it is hawk as little Feice that the Hopi use to help us bring up this issue in the council. Without hawk, there would be no start in healing.

Vision-questers ask hawk when to go up the hill and when to come down. Because hawk's message is only about some action needing to be taken, the recipient of the message is usually aided by another animal's medicine as well. If there is no action to be taken other than walking, like on our big trip, hawk usually signals... "All's well, continue."

The sounds of a hawk's cry are very distinct and only of two kinds... action and continuance. Today a hawk cried, "Kirr-ee, kirr-ee, all's well." Yesterday, I remember going into the lodge with Feice and hearing, "K-e-e-e, be alert!" Feice delivered her message to the old ones. Healing will now begin.

Swallow... now, you say, you couldn't have swallows in the prairie. But I tell you, we do have swallows. We have little areas where there are cliffs and water and mud, and them swallows build their nests in those cliffs. Swallows carry visions. They're like the delivery service. They're very fleet. And to prove their willingness for this fleet service, they'll even deal with the rock people. They'll go deep into the earth and use those soils and those muds to build their homes with. They're in agreement with the underworld as well, so the swifts or the swallows bring deeper visions. They're very fleet, because to carry such heavy visions you must be very quick not to get stuck in them. Visions of impending danger or death require a light and quick touch in their delivery. I think it was swallow who gave this vision of the big cold to Shuhinono on our walk.

Rabbits... well, we've talked about them before. It's kind of tough being the medicine that is everybody else's food, so rabbits carry fear, either to us or away from us. Someone gets it and we all take turns helping those who might be temporarily afflicted with it.

But I will tell you something good about rabbit. Fear is in place for two reasons. The first is to make you aware of something of importance, like to warn you of danger to your physical self. The second is to warn you of danger to your spiritual self. I'll try to explain by saying that the only importance fear has at all is to be gone through and overcome. Fear is in place to challenge your awareness of what *will* is for.

Now, simple awareness of fear's presence in you is not enough to save you if your will is not intact. And simple awareness of will to push fear aside most probably will not save you either. It is the expanded, spiritual awareness of the purpose of will, the certainty of your true function as a spiritual being that will save you.

Rabbit, then, as a teacher, can deliver to you the lessons that you need to understand about will and its function. This can only be done through the facing of your fears with the help of a Spiritual Guide.

Therefore, fear is a great teacher and rabbit is to be honored, especially at the moment you are able to enter, go through and understand any fear. At the doorway of this vision for our tribe, stands rabbit.

Next, I see bear is big medicine. Bears dream. They dream reality though, not the dreams of fantasy like we have as humans. Bear also knows all the medicines, plant and animal, so we come to the bear to ask them for help with our sicknesses. You see, bear dreams wellness, dreams those herbs, helps us find them and get back to health again. Through the spirit of bear, we get answers to our questions, to our introspections. If you ask and have a need, bear dives really deep, sometimes goes into meditation, into hibernation, and comes out in the spring with the answer.

Some questions may take longer to answer than others. For instance, is a person supposed to get well or not? For that, bear may have to dive deeper still. That's bear's job. It's very important, big medicine for us, asking the bears. So, what is this sickness in our tribe, this fear? What is the solution? I asked bear.

Next, I see coyote as trickster. And truly, coyote is a trickster, but beyond all that, coyote teaches family. Coyote has the strongest family bonds of any creature on earth. Coyote knows how to love. Their playfulness and their trickery comes because they have agreement among them that this bond is unbreakable, unshakable. They can afford to play because of all that certainty of family bond. With such heavy burdens on my mind, I ask coyote for humor and reminding of love's undying bond.

Now, coyote like mice for dinner. They like rabbits too, but rabbits take a lot of effort to catch. Mice are easy eatin'. They've got their noses down to the ground. They get to lookin' all around outside their hole and forget where that hole is. They get to lookin' around, and they forget the bigger picture. They get so caught up in the details of what they smell and what they see with those little nearsighted eyes that they forget, and they become... **Dinner!**

So I think it is with us. We must not get caught counting the grains of sand and forget the bigger picture. We must not scrunch our lives down to small worries ahead of time, or we'll forget why we're here, why we're alive now. We'll be dead before our time.

In this picture show that I was getting from Shuhinono about the animals, about all the Mother's children, I think I learned everything that you would ever learn in all your movies you watch. But I think I'd rather have my lessons of reality from the Mother about what these creatures are for, than to try to get reality out of all your stories that you tell about humans. Seeing a creature behave a certain way, live a certain life, demonstrates to us some characteristic of God, some characteristic of ourselves, and it is up to us to ask our brother and sister creatures for their help with characteristics that we may not have at the moment. That is much more helpful than looking at people, seeing a characteristic that they may have and we may not have, then envying them for it. All these creatures were put here, so you could have that characteristic as part of your learning, as part of your own character, if you but spend the time to observe and learn it.

Now, you may think this takes a great deal of time, but have you truly asked what your time on this earth is for? Algebra is okay, but what about earth? The animals and your lessons about them are being pushed farther and farther away from your lives. I think your rush to make movies is because you feel all will be lost if you do not document what is left. What you're doing is trying to replace life with your documentaries. I tell you, when the animals are gone, the free ones, your freedom will be gone too. And you will follow your own story to the end that you write now.

I see you watching *As the World Turns* or *Days of Our Lives,* and I wonder what you learn from those characters. What are they teaching you? How has it enhanced your life? I think I'd rather sit on a rock and watch a squirrel. I think I'd rather be taught by eagles who do not say one thing and do another or do one thing and say it's another. These visionary experiences are available to you, just as they were for me.

That day, I was taught how to breathe into vision by a butterfly. My son, John-Mohinono, was also led into vision by a butterfly's breath, using only one tiny muscle in his diaphragm. He let the butterfly breathe for him. I've never noticed a creature have more certainty and utmost lightness of spirit than a butterfly. To have such certainty and such lightness is a tribute to God. I still don't know how a butterfly floats on the air like that. It's totally amazing to me... to live other lives, one as an egg, one as a helpless little larva, then one as a caterpillar with twenty legs on each side, eating all the leaves up, then to pupate and be so totally different as a butterfly. Perfect certainty... an egg, a larva, a caterpillar, a chrysalis, and a butterfly. Spectacular! Creation is spectacular! And I know you, too, can have vision because a butterfly can show you how to breathe into it, just as we did.

You know, the body is so busy, heart pumping, everything moving, breathing, doing this and that... the mind doesn't relax. It fears the body. Give your breath to a butterfly, and have your breathing be so light and certain that you pop into vision. I recommend it. Trust the butterfly to breathe for you with perfect certainty and lightness. You, too, will have vision. Who on earth could fear a butterfly?

I know dealing with your mind is difficult, but I'll let you deal with your own mind. When you know who's in charge, vision will start. Let the butterfly breathe for you... unless you think God's not in a butterfly too.

I could go on and on about these animals. I saw hundreds of them that afternoon. It was Shuhinono's library. She was sharing it with Feice too and whoever else might bump into this space, like I did today. You see, I didn't know who to ask to get answers. The Hopi gave me confidence that Feice and Shuhinono would do their part, but here I am asking what mine is, and I didn't know who to ask to get the answer. So today, I give myself to bear, and I ask butterfly to help me breathe into seeing the answer.

I see that all the answers are there, somewhere. I see that truth must be available to you too. God does not make mistakes. Attempting to perceive the truth about yourself is like looking into a pool of water, and all you see is your face looking back at you, just a reflection. It's hard to focus your eyes beyond the dance of illusion on the surface and get to the truth. So I ask dragonfly to break the illusory surface, that I might see deep into that pool and use vision to know the truth. And he does.

I see in the pool, there is a fire in the below of human consciousness that makes us say and do crazy things. The power of this fire is greater than our understanding, so we struggle to make sense out of the darkness, but we cannot without the Light. That red fire of passion in the below is mostly out of control with deception, fear and anger. Without the cooling blue fire of Spiritual Reason in the above, there is only confusion, separation and searching. You see, the modern world divided creation into heaven and hell, when it never had such a separation before.

For instance, you imagine pleasure and pain as different, though the simple sensations that your skin provides are the same... just sensation. What is different is simply your interpretations of them.

You made a god out of sensation and asked it to guide your lives. This is upside-down looking into the pool, I see. So I ask bear, How do I get my perception rightside up in this pool to help my people?

And bear says, "Ask swan." So I do.

I see that this swan is black on the topside and white underneath. It is a symbol of both Dark and Light together. Swan joins me in that pool as black swan, wings folded and says, "Black is Creative Void, not negative space. Light reflected on this Void is creation. The Void is where you decide what will come into the Light. In this darkness, your thoughts are born into the world. Decide if in darkness, love is still present or not. If you decide love is not present, then only sickness and broken dreams follow. If you decide that in this darkness you are unafraid because love is ever present, then wellness and happy dreams accompany you."

In this pool, I see that my people's fear of dying is so great that they see no love in the darkness. So I ask swan to show me what is in this darkness. Swan opens its black wings and its underside is white, and we walk into the Light together, all of our people, together, under its open wings. And I cry tears of joy that we are delivered from our fears.

Creation is the Whole of it, Light and Dark in harmony. It is our bodily senses that we fear. It is the disharmony of pain and pleasure that confuses us. The Light doesn't even represent pleasure to us as it should because in it are revealed our trials. And when we close our eyes, it is dark, and we imagine fears and feel pain. When it is cold, we imagine freezing to death. When we imagine freezing to death, we project pain and become cold. When it is hot, we imagine burning to death. When we imagine burning to death, we project pain and become hot. Our fears are of death only, of pain only. Our fear is that there is no God in the dark, that there is no love in the dark. And we try to live happy lives, but it is our fears that we are worshiping, not the love that dispels them. The fear of pain is what runs our whole perception of creation, not the love that creation is.

I thank swan, and I thank dragonfly, and I thank bear, and I thank coyote, and I thank butterfly, and I thank all the other creatures who play a role in our awakening... that we are not alone, that Love is here guiding us, everywhere, for all times... that our fear of death, our fear of God, and our fear of godlessness are all unwarranted.

I can go back into camp now, calm, peace restored, trust in front, living in love. I am not disturbed by our vision of death. Our people will live, even if only under the wings of the swan, by some grace uplifting us. I know the Hopi will live too. I know it because they are the ones that are teaching us how to go through this problem, this fear.

Today, I learned Feice had pointed out to Shuhinono several people who were part of this fear problem. She did it easy, little Feice, walking right up and smacking 'em on the knee. When she did that, Shuhinono could see it for herself... the fear in their eyes. Just for contrast, Feice went up to an old man sitting by the fire, working on a moccasin, and she smacked him on the knee. And he scooped her up in his arms and kissed her little face and said, "Good to see you too." And she smiled the widest smile to Shuhinono, to show Shuhinono that she did know who was who and what was what.

And Shuhinono said, "Fine. Keep going. Doing a good job. No problem." And on they went.

We could easily see the next day that there was going to be a big polarization between the people in the tribe... soon. We could almost perceptibly feel it. It was like a great storm cloud building, with the air pressure dropping. It was getting to the point where it would almost make your nose bleed. That's how strong the feelings were in camp. To go from such high joy at reunion, such playfulness, to such intense concern on everyone's face, was one of the fastest and most severe shifts I've ever seen in nearly two-hundred people.

So out comes Six Trees, the ambassador. He starts speaking to everyone, walking through the camp saying, "There's to be a big meeting tomorrow. It's time we all got together and talked these things out. What do you say?" And like a good ambassador, he didn't get into any arguments. He just got agreement that they'd show up.

Now, we're all highly independent people... we think. We all pride ourselves on our individual perceptions. So, for Six Trees to get everybody to come was darn near a miracle in itself. We got some strong folks. That's like you trying to get the leaders of all your different nations together to sit down in one place. And I'm not talking about representatives either. I mean the leaders.

That's kinda' what our tribe was like. Everybody was a leader. And they were, *truly.* We were independent sorts and we were heads of our families. But we were associated in the tribe by agreement, and that agreement allowed the love to bind us. It strengthened our commitment to stay and understand each other, not just to tolerate each other but to truly understand each other... to see each other's gifts and value.

When people separate, it is because someone doesn't see value in the other or appreciate their gifts. You try it. If you're not appreciated at home, you'll leave, I'll tell you that. Pretty simple, yes? That we stick together and see each other's value makes us a tribe, bigger than family, not more important than family, just bigger than family. Because we are willing to work on our own individual perceptions that keep us separate in our minds is what makes us one family, one tribe, one nation. Because we want to be together is why we are together... one mind.

Now, we may have individuals that exercise their will apart from the tribe. But I tell you, it is only a test, a way to learn why we have a collective will. We tolerate those with strong wills who try to go outside the collective will. We tolerate them very well, and we teach them from where they will hear us. We also learn from them. It is our willingness to hear that bridges the gap between their separate will and the collective will. When they see that they lose nothing real by joining is when they give up defiance and aggression. They realize they still have free will to think and speak as they please... within the constraints of the collective will that is simply there to protect others from harm. That we rally to each other's needs and help each other is not blindness. We are aware of who is in need and the reason for the need.

Conscious love is not blind. You see, because we are joined, we know these things. Because, truly, at any moment, we could also slip into that need within ourselves if we thought we lacked something. I say, the only thing you can lack is understanding. I say, the only way to have understanding is to gain experience... direct, for yourself. This is why council members have council positions... because of their experience, not because of age. The more experience you have, the more you *feel* what the people feel. The more you allow yourself to have feelings, to have them deepen and ripen and mature, the more the people around you will allow you to speak for them.

I see today, the only way through fear is to step into it and face it, not avoid it. You can push fear aside and walk ahead and let it follow you all your life, right at your heels. Or you can stop pushing it aside, put it in front and step into it, learn what it is, see that it is a sensation that the body feels when your mind is confused, see that it is the dark pool, undefined for you, the looking glass, the smoking mirror, the blackened bowl. Look into it. Step into it. Learn what it is for yourself and your fears will disappear, just as they strangely appeared.

I think what you're afraid of is that you really *can* know what the truth is. You really *can* know what another person thinks, if you are willing to learn what *you* think... what is thinking you.

196

And certainly, it's a more conscious kind of love that knows what minds are doing. I think you're afraid to know what your own mind is doing.

So give it to bear. Bear can take you to the pool where you can ask dragonfly to break the illusory surface and show you the depth of the pool that is your own creative mind, that is anyone's creative mind. It is there, in that dark pool that swan will show you the Light. If you get scared, ask butterfly to breathe for you, and relax again and look again. You ask coyote to run that rabbit off... if it's there.

So there will be a big meeting. Everyone's to attend. Most meetings, big hunts go on... get extra food, make big meal, have dance, have ceremony. None of that took place. I saw no preparations whatsoever. Tomorrow, we will face our fears, I think.

Chapter 3
The Power of Life

Today is the big meeting day for the tribe, so I'll picture you the whole camp. I'll picture you the meeting place inside camp and the medicine circle inside it, with its four directions, four colors, and I'll tell you their meanings.

All the lodges are placed in quarter moon arcs around an open circle. All our doors faced east. The old ones are camped to the north, outside the large circle of lodges. People were camped in the south and in the west and in the east and in the north... big arcs forming a big circle, with a smaller open circle in the center. In the middle of the smaller circle is a medicine wheel with a great fire pit in its center. Why such a system of circles, you ask? Because within a circle, there's no beginning and no end, and everything's all connected by the four directions, is why.

You fly in an airplane high above the earth you live on now, and the land is all divided up into little squares. Each square calls out, "Mine! Mine! Mine!" And you link all those squares together with little ribbons to get to each other without steppin' in the mud. You have fences and gates and walls, so you don't step on each other's square. But I tell you, squares separate. Circles connect.

I'll show you why. Draw a square. Now put a circle inside. You see, the corners left over are where the dust collects. In your psychic life, the past, old experiences and decisions get stuck in those corners. When you become whole, your energy is more like a circle than a square... no more dusty corners. And the mud below is a friend that grows life again.

I don't know about you, but when I was a kid, the greatest feeling there was, was a spring rain, your feet in the mud, squishin' around, squeeching between your toes. You see, before your soaps, there was dirt.

Nowadays, you get grease on you, and if you use soap, you got to use water to get them both off, yes? When we got grease on us, we used dirt to get it off. Worked better. Didn't even need to waste water. Dirt's clean stuff compared to grease. What you give up by using soap is your connection with the dirt, the earth. You're always trying to wash dirt off with soap because you're *dir-ty,* you think.

Body oils are what causes stink. Dirt gets grease off. Fact. The scientific among you will say it's the bacteria on your body that makes you stink. I say, it's those bacteria that live off those body oils that are removed by the dirt. Dirt does not contain human body bacteria or oils. Therefore, dirt's cleaner than body oils. Soap is made from alkali and grease, so it cannot be a cleaner environment than dirt. Earth wins.

The only thing we didn't put dirt in was our hair. Too hard to get it out. For that, we used soap roots, yuccas, aloes, even fermented grains. You use slaked wood ashes mixed with fat to make soaps. But the vegetable soap root, the root the deer eat the tops off every spring 'cause the shoots are so tender, that hairy old root, we used to wash our hair.

Now, for big occasions, everybody would get washed and come to this circle with clean hair. Never mind the dirt on your body, but your head and mind had to be washed clean. It was a sign you were ready to hear everything with an open mind. I don't know why, but no one showed up to that big circle that day, washed, except Shuhinono and me and Feice and the council. The general population was in a state of depression, worse than anything I'd ever experienced in my personal life, even with Mohinono when we had to give him up to Creator.

So, they all straggled in. Normally, we all stood. This time, around this great circle with the fire in the middle, everyone sat. And they all sat in the southwest and west. This is not normal, I say to myself. Everyone has their position in this tribe, and that is why they are in the south or the east or the north or the west. They recognize their station or position and the reason for it. But this day, the entire tribe was sitting in the southwest and west.

Shuhinono and I were standing in our station, just inside the outer circle in the northeast, facing the great fire. The council members were standing in their places in the north, but the tribe members were sitting. This is different... sitting for a ceremony. Must be this is not a ceremony, I think, so I am intrigued further. It's unusual behavior to have the entire tribe act as a group and decide this is not ceremony and all align themselves to face northeast and east.

Feice was exceptionally quiet. I think she was expectant like we were and wondering how this was going to turn out or even start, for that matter. Since it wasn't ceremony and the great fire wasn't lit, there was no formal speaker. But it was Feice that finally broke the silence. She said, "I love you" and sat down. Shuhinono was wordless and sat down. The seven tribal council members were silent and sat down. It was only me standing. I guess I was too stupid to sit down, so I stayed standing, and I asked butterfly to help me, as I was not breathing well. I was not afraid. I was just... cold. I did not feel warmed by my big tribal family's presence. I felt cold. So I spoke to that.

I said, Your fears are making me cold, and I don't think the big cold that's coming is going to come in this springtime. You are freezing me to death with your fears, and it is spring, not fall.

A young woman spoke. I did not know her name. We have been gone too long. She said, "This prophecy has stolen our spring. We don't know how to live our last days." And she sat down.

Six Trees stood up and looked me in the eyes. I nodded to him and sat down. He said, "We have let the unknown frighten us before, but it has not divided us. I would hear now from you who feel strongly one way, then we will hear the other way after that." And he sat down.

A young man jumped to his feet, strained to control his voice and said, "Whoever's prophecy this was, is no friend of this tribe. Whoever knowingly goes down the path to death is a fool, and I will not follow him or her. I think you all are too old to do us any good anymore. You lie down with your long years. We need someone else with visions of life to lead us." And he sat down.

It took a lot of guts to stand up there like that to those old folks. I was proud of that young man. He was fourteen. That young woman was twenty. And these seven council members might as well have been seven-hundred-years old and dead many times, to those two. The seven council members stayed sitting.

Shuhinono got up. She said, "You are right, of course. Life goes on regardless of who stumbles and falls and perishes. I agree that this vision was given too much importance. One should never ponder their own death anyway, except to accept it as inevitable someday. And that should make us love each other even more. That should make us bond in this larger family we call tribe, even more. Will you not all again agree, or will you carry this problem to a final split? Will you not accept the wisdom gained from the experience of these old ones at your service, but now include your new view, your new courage, your new strength?" And she sat down.

It seems a compromise is struck. If the old ones stop being so gloomy, they can keep their places. Simple, huh? But I tell you, in our tribe, not so simple. You see, everyone knew a pretender. If you could fake it, you *couldn't* make it. Now, that's self-explanatory, isn't it?

You see, in your society, you give your actors accolades and great wealth for pretending. And the better and more convincing they are at their role, the greater you recognize them. But I tell you, some of your fine actors get stuck and can't get out of their roles 'cause they shift out of themselves and have a hard time shifting back to live their own lives again. Shifting is serious business. So, for an old one in our tribe, to shift out of themselves in order to keep a council position by trying to fake their feelings is a death sentence.

So, okay fine. We've got seven council members, about half of which are gloomy. And I know this day, those seven members got a big job ahead of themselves... getting a new vision to guide them about the big cold that is coming. I can see, like me they are wondering... How do we know a prophetic vision is true unless it happens? And yet, we also are aware of the power of the collective mind to make things happen to prove prophecies.

In your culture, you too have prophecies of doom and gloom... apocalypses. We "wrote" our prophecies down too, before the written word... with pictures in our minds, with stories.

The Hopi, too, have a prophecy that evolved over thousands of years. They shared a mind with the Mayans and got to see into the future. They got to see through the illusion of time. They got to see the seven different worlds come and go, up to the eighth.

These worlds speeded up are what I'm trying to show you with the symbols of the seven chakras. This succession of worlds, life going round and round, again and again, is what is symbolized by the Tibetan wheel of life. The Hopi and Tibetans saw that they could get off this human cycle, this ever-moving wheel of life. They saw they could step off to take a good look to see what was ahead and what was past. This seeing shaped their choices.

When your English time was born with Jesus, your ancestors, too, made choices which shaped your views of the world and its meaning for you. But even before Jesus, you had prophecies of doom... the apocalypse. Your prophecies even had the same color horses as Black Elk's vision did for the Sioux... long before the Spaniards and Englishmen brought them horses here.

And before them four horses were the four colors, a red, a black, a yellow, and a white color. They represent the four, unified races of humans and the four directions to which they went. So the four races are not different, except in your perception of them. The four directions are not different, except in your perception of them.

All colors came from the One Light. This One Light split from Wholeness into the many colors. Light is energy. And all your energy centers are affected by different colors of light. Just as the One Light split into different colors, the Whole of Creation just expanded from a point of Oneness. In that Oneness was Light containing all the colors and all the possibilities of movement. Your time now is the time for the coming back together of all the races from the four directions, back from the different colors, into the One Light again.

The circle connecting these four colors and four races and four directions represents the unity of all life. Within this circle, there are three more directions... above, below and within. Each of these seven directions represents an aspect of a person's specific psyche and their relationship with the planet and Spirit. Imagine the core of your being as the within and your life as a bubble within larger bubbles. Your orientation within the largest bubble is your relationship with all life. The above is your relationship with non-physical Spirit. The below is your relationship with the lower aspects of physical life and your connection with the body of the Mother... the earth.

There is plenty help in this sacred circle, this medicine wheel. It represents the first church ever, and that is *you*. Draw a circle in the ground anywhere, declare it sacred, and that is your church. You can pray from inside there and receive guidance if you ask, since you are never outside of love, except in your imagination. The circle you draw around you is to remove the effects of the world of ego from your inside bubble. If you order your ego to stay outside, this sacred circle is a safe zone where only you and Spirit reside.

Everyone seems to use color the way they see it, but this is one way the colors in the medicine circle can be used in your day and age, in your time.

The east is yellow for the rising sun, a place symbolizing your physical birth, then your spiritual rebirth and enlightenment. It is always a place of renewal. South is red, a time for the growth of the blood, the body. It is where in adolescence, a child can lose innocence by becoming aware of the psychic influences of the body... the beginnings of ego. The west is black for the disappearing sun, a place of the void and the relinquishment of ego. This time is the beginning of spiritual awareness and the place of transformation during the ego's death. The north is white for the return to purity, a place where the innocence of childhood is turned into wisdom. This is a place ego would pretend to have achieved but truly cannot accomplish. That is why the world is such a mess... everyone climbing a tall tree and pretending to see far.

Every human takes two cycles on this wheel of life to become real. The first turn is the turn of learning the body life, the red road. Taking a body is taking the lessons body life teaches. This is compulsory. The second turn is learning the spiritual life, the blue road. This also is compulsory. Free will does not mean the will not to learn. The will that wishes to change the truth is not free. It is the source of fear itself.

The second turn on the wheel of life involves the total giving up of erroneous human thinking and trying to lead oneself in the world. It is the result of a true request by an individual, asking to be reborn in the world as a spiritual human being, to become *real,* as the old ones say. It is this true request that brings rebirth and the second turn.

Initially, you are born in the east, and as an innocent baby you travel toward puberty in the south. At some time, innocence is lost and the ego begins to run the mind. Death is, then, in the west. Most people spend their entire physical life traveling from the south to the west, toward their mind's image of their physical death. Through prayer and true desire, one faces the fear of physical death in the west with Spirit, then travels toward the north, alive, released from fear. In the north, the wisdom of the Ancients is available to help us recover our lost innocence. From the north, we again see the south, and with innocent eyes we become wiser. With this wisdom, we travel back to the east for our spiritual rebirth in Creator's Light, where we first came from. This rebirth transforms us from the red road of physical life to the blue road of spiritual life, while remaining in the body. It is then that the wheel of life is seen in its entirety, including the above, the below, and the within. It is, then, the seven directions are traveled with conscious Spiritual guidance, and we can become truly helpful to others. We are free. We are all the same.

The only reason any of us ever see ourselves as different from anyone else is that we would rather our God-given uniqueness not be sameness. I'll say it again. **We are all uniquely the same.** You may "appear" different, but your God-given essence is the same. If we persist in being different, we will persist in not knowing our True Selves or our true purpose. The ego was born out of this desire for differentness, rather than sameness. This is how the devil got imagined, I think. But how could anything *real* of creation be different from the Creator?

So what color is your devil? Some places are afraid of black, so they use blue. Some people think the devil is blue, so they use black 'cause they don't like the blue devils. Now, if you're a black man, you may think white's the devil. If you're a red man, you may think... could be black or white, maybe yellow. If you're a yellow man, probably the red man... or maybe it's white or black... or maybe it's brown. Anything brown is suspicious. Devil's always somebody else, you see.

Now, not feeling what you're feeling... that's bedevilment. That'll get you into terrible trouble... blocking feelings or deciding what you're feeling you don't want to feel or that those feelings aren't true, then trying to change them on your own without Spirit... makes you crazy inside.

So returning to our problem, I see four council members feel positive and three council members feel negative about our future. I think we're doing pretty good. At least it isn't four against. And I look at these three gloomy members and I see that it isn't the vision they're in agreement about. It's not *the vision.* It is their *interpretation* of the vision they agree on. You see, if it was *the vision,* you couldn't get attached to it. There it goes, big as life, all by itself. Didn't have anything to do with your thinking or anyone else's. The fact that those three became passionate made it their *own* vision, their *own* belief, their *own* perception of truth.

So I ask bear, What's the remedy here? I see the sickness. How can you take the personal vision away from those three members, so they will see they are driving their own perceptions? And I think this must be a hard question because bear doesn't answer right away.

I wait three days. After those three days, I asked Feice what she thought about that big meeting. She said, "Silly."

I asked, Why you think so?

She said, "Means nothing."

I said, How come you feel that way? There's two-hundred people that show up for a good meeting and find a solution.

She says, "No solution."

I said, What do you mean?

She said, "Silly."

I couldn't get it out of her. She was perfectly clear within herself about what she meant... "silly." But I couldn't see it. So I asked Shuhinono, Do you know what she's saying? Shuhinono smiles, kinda' one of those–Ohhh, I got to explain it to you–nice like, but a little bit pestered kind of smiles.

So I said, Well, excuse me. I was just trying to figure this out.
She says, "Haven't you learned your daughter yet?"
And I say, What do you mean?
"Don't you know what she's trying to tell you?"
I says, No, of course not. Otherwise, I wouldn't be asking.
She said, "Look at yourself. What did you get out of that meeting?"

I said, I got a deeper look into those seven members. I got a deeper look into the problem, and I asked bear what the solution was.

She says, "Oh good. Glad to hear it. Until you get your answer, you're the problem as well."
I said, What do you mean?–I'm the problem.
She said, "It's a male thing... not knowing. It's a female thing... knowing. But our knowing comes with an ounce of doubt, so what we need from men is confirmation of what we hear from Spirit.

I said, Well, I expect I'm living proof of not knowin', but how does that make me the problem?

"Oh," she says, "don't take it so personally. As I see it, you can either study the problem or hear the solution. Yet, neither one contains the other. While you're studying the problem, Feice is *being* the answer. The failure comes not in asking the question but in failing to receive and *be* the answer."

I said, So male is slow. That's the problem, yes?
"This is the difference between men and women that I see," she said. "You men carry your energy out in front of you to deal with the responsibilities of the physical world. Though we have physical duties, we woman are more concerned with the Spiritual and psychic world. We are aware that the physical world *follows* the psychic world, that everything physical is a direct effect of the world of mind, the cause.

Since women's energy levels cycle high and low monthly, we generally carry our energy lower. Because you men push your energy high up and out in front, you blind yourselves for a time, whereas we women usually do not, at least at moontime. That is why I think women get their messages from Spirit sooner and tend not to interpret, change or use them, like men often do. Because men do this, they tend to seek power in the physical world more readily than women. That is why I still feel this problem over the vision has to do with the men on the council, as well as the women.

Perhaps what got some male members into trouble was entertaining the possibility that the vision could be *used* in some way. That's a male kind of thing, to try to use this vision on the physical level, like wanting to become chief or splitting the tribe. It's a female kind of thing to try to use this vision on the psychic level, like wanting to manipulate relationships or unduly influence decisions. So what's wrong with this whole picture is that it was born out of fear and needs to be turned into love again."

I said, I agree with you there, but what is Feice trying to tell us?–'silly.'

"Let's see if I can explain it to you. Feice's female, yes?"

Well, that's obvious, I said. Warrior like, but still female.

"I think she said silly because the proposal was taken at face value by nearly all of the members of the tribe as being accomplished... that the old people would just change their minds and that's that. It's resolved."

Oh, I see what you're saying now. You're saying that there was no solution given, so the whole meeting was silly.

She said, "Well, I proposed a way to reach a solution, but the proposal itself wasn't the solution. But it was accepted by the tribe as if all was resolved."

Now, there's the illusion. There's the reflection on the pool, I think to myself. So I ask dragonfly to punch that water one more time for me, right then and there. I turn my eyes to the ground, and I can see that pool of water again. And there's that dragonfly, slappin' the water for me, and in I go. And you know who's in there waitin' for me? Feice!

Feice looks up at me and smiles and says, "See? They all silly."

I said, Yes, daughter, I see.

She says, "So... I love you." And that was her solution. I could see her lookin' out at all those faces, two-hundred of 'em, telling 'em, "I love you." She gave the solution before the questions were even asked. And you know what? That's what everyone had taken home with them... what Feice said. They went back to love again. They were willing to expect and accept that the old ones' guidance would be love again, not fear. And they went home satisfied... 'cause Feice loved them.

Most tribal thinking is very simple, just like Feice's was when she was very young. Am I loved or am I not? Am I comfortable or am I not? This vision made them damn uncomfortable and they didn't feel loved.

So I asked bear, Who spoke this vision to the people in such a way as to cause this great anxiety? And in that pool, I saw that old woman, Flowering Tree, with Feice's finger stuck in her back.

So I asked bear to tell me what the cause of this illness was, this fear. And in front of us in that pool, we saw that The Flowering Tree never made fruit. It stayed just flowers and never got fertilized and joined creation. It was standing alone too long.

Now, this union was important because we're all connected. Everything is interconnected. And if one thing stands alone too long, I'll tell you, it will wither and die. So it was clear to me then, that this old one who had influenced a few minds must change her name to Fruiting Branch.

Funny how in those deep pool spaces a thing can be decided and it's done. To see a thing clearly is to see its cause, to see its form of presentation, and to *feel* its solution. Dear brothers, it is the *feelings* you have for each other that is the problem... and the solution.

For a thing to come to pass in actuality, it only needs the seed of thought and the willingness of action. In this woman, Flowering Tree, was a strong image. In her mind, that tree never stopped flowering. This was why we were so careful to take certain names at certain stages in our lives that would help us onward. And in this woman's case, she was in the fall of her life, and she could not let go of the image of The Flowering Tree. To think that the tribe would experience its death, to her was not The Flowering Tree.

So, was it the fearful musings of these three people on the council thinking about death that was the problem? Weren't all three disturbing us with the energy of doom and gloom? Or was the problem more that the Flowering Tree could not bear fruit with this vision? She was supposed to be a life-giver, full of positive thoughts.

Well, I tell you, it's not doom and gloom that's the problem. It's the failure to *recycle* the energy of doom and gloom appropriately that is the problem. Always death was present and always we responded appropriately to it with prayers for guidance until now, perhaps because the possibility of death came in such massive proportions. Flowering Tree would not enter that deep pool with me and see the swan carrying the people into the Light. She could not bear fruit with this vision, so she became a large part of the problem.

That night, after Shuhinono and I spoke about all this together, Shuhinono decided she would go see Flowering Tree the next morning. But I'll tell you what happened instead. Feice had that old woman by the hand, first thing in the morning, before we were even awake and had brought her to our lodge.

Startled, Shuhinono and I both sat up. And I was even more surprised that Feice could catch Shuhinono by surprise. That little one is something. We welcomed them both in and asked Flowering Tree how come she was up so early, and how had Feice found her anyway? And where had Feice gotten off to without tellin' us, in the first place?

Flowering Tree sat down, smiled and said, "I haven't slept all night. I've been wandering around. Sometime in the middle of the night, Feice found me, so we became buddies. Your little one's been up half the night with me."

We were both stunned, silent. Couldn't believe our ears. And there's Feice smiling all the way.

"Sure," she said. "We had good time."

I asked, How can you see anything at night, walking around? Then I remembered it was darn near a full moon.

Feice says, "I see fine."

Flowering Tree smiled and petted Feice's head with genuine affection. Now remember, this is the one that got poked in the back and vowed to fight Feice to her last breath.

I said, I see you two have come to some understanding.

And Feice says, "I'm hungry."

And Flowering Tree says, "I'm hungry too."

So Shuhinono's scrambling around now to feed these two. And I ask her, What do you suppose went on last night between those two?

Shuhinono says quietly, "Love... back to love again."

I asked Shuhinono, Didn't Flowering Tree have a husband and children?

Shuhinono sighed and said, "A husband once, killed early. No children."

I said, Ohh–not really understanding what I'm pretending I am.

Shuhinono said, "She's a woman without a mate, a barren woman."

I said, Ohhh–pretending to understand more than I did... again.

And Shuhinono shakes her head saying, "I know you don't understand these things, what they mean."

And I said, Well, I think I do.

And she said, "When you *feel* as she feels, you will understand."

So I reached that day to try to understand, and it was Feice that gave it to me. The woman herself would not join me. It was through Feice I could join Flowering Tree, however. I asked to see with Feice's eyes, and the bear said, "Yes."

I saw that Feice poked Flowering Tree in the back because she had fallen into a great hole. The difference between her life and her name was so great that it caused this woman to die to herself when that vision came. It took Feice's poke to wake her up to what she was doing. She was dying, and with her went The Tree that Flowered. She didn't think she could live up to her name and keep hope alive for the people in the face of this disaster. She was reliving her husband's death and her own barrenness, and the tree was not bearing fruit.

I saw that Feice fixed it easy. Feice said, "You be my mommy too?" And there was a flood of gratitude and tears that poured through me, as I saw that woman through Feice's eyes. And I thought I would nearly fall over from the release, the exquisiteness of it.

We do these things for each other, you know, without even knowing what it is we do. Feice, because she's so clear, is able to do these things for people, for this woman, quickly, simply, efficiently... give her back life again.

That morning, around a warming fire and a little something to eat, we joined Feice in her love for Flowering Tree. Shuhinono was especially sensitive. She thanked her for taking care of Feice and for being a good mother to her. She said she could see Feice loved her very much. We offered Flowering Tree our home, any time she wished to come. We asked her if she would be our family from this day on. We called her, sister, and we meant it. And I'll tell you, the gloom and doom vanished.

Now, the council members who still couldn't get out of that vision of doom didn't hardly matter anymore because this woman carried The Flowering Tree, not them. They're just grumbly old folks, pissin' and moanin'. But she had the medicine of The Flowering Tree. With her change, perhaps they will follow.

So you see, Feice found the solution and called the whole meeting silly. Now I know what she meant. And she's only a little over three! I can see why the old people worry about her... being powerful like that. But I see good things. I don't know what they're lookin' at, but I see good things. Funny, perception only exists in the minds of the fearful. With fear comes separate perceptions. Without fear, there's only minds joined in love, trusting, living their trust in front, instead of pushing their energy in front. The fearful, however, trust no one and nothing and push everything.

I tell you, this is the only disease there is... fear. There is none other. And all the bear's medicines are there to counteract human fear. You ever seen a bear afraid? You ever seen an eagle afraid? Now, you see rabbits and mice scurry around, scared lookin'. Well, I would be too if I was everybody's dinner. Truth is, you aren't dinner for anybody, so what are you afraid of? The dark pool, maybe? Well, you enter the dark pool every night when the sun goes down and you close your eyes and go to sleep. You keep wakin' up, so what are you afraid of? Afraid you won't wake up? Afraid you'll be caught in one of your own dreams? Well, depends on what you dream... whether it scares you or not to get caught in it. The end of fearful dreams comes with the recognition of what illusion is. With that comes a return to love.

There are none who do not long for love. But I see longing for love is not being love, is it? Thinking you are without and wanting to get it is not having it, is it? Feice just gives it. So I see she has it. I also see, she's not looking for it anywhere. I also see because of her certainty, she's as light as the butterfly and is not confused about the how, when, what, why, and where of it. I think she's a good teacher, and I thank her for her many lessons to me this day.

We didn't see Feice the rest of the day. Her new, second mom had her. Lord knows what little journeys Feice took her on that day, but they seemed to be having a good time. The Flowering Tree that had never born fruit, through an act of love that day by a little child for a lonely woman, was delivered from gloom to life again. The fact that nobody thought this out in advance as a solution is what you call a miracle.

So you want to know what a miracle is? A selfless act of love, anywhere, for any reason. Because we are such selfish creatures, it's a miracle anyone ever does that for anyone else.

It is yet to be seen if the solution will spread throughout the tribe, but I think it will. And, sure enough, as the days go by, the tribe members do accept it, but the council still has not reconvened.

Many weeks go by before that council of seven got back together. It was relatively calm in the camp. There were no highs or lows. It was just life as usual. I wanted to ask Feice why they took so long to reconvene, but she seems totally unconcerned and is enjoying her new playmate and mother. They don't tire of each other. It's the darndest thing I ever saw. We're talkin' about a woman who was very nearly fifty, Flowering Tree, acting like a little child again with Feice. They were having great fun. New life went with them, all around.

The seven didn't sit for many weeks. Why? Feice showed me why, so I'll tell you why. Flowering Tree's name is no joke. The Flowering Tree image to our people has power. Within this woman was carried the power of The Flowering Tree, and everyone was waiting for her to fruit on her branches. So, it took as long as it took, and that's that. When Flowering Tree was ready, the seven would reconvene.

Power is a funny thing. In your society, you tend to think somebody has to wrestle it away from somebody else, and whoever's got it has got it, and they wield it whatever way they want. But I tell you, true power is the power of creativity, of rebirth, of renewal, of regeneration. It's the power to live again. That's love.

So without love, the power of life, the only act left is one of defying death or the pitiful act of using death as a threat against life. Well, I tell you, the "death-callers" make a terrible mistake, not just for the others around them but for themselves. They must be in such terrible pain within their own minds... in conflict about love, power, the value of life, and the absolute permanence of it. You see, regardless of what you perceive through your eyes, the spirit of life goes magnificently on. Please do not mistake form for essence.

One simple, courageous act of selfless love... now, that's powerful. Sick people hold Creator hostage in their mind, threaten creation with death, as proof that God is not real or loving. And yet, those people hold only themselves hostage, for love cannot be grasped in anger. Love's still there, regardless of what war went on... waiting for us to come back to sanity and drop our pain and suffering as something personal. You see, it is only the thought of pain and suffering that makes us follow it in the first place. All we need is to put it down and walk away and forgive it the thoughts it thought, the deeds it did. Love's good like that. Damn glad of it too.

I think almost seven weeks have passed, and it's time for the council members to reconvene. That will be interesting, I think to myself.

Chapter 4
Back to Wholeness

It is appropriate, I think, that it is the end of spring, that Flowering Tree go back to the council and ask for a resolution. You see, the end of spring means the flowers that are blooming must now be pollinated and bear fruit.

Flowering Tree asked Shuhinono and me and Feice to join her in that council meeting. I can't remember any circumstance in which a council meeting called for the purpose of regaining harmony would be attended by anyone other than the council members themselves. Usually it was a private affair between council members only. But in this particular case, I think because of Feice, we were all invited. And I was pleased, as I still had not yet figured out what the men's part could be in the conflict. That isn't to say I couldn't imagine it, but it is to say I didn't truly know what it was.

It was late afternoon when the lodge was ready to include extra guests. This lodge was prepared a bit different, not like a Medicine Lodge or a Sweat Lodge. The Medicine Lodge was always very sparse in decoration, very plain, with a central pit dug to hold hot rocks. This freshly prepared ceremonial lodge was not like a normal live-in lodge, either, that always had a fire pit in the middle, vents at the bottom of the lodge to let cooler air in, and a hole in the top center to allow smoke and sparks out. This lodge was larger, had no central fire, and the roof was taller than a live-in lodge... plenty of room to sit up straight. You could even stretch your legs out, if you cared to.

I tried to make sense out of the seating arrangements. But, truly, I think in this moment of coming back together, there was no rhyme or reason to it. The chief sat in the west as usual, looking out the eastern gate, the doorway, and the rest of the council members sat in random places on the sides. We were the last to enter, so we sat near the doorway on the southeastern side. Everyone was cordial. There were no apparent feelings of disharmony. In fact, everyone seemed quite jovial. So I began to relax a bit. I thought maybe there would be some sort of confrontation here, even though I knew that Flowering Tree herself was full of love again. I thought maybe there would be a male who was still annoyed or irritated or not able to hide his true feelings. But within the space of that lodge, we all felt like family.

Feice made the rounds before anyone got serious. She walked around the lodge floor, looking in the face of everyone there. Some people would make little comments and try to touch her or pinch her or tease her. But Feice was totally unconcerned with their thoughts or actions. She seemed to have something else in mind, thoroughly occupied within herself about her duties. So around she goes, and she comes back to that doorway in the east from the north and looks out that door. She just squats there and looks out that door. The conversation finally stops, and when it does she turns and sits right in the doorway, which is very unusual. Shuhinono tries to move her over away from the door, but she sits right in the doorway and won't get up.

The chief says, "Oh, that's okay. Leave her there for now."

So here we go, I say to myself. We're off again. Feice sits there all content lookin', kind of puttin' her finger in the dirt, drawin' around. And everyone else is watching her. She has what you would call in your society, "charisma"... psychic control of the situation. To us, it was just curious... the power this child held over everyone.

During that time in our society, it was not necessary for anyone to say, "Shall we begin?" Everyone knew who had to begin. It was already confirmed that Flowering Tree was to have the floor and was to begin this ceremony. So Flowering Tree began a song in which she prayed to the four directions, then to the above and the below and the within. She thanked all the creatures that lived everywhere and all the spirit helpers that had guided her along her way. She blessed all the people in the lodge, then she stopped at Feice. Her speech was very simple and very clear. She said, "This child whom I so desperately feared would be the demise of our people has turned out to be a powerful reminder that the salvation of our people is our ability to love. Where we have had unresolved conflicts among us is where we have failed to learn what this child comes to teach. I now have the power of my name restored to me through the love of Feice, but I can no longer do anything to make it come true while there is still conflict in this council. There is one among us who has not spoken their mind. I will not point this one out, as it would only engender more fear and anger and resentment. And though I have accepted the solution for myself, I certainly cannot accept a solution for anyone else."

She took that stick she was holding, which we call the Talking Stick, and stuck it next to the fire pit, farther to the north of where she was sitting. She was sitting in the northwest. No one seemed to want to pick that stick up and continue the conversation. I think it was hard for the person who was being called out to truly face their own part in this mess. But as always, Spirit has a solution to an impasse.

Feice got up, walked around, grabbed the stick and took it to Yak-Yak, and stuck it in the ground in front of him. You know, I expected to see fire in that man's eyes, being called out so directly like that. But he looked at that child, and he looked at the sweetness and goodness in her, and he started to cry. And he cried and he cried and he cried. There was something about Feice that just wouldn't let the walls stay up.

After some time, cedar was thrown on a hot rock that had been brought in for smudging, water was passed around, and Yak-Yak picked up the stick and said, "I'm not sure where all this went wrong inside me. I do not hold my family members responsible for anything that I thought. It was my choice to have thought the thoughts I thought. I wanted to split our tribe in half, as I judged many of you as being too old to deal with this vision. It was my thought that the simple solution was to find a new homeland, go south, go east, even go west. I fought this vision of the big cold, although I myself saw it. Like the young man in our tribe, I could not accept that death was inevitable. I blamed Flowering Tree for not having the power to show us the way to life again, and I did not like the power that was coming to this camp from the Hopi. When it arrived in the form of Feice, I was sure that that power was going to destroy us. I feared the influence of those Hopi on our family here, Hinono, Shuhinono and Feice. I still do not understand what these travelers have learned and I don't trust it. I truly don't know how to interpret the vision, but I had many plans for avoiding it. I see now, through this child Feice and through Flow-

214

ering Tree, that one cannot avoid the next moment. One simply has a choice to live it or to die before it comes. I thought I was choosing life, but I see now that by running from death I was dead already. Watching Feice and Flowering Tree grow in their companionship reminded me of what we hold most dear, and that is our children... anyone's children. It is for them that we try to grow in our understanding. It is for them that we save our stories, so that they may grow beyond our understanding. And I see it is the love that evolves us. It is the trials and hardships that change us, but it is the love that evolves us. The fact that we accept these changes and go back to love again is evolution. So, although I don't trust the Hopi, I do trust the love that is helping us evolve. I thank Hinono and Shuhinono and Feice for their gentleness with me. I think I am changing quickly because there is nobody to argue with. No one is forcing this change on me. We all asked for vision, for guidance, and we got it. I just didn't know what to do with it. I needed to *do* something because I was afraid for us all, but I see now that a fearful leader cannot lead anything. I was angry because I was helpless to change the vision, so I projected the failure onto Flowering Tree. Forgive me for that, Flowering Tree, for you have always served this tribe well. You have given your name life, and your name has given this tribe life. And I see now, what you lost was returned to you by Feice. And I see my error. So I thank you all." And he stuck the stick in the ground to his left.

Well, I'm thinkin' to myself... another miracle, no doubt about it. It's true, we are not a warring people, so communication among us is much easier. We don't have so many angry ones. We don't have so many interested in grabbing power... being important. It is this communication that is our lifeblood. We are able to speak to our feelings because we are present to them. We have not split our minds off in an attempt to prove that we are not thinking what we are thinking or doing what we are doing.

This man Yak-Yak was humble before this child in this council. With that talking stick in front of him, he became humble. He knew that his words had the power to build or to destroy. And he was able to overcome all his fear and anger at being called out by a three-and-a-half-year-old child, in front of ten adults, including himself.

There were no eyes in that group of people that did not look upon this man with understanding and with respect. The respect was due him because he spoke the truth. He could have tried to hide his feelings, but he did not. He could have said nothing, kept his feelings to himself and refused to speak, and nothing would have changed... except Flowering Tree was flowering. He, then, would have been alone in his sickness, his fear. But because we loved each other, the environment we made was safe. Because it was not possible to be a self-elected chief or a self-elected medicine person, we could all relax into the positions that Creator designed for each of us, and no one was pretending their medicines. No one was pretending their roles. All positions were seen as having equal value because all knew that each part was vital to the interdependent whole. Even shamen healers were not envied. Everyone knew that medicine people were given their knowledge and their medicines by Spirit, were trained by Spirit, so they were supported by the people around them who knew that was their purpose, that was their role to play.

I think it is hard for you in your society to find your true purpose because you have no old stories to guide you into what is important, into the way to talk to Spirit, into what is your true role.

So you have schools with many choices and you study hard. You get out of that school and you go into a job, and you have no power in that job, perhaps because it is not your true role. So your life is filled with uncertainty and confusion.

Now, you say, "Oh well, my bosses know the path to go and I follow my bosses." But I tell you, your bosses got to their positions, most of them, not all, but most, by the very same confusions that you did. They have just settled for position or money, instead of their true role and the truth. So there is no peace felt by them, and whatever they produce offers no true enjoyment either. Only Spirit remembers for you the agreements you made with Creator before you came here. Only Spirit can reveal to you your true role. Only your fulfillment of your true role will bring peace and joy.

In our big family, the boss was love. Love was something the Creator bestowed on us before we had consciousness. Love is something the Father and the Mother have together, for there to be harmony on the earth. So it was our love of Spirit and our love of place that allowed us to live a peaceful and harmonious life. And in that love and in that place, we trusted. And in that trust, we had joy.

The fear of the big cold coming to this place is what destroyed our joy and our peace. To us, this coming cold meant that the Mother and the Father were not in harmony with each other. For there to be such a deep cold in winter, there had to be a reason for this to happen. So we looked to ourselves and to Spirit for the answer.

We saw that Mother Earth is like Her children, that there is a spring and a fall and a winter and a summer, that these are the ranges of human emotions... Her seasons. Fall is the dropping of seeds, the planting, and therefore the beginning of new life. All human emotions that have to do with hope are stored here. Winter is the relinquishment, the deep rest, and therefore the building of energies to support hope. All human emotions that have to do with possibilities are stored here. Spring is the action of stored energy. All human emotions that have to do with growth and fulfillment are stored here. Summer is the full basket. All human emotions that have to do with acceptance are stored here. For the Mother to give us a winter without hope and support was the worst fear we could imagine.

So now we have an apparent emotion that comes outside the range of hope, possibilities, action, fulfillment, and acceptance. And it stresses us to have the maximum feeling for this place, for our people and for God, both male and female, both Father and Mother, both Spirit and body. And it stresses us to grow.

This growing from a physical human being to a spiritual human being is no small matter. It requires you experience everything before its time. It is a speedup of the curriculum of being alive in the body, so that you may have no fear of death before you die. But now you say, it's not possible to live this before you actually experience it. **In vision, with Spirit's help, you can experience everything before it happens.** You can have answers to your questions before you even know what the questions are. You can be led, guided, protected, and nourished.

So in this lodge, we are in a reverie with each other, where no words are spoken. But there are minds communicating with each other, continually lifting each other up, encouraging each other, loving each other. And I'll tell you, I got so high myself that I thought the whole top of my head was going to come off again, like it did on top of Great Mountain... my first big experience with Spirit. So, Feice, sitting there all glassy-eyed, looked around at everybody, and she had the biggest grin on her face I'd ever seen. Hard to imagine a child so conscious, so young.

The chief put sweet grass on the rock, just on the edges so it wouldn't burn. It just smoked. And a sweet smell filled the whole lodge, and everyone's eyes came back to looking at what was in front of them again, instead of what was inside of them.

That stick was passed to the elected chief, this chief elected by the elder women in our tribe. And he spoke to us, "I have never seen a circle that was completed that could ever be broken. We have completed our circles many times together, so I have faith that this circle will be unbroken forever. To put to rest any fears that we may have, I ask Shuhinono and Hinono and Feice to tell us

217

more about those Hopi and their medicines."

The stick was passed to me and I passed it to Shuhinono. I fully expected Shuhinono to pass it to Feice, but Shuhinono started. And I'm happy she did because, truly, I haven't heard her say much about what went on with the women in those pit houses.

Shuhinono quietly put the Talking Stick in her lap and closed her eyes. I could see that she was praying for guidance. After a few moments, she began to speak. "It is hard to know where to start. We were taught so many things in those pit houses, in those underground ceremonial houses. I will try to summarize what I learned. I'll start by saying that it seems as creatures on the earth, we are a bit strange. Our minds are divided up into many small pieces. Because of this fragmentation, we cannot remember where we came from or what we really are. What the Hopi attempted to do was to bring all these fragmented aspects of our collective being together, so that we could get a larger picture, a whole picture of what we are, what our responsibilities are, and why we are here on this earth. They used the corn and the pollen as a symbol to teach that each of us are both male and female inside, even though in our physical forms we appear as only one or the other. The plant kingdom knows nothing of this division into male and female in appearance. Even the animal kingdom seems to have an intact mind, in the sense that they are not confused, male or female, about what their purpose is. It is only humans who do not remember what they are and what their True Self is.

"In those kivas of the Hopi, we went into the below to dive deep and to gather as much information as possible about our different selves. I saw that within the psyche of woman, the feminine mind itself could be split, in conflict with its purpose and not know itself. I saw that within the mind of woman, within a person whose psyche, whose mind was more male-like, there could be a possibility of a split from her womanness.

"This splitting from the female self occurs in man as well. Nearly all men have the additional burden of being split from their female side, as well as the responsibility of awakening to what true maleness is.

"I saw the importance of the role of the woman in helping her mate to awaken to his female self. While awakening to what true female is herself, she teaches it to her mate. Within her is also what true maleness is. Deep within the seed is the memory of oneness, but woman must find this experience within herself before she can share any of it.

"I got to glimpse pure Spirit, not as my physical self, but as if I were another. And within that Whole Self called Spirit, there was a first I, like the Creator, with a negative and a positive potential, a female and a male self... like the Creative Void and the energy that acts within it.

"I saw the earth as a blue ball within a black sky, stars all around. I saw that all life occurs on the surface of that ball because of the love between the Mother and the Father energies of creation, and because of the joining of their two energies within its One Self. The Mother and Father energies are halves that when joined is the Source of Creation.

"As humans, we mirror the Creator, both God the Mother and God the Father. Yet, to be fully convinced that Each is within us, we manifest male or female bodies to mirror the illusion of separation, in order to truly desire a return to wholeness within our spirit that is from Creator. In this process, each of us is unique and yet the same. That we seek outside mates as a substitute for this internal process of spiritualization is no credit to us. And yet, we can still awaken to the spirit within us when we come together as physical male and physical female, and have families.

"We saw within each person is the energy that is spirit, and that it is this energy within us which helps us grow. And while we are in physical form, our single purpose is to evolve our consciousness from physical awareness to a consciousness of ourselves as Spiritual. Without that process taking place, love on the earth would be impossible. We are all unconscious love becoming Conscious Love.

"We also saw that it is our thoughts and our actions while we are here that affect the health of the planet. Negative emotions based upon fear make the Mother sick. Gratitude based upon love make the Mother well. As a negative emotion, fear is an illusion, but it does have an effect on the physical well-being of the Mother. If we are unable to awaken to Love as a Reality, then the Mother receives no love or gratitude from us and She Herself becomes ill.

"So it is with our grandmothers. If they are not loved and cared for, they become ill and die young. Our grandmothers have a special bond with our children, with their grandchildren. And it is this feeding cycle of love from grandmother to grandchild that keeps the generations going. So I see, we are split once again into child and into parent and into grandparent. I see that our babies are the reflection of what our grandparents have learned and what we have learned and passed on to our children and grandchildren. And so it goes, down the generations.

"The medicines the Hopi used to keep you out were there to keep out other unhelpful minds and were not aimed at you directly but were designed to keep confusion to a minimum and silence to a maximum. They dove very deep, so what they learned and what they translated into their intent is powerful indeed. Feice was born there in Hopiland, near the great chasm, and I see she brought the depths of the Hopi's intent back with her. I don't know how they transferred their knowledge to her, but it appears that they have done so. I think it's just love that does it. I don't know.

"The Hopi saw that if you can return to your beginnings, you can get back to your Original Self, before the world confused you. It is from this deep place where you are connected to your Spiritual Self, that guidance comes. We saw that ego is born of fear, and that no matter what the cause of anyone's behavior, if they are willing to go through the correction process, their fear will diminish and their understanding increase. We saw madness cured. We saw snake bites healed. We saw many forms of emotional distress eliminated. We saw an abundance of knowledge about nature and about the creatures. And, above all, we saw a kindness and a playfulness that showed us these people had deep understanding and were not going to harm us or our minds in any way.

"Those people had gotten the turkeys to stay around because of the corn that they grew, and they even farmed those turkeys. We'd never seen a wild animal want to be around humans before, so this was a surprise to us. And we thought, only love could do something like this. Life around them volunteered and sprang from the earth. They stored this grain called corn for the winter months and for the animals. They had a unique response to their environment, and it is this that I learned... to seek understanding and knowledge through all the creatures, rocks and plants around us.

"The Hopi's medicines come from the plants and from the spirit of those creatures around them. We saw their whole environment respond to them through prayers for rain, through prayers for light snow instead of heavy, prayers to keep the lightning away from their village, and prayers to keep marauding, warring bands of other peoples from ever finding them. Their whole society revolved around remembering the stories of how they got there, how they come from Spirit, and how they go deep into the earth to rise again as spiritual beings through a small hole in a rock, to begin new life here as Hopi.

"Their society was organized into clans, and each clan had ultimate responsibility for a certain medicine and for a part of their creation story. And so it was that every individual was totally involved, had a role to play in tribal life, and knew their purpose for being there. It is that sense of purpose, I believe, which kept those people whole and happy.

"So if we brought anything back from the Hopi that you fear, I would say it would only be love that you fear, for that is all that we brought back. I think they gave Feice their knowledge to help us through this dark time when the big cold comes... if it comes... when it comes. But as you can see, Feice just brought back love to help us deal with that.

"The other gift they gave within that love is the knowledge of how we are split in our minds, where sickness comes from in our minds, and how that can be healed through ceremony, through understanding. I will share that with anyone on this council, individually, so we may all benefit. Perhaps you and I, Smiling White Hair, will sit many hours together, and I'll share some details of our journeys with you."

Smiling White Hair nodded, and Shuhinono turned to Feice who was playing in the dirt by the fire pit to see if she wanted to add anything. Feice looked up and smiled and shook her head no. Though no words were spoken, everyone in that lodge could see that Feice was an equal in her ability to join minds, to read minds, and to communicate without words.

It is our intent, I see, that is communicated, and the more words you use in your daily life, the less clear your intent is and the more confusion your mind will have... searching for words, searching for words to say what knowledge already knows. By searching to say it, you almost have to forget that you know it, because language is from the split-off part of your mind that doesn't know.

After the council meeting ended, I don't remember what happened. I think we just chitchatted, and there was a meal served. There was plenty of backslappin' and good humor. I did notice that Feice had snuck out the door. And I wondered, did she sit in front of that door to hold the meeting together, or did she sit at the front of that door so she could get the heck out of there quick? Well, I think she had both thoughts, 'cause out she went. Didn't even know she was gone.

The very next day, Smiling White Hair showed up, Feice tugging on her hand. Increasingly I'm becoming more and more aware that I don't know where Feice is half the time. And I'm still surprised that she shows up with people. But this one I was kinda' prepared for. I didn't think Smiling White Hair would show up so soon, but it looked to me like Feice retrieved her... had her get on with it quick. And I see now that the third person who was having difficulty was Smiling White Hair. Because she is our connection with our children and she herself is young, I can see why she would have difficulty with this vision of the big cold.

So in they come, preliminaries dispatched, then they sat down.

Shuhinono told me I was welcome to stay, since Feice had voiced her desire to stay with Smiling White Hair, and I had agreed earlier to look after Feice. I sat out of the way, so I wouldn't be a disturbance, since I was the only male. Then they began.

Smiling White Hair said to Shuhinono, "Your young one has collected me up, and I'm glad to get started. I'm willing to learn what you have learned. My mind is yours."

So Shuhinono began. "I learned from the Hopi the value of woman. I learned that the seasons dictate her moon cycles and her emotions... that her menstrual cycles are the speeded-up cycles of earth's seasons. And I see that without woman demonstrating these cycles monthly and the Earth Mother demonstrating them yearly, man himself would not be able to evolve because he is less connected to the earth in his emotions. It takes effort on a man's part to become connected to the Spiritual Mother. It is through family, through the living of his entire life cycle of birth, growth, maturation and decline, that men form a connection. The connection is love, and it is woman that carries the seed of the memory of what love is. Woman must demonstrate love for man to learn what it is.

"Most men are connected to their fathers through the bond of mind, and it is the guidance of truth men seek from their fathers. It's very easy and natural, this bond of mind. But with their mothers, there is always this big gap to be bridged between mind and heart. I see that a woman's moon cycle and her bleeding on the earth is her connection to all womanness. It is her connection to the Mother's Voice, this deep humility.

"So I'm grateful that you are here to share in these visions given to me by the Hopi people, so you may see deeper into life, as you are young and you influence all the young people in our tribe. Thank you for your innocence."

Then Shuhinono began what I know as an induction, a form of communication that is designed to have minds join. She took out a pouch she'd brought from Hopiland, opened it, and spread corn pollen and corn grains in a circle around the three of them. She sang a Hopi song, thanking the Earth Mother for her life and asking the Mother to join them this day.

As Shuhinono sang, her voice got younger and younger and younger, until she could barely sing... singing in a tiny infant voice. I saw that the two women were carried backwards in time through vision, to their births with their physical mothers. They saw many births of all mothers, and they were carried back farther still, until they saw only a Great Desire to have company... innocent company. Then they went back farther to a time when Love was Whole.

But there was a loneliness that came out of that Wholeness because there was no movement, no change. And from that was born a being which was both male and female, inside and out. And within itself, it had a conversation and kept looking at each part, male and female. But because it was the same mind and body, there was no fulfillment in its joining because it was not separate. So that being split itself in half, into male and female in its mind. And it cried out to Creator, which was itself as well, to give each part freedom, that it may express itself outside the one body. When this desire had agreement from the Creator, it became so. This first being passed away and was reborn into two entities, a male and a female.

The shock to these first two was quite great indeed because they never inquired about what would be lost to their feelings and understanding by the separation into two forms from one mind. And what was lost was certainty within itself of what the truth was before there was this separateness. But they worked hard together and formed a language that was able to keep them together in their individual minds. This language was born out of love. And so they flourished because they behaved as if they were one person. But what they lost was that the God Self was no longer apparent to them within their minds while in their separate physical forms. Because they split in half, their one God Self was no longer visible to each of them in Wholeness. Their eyes saw only separateness, yet their mind remembered Wholeness.

Over time, children, both male and female were brought into the world. But still there was one race, and there was no other than this. Again, two beings, one male and one female had a thought that there be something different, so the mind split again and imagined a world other than a perfect one in perfect relationship. So children born into this world were born with minds other than perfect.

Now one place was not sufficient, so they went this way and that way because sameness was annoying. They went in different directions and even changed to different colors, according to their desire for differentness. This single desire for differentness went in four directions and became the four races. And so the human world has evolved quite independently from plants and animals, with minds so different that they hardly recognize each other at all. That one thought has evolved into the complex world that we live in. It will be worse for others yet to come. So it is up to woman to remember the sameness. And it is up to man to overcome the separateness.

The vision continued as Shuhinono spoke, "There is a One Creator that is the Whole, a part of and yet apart from this process

223

that we are going through, this body life. And it is to this Power of Love which created the world we live in and these forms we've taken, to which we appeal for our visions to guide our lives. Because humans have split their minds and become afraid even about the Creator, rather than trusting, we are given visions to guide us. We don't know how they come to us and what we are to do with them, but we must ask for them to guide us.

"The Hopi speak of great changes to come to our way of life, great changes to come to ways of life after us and after that. Always these changes are accompanied by physical changes in the environment, in the wildlife, and in the humans inhabiting this place we call home. Many things they show us we do not understand because this future time will be so different from ours. The images we see do not make sense to us.

"What we have learned, though, is how to get back to wholeness within ourselves and how to get our tribe back to wholeness as well. It is these children you care for, Smiling White Hair, that will lead our tribe into the future. So it is toward them you need to give your love and attention, while we are waiting for guidance about where to go and when to go there. My husband has seen a great black swan in the pool lift its wings around us and lead us into the Light, through whatever peril this vision means for us. We know that some will survive. We know that all will *live*.

"It is the nature of the Medicine Lodge to transform us. And the Hopi taught me, it is up to us to face our transformation and to seek it in our daily lives. It is this truth that we are spiritual beings which gives us courage to face these changes. I think the Mother will let us know what we are to do and what we are to say and how we are to help each other."

Smiling White Hair said, "I was very much afraid to die in the cold, not because that would be painful but because I am so young and have not lived enough. My hair turned white when I was very young, as you know, not because I am so wise but because I took on all the suffering of our people. I was sick many months and came out of that experience an old, twenty-year old. I saw all the things that men do to women and women do to men, their striving for balance between them, their trying to be right in their perceptions. I had to die to being only female, and I had to die into being male as well because I could see both sides. And it was this early death that gave me my connection to Spirit. But when this vision of the cold came, I was not able to go back to remembering those lessons. So I think I became greedy about my own life and stopped sharing it. I tried to possess life to protect myself from harm, and I think I only pretended concern about anyone else's life. So I took a position on that vision. When I took a position, I lost my objectivity and I became fearful. You know, I had that one powerful experience in my life, and I held it close to me for as long as I could. And then, one day I found that all my experience and all my memories no longer guided me anymore. I was able to understand the people in this camp because I lived through nearly every human conflict possible in those few months of illness. But now I see that Spirit has given us this new vision, with the possibility of all our people dying. I was unprepared for that. I thought I had prepared by accepting my own death and my own unreality as a female or a male, but I had not. It is one thing to arrive at a place in your mind and quite another to have your feet get there. So here are our feet arriving near the place of transformation, and I have no experience to draw upon. It was by watching your Feice with Flowering Tree that taught me to look toward the children again for the answer. I have been guiding the children with my vision from the past, rather than learning from their vision in the present. And I see now, I can never stop learning or I drag everyone into the past with me, and we are doomed to repeat all the errors of that past. The stories handed down to us are good. They save us lots of time. They save our children many years of hard experience. The stories keep love strong because we have something of it to give our children. But I now see, our children have something to give to us as well."

Shuhinono nodded. There was a period of silence, then Shuhinono said, "Those Hopi showed us lots of beings who in their society had great power, for good or for harm. They also taught, it is your belief about your own will that allows another to do good or harm to you. They taught their children that their will is no less strong than the will of any other living thing, and that the path of truth within love is the only path that is certain. So it is up to us as individual human beings to find that path of truth inside love, or we will wander aimlessly at the push and pull of every will that exists in this time or in any other time, in this place or any other place. We saw there is no truth outside of love, anywhere, in any time.

"The Hopi showed us that a mind can join good or evil, selflessness or selfishness, but it is up to the individual to choose what they would learn, which path they would go down... the path of empty feet or the path full of love. They showed us that there are so many distractions, even in Hopi life, that this process is being dragged out longer and longer and longer... this one of choosing, this one of arriving. The time of choosing and coming back to the truth again is getting longer and longer and longer, no matter what medicines are used.

"They showed us that the very first problem that humans have is this idea of sex, and how the first choice of separating into male and female meant that the two forms now had to copulate in order to extend themselves, just as the animals had already done. The question in the minds of the Hopi was, 'If we are to populate the earth, is it God recreating, or is it just us copulating?'

"I tell you, the Hopi were a spiritual people, and they looked at this issue with great depth and carefulness. I don't know whether you want to learn more today, so I will stop now until you are ready for more, if you wish."

Smiling White Hair said, "I do wish to continue, and we can do it this day or another."

At that moment Feice and I bumped sideways onto the lodge wall because she was climbing on my back. It was that badger of hers rarin' to get outside. From the looks of things, it was a good excuse for everyone to rest. Good as any. So Smiling White Hair excused herself and said she would be back tomorrow for the lessons on sex. And she laughed.

Shuhinono cracked up. She was laughing so hard, she was fallin' over, and I know it was because of the look on my face. There's that word... sex. Together they were havin' a good laugh over my shock at her frankness.

Maybe tomorrow, they'll let me sit in again, and I'll learn something new... about sex.

Chapter 5
From Thought to Knowledge - Four Stages

There was a time long ago when man and woman didn't have a sense of separateness like they do now. There was a time within that time that male and female acted as one. Separation begins thus. Somebody is made to feel guilty, so they withdraw. Now it really doesn't matter who. Separation is separation. Whether one leaves or both leave in a huff is pretty much irrelevant.

So for lessons in joining, we need to look at the children again. They are the unconscious teachers. They don't have choice about joining. They join their essence to their parents, regardless of whether they are abused or not. And it's not until they go into puberty that they come into choice about their own emotions. Before puberty, children are all very forgiving. They adjust. It is only after puberty that we as children start holding grudges, we learn to separate, and we learn to have private thoughts.

Before that, we absorbed all that was given, for better or for worse. As adults, we spend the rest of our lives sorting out our feelings, trying to join like we did as children... innocent. It is in innocence that all things are joined. It is in conscious forgiveness that our emotions are changed.

Shuhinono and Feice are preparing the lodge today for Smiling White Hair. I haven't exactly been told I can attend, but I haven't been told I can't. Naturally, subjects of sex always interest me.

But if I'm prevented from staying for that talk, that will be fine. I understand that sex is the woman's purview. It is her domain. It is for her to choose or there will be no harmony. A man can court a woman, but in my day, until the woman chooses to be a wife, there is always withholding, suspicion, watching, learning.

That yielding barrier between the man and the woman is there because of the need of respect, honor, trust and sharing, not because love doesn't exist without those things but because it cannot exist long without those things. You can be in love with someone and have no idea who they are until after a year or more of marriage. In fact, that's the way modern marriages go. You see, with us we were all the same, so people were prepared for marriage by the time they were nine years old. There were no families that were unavailable to us for learning. All children were the children of every family in camp. There were no secrets. Sure, everybody had their squabbles, but even those weren't kept secret. Ideas of secrecy in the tribe were absurd. Why would we withhold anything from another person if they asked?

So the children learned respect, honor, trust and sharing, early. Within that context, love always grows. Very rarely was anyone disciplined harshly for anything, including what you call in your society, molestation. Only if those offenses were repeated and nothing was learned from them was the offending person then shunned from the tribe.

You see, our simple explanations for why you didn't diddle your sister or diddle your daughter or diddle anyone else in your close family were because of the big troubles that come in those births. The dark passageway of sexual misconduct can lead only to greater and greater madness.

Humans are just like a common plant of an open-pollinated variety. If a plant self-pollinated for a few seasons, its seed would have no new information to grow into a new generation. Its evolution would not be creative and would end way before seven cycles. That is to say, creativity would not be involved in the pollination process as required, and that species would surely fail. All other species would continue to evolve without them.

Each plant needs the diversity of new pollens, brought by the movement of the wind and insects, to grow strong into the future. By tossing its future to the wind, it gives up *control* to God. It trusts the process and it understands interdependency. And just like you, it makes a leap of faith. And so it grows.

So, to knowingly impregnate a direct relative doesn't include God in the cycle, doesn't include Spirit. It's harmful to the spirit and to the soul of the person molested because that molested person cannot understand why someone they trusted, they honored and they respected would break the laws and do such a harmful thing. This is where the boundary of sharing is drawn.

Now, I tell you, real laws, God's laws are there because they work. They are the truth. And you can cite your sciences to prove what we say, that incest causes genetic difficulties. Well, that's true. But worse than that, it creates a sickness in the spirit of the people involved, which eventually can destroy the whole family. It does that not because it is law and law caused that to happen. The law is there, stated as law, as a result of all human behavior... the experience of all those that went before. Law is there to say, we tried it. It's not good. Don't do it.

*

It was midmorning when Smiling White Hair showed up bringing a basket of berries and seeds and roots, even some jerky. Shuhinono put those aside and invited her to sit by the fire. I looked at Shuhinono and she nodded to me as if to say, "Yes, you can stay." So I told her I would look after Feice, in case she became a disturbance.

Shuhinono sang a beautiful song. It was about the bluebirds that occasionally come through our area, how the sight of them always made her happy. She thanked those bluebirds for their cheerful song and happy little spirits. She prayed to the four directions and offered what you call celery root, then put it on a hot rock, next to the fire. It filled the lodge with a fresh, clean aroma. She laid out a circle of cornmeal and drew the cardinal directions, then prayed to the four winds to give her help. She asked them old Hopi people to induce her back into that underground kiva, to relive and share her learnings with Smiling White Hair.

After some fifteen minutes of chanting very softly, rocking back and forth, Shuhinono opened her eyes and looked at Smiling White Hair. I noticed her eyes were a bit glassy, and she looked deep into Smiling White Hair. I could see there was a bit of embarrassment, as Smiling White Hair dropped her eyes and looked at the fire for a moment before reengaging Shuhinono's eyes. I saw that we are all shy creatures, but we want to learn, so we face our discomfort at being seen inside.

Gently, Shuhinono said, "Dear one, let's close our eyes. Take a few deep breaths and relax all the muscles in your body. Let your mind release its grip on your body, release you from all worries and concerns. Relax deeper... and deeper... and deeper. Trust in Love to be your Guide. If you will follow my words, I'll take you to that underground kiva of the Hopi. I'll try to go slowly, so as not to rush you."

Shuhinono began to speak quietly in a slow, rhythmic tone. "We are standing on a flat mesa, trees all around. Now look to your left and see where the great, stone-lined pit is dug in the earth, with a ladder going down through the hole in the roof. We are going to go down that ladder into that underground kiva. But first, the keepers of the kiva are going down to help the elders inside. Do you see them?"

"Yes, I can see them," Smiling White Hair answered.

Shuhinono continued. "Now some older children are going in... now the women... and now it is our turn. Feel yourself descend slowly down this ladder into the kiva. Feel your feet touch the earth, then sit down next to me. This day is to be a woman's ceremony, an induction into womanhood from puberty for some of the young girls attending. There are all ages of women here, and there is one older male helper to keep the fire and to help any of the children if they have difficulty. It's very dim in this kiva... only a faint light coming through a small hole in the top, only the glowing embers here below. It's warm inside, even though it's winter outside.

"An old woman is shaking a rattle and singing in Hopi. A very strong, earth-smelling powder made from dried cactus is poured onto hot stones around the fire pit. The smoke burns our eyes and makes us cough a bit. The women begin joining the old woman singing, one by one. The song progresses in a clockwise circle by twelve women in succession... one starts, then the next, another starts, then the next, 'till there are twelve women singing. Then they take turns singing phrases in succession in reverse, only a few words at a time, until the song is going around in a reverse circle. We are going counter-clockwise to reverse time.

"It is the singing of this song in this way that causes our small minds to lose predominance. This song in reverse makes us dizzy, so our minds cannot comprehend what is being done to them, and we have to give up trying to think. Instead of being hyper-alert and on guard, we relinquish our sense of separate selves... lose our sensitivity to external influences. We give our full attention to the movement of the song. The singing makes us spiral into ourselves, turns us inside, and joins everyone here together as one. This goes on for some time until the song is abruptly stopped, and we are aware that we are no longer seeing with the eyes of our body.

"The whole top of the lodge is covered, except for a very small opening. The glowing embers on the floor are spread out into a pattern, the pattern of an eagle. Now someone comes in dressed as a large eagle, a headdress covering their whole head, feathers hanging all over their arms like wings, and a large bustle for a tail. The women are chanting very quietly as that eagle dancer floats around the fire pit in a circle, counter-clockwise. The light is very dim and we cannot see details, so that person becomes an eagle for us, flying around inside that lodge.

"As the dancer spins and dances counter-clockwise around the fire, the smoke in the room begins to spiral up to the ceiling, up to the roof, up to that small hole. We are all spiraling down a chamber once again, deeper than the deepest hole we have ever been in in our lives. It feels like we are in another world now. It is very dark and very quiet. Even though this person is still dancing, we can't hear a thing.

"The old woman's voice speaks to us very rapidly, then she lets out a yell. It sends a shock wave through us, and we pop into another room more brightly lit, a golden color. Within that room, another much older woman is standing, talking to us inside our own minds. Since we don't know Hopi, she looks at us and points off to her right.

"We look in that direction and see a man and a woman standing there. They are all golden color and their hands are joined. The energy surrounding their bodies is combined into one form, one egg-shaped form. As they let go of their hands, their shape remains as one. And as they step apart from each other, one back and one forward, their egg-shaped energy form is still around both of them, but it's much larger now. The color in this room was a golden color, but now it changes to a reddish color. Orange, I'd say.

"The expressions on their faces change as they come back together. Mistrust is on their faces. Their egg-shaped form was whole, but now it's changing and becomes two individual forms. Now they are only connected to each other from their navel down to their crotch by threads of energy that are murky orange and a dull, dark red. Their entire bodies are not conjoined in the energy of that golden light anymore.

"Now that woman and that man are lifting their energy up to their diaphragm, and the color of those energy threads change to a kind of yellow color. Then they raise it to their hearts and the threads become green. They raise it to their throats and the threads become blue. Now they raise their energy so the threads are connecting their minds, just above the bridge of the nose. And there the threads are a pinkish-lavender color. When they join at that level, their two energy bodies become one again, and all the colors become brighter. They smile at each other and take each other's hands, and out the top of their heads comes a fountain of light... sparkling gold and silver with threads of blue and lavender, green and red and yellow... all colors. Then those threads cover their one energy body again.

"Now this woman in energy body form begins speaking to us. Her words are coming out of her throat and heart and forehead, rather than her mouth. Streamers of color are being projected into our hearts. As she does this, we nearly fall over from the love of it. Such pure energy of love... the world has little known.

"While in this exquisite state of love, we see that we are spiritual beings, and we see that our separation from each other is only due to the confusion of our senses while we are in the body. The act of taking a body means forgetting what we are. The act of making love and having children is a further forgetting of what we are. But through the hardships of life, we are brought back to this memory of ourselves as pure love... as pure energy."

With eyes still closed, Shuhinono asked, "Smiling White Hair, are you in this kiva with me? I feel you here. What do you see?"

A faint voice said, "Yes, I'm here. I'm looking at the radiance of that man and that woman together. I'm seeing that our thoughts affect our energy. As I think a certain thought, the energy within my form moves. I am also seeing that my mind does not like to have the awareness of this in itself. It's trying to run and pretend that it doesn't know what it's doing. I see that there are two or three of me doing different things at the same time. And as I do this, I see that man and woman mirror my thoughts and show me what my thinking does to the energy body. I see this man looks as if he is two different people, and instead of there being the single light body, there are threads of different colors moving throughout him as a result of his thinking, as a result of *my* thinking. And I see the confusion on the woman's face and the confusion in her energy body, as she is trying to figure out which one of him she is talking to. I see she becomes afraid, then splits herself. I see that we are all joined in love as a natural state of being joined to all living things. And I see that it is only our mind, by itself, that searches for the answer of what we are but cannot find the answer alone. I see that the mind cannot be by itself and know wholeness. I see that it must return to wholeness, and I see that this is the only sickness there is. This is where all sickness begins, this splitting off of ourselves in response to confusion or fear."

There was a long pause and Shuhinono asked, "What else do you see?"

Smiling White Hair said, "They are copulating. I see their energies join, but they are joined only at their sexual centers by those red fibers. I don't see the other energy centers join. Now they are talking, and I see their hearts join and their throats join. Now their minds are joined, and now their energy bodies are together again as one. I see by this simple act of making love with their whole being, not just with their sexual centers, that they are in harmony with each other again, and share love and respect and trust."

There was another short pause, then Smiling White Hair spoke again. "Now it's as if it is the next day. I see they are still joined at their hearts and at their sexual centers. But I see that confusion has entered again because their minds are not still joined. I see that sex is not enough to keep minds joined. I see that it is only meaningful communication with each other that keeps us joined in mind and in heart. It is what we say and do with each other that keeps our energy in balance or creates imbalance. And I see that both male and female are equal in their ability to return to harmony or to separate in confusion."

Shuhinono asked, "Do you see that the male is no different from the female, except in one significant point? And that is, the woman carries the seed of life, and within that seed is the memory of what love is. Man does not carry the seed and must look to the woman for that memory. This, the man learns through the woman, through his children, through his grandparents, through his tribe.

"And do you also see that a society that does not respect their women and honor them will not have peace and trust in their tribe? I see that a society that does not respect and honor their men will not have peace and trust either. I see Creator was very smart to make us need each other so much. And I see that Creator gave woman balance by putting truth in the mind of man, in front of love, to lead. Man must, then, look back to woman for the memory of that love for his truth to be true, since there can be no truth outside of love. The truth does not exist without love. Without love, there is only the separation caused by individual perception. Therefore, the Gateway to Knowledge is the joining of truth and love.

"I see that love not joined to the truth, if left to its own devices, would return too quickly from whence it came because it had no mirror to give itself knowledge. Love without truth would retreat too quickly to the Source and not extend itself through form into creation, because it has the power to do what it wills.

"So Creator put truth in front of love to lead, knowing there was no truth outside of love. The woman, though she has the seed of the memory of love, was given an ounce of doubt. So Creator gave man the job of mirroring the truth for her. But if man does not see the love in the woman, then he surely will not see the truth within himself, nor will he be able to speak the truth to anyone. Man's difficulty, I see, is in not having the seed of love in the first place. And because he does not have the seed, he cannot touch love directly, except through the heart and mind of a woman."

Both women sat quietly in deep silence for a long time. Then Smiling White Hair said, "I asked that oldest of women, 'How are we to return to wholeness? How do we know who our mates are?' And I heard that old woman's mind say, 'Stay in balance with the Earth Mother. There is one in your tribe that will go on to become a guide. There is one who will understand people's energy and will help to make happy matches. That one will hear the Mother's guidance.'

"So I asked, 'How does one get in touch with the Mother, the Earth Mother? I have not heard Her before, so I would know Her voice.' And that old woman said, 'You hear just fine. You afraid your mind by thinking you do not hear.'

"Then I saw this old woman, in my mind's eye, turn into a beautiful young woman from a distant place. She went through a hundred changes to be everything on the earth, all peoples... yellow-haired people, blue-eyed people, brown-haired, black-haired, big and little... all the races. I was shown that the Mother loves all Her children... from the ants to the blackbirds. She turned into everything. She always had a smile on Her face, even for the poor, pitiful ones who were born deformed or were born female in a male body or born male in a female body. She loved them all, even the crazy and wicked ones. She showed me so many faces I thought I couldn't stand to see anymore, but they kept coming. I very nearly hollered out in my mind... "Enough!" And the old woman, the Mother, spoke without words to my mind, even as the faces were changing, and She said, 'You don't know what enough is.' So I kept watching, even though it was hard going through the changes of feeling each person's life.

"I asked the Mother, 'How does anyone know who is a match for who? How would anyone know such a thing?' And She answered, 'I'll show you in your mind. You will see their faces, then it is up to you to wait patiently until those faces come into your eyesight. It's all arranged. You don't need to do anything. I will help you.' And I said, 'So it is *me,* the matchmaker?' And She said, 'Yes, Smiling White Hair. You will be given this chance to help your people.'"

At that moment, Smiling White Hair gasped for air and slumped forward into Shuhinono's arms. She said weakly, "I must have been standing in that kiva for nearly a day. I could see every detail in it perfectly. I got sick to my stomach, thinking, how could I be

234

so far away? So I popped back into this lodge, not in Hopiland but here in our own land." Then Smiling White Hair slipped into the silence of sleep.

Shuhinono said, "I think she will sleep a long time. Shall we keep her here or put her in her own lodge?"

Feice said, "Keep here. I look after her. Okay?"

I said, It's up to your mom 'cause she's too big for you to look after.

Feice jumped up and looked at her mom with a big smile on her face. "See, I bigger now. I help."

Shuhinono says, "Okay. It would be easier to care for her here than moving her and checking on her so often. Okay, Hinono?"

Sure, I said. Besides, we don't know what state of mind she'll be in when she wakes up. That was some journey. I'm glad I got to go with you. I learned a lot.

Nearly two days went by. We had to roll Smiling White Hair over every couple of hours so she wouldn't wake up bone-sore, like you would for somebody who was paralyzed. I don't know why we didn't worry about her, but we didn't. Our life went on quite normally. Only once on the afternoon before Smiling White Hair woke up did Shuhinono scoot me out and bathe the sleeping woman. Perhaps it was that bath that brought her back.

"You sure sleep long time," Feice said. "What you dream?"

Smiling White Hair smiled weakly at her and said, "Oh, good dreams. I think the Mother of All was there teaching me. I'm hungry. I'm thirsty. How long have I been asleep? Is it the same day?"

Feice said, "You sleep two days. The Mother makes lots of faces, huh?" Then she went around the lodge making lots of funny faces, being tall and short, wide and skinny, flying like birds and crawling like insects. And we laughed while we got water and food for the sleepy matchmaker. After so much work, it was good to see everyone laugh and be silly.

Smiling White Hair asked Feice, "Did you dream too? And did you fall asleep for two days afterward?"

Feice said, "No, I dream some. Not much. I'm too little. I look after you two days."

And Smiling White Hair said, "I thank you for that. Right now I feel like a newborn, a little bit stranded, floppin' around. Shuhinono, just tell me one thing. How does it happen that you go to a different place in vision and end up inhaling the smoke of their medicine and are gone for two days, not really having been there at all? I really wonder for my sanity."

Shuhinono put her head down, thought a moment and said,

"What we learned in those kivas is that time goes in many directions. Your visionary experience is no less valid than the ones we had in Hopiland and relived again here with you. Your willingness to join the experience made it complete for you."

Smiling White Hair said, "I sure didn't know where I was. It was so real, but I don't know if I was really there or not."

"I don't know how to explain it to you, but you were there and you did experience what we experienced in that place," Shuhinono said.

"Strong medicine," Smiling White Hair said. And after a moment she asked, "What I would like to know is, how do you enter this visionary place? How do I regain it to talk to the Mother again? How do I make a place in my mind and heart for Her? I've been told what service I will perform, but I don't yet know how."

Shuhinono suggested that Smiling White Hair just sit very quietly and sing a song that would take her back to that kiva each time... that she use that kiva for her meeting place with the Mother. Smiling White Hair asked her if that's what she did for herself, and Shuhinono said, "Yes, and I will teach you a song that will return you to the kiva when you wish to go."

Smiling White Hair said, "Thank you," then turned to me and asked, "Did you see what we saw?"

I said, Yes, I think so. You mean the man and the woman who were golden color and changed all their energy around for us to see?

Smiling White Hair said, "Yes, the very ones. Did you see the Mother also, that old woman change into many people and many creatures?"

And I said, Yes, I did.

"So what work have you been given to do here?" Smiling White Hair asked Shuhinono and me.

We both said in unison, "We don't know yet. We are waiting."

It was at that moment Smiling White Hair began to rock back and forth and her eyes turned up in her head. After a moment she said, "I see the Mother again, and She is showing me that before the great storm comes, you both will dream of a place of safety for the members of the tribe that remain here. I see that others will decide to leave and will divide into three bands and go in three different directions. She is also showing me what was revealed to you... the great swan, wings outstretched, taking many of our people into the Light."

Shuhinono and I nodded and said a word of thank you.

Feice spoke, "Oh, they know. They just pretend." And you know, I think she was right. We did know our role, but there was

236

still a part of us that doubted. Because we did not yet have the tools to do what was being asked and it was not yet time, we doubted that we knew.

I think part of this doubt was healthy. It is better not to try to do a thing before its time, so we put it out of mind. Besides, Spirit could change the plan at any moment. And if we remained rigid, we would stop learning. So we would rather doubt our minds a bit and remain open for the next clue or lesson, rather than to claim ourselves to be something, truly wanting to be it but not being it at all. By not rushing to conclusions about our experiences, we remain open to changes.

Many of your modern students go to medical school and come out being called doctors without any experience or true calling. They've rushed into being a doctor so quickly that they truly are not healers for many years to come... maybe never. So rushing ahead and believing you are something before you are, I see, is not helpful. Trying to dream up your role is not helpful either.

We talked for many hours and shared a great deal about this vision and the ways of the Hopi. And I think Smiling White Hair was very peaceful again within herself. I knew it would take many more experiences for her to completely rid herself of her confusion. But I felt she was in good hands, that the old woman speaking as the Mother was going to show her a great many things and help her heal within herself, so her mind would be whole again, not confused, not afraid.

It's a process, you see. You begin, and you go a long way before that beginning is the middle. And perhaps, when you're at the middle of your journey in your understanding, you can look back and say you've learned something. But before then, before you've reached that center point, honestly you can't say you know anything at all.

As a matter of fact, the first part of the journey is the erasing of all the errors that we have made in our thinking that prevent our mind from being whole. It is the time of relinquishment, and it is very hard indeed. If you prize your infant mind above the truth, you will feel loss during this time. And yet, it is only at the middle of the journey do you see there is no loss at all, and what was left behind is being rebuilt for better function, for better usefulness, for better helpfulness.

I myself am very old now, long dead to your world, and I learn still. Perhaps I am at the middle of my journey, perhaps a little farther, I do not know. I do know that once your path has been consciously chosen by you, there are a great many Helpers to ensure your completion. It is only your willingness to walk this path that makes it easy. It is only your unwillingness that makes it difficult. For some people who are split into lots of little fragments of confusion and conflict, the undoing will seem very difficult indeed.

I will say this, Spirit will use anything and everything to help you. They will move you quickly through this trial time where your misperceptions are being healed. You will relearn what everything is for. You will relearn that you are not the body that you inhabit for a time. You will relearn that time and space are not fixed or rigid, except in your own perception. And when you are ready, the universe will expand in front of you, and you will be shown things you never imagined about the world or about the beings that inhabit it.

I talk to your twenty-first century minds in this old way and share these old stories, so that your journey to awakening is swift. Spirit's job is to help you become unstuck. To do this, you must be willing to have your perceptions changed and be willing to learn to watch your energy move, according to Spirit's direction. Your Guides will help you with your energy. They will help you understand what you are.

My energy and perceptions changed after my experiences with the Hopi. My mind expanded beyond my personal concerns as a human being, within my family and within my tribe and within my country. I learned to travel to other times and other countries and other families and other individuals' concerns. I learned to extend myself through time. And, as a result, one of the greatest pleasures in my very long life, after many generations, has been to reconnect with my son and his wife, the twins... my children.

Because they are in your time, I will now speak to their concerns and speak to their travels and speak about their path. And I will speak about the world you live in. These words that follow will take you on a journey of your modern world and show you how you make your world by where you place your energy and by what you value.

This land you call the United States is run by two minds. There is a public mind that says it is whole... all these separate states, separate cities, separate people living in separate environments with separate concerns. And there is the private mind of each individual that is lost inside of its own physical, living self, having separate ideas within it about its experiences here. I'll not talk about the public mind until much later, in another book, perhaps. But I want to talk to you of your private mind. And I will try to show you how that mind gets split and how it can get back to health again. And I will tell you of the many pitfalls along the way.

238

When a baby is born, you look at that baby's face, and it will either smile or cry or just be astounded. And I ask you this simple question. Why does a child smile when it can't even really focus to see your face? And why does a child cry for no obvious cause when it's not in pain or hunger? Why does one child perceive pain and the other perceive joy, without little outside stimulation whatsoever? Why is one person in wonderment with an open mind and another apparently crushed by some unseen force within?

I'll give you this one clue. Everything that has come into existence on the physical plane has always been alive, has always experienced something before its birth into physical form. And how is it that a person can go on living beyond this body and have more experiences? And how can any person be so profoundly split that they can be in two places at once, in two different times, living lives simultaneously and not be consciously aware that they are doing so?

It's like this. To take a body, you must split from the Whole in order to become distinct. To accomplish this, there are two kinds of agreements made with the Creator. The first one you made consciously and directly with Creator, with full knowledge, before you split your mind in half and forgot your agreement. And the second agreement you made indirectly, as a result of the first. The second one was agreeing to be taught through the laws governing body life. Before the second agreement, there was always the first.

The first is your Spiritual Self that made the agreement, and the second is your body-mind that forgot it. Thus, there is two of everyone, one awake and conscious and one not. There can be more selves, based upon the laws of disassociation that govern human body-minds.

An unhappy soul, not wanting to take form again must do so from the first agreement because they are not finished. An unconscious person–as we all start out, except for the very few–will never remember his original agreement and will often curse his life. If that person is born with pain and unhappiness, it is because they brought it with them, unfinished from a prior life or lives. You take one ticket in the beginning, and you take but one ride to the finish, regardless of how many lives you live.

And there is no point in discussing any prior life, as the work to be accomplished can only be done in the present. Looking back is looking away from the present. If it can be helpful, Spirit will remind you of a prior life, but to seek out yourself in a prior life of your own volition is again trying to teach yourself what you do not know.

Eons may go by, but in Creator's time, you have but one life living, consuming days and weeks and months and years and decades and centuries, but for one purpose. And that is... **to learn what you are in truth,** not what the world tries to tell you you are. To take a body is to become vulnerable and subject to the laws of the earth. At the same time, God's laws are forgotten. What would be the purpose in this, do you think? Why would one want to leave God in the first place... to be "born?"

I think it's very simple. Life has four stages. The first is *the thought,* the possibility. The second is *the request,* the desire. The third is *the acceptance* and the fourth is *the knowledge.*

The first impulse is the possibility that creation could expand at all. What possibly could be the reason for this except company, reflection, entertainment, play? The second impulse can best be described as the desire. In your language you call it, "the yes." That yes makes your energy separate and become distinct from the Creator's energy, that we hide inside of as embryos. The request, then, is your asking to learn from God what you are in terms of your powers of creativity. In other words, "If I was created in the image of God, then how do I get to be like God?" It follows to wonder how God got to be God, how Creator got to be Creator.

At that point, you are given integrity and you are asked if you wish to go on this journey to find out, as before then you are barely even recognizable as distinct from the Creator. You are told all the conditions that you will have to go through in order to find your way back to the truth inside love. And you are given a center to hold onto, to help you remember that you are the love that sent you, so that you might remain connected to Help. You are told that all you have to do is ask sincerely, wholeheartedly, with all your being, and you will be helped. You are also told how difficult this might become because of the confusions of the mind in the body. And if you agree, you step into the third part. The third part is your emergence into a form... your acceptance of the lessons that now are coming to you.

You know, it doesn't matter whether you are born a happy child or a screecher. You get all the same lessons whether you are rich or poor, whether you are black or white or red or yellow or brown. You get the same lessons whether you are a good witch or a bad witch, whether you are a warring person or a peaceful one.

But I tell you, what is "random" is the body life you are grown into, thrown into, the place of your birth, the parents that you have, the country... the life is all random or it would not be fair.

There is no other way to describe this appearance of randomness other than to say, it is like a great churning. And within it is this reaching that happens... Spirit to you, and someday you to

240

Spirit. Those that speak of karma refer to the spiritual laws that govern our lessons and express themselves through the physical laws of attraction and opposition. Random refers specifically to the material appearance of your life before you are able to perceive the very improbable but absolutely impeccable order of it... from the beginning of the stars, to the dust of your ashes after you return home.

So, some children are born into extreme boredom and some are born into extreme busyness. Oftentimes a genius finds himself in with idiots. And, truly, those idiots are now within that genius. The play of opposites within the world is sometimes very extreme.

The first major split that occurs in the personality of a human being is finding yourself in a female form or a male form. Now, not only do you feel separated from God by being in a body, but you feel separated from your Whole Self. All of a sudden, when puberty comes, you find that you are female or male, and not only are you vulnerable in your feelings, but now you are vulnerable in your physical self as well.

With the arrival of puberty, love seems outside yourself. And yet, your whole struggle is to try to own it inside you again. Your memory of your Self, if you retain any at all, might tell you you were something before, not what you are now, and this may set up deep conflict.

You see, the concept of love was born out of Wholeness, so if you now perceive yourself as split from your female side or your male side, you will certainly not be comfortable and will seek love outside, from the other half in order to be whole. This is great for body life because it makes lots of bodies. But it's not so great for spiritual life, unless you find someone who is willing to be your perfect mirror or mate. Even then, the odds are very much against that because your memory of Wholeness dictates to you what love is supposed to look like. You have an expectation by your very nature of what love is supposed to be. Even if you had the most perfect parents in the world, I think a natural human being would still not see love in themselves first but would first seek to see it in another.

Because you come from Spirit, you will eventually tire of the confusions of being body. Foremost in your mind becomes the one question, "Who am I? What am I? Where did I come from? Where are we going?" You see, all questions are but one question. There is but One Answer, just as there is but One Source. All children ask this question of themselves. Some ask it of their parents. Some ask it in the world. Some ask it from Spiritual Masters.

If we do not have too many distractions, we will probably ask these questions enough times to find our other mind. And in that right mind, we will hear One Voice. But before we hear that One Voice, we will probably hear several voices. And it will sound like this. "There is a God–there isn't a God. God is blue–God is red. God is a body–God is not a body. Love is safe–love is unsafe. I am beautiful–I am ugly. Too tall–too short. Too hot–too cold. Too far–too near." And a slip will have been made back into objections, rather than into possibilities. It is easy for the mind to slip into its objections.

In our time, we didn't have that luxury. If it was too cold, we had to go gather wood to make it warmer. We had to quickly do something in a positive solution direction. If somebody hurt our feelings, we would speak to it directly and find the solution. We would try to get past our upsetness. Because we depended upon each other for survival, we could not afford to make an enemy of anyone in our large family.

But your families, for the most part, are very small. You barely know what each other thinks because you do not talk your feelings. You talk your mind. You have so many distractions and so many comforts that you don't even need to look for a solution. Nothing is at stake. So you develop a private mind that has decided all kinds of things about the world and the people in it.

You're taught these confusions, distractions and objections by your parents, your teachers, your churches, through radio and television, through popular songs, through movies, and through the actions of your peers when you're in this environment you call school.

This past thirty years, your whole population has been trying to decide if love is free or not. But you fail to ask the question, "What is love, who has it, and where does it come from anyway?"

One group of people decide early on that the body can be used for whatever the mind wants to use it for. And they determine that love is sexual, and they began to follow that energy in search of love. Another group might decide that love is providing the richest, best home possible by whatever means necessary to get it. Another might seek power as an aspect of love, and they might follow that route of "looking good," being successful in the world, being powerful.

If you make decisions without Spirit, then you follow the path to which those decisions point, to the goals that they serve. If you make no decisions and develop no will for any goal, you will follow everyone else's decisions. If you use your will to decide that you do not know what to do or what to think, and that you are going to discover what the truth is in every circumstance, then you have

242

come closest to finding out what you are.

A leader in the world leads only their own ideas. A follower may know the wisdom of not having their own strong opinions to follow, but they may never know what the truth is if they don't seek it. And they follow leaders anyway. So, is it better to be a leader or a follower? Is it better to be aggressive or passive? Is it better to appear right than wrong? Is a right man less guilty than a wrong one? Is the lawmaker also the jailer and the jailer also the prisoner?

If your desire for the truth is no stronger than your unwillingness to be separated from falsehood, then you go nowhere. You may sound good to others and to yourself, but you delay.

Is a distracted person who is very busy in the world with many lessons delaying by having so much activity, by appearing so involved and busy? Is a person who meditates and is generally not busy, making faster progress with their unbusyness, or are they delaying also, not wanting to appear to be distracted? Do they still delay? Is a life of apparent peace different from a life of war? Because one rushes toward death with feet moving, does that make them less conscious than a person whose feet do not move and who shirks from the world by claiming to be at peace?

If a person persists in the game of being right and someone else being wrong, then I assure you, they will not know what the truth is or what their purpose is. **You cannot polarize against life in any of its forms and know what life is.** And if you are trying to make yourself be something, then you have forgotten what you already are.

I'll ask you this. If you are female, do you believe that the source of love and safety is a male? Or are you just willing to settle for the appearance of being safe and the appearance of being loved in this world? Is that all that you think you can hope for in this material world you have made... comfort, safety, maybe loyalty, perhaps respect?

If you are male, I know puberty is harder for you because you do not carry the seed of love, and you do not cycle your energy monthly. And if you see a female as the source of love, then you surely will get stuck in a sexual space in your mind and may very nearly never get out of it, except when you are old. And you will be so blinded by this sexual energy that you may very nearly be used up by it, and you will not be able to see what an unconscious female is doing to you with her energy and why. Therefore, after a time, you will be astounded that you did not know another person as you thought you did. And love will change its face for you, and you will have to scramble to keep up. You see, you loved a body and a behavior in it, and when that body changed, that behavior also changed.

So if you are not prepared as a young person for all these changes and all these emotions, you will either prefer the perfect picture in your mind of what you thought love was, or you will look deeper into the spirit of that human being who is also struggling to understand what love is.

I've told you before the woman holds the seed that contains the memory of love. And I have said that Creator put truth in front of love to lead, knowing there was no truth outside of love, so man must complete the circle back to love again for both to return. So the woman often feels, especially at moon times when her energy cycles very deep, that she does not know what is true and will question everything. It is during these deep times of questioning that the male is challenged to communicate what is true. This is hard for any man because, unless he has faced his own death and has learned what love is, he won't know what the truth is and will start pretending he does.

Your culture is not used to deep metaphysical questioning. And instead of saying it doesn't know, it pretends it does and lies about it. A lie reverses your energy, half of it, and makes one part fight against the other. It is the liars who break themselves apart into little pieces, small conflicts unresolved. Everyone retreats into a material world of encyclopedic answers, so that they can appear knowledgeable and appear useful for the sake of comfort. But you see, **the truth is always beyond your ability to be comfortable with it**. So if you seek comfort in the world, be sure you will not know what the truth is.

It is the *deep* questioners that have only one conflict... between what they know and what they don't. That is not the same conflict as what you *think* you know and what you don't. Pretending to know is what built the ego's tall tree. And in your mind, you climb that tall tree and pretend to see the truth that is so far from your eyes. I think two doodle bugs in the sand are more honest than most modern people.

You all have so many comforts that your one goal in life is to stay "happy." Your schools have burned you out with lies so much that you aren't even interested in learning anymore. You just want to, "be happy." In fact, you want to be so happy, you don't even see anyone else's pain or confusion or sickness or mental illness. You don't even look at death at all, in any form. Sure, you go to movies and see people get chopped up, but that's not the death I'm talking about. You see, the body's irrelevant and you know it.

You look at that fantasy of torture and you see scary images, maybe of the devil–because you were taught there was one–and you try to shut that out of your mind because you think those images are real, because they evoke sensations and feelings in your body, your emotional body... mental images made in fantasy.

So, what's real? Physical body? Emotional body? Mental body? Or Spiritual embodiment? Is there an opposite to God? Is there a devil?

In our time, Spirits who used their energy for good, we called Deities, Helpers, Guides, whatever. But spirits or people who used their energy for harm, we called witches or devils because nothing good ever came from anything they did or said or thought.

So it is with your society. You, too, have made a positive God and a negative god. So there is another split from the wholeness of what you are into a negative and a positive self.

Then, once again, you confuse yourselves. You say female is negative in her energy because she is receptive in her physical self. You say man is positive in his energy because he is outgoing in his physical self. So you call male, positive, and you call female, negative. I tell you, you do a great disservice to each other.

Energy works this way. Any energy given by any living thing will be returned to the sender, whether it's positive or negative. You see, all your decisions and thoughts are images that give or take energy. So the law of giving is a cycle that dictates that you receive what you give. And if you take and do not give, the law of taking dictates that you will never feel as if you got anything. Therefore, these laws dictate to you what your experiences in the world will be and what you have decided about the entire concept of creation and the Mind that created it.

Your difficulty is, you haven't been able to determine what is illusion and what is truth, from what love is and what fear projects. So the decisions you make about things, positive or negative, are meaningless because your decisions cannot discern what the truth is. **You cannot decide truth. It already is.** Your taking on of judgment, this active taking of a stance, prevents you from remembering what the whole truth is. And those who claim to know it and are strident and well convicted, often are the most deluded. So the modern world makes a god out of pretense, and they are positive they are right. And you call them leaders.

The truth is you don't know what love is. You don't know what death is. You don't know what the Source of Creation is. For human beings to be so strident about how one should live or behave is an attempt to make their world safe and comfortable. If you are seeing only the things that you must do for safety and comfort, they are your gods, not love. You may claim to do this in love's name, but I tell you, it's fear, not love.

You have made your society so complex because of your complex fears that you have forgotten why you are even here and what you are to learn by coming here. You have split your mind into so many rights and wrongs, goods and bads, positives and negatives, that the very thing you fear the most is what you worship... and that's death of the physical body.

Because you entertain the possibility that God doesn't love you since "He" made death a part of life, you believe God is not love and is not real. Therefore, while you are here, you think you can do anything you want to anyone... because you're just going to die anyway. I tell you, Love made no mistakes and death is not real. Fear is not real. I'll show you.

You love children, do you not? How hard is it to get a child to come home on a warm summer day or evening and abandon their play to come inside? I'm sure most adults get a big argument trying to get kids to come in. Plenty threats. Well, what if God was our adult, and we're still out here playing, being children, thinking we're adults, and we've been asked to come Home from our play and won't? Because we know in our hearts that God is love, we just keep playing... because we know we won't be punished... Love never punishes.

So you see, even as insane as we are, we know the truth. So on and on you play... infant gods playing... because Love doesn't punish. But what's the cost? When does patience become indulgence?

A child steals something, beats somebody up, hurts someone, and because long time ago in our memory, we heard that Voice say, "Love doesn't punish," we don't discipline our children... because we don't discipline ourselves. So we grow up to murder someone or rape someone or steal something big time and go to jail or just get killed in a fast car while being defiant and crazy. No, Love doesn't punish, though. But because we didn't discipline our children and teach them discernment, we had to experience our child's death. And now, here's God punishing us for not disciplining our children... we think.

We get angry because it's so hard to know what decisions to make in life about dealing with our children, dealing with our spouse, dealing with the world at large. We withdraw and we refuse to make any more decisions. This is good. This is a time in our lives that we are ripe to actually receive. That is the third part. Remember, the first part was *the thought,* the second was *the request,* the third is *the acceptance.* To accept means to allow replacement of what you hold instead of the truth. Yes? But if you value what needs to be replaced more than the truth, you will feel loss until you reach the fourth part which is *knowledge.*

We often have to lose something in order to determine its true value to us. And yet, because we now want to understand true value, God tells us we haven't lost anything real at all. So we think God is insane too. And yet, what are we to do? We realize the time of our playing is over, and we must make an accounting for our decisions, our choices. And we see that to not choose is delay and to choose in error is delay. And we see that there is but one choice and one choice only... to ask what the truth is for everyone, for all living beings, and to accept a whole concept of life. To do this, we must ask some source outside of ourselves, outside of the human form, for knowledge that is beyond form, and wait for the answer with an open mind and an open heart.

You find this path hard because there seems to be lots of noise and disturbances, both outside and inside. It occurs to you to ask Spirit, once again, to resolve all these difficulties so you can hear the answer, the truth. You no longer want to delay having knowledge until the very end when there are so many more obstacles to having it. It's harder to develop enough energy to break through the density of being in a human form when you're old and feeble and sick, when you've collected so many habits with so much weight that you're nearly crushed by it.

So you begin to hear a Voice, perhaps. You begin to have dreams, and sometimes the dreams will bring you experiences. And those experiences will become real in your psychological makeup, in your emotional body. Even though, perhaps they didn't happen on the physical realm, you can learn the same lessons from them without having to live through the actual physical experiences.

For instance, I helped my son learn in dreamtime that he is not the body, by taking him up into great flights into the air and dropping him on a stone floor below. Many times before, he would conclude he was going to die and would stop the dream or wake up. But on the final occasion, he accepted his apparent death and the possibility that only the body could perish, and he went through that floor into the rock and dirt below. He felt what it felt like to be all those materials... not dead, even coming up into a tree to know a tree's feelings, sensations, concept of self, and even its purpose.

Later, in another dream, he experienced the death of his youngest daughter through accident. This dream was given to him when he had been asked to give his children to God, just prior to going through a divorce. The dream brought the experience of grieving for a living child. It allowed his possessiveness of his daughter to die, without his love stopping for the living child. He found that his love for his children is what he gets to keep, not his imagined loss or fear for them.

It is Spirit that can separate love from fear. It is Spirit's job to do this and to prepare you for your return to Creator, as well as to help you have a good life while you're waiting... if you but ask. Why wait?

I tell you, the two, love and fear cannot touch each other in any way. Even light and darkness are more closely associated with each other than love and fear. There are many varying shades of lightness and darkness and all colors in between, because they are not opposites like love and fear. Colors have the same perceptive quality, eyes open, eyes closed. Like the illusion of total darkness, fear seems to go on with eyes open or eyes closed. But the huge bubble of love, I tell you, encircles the tiny concept of fear, a tiny bubble within love, eyes open, eyes closed. You see, you make gods according to your fears first, before you develop will to have God exist according to God's plan, not your fears.

So we have talked about the two thought systems, love and fear. Because they begin in *Fire,* they're resolved and worked out and made seen in *Earth.* They are cleansed and washed away in *Water.* And in *Air* is the known truth made available to you. And it is the truth that rekindles the fire and completes the Sacred Circle of Creation.

Chapter 6
Life in the Balance

Too often we are quick to judge, quick to anger, quick to defend, quick to attack. And we do this to confuse everyone else, so they will not see that we ourselves are afraid and confused. This is not honest. So I will attempt to unconfuse you. I'll begin by telling you what happens with energy.

A baby is conceived and the energy to animate it enters sometime before birth through the crown chakra. There's much discussion about when an embryo is considered alive, but I will not enter this discussion, as there is great variability as to when a spirit enters a body. Suffice it to say, life is always alive, regardless of whether the form is tiny or huge, and regardless of whether an embryo survives in form or not.

This spiritual energy that enters an embryo, enlivens the form and makes it ready to live on its own outside the womb. As this energy enters the form, it enlivens all of the organs from the brain downward, through the spine and into all of the other energy centers which feed all of the organs, then returns to the brain to complete the circle of sensation. These energy centers also receive psychic energy from all those around, as well as from the environment itself. All of this information is returned to the brain for the mind to sort and interpret.

What a relatively mature human will experience about this energy is that the emotional life evolves from the various sensations evoked from thought and action, both inside itself and from outside. What will be memorable in all this is, thought projected outward produces a downward flow of energy, down the front of the person. The emotional challenges a person encounters, therefore, is to take this downward flow of energy that modern life engenders and find some way to reverse its flow up the spine, to find true joy in such a chaotic environment.

An example of sensation as energy is as simple as feeling your swallowing of food going downward until waste is finally released. Colic, for example, is the uncomfortable sensation of digesting food going through a sensitive colon. This, as anyone knows, makes for a grumpy child.

You see, the sensitive colon is a second chakra problem with the child receiving projected negativity from the world around which affects its digestion and disposition. Most young children, still at the height of play and discovery, aren't the least bit concerned with this downward movement, except that it is a delay in getting back to play and discovery... a minor inconvenience. Adults have lost the thrill of discovery and fail to rise to play, so are more concerned and stuck in the downward journey than children. This can be proven easily by a simple exercise.

I would like you to draw a line at the center of a piece of paper from left to right, then draw another line down the center of the paper from top to bottom. You will find there are two spaces in the below, two spaces in the above, two spaces in the right and two spaces in the left. Let's say your spine is the vertical line, your balance point. At the bottom where the vertical line touches the bottom of the paper is where the fire in the below is located, the Mother's root fire, your first chakra. The front of that chakra corresponds to your pubic area. The rear of that chakra corresponds to your tailbone.

Above that fire and to the left, we'll call the front. So picture yourself facing left. The first energy center at the root fire is about sexuality, the compulsion to breed. The second energy center above the first is about survival in the material world. This corresponds to your intestinal area and, for female, also includes the womb.

So now, on the left, the front side of these two chakras in the below, write all the negative emotions that humans have and project outward. Now look to the behind in the below, on the right. What single emotion do you think it would take to change all of those negative emotions in the front side of the below... to have them healed? Do you know?

Face your fears. Find out. By consciously following your energy as it goes downward, as it goes through the first chakra, through the Mother's purifying red fire in the below, through that root fire and comes up the spine, you can be shown what emotion is real and not based upon fear. This back side or rearward journey up the spine through the energy centers is the process of transformation from the lower emotions of the body, back to the creative blue fire of the Father.

Ultimately, you should be able to cycle all of your energy through all of the chakras, from the blue fire of your first enlivenment, down through all of the illusory emotions of physical experience, to the root fire of the body life you borrowed from the Mother, then back up the spine, and through an act of will, redeem all of human thought, then return your energy back to the Light from which you came. This is the Sacred Circle of Life.

There you have it, all at once, but I will continue with some details to help you along. The third energy center is located where the center lines intersect on your drawing. This center, encompassing your solar plexus, is your power center where your will resides. Your ideas of power and your use of will depends upon whether or not you project your energy outward from the front or are guided by Spirit from the back.

The fourth energy center is your heart, your mind's feelings. Projected outward is a life lost in the softness of one's concept of what they think love should be, without an anchor point anywhere. It's like a life with too much ice cream, too much honey, very sticky, and doomed to rot in the lower chakras. This truly is a defense and retreat to a world less hostile, yet hides the most hostile feelings anyone can feel. A heart that has been delivered through the fires of truth into the light of expanded love becomes a beacon of leadership to those in need. This is God's goal for us all.

The fifth energy center is your throat, your speech. And truly, this should be obvious to all of us, since now we are living in the fifth world where our words manifest what we intend... love or fear, healing or destruction.

The sixth energy center, encompassing your pineal gland, is your inner vision, your mind's eye. And to the degree you prefer your body's eyes, you will never develop spiritual vision. Notice the frequency with which your television is describing to you extrasensory perception and spiritual vision in your society. It is not a new phenomena but only a new interest in an original capability of an open-minded human. Until you can be led in inner vision, you cannot heal all of the perceptions that prevent you from having an open heart and an open seventh chakra, the crown.

251

Now, above the will center, on the front side or left of your paper, please continue to write all of the emotions and thoughts that can be projected onto the world. Do this with power, feelings, words, and with perception, all the way up the chakras. If you missed any emotions that have to do with will in the below, write them down too.

In the above, on the right side of your paper, list what emotions you might have if your will was to be joined to the Mother, then to the Father, then to Creator, energy rising up the back. Recognize that if your energy is in front, it will always go downward, unless, of course, you are pretending you are above all this or are trying to turn it around by yourself, without first going through the purification of the Mother's fire in the first chakra. Pretending takes your feet off the ground, off the Mother, so your energy rises up the front of your body to the top front of your head... thinking and pretending your life... frontal lobes, you know. Occipital lobes, you don't. Ancient memory. Remember?

You can't get to the Mother without first going downward, clear down to your feet. You can't get to the Father without first coming back up and going through the Mother's fire in the first chakra. How long you sit in Her fires of purification is up to Her. Only then will She guide you back up the back, up the spine to the Father Who waits for the Mother at the crown chakra, the center top of your head.

In and above the crown chakra, represented at the very top of the line on your paper, is the blue fire. It is this blue fire that transforms you. And, together, the Mother and the Father, joined, take you, purified and joined, to your Creator, the Source of what you are... love.

What does it take to undergo transformation from all our fears and negative thoughts, from all our feelings, judgments and projections onto the world and those around us? What simple act delivers us from fear to love, to truth, to seeing, and to experiencing our union with all of creation?

Forgiveness.

If all those negative emotions on the front side, all those questionable actions in the world were to be delivered to the blue fire from your will center in front, down to the Mother's fire, then back to your tailbone and up to the top of your crown, what would you experience at that blue fire? What emotion?

Joy.

What prevents any of us from offering forgiveness to everyone, including ourselves, and experiencing joy?

Damned if I know.

252

You figure it. I think people would rather have life act upon them, rather than take responsibility for acting within it. You suppose everyone's waiting for the Second Coming, rather than becoming the next second?

*

Be deeply honest with this exercise. It is designed to show you that at any moment you could decide not to be the negative emotion you might be feeling, first by letting your energy drain beyond your feet, by giving all your confusion to the Mother, to the earth. You deliver everything you are feeling in your front side–lust, shame, anger, greed, guilt, fears of any kind, you name it–through an act of willingness, to the Mother for Her to cleanse. Allow Spirit to help you. It will be done. Withhold nothing. By thanking Her for helping, the negative emotions are transformed into the energy of gratitude. Gratitude will move back up your spine from the earth, through your tailbone, up to your will center in the back. Sing a heartfelt song, using your will to deliver yourself to Spirit, and you will find out what will is really for. Try it.

In the below, you need your own forgiveness of yourself to transmute negative energy into humility, into compassion and into understanding. Willingness to forgive is what opens the trap door to deeper experience, to deeper understanding, to change. Forgiveness pulls back what you have expressed onto the world. And, by an act of will, combined with your new humility, compassion and understanding, you are delivered to Spirit via your backbone, drawing in energy through your heart center, throat center, vision center, and finally your crown where you are released into the purity of joy once again. And your thanks of gratitude for each step in the process returns to you the energy that you expended for your willingness. Your gratitude to the Mother brings energy into your feet and up to the heart. In your heart is where the Mother waits for the Father, in love. The gratitude to the Father brings energy into your head and into your chest. You join Them there, in love. Each time you do this, each time you the beloved child join Them together, you feel the love of the Mother and the heartfelt gratitude of the Father. He misses Her... She misses Him. And you are empty and filled like this at any moment that you choose. If you never try it, you will never feel it, never know it, never benefit from it. If you prefer to live your life in defiance of love and truth, being your own god and guide, then your ego is the problem you own. Indulging in it is not your solution.

Men have big egos and are approved to use them in the world, the modern world. In our times, a hunting party with big egos

253

was a dangerous affair. If we didn't work together and communicate honestly, someone could get hurt or killed, or the whole party could be lost. So do not be afraid of sharing your innermost thoughts and feelings with another, not of course as a verbal addiction but in all honesty, for if there is anything ego can't stand, it's honesty.

The only reason these negative emotions remain in place is that they are not brought up and made public enough to find out what the true error is that made us have them in the first place. It is only the private mind of ego that makes us feel guilty and alone, because we think we are the source of this negativity and fear. It is in revealing that Help comes. So risk being judged, but please, risk.

It was our communication with each other and with Spirit that kept us alive. And I tell you, this connection to Spirit will change the world you live in too. Do not hide behind closed doors. Your fear of the world that you made is getting acute, and you are passing this fear onto your children. Pretty soon it will be hard to tell whether you are the guard or the prisoner.

I say again, it is the Spirit of the Earth Mother and your need of gratitude for Her that will heal you of your fears. Step outside and face them. Understand what impulses you have inside of you, so that you may choose the ones you would keep, the ones that are life-giving. Face the ones that are not. Face your devils and decide what you would worship, creation or fear of destruction.

Too many of you have decided that life is not worth living, at least not without a lot of meaningless distraction. That is because you have not chosen the most honest path. Everyone was meant to have it all, the whole truth. And you would have it, except that you deny you want it. Busy, busy, busy... the world is very busy indeed. How long will you delay your quest for true knowledge? How long will you be satisfied with temporal facts and skills that only serve you until you are old and no longer have the energy to awaken? What would you teach your children and grandchildren about what the world is for and why we are here and what they are with you?

I'd like for you to make your lives very simple. It's easy to do. Just recognize in your mind which thoughts bring peace and which thoughts bring conflict. Don't bother to look at anyone else's mind. Focus on your own. If you would choose peace, then the actions and words and behavior of everyone around you will begin to change.

The two thought systems of the human mind, again, are this: love and fear. Since you are a part of creation, you naturally hold within you a spark of the blue flame and a spark of the red flame.

254

The blue and the red flame are essentially related but serve two different functions. We'll call the blue flame, the Reason for Life, the essence or Spirit of Reason. We'll call this red flame, the Physical Accomplishment of Spiritual Will... the Word made flesh. We'll say the red flame is the blood, the bone marrow and the womb. Therefore, it is natural that a male who has no womb would have less connection to this red fire, so would fear the downward journey more than a female. It is this fire of the body that we mistakenly fear, even more than we mistakenly fear the very blue spark that is our spirit.

It is good to note that without the love of the Mother to provide the materials of physical life, the spark from the Father would have no experience of itself at all. To call God male, I think, does a huge disservice to God the female. It is this distinction that Christianity has not fully resolved that makes males more warring than loving.

Note that a male cannot even enter physical existence without the willingness of a female. And you must also note that a male cannot return to the blue flame without going through purification by the red flame. Better said, **no man gets to God without the aid of a woman.** If man persists in fearing the power of womankind, he will persist in the path of destruction. If man is willing to acknowledge the destruction wrought by his quest for power and knowledge outside of love, he then may be forgiven and return to the only circle which has purpose... the Sacred Circle of Life. By returning to woman the power that love is, man is returning to himself his usefulness as a communicator of truth. Be sure love will feel the error in untruth, though human love may not always be able to speak what is truth. What is important is that you see each other's value and depend upon it, for the whole depends upon the halves.

As you can see, it is in overcoming all that the ego says you are or aren't that you become aware of what you truly are. Since the second thought system of fear is not reasoning at all, it can be overcome and changed. You see, fear has no logic and truly understands nothing.

Because the ego as the body can die, we must all face our fear of death, our fear of God, our fear of godlessness. Any thought of the body produces a vibration called fear. So when you take a body, you take on this returning to love through fear. The two thought systems, Spirit (the quiet Voice for God), and ego (the loud voice of fear), are totally opposite and do not mingle in any way, other than to be opposed to each other at every turn. The truth is, even the red flame is Creator's. The Mother's red flame is the Physical Completion of the Intent of Creator to provide a physical reality for creation to learn in. All fear, then, is illusion, and therefore not really a true thought system, being not true at all. Ego doesn't really think at all.

The fear bubble within an all-encompassing love bubble is your human mind in the balance between two thoughts, one real, one not. It is your separate self, male or female, separate from Creator, that has to catch up to the truth. This balance point, this fulcrum on which our neutral mind stands, is where we all learn. The goal is to expand to the larger bubble and see fear for what it is.

I think a human being can make only one error, and that is to shift from the neutral point where Spirit is present and take a stance, alone, without Spirit. It is when this shift is made that learning stops.

Contemplation includes Spirit. Introspection does not. So introspection on a higher or lower level, being alone, is not direct experience translatable into knowledge, and therefore is not learning at all. Introspection is an art and tool of the ego, and perception is its main function. Perception is based upon an individual point of view, looking at a single idea, then shifting points of view all around the idea in order to get an understanding of it from all directions, outside the idea. The flaw in perception is that there is no foundation point or joining in love from which to *experience* the idea from within it, so it cannot lead to truth. Ego, then, is a device for judgment, deciding what is true based upon external perception, apart from any real experience and from any ever-changing point of view.

Our errors, then, are the judgments that we make about this world and about the living things in it, especially about each other. Because perception has no foundation in truth, no part of it is true. So how do you shift from perception? It is a good question.

First, you must return to your neutral point, in between the conflict called love and fear. To do this, you must realize all of your self-concepts and your world concepts are based on fear. You must also realize that you are not the sensations that you feel. You must recognize that you are not a sexual being, and that the sensations may be happening to you as a *test,* and do not come from you at all. To recognize this by yourself would take many, many years, but it can be done. It is better to ask Spirit to help you learn discernment about all of these sensations and emotions. Takes less time. Goes faster.

People that have a negative view of life have that negative view because they have taken a position. They have made judgments. So, to change your world view, you must allow your judgments to be reviewed. This takes contemplation on a deep level, from a neutral point with Spirit.

Most people, however, are habitual and have practiced their ideas, their decisions, their judgments so long, they have forgotten where in the mind they are even stored. Some decisions are so old, they are stored in the bone marrow.

For instance, anger generally is stored in the intestines. It's a recent thing and is kept active in that place. Rage, however, is a much deeper, older phenomena and is stored in the marrow. Bone tired. So how do you recover something you decided twenty-years ago, thirty-years ago, forty-years ago, even from the beginning of time... ancient memory?

Well, there is a fast way and a slow way. The fast way, I will speak about later. The slow way, I see, is to dedicate at least four hours sometime during the week to a long walk at a very slow rate, perhaps by the ocean, perhaps in the country. It does not matter. Since your modern world isn't geared to having such long time blocks given to you, you must learn to take those opportunities for yourself. On these walks, you will pray to Spirit and ask Them to help you in the undoing of the effects of your thoughts and decisions and behaviors and judgments. As these things are brought up to consciousness, they are undone, and you will experience new freedom and spaciousness in your mind, new health in your body. You will learn how to forgive yourself and others for what was thought. And in doing so, you forgive the world what it thought. And by such a process, you are released from judgment and its effects... fear, conflict, guilt, and disease.

At some point in this repair process, you will eventually come to the realization that you don't know what love is at all. It is much bigger than you imagined. And it is at this point, your mind opens to seeing the lessons that love would have you learn. You will begin to see a world where people help each other, instead of a world view of selfishness, strife and sickness.

It is from the balanced center point, between willfulness and willingness, that I will speak to you for the rest of this book. I will speak to you of these two minds, love and fear. Because you all have an idea of what you think love is, I'm going to begin with fear.

When children have a bad dream in the night, they run to their parents and ask to be comforted. I'd say, half of you bring your children into your bed and half of you do not. Now, there's an interesting decision. What's the right thing to do? Here's a child in fear, and some believe that loving the child will dismiss the nightmare, so they snuggle them up in their bed. And there are those who think that will make them weak, so they put the child back into their own bed and discipline them. They tell them, "It's not real. Don't worry about it. Go to sleep." Now, the person that snuggles the child through this nightmare says the same thing. Do they make their child weak by putting them in the bed with them? Is the child who is left in his own nightmare stronger for it? Interesting questions.

If the nightmare is not real, then why is the child afraid? Because a child watches a murder on television, then has dreams of being chased all night, is his fear less than a person actually being chased? Or is the vivid dream of injury or death more fearful than actually facing your own injury or death? Is the dream world less real than the physical world you play your dreams out in? What are you running from? What are you defending against?

So what is it about fear that we run from, that we seek solace from, or that we seek strength against? Now, you can say, people on the street in Los Angeles are in fear because they get shot at. Well, they get shot at all over the world. Everyone's still shooting at each other, either actually or in their own minds in fantasy. Is the fear you feel in L. A. the tension? Is the aggression the cause or the effect? Is one kind of fear different from any other?

The only difference between a skydiver and a person who will not skydive is that he jumped. He faced his fear. But he took lessons from people who had already done it. Somebody had to be the first skydiver. Somebody had to be the first astronaut. Somebody had to be the first person to jump on the back of a horse and try to ride it.

I tell you, all fear is the same. It is simply the energy of conflict. And you say, "That skydiver, he's a brave man. He's fearless." Oh, I don't think so, but he's already proven to himself, perhaps, that fear is just the energy of not making a decision. Once you make it, well, that's it. You jumped already. Deal with it.

Some guy hung onto the back of a horse long enough for it to wear itself out, until it decided not to buck off that fool riding. And once that horse was subdued, then perhaps that person and that horse had a friendship which developed. Once the horse realized it wasn't being eaten or attacked, perhaps it decided this idiot on its back didn't weigh that much anyway, and when the horse got pooped out, it just decided to leave him there. Tricky. Took a lot of guts to do that, to tame a horse. Took somebody who was willing to get past their fear of being kicked to pieces or bit to pieces, and it changed the face of the world... riding horses, using oxen to pull plows.

So always, we are faced with big and little fears, conflicts. Where does conflict come from? Two opposing ideas: I'm gonna' do it–no, I'm not gonna' do it. I'll be successful–no, I won't be successful. I'll get out with my hide or I won't. Always it has to do with confusion of purpose. And almost all human thought has to do with justifying or resolving conflict, in an attempt to get back to balance, to feel good about themselves.

I'd have to say that the ultimate challenge to a human being has to be facing their change from an alliance with body to an alliance with Spirit. All male acts of bravery on the physical level are really leading him up to facing Creator. All life's lessons are to bring us to this point of balance before the Creator. That is why some feel the pressure of guilt, and others feel the pressure of striving. It is an attempt to tip the balance and keep the lessons coming. In this way, Spirit helps you face Creator.

If a thief spends a lifetime in deep thievery, why didn't Spirit shift the balance the other direction, you ask? And I will tell you. It is *your will.* We will not take it from you. We cannot take it from you. Creator gave it to you. It's free. If you go down so far that you have not the will to return, then without asking for help from Spirit, you will not return. However, your will, as poor as it may seem, when joined to Spirit has the Creator's will joined to it. Until you are ready to accept the full journey, you will not be rescued. It is you teaching yourself the limits of your life apart from Life.

Some people believe in reincarnation, that it takes many lives to reach balance. Some people even think they remember their lives. If it served a purpose, you would remember them, all of them... if you had any others. Because the human mind has within it the ability to create its own idea of reality by using the mechanism of perception, it must go through cycles of shedding in order to get another mind, perhaps more useful. We'll call them rebirths. You don't remember other lives because the mind you used to think them with is not spirit.

People who have a difficult time facing their death, do so because they've never used the part of their mind that is spirit. Their eyes and their senses all tell them that they are the body. And it is only at the time of death or near death, or anyone else's death or near death close to them, that they begin to ponder what they are at all. Otherwise, they run around with ideas and self-concepts like, "I'm a baker. I'm a stockbroker. I'm a housewife. I rear children. I make money. I look good." Always in it is someone trying to be the best... best of whatever. Where's the balance in it?

It was much simpler in my day. Our occupations were food gatherer or ceremonial leader or storyteller, healer or warrior. Everybody sang.

Nowadays, you've got occupations I can't even conceive of... assistant secretary to the secretary of defense of the whatever of the country of the best. We didn't know best. We didn't think in terms of varying degrees of having or not having. We had abundant years and we had slim years. And still, everybody sang. In our songs, we balanced our lives.

You have given up your relationship with the earth and have lost your sense of abundance. And very few sing songs of gratitude. Abundance to you is the grocery store, assuming you have money to buy groceries. And your sense of abundance can change as to whether you're employed or not. You can even lose your homes if you're not employed. The whole earth was our home, so our gratitude never changed.

It is a fact that the seasons come and go, and that for the Mother to continually replenish Herself and provide you what you need to live on, She must go through seasons. So there are hard places to live and there are easy places to live. My brothers who chose the desert did so because they weren't so attached to water. My brothers who chose the north weren't so attached to warmth. My brothers who chose the south weren't so attached to low humidity. But now, everyone's attached to everything. You've got to have endless water, air conditioning and central heating, with a seventy-degree house in the winter and a sixty-degree house in the summer.

I'll tell you what the cost of that is, though. Something has to run your energy systems, yes? And you use so much energy that the resources required to run those energy systems are taken from all over the world. You've taken so much by so much deception, people don't trust you anymore. You're greedy. You're comfortable. You're rich. And now, others believe they are poor and uncomfortable. It has created a very great imbalance in places of the earth and in the peoples that inhabit these places. The only ones that haven't forgotten what true balance is are being wiped off the face of the earth, so you can get the raw resources you think you need.

So fear, it's a funny thing. Face it now or face it later. We were lucky. We had to face our mortality every day, every winter. You, you only face mortality when the money runs out. I know many of you, your greatest fear now, instead of it being nuclear war, it's being a homeless drifter, a bag lady. I tell you, the nuclear war is over and you've lost. It's already in your water. It's already in your air. It's already in your land. Cheap power, they called it. Humm, not so cheap.

In your deepest fears, you cry out for God to save you. In your deepest terrors, you are afraid of God and blame the imbalance in the world on It, the Creator. Why aren't the destroyers being stopped, you ask? Where's God?

I'll break it down for you, so you can understand what is taking place on the earth now. The Whole of Creation Is One Bubble, Unlimited. And within this Creation Bubble is a smaller bubble, your universe, limited. And within this limited universe bubble, you have another bubble called a galaxy. Within it is a sun with planets spinning around, one called earth. This earth itself is yet another smaller bubble. Each person, each creature, each living thing on the earth, each inorganic and organic thing on the earth is within one collective bubble called life... as you know it. Within that one collective bubble are yet smaller bubbles. All sparrows are in one small bubble. All horses are in one small bubble. All dogs are in one small bubble. All human beings are in one small bubble. All pine trees are in one small bubble. All cedar trees are in one small bubble. All buffalo grass is in one small bubble. All sandstone is in one small bubble. Each bubble is a smaller collective consciousness, all within another larger collective bubble, expanding to the Whole. Each of the smallest bubbles can pierce their own bubble to expand their consciousness, even to the largest bubble.

Human beings seem a little different. They are all in one collective bubble, human. And yet, because they believe almost entirely only what their eyes see, they form a separate bubble around their separated consciousness called ego self. Modern humans seem to prefer their illusory, separate identity to the collective truth. This makes them feel afraid and alone.

The fact that one bird does not separate from any other bird in its species creates perfect communication between a flock of birds. No eagle flying is unconnected to any other eagle flying. No dolphin in the ocean has a mind separate from any other dolphin.

Any of the major languages of the world have many different dialects... the same language, yet expressed uniquely in many ways, often unintelligible to each other. The English language (American style) has only been around on this continent, the U.S.A., for a little over three-hundred years, so it only has a few main dialects recognized. Some people have tried to identify all the nuances of expression. For example, some call one part of New York speech separate from another. And to some degree, this is valid. Left to itself, it would continue and perhaps grow in separation.

The original purpose of language was to create a common form of communication, a common understanding, a common knowledge, a common joining to create balance. And yet, when we speak to each other, are we trying to join by recognizing each other's intent and overlooking our differences, or are we trying to encourage separateness by pointing out our differences, our so-called uniquenesses?

It is the separation you feel from the people around you, from their judgments on you that also cause you fear. Watch any child in a school yard become upset or angry when they're rejected by another school mate. They got their feelings hurt. Somebody said, "You're fat. Your hair's weird. Your skin looks dirty. You're all brown." Or somebody said, "You're Indian. You worship the devil."

It is that you justify your turning to use their judgment against them in your own defense, that makes you just like them. And so it goes. What was the thought of separation now becomes deep conflict. And with your joining in the error, it becomes the demonstration of separation, the belief in differentness.

That we do not seek to join in our humanness creates separation and fear. Anger, hatred, any violence of the mind is created out of fear, out of judgment, out of unresolved conflict, out of a simple misunderstanding about what you are.

I'll tell you how murder happens. I'll tell you how rape happens... from a simple misunderstanding. A male who is terribly afraid of approaching a female, because of the pressures of puberty, because of the belief about love being in the body, may fear rejection. And because the energy of fear doesn't feel like love to the woman, to the girl being approached, she probably will reject his approach, and he may turn to violence as a form of inadequate communication. The nervousness, the anxiety of having to approach the subject of sexuality directly, creates the energy of rejection. So now you have a young person in puberty who has been rejected, is hurt and is angry, and yet terribly fearful of doing anything positive about it. A positive solution would be trying again, perhaps this time being more relaxed about it, taking another chance, and not putting so much pressure behind it.

All deviant urges are born out of a fear of facing the very same thing that you're attracted to. It's a very deep conflict. Conflict left unresolved creates a form of insanity, a personality that is split in half and will flip from one side, the side of wanting, to the other side, the side of wanting to kill the desire to want.

A person who desires money and doesn't have it will eventually, if left to their own devices, steal it, either by learning how to do it almost legally or by literally robbing someone. The shyest form of a thief is a burglar who sneaks in the night. The most dangerous thief is a very well-educated one that uses what was meant to be a benign system for his own benefit and robs thousands and millions at a time, coldly.

There is a mechanism at play in this world that is a function of the creative energy of the earth itself. It was planned this way by Creator and Spirit eons ago... that there should be a reflection of the energy of collective thought. All thoughts are reflected and have consequences for each being responsible for adding to or detracting from that collective thought.

For example, give love and you receive it. Project anger and it is returned. Lie and you are caught in the web of deception. Seek honesty and meet the conditions of truth, and you will be freed from this web.

So the only way to get to the truth is to follow the path of yielding love, for love to show you correction to help you find your neutral point. Your neutral point is the balance point within your center, your True Self.

This is Spirit's job. Without this correction, you could no longer even perceive the path necessary to get to the truth. You have developed a mind called ego which is separate from all other minds, which has its own plan, its own identity and its own energy to run it. And you have given it your allegiance and lost your will for anything but what it dictates to you. If there were not limits and consequences to this deviant behavior, it would go on until the end of the earth. It would consume the earth along with itself.

So the mechanism is very simple. It is that each deviant thought the mind can conceive of can only have but one outcome, and that is fear and the destruction of physical form. Each thought Spirit hands you in correction is a surefire, easy or hard way of returning to the path of love.

Now, you say, love is a physical path. No, I say, love is the connective tissue that constructs the existence of a bubble. It is the conduit within and the connection to all other bubbles. It is, as you would say, the very air with which it expands itself within life. Love is the purified mind of all human beings joined to all living things. Love is the only Source of true creative energy. And you should see by now, all energies are definitely enjoined in the dance called life, whether you know it or not.

This may be difficult for you to understand because you are looking, perhaps, with your limited perception. And yet, it is Spirit that has come to this earth in this time to help widen your perspective, to show you that the mind that can fear is not the true mind. The mind of ego was invented from the body. It is only because you prefer the five senses of this ego mind to guide you that you do not know that Spirit is already here guiding you.

Within this core of the earth is a fire brought on by tremendous pressures from what you call gravity. I'll not call it gravity. I call it, the within. The earth does not burn like the sun, and yet the fires are the same. They are from different forces, but they are the same. On the earth, this fire is caused from the pressures of rock and minerals and core material that vibrate and liberate a certain energy. Many of you fear these lower vibrations, this core fire under great pressure. Because you do not understand this energy that is basic to life, it causes you confusion.

I tell you, the lowest energy known to mankind that can be felt isn't fear. It's the earth, the Mother. **You only fear your fear.** You fear your lack of understanding. You fear your misperceptions. Most of all, in your ignorance, you fear not knowing. Ultimately, all you fear is God. You fear Creator. Because It created you, It must be very powerful indeed. So you think It has the power to destroy you, and you "know" that's true because everybody dies. Go ahead. Fight death. Have a good try. By fighting in life, you are trying to face your own fear of death.

I'm long dead, and it's because I'm not really dead at all that I can describe what you'll go through. So you want to know what death is, I'll tell you. You won't find it any easier, but I'll tell you. Dead is the separation between truth and illusion. It's the end of the game of learning you are spirit in the illusion of a physical life. Those who have not begun to see what the truth is before they "die" will surely think they are going to hell and will be fearful. So, if there is a hell, it is only fear. And if there is a heaven, it is release from fear, from all fear, any fear, from any doubt whatsoever. It is absolute perfect certainty. You say, certainty of what? And I say, certainty of what you are.

So it is with us, in our time, in our camp, faced with our vision of death. We are more acutely aware of Spirit working to help us to stay in balance while we are dealing with this vision, this vision of change.

In the Hopi camp, we were given a glimpse of the world as it would change and the way it would change native peoples. We were shown it was only through the connection with Spirit that native peoples would survive to this day.

Interesting, native peoples in balance don't have any trouble embracing the truths of what Jesus taught. But Christians seem to have great difficulty accepting the old teachings of native peoples about Spirit and the earth that they shared.

Today, there is a resurgence of the honoring of the Mother, of the planet you live on, of the interrelatedness of all living things. And with that resurgence of interest and respect for the Mother which gives physical life, comes the teachings of native ceremonies. These ceremonies were developed over the centuries by the natives to awaken their people to Spirit. The only way to awakening for anyone is to remove the grip that the small identity of ego self has over your whole mind. It was fear that made your mind small, and it is in facing your fears through ceremony that your mind can become large again.

Fasts are designed to challenge your mind about what it thinks it needs. Vision Quests are fasts requiring physical endurance and focus of mind. The challenge to any aspirant is to first understand the forces at play within themselves. Once these forces are seen, then one can begin to understand the aspects of mind that are controlling and are born of fear, versus the aspects of mind that are liberating and are born of love.

In your modern society, the central theme is the externalized battle between good and evil. But I tell you, it's all happening in your own minds, daily, every moment. Were you to confront your own mind, you would not have to play these thoughts out on the world. By seeing good and evil as outside in the world, you project your thoughts outward, rather than confront them within yourselves. This, your mind, is the battleground. This, your mind, is the fertile field to plow. Nothing internal can ever be fixed from the outside. **That you seek permanent respite from the relentless mechanism of your ego mind is the only work there is. Everything else is a distraction.**

Now you say to me, the world is in automatic. No one can do a thing about it. And I say to you, it is that way because you would have it be that way. Your mind, you feel, is in automatic and you bless it. You think by your approval of it, it will not harm you. That you appear to lead a righteous life and hide from the devil is what gives it power over you. That you do nothing with your will to understand your own mind makes you helpless.

You come home from a hard day at the office and have a drink. The office is artificial. It is one tiny aspect of the whole soup. And I know, even you at the office have your mind open, working on the larger issues anyway. But devoting direct time and effort... you almost never do it.

Those who study the Bible and exclude other religions, other views of creation, those who cling to a single source or a single idea or a single doctrine, do so out of fear. I think creation is bigger than all of it. But because of the immenseness of creation, you feel like you're drowning in an ocean of knowledge or experience, and you grab some single point for your anchor to try to achieve a balance. That's fine. Call yourself white and go to one church. That's your anchor point. Fine. But leave your mind open and learn everything there is to be learned in this world about its beliefs, about its desire to know its Source. Do not exclude *any* human viewpoint, and you will find, though the sounds and colors differ, the conclusion reached by each and every religious faction on the planet is in essence the same.

Now, some may break down the Absolute Creator into aspects called deities or gods, but you'll find that that religion does not teach you to look at one aspect only and call that the One God. Because we are simple creatures, religion may offer us one bite at a time. Any religion's foundation will ultimately be some aspect of love. So it is love we turn to for understanding, not fear. And yet, for love to be known at all, we often cling to its aspects, its results, its feelings or sensations.

To get out of the small mind concerned only with its physical or emotional well-being is a great challenge, but it is the only work there is. So I will help you on your way, face your fears, face your illusions.

What is illusion, you ask? Easy. Everything you see with your eyes or feel with your fingers or smell with your nose or hear with your ears or taste with your tongue. Physical life is a device to awaken you slowly, gently, to the truth, from being asleep within love, to being awake within love, within God.

The new world you aspire to is here too... if you are tired of this one. And the knowledge of what you are afraid of is what you must have in order to achieve the shift from this world to the next. Were you interested in helping anyone else, you would be learning this for yourself.

And so it is, those who are interested in facing their fears and getting to the truth by the path of love will find it. Those who are afraid to face their fear will not make the shift, as of yet. But they will surely reap the effects of having *not* chosen or chosen to delay.

The ultimate horror, you say, is the apocalypse, where everything is destroyed... Creator's way of saying, **"Enough!"** So whether it is true that God "seems" vengeful or not simply depends upon whether you face your limited self and become less limited now, or you save it up until it has to be done for you.

The atheist believes God isn't real. That's fine. It's a way of rebelling and being defiant and saying, "If God was real, He'd show up." Or, "If God is real, where's the proof?" Well, I don't think atheists are asking for God to show up. They'd rather be right. And yet, I wonder.

Now, you say, "How about the theory of evolution?" And I say, what evolves? I think there is less meaningful life on the earth now than there ever was. How is that evolution? Is creation more... or less? Did man come from apes? Were you animals before? Are you more highly evolved?

If you have not even faced death, how can you say you know what evolution is at all? If you still are afraid to even live, then how do you know what you are? Philosophy and psychology are for people who are studying what they think they are. Now, if you think you don't know anything and you get depressed, and you know you'll never know anything, that's still the ego telling you that you better not know anything because you might die... because true knowledge makes you shift out of your small mind into a large one.

By now, you're familiar with the psychic world as it's written in all the books, and maybe you've had a few experiences too. But what kind of perception is beyond your eyes and your ears? What you are afraid of is tapping into the abilities that you *could* have, if you gave up the ones you think you *already* have. If you have a vested interest in what you already have, you will probably never have more. If you turn your eyes from what you've learned to what you haven't, then you must give up what you *think* you've learned for what you *can* learn.

At this point, your worst fear is that you think you're gonna' go crazy. But I tell you, the mind that you're giving up is the one that's crazy, not the one that you're turning towards. Relax, you cannot go crazy, since you've already been.

The mind of the ego is so well defended by fears that you will think the only way out of this turmoil, out of these crazy pictures, out of these crazy images, out of these urges, is to blow your brains out. But it's pretty hard to get a new mind if you blow your brains away. There has to be something to work with, some mechanism to receive new information with while you're on the planet. Since you are not yet completed in your light body, you still need the physical brain in order to receive. Later you won't. To blow away your physical existence is to remove the chance to fix the mind you get to keep.

You see, your Spiritual Self, your light body is being created as you grow into it. It is a response to your desire to be Spirit that will have it be so. It is the function of the earth to teach you that there is no freedom in physical form. And without a completed mind, you can't know what freedom is, so you can't have it. So the earth is a place of trials, of tests, of challenges. And it is through these trials and tests and challenges that your mind begins to grow beyond itself, its reactions, its fears, and begins to seek for understanding. And it calls to itself the experiences that it needs to have that understanding.

It is a glorious journey, but do not be impatient. Do not be indulgent. Do not cling to the tall tree. And don't sink to believing or acting out the lowest urges. Find your neutral point, in balance. **Judge nothing.** By recognizing that discernment is not judgment, you will expand your awareness and learn what is truly helpful from what is not. Trust Spirit to help. When you have done that, your fears will diminish. And your need for some physical person to be with you as guru or guide will decrease. Your new sense of independence and your new understanding of what will is, will guide you on.

In your society, you need each other so much because you fill each other's emotional gaps, because you are *dependent*. In the Spiritual world, you are joined with all living things because you are *interdependent*... because you share the same mind and have no needs apart from that Single Mind. Communication in the One Mind is perfect. There are no misunderstandings. In this Light, you become *independent*.

Until you achieve this, you are part of the mechanism of awakening, and you will not escape it. Until you develop the energy and the desire to learn, you stay within the mechanism and are affected by it. This mechanism, I call the laws of the earth.

Now, Christian religion has divided creation up into God's world and the devil's world, heaven and hell. And it teaches that the earth is the domain of the devil for a time. But I tell you, the devil is nothing more than your collectivized fears and the physical urges to which all are subjected. It is the purpose of the earth to have your mind grow from its tiny, spiritual beginning... from the body where the memory of what you are is hidden in plain view, back into a Spiritual entity with full memory of the All of Creation.

The reason why the earth is so crowded is because everybody is so damn comfortable. Everybody is living to a ripe, old age, having gotten very clever... they think. But cleverness will not save you from what you need to learn. You delay. And because you delay, the earth grows old and polluted and tired. And species of creatures who were put here to help you awaken are choosing not to come back, once extinct.

Because of this delay, the earth grows warmer, more unpredictable. Water tables drop. Land subsides. Earthquakes shake. Volcanoes erupt. Weather patterns are disrupted. Cities are more violent. So you think apocalypse is beginning. Well, some thoughtful person long ago sat down and glimpsed far ahead and said, "If we continue living out of balance, these things are going to happen, I see." And so they are.

The demise of the earth is not too hard to imagine. There are no native cultures that don't have prophecy. Spirit's been around a long time. These things will happen as slowly or as fast as your awakening proceeds. The slower you awaken, the faster apocalypse arrives. The harder you work on yourselves toward your awakening, the slower the arrival of the apocalypse.

Since no one awakens alone, it is helpful to share your process of awakening. Those who are farthest along should return to the beginning to help those who are asking. So make books cheap and maybe somebody in the ghetto will buy one. Choose a larger picture of the world, and help those around you to choose it too. Give your books away to those that have true desire but no money. Sit with them and help them understand. Help them have the courage to have their own experience with Spirit. What you give, you get. Trust Spirit.

When you become afraid, your physical response is to grip down and resist. And I tell you, in order to have anything beneficial happen, you have to relax and trust to allow the changes to happen. If you ask Spirit for help, you must at least *allow* Them to help. If the difficulty is your perception of fear, then you have to allow that fear to come up, so you can perceive that fear differently. If you continually control, using resistance or denial, then your form will wear out sooner, and your chance to face your fears will be over sooner. **Left to the last, the process of dying is the release of the resistance to knowing what death is, to even knowing what life is.** You can't hold yourself in tension when you're dying. You cannot resist it. So why not stop and learn now, rather than later? Trust.

I'm having a hard time staying in your time because your world is so absurdly complex. Even though the issues always remain the same, there are few of you that are of like mind. Your interests and concerns are so different that it's hard to know where you are in your mind in order to join you. So this is Spirit's dilemma. How can we help you while you're in hiding? If you feel guilty for something you perceived as an error, which you call an "unpardonable sin," then how are we to get to where you are? If Spirit is real and where you are is illusion, then you must first make some effort to come to some real place where you can be met by Spirit. Illusion must be brought to truth to be corrected. Hollering to God out of fear will not bring you to the truth. Hollering to God out of anger will not let you see the truth. Hollering to God out of despair is closer but still behind the wall of illusion.

Praying while descending in vision, using the image of the trap door at your feet, is a beginning. There is something beyond despair, something beyond anger, something beyond fear that is the truth. To at least be humble, to ask sincerely, to stand in a place without judgment, with only a clear question, is how you hear Spirit. But you have to meet the conditions necessary for that kind of communication to happen.

First of all, you have to perceive your own mind as way too noisy to hear anything. When you can hold one question in your mind long enough, recognizing you must ignore all your own attempts to answer it yourself, then you can begin to hear Spirit. That very first time you actually hear Some One respond to you will probably make you feel like wetting your pants, like it did me the first time. To hear, though, you must cultivate quiet. In quiet, you must begin to grasp the devices that your ego uses to deceive you.

Every person has a Guide, maybe several, can be hundreds. Until you are sure that you are being guided to an awakening that you desire, you will resist. As long as you believe your fears more than your desire to know the truth, you will delay. As your desire to know the truth grows, so will your strength of will grow to bring you to that neutral point. Each time you pray, each time you meditate, each time you contemplate, each time you act or speak with Spirit in the world, you strengthen that neutral point, your True Self.

As your strength of will grows, you find that the mind that you have created apart from God, apart from Spirit, is not your friend. You begin to know it is your own mind that betrays you. And it is then that you earnestly begin to desire the healing of the splits within your own mind. It is when these splits are healed that you begin to understand the purpose a whole mind has, within peace. It is in God's peace that you find out what true creativity is.

A simple explanation is this. A seed is life. Put in the ground, warmed and watered and sheltered from the hot sun, it will grow into a seedling. If nourishment continues, that seedling will grow into a fine plant, and it will flower and fruit and produce new seeds for its species survival. A single plant can produce anywhere from one to fifty-thousand seeds, depending on its species. If every seed had a chance of having a perfect bed and environment, and each one grew to maturity, the world would strangle from the growth. The soil would be depleted. The atmosphere would explode from the purity of the oxygen in it.

So it is with human beings, and so it is with the place that was designed to support them. To hold your physical being so sacred in your mind that you seek only to extend your life-span at all costs, or you will not abort a child under *any* circumstances, and yet with the same mind call other people savages while you try to destroy them so you may have their place, is an insane mind, is it not? To say you are not split is an insane statement.

To desire to end duality within your mind is at least an attempt in the right direction towards sanity. To wait for the Mother to die, to imagine that God is punishing you, so that you will grow up and discover what you are, is insanity. To continue to overpopulate an earth and hold one part of life sacred, according to your views and not any other, is insanity. **Either all life is sacred or it is not.**

Either there is a God that loves or there is not. That anyone would choose a mind that was Godless and hold nothing sacred is insanity. This is the point to which your society has come. And to show its insanity, it kills the insane who kill. Because by itself, society does not know how to cure its own insanity. And it will not look to the cause, especially within itself.

Is this arrogance justifiable or is it insane? Ask the semi-powerful while they're on their deathwatch. Ask the influential when they have no influence against death anymore. Ask the proud when they have fallen to their sickbed. Ask the fat when they can no longer absorb anything. It all goes. All illusions go, every one of them, all at once or one at a time. You choose.

Any argument you may have against anything that I have said is useless. I think if I were you, I would rather die with my eyes open and with my heart open and with my mind open, so that I would not have to sit and rot in my form in the ground. I'd shed it like a snake's skin and say thank you for your good service and your many lessons. And I'd go on to the bigger mind and learn more, because if we are not here to learn, we are only here to die. I wish better for you than to have lived, only to die.

Our ceremonies were to celebrate life, even when somebody died, because we knew they would have another life, a bigger one. And we made songs that opened our hearts, that opened our minds to Spirit to guide us, to the Mother Who cared for us, as we were grateful for the help. We had songs to the eagles, we had songs to the buffalo, we had songs to the hawks, and we had songs to the butterflies and the bugs. We didn't sing to fish very much because we were land creatures. We didn't understand the water world, so it made us nervous. But we did appreciate fish in our small and simple way.

There were those on the coastline who prayed to the fish and dolphins and whales better than we did. And them Hopi prayed to the Mother and to the corn maiden for her fertile grain, for her symbol of fertility. We appreciated everything on the earth. We were connected to it all because our feet were grounded, and our hearts and minds were open. We received guidance from Spirit. In balance, we understood what was coming to us and why.

Nowadays, you have interest payments, depreciation schedules, amortization schedules, and you know what's coming to you or going away. But you don't have feet that are in balance on the earth, and your minds and your hearts are not open. One day, perhaps, you will have to learn to share by having nothing and having to ask.

It is only when you have nothing and have to ask that you will understand what a gift is, perhaps. If you pray for a gift, how do you know you receive? How do you know you talk to Spirit? Some people have a vision, and they think that's God "Himself" talking to them. Yes and no. Some people get all swelled up because they had a vision, because their prayer was answered. They see most people don't have that, and they become special... in their own minds. This is another form of self-trickery and becomes only a lesson for the vision-getter. The mind has tricked itself into being separate once again... special. And so, the lesson comes.

With a gift comes a responsibility. And it is that responsibility that will bring you back into balance on the earth, out of that tall tree, with a heavy thump. And you may perceive pain because you climbed so high to get away from that responsibility. So you're brought back to balance again. Thump!

A true leader with vision is a humble being indeed. That servant knows it is not the Source of its visions and seeks to gain nothing at all from having them. If there is a motive of gain, then the vision-getter is going to get a lesson, to be sure. Do not even judge that, for we are here only for our lessons. Add nothing, imagine nothing, detract nothing. Speak clearly, explicitly, impeccably, only the truth as you know it at the moment. Do not imagine that you know more or can reach a conclusion for which you have no guidance. Be humble about your experiences, and serve well what Spirit would have you do. I will say again what I once told my two children here. **Be humble before your ignorance, and you will learn like the comet's path. Think you know and you crawl with the slugs.**

You see, perception is like a lake in the middle of the prairie. The animals use the lake to drink from, and the humans use it to bathe in. And one will fish, and one will make a boat and float it. And birds will dive in it and fish will swim in it. Predators will hunt around it and bugs will breed in it. And plants will grow around it and in it. But I tell you, you don't know a thing about the water that's there. No matter what use it is put to, you know not what it is and why it is there.

How did there come to be a hole there for water to leak into? What is its purpose? You see all the activity around it, and yet water itself you know nothing about. All you do is see with your perception. All you can do is describe its properties and the activity around it. But knowledge of water isn't possible with the mind that is still trying to figure out what itself is, while it is out of balance.

I tell you, you can join the meaning of water. I tell you, you can join the meaning of earth. I tell you, you can join the meaning of fire and of air, if you would but give it time and give it your true desire to know.

Chapter 7
The Fall

It's late summer in camp, and everyone is beginning to harvest for the winter. Seems like there's extra activity, a little more anxiety, a little more purposefulness, a lot more seriousness. I see that everyone is making shields. I see that they are asking to draw on the medicines that they already have, and they are also asking for new medicines to help them with the challenges ahead. No one knows if this is the winter or not, but it is foolish to assume it is not.

More than ever, I see that the people in camp, particularly the older men and women have begun to spend time in the old ones' lodge. The old ones are helping them to review their medicines, their gifts, studying their weaknesses, looking for new medicines and new ways to strengthen their stamina, to strengthen their sensibilities and awareness and alertness. It is as if we are getting ready for a war between weakness and strength. The war, I see, is against our sinking energies, sinking emotions, against our fear. And we do this by facing them in ceremonies, by fasting and prayer, in Vision Quests and in Sweat Lodge. We sink beyond our fears in these ceremonies in order to find strengths that are the gift of passing through them.

In this war of emotions, all our petty differences, all our petty concerns, all our childish and foolish emotions are being faced. And in their place, we are given communion, companionship, caring, compassion. We are given a sense of oneness among us that only the children, the youngest don't notice. The youngest are in innocent joy and awe already.

There are two kinds of warriors on the earth. The first are those that face fear with tremendous energy, are angry, and use their energy through vehemence. And there is another kind of warrior who sinks through fear into acute alertness and waits for guidance from Spirit about what to do and when to do it. The second warrior is one who leads us *through* tragedy, not *to* tragedy.

In your last two generations, your emotional war has been about sexual energy between male and female. It has been about the discovery of will and about the arrogance of ego. I will give you an example from our time that was a rare occurrence of this kind of thing.

During the spring reunion with our people, after our walk back from Hopiland, a young woman had a child born between the confusion of two fathers. This created a great disturbance in our tribal life because this young woman never communicated to her parents that she was courting. It was done secretly. So you will see here the damage of lies and secrets.

To get one man, she used another. While thinking the man she would not get was the one she wanted, she used the one she did not want, to try to get the one she could not have. With her many lies and deceptions, she disrupted the family life of the man she could not have and used the man she could have. So it created great antipathy in those families. Her own family viewed her as a secretive, silent and mean-hearted woman who did not marry young because of her violent temper. The weakness of the married man, the susceptibility of him to manipulation through sexual torment, virtually destroyed his family life. The weakness of the unmarried man, the disregard for tribal law, and the lack of respect and honor for his family made him look foolish and pitiful as well. For until this difficulty became obvious through her pregnancy, no one spoke directly to the ones involved. And only a very few who observed the three in their difficulties said anything to anyone at all about any suspicions.

Now, since we don't hold secrets in our tribal life, suspicions, although observed closely, are never taken seriously. Just like in your society of today, everyone is considered innocent until proven guilty. We have no system for which we spend time investigating suspicions. We assume that respect, honor and trust creates communication, and therefore resolution. We never seek to punish but to understand.

The desire for sexual coupling at a young age is so intense that without communication to elders, there's no telling to what depth and extremes a person might go in their fantasy. Fantasy coupled with strong will creates projection. And projection creates action. The thoughts you have, if not understood, will create behavior. The behavior, if not understood, will create compulsion. Compulsions acted out create addiction. And the road back from addiction is intense and difficult. There is a very large gap in time for most people between addiction and healing. In the wake of defending our behavior, we create very strong emotions coupled with belief. This coupling of personal energy to belief creates a split in the mind. This split becomes an invisible chasm between belief and the truth. How far you walk down the path of deviation is exactly how far you will have to walk backwards in the undoing, to get back to what's true, to bridge the chasm in your mind. Here, you begin again as a child, to relearn what a whole mind is.

We did not live long, so most never stepped into deviancy too far. We didn't have time. We worked things out much quicker than you do today. Our life was virtually over at forty-five, whereas yours at forty-five is only about half over in your comfortable time. A shamed, married male member in our day would probably have to leave the tribe for some time under supervision to do Vision Quest, to do Sweat Lodge, to do penance to become penitent. Fortunately, we had extended families, so a missing husband was not a survival issue. And because we were a strong matriarchal society as well, that husband still might not be accepted by his own wife or family when he returned. He could be shunned.

Medicine work, council meetings and family meetings would all take place until the issue was resolved. And the woman with the child would certainly not be shunned but would be known as the crazy one, as it would probably take many years for her to resolve these deviant issues. The elder women of the tribe would help. And for the unmarried male came many lessons too. Much to learn. Much growth for everyone. And it is our stories that we tell, in actual or in fable form, that are meant to ease the confusion of our individual journeys, so that we may come together in the truth and understand why boundaries are necessary.

In your time, you have quick divorce and virtually no extended families to help, so a missing husband can spell disaster for his immediate family. Worse yet, this makes women inordinately dependent upon a missing husband, both materially and emotionally. The effect of this isolation frequently makes both men and women emotionally and sexually weak and devious. They cross all boundaries of sensibilities about sex. Straight up, everybody screws anybody. Where people gather in large numbers is where you feel the greatest energy of deviancy, and this energy is what teaches the children who are your future.

What are the boundaries that each individual must have, whether they are female or male, in order to live in harmony with other people? Your society of today has those boundaries, and yet purposefully goes beyond them or breaks them or dissolves them in the search for the meaning of them being there in the first place. Whether you live a life of deviancy without God, having to justify everything you think or say or do, or whether you live a life of a spiritual aspirant or the spiritual leader, depends on how far you have gone down the road of deviancy and returned to sanity.

We had ceremony and Sweat Lodge, Vision Quests, medicine sessions, stories, and counseling. All our practices were designed to have us learn about these deviancies through contemplation, through vision, through internal teaching, through telepathy. Those who were least fearful and learned the most through the depth of their visionary lessons, without acting them out within the tribe or upon another living thing, rose higher and saw wider and became more helpful to the tribe through their spiritual service.

The key component, the key aspects that we looked for in all our children were respect, honor, trust, and sharing. We taught our adults to give our children these things, so the children learned to give them from themselves to each other. If those four aspects weren't present, the child could not learn the stories and would have to live a life of acting out in order to learn them. This was hard on everyone around them. It was a slow process and could lead to an early death. If a child had internal damage because they had not been respected and honored and trusted nor taught the value of sharing, then the actions of all our medicine people and council members were directed toward the individuals responsible for teaching that child those aspects. If the offense was great enough, the child might be adopted and the parents shunned. And to be shunned in the wilderness was a very great challenge to your survival.

To be shunned in your society is to create another society separate from the other, living in darkness, with virtually no chance of reentering acceptance. Shunning in our tribe was not meant to permanently erase the memory of the members shunned but, in essence, to put them out into the snow. And if they appealed to Spirit for guidance, then they would survive and return. And they would have learned to connect with Spirit, rather than connecting with insane guidance from their own ego.

In your society, sin condemns the person and the state punishes that person, without forgiveness, without Spirit. And the condemned person, after punishment, is returned to a society that has not taken responsibility for the punishment. So there is no real return. There is no undoing of the errors that created their mistake. There is no communication between the state and the church. Though you may have a forgiving leader in your Christian religion, the rehabilitation of a sinner is not accomplished through handing the erring one to the state to punish or correct. So you breed a society of liars and cheats and secret-keepers who live split lives because they don't know how to stop their behavior. The system of correction doesn't know how to undo the perceptions and the experiences that the error-maker has made. So you have split minds, broken in half between the desire for love and the guilt that one hasn't any understanding of what love is.

If a young buck in our tribe has too much energy, too much sexual interest, too much disrespect, too much arrogance, then that young one is not shunned but taken in by the elders and taught why we check our arrogance, why we check our urges, why we work on having respect. An older warrior, a spiritual warrior will take him out hunting with a small party, and there will be great hardship and difficulty. There will be great discipline and stamina required. There will be great teamwork necessary to accomplish something as great as downing a buffalo. And, truly, if that young one does not learn the lessons, death may be present.

So the teacher risks his life to show the angry, young warrior what life is for and what demands the Creator has put on us to grow us up. I'm afraid you risk nothing when you try to teach your young people, so they test you constantly to see if you are weak or strong, to see what your boundaries and limitations are, and to see whether or not you have respect, honor, trust, and sharing, yourself.

Because your life is not at risk in your job, your lessons seem somewhat flat. This is the purpose of the old stories, to take you back to a time when we risked our lives to bring food to our families and to bring children into the world. Without these old stories, being a car salesman or a bookkeeper or any other non-risky occupation will seem flat and meaningless, and your children will rebel and look for meaning elsewhere. Until you understand your own life, how can you communicate the meaning of life to anyone else, especially your children? They will challenge you at every moment.

I have taught my children that it is up to the women to teach the female children respect for the men, and it is up to the men to

277

teach the male children respect for the women. It is up to us all to honor life, all living things, to have gratitude for what we are given. And it is up to us all to trust in the ultimate power of the Creator of all life to be good and helpful and loving and forgiving and compassionate.

With that outlook, you can have peace in your life. But if you view Creator and creation as mean-hearted and fierce and unforgiving and judging and condemning and punishing, then your life will be stingy and meaningless.

If you make sex a god, if you make money a god, if you make fear a god, then you will find no fulfillment, no peace, no rest, no sanity. If you but ask the single question that is valuable to learn the answer to, if you are humble and recognize that you do not know anything in fact, if you ask humbly to be taught what love is, then you will begin to emerge from the darkness beneath life into what Life is in the Light.

Then, if you ask what Spirit is and you take a neutral point with your life, you will be shown what Spirit *isn't*... first. After you have been tested to see if you have disbeliefs, addictions, desires, then you will know where you are on this path. If you have given up disbeliefs, addictions, compulsions, if you have given up "thinking" your life and given up deciding alone what anything means, then you will be ready to face your fears, your fear of the unknown, your fear of the truth. It is through the facing of your fears that you begin to stop being afraid of fear and see it simply as confusion, conflict in the lower energy realms of the human mind, in the human body.

In short, when you are afraid to grow, you will not grow. **When you no longer are afraid of change or growth, the truth will dawn on you of its own. You cannot seek to find truth.** For it to be revealed, you must *allow* it to be revealed. You must meet the conditions necessary for revelation.

It is through experience that the truth dawns on you. It is through rote, superficial learning that you are confused. The purpose of our stories is to induct you into a deep place of contemplation and relaxation, so that your mind might open to the Light of the Truth dawning on you. A gentle dawning can be a glorious explosion. It simply depends on what you will allow and how much effort you have put into your learning, into your willingness to ask real questions.

If you are distracted, it is because you do not yet see the value of focus. And yet, it is only through true desire and intense focus that you will break through the surface of illusion, deep into the pool of experience to ascend into the Light of Knowledge.

The fire in the below, if left unexpressed, builds exquisite energy that is no longer heat but is light. And it is through maintaining a neutral point during your training, during your undoing, that you will understand the trials and lessons and experiences that are there to show you the illusion and the truth of what you are.

The rising of this energy from that root fire will awaken and enliven the energy centers in your body, and when seen as a whole system will bring you knowledge and understanding and compassion, and make you aware that creation's presence is love.

The prize, my friends, is conscious peace and joy, simultaneously. It is total absence of fear, total trust in the perfect plan. It is the knowledge that is life itself.

Now, how are children to know these thoughts are possible, these accomplishments are real or that life is valuable, unless *you* work on these things and ask these things for yourself, and *you* seek the stories that help you comprehend the path of joy and love? You cannot bypass human experience and human failures to get to joy. You must experience all of life, both its illusions and its truth, to become whole and to become certain. And it is easier to do this in vision and not have to spend lifetimes in different forms for the same knowledge.

Believe me, creation would not exist in its forms without the Creator's absolute certainty. Have you ever seen a "maybe" frog, a "maybe" eagle, a "maybe" buffalo? Seen lots of "maybe" people. Even an ant doesn't contain a maybe. Even bacteria are certain. So if you lack certainty, it is because you have not sought the truth enough.

It is through the dreaming mind that correction of your perception takes place. There is no correction in the world because the world is about *doing.* The dreaming mind is about *undoing,* then repair, and then doing within love. Songs are written from the dreaming mind. Prayers are said in the dreaming mind. Aspirations and hopes are visualized in the dreaming mind. A dreaming mind that is sick, dreams fear, dreams guilt, dreams vengeance. A dreaming mind that is well, dreams harmony and peace, dreams love and gratitude, dreams compassion and forgiveness.

The Creator's mind dreams only possibilities. And in this love, the effects of illusion are limited. If the Creator was not real and did not dream with love as the intent, your demons would face you in physical form as you create them in your minds. All the ghoulies and ghosties would be a reality. So the Creator limits the effects of your fantasy and imagination. The energy, however, that you imagine them with is real and does remain. The effects of this energy are numerous and devastating to your children, to the life on this planet and to the planet itself.

You borrow from the future to assuage your feelings of lack in the now. Your fear steals energy from the future and expends itself in storage and collection of what you do not need in the now. You drain your children of their physical future and prevent them from having a possible present, by warehousing what you fear you will lack. And to overcome your fears of lack, you have valued the goals of safety and comfort, and you have placed their cost so high that very few can ever attain such goals. To make safety and comfort out of reach, creates distrust of the society that purports to care about you. Even your money says, "In God We Trust." And yet, you collect your money as if *it* were God, and you trust in its power to save you. Were you to trust in God, you would know you are saved, and fear would be meaningless, yet your dollars symbolize your fear instead of your trust. It is in gain you trust and in loss you fear.

Your government's desire to shore up the value of the dollar against all influences is proof that they're trying to get you to trust the dollar. And yet, the very environment it is to serve, the earth you stand on, you do not trust.

You fear winter because of the cost of heating. It is not the heating that you fear or the cold, but the cost. It is the cost of living that you are so involved in, rather than knowing the meaning of life. You think, oh, I'll get meaning along the way, as a natural result of having to live. But I tell you, most people miss the point. They might give cursory knowledge or cursory attention to the function of life, to the purpose, to the meaning, but are they transformed by their knowledge?

You say, only saints and scholars, artists and spiritual leaders ever get to the meaning of life, and the average person never gets there. Well, I tell you, your young soldiers coming back from Desert Storm got a deeper glimpse into human nature and the sacredness of life. Something was put at risk, and there was a cost and it was seen. But the gap between being there and watching on television is too great for the average person, I think.

All over the world, Christians and Muslims, Hindus and Buddhists, Socialists and Capitalists, Communists and Imperialists, Republicans and Democrats, Fascists and military dictators all align themselves in beliefs that are convenient for the purpose at hand. The purpose is power, influence, control. The desire is for wealth... to somehow climb above life and look down upon it and not have to live it in its simplicity, in its directness.

Take off your shoes. Come out of your homes. Reconnect with the earth that you're standing on. Give thanks for the abundance and count the gifts you get. Count the times you have been grateful, and you will begin to see what has value and what does not. You will begin to see that all living things share equally, and that humans are just barely among the "living," the aware, or the conscious.

When you desire full consciousness and go in the direction of the goal, you will have it. But do not pretend and do not assume, and do not aspire without sincerity and persistence. The number of fools is greater than the number of simple, honest human beings. Would you be counted as a fool, or would you be counted as a human being, simple and honest?

*

Returning to our story.... This is the first moon of the season you call fall. And it is noteworthy that the human part of your creation story begins with "the fall" from grace. It has never been fully explained what this bite from the apple symbolized, but I will clearly tell you what happened with the vision of our fall.

I'll tell you how you know a vision is true. It's very simple. It happens. With the first cold rain, the first morning frost, a bone chill went through our entire tribal family and created the desire for a large gathering. The gathering was spontaneous and attended by nearly everyone, except for the one hunting party that was out. This gathering was precipitated by the appearance on the horizon in the very early morning of a cloud form that looked like a swan. It was white on the underside and dark grey to nearly black on the top.

Shuhinono was called outside by me to look at this phenomena. She merely shook her head from side to side, looked at the ground and retreated into our lodge.

By midmorning there were nearly a hundred-and-seventy adults gathered around our central council fire. The seven council members showed up shortly and began to talk with the people, individually. By noon, the warming sun had defrosted us, but our concerns were all apparent. Was this an omen? Was this our winter to face our fear? Was this the fall or was this just the precipice?

As was not customary, Shuhinono spoke first. She said, "What shall you look at, the white underside or the black pall on top?" And we were once again reminded to question whether we would walk into our future in fear or with faith.

Since this was not a formal meeting, we watched carefully the people's moods and movements. Who would depart? Who would depart first? Who would depart in peace? And who would depart in anger? And who would hang to the very last? You see, **all people are images and reflections of our own mind, each one of them.** We are all fragments that make a whole. At stake was, where was this whole going? And would it stay whole or would it fragment?

The council was not interested in making all the tribal members proceed down a single path, if it was their intention to separate. But, to be sure, the council members were acutely aware that we would no longer be a whole people if any of us chose a different path than any others. You see, the land around the globe was already populated by different fragments of our Whole Being called Creator. Would our fragments now become smaller yet and disperse farther and wider across the planet? This fall was the thought of separation, our bite out of the apple.

In the weeks that followed that meeting, some small bands or families decided to leave, then packed and left. Of one-hundred-and-seventy adults, our tribe dwindled to seventy-five adults. We all stood at the perimeter of our camp in abject sadness and watched each family member depart. To us, their fate would be unknown. To them, our fate would be unknown.

During the three months of the fall, our tribal family further dwindled to thirty-five adults and seven children. There was one sure bet. Everyone who left knew that when this trial ended, we would reassemble in this exact spot, if there were any of us left.

Not once in all of our many nights of intense dreams was Shuhinono, Feice and I called to Hopiland or any other place. One night I had a particularly strong dream that made me sit up suddenly to find Shuhinono already sitting up. Did you dream the same dream? I asked her.

"Yes, my dear Hinono. So now we know where we are to take our people to safety," she said.

Once again I am reminded, we dream the same dreams, my wife and I. Smiling White Hair was right. I had almost forgotten that she had told Shuhinono and I that we both would dream of a place of safety for our people, somewhere in a box canyon.

"Do you know where this place is?" Shuhinono asked.

Yes, I know the place. I remember seeing it when I went on my two day walk when we found out about Mohinono. I think it's about one day's walk from here, I said.

So this dreaming vision was why we chose to stay with the remaining tribal family. If we were the ones who were chosen to lead our people to the box canyon, then we would stay and play our part. Feice summed it up very quickly for us one morning. She asked, "Where is everybody going?"

We don't know, I said. Maybe they feel safer walking. Perhaps they feel the pull to go somewhere else but here.

She said, "I like here."

Shuhinono asked her, "Do you know the big cold may be coming?"

And she said, "Cold everywhere in winter. Winter is cold."

"Must be, for all we know. We heard tell once from the Hopi that there is a land south of where we went, a thousand suns away from here, that never gets cold. Stays hot all the time," we told her.

Feice said quickly, "Too far."

We agreed. And since we trusted this guidance of Spirit to give us dreams, positive ones to follow, not fearful ones to resist, we stayed. All our dreams, all our conflicts didn't have our feet moving. And yet, we pondered the decisions and the dreams of those who had moving feet.

If will is free, then our desire for a complete, whole family had to include the will of those who had moving feet. So our hearts expanded to include those who had to walk away, and we did not judge them.

What is freedom and what is will? And if you are guided by your fears, is your will free? If you are guided by Spirit, is your will free? Question deeper what freedom is. Question deeper what will is.

Our hunts were successful and we stored much food. The air was damp now, and it was difficult to store this food so it would not spoil. We had shared our vision of the box canyon. And, by now, everyone remaining in camp had moved there. Lodges had been set up, and inside our lodges we hung strips of meat and baskets of grain. Roots were packed with straw in the cold earth and stored. We all felt confident that we would be able to sustain ourselves through a deep winter. And we had agreed, because of the small number of us remaining, to create shelters with more people in them, to share our warmth and space, and to help each other maintain good cheer in hard times. We pulled together all our resources and all our energies. It is in these hard times you realize what family means and how big that term is or how small it may be for you in a moment, in a moment of exhaustion.

If this was a simple story, it would end with our deaths, would it not? But I tell you, this is no simple story. This story goes beyond our mortal fears of physical death. This story spans nearly three-thousand years. The trail-off of this story goes beyond your twenty-second century into the future of humankind. So do not be discouraged when you find us frozen in our places.

A trial is there to awaken you to a larger being within your form. A test is like your pencil that writes and erases. A test completed, erases misconceptions. You have a chance to rewrite your life when you allow your misperceptions to be unwritten.

Of course, the most fundamental misperception we have about life is its apparent, perishable nature. And yet, we look to the earth to teach us that where you harvest grain, if you do not take it all, some falls to the ground and next year allows you to harvest more. If you do not kill the largest buck or the strongest females, the next year you will have new ones, strong ones, vibrant life spreading everywhere. If in your fear, you store too much food and take too much grain and take too much game, it will not return to your place, and you will chase your lack of abundance across the earth.

If a farmer does not kill his soil, he will have wheat. If a farmer does not let his soil rest, he will have weak plants. If a farmer plants a single crop over and over and over without rotation, he creates soil deficient in nutrients and weak in structure. And if a farmer does not pray, he does not learn the error of his ways. He does not learn any correction and repeats his errors endlessly.

So you have it. An umbrella without a handle is useless. A circle uncompleted is not a circle and is useless. What good is half a bowl? How many balloons can you fill with air without closing the hole at the top where the air leaks out?

Your bubble is a life. Your life is a balloon. And without prayer, it leaks vital energy and deflates quickly. Because you are free, you can experience anything you want. Because you have will, you can use your life freely, any way you want. But without prayer, you will not know what it is for, and you will wander aimlessly and never learn anything at all... except what doesn't work.

If any of us were to survive this time of winter, it would be because we loved each other and we would help each other. And we would each do what was necessary to save the children, both male and female. So during this time of cold, we took turns, and in story form we taught the children everything we knew.

In our group of forty-two remaining, we were blessed to have all seven council members. Not one chose to leave this place. Between thirty-five adults and seven children, we had three lodges close together, all walled against the northern wind, all in this box canyon where a southern sun might melt snow for water. There the animals gathered to drink and have shelter in the deepening cold and snows. We were blessed with such a good place. We had wood for fire. We had walls of rock to collect southern sun. We had abundant wildlife. And we had dry caves to store food stuffs in, much like your icebox. The deeper the cave, the warmer the ground. The shallower the cave, the more deeply frozen things became.

It was in Sweat Lodge, in great thanks and prayers that we gave ourselves to the Mother of Creation. It was on the high cliffs above us, in Vision Quests and in fasting and in singing that we gave ourselves to the Father of Creation. And it was to our dreamtime animals that we prayed for guidance, that we would not make faulty steps through this perilous time.

We noticed all our petty irritations, all our personality differences that we cherished in ourselves began to fade. And in the intensity of the winter bearing down on us, we became a single mind with no separate personality. The children laughed and played. Life continued. But there was not one squabble or distraction among the adults. The focus became singular. There was little snow, but the winds howled and the temperature dropped. At times, it was even impossible to leave the lodge to urinate.

Your culture has down and Hollowfill blankets and many other manufactured ways of keeping yourself from feeling chilled. We had wood. We had animal robes. We had simple moccasins covered with layers of fur. We looked a little bit like a hedgehog rolled up in a ball, fur sticking out all over, two little peep holes for your eyes and nose to stick out. And even the children began to be silent and not play. It got so cold it was not worth a complaint.

I know you have thermometers, and I will guess what temperature it was for our time. We spent two-and-a-half months in those three lodges in ten-below-zero weather, with alternating ten-and-fifty-mile-per-hour winds. It was life threatening to go forty yards to food storage caves. To remove cover rocks from the cave face and retrieve a basket of our frozen meat was cause for alarm. No one left the lodge alone for any reason. No young person or elder was allowed to leave at all.

There were many songs, many prayers to keep our spirits alive in this time, and many stories for the children. Usually, we had winter projects to complete, new clothing, new baskets. None of this was done. There were hours, endless hours of rocking prayers. Sleep came in two-hour snatches, for if any of us fell into a very deep sleep, we would surely freeze and die. If the numerous firekeepers who rotated their duties throughout the days and nights failed, we would all die for sure. So no one slept in long, even-flowing, dream-filled quietude. Movement was necessary every two hours, or you would lose part of your extremities.

At the lowest point of the southern sun, an elder died. As the sun began to come up past winter's solstice, more died. Some accepted fate and refused food or water. They blessed us to continue and not to become disheartened, for they knew it was their time, and they passed on with smiles to those left behind. No one could leave the lodges at all, anymore.

Within a week of the passing of seven more members, young and old, the snow began to fall. Within three days, we had to push a hole through the snow, two feet higher than our lodges in order to get smoke out and air in. It was this snowfall that saved our lives... this time. It created a blanket to insulate us against the wind and keep the heat in the lodges. But with the moisture that melted, ice sickles were created that let a sickness stick to our floors. It was the dampness that wracked our bones.

When the first melt came, there were eighteen members left in two lodges, and the dead were stacked outside like cord wood. After two-and-a-half weeks, we were able to go out again to retrieve frozen food, to gather more wood, and to scout the landscape for the possibility of hunting for fresh meat. Ever present was the danger of a fierce wind freezing us as we walked. Nowhere was there a memory in our people of a cold that was so deep and so long.

Now, in your lives, your lessons of endurance and patience come in much the same way. The subject, the test may be different, but the function of a trial is to make you stronger and more humble. For some people, the test of patience makes them angry. The test of endurance makes them vengeful. And for other people, patience shifts into indolence, endurance shifts into hopelessness.

Is a person who survives a trial by indolence or hopelessness free? Do they have will or did they merely survive by not dying? Is the will to survive useless and absurd in the face of "destiny?"

Weak and emaciated, bone sore, sick and tired, we thawed and thought. Such a hardship must not have been all that vision was, for we are alive. But Shuhinono spoke one morning to say, "This is not all to come. Be careful."

We all agreed, and yet we were stupefied. We were paralyzed and numb with lack of activity and stimulation, with lack of movement. With such discipline, we were exhausted.

Because of our being indoors so long, the terrain around us became invisible, unknown, treacherous. What looked like a ledge overhanging a small precipice was just three inches of ice, rapidly melting from underneath. What appeared to be a wide foot ledge was only a narrow three inches of rock, widened by six inches of ice.

Two members of a hunting party were killed by slipping on the ice to their deaths. Two more members of a hunting party froze to death when a fierce wind blew from the north suddenly and was sustained for two days. They had wandered too far in their search for food and could not get back before their muscles no longer moved them forward in the deep snow. Two children died of croup from the deepening cold and high humidity. Two women died of despair when their children perished. With no husband and no child to care for, they gave up. A rock fall from the canyon wall demolished a lodge with three people inside. And then the wind blew again and blew again and blew again. And although we had food and we had fire and we had each other to huddle, the temperature dropped so low, it was not possible to keep the damp wood lit.

We blessed each other and sang to Creator. I tried to cover my wife and child and two others with my body to hold out the cold during the night hours. And we asked Spirit to take us into the Light with them, not because we were tired of living but because we knew that most of us would not live the night.

The swan with white underwings came for us. My child Feice lived on with four others that survived. My wife and I departed that night with love in our hearts for everyone. With power in our prayers for those left behind, we filled them with our energy of love and protection. We stood and watched them all night, in a different form from our frozen bodies, and watched them wake to a bright, sunny morning, windless, calm, perfect in its silence. We watch them still because love knows where it is and what it's doing and where it's going.

I will tell you of holiness and sacredness. And I will tell you of unfathomable love. I will tell you of certainty and perfection. And I will prove to your doubting minds that you are never alone and that you are deeply cared for. And I will show you in your dreams, if you want, what part of mind is real and what part is not. And I will teach you again what you have forgotten about how to live and how to die... and what life is and what death isn't. And I will give you all the strong and good stories. And I will explain the meaning that is in everything you see or touch or hear or feel.

We are all children, dead or alive, Spirit or body. And we are endlessly connected in truth. And my breath in my day was the same air you breathe into your lungs to enliven you today. And it has gone through billions of transformations, billions of cycles, in order to be as good for you as it was for me. And the water you drink that enlivens you is the same water we drank. And the earth you grow your food in and rest your feet on is the same good earth that supported us in our time. And the fires you feel are the same fires that warmed us and moved the air around the earth and made the waters fall to nourish the land, to cool its hot core. It is the same fire that is within you now. And the Love that sustains this fire is the same Love that animates you and animates me now.

Chapter 8
Love Knows No Barriers

I will not tell you details of our reality as Spirit because I would not taint the creativity that is your life and have you choose a reality other than that one which is co-created with you. I will not try to describe the indescribable. I will not influence you or manipulate you into having a reality that is not wholly yours with the Creator. I will, however, intermittently help you with the meaning of the things around you and show you their purpose, so you can use them for your benefit. And I will continue to tell you the story of my children as they evolve through your present day.

Because you hear the sounds that make up this language as you read my words, you will know that love knows no barriers. Because you have physical form and feel contained within your skin and within your mind, you can see that physical life in its distinct appearances has boundaries, and that they are even necessary for the maintenance of a harmonious physical life. But I tell you, Creator's love has no boundaries, and the sensibilities of physical life must be learned and grown beyond in order to have a Spiritual life.

Shuhinono did not maintain her form as human because she found her purpose in formlessness. I maintained my physical appearance in light body form because my purpose is to transduce life's meaning into formlessness and love. I use language to communicate the incommunicable. I bring you to the threshold of understanding by using words as footsteps to the Threshold of Knowledge. And Shuhinono uses wordless pictures, energies, and the Power of Knowledge to break through the barrier of unknowingness, of incomprehension, through your dreaming mind. I stand on your left side and she stands on your right. I mumble your words of familiarity and point to the bridge to truth by experience... your experience. I help you shift from your left mind, where words are left behind in dusty little piles, to your right mind where the new bird flies. I feed you nubbins to give you strength. Shuhinono lifts the courageous fledgling into formless flight.

It is the formlessness of the Creative Mind that is the One Reality that we all share. It is our misuse of the powers of imagination that perceptually keep us from understanding creation itself. The bonds of fear belong to the realm of imagination and a vague awareness of the complexity of physical form. It is this bond between perception or imagination and the physical form that must broken in order to understand that death of the form has nothing to do with the phenomenon of life itself.

Life is this. The act of leaving physical form is another birth. The act of facing physical fear, psychological fear, spiritual fear, is labor. Becoming pregnant in this process is the desire to know. The coming of puberty to prepare for this pregnancy is the willingness to learn. The beginnings of consciousness and the growth of willingness is the admission of not knowing. Physical life is the beginning of consciousness. To be born as a physical entity is the impulse to self-awareness. Love is the vehicle for the impulse. And love is the overcoming of the fear of death and the return to knowledge.

We watched over Feice and the remaining four members for the next seventeen years. At the end of those seventeen years, Feice gave birth to twins, two boys. Her husband was the son of Two Secrets. Of all the council members, only Smiling White Hair, Two Secrets, and Whistling Woman lived. And of the remaining members of the tribe who had walked away, fourteen returned. They returned in two different groups, six days apart, the same summer that Feice gave birth. Twenty-two people, including the twins, were all that remained of our tribe of nearly two-hundred.

During that time, Feice remained in contact with her mother through the animals. The deer would come to Feice in the night and stand by her lodge until morning. Her husband vowed that summer to never hunt deer, to never eat deer meat because of Feice's certainty of her mother's presence. Other members of the tribe, because of the marvel of this act of the deer, would only hunt to the south and to the west and to the east. But they would never hunt to the north for deer because those deer stood in the north of Feice's lodge regularly for months and periodically over the years to follow.

Feice was renowned throughout the northwest because of her ability to call the animals to her. She became a great medicine person because of her willingness to love her mother through the creatures and to continue to receive guidance through visions and images that were wordless. In those seventeen years, I said only two words to Feice... *It's love.*

To me, you are my child and children, my mother and father, my grandparents and my wife. And I give you all these words I could not give my child nor my earlier son and his mate while they were here. I give them to you and to them now, as you would give a warm blanket to a chilled soul.

The colors that arise from the east and bloom in the west, that dance across the landscape and move in your dreams... *It's love.* Do not be afraid. Do not even be afraid of your fear... *It's love.*

Our original tribe grew over the centuries to nearly thirty-thousand and traveled enormous distances to become named. We even went south again and visited the Hopi. We exchanged goods and exchanged medicines and exchanged ideas. The world was a good place, full of bliss and enterprise, and the land was loving and warm, filled with abundance. The stories were told in cycles, twice a year, and the ceremonies were performed in regular cycles all year long. Help was everywhere. All the ancestors and all the medicine people and all the storytellers and all the teachers and all of the song-makers shared from across the veil, both directions. Everyone's needs were met. There was no mind for war, so all squabbles, all conflicts were minimal and just symbolic. No one had tips on their spears for each other. We would just tap each other, count coup to demonstrate our courage and our bravery. And because our spears were not tipped, we acknowledged the possibility of the depth of our foolishness. Therefore, we did not build courage from death. We built courage from love.

All well and good you say, but that was then and this is now. I'll tell you how you got from then to now. We built on the land, and we expanded our relationships with the land through Spirit. And from all the peoples that we met, we learned.

Now, you ask, why do I include myself as "we?" **Love knows no boundaries.** I could speak to you as if I were a dead person and tell you the story of those living. But I tell you, death is not real and I still live with you now. If all that we are is ideas, then all that we do is in belief of them.

New peoples came to our land from many directions, with three predominant languages but very similar ideas among them. It was the introduction of these new ideas, the introduction of seduction and deception within those ideas that has very nearly wiped out the memory of an entire race of native peoples. It is the cruelty to which those modern ideas were forced to dominate that has very nearly murdered the native spirit.

Now, to be sure, you cannot murder "life." Were you to obliterate the entire surface of the planet, just beneath the surface would be the seed for new life. But ideas whose only goal is to replace life... that is the enemy. The desire to categorize, to accumulate and to store knowledge cannot be put in front of life. Domination and control cannot be the goal. Life must be the goal.

These ideas, European in nature, moved to this continent because of the lack of room and the lack of resources in their own countries. This has occurred in various ways in every country on the planet, with every civilization and every species of man, whether in small degree or notion or in grandiose and expansive form, through conquering other peoples and through imposition of rule. So wherever there is disagreement, there is war and death. And in its wake comes weak alliance and suspicion, rather than harmony and peace.

It is because of these conflicts that what was left of spiritual knowledge was temporarily placed in the protection of organized religions, simply because dedication was required to remember the stories. Dedication was required to teach them. Dedication was required to carry them forward to the written word.

It was six-hundred-and-thirty-six years after my physical death that your Jesus was born. It was nearly forty-thousand years before that, that the Aborigines formed an organized religion, a language and pictographs to demonstrate their stories. Islam was born and Mohammed taught a hundred years or so after Christ. Hindu and Buddhists religions, though modern in style, had concepts nearly as old as the Aborigines.

So ideas persist. Truth is stored. Aspirations are cultivated and learning enhanced by all our practices to awaken to ourselves as spirit, by any means, in any place, with any people. It is the worst and best in being human that our stories preserve. The one common element in all of it, in any expression, in its mature form is that we are all one thing. There is one whole being called, Creation.

Now, I tell you, this whole being is not as big as the earth, and yet bigger. It is mind. Mind is bigger than all the universes put together or any conceived of outside of space and time, before space and time, in formless eternity.

So how should I tell you about eternity? Where to begin? Your trials here on earth are because you need to work out in your mind what is true and what is not true, what is valuable and what is valueless, what is helpful and what is distraction, so that when you enter the Mind of Eternity, you will not miscreate with your mind. Heaven would not be heaven if there was war, if there was conflict. And yet, here on earth you are entertained by your conflicts and bored when you are in peace. Were you to sit out in a field, far from the busyness of your modern world, you would easily enter the dreamtime, the World of Mind, the World of Creativity. It might take you many weeks, but your mind would shift and would align itself with the natural world around you, unaffected by man's desire for change. If you were to sit in the changelessness of an open field, you would begin to open to the spiritual nature that surrounds you.

Our people in our time had it much easier, and yet their world, too, was to change with the coming of the Europeans. Certainly, the most powerful, changing force to affect all the natives of the "American" continent was the bringing of the horse by the French and the Spanish.

I will skip quickly over the age of distrust, disrespect and war between the natives and the immigrants. Much has been written of it. But, until recently, much that was written was a lie. With your new generation of young people and an unfortunate war in Vietnam, public opinion began to change and the truth began to emerge. The truth of those dark times, from the 1600's toward the present, began to emerge with the young culture of the 1960's and their interest in the old ways. When more native stories were allowed to be told and were published and distributed, then the value of the balance with nature began to be appreciated again in the modern world. That's what native peoples have saved in their stories... balance. And as more of the *supposed* conquered are sharing with more of the *apparent* conquerors, the idea of conquered or conquering is being erased. The only line that stands between the two is the line of property, of owning the earth.

Settling of this new land, United States, was accomplished by the promise of being able to own or possess a piece of land. The single idea that natives fought against was the concept that you could *own* your Spiritual Mother at all. It was a dangerous concept which meant the end of the freedom of movement of both people and animals.

A modern person cannot easily or freely move from one place to another without a great deal of money, without having to rent or purchase another home to replace the one they left behind or sold.

This idea of ownership of the land under your house is not freedom. Your government retains the right of imminent domain to prove to you that land cannot be owned by you, even if you pay for it. The animals, of course, have no rights... many think.

Paradoxically, the minds of the conquered are still more free than their conquerors. And yet, even this is just a parenthetical idea. In the eyes of eternity, is one house better than the other because it stands longer under one man's laws or another? Can the truth exist in time and place, or is it forever outside our reach, and must we then resign ourselves to living within man-made laws as protection for our ideas? I say, there is a way to have truth here now.

The native ceremonies that have been saved are to maintain a place where eternity can be reached without the aid of a calender or a date book. Ancient ceremonies are important to be kept alive as a reminder of what is true as a foundation. Any house can then be built anywhere, moved or sold, left to rot or repaired if it has a foundation in truth. A house with no foundation is a prison to keep life out. Ceremony is a time given to let life in.

It's time, I think, to pick up the story of my children, all of them. I think I will go all the way back to the time of my son, to the release of my son to his twin in the Creator's world. Because I am on the other side now speaking, I can give you a clue about other realities and what took place when these two split.

What Smiling White Hair saw with Shuhinono regarding the male and female and their energies together was much what happened to my son and his other half. Mohinono returned to the Spirit world because he could not bear to be apart from his female self. And yet, their life together in Spirit had lasted many hundreds of years before they returned to the earth again, this time as separate entities, in separate places. Much experience was gained by them, and their lives were very different. They have come and gone in this beautiful cup or crucible called earth. They have spent many lives apart, searching for each other.

While our single tribe built to thirty-thousand and spread across the northern and western part of the United States and Canada and became known as the many sub-tribes of the Sioux nation, Mohinono spent lives of every color on every continent, always as a male, and his partner spent lives always as a woman, one black, one red, two white, within three cultures but never to leave this continent. It was many more hundreds of years before the two were allowed to come back together. Because of the nature of the split, it was the Creator's desire for this process to not continue with other people. A way home was planned for those who did split because of the severity of the idea of the separation between man and woman. There were many other pairs or entities over the last two-thousand years that had split themselves in two, into male and female. Others who had not split, the vast majority of people, were both male and female inside themselves, and their being born into one body or another was simply emphasis for one experience or the other.

To bring this split pair home as one, it was necessary for them to burn out their desire for single identity. It took five turns for Mohinono and four turns for his twin, Shuhinono, to come back together. It was their desire for union again that brought them back together in their present life. It was this desire for wholeness that gave me a chance for contact with the two of them again. It was their desire for guidance from Spirit that allowed me to enter their lives and help them.

The general reader will ask, "Well, what does this have to do with me, since I am not one of the twenty-three pairs that are split?" I tell you, being physically split into two entities, male and female, without the other half inside is symbolic... strongly symbolic of the division between male and female within each human psyche.

So the reconnecting of these two, Mohinono and his twin Shuhinono, can prove that you can achieve a balance between male and female within yourself, if you will allow it. The first hurdle is getting rid of the idea that what your eyes see is more important than what your heart knows.

I will very briefly tell you the story of their coming back together and what it took. I will begin with the daughter not born to me, the female self, Shuhinono. This present birth, she was born to a poor family, simple, no conveniences, no entertainment, significant hardship and lots of work. She was given a strong will by the Creator from her first birth. She was given the seed of the memory of love, and she was given the courage that goes with that understanding. She was born into a white family and into a religion that taught fear of God and fear of anti-god. With the seed of the memory of love, she fought not against those who were ignorant but against ignorance itself... not to change the face of the world around her but to understand it. Her whole life was a medicine walk from lack to abundance, with only will and the seed of the memory of love inside her to guide her. She had many relationships and traveled across two continents but never married. Like all young women, she wanted to be loved, but later discovered the gift of love is in the giving. It was her willingness to give love that finally led her to Spirit. It was her understanding that to settle for less than what Creator promised would only lead to deeper depression and death. So she continued searching and learning, until the world no longer frightened her, until her mind was as strong as any other mind, capable of any learning or any teaching. And yet, she was waiting.

Meanwhile, her male self, Mohinono, had been to the ends of the earth to experience lifetimes as a native in each of the four continents, each of the four colors. And too, he waited... desperately... to be returned to his Whole Self. In this life he got to be white, as did she, on the same continent as his twin, and he went through the same trials as she did. And yet, with less will in his waiting, he settled for less because of the pressures of the society around him. He was not born poor with a better perspective on the world. He was born middle-class with middle-class views all around him. He lost himself and split many times. You see, as only male inside, he had no seed of the memory of love. And in a society that lies, he had no truth.

There comes a point in everyone's life when the failures outweigh the successes, when the pressure to change is so intense that nothing can stand in its way. They both reached this point simultaneously, and both began a spiritual journey, one through force of will, the other through drugs, medicines, and through disintegration.

While Barbara-Shuhinono breaks through the crust of unawareness through fasting, through herbal cleansing, through high fevers, and begins her journey to spiritual understanding, the other, John-Mohinono begins to disassemble the material life that he led... through physical failure–a heart attack–through bankruptcy, and through divorce. It is at the bottom of our lives that we ask for help, is it not?

For a woman to go on a spiritual quest to India, from a background of extreme religious Christian conservatism, was an act of will. For a man to totally reevaluate the arrogant culture that he lived in, to admit finally that he knew nothing and had been pretending his life, took little courage and only a moment of deep self-examination and admission.

One knew what love was but could not sit in the largest form. The other one admitted he did not know what love was at all but was willing to learn. So he asked. Both wanted the truth. Both were willing to work to obtain it. One had significant discipline. The other had none. One had good will. The other had none. One of them had awareness of love. The other one had none. Both sought the truth in their different ways, and both asked simultaneously to learn what Big Love was, to learn the Truth of what

Love was. And they asked Spirit to show them. It was their asking that brought them together again. It was their asking about the Truth of what Love was that brought their spirits into alignment long enough for us to pull them together to a single place.

So Barbara was led by her dreams. And John was led by his nose. Sometimes we even pulled on his ears. Once in awhile, had to kick him in the rear. Most of the time, had to have him take medicine because he was so split inside. They were a humorous pair... fire and water, for sure. It was a big job, but Creator was kind. He gave the job to somebody who already loved them in a personal way, so their path would be full of good humor and friendly conversation. It wasn't as if there was an outside force acting upon them. It was as if something inside them was tickling them back to reality. Who better to do this than their First Father? And then, their second father... me.

So I guess you'd call me a Holy Ghost. I was wholly ghost, for sure... because I wasn't "alive." And I am holy... because of my love. I think true love is the only thing that is holy. What do you think?

So we got them together, as quickly as their learning would allow. And I tell you, they were not too quick. But I'll tell you this. The pressure was on. And so, it was a lot quicker than if they were left to find each other by themselves. Good thing they asked. This could have gone on for another two or three centuries.

Now, Spirit doesn't plan your life out. You do. All the decisions that you've made set the conditions for your return. The good part about this split pair is that each time they returned to Creator from a different birth, they renewed their commitment to coming back together in this age, today.

Time is running out for the Mother. We have entered a new sun, and She is full to bursting with the illusions that have to be stored within Her until they can be transmuted. And there are not nearly enough people left on this planet today that know how to transmute this energy.

So it was agreed that Barbara-Shuhinono and John-Mohinono would take their place of learning. They would learn to transmute. By helping other people to reach inside past their fears and connect with Spirit, they would do so for themselves as well. They would again be joined, and the rift between male and female, the perceptions that separate them would be dissolved.

I tell you, the only loneliness there is, is between the halves of your split self. All of the confusions of your lives have been a result of this split within you. All life is recycled and each animal knows itself to be male or female, male *and* female. They have a collective mind... called bird, called dolphin, called dog or cat or horse or buffalo. To be born one, female or male, is to them the same experience. Physiologically, the differences are irrelevant. But to humans... wow! All of the misperceptions of being male and all of the misperceptions of being female, stacked up together, create enormous barriers instead of joining.

There is a simple solution. Honor each other's gifts and you will no longer see each other as physical at all. Focus on each other's failures, and division and separation is certain.

It is at this point I will attempt a controversial explanation of the use of drugs in your society. I'll begin by telling you that native peoples all over the world use medicinal herbs in many forms to produce ecstatic states in which a humble questioner can be given dreamtime guidance.

Your modern society lumps all drugs into one category, but I will separate them and show you their difference. I will call the first category ego drugs. And I will call the second category medicinal aids or tools or just medicine. The distinction is clear. Anything used without the care or guidance or desire for Spiritual connection is an ego drug, whether it be sugar, coffee, alcohol or tobacco, whether it be speed, crack, cocaine, heroine, marijuana, hashish, opium, or any other psychoactive drug that you can think of, whether it be L.S.D., mescaline, peyote, ayahuasca, or a designer drug like ecstasy. All of these without Spirit are useless for anything helpful. It is your society's immaturity with these questions, its lack of directness about drugs, and its lack of understanding of what mind is at all that creates chaos.

Within the mind is the voice of either truth or illusion, Spirit or ego. The first choice, then, should not be what drug or medicine to use or not use, but what voice to listen to and for what purpose that voice would have for your using it or not using it. To seek a thing without Spiritual guidance may not always be dangerous but truly would be foolish.

The truth is that your society has not outlawed ego or illusion but has made some truly helpful, physically nonaddictive medicines a drug, and considers all of those illegal except the most commonly addictive like sugar, coffee, alcohol, and tobacco. If your society cannot guide its children in the use of sugar, coffee, alcohol, and tobacco, then surely you see you have no way of guiding your children in the use of medicines or the nonuse of drugs. Your biggest concern should be finding within you your Spiritual Guide, so you may help your children connect to theirs. Without this, ninety-percent will probably never reach maturity in the next thirty-five years.

I could even tell you that your society uses sex and orgasm like a drug, and that you could be as addicted to it as heroine or methadone or speed or ecstasy or any other drug. I can tell you that sugar, nicotine and caffeine in your society are drugs, and that there are hundreds of millions of you addicted to it. I could even tell you that your young people are addicted to driving cars, and that central heating and air conditioning is a drug. Whatever weakens you and makes you farther from the truth of what you are is an ego drug. Whatever you place in front of truth is not helpful, except that it becomes a lesson to bring you back to the truth.

Because of the speed in which your society operates, my first difficulty in dealing with these two children, not yet brought back together, was trying to get them to relax, to go into a deeper state of relaxation than your society knows as a general rule.

With my son, it was easy. He was so unhappy. The most entertaining thing he could do was to walk on the beach at night, alone. And it was there that his mind began to open and to question. His responsibilities in the world included supporting a wife and two children. And even though separation was imminent, he worked diligently, both to support his family and to awaken his right brain... his interest in and awareness of the Spiritual world.

There was one difficulty with his awakening. The nature of his first marriage was such that he would not allow himself to dream when at home. So, to open his mind, he had to use medicines and pray to Spirit. He had to walk hours on the beach and spend time alone in the mountains. He had to go to Sweat Lodge Ceremony which opened the channels to Spirit. And he was much like me in that when Spirit answered him for the first time out loud, it frightened him so badly that he didn't ask again for months to come. But it was because we used good humor in answering him that he began to trust, slowly, that Spirit was real, that you can hear a Voice other than your own. It doesn't always have to come from inside your own head. You can hear it outside too, as if Spirit was standing right next to you. We are.

Barbara's dreaming mind was so developed that we enlisted the help of good teachers in India during her year stay. With their dreaming minds, they filled hers with possibilities. They also taught her not to get stuck on having to have an outside teacher in physical form.

It was the getting of these two together, Barbara and John, that awakened in them the idea that miracles are real, that synchronicity happens, and that there is a Higher Plan. They learned there are Helpers everywhere to help you complete your part in it, that everything in time and space can be arranged for the accomplishment of an agreed upon goal, and that the whole of creation will bend to assist you in attaining the truth.

To admit you know nothing, to stand in this uncomfortable place of not knowing, to learn to be comfortable with your questions, to wait patiently for the answers, to be observant and alert, so your questions can be answered in any form, to have the courage to walk a spiritual path, is not hard when you have burned out your attachments to the illusions of the world. It is the most natural thing to do. What is unnatural is to avoid, through the distractions of the world, the facing of any fear that prevents you from being on a spiritual path. Children playing.

So we were grateful when these two young ones had run their games, seen the cost of further delay and stepped on the path. They were then put on an accelerated learning course. They were given responsibilities for other people, and they were continually taught and tested. In three years, their bond grew and was rendered, virtually destroyed, and rebuilt again.

This was done for two reasons. One, these challenges were put to the both of them to test their willingness to learn and their desire for the truth, and two, to test the level at which their personal mind was more valuable to them than the intent of Spirit. It was this period in which all splits would be revealed.

Now, I want to tell you, the average reader, that this is a fierce process, uncompromising, unbending, because ego is so slippery that it cannot be caught out and revealed unless the stakes are very high and absolutely clear. It is only when ego is revealed that the personal attachment to it can be ended. And it is only this that the aspirant has choice about, whether to yield it up for change, for transformation, for transmutation, whether the mind can be used for something other than the use the ego has put it to or not. That is your choice. To this point, *everyone* will come and it will be fierce indeed, whether you use medicine or not.

For your understanding, I will tell you one secret of Spirit, but only one.

It is to the test of your words that we put your lives.

It is in these tests that you will redefine and re-understand and reconfirm what everything means.

There are times in this process that it will look like you are abandoned. And it is during these times that you will develop your most strength of character, that you will develop an awareness of what will is for. Were it not love doing this, you would not learn. It is only in love that you can learn anything at all, regard-

299

less of the hardships you endure. It is not enough to be told that something is not real. It is essential that you make the connection yourself, in order to have self-respect and knowledge within you.

If a child cries because his bottle is taken away, he will either become a greedy person and make sure he has plenty of bottles when he is older, and have control over his own life, with his own refrigerator for the bottles and his own house for that, and his own bottle company to own so he can't be fired, and so on and so forth, or he will find out that he never needed the bottle at all. And it is through the loss of the very thing you value the most that you find out that your value is misplaced, and nothing at all was lost.

If I were to be too specific about my twins' experiences, I would only entertain you. So I am not being specific, except about the process of learning and what was learned, so that you may have your own experiences, untainted by anyone else's.

Everyone is unique and yet the same. We are all uniquely the same. That you are all on a spiritual path is the question. If you are not, then clearly look at what you'd prefer in the moment. John's split was about seeing women sexually, at the same time as he was seeing them spiritually. To hold a thing in high regard and want to seduce it is a split mind. So the first order of business was to get this healed.

Now, you all know how hard it is to break a thief of stealing, to change a liar into an honest man, to get a drunk to love God better than the bottle. So the only person that could help this be accomplished would be his other half.

You see, God likes you to put something at stake. And in this day and age, what is at stake is love, is truth. If hell were to be something real and present, there would be no way back to the truth or to love. If heaven were to be present, there would be no way to fall out of truth or out of love. What mistake would be great enough for heaven to toss you out or for hell to keep you in? You all make judgments all the time about each other, and yet you cannot put each other into heaven. You can build each other's egos and make each other feel important, but in the world you do this and it is illusion. One mistake and you could be in hell. I tell you, you all make up what hell is, but only the Creator makes up what heaven is. And there is no mistake so big that there is no way back into heaven from hell. If there were, love would not be love, would it?

So if you do not forgive, you create hell and keep yourself out of heaven as well. If you prefer to judge anyone for anything, then you are the jailer and the jailed. You are the condemned and the condemner. You are the guilty along with the guilty you judge.

You see, the path of healing, though it walks everywhere in the world, is not a part of the world. Health walks here, not as a part of sickness but distinct from it. What is helpful can only arrive at the only goal there is... to Help.

If you are confused in any way, it is because you perceive conflict inside and still see two opposing viewpoints, having not chosen the one beyond both. If you think you do not have choice here, it is because you do not see the choice was already made. The conflict was illusion to begin with, because what is eternal remains so. What is in time belongs to the laws of the earth and is for lessons only. It does not change the truth at all.

So, separating God in half, into male and female, is only for lessons to get you back to joining again. Joining is the only purpose for lessons. That is what the world is for.

It is easy to get to the truth, to overcome the fear that the truth is not true. By overcoming your fears, you make the truth true for you and you see its value. If you prefer illusions, it does not change the truth, but the lessons that you receive will be much more difficult, much more intense. It is easier, I think, for me to tell you that death isn't real, so you don't have to go out and test yourself against your fear of death, trying to find out what's beyond.

I'll answer you this. You are already beyond death, and so is all of your foolishness. Take comfort. Your mind is your *own* judgment day because it is not apart from God. Your mind is a part of God, so you know the truth, and therefore judge your own actions accordingly. It is notable that in your times, your murderers are asking for the death penalty. It is because they know the truth, and they are tired of their behavior and tired of the world.

I say, it's far easier to change your behavior than to live extreme lives. It's easier to appeal to Spirit to help you remember your True Identity, than it is to believe in the world around you and what it tells you, you are.

Barbara had to endure John's extreme behavior. She had to risk the loss of trust of Spirit and trust of her husband, the loss of the final union between two split souls, in order to wake John up to what was present, to what was at risk, to what he truly preferred.

Your splits are from waiting too long to talk to Spirit, to ask questions for you that are deep in conflict. You do not bring your troubles to Spirit. You try to resolve them yourself or stuff them away. And deep conflict will cause a split in your mind to become nearly permanent behavior.

Certain medicines, when used through the guidance of Spirit, are virtually the only fast way to ever see one's own psychic split, to have it healed, and to retain a consciousness of that healing process. (And incidentally, this is the only way to train a modern-day shaman who is not presently native or being trained in ancient, secret native ceremonies. Traditionally, such training takes a minimum of sixteen years. With medicines, learning can be accelerated, assuming the student does not flee from the challenges.)

So, any discomfort you feel in your physical form is from psychic conflict. Simple tension is conflict. A pain in the neck, a runny nose, burning eyes, ringing ears, stomach pains, menstrual cramps... it's all conflict. Every thought you think, every thought of those around you for hundreds of miles affects how you feel.

Now, you can climb above this in your mind and go on, you may think. And you do. But the conflict is still there. Unresolved conflicts eventually wear the form out. All the dual concepts that you carry within you as a result of the culture in which you live, create deep conflict and eventual significant splits and sickness. That you never speak to your conflict is no credit to you at all.

A whole generation of young people began to take drugs and medicines in the sixties, and they began to see and choose who they would work for, love or fear. What you call the "love generation" was born, born out of fear, out of the ashes of the threat of nuclear war, into a desire for non-judgment, peaceful harmony, free expression with loving intent. Though there was much immaturity expressed in these views, the intent was often pure... no more lies... no more war.

What has come out of this generation is more openness, more real discussion, and more real communication about the issues that face this world. What has been left unresolved, however, is a clear understanding of the equality of male and female, a clear commitment to spiritual communication, a real understanding of each other's role, and the role of male and female self within each one of you.

If you want an example of an outward behavior exhibiting male and female inside, I would have to say that bisexual behavior is closer to the experience, except that it's still behaving rather than being integrated into any actual One Truth. The bisexual mind still sees itself and others as the body. So in that state, the mind does not know the truth of what it is any more than any other sexual orientation.

Transformation to a spiritual awareness will begin to occur when you have mastered your mind enough to stop being sexual to each other long enough to recognize what you are *not*. Thinking you experience your True Self as heterosexual, homosexual or bisexual is not remotely relevant to the Spiritual Mind. If you do not master the undue influence the body has over your minds within your cultures, your populations all over the world will continue to grow, until the horror becomes so intense and the conflict so clear that you do change your minds or perish.

A good example of this conflicted mind is any religion that teaches abortion is abominable and is an unpardonable sin. The loss of one life, while the overpopulation of the planet is threatening to wipe out millions at a time through famine or disease, or clearer yet, the insane belief that killing abortion-rights doctors or supporters is going to save a baby's life, and that one life is somehow different from any other, is absurd.

You're saying to me, how do you answer such conflict in this world? And I tell you, the answer is to see that there are not separate conflicts. If you perceive things as separate, then you will not see the One Answer. The truth joins everything. It does not separate anything. If you were to see you are both male and female, if you were to see fully the truth of that, then there would be no conflict.

Now, to bring these two children together who have been separate for centuries and to bring up all the issues between them, all the misperceptions, doubts, confusions and suspicions, many difficult tests were given to them to find out if they really wanted the truth or not. Though they had been asking to come together, we knew their coming together would be explosive, to say the least.

But I tell you, *it's love* doing it... the bringing together is love. For two people to be joined psychically, mentally, emotionally and spiritually, requires that all the misperceptions which separate be healed. And it is only the desire for love and joining that will heal it. But if you value your own mind as a separate entity more than the truth, you will never know it.

So my ancestors rejoice and your ancestors rejoice when any two people overcome all the obstacles in their path to get back to wholeness again, to join each other in perfect union. It makes the world have value again, have purpose again, have meaning again... that something real could be accomplished from all this activity, all this energy, all this giving, all this taking.

It is for the purpose of healing that these books be written. It is through the example and willingness of these two people to undergo this process, as difficult as it has been, that allows these books to be written. Perhaps they have no more importance than any other book, I do not know. But if they lift your eyes out of illusion for a moment and put you on the path to the only goal that your life has, then these books have achieved what they have set out to do.

Renew your relationship with the earth. Renew your relationship with the spirit in all living things. And renew your awareness of yourself as spirit as well. It is in Spirit that all things are equal.

Chapter 9
The Gift Of Consciousness

I think the hardest thing there is for a human being to come to realize is that the mind that they identify with as "self" betrays them. If your mind is in conflict and in pain, and yet you cannot stop the conflict, then you must begin to realize, albeit very slowly, that your mind is not necessarily your friend.

Now that you're aware of the fact that the mind is the source of all the difficulties, what do you do with it? Now that you're aware that conflict exists, that you no longer wish to be at the mercy of the impulses of the body running the mind, how do you stop it? Now that you're aware that this worldly mind called ego runs of its own accord, regardless of your wishes, how do you take back this space you call your mind? How do you take your will back?

When your relationships are no longer helpful, you leave. Yet, how do you leave your own mind? This conflict, though it appears to be just like every other conflict, is much more serious because it pits one powerful adversary against a relatively weak one, the new self.

First of all, be aware that it is your mind that deceives you. Second, be aware that all your past behavior is due to the fact that you have given the mind your power and your will to control *you*. When you see something has been behaving your life, even though it is not the behavior you would want, you must then begin to take your will back from the mind that behaves you.

Simply said, don't do what it suggests. Begin to put your awareness at a bit of a distance from your mind and watch it. Be aware of the thoughts it thinks. Be aware of the judgments it makes and the decisions it would have you make. Become aware of what is motivating that mind. Be dispassionate. Study the mind that you thought was you. As the strength of your focus grows, your awareness becomes split from the automatism of this ego mind. But unlike the split the ego made from the truth, your new awareness split from ego is a *return* to truth. Without awareness being developed, there is no chance at becoming conscious.

While developing your awareness, I recommend that you do not study the world around you at the same time. This is one of the mind's devices for distraction. If you have a characteristic that you do not like, then the only way to change that characteristic is to not indulge in it. You will then begin to create a personality that does not include that characteristic.

I will use one characteristic as an example because I believe it is a cornerstone in the foundation of ego. And that is to lie, to misrepresent, to twist, or to shape a perception that is different from the truth.

Jumping to conclusions is the first form of lying. Assuming you know is not knowing. Jumping levels, blaming, not speaking to primary motivations or only speaking to secondary motivations when answering questions are all forms of lying. All are deception. So if you don't like lying, don't do it. When you lie to others, you lie to yourself and so split your mind.

For instance, the conversation a thief has in his mind to justify stealing requires significant willingness to lie and to believe his lies. It is the desire to believe the lies that will finally cause the mind to split.

All human traits we consider undesirable, like lying, are born not out of strength but out of weakness. To prove this, take an obsession or an addiction and stop it, and see who is weak and what is strong. To develop will against an undesirable behavior requires that you do not indulge in that behavior. That's the first level. The second level is, now what do you do with the mind that still thinks the thoughts that created the indulgence and the behavior? How do you stop your mind from seducing you?

It's very simple and difficult. You must train your mind to have a thought you would prefer in place of the seduction. To do this, you must call on Spirit to help you at the moment of seduction. As an example, I will use caffeine or alcohol or smoking or candy or

305

the pursuit of money or sex or any other such sweet device the ego uses to seduce you. When you think you need something, say you don't, then turn your thoughts elsewhere, and you will see the struggle you will have. Because you are weak, you cannot turn your thoughts, and the mind of the body, the ego, controls you. If you can turn your thoughts easily, then your mind is still relatively free. Always in this process, ask Spirit to help you if you find you are struggling against the body's own impulses, the ego-mind's desires.

My daughter here reminds me that this struggle is between the small mind and the larger mind that is connected in love to everything around. She asks how one gets out of the small mind. And I say, when it starts to seduce you, you start to pray, not against the mind you have at the moment but toward the goal that you would reach, toward peace in the moment, then toward God's peace.

If you turn and fight your mind, other than to say "No, thank you," the very will that ego uses is sucked from you again. The "No, thank you" is a door that closes on the ego's use of your will. But then your attention must be pointed toward the goal, not toward the battleground.

So how does one get rid of the battleground altogether? Good question. It is when sufficient will is developed and sufficient trust in Spirit and lack of arrogance about this process is gained that Spirit will come to help you put a permanent end to the mind you do not want. Spirit cannot do this until you truly and absolutely do not want it. If there is any attachment whatsoever, then when Spirit begins the undoing of these errors, begins the process of cleansing, you will resist.

This testing process, this testing of attachments to the small mind we each co-invented with the ego, will go on until every hook is relinquished. Spirit will not go faster than you can stand. And as you progress, you become more diligent, more aware, more willing to have these errors undone. And eventually, the small mind is replaced with the large one. Pretty soon your mind is quiet and peaceful, and no longer your antagonist.

Spirit will not do the work for you. We would not make you weak. In the very beginning of the process, Spirit will take your willingness and help you as much as you will allow. In the middle of this process, your initiative is required. Toward the end of the process of the undoing, it is your initiative alone that has the repair continue. In this way, your autonomy is strengthened in the truth. It is not the function of Spirit to do everything for you as if you were a baby still in diapers and at the breast.

With those persons who have deep splits in their personality,

Spirit helps a bit more, puts on the pressure, brings the conflicts up to awareness, even catches you out in your behavior, so you realize that your mind betrays you. If nothing was at stake, if the betrayal cost nothing, you would never look. You would never take a neutral stance with your own mind and look at it as if you were another person viewing it from inside.

The value of medicine work is that this process of seeing the errors, recognizing the splits and allowing healing, occurs in a state of awareness that leads to consciousness. Your new mind is developing as you watch. Your watching mind then blooms into full consciousness. The value of consciousness is its permanency. Another value of consciousness is that you begin to help others around you with the same issues, problems and solutions, through the mere fact that you are no longer adding to the confusion.

The religious will say, "It is the Holy Spirit, the Holy Ghost, it is Jesus, and it is the Father that affect these changes that help us overcome addictions and weakness, that help us overcome being sinful."

The Latin root word sin means "without." In Christian terms, it means "without God." The essence of what Jesus taught was that sin was not unpardonable, that misbehavior could be forgiven but not condoned. The purpose of a mistake is to learn and not to remake the error. Therefore, the circle of forgiveness is completed when learning is achieved. So it is, a way to healing through forgiveness, through consciousness, through the joining of your will to Spirit, is achieved.

Now, you ask, what does this have to do with indian spirituality? Well, we pray to the same Creator. We ask for forgiveness for our pitiful behavior. We ask for help in changing ourselves from weak to strong, from fear to love. So Spirit uses tests and trials to uncover our minds' self-deceptions, to break through the web of illusion to truth. And we willingly challenge ourselves as well and put ourselves at risk. That is the path of native healing.

I will tell you the path of error. All our adult perceptions and all our adult behaviors are based upon decisions we made as children. All of those decisions were based upon misperceptions we accepted, while trying to interpret a chaotic, adult world. Therefore, all of the world's behavior is based upon misrepresentations, misinterpretations and misperceptions accepted when all were children. So we have children with children's perceptions teaching children.

It would not be necessary to have a Holy Spirit if you were not so confused. Jesus would not have to come back to save you from your sins if you had a way of dealing with the mechanism that runs your own minds, if you had the will to change the mind that errs. But it is necessary for Spirit to help, and there is a way to take your will back from the mechanism called ego.

When you allow Spirit to return you in vision to the place and time where you made the errors in your thinking, you will laugh because your mind has evolved in its understanding since then, but the decisions you made back then have not. And I tell you, you are guided in your personality, in your definition of yourself by the decisions that you made earlier.

Some of these decisions can be very helpful to get you to adulthood, to get you through the trials that normal life brings you. And yet, when you are faced with circumstances where those decisions are no longer helpful, you find you cannot change your mind. You have never learned how to change your mind. You have not even discovered the reason why it would be helpful to change your mind. Most people would rather be right to the death than change their mind.

Is God creative? Would creation be creation if there was not a mind that was able to expand and grow? The definition of creativity is an ability to learn and to evolve beyond an original state. So, it may look hard to do... change your mind. And I tell you, without your awareness of the influences on your mind, without your awareness of its mechanisms, it is hard to change.

So talk to yourself. You have a mind that will listen to you. Shift your eyes up and to the right, and ask your mind where a certain behavior came from. Why do I believe, for instance, that the devil is blue? Why, for instance, am I afraid of policemen? Because they wear blue uniforms, because of the guns that they carry, they must be evil. This was my son's thought as a youngster. But as an adult, while walking down the street, he began to laugh to see that this thought was a child's thought. As an adult, he could laugh and see that a policeman was a human being, not the devil. So he began to respond to them as human beings. And his relationship with policemen changed... from fearing authority to talking with a human being.

So if you have a fear, ask how come. If you have a core belief that is causing you fear, speak to it. If you cannot go up in an elevator or come down an escalator, put yourself in those places and speak to your fear. Do not give up until you get to its cause. When you are no longer afraid of being afraid, you will recall why you were afraid. And, I tell you, it will be something that you decided a long time ago, something you no longer need in your life. And what made you weak with fear will transform to make you strong in peace. You will have faced a fear and recovered some experience from your past. And you will forgive it this time, and it

308

will be changed forever. When you are afraid, call on Spirit to help you. They'll come because They love you. They will always help you face your fears and find the road to true freedom, back to love again.

If you believe that love can be lost, then, be sure, for you the world is a treacherous place... and maybe even God's not real. If you trust only your thoughts about what love is, then your fears call to you the lessons needed that prove you are mistaken. If you judge the lessons that come to you, then your life will be hell. If you embrace a larger concept of love, then you will learn from your lessons and grow toward fulfillment. If the core belief that love can be lost is cherished more than having love, then you will not have it. If your ideas of love are designed to protect you from being used by unconscious people, then you are not giving love but defending against the possible loss of it, and therefore aren't in it.

The true enemy is not love lost but ignorance, ignorance of what love is in the first place. If you seek to be taught by the world about what love is, I think you will be disappointed. I think it is just Spirit who can help you. Being lonely for a partner and having one in ignorance will not fulfill you in your desire for love. So ask Spirit what partner is for you. Be diligent by working on yourself, and be honest with all those who come to you. Spirit will show you who is your teacher and who you are to teach. This marriage Spirit makes with you and another will be helpful. If you are in a marriage, the only criteria you should judge it by is, are you helping each other or not? Is your life creative with each other toward the truth of what love is or not?

You see, you are meant to enjoy, not to think alone. If you are thinking alone, it is because you are not in joy, not enjoined. Thinking is not having. Thinking is not knowing. The only way to knowing is to give up thinking you don't or can't or won't or shouldn't or couldn't or wouldn't or couldn't possibly or wouldn't ever or couldn't barely begin. Begin somewhere, please.

If you defend your perceptions, then you are not learning. If you are open to your perceptions being changed, then do not defend them. If your mind remains open and you ask for Spirit's help, you will not get lost. You do not have to believe the words that people speak. You do not even have to believe the words that Spirit speaks. You simply, like a new shirt, try the words on and see how they fit. If they don't fit, you take them off, set them aside or give them away. You recycle the words that do not fit, continually. And as your mind evolves beyond the words, the truth will dawn on you of its own. The truth is not contained in words given as possessions to one another, traded as gifts, or offered as debts. The truth will stand clearly in the present, in your awareness, all of its own. And it does not sit in judgment on a throne and does not point anywhere.

Now, I said a great many things earlier in this book and in the book before it, in the way of provoking thought, stirring the pot. I do not profess my thoughts to be the Absolute Truth. I do not claim that my words come directly from God. I simply tell you, I'm an old indian who loves his children, and I am working to set their minds free, so that they may see the truth and know God for themselves.

I did not say, don't eat cow 'cause they're too slow. I did not say taking soy milk from a bottle instead of the female breast is bad for you. I did not say your government doesn't love you and only lies. I did not say you cannot live in a square house and be spiritual, or not to eat hamburgers or fried chicken. I did not say you had to be indian to know the love of the Mother. I did not say ceremonies are the only way to test yourself. I did not say medicines are the only way to awaken your consciousness. I did not say that the earth will be destroyed by one government or another, by materialism or asceticism, by fire or by water. I would not say these things because they are not true. And yet, within them is a grain of the truth.

I will tell you, for sure, that you do not need your language to know love, to know truth, to know God. You do not need your sensations, your sex, whether male or female, to get to true knowledge. The more you shed of illusion, the closer you get to truth.

So, like a good meal, I stir life up pretty good. Because the Last Supper is all supper, it's a huge soup. In it is the acceptance and the relinquishment of everything it took to get you to the place of transformation. It is the acknowledgment that it took all of that to get you there. It is in receiving that you give away. It is in gratitude that you turn your eyes from not having to having. You will never get to God by being disgusted with creation, the world and any life in it. Neither can you renounce your disgust before you accept you had it. You cannot give up something that you have not "received"... in honesty, admitted you had.

All change comes this way. All liars are healed as soon as they admit they lied, not for one lie but for all lies... everyone's. When the function of lying is understood to be universal and accepted is it finally put away. First, you must not lie in order to accept the fact that you have been lying. When you accept the function that your ego had for lying, that's when you get to see it. When you get to see it, you get to forgive and change. You cannot kill it off by not wanting it. But you can stop it and bring it to the place where it is embraced, so the error may be replaced.

Thinking of ourselves as a physical entity, human, can be replaced with the truth... spiritual entity, human. Thinking of ourselves as male or female, singly, rather than as one... these thoughts that divided us can join us. **You cannot truly love something if you think it's different.** The thoughts you have follow the decisions you made, based upon the perceptions you projected from your eyes onto the world as judgment. And I tell you, your eyes don't know anything about the truth. So use your mind's eye to look at the sameness. And retrain your mind, so that it doesn't take the five senses and life's appearances as God's Word.

That you perceive with your five senses makes you vulnerable to the illusions of life, not its truth. The world you see will change in front of your eyes as your mind changes. It is your perceptions that make your reality, and it is the correction of these perceptions that will change your world. Everything that comes out of your mouth, everything that you do, I tell you, is based upon your individual perceptions of the world and the ones that you've agreed upon with your neighbors. That is why the world can look so different when you visit different cultures. That is why there are different religions, ceremonies and traditions. But look at what they teach, look at their function, not at how they're done.

Let's say, dancers in the southern hemisphere are dancing clockwise, while in the northern hemisphere they are dancing counterclockwise. Is the world twisted in half with this movement? No. Why? Because our perceptions are powerless to change the truth. It is only the truth that has power. None other. And I tell you, you didn't make up what the truth is and have barely even begun to ask what it is. When you discover and become aware of what is true, your words and your actions begin to have power. But remember, only in love does the truth exist at all. Nowhere else.

So, it is easy to be psychic. Just be aware of the *intent* behind anyone's words or actions. Do not get caught up in their words. Listen to what is meant by them. Their intent drives their meaning. Their meaning or lack of it drives their words. And there are only two kinds of intent, constructive or destructive... to build or to tear down, to reveal or to deceive.

You may draw a line and list all that is love on one side and all that is fear on the other. And, as I have said before, the two do not touch each other in any way. They are a simple choice of mind. What would you believe?

God is not a marriage between love and fear, nor was humankind made in God's image out of a marriage of love and fear. What would love birth? Love? What would fear birth? Death? Look around you. See what love created. See what fear made. All *life* comes from the completion of the Sacred Circle of Love between male and female, a circle of giving and receiving and giving and receiving and giving and receiving. No fear in it anywhere.

From within this circle, a thought was born that to prove love is true, to prove that love is real, it would be put into an arena and tested. The test was to give the *appearance* of separation, by giving separate bodies to male and female. The truth to be proven was that bodies could not separate love from love. So what is, came to be. Bodies were born into the world. The thought of creation was not enough. Demonstration was necessary for proof. So it is being accomplished.

And because mind had to be born into a body, because spirit had to be born into a physical brain, the body responded and grew around the mind that willed it. All the materials of the universe came to be at life's disposal, for life's use. So sprang around you a temporary device called body. It sprang around Life's Intent, out of love, because Love sent it on this journey to prove that love is real.

It is the nature of being born to forget. Life being born into two different bodies, male or female, split itself in half, so it did not know what it was anymore. It forgot. So man looks to the woman for love, and woman looks to man for truth. And in this whirling circle called life is a single gift the Creator left as a birthday present at your feet between you, a little, tiny package.

Now, what is this present that follows you everywhere, this gift? And how is it opened? Your thirst tells you it's there. You know it's inside because the world outside doesn't reveal it to you, though you search everywhere and try everything.

Humanity has gone through four suns, through four worlds, and it is the spirits that are born into bodies that are growing up the world's mind. It has been a long process of many births to get the world to evolve to where it is now, to where it can actually begin to see the gift that the Creator left for each of us.

To open this gift, each one of us must learn to give up the separate mind, the mind that keeps us separate from each other, the idea of differences between male and female. That you prefer your small identity as safety makes you push the gift aside. That you prefer past grievances pushes the gift aside one more time. That you prefer judgment and anger pushes the gift aside. That gift cannot be opened until you have joined male and female inside yourself, as you were before the earth rose to greet you out of love.

To the degree that you prefer your differences is the degree to which you push that gift away. To the degree that you value your own mind more than the truth is the degree to which you will not have it.

So I ask you, do not hold onto one thing that you now mistakenly value, and that gift will come into your awareness. To the degree that you are able to relinquish your attachments and fears, one by one, is the degree to which this gift will come closer and closer, and you will become more aware in your mind of its value.

So, possess nothing and give it no value of your own. Don't even possess one thought in your mind, or you have pushed the gift aside and preferred something else in place of it.

In *Fire,* I have attempted to open a discussion and to create a vague awareness that you are energy, that the material fire, red, runs the body. That this material fire would run your mind is an error. The ultimate purpose of this material fire is to transform you into the awareness that your body is an effect of this red spark, that being an adult is coming to the full awareness that you are not the body. That you would choose to awaken to Spiritual truth, through the trials of this physical fire, is your function.

It has been said previously that no man gets to God except through woman. This is not an active journey to be pursued. It is a passive one of realization that you must return to your beginnings to understand. You cannot be unborn in physical form, but you can be reborn from physical into spiritual. You need *do* nothing. It's love doing it. Only your willingness and true desire is necessary to achieve this awakening. If you stop along the road and pretend to *be* something, then you once again have pushed the package aside and not received the gift.

That you would use the energy of the physical fire to try to achieve a spiritual awareness is the ultimate in self-deception, and your mind will betray you all your life. That the truth is true is your salvation.

To awaken to your understanding that all life has a God Self is not enough to save you from the betrayal of your own mind. Knowledge cannot be had without love. What you possess is useless to you and more than worthless to anyone else.

A sure note of anyone who has slipped off the narrow path to awakening is their claiming to *know* anything at all. Any pretense to ownership of knowledge is not knowledge. The tests that Spirit will provide you in your growth will never end until you are truly awakened. And it is not until this awakening takes place that you could be useful for any purpose at all. You see, your life is a gift and it is free. However, it is not eternal until it totally understands what it is in truth, not what it thinks it is.

The most pitiful, philosophical statement ever perpetrated on the minds of mankind is, "I think, therefore I am." The last arrogant step that an arrogant mind can take is to claim, "I Am that I Am."

Am what?

Pitiful! Pathetic! Nice try. But it won't get it, will it? To claim something without knowledge is a waste of time. This is an act of a mind caught in the midst of trying to create itself, to be its own creator. What fool could imagine for a moment that it is the God that created itself, unless it was deceived? This is the mind of ego. It betrays the truth. And I tell you, even in your confusion, the truth is within you. You do not possess it alone, however.

The fault of language is simply this. It is spoken alone, inside its own thinking. And if its purpose is not love, then it can't even conceive of any truth within it. Silence is closer to the truth, but I'll tell you how hard it is to achieve. Stop talking to yourself inside your own head. Go ahead. Try it. You don't even know what silence is. And with all that chattering going on, how on earth could the truth ever dawn on you?

Within love, within truth is this Sacred Silence. Before you speak, before you act, even before you think, you would do well to remember this one thing. **Silence is the Womb of God, and everything that comes forth is God's children.**

It is your own mind that frightens you because you are not in control of its images, thoughts and words. You don't even know what it is. And to make matters worse, you get sensations all over your body... hunger, thirst, pressure, pain, pleasure, and the most confusing of all to you... sex.

The second most confusing to you is anger. You don't even know that your anger is the sign of the most violent betrayal of the ego against you. It is ego defending its perceptions which made alone in error could never know the truth. It is a device for self-destruction and the destruction of life around it. It is the most arrogant device man has ever conceived. And it is responsible for the destruction of goodwill on this planet. And yet, you think it protects you from the world.

Now I will confuse you further. I will tell you that all temptation is a device of Spirit. What you think is the devil is a teaching device of God. Let's call it the "negative teacher." I'll even make you angry. Perhaps you'll even throw this book into the fire. I'll tell you, the devil is god too.

If God is omnipotent, omniscient, omnipresent, and all them things, if the Creator is the Creator, then evil is part of creation. It

314

is still in the service of Love. And it could easily be recontained by Love, put back in a box as it once was, if that was the plan. Evil will be undone in God's time, as there is no opponent to God's Will. If evil had no value or purpose, it would not be here as the negative teacher. The lessons it teaches are there to develop your will... your will not *against* evil, but your will *joined* to Creator's love. It is love that will dispel any illusion about truth, and it is the truth inside love that will dispel any illusion about love. This cannot be accomplished in war or opposition of any kind. The trick is not to believe or do anything that evil suggests.

Because humans demand an Armageddon to win the battle between good and evil, it will probably come to pass. It is that they don't know they can simply just open the gift and give it around in its truth, and the pitiful thought of devils would be gone. Any weak power that negativity would have would be useless. It is the Creator letting the children play this out for themselves that births them into Spirit. That they learn to choose love and peace is what the earth is for.

Many people think the earth is both heaven and hell, somewhere in between perhaps, maybe just a huge hospital for the temporarily insane. But I tell you, **Love is All there Is.** The earth itself is an alive, complex system designed to support physical life. The whole thing demonstrates love in every instance. But you say, "Oh well, it's winter and then it's summer, and it's hot and cold, and sometimes there's rain and sometimes there's not, and all in all, it's a big challenge." Well, I tell you, God would not make you weak. What good is a sixty-year-old baby? Because of your self-indulgence and your resentment of the experiment at all, you will call hard times to yourself. But it is *you* trying to wake *yourself* up that does this because... **you love you.**

I'll give you examples. Two people can say, "All we have to do is consider each other, make a place for each other in our minds, honor each other's life as our own and we will be joined."

All well and good. But Love will test these two, to see if their desire for joining is a conviction or not. To desire to love one another is not conviction. To what degree do you love me and I love you? When would love fail under stress? Or would it?

In this world, it is not what you would give up to have love. It is whether or not you would give up loving at all. You can love another human being, and they can say they love you and every day prove they don't. And yet, it's love doing it. That two people would want equality between male and female is a result of giving love, not a demand to get love and not a prerequisite for having it.

If offered to Spirit for correction, any obstacle to having love

315

becomes a lesson in giving love. Backwards, that's to say, because you have pressure to find love, that makes you think it is missing, somewhere else, in someone else. Yes? The illusion is that love is always outside or that you are always outside of it. Yet, how could that be true?

This age of insanity that you're in is only there because you prefer illusions to the truth. You prefer complexity to simplicity. You prefer conflict to peace. You prefer to scare yourselves to entertain you, rather than to learn what love is. You prefer to stir up and test love, rather than to give it. You prefer to walk and look away, rather than stand still and look inside. You demand to be loved, but you prefer to war.

Another example. Is the Christian idea of God different from the Muslim idea? Do you prefer to believe it is? Are there thirty-five religions or seven big ones? Are there seven Creators or even two? Can a woman have a baby by herself? Prove it. If you be God, do it. So is woman, God the Creator by herself? Well, if you make man God, then maybe she can have an immaculate conception. Nobody saw it. Nobody will admit it. But is man by himself, God? Okay, birth yourself, sucker.

There is no male or female God, alone. There is One Creator, one creation, and They, the Mother and the Father did it together as One. Now, I ask you, what did They do it for?

Look in the package... please. End the age of insanity. Open the gift. Ask questions.

If it did not rain, the seed would not grow, yes? Without water... no life, yes? Is water, God? Without the fire of the sun, there would be no warmth and the seed would not grow. Is the sun, God? Without the trees and the water and the sun and the earth, there would be no air, yes? Is the air, God? Without all these things, there would be no physical life... mammalian life, insect life or any other kind of moving, living, breathing, flying, swimming, walking, crawling thing. Are they, God?

Pray to a spider. You might learn what the heck a spider's for, what it teaches, what its purpose for being here is. Ask it. Be humble. It will tell you because... *it's love.*

What is a tree's life? What is its purpose? What is its consciousness? Be humble. Ask it. It will tell you... *it's love.*

If a tree angered itself, it would pull its roots up and leave, yes? If a bug did no longer like its skin, it would rip it off and leave, yes? If a being no longer likes being human, it will be something else... if it is God. Yes? All these things and more are God.

I think a tree is more conscious of what it is than a human. I'm sure the bugs are. Feice proved it to me. I know most animals have no confusion in their minds about what they are. I look at humans and they are nothing but confusion. A human can be all of it and is, but to know that you are God, you must ask Its creations to teach you what you are. You must ask love to teach you what you do not know. Because you grow to physical maturity does not mean you grow to direct knowledge of the truth of creation. You've got to be interested in finding out, first. You've got to be teachable to learn, yes? Thinking you know is not knowing. Thinking you have is not having, is it?

You are God. And yet, you are a human being awakening to your small position. If you cannot accept that humble spot, then how can you expect to be all of it? If you cannot accept your experience as human in all humility, with all the feelings, thoughts and sensations that come with it, with all the illusions and recognition of them, then how can you know your God Self?

Begin with yourself and what you know and do not know. Be honest. Do you know what love is? If you do, you know all there is to know.

Now, I think there's some people walkin' around on the streets that sure act like they know it all. But they're just human. And to the degree that they're arrogant is the degree to which they do not know what love is. To the degree that they are insecure is the degree to which they do not even experience their own life.

To behave is an attempt to understand. To behave without self-examination is an attempt to live without understanding. To behave without understanding is pitiful. To behave with some understanding but without knowledge is sickening. To behave with the pretension of knowledge is evil.

I'll define evil for you. It's very simple. It has two levels. The first one is deliberate cruelty, without conscience. The second level, I'm afraid to mention it to you. I don't want to give you ideas.

As a matter of fact, I will withhold this one because it deals with the area of knowledge, and therefore extends into the area of Spirit. And I would not poison your mind against Spirit. Suffice it to say, everyone is innocent until they have a thread of knowledge. You see, any thread of knowledge contains the entire thing, the whole truth.

So when a person has begun to awaken and reverts and pretends they did not learn, they fall into a great chasm called evil. A great many acts have been done to people and to the land and to all its creatures out of ignorance, without a thread of knowledge. Because this level of understanding was achieved and these acts were done without true knowledge, they can be forgiven. But when humans learn the truth and choose a path of evil, then they

317

have already rejected the only return to sanity that is available. Their lives will be taken from them. Their spark of truth, the God Self remains, but the life that knowingly tried to live itself outside of love will end.

Now, you say, if God is love, why would that happen? Because only what is real is inside love. God never stopped loving. It was not God that ended that life. It was the God Self within the split mind that ended it.

I will tell you this about second level evil. Love throws a bubble around that spirit self when they're out of line and do not serve Love's purpose. There is quite a bit of leeway here, and it depends on whether this spirit self is on the earth plane or another, whether or not a bubble can be thrown around it quickly or not. There is a transition zone very near the earth's surface that Spirit can do little to influence without direct asking. Even then, a great struggle can take place for the small spirit that was evil, to get help from love. Many times, a living being in body must help, for the dead one stuck in evil to be released.

Now, I tell you these secrets in *Earth* because we are soon to begin *Water*. It is in *Water,* I will reveal to you the ways of healing, the ways of undoing the effects of a split mind, the ways of rejoining the separate male and female self, to get to truth, to stand again within love, to return then to One Self, All Selves, All One Everything... God.

Now, after what I've said about everything being God, you may want to throw your gift of consciousness in the fire, or you may want to bury it under the earth. But if you do, I'll pour water on that fire, and in the dampened earth this seed of consciousness will grow again anyway because... *it's love.*

Chapter 10

Summary of Fire and Earth

All life began at a certain point and expanded to what you see in front of you, to what is behind you and beneath you and above you, to what is your north, south, east and west, and to what is your within space.

I wish to tell you that the seven directions apply not just to space but to time as well. A person that travels, yet does not know north, east, south and west, must use a guide or a map to read. Those that do not use guides or read maps well cannot orient their own mind within the universe. A person that cannot orient themselves on this planet, on the surface, does not know where their within is. They do not have any reference point from which to orient their own mind in space or time.

The only purpose in learning to orient yourself in the universe is to find your *within* moment in space and time called **Now.** It is only in the oriented within moment called now, collecting both past and future, that you can understand the purpose of your center. It is in the now, within your center, that you have an open and neutral mind. The open and neutral mind is the point at which your will becomes aligned with Creator's and changes from the willfulness of ego to willingness in Spirit. It is in this state of willingness all your words are redefined, so you can see value and helpfulness in everything.

The words I favor for this centering process are courage, patience, endurance, and alertness. I put those words in four cardinal directions, east, south, west and north, and I draw a circle around them and draw lines from top to bottom, side to side. And the words I put around the circle in the open spaces between the cardinal directions are relax, love, communicate, and trust.

The attributes of a human being who can complete the sacred circle are courage, patience, endurance, and alertness. These qualities or attributes are required for joining the red and blue flame, for joining love (red flame) to truth (blue flame), and finding the One Creator beyond God the male and God the female, within.

THE CIRCLE OF LOVE

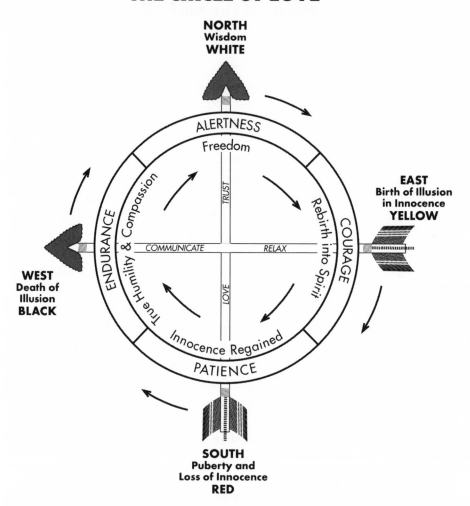

NORTH
Wisdom
WHITE

EAST
Birth of Illusion
in Innocence
YELLOW

WEST
Death of
Illusion
BLACK

SOUTH
Puberty and
Loss of Innocence
RED

ALERTNESS

Freedom

TRUST

COMMUNICATE   RELAX

Compassion

True Humility &

ENDURANCE

Rebirth into Spirit

COURAGE

LOVE

Innocence Regained

PATIENCE

BODY • First Turn - Outside • Red Road
SPIRIT • Second Turn - Inside • Blue Road

*

To join male and female within yourself, a major shift in consciousness must be made from having your perceptions dictated to you by your sensations, by your body, to returning perception to Spirit to give you guiding visions. These visions will eventually put you in correct relationship to the world, and you will find all living things are your relations.

You will, then, begin to understand you do not know what has value, so you will question the value of everything through prayer. You will ask Spirit what the value of everything is. Then you can have a healed relationship with the natural world.

When you do this, you'll begin to give up all forms of suffering. You'll begin to give up guilt, remorse, anger, and the attempt to be right and determine wrong through judgment. You'll give up failure and the state of depression. And you will give up attack and defense as a form of safety. You will walk from not knowing to knowledge, through the *thought*, the *request*, the *acceptance*, and the *knowing*.

The thought is determining what you want. The request is developing true desire to have it. The acceptance is the willingness to have your perceptions transformed, so you can have it. And the knowledge is the event itself, is the revelation, is what is revealed to you.

Your biggest challenge is finding agreement within yourself to ask these questions. The only way to find agreement is to accept the powerlessness of your position and admit not knowing anything in the first place... your humility.

A reference point for the maturation of a human being is when one does not stop at not knowing but continues on, desiring and asking to know. An immature human being will endlessly review details over and over and over again without resolution, whereas a mature human being will take all those details and find the clues that are there. They will use their own mind and ability to inquire, to crack the code to understanding. That understanding is the platform to the next level of the expansion of that person's being.

In other words, thinking becomes meditation. And when the goal is more important than the distractions, meditation will find time to become contemplation. In meditation is the discovery of your energy centers and the understanding that it is your mind which can only react or remain neutral and aware. Contemplation is in neutrality with Spirit.

The energy of control then disolves into the power of discovery. When control is yielded, revelation is possible. When trying is put away, the clockwise flow of energy caused by trying, now begins to move counter-clockwise. Allowing, produces vision and revelation.

Doing in the world moves your energy clockwise to the right and projects it forward, because in the world doing is really trying. The world of control or power or manipulation moves energy clockwise and makes the front side of the chakras spin that way. Spirit's reversal of your projected, clockwise energy is the undoing... the Atonement, the receiving of your healing.

When you are able to take any unhelpful energy and ground it to the earth and join the energy that is the earth, the Mother, then that clockwise energy in you will reverse and go left, counter-clockwise in its undoing.

When your will is finally rightside up and changed from willfulness to willingness, your other energy centers that moved clockwise in the front can now connect to the chakras in the back and move counter-clockwise. When the undoing is complete, your chakras can again reverse and spin clockwise, and allow you to "give" and "do" in the world in a balanced and conscious way.

You cannot receive until the back of your chakras are open to Spirit and open to the undoing of any errors in your perception. You cannot do anything of true value in the world, until you truly know what has value and what is there for you to do. Without Spirit, clockwise doing will always need to be counter-clockwise, undone.

Once you've got this, you will then learn to move your consciousness down the front of your body, through the root fire, then up through each chakra and see what the teachings are, from below first level up to seventh. You will find out you are a communication device of the highest order, with the most ancient memory. You will even learn to read your blood and bones like a radio transceiver.

Remember, it is your *descent* which grounds your mind and heart to the core of the earth, the red fire, the heart of the Mother, that makes *ascent* possible at all. It is only when a human comes down out of the tall tree, pretending to see far, that they see their Tree of Life grows roots to the core of the earth. Reversing the ego's energy grounds you to the core of the earth. And you receive as the gift of accomplishment, the ascent to Spiritual understanding.

Done willingly, the gifts of accomplishment are expanded awareness, expanded sensitivity, expanded helpfulness, expanded creativity. That means that though you are still in form, you have freedom in your bondage. Though you must go to work every day to put food on the table, you are not cursing your life but blessing it.

After many years of finding the good in everything, of being helpful and seeing helpfulness everywhere, you might be ready to face the mechanism of ego itself. And in facing that mechanism, the facing of evil, madness and death, you will get to glimpse the Great Mystery and know God is real and love is real, and know the truth that burns away all fears, compulsions, obsessions, and addictions.

Fire and earth have been given the association as female elementals, the red flame. And that is because women carry the seed of the memory of what love is and the ability to reproduce, using that red fire. This links her close with the materials of the earth to grow a new form within her womb. This child that emerges links her with all mothers, for all times, beginning with the First Woman.

The elementals of water and air have been given the association of male. That males run, makes them like water. That they are difficult to get to commit, makes them like air. That they walk on top of the land and are always hard to pin down, makes them like water. That their feelings are unknown to them, makes them like water vapor that never touches the earth, like clouds. That they often seem to be above the earth, not looking at consequences, makes them like the vapor in the air. That in their purest moments, they reach for the highest truth which seems so illusive, so difficult to speak in words, makes them like air. So it is man's remembering that must come, before his words have any value to woman. And yet, it is woman that has deep within her the memory man needs.

All of the difficulties between male and female come from the fact that as air feeds fire and as water nourishes earth and cleanses it, water also must quench the raging fires and cool the overheated earth. And though the oceans and rivers and lakes and streams run across the land, just as the hot wind blows and carries the vaporized water back to earth again as rain, the relationship of water to fire seems unclear, ill-defined, unfinished.

So I will tell you that fire and water are not opposites, just as the density of earth is not an opposite to the lightness of air. The air you breathe is a chemical fire that is blue, the cold fire. The weight of stones makes the red fire. This mass of stone, along with the growth of life on the surface, gets broken down by the solvent of water and is recycled endlessly to cool the red fire within

323

the core of the earth and the yellow fire of the sun on the surface.

At the extreme point of the relationship between fire and water, what is essential interdependency appears to be irreconcilable opposites. At the balance point is where one learns what relationship is, not at the extreme ends of an apparent opposition. A teeter-totter is cooperation and the creative play of relationship.

Examine the relationship of these elementals on your planet, to you and to each other. Examine your emotions in relationship to nature, to body, and to each other. Learn that you cannot but communicate something all of the time. Learn what it is you are demonstrating. If you are angry, go look and see how come. Don't stop on the surface, but continue deeper and look for the source of your anger. Look for the source of your projection, your depression, your guilt, or your defense. Dog it down.

If you do this, you'll be surprised to find the source was illusion. If your life is like a barren desert, dry and fierce with strong winds and burning sand, pour water on it and let the earth you are grow life again. If the fires in your earth are out of control, remove the air. Take the belief of truth away from anger and judgment and projection. Starve your belief in illusions by removing the air, and the fiery energy of fear will die. And with the death of fear as fertilizer, you pour the water of forgiveness. Earth will grow life again.

Water

Book Three

Introduction
Water

Healing, cleansing, awakening, remembering is as simple as drinking a glass of water. No more complex than that. But I will warn you with this introduction. I'm a shaman. I come from shamen families, and if you read the *Water* book, I will be working on you. I'll be describing what you can expect on your way to achieving a readiness for God.

On level one, my words communicate straight-up, left and right, above and below, but I have another mind on top of this one that I am speaking to you with. I'm using it to work on your psychic self at the same time you're reading. I'm planting seeds with words, and I'm cultivating and watering the ground in your mind while you're reading, so you will grow deep roots and high branches, so you will not fear going into the below (subconscious), so you will not fear going into the above (superconscious), so you will not be afraid of the Mother or the Father.

This is not ordinary reading. By reading on from *Water* to *Air*, you are giving me permission to help reorder your mind, to make it possible for you to see all of the land's history, to see how this natural history has influenced you and shaped your thoughts, to see how all the thoughts that shaped the modern world have afflicted you with a prejudice toward a new future. By the end of the *Water* book, the seedling will be ready to emerge into the *Air*.

Because time is short, I will be very direct with my words. You either catch the bug and read on... or not. If you get perplexed, I suggest you stop and pick it up later. Don't read on like this is a novel, a work of pure fiction, and you're waiting for the punch line, the solved riddle or the pretty ending. Read it like your life. Read it like your grandparents' life. Read it like your ancestors life, back in their old places and times. Read it like those ancestors would, and wonder like them where they came from and how they came to be there. Read it like the first people would who invented the first language, and wonder why they did that... language. What was the purpose of them creating a language together? Go back to the beginning of everything and everyone, and ask questions.

We're going to cover a lot of territory in this book. It's necessary and I hope it won't bore you. In later books, I will go into more detail on single topics. I'm going to take words you use and give them specific meaning. Check the glossary (pg. 457) to refresh your memory. We are going very deep, because at your core is where the confusion began. The world didn't confuse you. People didn't confuse you. The only thing that confused you was this. As you grew, you lost touch or connection with your own core. You weren't supposed to store all the knowledge of the world in such a small brain. But within your core is a connection through which you can receive all the knowledge there is or ever will be when you need it.

So, if you're confused, it's because you forgot how to get to your core. But with my words, I'll take you there, if you'll go. I'll tell you what to pour water on that needs cleansing. I'll tell you what to pour water on that needs nourishment. Maybe they're the same thing, cleansing and nourishment.

If you stick with it, you'll know what a shaman is, and I won't need to draw a box to put around it and limit it. I won't need to define it. If you stick with it, you'll know what a medicine person is, whether they ever put medicine in your mouth or not. You'll know why and when to ask for help from Spirit. You'll know what their domain is. You won't need to go to a doctor for a nosebleed that won't stop or an infection that won't go away. When we're done, you won't worry yourself about disease. You'll know what healing is. You'll know what wellness is. And you won't have much need for sickness anymore.

So there you have it. That's my ulterior motive for your mind. That's what I'm doing to you psychically while you're reading these simple words. Oh, you think, read anything you want. Thoughts have no power. Words are nothing. Humm... think again.

With your decisions, you make yourself sick or well. Those decisions are made based upon the thoughts you think and the words you speak. You may not remember having made those decisions, and maybe you didn't make them with words at all, but those decisions are now what form the words that come out of your mouth or remain hidden as you sit thinking.

I give you this strong introduction because I want to warn you, once again. If you don't want healing, don't read the *Water* book. If you want to be entertained, well, go to the movies. If you like the two books thus far and think there's a story in *Water,* well, forget it. I told you my story in *Fire* and in *Earth,* so that you would know who I am. Now that you have read my story, perhaps you can trust me as you would a physician whom you know far less about, who treats only your physical self and never anything more.

If you just want to be physical, don't read on.

Chapter 1
Meaning

Let's face it. Physical life is messy, full of inconveniences and distractions. Nowadays, only children don't mind the dirt, yes? They eat it. They sit in it. They roll in it, just like the animals. And they have no concern for what they look like. It's play. It's God's play in the Garden of Eden for them.

When did you die that you are not a child inside anymore? Who told you that you wouldn't be loved if your shirts and skirts weren't pressed and clean? Who made you believe that dirt was dirty?

Okay, I'll humor you for a moment and consider that you believe you need cleansing because "something" got dirty. I could tell you how to make soap, but that isn't what you mean by dirty, I think. But if you are unhappy, if you are in pain, if you are confused, if you are not conscious of what you are, if you are not in joy, then you do need healing. If you are in judgment of the world, you are in need of healing. If you do not know what to do with your life or know what life is for, then you need healing. If you are motivated by anything but the desire to serve love, then you are in need of healing.

Some people's lives are like the desert. There is a little bit of life there but not too much water. It's a hot place. Those who are in it and see abundance, live. Those who are in it and see lack, die. There are those who live in the lush prairies or in the verdant mountains, and though there is life all around them and abundance everywhere, they feel lack and they die, or they feel abundance and they live. There are those who have millions of dollars saved and spend nothing, and they are always searching to save more because inside they still feel lack and are dead. There are those who are materially poor, who have no money, no possessions and no land, but feel abundance and live. Understanding the difference between lack and abundance, between poverty and wealth is as simple as understanding a glass of water.

You know the old story... one person looks at a glass of water and says it's half full, while the other says it's half empty. But I tell you, there is more to it than how much you've got or think you don't. That's perception. What about the *meaning* of water?

One person who lives by the body sees water as quenching thirst, nothing more. The capitalist looks at the water and sees that he could sell that water to folks who have less, and make money. So water has no meaning at all, just some arbitrary value.

That you have a need for water makes it valuable to you. That you cannot live without it makes you vulnerable. That it is heavy to carry makes you dependent upon the places where it collects. That it always collects on the land makes you susceptible to war over water resources and ownership and use. And yet, this water still has no meaning to you. You now are afraid of not having it and see those that do own resources as wealthy.

Maybe you move to places where plants grow naturally because you love the green, because it rains in those places, and there is plenty of water. You grow food there and sell it. You have a living with water. Even the cactus wren sets up house in the cactus, because in the heat of the desert there is water inside that cactus. And yet, does the cactus wren truly know the meaning that water contains? Only plants truly understand water. Only fish truly know water. Even the whale does not know water like the fish.

Try this. In the summertime, put a blanket out under a tree. Take one glass of water, and set it on the ground in front of you. Live for three or four days and nights on that blanket, and do not drink the water, but honor it. Ask it what it is. Learn for yourself firsthand the value of water and its meaning. And at the end of that fast, do not rush to drink that water, but pour it on the ground and ask yourself what you have learned. Do this over and over each year until you know the meaning of water.

I will not tell you the meaning of water because I would not steal your experience. I will not make you weak. If you hear someone's conclusion and accept that person's results without your own experience, you attempt to borrow or steal understanding, so don't have it. You cannot borrow knowledge. The mind can't have knowledge it didn't earn for itself. If you want to know what life is, don't live your life by anyone else's experience but yours. This is not to say that you cannot appreciate someone else's experiences. Just don't pretend they are yours.

The most colossally inept and shallow people in the world are those who try to get to knowledge at school through books. The books will not give you the experience needed to be able to know the meaning of or understanding of anything. Direct firsthand experience of true meaning is all that will give knowledge to you. Only Creator gives meaning. You can't make it up.

Now, you may know how to build a bridge or fix a radio or build a house or do taxes or send a rocket to the moon, but you still don't know the meaning of water. You still don't know the meaning of fire. You still don't know the meaning of earth.

There are people who have participated in ceremonies like Sweat Lodge, Vision Quest, and Sundancing. And I see that some people come back from these experiences being very proud of having had them. And yet, many never asked one real question during their trials. They never sought for truth. They collected the experience for more pride and more arrogance.

It is a pity that consciousness is not more prized, that awakening is not more sought after in your experiences. It is a pity that life seems to be more of a series of unconnected events and experiences that teach you something in spite of yourself, not because you are consciously asking to be taught. It is a pity that most prefer to learn through endless errors, rather than by direct questioning. Most would rather behave their lives and learn from all their mistakes made in abject busyness, than to contemplate or meditate on life's meaning at all. I can see why people try to blame God for their bad experiences. It is an unfortunate trick of ego to always blame someone else or something else, yet all the while never being conscious of the power of one's own thoughts, and therefore one's own actions.

It is even more pitiful that your religion teaches you to be **weakly** forgiving and always turn the other cheek. You can easily forgive the innocent for their mistakes if they learn. It is much harder to forgive the insolent when they have no intent to learn. Forgiveness was never meant to condone vileness or villainy. It was meant to give back innocence to the "redeemed." (See glossary.)

It was the highest moral code of our tribe to protect the innocent. It was the next highest goal to educate those who were no longer innocent. The education of a natural human was intended to allow the awakening one to investigate and experience within certain guidelines designed to protect the innocent. Honor and respect were essential. Because our lives were put at stake, we paid attention and learned quickly. If we didn't, we died... either by someone else's hand or by the process of nature itself. We learned early, you don't go courtin' without the awareness and permission of the parents. You don't piss in the creek. You don't crap in the water. You don't throw trash in the water hole.

The odd thing about modern people is that they gather so intensely in such small places that they never give the land rest nor the water respite. Cities become huge sucking devices that consume everything in sight, so much so that they have to recycle the very same water they piss and crap in.

Your water is not yet sacred to your sciences. And if your

water is not sacred to you, you will die in the filth of the lies you dumped in it. You swallow your own ignorance. You swallow your own arrogance every day with every drop you drink.

Fast with that water. Pour it down on the earth, rather than let your body-mind force you into anxiety for that drink. Don't take it from the earth for yourself, then piss on the earth unconsciously because you really stole that water. If you did not ask the Mother for it, you stole it, even though She would give it to you freely. Pour that water out and give it to the earth from which it came, back to the air that's birthed through the plants. Breathe in that moisture with that air, or drink the falling water when it rains. It is when you do that, you make water sacred to you, and you begin to learn its meaning.

I will not lecture you about the physical aspects of fire because everyone's been cold before. Everyone knows during winter when the sun comes out how good it feels to absorb that warmth while you're standing in the snow. Everyone knows how good it is to eat warm food cooked, rather than cold and raw... because of what it feels like, not because of its true value to you. Everyone associates warmth with love.

I do want to talk to you about the physical aspects of water. In your modern homes, you take showers every day. Ten-to-sixty gallons of water per person goes down the drain every day. You don't even have to concern yourselves with where it goes. You say, "Oh, the Mother is endless. Water goes down the rivers to the oceans, is evaporated and rains out again, endlessly." You don't even know why you're taking showers at all. You say, "To smell better." You don't even know why you smell bad in the first place. You don't take responsibility for the causes of anything, especially your bad smell. But you would ask water to cleanse you of it... endlessly.

It's funny. Indians don't smell. They don't smell good; they don't smell bad... in our time. But you see, we honored the food that we ate, and we honored the water that we drank. We took the simple food as it was given us. Some tribes farmed because they learned how, and they preferred not to wander in search of food. Later, some tribes ranched and herded their goats, sheep or turkeys, wherever they went. Some tribes hunted and followed the animals wherever they went. But those animals were honored. They were seen as partners. They were loved and protected. They were respected for their ways and their meaning. We didn't smell bad because we didn't have bad thoughts. We didn't eat bad food or drink bad water. Because all aspects of creation were sacred, we derived their benefits... life feeding life... true nourishment.

You folks eat to entertain yourselves and know nothing of where that food came from or what life was in it. You are not truly nourished by your food. You eat more and more because you are starving. Huge, fat people who eat compulsively are starving to death... they think. They see no meaning in their food, and therefore can't stop trying to fill an empty heart.

Sure, take showers. Wash your body. Put perfumes on. Cover up with pretty clothes. But the stench of meaninglessness still pervades your whole life.

Try this. First, learn to relax. Stop arguing with and defending the mind that you have. Stop fighting within yourself. Then, in that conscious mind, step into the shower and ask the water to cleanse you of all your worries and doubts, your fears and sense of lack. Ask it to help wash away the illusions that pervade your own life and your own mind. Give yourself to the water for cleansing, and ask it to honor you this way. It will.

But do this for water in return. Do not take the meaningless mind back as you dry off. Thank the cotton fibers in your towel. As you dress, thank the wool fibers, the leather, or even the synthetic fibers made from the materials of the Mother, for protecting your skin from sun and wind and rain, from chaffing and unwanted embarrassments. Then you will understand the function of clothes, of shoes. If you honor the things that went into them from the earth, you then are connected to the earth and can feel gratitude.

Continue this mind to your kitchen, and catalogue everything that you have ever eaten. Trace all your foods to their origins on the earth... your apples, your lettuce, your potatoes, your rice, your bread, your butter. Remembering where a thing comes from, remembering the people that work in those fields, is honoring that which gave its life and That which gave it life.

Then, jump into your car and go to work, aware of the life of those metals, those fuels, those plastics and glass, and remember the ingenuity of all those who gave you the horseless carriage. Remember the horse.

And, above all, remember your ancestors' footsteps. Walk again in the fields of your ancestry, and honor the lives that gave you yours. Stop along the road and pour a few drops of water onto the ground, and thank them all for your life. Then, thank Creator for *all* life.

It is the Source of Love, through your gratitude, that gives meaning to your life. It is the meaning in life that will teach you to love. It is a simple glass of water that can be your Christ... forgiven.

Truly, modern life has forgotten how to walk, has forgotten how to be grounded and how to know anything. It values "useful" information to store and recall, but the people have no true knowledge. Because folks buy and sell land and put up barriers around it, your children cannot even go to the riverbank to learn the life that's there. You put your children in closed buildings and teach them mathematics and some "politically correct" version of history, and never talk about the mistakes that were made and what was learned. And you never talk about love at all. You show them how to make steel and pottery, how to work computers and play games, but there's no love in it. You keep them busy like you and cut them off from deeper meaning, like you. Most marry so they won't be alone. And then they sit and defend their perceptions in their aloneness. You separate everyone, yet call them family. You possess your children like dogs and feed them nothing at all of any value. You cripple their thinking, so they will not find out that you know nothing. You fill them full of beliefs and desires, and you demonstrate to them that love is not enough.

When did you stop going to the pond to catch tadpoles? When did you stop honoring life, just for itself? When did you stop drinking a glass of water and remember how good it tastes or recall its meaning?

You hate the world you live in, and yet you made it. You made it by forgetting it was already perfect. You are too busy enjoying your ability to rearrange the land for your comfort and gain, rather than honoring the perfection of its being as it is. Because you have built yourselves into a prison of your own perceptions, you now know your life is meaningless. It is this pain that blinds you further to any meaning. And it is the agony of this blindness that I hope will awaken you to your need for the earth and its lessons for you on an intimate level.

You must reevaluate by going back to the beginning of time, by looking at fire, by looking at earth, by looking at water and by looking at air, so life may again bloom inside your mind and heart, so meaning will come back into your life. It is the recognition of and responsibility for all of the destruction that you have wrought that will be your road back to health. What do you want, a stand-up life or a lay-down death? You decide.

Has humankind produced anything that is alive, except children? And is even that done with much consciousness? Are all the fruits of the labors of humankind, life or death? Are they fear or are they love?

Do you plant grain and fear no rain? Do you plant grain because you fear having no money to buy meat with? Or do you plant grain because you love the Mother and the earth and the water and the rains and the fire of the sun? And do you eat what you grow in gratitude? Or do you just sell the shit off and buy what you want? Do you grow melons because they're sweet and you love them? Or do you grow them like rocks, in trade for coin?

I tell you, a conscious human can tell when a thing has been grown from love. When they eat it and it feels like a rock, they know that's not love. You have been duped by your grocery store's convenience. They are selling you a lot of rocks, "for your convenience," of course. "Customer satisfaction is number one."

How many of you are old enough to long for an old style tomato, fresh from the garden? Most kids have never even tasted a real tomato. Most kids don't even know what fresh garden vegetables taste like. Most kids have never caught their own game, dressed it, cooked it and eaten it, either. Almost no one remembers how to spin and weave their own cloth.

And most people's ideas of healing come from a drug store. Most never inquire as to how come they're sick in the first place. And God forbid should anybody die. Hide 'em quick. Don't want nobody lookin' at no dead bodies. Too hard to do because, by God, it makes you think. What's it all for anyway? What's it all mean?

When people start gettin' old and askin' hard questions, it's easier to send 'em to the nursing home. Let other folks deal with 'em. Pay someone else. And yeah, if those old folks get to be too much trouble, drug 'em. Back in my day, old folks got taken care of like they took care of us when we were young. Difference is, they didn't try to hang on past their time, and they contributed to the education of the grandchildren every day.

Nowadays, you disrespect everything around you, so you deserve no respect. You honor nothing, so are not honorable. You care for nothing but yourself, so your "self" is all you get to keep.

How would you like to be locked in a psychic prison where the only person to talk to is your small "self"? That's what you do every day. The old ones talked to each other over hundreds of miles, without words, because they loved each other and were honest people. No big deal. Telepathy is a natural state born from love that is fearless and from the honesty that allows that joining.

Nowadays, only the littlest children remember what God is. You know why? Because nobody confused them with words yet. There's no clutter or distraction. They're just wholly, one-hundred percent present... and God's here already, waiting for you to wake up out of this crazy fog you're in.

Splash some water on your face, and ask yourself to wake up. Ask the water to wake you up. You do it every morning... splash water on your face. "Wake me up, water!" You take it for granted, don't you? It wakes you up, doesn't it? Ever say, thank you, water? You say, "Well, I pay the bill." There's a bigger bill comin' yet for all that you take for granted.

Go down to the river. Dip a bucket in that river. Carry it a mile to your house. Use it for everything. If you carried that water, you'd honor it more, wouldn't you? Or you might have the personality that would curse the water for being heavy. Which one are you, the thank you or the damn it?

People built elevators and escalators because they damned the stairs. People damned the ground and long walkin' when they found out they could jump on a horse... when they got over their fear of the horse. Then people built cars because they damned the horse. And what people lost was their *ground*. Folks don't honor the place they stand on anymore. They're too busy gettin' off the ground with high heels and pretending to be God already, all by themselves. Folks need to come down to earth again, I think, and honor the whole place for the love it gives and the challenges it provides which make us strong.

But that's okay. Play your video games. Don't let me take you away from them, 'cause I'm sure they have value to you. Those of you who would rather have your kid sit in front of the video monitor or the TV, than talk with them or go outside to discover the beauty of nature, haven't offered your child anything but the misery that you cultivated yourself. If you are just into "looking good," you're really just lookin' bad.

Because the human mind is capable of reaching great heights in imagination, does not make anything it thinks true. Because it can go to incredible depths and even take its own life or the life of another, does not make it evil. You are given these heights and these depths... within limits, so you might understand the futility of a single mind, all by itself, trying to figure out what it is. Please see there are only two systems of thought, love and fear, and that you must choose what you would rather be and learn from, truth or illusion.

If you know what love is, you cannot be deceived by another mind. You would know its intent. You would know its pretenses. You would know its limitations, and you would know its gifts. In love, is nothing unknown to you. In fear is nothing known.

Please know the only thing that could betray you in your whole life is your own mind.

Love is not your enemy. Fear of fear is your enemy. Facing your fears is your only battle. This is the only battle that can be won. The thought of water will not quench your thirst, but water will. If you are spiritually thirsty, you can drink the water down, and it will not quench your thirst. The *meaning* of the water will quench spiritual thirst, not the water itself. So pour that water out onto the ground after you fast, and ask once again. What does it mean?–water.

Chapter 2
Cleansing

What does that mean exactly?–cleansing. I will save you time, save your mind a bit of trouble, and I will tell you that cleansing is the correction of all the thoughts that prevent you from being aware of the presence of love. Sounds like a tall order. I would say so, considering the present condition of your world.

I will tell you something of the situation that you've all gotten yourselves into and explain to you why water is so important. Of the different cultures past and present on this planet, worshiping the same Creator today, three of them have enduring, written prophecies of a Great Cleansing that's to come to the earth. The earliest known prophecy is Mayan in origin. The next to follow are the native prophecies of North America. And following that, or roughly at the same time, are the New Testament prophecies.

Other cultures speak of the many aspects of the Creator, the One God, but don't speak of a cleansing in the future. They refer to God-like aspects of positive and negative, of creative and destructive, of peaceful and warring. Yet, for the majority of people in the world, these God-like aspects are only mythical.

But for the modern mind, war is not a matter of the gods. It is seen more as a distinctively human activity for gathering and managing the resources of the earth. And yet, behind all this is a tentative awareness that nature contains certain powerful forces and that catastrophes do happen. Always in the back of a human's mind is the question of whether nature is at war with humankind or not.

There are two kinds of nature: one, the natural flow and ebb of the cleansing forces on the earth, and two, the essential nature of humankind and the nature of the mind of humankind.

Because heavy rains or snows fall in one place, making a river change its course, taking a house, some land, animals and humans, some think there is a negative force in nature, and they fail to see that it is often the land cleansing itself, rather than warring on us.

Great effort is put into controlling the course of rivers, controlling flooding waters, reducing earthquake damage, and so on and so forth, to make the land stable and predictable. Yet, no one sees it is only us who make war on the natural earth with all our selfish activities.

Now, don't get me wrong. I'm not condemning sewer systems and storm drains and aqueducts and irrigation ditches. It is not my purpose to condemn. It is only my purpose to have your inquiring mind ponder for a moment the forces that are at play here. The intense activity in large cities, the thousands of square miles of concrete and asphalt, the many hundreds of tons of fuels consumed each day, produce conditions where heat cannot escape and places where water cannot go into the ground, and the natural cleansing rains, instead rain acids. Because of the huge concentrations of people, the consumption of water is such that it must be piped in from thousands of miles away or pumped from deep in the ground. The effort to recycle waste from large cities is admirable but insufficient. The single function of a city appears to be to sustain more and more people and industry. The cities can be likened to a cancer which grows uncontrollably by some strange mechanism, much faster than the rate of normal cells nearby. What triggers such a mechanism?

The lives you live in these cities should tell you. Observe. Every large thing is something smaller. Every small thing is something larger. There is nothing that is not the whole thing. If a cell speeds up its replication processes, then you need only look to see what your cities are doing to tell you how this cancer comes to be.

People who are not completely numbed by the intensity of life in a big city, seek quiet, seek to slow down by going to the country or to the beach or to the mountains or to the lake. And maybe they hike around and even camp out just to soak up the peace that's around them, so they are able to go back into their city and work once again at its frenzied pace. If your society has cancer, it is because it is split between going too fast and wanting peace. Where are you rushing to? Like the water that falls, you will just run back into the ocean once again. What's the big rush to get to the sea?

Religion's intense desire to have cleansing come is admirable, but to cleanse by hellfire is not the same as cleansing with holy water, is it? The prophets of doom say their calls to people are to awaken them. And yet, have you ever awakened through fear yet? You might awaken to the importance of stopping at a stoplight after once going through one while traffic is crossing. And you might get a vague awareness through fear that you have a physical life you can lose, but losing life is not the best way to learn to value it.

But as I said once before, worse works. Okay fine. Creator gives you what you want. It is best to become consciously aware of what it is you truly want because you *will* get it, even if you are not conscious of having a subconscious which undermines your best intent, or of having a superconscious which can pretend not to be influenced by your subconscious. You are co-creating your way back to God. Best to be conscious and alert to the mechanism of the mind.

This is the fifth world just beginning. The transition period between the worlds is virtually over, and the census was taken as to whether the world will be cleansed on a psychic level only or on both a physical and psychic level. Because it appears that the human race has not taken full responsibility for the effects of its own mind, both individually and collectively, you therefore will experience changes, both psychically and physically. Your planet will experience climatic and geologic activity, based wholly upon your collective desire to judge and punish each other, based wholly upon each person's desire for some small vengeance.

But I tell you, love knows nothing of vengeance. To claim you love your own family and want vengeance of any kind on any other, to want revenge for a family member's death, for instance, is a fallible, small version of what love really is.

You don't even know what you're angry about when you're angry. If you searched out the cause in your mind, you would never be able to find it. Anger is the energy of conflict which produces a sensation and reaction that is preferred to the communication of truth. It is a misunderstanding and inability to truly communicate or accept truth that causes anger. Were you to understand life at all, anger would be impossible.

Armageddon, you think, is God's anger on the world. How could Love be angry, unless it was not love? Why would you be placed here to work out what love is, unless Love did it? Do you think "life" is a sentence passed upon you in judgment, and you are here serving this natural life sentence until your death... then you are free?

I think you're not sure if God loves you at all or even if there is a God. And in this confusion, you barely live your little lives, clinging to each other for reassurance. And your families become hovels of sickness, well defended against outside intrusion. It becomes easier to remain passive and distracted, than to make any real effort to receive any true answer. No one loves the truth enough to risk discomfort long enough to break out of the illusory restrictions of ego and "find" God.

Go back out under that tree, and sit on that blanket with that glass of water. Maybe you'll remember to ask again and listen once again. It is only when your ego mind is quiet that you could hear an answer that would satisfy you. Put something at stake. Win the battle against your own mind. Get quiet.

The energy the fire builds for you in irritation and agitation is to get you to ask a real question... with the force of your whole being. That is the value of fire. It got you there. Now, pour water on that fire. Sit. Wait. Show some determination. Show some willingness. Show some courage. Put your small self at risk. Endure some small trial, but pay attention. Be alert. And remember, you can't hear while you're talking, so be quiet. Time will change for you. Your clock will slow down. Your city time will be put aside, and you will drop into the rhythm of the natural world of a natural human being. It is at this slower rhythm that your right mind opens. It is the soon-to-be-quenched fire of your desire to experience the truth that will move you peacefully into the state of awareness of love's presence. It is only in that state of purified air that your question can be answered. None other. You must be willing to join the state of being in love to get the answer that Love gives. And it is only Love that can truthfully answer the question of what love is. Yes? You must deliver your real self to the Source of Meaning to ever have any.

This Great Cleansing that is coming to the earth, that is coming to the people, can be easy because you would have Love do it. Or it could be difficult because it would be fear resisting it.

Make a ceremony for yourself with the four elementals. Make the first elemental the earth you stand on, the love, the Mother. Make the second a warming fire you build from the earth, from that love. Make the third, the water you use to cleanse the ego from yourself. And the fourth will be air, the truth and essence that is breathed in by all life to sustain and carry its spirit. Even the life of the fire has breath. Even the clouds are the vapors of earth's life and its waters. In each elemental is the recognition of the interconnectedness and Oneness of all things that allows each participant in any ceremony to open to Spiritual awareness and guidance. It is during these ceremonies that sorrows can be lifted, that confusions are undone, that conflicts can be mended, and that sickness can be healed.

It has been said that native peoples looked seven generations ahead and made their decisions based upon continuing life through the seventh generation and beyond. The wisest did not steal from their environment, so they were not afraid of it. They did not overpopulate one place, and they accepted as natural, their death. They did not stay on one piece of land so long as to denude it entirely of its resources. They moved in natural cycles. Many did not build permanent dwellings nor hold permanent possessions because they recognized that one cannot permanently protect oneself against all change and movement. They kept themselves from the weakness of excessive attachments. They did not see God in only one single idea or only one person or only one place. They saw God everywhere, in all things... omnipresent. They honored and respected and gave gratitude in their hearts for everything they saw or took for their lives and livelihood.

It is the dark mind of humankind, the lower emotions, the fearful mind that is cleansed. It is the high-rise, off-the-ground arrogance of specialness that is cleansed. That we human beings have placed so much fear into the earth may soon cause the earth to tremble and shift on its axis. The warring things we do in our mind, whether we are physically at war or not, create the collective energy of ego that causes destruction. Remember, it is you who are moving and changing with the earth, while the sun and stars stand still for you.

You live in a chaotic time, with great hope and promise. And the questions asked all over the planet at this time are, "Is humankind worth the effort of the universe or not? Is life worth redemption or not? Is love enough or not?"

Well, I tell you, it has been decided already that life is worth redemption. Love is enough. But to make the effort to get to the beginning of your cleansing and all the way to redemption is what you fear. To be like Christ, maybe you think you have to physically die for love, in order to be reborn in spirit. I tell you, to be reborn, you need only die to the idea that you are the body, and die to all the ego tries to make you think you are... when you are not.

Sundancers know this, many of them, for they go through a small death in order to learn more, in order to join more. All ceremonies that are spiritual in nature are for this purpose. The elementals are for this purpose. All hearts and minds are for this purpose. All wills are for this purpose. Were all of you to do this, to die to yourselves as body and learn to join in love, Armageddon would be a hiccup. To the degree that you are not able to be this purpose, the Cleansing will be more dramatic. All of your false beliefs will be challenged, so you might as well challenge them yourself voluntarily. Why wait? Why wait to be forced to accept your healing in the truth?

Everybody's waiting for Judgment Day. Everybody's waiting for Christ to come back. Everybody's waiting for a teacher to show up and stimulate them into growth. Everybody's looking for somebody else to ask the questions and give them the experience of what true love is.

Maybe you say, if a human being isn't already giving love, then why ask them what it is? They surely would not know. I challenge you to ask each other and help each other find out. You think Spirit's spooky, so you don't ask Them. You think you'll go crazy because the mind's so vast, so you don't even ask inside yourself anymore. You leave that part of your mind closed, and you wait and wait and wait. And while you wait, you destroy the place you're waiting in, both inside and out. You play and play and play to distract yourself from the real questions which torment you. "What is all this for? What am I? What is God?"

The mind has billions of questions. But I tell you, there is only One Answer to them all. Yet, to receive that Answer, you must meet the conditions for its transmission to you. You must actively wait with a peaceful and open mind, with true desire and real intent to receive. You must not become distracted and forget. You must be diligent against the ego mind, the doubting mind, the mind of conflict, of illusions and tricks. You must find your true mind and give up the insane one caught in a sick and busy world. You *will* outlive the small mind, I guarantee you, and the sooner the better because the small mind is death, death in all its many forms.

So why wait? Face death now. It's there talking to you in your own mind every minute. It's your fear talking to you, but you will not find the answer to any of your riddles in the fear. So face your fears. Don't do battle with a pitiful enemy. Forgive the body its pitiful weakness, and learn from the Voice of Truth what truth is. Fear cannot teach you. Pour water on your fire and learn what is beyond fear. Be quenched in your search for God and let God find you.

In this state of readiness, you will learn to speak gratitude to all that helps you. You will review your life, and you will recover all the experiences that were love. Your mind will be rebuilt for you, gradually, erasing all misperceptions, all fears and sorrows, all worries and concerns. And as you allow it, you will relax to yet deeper and deeper places in your mind and body, to receive new gifts to give away.

The flowers that grow by the wayside won't be outside you anymore. They'll be inside. Noises that used to cause you pain will no longer cause resistance in you. They won't touch you at all. You will stop imagining yourself as a dartboard for the game of life. You will flow like water where love would take you. You will find that you could be the four winds or the gentle aspen. You could be the cleansing rain or the warming light of fire. You could be more like Spirit than the limitations of body. And your dreams will change your mind's eye to guide you and show you other worlds different from this, other people different from this, and yet all the same.

You will begin to see essence instead of form. You will know intent and energy, and you will read them better than words and language. The effect of communication will be union, the sharing of images and pictures that cover millions of words in a second. You will, then, begin to understand the true purpose of a human mind, the true purpose of a Spiritual mind, and the Plan of Creation will unfold before you. The Cleansing was for joy.

Chapter 3
Disbelief and Belief

Disbelief and rigid beliefs, I think, are two of the worst obstacles to overcome in a human mind. Superstitions, maybe, are next. But I won't worry about superstitions at all. Let's talk about disbelief and belief.

Incredible amounts of money are spent in American society persuading consumers. Billions of dollars are at stake as to whether you believe one thing tastes better than another, or that this soap works better than that soap. If customers are this easily swayed from one product to the next, then why can't consumers of the many perceptions of love, who switch partners as easily as switching soap, switch their minds as readily from some crazy idea of love to the truth of love?

It is ingrained in your culture to enjoy being defrauded by love. Whether you believe me or not doesn't matter. You see, it is the chase you relish and the conquest, but there is no love in it and no truth to be found anywhere. Everywhere is this talk of betrayal, especially on television talk shows. The talk, shows no one knows what the truth is or what love is at all, though you all fervently believe you do. You would rather believe yourself than disbelieve yourself. You would rather disbelieve me in this, just as you would rather believe the state of love Jesus attained is totally unattainable for yourself.

So when I talk to you about cleansing, about truth and about love, I'm not talking about made-up stuff here. I'm not talking bogus. I'm not telling you to go join some movement you believe in or to gather together for a common good. You can have a healing Sweat Lodge in your own bathroom to return you to love. You can have a Vision Quest in your own backyard to get you back to the truth.

You see, if some one thing is true, it will connect you to everything else that is true. It is the nature of truth to join. And if truth is real, then it should be apparent to your five senses, but it isn't... not in your present state of awareness. The shift of awareness that is necessary to get to the truth is the same shift of mind that is necessary to get from seeing with your eyes to knowing with your mind, not your thinking mind but your visionary mind... the One Mind that is connected to all Truth.

That humans remain stuck in their own limiting beliefs and entrenched in their disbelief that something good will catch them if they take a leap of faith, makes them unable to shift. To the degree they are fearful is the degree to which they would put their belief in death and their disbelief in love.

So, we all have mistaken beliefs. But believe me, the only purpose of a mistake is to get you back to God. In that plan, fear and guilt have no purpose. Is it not better to understand what you have learned, than to condemn yourself for how you learned it?

In an earthly perception, our errors are like a flood of water... our judgments are like a stony earth... our punishments are like a fiery hell. I don't know about you, but I prefer to see not all our errors but rather all our lessons. I prefer to see that forgiveness is the holy water, that the arena for our lessons is the blessed earth, and that it is the sacred fire that transforms us in our learning.

Perhaps you think you have completed your lessons here. But remember, it is this sacred place, our Mother Earth, on which *you* learned *your* lessons. So if you now condemn the world as valueless, you condemn those in it and do not give them the same opportunities to learn their lessons as were given you. If you think you are the one that has run the world through, tried everything and are now ready to put it all aside, do so in your mind. Then put the mind aside that's part of the world as well. If you've learned the world's purpose, this should not be hard. If you still have attractions to the world or anything in it, the mind you have will not be so easily put aside. Your fight, you see, is not now with the world whom you've forgiven because it has served its purpose, but your fight is now with the mind that will not give you freedom or peace, nor will it give you truth or love.

To the degree you still blame people and the world for your problems, is the degree you still prefer to project onto others what your own mind is doing. Blame. Blame who? Blame who for what? If there is still a drama going on inside your mind, then you have not recognized that it is not the world or your concept of it that is the issue, but the very mind that you think with that is the issue.

And to imagine you can fix the world by acting upon it from the outside is ludicrous. It is the very mind that humans think with that is the difficulty. It is their beliefs that they prefer over the truth that is the problem. It is that they prefer to project onto the world what they want to believe and what they choose to disbelieve that is the problem. So it is not enough cleansing to wash away your erroneous beliefs about the world and what it is for. It is as important to wash away your disbeliefs about what you think the world is not or will not be or could not be.

Disbelief can be used for protection, you think, to keep unwanted ideas out, but it doesn't. You hope your disbelief will separate you from your fears. You choose not to believe that vampires are real. Good idea. But it isn't whether a vampire exists or not that frightens you. What frightens you is the mind that could think things up like that at all. Nothing could be worse than a devil in flesh, that's what you think. Well, vampires don't exist, do they? And yet, you believe the devil is real.

How many of you have seen werewolves? Not me. Seen a couple of crazy dogs once, but they had rabies. Rabies existed a long time ago, before werewolf stories, before vampire stories. Bats get rabies. Bats bite people... probably people catching them for who knows what. People get rabies, go crazy, act like vampires. It's your stories and the mind that thought them up that scare you. Just don't grab no bats or no crazy dogs, and you'll be fine.

The worst idea you've got going in your society right now is about whether alien space creatures exist or not, and whether people are being abducted or not, and whether those aliens are here to eat us or help us... to see if we're fit to eat or if we contain too many toxic chemicals. Who knows? Maybe even worse, a greater fear is that they'll mess with our minds... that they're the ones causing all the fear and insanity in the society.

Well, I as Spirit would never tell you in a million years that what you think exists, does not. I'll tell you why. **Collective consciousness has the power to manifest any illusion it wants.** It can even manifest something that appears totally real in physical appearance, in material form, the whole bit. Swamis in India materialize things, plenty times. No problem. Medicine people in my own tribe could make things show up or disappear. No sweat.

Modern people, of course, are terrified by all of this because they've been trained to believe only their science explains their physical universe. But, look deeper. Nuclear physicists have no idea why their laws even appear to work. Don't forget, those laws were modeled mathematically by observation of energy changes. You ask a scientist how come a chair stands still when you put it there, and they can't tell you how come. Maybe it's just by agreement. Maybe the chair agreed to sit there while you're acting like you put it there.

The thing that frightens you the most and causes the most disbelief is in your own dreams. Believe me, in vision when I saw hands coming out of those walls where them skulls were stuck...

well, I had a hard time with that one. Scared me pretty good. And to make sure that I wasn't going cuckoo-beans completely, I opened my eyes. And there I was sittin' next to this great old woman tellin' me to go back. She was inside my dreams, my vision.

So what was this vision? A tool? Yes. Vision is a tool, a transition tool to get you used to a larger reality. And it's good while you're doing that to keep your eyes closed because your eyes will still want to believe the physical reality that they see outside, rather than the psychic one inside.

But I'll tell you again. If you want to know what your mind is doing and what it's for, you have to go inside. You can stay outside and study people and call it psychology or psychiatry or philosophy, but that's still like science... outside, observing, not knowing, just observing.

Go inside and the arena gets bigger. This is the place that you find your fears. Inside is where you face them, not on the street with a baseball bat or a gun or even a college degree. And still, at first, you'll return from this inside psychic space in disbelief. This disbelief is natural. It is natural because your eyes are always trying to train you to think that only what they see outside is real.

And yet, your eyes and your sciences can't tell you why the material universe stays as it is, why one molecule has attraction for another, and why there is so much space inside a nucleus. Scientists can try to explain why everything is stable, by measuring electrical charges and spins, but they still don't know why atoms on this world stay so close together, any more than they know why the atoms outside this atmosphere stay so far apart.

Old people close to the earth were more interested in the direct experience of the fact that you *could* change shape and place and time, rather than trying to find out *how* that could be true. Some shamen knew how, but only as a result of being trained in the practice. What they learned as factual came in an experience, before any desire to discover how it could be true. Most of present day science, regarding psychic or spiritual matters, would still rather try to prove what they disbelieve, rather than starting with a possibility of truth and their own direct participation and experience. Until law and science are willing to alter their rigid perceptions, they will never perceive the truth. Most are afraid to risk themselves to find out. Shamen types, therefore, are the true pioneers in this realm. They risk everything for the truth. Their only error, in the case of sorcery, is forgetting to let Love lead them and in being in such a big rush for power.

What you're really afraid of is that if I tell you how to shape-shift into a crow and you believed it could be done, then you tried it, you might not be able to come back as human again. You're still afraid of shifting into anything, so you maintain your personal perception to the death, as if this gift of shifting that begins in vision is a cruel trick. The trick is that you were never solely your personal form to begin with.

What you're afraid of is that your body is alive and not you, and that it, being you, will die and take you with it. You think you are the body, so you think it has all the power to kill you or keep you alive. So you are afraid of its death. And in this illusion, you are asleep and dreaming fearful dreams.

To counteract your fear, you may think it is necessary for you to believe all your life that you are special, that somehow your life is better or different from anyone else's or any other living thing. You may even set out to try to achieve specialness. In this way, you separate yourself from everything. And in that illusion, you try to justify your life. In that illusion, you take what you need in desperation and don't even know what a glass of water is or what it does for you. You bathe constantly and are never cleansed. You even heat the water up to do a better job because it feels good too. And you might almost relax in that water, but you don't really.

Now, I know most women do a better job of relaxing than most men, but that is imposed on them. If they never menstruated, they'd be just like men, except perhaps a little bit less strong physically. So, since a woman bleeds, she runs out of energy quicker than a man. She can't hold up the illusion of life as long as man. She can't play silly-ass games as much as man. So she relaxes sooner and frequently wakes up faster than man.

Though woman does tire more quickly, even this tiredness is ultimately an illusion. Even that is still believing you're a body and that all your energy depends upon it. Relax into this tiredness and vision will take over. The drop in energy interpreted as exhaustion is a door to vision that can open to greater learning. Extreme physical exertion for man is the door... risk taking. Going beyond his supposed limits can create a deep relaxation that is the Door to Knowledge.

This shift to knowledge is radical and complete. The preparation to shifting goes on a long time, many lifetimes perhaps, many helpers, lots of experiences. But the purpose is to wake up. How many more experiences of wine do you need? How many more experiences of sex do you need? Well, probably thousands and millions if you've never asked a real question that challenges your beliefs or disbeliefs.

And the reason why you aren't healed immediately when you ask to be is not because it didn't happen, but because you have a mind drenched in disbelief. You stand in it like tar... stuck everywhere, can't move. Go ahead, walk through tar over your head. That's what your mind's like. I can see why you cry out for help... on occasion. I can even see why you might want to assassinate it... that mind, in desperation. But the answer to this negative mind, the answer to this tar pit, this shit hole of the universe, is not to commit suicide. To commit suicide is a useless attempt at escape. And unfortunately, it was done with the mind that wanted to kill itself. Where does that mind escape to? Itself? It thought the hell up, lived it, hated it, judged it, and killed it. So where is it? What's dead? Where did your mind go? Is your brain your mind? Suicide's like shootin' your car 'cause the road's rough.

Okay, so here we are in this realm of mind and I know you're scared. You don't have to pour water all over the place. I know you asked for healing. So how do you get healing inside of a mind that's full of fear, full of projection, full of disbelief as a defense against what it thinks? Well, the first incredible hurdle to get over in healing is your not wanting to arrive at the conclusion that *you* caused your own sickness... your not wanting to stop blaming it on "the devil."

All these thoughts that created an environment of fear must be relinquished for you to be healed. To be so afraid of death that you do not live life is to be dead already. To be afraid of going crazy or being manipulated by dark forces is a deep-seated fear that must be removed for you to see that the unhealed mind itself is the dark force. **The misuse of your own creative potential is what makes you afraid.**

Being afraid of a dog because it barks, thinking it will bite, is a form of miscommunication to the animal that you want to get bit. Your mind need only image what you *want* in order to receive. This is a law of mind. Fortunately, most dogs are smarter than you. They already know that humans are crazy, and that their minds often project what they *don't* want. But those are the animals that have lived around humans enough to know they're a bit strange. To an animal, the mind's only purpose is to project what it wants, not what it doesn't want. That's communication. That's how it knows what is friend and what is foe. Fear turns everything backwards and often gives you what you don't want.

It's easy to know what is being communicated. It works like this. When a rabbit sees a wolf, the wolf goes... **"Dinner!"** The rabbit gets the wolf's intent and runs. So when the rabbit sees a human, it's like with the wolf. If they're used to being around peaceful humans, they won't run anymore, until hunting season when that human mind set "**Dinner**" comes out.

In places where there's no hunting, ever, like national parks and wildlife sanctuaries, where there is nothing but pedestrian traffic all day long, the rabbits and the chipmunks and the birds come around, and they look at you having lunch and they say... "Dinner!" They come around 'cause you feed 'em, and you don't mean to eat them.

The mind is a powerful instrument. It has the capacity to lift you beyond the stars, if you so desire it. It has the capacity to take you to different worlds, to imagine people different in appearance. But when *you* try to imagine something other than human, not just in appearance but in mind set, you make it fearful. You make it vicious and dangerous, and you call it an alien. You give it a mind like you've got.

Well, I tell you, if humanity was so fit to pick like a ripe peach, they'd be here, those aliens. But the harvest from this planet is insanity. If you're visited, it's because they're trying to figure out what the cause of this insanity is, so that it won't spread anywhere else. So don't worry about *them.* It is this planet that's still behind the times, still living with a mind that's in the dark ages, in the dark, in the fear, and in the disbelief.

It is your culture that doesn't know how to heal itself. And you can clean up the environment all you want. You can honor things as much as you want. You can even have intense gratitude for creation as it's meant to be, and you still might not take responsibility for the part of your mind that you made collectively along with everyone else.

Do you believe that Creator is both negative and positive, and that there is a male God, positive or negative, and a female God, positive or negative? It's okay if you do, but I'll give you this image to work with that proves it's not true.

Take two poles, one positive, one negative, on a big battery with two wires coming off from those poles. Then, stick those two wires together in the middle and what do you get? You get a spark. You get an arc. You get an intense exchange of energy between positive and negative. And it either melts down the wires as it releases light and heat, or you hook up a tool that helps you do some work. But nobody ever looks back far enough to see how and why these two energies got separated in the first place.

Look at it this way. The natural world is constantly adjusting and balancing between positive and negative energy forces. If it is not able to balance chemically, then electrical exchanges take place in the form of lightning to restore some of the balance in the air and shallow subsoil. In nature, there is virtually no mineral source that is pure acid or pure alkaline, without forced oxidation or reduction, without someone making it so by reversing some law of energy or by removing some mineral from one place on the earth and taking it to another. It is the unnatural world that undoes the balance in nature to make the unnatural battery.

So if male and female are separate in your mind, then like the unused battery with separate poles, you've got work to do and need enlightenment. You are both positive and negative, both male and female, and yet you are neither. After all the paradoxes (like negative and positive) are resolved, you are most like Creator.

If you look back far enough, past all the contrivances of a modern society to see why there is male and female, to see why there is a separation into positive and negative, you will see it is only for the two to come together again as one. That is the spark and the work to be done. Creator did it like that on purpose, so you would learn how to *know*. Thinking you know or being afraid to know won't get you there. This knowledge is saved for you by Spirit.

You can either feed the fear with strong belief in separation of male and female, or you can release that stored energy between you and between your two separate halves, by pouring conductive waters over your own disbelief, and you will heal and join. When you do, knowledge will come. Enlightenment will come. Love and truth will join.

Chapter 4
The Tree of Life

Fire and earth belong to the domain of female. Water and air belong to the domain of male. They are the characteristics of the God Self within us, both male and female. They are the elementals that most closely give us a sense of the mind that we are born with. So, if you are born female, then the sense of self will come from earth and from fire. And if you are born in a male body, your sense of self will come from water and from air. That is not to say that you cannot have the characteristics of both male and female, because you truly do. But the emphasis for the majority will be placed according to their physical self.

Homosexuality, whether male or female, is simply an indication that within the mind there is this other self, male or female, and that in accordance with your agreement to come to the earth and be born into body, to rediscover yourself as spirit, you might find yourself in a form not to your liking, one that may feel foreign to you. These "foreign" births are not mistakes of nature. They are a purposeful experience of both halves of a single self. It is a demonstration of a fundamental truth that you are both male and female in psyche.

So the fear of homosexuals or the hatred of homosexuals or lesbians is unwarranted. It is a mistake to fear or hate anything. If you fear something, you could never begin to understand, and you remain divided within yourself. It is an error to judge or to believe that you are simply male or female according to your form. You are both.

In rare circumstances, a single spirit will split entirely in half, creating two beings, one being, male only in form and consciousness, and the other being, female only in form and consciousness. There are twenty-three such split pairs in existence on your planet as this book is written. These are true twin souls. Contrary to popular belief, most people carry their twin inside themselves, but they look outside for someone to mirror their twin inside. This is because there are very few who have been able to pierce the veil between their two inner selves, without external help or strong medicines.

Spirit's purpose for these twenty-three pairs is to find their other half and to rejoin their psyches on earth, so when they return to the Spiritual realm where bodies no longer separate, this error of splitting will be erased. When this is accomplished, whether by one pair or by all twenty-three pairs, it will reverse the laws of the world and make them align with Creator's Intent. It will bring about the healing on the earth for the psyche of male and female, regardless of form.

It was never Creator's intention to have male and female be so separate that they could not understand one another, communicate with one another, and join one another in their hearts and minds. To have both male and female within you and to have them join, is the Sacred Spiral of Energy that brings you to full consciousness. And it is the partners that you seek that help you achieve this purpose. To the degree that you help each other as partners is the degree to which you will be *together*.

A holy relationship is one in which you can be together for eternity. Because the learning and teaching exchange between you is equal, the balance is perfect. This is a rare commodity in your world. How can you achieve perfect balance while so much confusion exists surrounding marriage and coupling and separation and divorce?

Separation between couples can occur when there is no growth, due to a fear of growth or out of a mutual recognition that your time together is over, and that your learning goes on elsewhere. Now, many will say this releases people from any commitment to marriage. But I tell you, the unconscious cannot commit to marriage. They can but imagine they do. They can but wish to do so. But it is unconscious love doing it, and it is the goal of any relationship to increase consciousness, not to condemn two people to a marriage that does not grow, except in grievances.

So, study your relationship first between fire and earth and water and air within yourself. Then study the energy you communicate to another. Decide whether it is fear of growth leading your life or it is desire for growth in love that leads you. See if you are male dominant or female dominant. Find within, your two halves. See if fear makes one half dominate the other. Find out what that fear is afraid of.

Too many men, I think, are afraid of the aspects of female, the fire and the earth, so they do not understand their mates. They do not understand how the energy of their own thoughts and feelings affects their mate. **It is the acceptance of the female aspects within the male that is the goal Spirit has for this age.** Female, then, can accept for herself the water and air that are the healing and truth man was made to embody. Love, then, can have truth inside itself again.

I will tell you that it was Feice who was born with the male and female joined within herself. She was the fruit from the mature flowering tree. With her seed, joined with the fire from below and combined with the nutrients of the earth, she grew spreading branches and reached her female arms toward the truth in Father Sky. With her male trunk and roots, she reached deep into the love in Mother Earth. There she found the cleansing waters and solid foundation that would steady her tree in any strong winds to come.

Feice grew thus into womanhood, married and gave birth to two twin boys. When the weaning of her twins was complete, Feice noticed after she bled on the earth in two spots for several seasons, that new life sprang vigorously from only one spot. She realized that the lifeless spot she'd bled on had been chosen in a dark mood when she felt sorrowful, woeful. This spot was rocky, coarse, and lacked enough soil to retain the blood. This was the reason it was lifeless, she thought. But it came to her in a dream that the mighty cedar grew from the cracks in the rocks, so she sensed it was her mood that was lifeless.

In her dream, she saw a lodge lit by a full moon, and she went in. In this sacred Moon Lodge, her mother, Shuhinono, sat with her and told her that woman's moods were life or death to everyone around, and that she should build a Moon Lodge like this one for other women to come during their time of bleeding when their moods were often dark. Here, in this lodge, they could rest and work and sing each other back to the lightness of love. They could honor their drop in energy brought on by their blood loss. They could mourn the loss of the seed of the memory of love, without affecting the men who experience no such memory or loss. They could be respected during this time of deep cycle and regeneration. They could even talk in prayer to their loved ones that had walked on. They could retreat and feel again, in vision, the closeness of the family of their childhood. Their Spiritual Mother could come to comfort and encourage them. And although during this time the seed of their last cycle bore no fruit, the next one could, and they would not lose their hearts to sorrow but would retain the fragrance of The Flowering Tree.

Feice learned from her mother that bleeding is a psychic door to the memory of love, that woman's blood is her connection to her family, both present and past, way back to the First Woman. Therefore, it is a door to the future, as well as the past, and her door to understanding all relationships.

It is the female that flowers, ripens and bears fruit. It is she that sheds her leaves or keeps them when it is cold and the hardness of winter is upon her. It is she that feels her psychic wound and those of others when the branches break from heavy snow or a tree is felled by wind, by age and by infirmity. It is she who picks up the bones of the dead ones and brings them to her fire to warm and cook food over for her seedlings. It is she who lives inside the consciousness of blood... before man can. In this awareness, she leads. Man must follow her to learn it is so.

In the dream, Feice asked her mother about this psychic wound. "I understand the purpose of bleeding for the body, but there seems to be a bleeding the mind does as well," Feice said.

And Shuhinono answered thus, "Bleeding is a psychic wound. The only way that life can birth life is if it can be wounded. Without a wound, you would not be vulnerable. Without vulnerability, female could decide against a life in form. Without birth, there would only be the Completion or the Spirit of Life. Then the cycle of experience through birth would end for everyone, not just you."

"Where does this wound come from?" Feice asked.

Shuhinono answered, "The psychic wound of woman's bleeding is from Creator. The price of carrying the seed of love and its memory in her being is her wound of the separation of truth from love. For her life to return to her each cycle, renewed and conscious, her blood must touch the ground in gratitude for the memory of love that is within the seed.

"And though man does not bleed monthly, man's wound is as great, for man cannot even conceive of love without woman. And though he carries the seed of the memory of truth, he knows it cannot create anything alive outside of love. He must first honor, respect and trust the woman to awaken him to love. He must be willing to give his blood in ceremony to awaken him to the larger family.

"So I give you this stick that you will paint red with a few drops of your blood each month of your moon. You will touch it to the ground and ask for the effects of all feelings of loss and sorrow to be removed from you. This stick will take all that is dead and give it to the earth to recycle. Let the heaviness drain from you to the stick and into the earth. Then give the Mother your deepest gratitude. In this way, whatever is dead goes through this sacred Red Stick, back to the earth to be transformed by the Mother into life again. Through your gratitude, you will feel new strength return to you through that stick, from the Mother. This is the way of woman, and this is part of the Sacred Circle of Life."

From her mother, Feice learned that each child is the Mother's

Tree of Life. Each person has thick male branches and a male trunk, with strong, deep roots reaching into the water and rocks, the blood and bones of Mother Earth. And each person has lighter female branches, with leaves turned to catch the golden light of truth in Father Sky, waving graciously in the air under the blue dome of Spirit. Above, stand all our ancestors, the stars.

And though each child of creation is the Tree of Life, only women *feel* it is so. That women bleed and feel the people is their link to Creator. Sundancing is that for man. When man is pierced and bleeds in this sacred way, he too can feel the people. Women bleed every month. Man can only choose to pierce and bleed this way but once a year.

So in the tree you have the female, balanced, standing in earth, standing in water, reaching for the fire in the sky, reaching to make air, combined with male, penetrating the earth, bringing the water up to the female. This sacred tree is a life-producing, life-giving and life-balancing sacred circle of earth and water and fire and air.

You, too, have a sacred circle to complete within yourself and with those around you. And what is it that you produce, like the tree produces fresh air? You breathe the air, you drink the water, you eat from the earth, yet you have no penetrating roots to the Mother's fire below. You have no reaching arms to the Father's fire above, no branches uplifted to catch the sun. You say, "Oh well, I breathe CO_2 for the trees to use." Sure, but are you in relationship to the tree? Are you connected to it? What waste does a tree produce? Well, nothing is wasted. What waste does a human produce? Oh, far more than we care to think about. So what is it that a human gives when their circle is complete?

I'll tell you. It's not so complex. The sum total of your produce to the Creator is what you give by way of your energy. Within you is a fire like the Mother's, to produce fuel and energy for your body. When that red fire is quenched with water, energy is released. You breathe in the blue fire that is the air. From the trees, you get fresh oxygen as you breathe out CO_2 to feed them... balance.

As with the trees, your relationship to all living things around you must be your *conscious* giving and receipt of the love that all is. A human being's energy is either fear or love, derived from their thoughts. Thoughts are images that get stored as the energy of peace or conflict, not only in each individual's own body but in the body of the earth as well. When stored in your body, fear causes sickness. When stored in the Mother's body, fear causes sickness on a global scale. What would you give back to Creator and to the Mother?

Nothing more has been asked of you than to complete this sacred circle back to Love again. While completing your circle and remembering the Source and your agreement to be here, you will overcome your fears and return to Love again... return to Truth again. And in this return, you will learn to transmute all that was fear... to cleanse your body and your energy that made the Mother sick. As each one does this, the Mother is strengthened again, and the Will of God is done.

To do the will of God is nothing more than remembering what you truly are. In remembering your will and God's are one, your tasks are fulfilled effortlessly, without conflict or constraint. What is more simple than this... to simply be what you truly are? All the struggling and striving and pushing and pulling and willing and won'ting are useless and absurd in the face of this knowledge remembered.

Spirit would not force you to remember. That is why this world seems to drag wearily on. That is why some human behaviors seem so outrageous. You must remember what you are in order to do what you came to do. But were Spirit to force you to remember, it would only create more fear and anxiety. And yet, because of the laws of body and the laws of God, all your experiences are communicated to others, and it is this that you teach. Decide whether it is fear leading your life or it is Love. What will you teach?

To remember, you will have to release your beliefs and suspend your disbelief. You will have to empty your cup and be humble, because your "already knowing" blocks the truth. Listen to Spirit, but make no attachments in your mind to specialness. Receive, and yet feel no need to go out and give before you have fully received. Allow your mind to awaken to a remembrance of perfection, to a remembrance of what was agreed would be your purpose. It is only the knowledge of your true purpose that will satisfy you. It is only your remembrance of perfection that will give you the foundation on which to stand in the midst of insanity and be sane. It is only standing in the eye of the hurricane that Armageddon will be a hiccup, that redemption will be instantaneous, that the concept of time will not be linked with vengeance.

The purpose of any elemental discussion at all is to give you a foundation on which to stand and be Spirit on the earth. What good is Spirit if it isn't on the earth too? Perhaps you may wonder if my usefulness to people has been limited by the fact that I would not and need not take another birth. I chose this path for myself, as I was not up to facing the challenges and distractions of a modern world. I knew I was better suited for helping others remember what they are during these challenging times, where again it is possible for you to awaken to yourself as Spirit while you are in form. From this side, I can help many others awaken, whereas if I were in form, I could only help a handful. But you are the courageous ones who risk. Spirit does not risk you, for we know how to help from here.

I bless these two who write these words down because they will reach more through books than by talking. By their asking for Spirit for themselves and by asking Spirit to guide them, they have opened a door from us to them, from their past and their future to their present, from eternity and the perfection of truth in it, to now.

If you wholly desire the truth, you will have it. But the only people who remember fully what the truth is, are Spirit. Yet it is Creator's desire for you to have the Truth while in physical form, to be Spirit within the body. It is this that will transform the world. To know yourself as Spirit and to behave it in the world will heal the world.

Many of you have asked, "Why is this process so slow, and why is the world evolving so slowly?" Well, it is because of fear, dear ones. So be not afraid. Use your mind for prayer and communication to Spirit, rather than avoiding your fears and projecting your beliefs. Withdraw your investment from the ego mind, from the world around you, from the distracted people in it, and from the place itself. Point your mind instead toward the only Help that you could ever receive. Ask Spirit what life is for and you will learn. Ask people what life is for and you will not.

Pour water on your fire. Complete your circle. Be grateful and put your feet deep into the earth. And in your breath, in the air around you, you will be delivered from illusion, and you will return to Truth. That you experience your physical death is not important. That you experience your Spiritual Rebirth is.

Take heart. You are deeply loved. You were never abandoned and certainly not forgotten. All is well. Join hands in your heart. Take courage from love. Take endurance from love. Be alert in love. Be patient in love.

You are the fire in the seed, dropped to the earth in the dust and ashes of those gone before. You are the water that rises and falls and runs across the land to collect and nourish the seeds that grow along the banks. You are the air, both hot and cold, that makes your seasons come and go. You are the cold flame gone hot and back to cold again. You are the circle of seed, dropped to land and back to seed.

Show a willingness to learn and you will. Show a willingness to share what you're learning, and Spirit will show you how to be honest and how to learn as you teach and teach as you learn. Make giving and receiving the same. Make them simultaneous. Receive as you give. **Regard no moment or movement of life as anything but a response of love to love.**

Spirit will, then, have you be where you are supposed to be, meet whom you are supposed to meet... as soon as your learning will allow. And maybe, you too will have a mate to help you, or maybe you will join the male and female together within you in the Divine Spiral to Wholeness, to Oneness within creation, within your mind and heart. And you, too, will be fulfilled in your learning. Would you have any other purpose first than this?

Put cedar on the earth in gratitude for what you receive. Pour water for people in pain and confusion and in difficulty. And as you pray for their receiving of help, accept help for yourself. Make your asking, everyone's asking. Awaken together.

Chapter 5
Awakening Together

Now that you have a familiarity with the elementals of fire, earth and water, and you have a clue about air, I will tell you a bit more about Barbara and John. And the only reason that I've been telling you anything about them at all is so you may see how Spirit is present in *your* life. When I tell you to what degree these two people were totally split into male and female and what it took to bring them together, perhaps you will take heart about your own relationships. When I tell you about the healing that these two have begun to accomplish within themselves and between themselves, perhaps you will begin to desire it for yourself.

I do not tell you these stories to glorify these two or to make them any more important than any other human being or creature or life-form on this planet, but only to demonstrate to you that in the midst of confusions and distractions, you too can find a sense of purpose and a sense of mind, that you too can have true desire in your life and reach the goals that you set. Besides, if they can do it, anybody can. (I tease my children.)

I will begin with Barbara who was born into a poor family, yet they were wealthy in that they owned the land they lived on. They did not have to move from place to place and find jobs in the cities. She was raised in a conservative, religious family, with uneducated parents, in an environment that was slow. The oppressiveness of the assumption of knowledge, without experience, drove her to look outside her environment for her own experiences that would teach her, without the fear and guilt, what the truth was. She was wholly female, with only the fire and earth within her. That she contained the seed of the memory of love, sustained her through her growth period, her trials in the world. She tasted all the world had to offer, and she watched the intent and behavior of those around her. And at the core of her being was the belief that love was real, that it was sacred, that between man and woman for this sacred truth to be present, trust must be present, honesty must be present, faithfulness must be present.

My wife and I followed her through her development. We watched her suffer the world's insults and confusions. We watched her sample the smorgasbord that life was in these wealthy times in the United States. We watched her grow in courage and daring, and we watched her grow in her despair, until one day she decided to end her sufferings, to end her involvement with the world as it was, not through death of the physical form but through death of her self-concept.

Her strength of will and her sense of humor kept her from death of the physical body while her mind switched. She went through high fevers during an herbal cleanse that lasted many days. And at the end of these days, she looked in the mirror and saw a new person, unbeknownst to her, a new self arising out of the ashes of the fire of transformation.

The depths of the suffering in the world had been taken on and endured. And in this deep connection to all life, she began to open to consciousness. And in the years that followed, after thirty-nine years of wandering misery without knowledge, came different, new years with a will toward the solution, rather than the problem of suffering.

A quest was begun for a Spiritual teacher that led her to India a couple of years later. The desire for an external teacher was still too strong to allow her internal teacher to awaken in her. Her mental growth was accelerated. Her awareness of telepathy, of manifestations, of distant healings, of miracles, grew. And yet, the arrogant mind that demands proof kept her in misunderstanding.

This seed of the memory of love sustained her through the nursing of her dying father to his physical death, though her feelings of love for her Creator and her Guides had not grown enough to overcome the negativity of the world and even judgment against the Creator Itself, for a world apparently filled with so many trials and so much suffering. Where was a merciful God in all this? She was still waiting for understanding, as was her mate.

During this time, she had relinquished any idea of finding her perfect mate, as she had never married. Relinquishing this search for a mate allowed Spirit to enter and help her find her lost half.

Meanwhile, John, who was married and had two children was just beginning the process of relinquishment at the time that Barbara was leaving for India. She was renting a room at the house of a mutual friend John just "happened" to visit. Spirit just "happened" to get them to talk briefly before she left for India. Nothing "happened," though a deep and very old memory slowly began to stir in Barbara.

John had tried in previous years to involve himself in the world in some positive way, as an artist, an inventor and medical technologist, to raise his family and to do the best he could in the world. And yet, there was the heart that longed for the truth. It was his involvement in *A Course in Miracles*, native ceremonies and in medicine work that awakened him to the possibility that Spirit and God and the Creator were real.

With a bankruptcy, a divorce and a minor heart attack, all at once, he relinquished his control of everything. And it was only his desperate question... *"What is love?"* and his willingness to give up pretending he already knew anything at all about it, that signaled to Spirit that the two of them were ready to be reunited.

When they finally were reunited through various tricks and manipulations by Spirit, what you call "coincidences," they began to recognize Spirit was guiding their lives, and they were no longer lost, without help. It was their joining of minds that allowed us to come in and reorder their reality. Though there were obstacles to be overcome and there were many trials and tests yet to be endured, at last Mohinono and his spiritual mate and twin were again together in the same damn room, actually talking, actually finding they had one single goal, that of awakening... and now, that of awakening together. Good thing too, 'cause they never could awaken apart. Each was a part... halves, now together.

They were put on an accelerated path when they asked, together, to learn. So it was Spirit's game now. Wanna' play?

I'll tell you how this game of awakening works. You ask. We start. Lots of fun for us all. Then, maybe somethin' happens and you get scared. We don't stop, 'cause we honor your first request. We won't stop for illusion, and we don't let up 'till you holler "mama." Then, maybe you rest some. Depends. Funny thing about knowledge. It doesn't come before direct experience. Yes?

So, while Barbara's love was being tested to the depths, John's split mind was being made apparent. Through their working with other people, together, helping others to heal their misperceptions, their own were being healed as well. Economical, don't you think? Equally comical, don't you think? Comically equal. Don't think.

I will tell you something of the split mind in John, so that you might see it in yourself or in others, so that you might understand that these difficulties can and must be overcome and healed, while under great pressure from Spirit and with good humor all around.

John had an addiction, like most men in any society, of seeing sex as the demonstration of love. He was split between good intentions and lust and fear. In his preteens, he learned to lie to cover up his thoughts. And in lying, he split off an alternate personality that desired to love, desired to respect and desired Spirit, to hide the one that lusted and worshiped sex, while using the energy of "the conscious one" to attract and to entice. So, which one was he? Or was he both?

The conflict grew and grew. And during this time that we were helping, many tests of mind were given him and many times he failed. It was his failures that taught him the depth of the split and tested Barbara in her ability to teach him what love was. It was her commitment to love him that taught him what love was. She told him after one of his more notable failures, "I don't need your guilt. I need your compassion." It was then he realized that guilt was the result of never having learned to join in love. And it was this that awoke him to his will. If he could not yet develop compassion, he would at least take his will back and stop the mind that tortured them both. It was then, his true desire to give love fully was born through this woman's demonstration of giving love unequivocally. He took his will back from the split ego mind, and he took a stand against the mechanism of ego itself. It was this act of will that opened the door for their joining to begin. He no longer invested in what he *didn't* want, but committed to what he *did* want.

Eventually, he was able to see with Spirit's help that the mind that was split in two was an adaptation to confusion and guilt. When he was able to take a neutral point in his mind and do nothing to defend or protect was when Spirit was able to show him this split, to show him these two selves he'd made in error when he was a youngster. It is this bringing up to aware consciousness of an error that is its undoing. It was this undoing that gave him back a quiet mind, unconflicted, undisturbed, able to learn once again.

The mind in the tall tree was the self-invented spiritual mind pretending to know, all the while invested in hiding and protecting the lower mind from discovery and shame. It was his willingness to be shamed by discovery that produced a forgiveness, even unto the beginning, as his intent was rediscovered to be pure. It was the regained honesty and innocence that delivered him from this entrapment of the soul.

It was Barbara that helped bring her mate back to wholeness. She, like her Spiritual Mother, Shuhinono, walks with feet deep in the earth. Yet it was her husband's love of nature that had helped her replant her feet deep enough to have the conviction of love that would teach him what he needed and to connect her to his air, his water. Through her deepening earth, through her fire, he gave her back the male properties of air and water that she needed, as she gave him back the grounded, female properties of earth and fire that he so lacked.

They returned to each other the gifts that each had saved for the other. From the liar that is loved is born the truth in love.

From the fearful of the earth who became angry because she felt that love was lost, comes the water on the fire. From the water on the fire comes the air, the truth. From the water on the earth comes love and life. From these two, we finally got some peace. Spirit actually got a short vacation.

Now, I can hear you saying, "Oh sure, big deal, but they still lead physical lives." And I'll tell you, sure, they're still human beings bumping along and learning what love is, just like you. They're still human beings tripping along, learning the truth and remembering their purpose, just like you. They are not ahead or behind. They are not faster or slower. So take heart. If they were a finished piece of work, they'd be gone, done, finished, outa' here. It is that they fulfill their purpose here that will make them a finished piece of work... just like you.

So, what is life? Well, you take the ticket, you take the ride. No sense in bitchin'. So relax. If you're on a rollercoaster, the harder you grip, the worse it will be. The more you relax and detach your unwillingness, the more you will learn. The more you learn, the more you will trust. The more that you trust, the more that you will be able to hear, be helped and be of help. What purpose is there in being here anyway, unless you are willing to be helped and willing to be helpful? Now, to all healers or would-be healers, all communicators or would-be communicators, I ask, what's helpful?

Go ahead, try to decide what is helpful by yourself. You will surely send confusing and conflicting messages, because they come from a confused and conflicted mind. Were you to join Spirit, Spirit could show you what's helpful in any given circumstance.

So I say this, decide nothing alone. Then remember you decided it. Make hearing Spirit your goal. Make becoming honest your goal. Make peace your goal. Make truth your goal. And, for God's sake, be willing to do whatever you are asked to do by Spirit. But make sure, it's a good Spirit... the Holy kind, the wholly kind, kind, whose only brutality (to the ego) is honesty.

Make whatever effort you need to make within yourself toward responsibility for your physical needs and toward responsibility for communication. Remember, communication is not just lips flapping with a bunch of noise. It's a joining of heart and mind.

Start listening and learning from the words you speak. Pay attention. Be alert. It is the intention of Spirit you be helped through your own mind, not just through others. Spirit would not have you be dependent on hearing their Voice through others, forever.

Chapter 6
Sacred Trust and Nine Suggestions

There is something called the valve of trust. And my son now knows what this is. He allowed an experience to come where he saw that his navel cord, when he was in the womb, was the source of food, of water, of air. He saw that this navel cord drops off in the first few weeks after birth, and that just before birth the hole in the heart closes to the mother's placenta, allowing the baby's own heart to pump the blood through its lungs and seek its own nourishment from its own blood.

So what was revealed to John and Barbara about this valve of trust, I will reveal to you. The psychic connection to the mother is a physical fact during development in the womb. After birth, the child transfers its psychic connection, what you call bonding, to whomever is the primary caretaker. And we're not just talking about physical needs. We're talking about psychic, spiritual and emotional needs.

Native medicine people across the world recognize that the navel button connects the psychic mind and the parasympathetic nervous system to the heart and all the organs of the body, including sexual. This navel button is your point of vulnerability for communication of feelings, both sending and receiving. It is also the point where sacred trust can be formed.

I showed my son that his navel cord, psychically was dragging on the ground. He trusted no one, not because he didn't want to but because he had never placed that sacred trust with anyone. He never knew he could or should. He did not recognize the value of this psychic reality. Therefore, he could not feel what other people felt. To him, betrayal or the breaking of an oath was common, to be expected in the world... everyone was really a liar and a cheat. So he had within him a desire to punish the world, to condemn it, to judge it, rather than to join the humanness of it. In relationships between people, this sacred bond of trust, this valve of trust is either open or it is not.

In our native ceremonies of birth, this connection to the mother was honored. This navel button of the male child was dried, saved, and put in a medicine pouch. It was then put in the safekeeping of an impeccable person, until that child came of age and wished to marry. Usually that impeccable person was a great-grandmother or a grandmother or a greataunt or aunt. Only women were entrusted with the job of holding the navel cord of a young male until he was grown. Only to women who had given birth was this sacred task granted. Only they were worthy of carrying the responsibility of keeping a child's psychic navel cord from dragging on the ground and being abused.

It was this sacred bond of trust through which a child received psychic nourishment, spiritual nourishment, and it was through this sacred bond that the male child learned what love is. Because female children have a womb, they already have the seed of the memory of love, so their navel button was later buried in a sacred spot in the earth, in honor of the First Mother, rather than saved. A girl child could carry her own psychic navel cord. To her, trust came with the seed. A male child, if carrying his own, could become unruly, distrustful or even crazy.

When a young male was courting, he was brought into ceremony, and the importance of this navel button was fully explained to him. He was presented with his button by its caretaker, and in marriage he gave it to his wife, symbolizing the commitment to perfect communication, to perfect trust.

It was in honoring the role of female that the male became connected to family. It was from the grandmothers and elders that he learned about this sacred bond of trust, whether audibly or psychically. It was to them that he appealed for explanation and understanding of what the larger family was and what commitment was. He was taught through his psychic navel cord by the dreaming of the elders and through visionary experiences given by the medicine people.

All the grandparents were responsible for basic education of both male and female children, by reciting teaching stories to introduce them to the importance of honor, respect, trust and sharing, and the way to lead a spiritual life.

It was the duty of the elder men to help young males overcome their fear about challenging the body, about the Spiritual realm, about the psychic world, and about the below that women naturally cycle into while men do not. It was in the handling of the will center, through this thread of life to every organ in your body, to which all the ills of the world, all the power struggles, all the wars, all the fighting... it was to this navel cord that we pointed all responsibility.

Cultures that have lost their understanding of the psychic nature of physical phenomena have lost their communication with each other. They have lost their ability to understand one another. They have become egocentric and selfish. It is this self-centeredness, this egocentricity that is the cause for much insanity and unhappiness in this world. It is in understanding the laws that govern physical, mental, psychic and Spiritual reality that you will begin to understand your true role and position, your true abilities in this world. It is through this understanding you will repair your relationships with the earth you live on and the people around you.

I recognize Christian tradition dictates the Ten Commandments as God's laws, and I do not dispute this for Old Testament times. I will only remind you of one law, the first. And that is, to love God with all your heart, with all your mind, with all your soul... with your whole being. All else will follow.

It is in this centered love, this neutral point of stillness, that you will recover your memory of God's natural laws. So I will ask you to be still and quiet, and read very slowly as I list a series of suggestions to help you achieve knowledge.

1. **RELAX.** The first thing you must accomplish is to learn to relax, relax beyond sleepiness and stay awake. God's laws don't need your invention or pushing to find them. God's laws always were. The only way to get beyond any obstacle in spiritual life is by peace. Peace cannot be had without relaxing. There is no love inside war and all conflict is war. Truth is not polarized against anything. Truth needs no expression whatsoever to be true. Defense of any kind is avoidance of truth. Anger expressed in any form whatsoever is harmful to communication and is never justified. Remember, you cannot search endlessly and find anything. Searching is not finding. Trying is not doing. Trying to be spiritual is not the same as being. Trying not to judge is not the same as the state of non-judgment.

2. **STOP.** The second suggestion is to stop. Stop doing. Stop searching. Stop running. Stop hurrying. Stop thinking you already know. Stop using. You don't know what anything is for. If whatever you did to get yourself here hasn't worked, stop doing it. Be still. Be quiet. Be at peace. Never stop taking the first suggestion with you... Relax.

The hardest part of stopping has got to be, stop judging. The Muslims hate the Christians and the Christians fear the Muslims, and the Hindus can't be understood... and the Buddhists understand everything... thinking and judgment, going on and on.

The game of right and wrong has nothing to do with God's laws. If everyone learned God's laws, there would be no judicial system necessary. All the laws written by man are there because the society somehow prefers a government to God. Yet, tell me one thing a government has created... besides the six-billion rules that no one can follow or make sense of anymore.

3. **ASK.** Ask anything you want, but make sure it's about your own understanding and development. Remember, you cannot ask for someone else, unless they are asking with you. I suggest you ask for an experience that will teach you what *you* need to learn. Don't forget your question, and only ask one at a time. Don't answer your own question. Wait. The answer will come. Relax.

4. **LISTEN.** That is the fourth suggestion... Listen. It is good to have a question. It is good to ask Spirit. But I promise you, you don't even know what questions to ask. And because you're not used to stopping anything, your asking may become incessant noise in your head. So I would rather have you say, "There is my question." Now stop. Now listen. Don't listen with your ears. Listen with your *whole* being. And if you get caught up in the world again, you will get uptight. And I will tell you to go back to the first suggestion... Relax. Then, stop again, remember your question and listen again. You can listen while you work. You can listen while you sleep.

5. **BE NEUTRAL.** That's my fifth suggestion to you. We are going to talk more later about being neutral, so I'll not cover that more than to say that this is your interim goal. You might think reaching God is your goal. But I tell you, without neutrality you'll never make it. Without relaxing, you'll never make it. Without stopping incessant behavior habits, you won't make it. And certainly, if you cannot listen to guidance, you will not make it.

6. **ALLOW.** The sixth suggestion is allow. Remember, don't try by yourself. Trying builds a wall between wanting and having. It is here in the relaxed space of allowing that you begin to let Spirit return to you what is yours. For you men, it is here that Spirit will pick your navel cord up from the ground, shake all the dirt and bugs and critters loose from it. And They will ask you what you'd like to do with it, who would you give it to, since you cannot carry your own and remain sane. It is here in safekeeping that the sacred trust which you give to another is returned to you, and you understand what trust is. It is not until you consciously give this trust, this sacred honor to another conscious and responsible being, that you can become a creative adult, that you can mature into the real world. It is not until you deliver yourself to another that you understand the horror and havoc that has been wrought on the earth by mankind to womankind. It is the delivery of this psychic truth and the honor due back to woman that will heal the rift between male and female. No one can learn to

create without trust... trust within any relationship and trust in relationship with Creator.

7. **LEARN.** So number seven is learn. You learn by opening. You learn by sacred trust and by balancing male and female within yourself, within your families, within your nations, within your cultures. And what is it that you are learning? What do the lessons teach? I'll tell you. You learn what love is, not what you thought about it but what it truly is.

I know there are people running the streets teaching that the Old Testament God is coming back, and that He is vengeful and vindictive, that He is selfish and egotistical, that He is not a loving, living God. But I tell you, each person reflects the God they believe in. If you see God as vengeful and all powerful, rather than loving and all powerful, then you are projecting vengeance and destruction onto the world.

And if you believe only the Hebrew-Christian view or only the Hindu view or only the Buddhist view or only the Muslim view or any other single view, then you are not seeing the Whole of God. And you will surely love your opinion more than the truth. Creation is bigger than any religion. It is a living, moving, breathing, expanding thing.

8. **STAND IN IT.** That means, stand in it regardless of the consequences. From Spirit you have learned what love and truth are. Now stand in it. Be it. Remember, love and truth are not solely a personal experience. They are shared by all. There can be no certainty until love and truth are joined.

Men without the desire to give love have no truth.
Women without the desire for truth have no love.

9. **GIVE IT.** That's the last suggestion. I call that the place of transformation... Give it. You learned it. You're standing in it. Now give it. Become a healer. Become a teacher. Demonstrate your life. Share it by giving it away. Don't be afraid that you'll lose anything, or you'll teach fear.

Take a chance. Put something at risk. Do what Spirit asks. Don't be arrogant and think you originated anything, or you forgot what love is already. And, for God's sake, don't try to be the Source of love. Be humble. Be honest. Receive as it is given by Spirit. Give as you were given by Spirit. Do no more and no less. Remember, it is only the ego that tries to give away something it doesn't really have or know anything about. Everyone knows how much one ego really loves another. Envy of a better act, perhaps.

369

*

The first thing that you knew for sure when you were born was that you weren't in charge. How come you forgot?

The second thing that you knew was that you were helpless and dependent. You had to have perfect trust. How come you forgot it?

The third thing that you knew for sure–and you couldn't possibly believe that this is wrong–is that you came from somewhere, and you're at least one year older than you think you are. Your intent to be born was born before you. So you were three months in preparation in the Spirit world, getting the act together before you found a womb to jump into. Then it took nine months, more or less, for you to get the physical form together enough, so when you popped out everything worked, so to speak. So I'm going to say, when you were born, you were a year old already and came from some place older yet.

Now, native cultures knew this. So when the decision to have a baby was made, the grandmothers began preparing for the birth, even before conception. There was a lot of talk, a lot of counsel about intent.

"Oh, you intend to have a family. Okay. Let's talk about that. What do you see around you? How do you see other people behaving? So you want to be a mother? And you want to be a father? Okay. Do this. Look seven generations ahead and see what kind of world you would have for your family."

Now, most people can see two or three generations ahead, easy. But I tell you, those old people made those young people sit down and look, for as long as it took, to see seven generations ahead. When they sat with the old people and the Spirit of the Ancient Ones, they got pictures of choices that lead to all possible ways of living in the world. They saw that the greatest numbers of people walking on the ground are in the first level of consciousness. This refers to the consciousness of the root fire of sexuality and all its many difficulties. Then, they saw that as people ascend in their learning about the other energy centers, they learn the different levels of living their life. Our young people were given this riddle.

"The higher the life you live spiritually, the higher the life you live emotionally, and the higher the life you live mentally, the higher the life you live physically. Is that true?"

No.

"Truth is, the more you are able to ground yourself, the more you are able to understand the planet you live on and all the living things around you, and the more you will be at peace and will trust. Is that true?"

No.

I'll tell you what is true. The more you stay in the center of your being, the more you will be connected to all Beingness. If you lose that, you will never reach knowledge. You will become afraid. You will not have a center with certainty of anything. And where is your center? I'll tell you.

It's the Heart of the Mother and the Mind of God.

You trusted when you came. Trust while you're here. You weren't in charge when you came, and you ain't in charge now. You can trust that you won't be in charge when you leave. Better practice now.

Chapter 7
The Nature of Perception and the Dreaming Mind

Having a flashlight without the energy stored in the batteries to light the light bulb doesn't do much good. So, too, human perception without the energy to run it would have no effect. By talking about the nature of perception, I will talk to you always about the energy behind it that is your life. It is because you do not know what to do with your energy that makes life for the western world or any other country as it is. To the degree that you admit that you don't know what to do with your energy is the degree to which you will eventually seek to be a spiritual human being, rather than a selfish one.

I will assume by your reading this third book that you want to know something about your energy, so I'll begin by saying that without love nothing is in balance, whether it's your own energy or your own perception. It is the nature of Love to put in balance the energies that drive all things, especially sexuality. But we're not talking about human love here. We're talking about the Creator. We're talking about big-time Helpers, like Jesus for the Christians and the Spiritual Mother for the natives.

The energy of your life is not generated by the food you eat but by the first chakra energy center, the root fire. It doesn't need food to feed it. It takes the energy of your psyche that you accumulated while dreaming, and it stores what you gained, like a capacitor, in the first center. For a culture that has adequate food and solid sleep, I can tell you, you store an awful lot of energy there. Now this is regardless of the anatomical differences in male and female. The base of your spine on the inside is the center for the distribution of this energy.

Now, if your energy is sexual, it's all pointed forward. If you point this energy forward, you will have an outgoing personality which tends to cheerfully or plottingly project everything it thinks, outward onto everyone else, and when confronted may withdraw, get angry and become defensive. Sexual energy can even become quite vicious and vengeful, because all of the energy of sexuality that is driving everything, all the way up the front of the energy centers, is affecting survival, will, heart, speech and hearing, and all the mental processes associated with perception, including projection as a form of vision. An example of this is an "inner-visual recall" of an old experience of pain or injury when involved in an extreme but unrelated circumstance... a flashback.

The root fire is a very selfish thing, very self-centered, very self-conscious. And it will use you and everyone else around, until the energy that is pushed forward and up the front side of the body is brought back down to the root fire to be reinterpreted and guided by Spirit to the tip of the tailbone and back up the spine. The choice is this–to project what you fear or learn what is true. It's that simple.

The hitch is that if you defend your perception, the very energy that you wish to turn around will be bound and stuck to the front by your fearful thoughts, by your control, by your defenses. This is where I ask you to take water and pour it on your own defenses, if you want to change. Even in the middle of a heated battle where you're actively defending all that you think you are, I ask you to take that water and go outside, and pour it across your hands onto a rock and say, "I don't want to be bound by old perceptions, by old behaviors, by hard thoughts, and I no longer defend or cherish them as true. What is true needs no defense."

When you pour water like that across your hands and you ask for a change of mind, your energy changes. And instead of it being a hook to keep things bound, that drop in energy goes down through the root fire and is turned around counter-clockwise at the tip of the spine, versus clockwise in the front.

So even in the middle of battle, you can ask for Spiritual guidance, and it will change your energy. Instead of rising to battle, you put down the sword, you pour water to wash away the feelings and ask the rock to hold them while you take time to see things differently, to decide what you truly want instead of war. That reverses the energy flow of your whole life.

So what you use to separate and delineate and identify you as a finite individual... your individual perceptions, when broken down by a simple prayer for peace and truth, begin to be an act of joining. Alone, perception is a device of the ego... destructive, selfish, greedy... whatever. And you might not think that you're really all those negative attributes, but when you're asked by Spirit what you really know, the test of humility will come to you. And if you defend your perceptions, any of them, no matter how gentle of a human being you are, you will find out what's been running your life and what's using your energy and how many grievances you've stored up. It is those very grievances and fears and beliefs and disbeliefs stored in your bag of images that keep your heart from joining anything.

I can say this, there isn't a human being walking that isn't addicted in some way to their energy being and staying exactly how they are used to having it or wanting it to be. The hardest thing for a young woman to go through is finding out that when she loves someone, her heart rate changes, her blood pressure changes, and she joins another's energy field. And when she does that, not only does she lose her own energy field–her perception of it, that is–she loses her perception of it to a man who may or may not be conscious and who may or may never rest or be humble, ever. And therefore, the hardest thing for a young woman is not understanding the consequences of joining or falling in love.

When you fall in love, you fall in love with your own identity intact. And when you finish joining, you often shift into the other person's feelings or psyche. Depending upon how strong of a personality you are, you may or may not lose your own identity. But for most young women, the draw of love is greater than the fear of shifting, so they learn early how to shift in and out of different people.

Now, I can say, most young men don't know a thing about shifting and joining. There are a few that are in touch with their female side, who can shift and understand. They learn that all you have to do–a shaman's trick–is to change your heart rate, your breathing rate, and match the energy of the thing you want to shift to, whether it's a person or an animal, and you're able to shift.

Women of old did naturally what sha-men had to learn... how to center and focus their energy, how to gain will over and control of it, and how to make it stop running their minds. They learned how to pray it to the back of the tailbone and, in all humility, to ask for help in transforming the energy of separation into joining again.

Women's energy cycles monthly, and it's during those times that her heart rate and blood pressure and breathing rate all change anyway. So she's a master of changing minds and moods, with the help of hormones and her female physiology.

Most men don't even know how to change their heart rate, not even aware that they have one. I have to say this–it sounds silly, but I have to say it–a man that's been seriously wounded is a better human being... if he lives through it. Awareness of physical mortality is a humbling experience. Whatever is humble can join. Whatever is vulnerable can join.

A woman is vulnerable and bleeds every day. I'll explain that by saying that the blood that she loses in menses is replaced from her bones and goes back into the womb to build a place fit for life to grow. She doesn't lose blood until menses, but she bleeds from her bones all month to rebuild that place, then cleanses that place if it's not fertilized. That place is where that egg goes to wait, the womb. Her whole system is one of building and waiting, then loss, then having to rebuild and wait. That's what the physical self does. The psychic self is either in accord or split between joining and separation.

All the different seven levels of chakras and seven directions–above, below, within, north, east, south, west–are about separation. They're all about perception and having a physical place to stand. When you close your eyes and dream at night, familiar ground is absent. And unless the mind builds something to stand on in this empty space, it has no foundation from which to view anything. Its center has no reference point. Mind is vast.

So the imagination has to provide the landscape. It is the fear of the dreaming mind that fuels perception. In the dreaming mind, water can be breathed, as do the fish, bodies can fly without wings or feather, and falling into the ground becomes a new journey, with new dimensions in joining.

Giving up of personal perception for the unlimited world of dreaming allows you to encounter all the fears that your mind has about drowning in the undercurrents of the ocean of the subconscious... the water. Giving up of personal perception brings you back into the fearless neutrality of the dreaming mind that is more creative and fluid. This is not the world of fantasy or of imaginary friends. The friends you meet here are real. The world of solid forms, however, is left behind. Some have called this experience "out-of-body." I would rather refer to it as "first body" or "light body" experience... the real body of experience. I say this because in this realm you are conscious. You can become aware of your physical self sleeping, while you are experiencing your real self that is awake in the dreaming mind. It is only the consciousness of your dreaming mind through which Spirit can communicate to you in vision and in soundless words... by telepathy.

It is fear that prevents joining and shifting and rejoining and releasing and rejoining. It is our fear of getting lost in this shifting and joining and releasing that makes us go backwards and defend what we think we are. It is in letting Love guide you and trusting Love to keep you safe, it is in taking guidance from Spirit that all this joining and shifting and rejoining and releasing and rejoining allows you to finally get used to the territory that an eagle or dolphin knows from birth, and that is putting itself in the water or air and trusting in the currents.

Now, you say, the world of mind doesn't have anything to trust.

But I'll tell you what you do trust. You trust that your creative mind can build a ship, and when you put it in water, there will be wind to blow the sails. You trust someone will build a wheel for your car and a plate for your food. You do trust in your creativity. Why would the Spiritual world, a world your dreaming mind can tap, be any different from the physical world?

When all fears of drowning, crashing, burning, or of dying by any way imagined are gone, it leaves a lot of creative time open. When fear of being attacked or overpowered or raped or whatever is released from your mind, you'll find you have all this energy and time to be creative. The energy expended in defending the perception of what you think you are keeps fear in place, keeps illusion running your life. When you face your worst fears, you'll have all your energy back. You'll have a mind that is capable of being creative. The energy that you fed perception with to keep things separate can now be used to join.

We'll talk about energy just for one more second. Just like in a battery, the energy can be high or low, intense or weak. Some people draw high current all the time, expending lots of energy. It makes you nervous just to be around them. And some people seem like they're about to run out... current is gone.

But I tell you, joining is in a neutral place, not strong, not weak, not high, not low, not here, not there, not right, not left, not right, not wrong. Joining ain't about perception at all, and it ain't about evasive maneuvers either. It's not about defenses. It's not about going anywhere. It's about relaxing. Just like in a battery, hook up a strong one and a weak one together, and you've got equilibration... equality. The only thing left to do is to look at why the high one might not want to be in the middle and why the low one doesn't get to the middle by itself. In this scheme, arrogance (high) and dependency (low) are equally erroneous. Love is in the middle.

Love joins all things. You don't have to worry about shifting into another human being and losing your "self" and becoming them. You already are. It's just that your lessons are uniquely for you. If your will is so weak that you fear losing yourself, then all your lessons are about developing more will and certainty of what you are.

There are two things life is meant to challenge you about: perception and will... all of your perceptions and your will, anyone else's perceptions and their will, and the mechanism (collectivized ego) and collective will.

*

If you are aspiring to be a spiritual human being and you are asking, if you are willing to receive and develop your own focus so your mind doesn't distract you to madness, if you can stay focused with a single intent, like getting ready for God, if you're willing to take water and pour it over your hands to let the past go, if you're able to pour this water on your own perception, if you are able to take what separated you and have it turned into joining, if you are willing to face your fears about the dreaming mind, if you're ready to understand energy... then you will be able to use your own intent and focus to open your mind, instead of using perception to keep it closed.

Pray it open. Pray the nighttime sky live inside your mind. Empty it of everything, then let Spirit begin to populate it for you.

That's my suggestion. You got one?

Chapter 8
The Natural, Open Mind

It has been said that when a Swami–meaning teacher–accepts a student, the first test is humility. The student walks up to the Swami and asks, "Will you teach me?" The Swami, right out of the blue, smacks 'em in the face–it's gotta' be the face–and that if that student rises to anger and smacks him back, the Swami says, "Come back later, you ain't ready." But if that student takes that confusion and asks a question with his mind, ignoring his own discomfort, the Swami will say, "Ah-ha, ah-so, I see you have an open mind, and that you do not defend your body as yourself. I see that you handle confusion well by asking a question with your mind, rather than jumping to conclusions, forming your own opinions and following through with some stupid and forceful action. I see you have self-control and discipline over the hardest emotion which is anger, so I will accept you as a student. And greater challenges you will have than this."

So I ask you, reader, are your fires intense, and do you never pour water on them? If you have never poured water on your own fires, whether they are judgments, trials and abuses, or simple frustrations, then, I can say, you have not harnessed the energy that runs your life well enough to become a Spiritual human being. I'd say, test yourself more. Put yourself in situations that normally made you angry, and practice pouring water on your own emotions.

For women, that could be purposefully sitting in an environment of machismo males... beer-guzzlin', football watchin', eatin', drinkin', smokin', fuckin' fools. Not that you haven't been doing that all along, but to sit in that environment and pour water on all your feelings, over and over again, until you can join their simple little minds and love 'em anyway, you have not developed enough distinction and control to meet God.

If you still think there's something to blame or something to use, then God eludes you. If you're still angry at having a physique, you will not find out what true strength is, and you'll be tested over and over until you do. If you're tired of the world and all its pretenses, I would say to you, pour water on all of it, family and friends, business, children, government, law, expectations from any direction. I would ask you to pour water on them all, and go sit out in nature. And instead of being afraid of being bitten by something, just open to it. Just open your mind to it. Quit being defensive and afraid. You will see that even in the dreaming mind, the ocean you are afraid would drown you becomes a place for dolphin and otters to play. Where you were worried about a shark, you now learn that a predator has to wait to eat, and that it only lives off the weak and dying. You would see that the dolphin with their pointed noses, when all together, are not the least bit afraid of shark. They go poke its underbelly until its liver bursts. So they go play in the open water and they don't drown. And the birds that fly in the air, once kicked out of the nest, learn the joy of the wind, and they ride the warm air currents from the earth that go up and all around.

That big night sky, instead of being a horror show, is just what it is... big, open spaces, little lights all around, love everywhere in it, full of creativity and adventure. Having so much space inside your mind will make you aware of the function of time, will make you aware of the nature of your open mind. And instead of fearing all the animals, all the creatures, you will see that they bear gifts for you, gifts of the understanding of their sweet, simple little selves. And in your collecting up of all the shifting and joining and rejoining and releasing and joining, you will begin to collect for yourself a vague awareness of what you are. And instead of thinking your life, you will start living it. The threads of time and experience that bound you to a simple concept of yourself, to a limited concept of your Self... when you give up your limiting perceptions, you will find that the timeline that bound you, now can set you free, that going into the past means recovering memory of other places, other times, other lives. When you join the love that's all around, your freed mind can point itself anywhere and go everywhere, unafraid.

This is the altered state which I call natural. Any child can do it. You can join any life and feel it. You can get its experience and knowledge by joining it, whether it be a bear or a deer, whether it be male or female, whether it be human or not.

When you are unafraid of shifting and traveling in time in this open-minded state while you're awake, you'll begin to find out what you are. Instead of using your personal will as a device of separation, you will find out you don't know what will is for, and you will give it to God. If you're trying to be used by God without first working on yourself and your perceptions, well, I have to say that everything you do in God's name is for *you*. And only your experience of God can be limited by what you claim God to be. And if you're worried about fate, destiny and the uncertainty principle, then I can't say that you're particularly aware of what the Great Mystery is.

It is when all the questions cease to interest you, it is when you give up the mind that thought them up, it is when you pour water on your fire, sitting out in the open with no one around that the Answer will come to you. Don't be in a hurry. Don't be cold or hot. Don't worry about no bugs biting your "self." If you're distracted, you forgot your question. If you could be distracted, then you couldn't hear the One Answer.

All the questions... fate, destiny, the function of life, the purpose of Spirit, the purpose of death, making the distinctions of reality–what's real and what's not–recognizing the purpose of illusions... all these questions will be answered all at once by a single experience and you'll be mystified. That one hungry thing will be fed, and all your personal insanity will be quieted. And God, again, will have the First and Last Word...

All is One. All is One. All One Everything, Everywhere, for All Time, All is One.

Chapter 9
The Breath and Land Remember Everything

Can't have understanding without knowledge. Yes? Knowledge comes with experience. Yes? Can't have experience unless you risk. Yes? Don't risk unless you have true desire. Yes? Can't have true desire if you're afraid. Yes? Can't put out the fire of fear without water. Yes?

If you withhold forgiveness for anything thought or done, the merciful bowl of water cannot be tipped over and will not put out the fire of fear and revive the dying land.

Now I'm going to tell you a secret which was hidden in plain sight. Your will is retrieved by your becoming conscious in the spaces between your breaths. There, and only there, can your *no* be changed to a *yes*. Your will is only this, no or yes, willfulness or willingness.

The energy you store in your body as tension is the fire of the *no*. With eyes closed, slowly stretch the muscles all over your body while you breathe in slowly, counting to ten or more as you inhale, holding for ten or more at the top, then exhaling for ten or more. At the bottom, hold for ten or more counts, then repeat. As you release that energy by stretching (called pouring water), watch your mind's eye and see the *no* images appear while you are holding your breath. Your will to hold your breath will strengthen. As it does, the time holding it will lengthen. And as it does, the *no* yields to a *yes* again. While you're practicing, it's okay to take catch-up breaths. Do not be cruel to your body. Be determined.

When your no changes to yes, go outside and pour a few drops of water on the land to nourish it. Give thanks for your life. Be grateful. It is only your gratitude and willingness of your mind and heart enjoined that can link you to God the Mother and God the Father. Creator is yet beyond.

*

The reason why you may not feel totally at home or secure on this land of the Turtle Mother is because the land remembers everything. Twisted perception and lies in books of history cannot change the truth. This land was taken over through deception and murder. That energy is stuck to the land until these mistakes are corrected. This unsettling energy is why your home may not feel peaceful and why your children may want to always move away. To correct this imbalance that past wars (hates) have caused, the Sundance Ceremony evolved to ease the future suffering of the children, through prayer and self-sacrifice now.

To explain, I want to now tell you about sundancers. But first, I want to say this. The Sacred Ceremony of Sundancing is each person's challenge of pouring water on the fire of their life and the earth's life. It is about will... bringing a personal will with sacred songs and sacred breath to the Tree of Life, for all the people. It is here a person takes a stand, offers everything, risks everything, goes without food and water for four days and nights each summer for four years, singing and dancing in the hot fire of the summer sun, and at the end of four days of ceremony, offers a little of their own flesh and blood.

This is strong medicine, and the dancers' intent is powerful. And because they were willing, they get some healing. To the degree that their motivation is pure and innocent, is the degree to which the Door of Knowledge is opened.

This is the path of purity. And it's done without drugs or medicines. The only drug allowed to this day, by most intercessors, appears to be tobacco. But why anyone on a fast would want tobacco–except that it does, temporarily, make you less hungry–I'll never know, because along with this good effect also comes a raging thirst. However, most indian folks consider tobacco, sacred. And it is, as an offering. Tobacco is an offering when smoked in a Sacred Pipe Ceremony and used as a sacrament. But rolled up in little papers and smoked in addiction, well, I think that even in sundancing, tobacco should be given up for four days. Then it truly becomes an offering again.

Now, I know many of you have great interest in the "Good Red Road," and that you want to be accepted into an "indian" understanding of spirituality, without really having to walk "the way" to get there. For you, this is the way I see.

Go now *in vision* in your mind to the edge of any reservation, and sit on your side without food and water until the correct someone comes for you. Ignore any attempts to dissuade you by anyone from either side. If removed, go back. Stay through the seasons, if you must. Sustenance will appear if need be, or not. Endure any deaths of the ego or assaults your mind or anyone else's could mount against you. Be pure. You only want to learn from their teacher. Someone will come, and does... when they are moved to.

So, here they are. You endure their questions and the intimacy of their language that you do not know. You are fooled by their intent with it, or not. You are not angry when their insults hidden by language are realized. You speak only to your intent to learn from a spiritual teacher, a medicine person. More abuses and insults come from the many who now gather to taunt you about past events, with the mimicry of the personality types of old tormentors that still try to overwhelm their culture and erase its spiritual nature. As you relive with them in vision those moments, all that they experienced in the past and still face to this day, you choose to run or stay. If you stay, you then see how you have insulted each tribal member by seeking a spiritual teacher without learning the lives of each member first, as if they had nothing to teach and were of no value in themselves. When you learn from each one, then maybe they will take you to the one they love and revere as spiritual teacher... maybe.

Afterward you can say, "I don't know why such a great people should waste their energy in anger and hatred on me anymore, for I see everything you show me is true, and I defend nothing that has happened in the past as if it were good for any. I do see how your energy of anger helps to keep out the ignorant and the foolish. You are wise."

After you can *be* your words all the way through, you will know that everyone in the tribe is the spirit of the teacher. In your joining them is the learning you seek.

Do this exercise for real in your psyche first. Then you won't have to go botherin' no people with your physical self and the weight of your ignorance. Psychic joining don't cost or weigh nothin'. Nobody goes anywhere to get it.

These are further suggestions, in case you have more direct involvement with "indian ways." Maybe you will have joined the spirit of the people, but remember you aren't it. Don't start thinking or acting like you're it. It's their history, not yours. Don't attempt to use the spirit of their lives as if you'd lived it.

You may be invited to a Sweat Lodge or an Inipi Ceremony. You may get healing in a Yuwipi Ceremony. You may even participate in a Sundance Ceremony yourself. All well and good. But don't ever try to own what you learn and posture to others that you've learned it, or you ain't learned nothin' yet!

You may even try to live as we once lived, dress or talk like someone red or brown, but you ain't foolin' nobody but yourself, 'cause the spirit of it ain't in the livin' like it. It's in the *being* of it. You can join it, and we're honored you would care enough to endure it with us. But be *you,* where you are, as you are, sharing and teaching as *you* do... honestly, truthfully, impeccably... like we are doing to the best of our abilities. It's good to share realities. We are all expanded with it. But, be humble.

Chapter 10
Challenges and Influences

This chapter is called challenges and influences. (It ain't my favorite.) The first section called challenges is very short. (It won't be your favorite either.) It's real easy. (Who says?) It has to do with a single question and a single answer. It's the difference between a full cup and an empty cup. The challenge is that you started with a full cup, and then as you entered physical form, it got poured out. So the one question you can ask that is of any value whatsoever is... What am I? (Who poured out my water?)

In that question, in that single question is every other question. What is life? What lives? What is love? What is truth? What is mind? What can you possess? What will you keep? What do you want? What is there to learn? What is time? What is time for? It goes on and on, thousands of questions, but they all stem from a single question... *What am I?* Find that out and every other question will be answered.

To find out what you are, you must be willing to return your self-made self to an original state, before your cup was poured out. The spiritual challenges you face in doing this are these. I will list them:

The burning out of the attachments to the sexual energy that drives perception.
The burning out of attachments to personal perception and the desire to defend it.
The burning out of selfish anger and the desire to murder.
The burning out of the desire for or belief in personal power.

The fifth book to be written soon will cover these subjects and will offer solutions to the temporary effects of these processes which are not much fun, but here goes... despair, depression, hopelessness and thoughts of godlessness; guilt, thoughts of worthlessness and suicide; insane moments of an out-of-control mind, racing pictures; assaults from evil intent not your own–or maybe your own; overwhelming sexual sensations imposed on you whether you really like it or not; feelings of being possessed, as if you had nothing to do with your life and knew what it was for anyway; hearing compelling voices telling you to do irrational things which may or may not be fun, and if you're having fun, it'll be ruined quick; bouts of intense fantasy, like you're the savior of something complex, like Hitler complex, like God complex, like Satan complex, none of which you are anything like and certainly don't like... unless you do. And if you do, then you certainly know why you're stuck and don't care nothin' about nothin', especially me talkin'. But hey, I'm just the Holy Spirit... you already God.

*

The rest of this chapter will be devoted to the influences you will see in the empty cup, if you care to look. The first thing you'll notice in the empty cup is that everything's got some kinda' fat, sweet smell to cover up the stench. Tip it over. Look what comes out...

... attractants, enhancers, magnifiers, expanders, lifters, compressors, repulsants, droppers, and general wrinkle removers with spacially special social maneuvers, which are holes, hooks, seductions, and conjobs that promise some immediate gratification. Rub it in. Rub it on. Rub it all over. Rub it all over your friends. Can you believe it? Can you believe in it? Canned believement.

I will go back to the beginning again. Wanna' come? It's okay if you don't. It's a rough ride.

So, what you did is to change the question, "What am I, body or Spirit?" to "Who am I?" Like now, you gotta' go find yourself, and probably somebody else did it better, so maybe you'll just be them.

You're born, and all of a sudden you've got to have a name. Ralph Bufkanufkawits. Surelee Shareme. And the ancestry of family lineage, the parents, and the whole culture's mind set become more important than what new being just popped into the world.

If we considered those babies openly, we wouldn't name a child before it's born. We wouldn't give it some conventional name before we knew *"what"* that person was and what their baggage was when they arrived here. You think because you come in a little skin with little lips and little fingers that you can't be carrying any baggage. Oh well, think again. The baggage comes within the soul of the person, within the spirit of that person, within the energy field of that person... in the empty cup.

Now, in our native culture, everybody born, same. Nobody gets named right quick. It's just, baby of so-and-so, until that baby develops its own ability to communicate what it is, what aspect of creation it came to mirror, to share, to amplify. Then this young being is given a name that he or she will answer to that has a larger connection to the world around them, than names like Joe or Betty. Usually, they are endearing names like, Little Bear, Little Feather. When they hit puberty, when this person's personality or soul is fully emerged, when through trials, through tests, through naming ceremonies, with the help of Spirit that person will discover their own name, the name that Creator or Spirit gave them to guide them in their true purpose for being in a body.

You think about your name you were given. What does it have to do with your purpose? What has it to do with your soul? How does it connect you to your life or any other?

In the sixties love generation, people got to be Rain, Oak, Love, or Freedom. People were named things that had a bit of meaning. Think of it, children named Stormy. Whew!

In your culture, if you were to trade names that had meaning and described a person for what their energy portrayed, over there would be, Sex Pot. Over there would be, Money Grubber. Over there would be, Looks Good in the Mirror before Noon. Over there would be, Selfish Cuts Throats.

Maybe over in the corner, watching carefully, there'd be some little person, and we'd call that one with the big heart, Redeemer. We named people for their gifts, for their talents, for their abilities, for what they shared with the people.

So, the worst mistake a human being could ever make is to say, "Who am I?" instead of "What am I?" then seek an identity that's private, that cannot be shared, that is truly an invention of one's personal perception, which is often formed in opposition to those around.

Because that name cannot be linked to anything real, it is subject to what I call, the mechanism. This means if something has no meaning, it can be used by anything. It can be influenced by anything. It can be subject to laws other than those that are God's because it is illusory, and therefore has no ground in the truth.

So what is this mechanism? I will explain it as best I can. This mechanism is a relatively, semi-intelligent collection of all the energies of illusion, i.e., collectivized ego. I call it semi-intelligent because it has intent and can manipulate, but it cannot truly create. That is, if a person believes himself to be, let's say a Rambo, let's say powerful in the world, physically powerful, then that illusion of self can be used by what I call a collective mechanism of illusion.

This mechanism is a mirror of illusion that reacts wholly and completely to reflect and test you on your own fears, thoughts, beliefs, and desires. It is the "negative teacher." It is the ultimate teaching device of what is *not* God, *not* love, *not* truth. It teaches perfect lovelessness, perfect horror, so whatever attraction one might have had to any loveless thing gets burned out when perfect humility is reached. Its ultimate teaching is that it has no power over God or love or truth or life... or *you!*

If you are on the initial descent of your journey to awakening, you will surely see it as a "negative" influence. People have called it Satan, the negative mind, the destroyer. They have given it a persona by calling it the voice of fear. But I tell you again, **there is no single person responsible for the use of illusion.** Illusion itself is a fearful, collective mechanism, and therefore is used by itself for itself... the ultimate selfishness.

To speak of it another way... love expands, fear contracts. If love is light and it expands at the speed of light, then what room would there be for a black hole which contracts at the speed of light? If love is all-encompassing, then how could the destroyer or the voice of fear create a vacuum so intense as to suck up all of life? If it is not creative, then what is it doing with everything that it is supposedly sucking up?

I will attempt to describe this reflective mechanism that rules perception. I will attempt to unwind this mechanism of perception for you. I will attempt to do the impossible, and that is to use perception to undo itself. I will attempt to describe to you the way through this dilemma of being acted upon by forces which now seem to hold you back from knowledge.

I will give you an image to hold onto, and that is of a bubble within a bubble, but having a common spout or opening. What must be done with perception is this. The smaller, inner bubble of the True Self must expand, as the outer bubble of fear contracts. The inner balloon must expand and turn itself inside out, over the now smaller and what used to be the outer bubble, through the common opening, thus changing places. What was large and controlled you, must now become small and controllable within you.

This process of turning inside out is what must be accomplished, in order for perception to be traded for knowledge. The external bubble covering your inner self is this mechanism. As belief in what the mechanism projects and fear of it are withdrawn, it begins to shrink. As your new awareness of self as spiritual begins to grow, your inner bubble begins to expand.

So, as you take your will back and stop feeding this fearful mechanism of perception, you reach a point where the bubbles are identical in shape and in size, and it is here that the most stress will be felt. This is the point at which your new self and ego seem to be equal in strength and size, almost indistinguishable.

This middle point is usually a point of great turmoil. You may feel mistrust for Spirit and a strong pull, back toward the devices of ego. You will feel very weak, and yet it is at this point that you must develop the most will. This is where denial is useful, but only against the ego, never against Spirit.

This point takes the most trust. Is God love or not? Is love real or not? This is the crucial point at which you can truly accept healing. This is the point you begin to realize that your entire personality was part of the mechanism that controls behavior, beliefs, actions, and thought. You don't know who or what you are at all. It is at this point you must ask Creator what you are, for you now know you don't have the memory of it and must ask for it to be returned to you.

Getting to this place of exquisite humility is for most people a very difficult journey, and yet all of you as children began with it, and were erroneously taught by the world to be a "who," rather than to experience and know "what" you are. But you must return to this place of humility as an adult to ask for the truth. You must become neutral in your pursuit of truth to learn that truth just is, that love just is. Knowledge awaits your arrival and your joining at the place where it is kept. But it is only the deepest humility and greatest desire that will bring you to this place. It is only within this Great Hall of Learning that truth exists anywhere. It is from this place that truth will be extended to the world, once again. It is here that the Plan of Creation is kept and shared.

We as Spirit do not allow casual visitors here. There is but one way to enter. All illusions must be given up. All desire for power must be burned away. The passing of certain tailor-made tests of character determines when entry is given. The memory of what you are must be regained. I am here to help you remember all that you are, to help you regain lost memory of what you are.

I will begin by telling you the greatest illusion the mechanism has to offer is that life dies with the form, that death is equal to creation, that there is power in destruction. Many believe that to be able to destroy is powerful, when in truth it is the exact opposite. Destruction is the lack of power to create or renew.

The only use the mechanism has for the human mind is to trap it in the diametrically opposing twenty-seven paradoxes or dualities. The only purpose Spirit has for the thinking mind is to eventually realize that it is totally an invention from within the conflict of the twenty-seven paradoxes. Therefore, the thinking mind is only the illusion of self as body, defined here as ego. All ego life is living inside the twenty-seven paradoxes. Sounds like prison to me.

In other words, its thought is split, dual. This thinking mind is caught in these paradoxes of ever-rebounding opposites... positive/negative, light/dark, up/down, left/right, forward/behind, here/there. It even goes into relationships–male/female, money–have/have not, responsibility–did/did not, and learning–will/will not. Duality is in every aspect of your life–active/passive, guilt/pride, success/failure, and the most seductive–right and wrong.

The function of the twenty-seven paradoxes is to take you beyond conflict, to show you where there is conflict, to help you realize that the mind that thinks does nothing but try to resolve conflict and attempt to win. Therefore, it is always in conflict. Peace does not exist anywhere within this thinking mind. Solutions are nowhere in the problems. Always in the mind of conflict is fear of the presently unknown Great Mystery and fear of the eventual undoing of all conflict. But in the face of the Great Mystery, all the categories of the twenty-seven paradoxes are in themselves totally irrelevant. Ultimately, they can't and don't exist.

I tell you this to help you simplify your mind. A complex mind cannot be at peace. A complex mind cannot know what love is or get the answer to the question, "What am I?" A complex mind cannot enter the space in which truth exists, where knowledge is real.

And the reason why you don't remember what you are is that you have split your mind in half, into opposing hemispheres, into opposites, into dualities. You have made left and right a reality to you when they really only mean something when in relationship to what's in the center. So what's in the center? Left and right of what? Don't make this an intellectual exercise where you choose what you think is the right answer and you win. If you don't truly know what's in the center, you're in pain, whether you know it or not.

Picture this. Everyone standing on the planet in the southern hemisphere is standing on someone else's feet in the northern hemisphere, no matter how much dirt or water is in between. Otherwise, the earth would wobble out of existence. That there are too many people, that they are changing the climate of the earth with their burning of fuels is obvious. That there is inequality is obvious.

So if you are going to "wobble" this planet back into a stable state, I would say that the haves and the have-nots have to come closer together, without light and dark and right and wrong getting in the way. As long the dark stays dark, as long as the dark doesn't let the light in, there will be opposites. But you notice that when the moon reflects its light to the earth, the dark doesn't oppose it, nor can it. The dark has no power. When you light a candle or a flashlight or a light bulb in your house, it takes power to light it. Dark doesn't cost a thing nor is it anything real at all.

So I'm going to say to you that ultimately the voice of fear has no power over you whatsoever. The mechanism, the destroyer, whatever you want to call it, the negative, dark, down, behind, away-from-here place that we fear, I promise you, it is not real and has no true power.

Though the mechanism that influences people *appears* very powerful on this earth, it is only because there are many, many people throughout the ages who have pointed their energy toward it and magnified it. It has grown into what the Mother calls an "unspeakable horror." She once told these two here, "You don't see what I see. I shield you from the horror, but I'm beginning to lose control. I can't hold it all anymore." So please be aware, your attempts to block out this horror show from your seeing will soon fail. What will you do then?

Let me explain. Horror films, we all know are not real. And yet we go to the movies, we get scared and we become fearful, and we expend an awful lot of energy being afraid in the movies. Where does that energy go? You go home and eat and sleep and forget, then come back for more tomorrow. It's all entertainment, so what's the difference, you ask? Maybe you never noticed where it went, but the energy of negativity and fear does, in fact, go some place. The reason you don't know what peace is, is that that energy of fear and negativity is never fully gone. It's stuck to the ground you walk on.

It works this way. You took your flashlight into the film. Your flashlight is you. You are the light. You took it into the dark and got teased around a bit. The energy of your batteries that expended your light in that space, produced the vibration of fear and released that energy. It's stuck to the ground. Just as there are holy places where people pray, there are other places where stuff is stuck to the ground.

This mechanism that is collectivized ego or collectivized illusion or collectivized fear has a certain psychic "life" of its own, based upon those who are involved in using that energy that you expended. Witchcraft at its darkest uses this energy. Even average people who try to extract what they want by the use of your fears or through the projection of judgment, anger and guilt use this energy.

So you agree there's a problem. And you agree that the energy that is generated in fear goes some place, just as the energy that you give out in love goes some place. But there's a big difference between the energy of fear and the energy of love. The difference is in usefulness. The ego would use everything, would use anything. Love *uses* nothing.

I'm going to ask you this question. Can the truth be used for anything? If you answer yes, then you still are on the side of seeking power. If you say no, then you realize that truth can't exist outside of love, and love doesn't selfishly use anything.

One of the first conditions of the truth is peace. The second is, the truth cannot be used for anything at all, at any time. **Truth just is.** The minute that you try to take truth into your possession and selfishly use it, the truth will appear no longer true. Using anything makes it a part of perception, with all the many opinions or points of view. There is no peace in the realm of perception, and therefore no truth. This is why there can be no truth outside love. All opposites collapse inside love's truth. You can learn what love and truth are, but only by first choosing peace.

Now, I want to tell you more about how the mechanism got its power. It works like this. The four richest areas where you have the most fears are insurance, energy resources, drugs, and law or lawlessness.

Now, insurance and energy you can understand. You can understand energy, based upon your society's consumption of fuels and its addictions to the automobile, central air, laborsaving devices, and its vast thirst for entertainment. You can understand buying insurance, based upon the possibility or probability that something might happen.

So that's one way the mechanism gets your power... from your fear of death, your fear of hardship, disability or sickness or injury, your fear of facing the elements of nature by losing your utilities or your house and all you've worked for, and by your fear of being overpowered in any way.

Now I'll explain how the mechanism gets its power from drugs and why young people are attracted to them, because that's what you have the least understanding about. It's real simple. Enhancers, magnifiers, expanders, lifters, compressors, repulsers, droppers.... Get the picture?

The older generation used medicines for the body. The young have transferred some of this interest to the mind and the drugs that play with it. The young take drugs out of a desire to overcome their own limitations as simple human beings. Rambo and other super-heroes all offer illusions of escape from physical limitations, and in some ways, even spiritual.

Now, overcoming limitations can't be the enemy, can it? Instead of teaching the young how to overcome limitation, the society has made all drugs the enemy and made the penalty of being put behind bars a further limitation. So now, drugs represent a risk-filled subculture that has powerful motivation in overcoming its limitations, yet with the threat of becoming more limited. So, in turn, the subculture sees the law as the very thing that it's trying to go beyond.

You say that the laws are there to protect and serve, that the limitations that they set are good. I have no argument with that. I agree. But your young people are growing up in a world where everything is owned and controlled and no longer free. Even nature isn't free. It's managed by the fish and game. The wilderness areas are there, but they are almost impossible to get to. Even as I speak, some states are now charging money for a permit just to hike on public land.

It seems every inch of land is possessed and controlled. Everywhere you go, there is limitation and control and possession. Young people are growing up inside this mechanism, this costly, rigid structure that is uncreative and does not reward expansion.

The books and the learning methods that you use, teach mostly without creativity. And instead of a life of endless option based upon your true purpose, you have limited choices based upon what earning capacity you wish to have, based upon how much money you have now, and how good your grades were, and what you went on to study. You have nothing but limitation and expectation. You say that creativity is rewarded, but when you get out of graduate school, you find out that it is not.

Many of the idealisms put forth in your society don't come true, and pretty soon you have a person who grows up aware that the society is more interested in its advertising than its fulfillment.

So now you've got gangs on the streets making quick money off drugs, driving fancy cars, owning cell phones, and they're seemingly unlimited in what they can do... until they get caught, of course. But, for them, the threat of limitation or punishment is no worse than the conditions for their expressions against it in the first place.

Now, you call those kids, "Satan's work," "the work of the devil," and say that they are throwaway kids. "Put 'em behind bars and limit 'em." And you say that this disease of the young is the scourge of the earth, that it's a result of abuse, poverty and ignorance. But I tell you, for these children, this is ultimately a spiritual issue, not just a physical one. For anyone who grabs power in any way, it is a spiritual issue. That these folks think that they are not being used, that they are powerful and are the users is an illusion, whether they're an adult selling bread in a store for 30 percent more than they should or they're kids selling drugs on the streets. Kids see no difference between sanctioned criminality and unsanctioned. The desire for advancement, above and beyond any other thing, living or dead, is always a spiritual disease, whether it's selfish capitalism or organized crime or street gangs.

Now, I can see everybody saying, "Oh, how you gonna' reform a sixteen-year old with a pocket full of drug money, driving a big car, with a bad attitude about society?" Oh well, we'll see.

You say, the very thing that that young one feeds off of has nothing to do with anything but the physical–clothes, food, sex, drugs, money, cars, music... total sphere of influence right there. Knows nothing else but those things. Not interested in anything else.

So you say, "Take away those physical things, limit their life some more and put them in prison." But do they grow up? Well, they grow up around other people just like 'em, with the boss man standin' there with a big stick or gun. And instead of being independent on the street and small, they join an organization and become more organized, 'cause now they really can't get a legal job when they get out on the outside, not one they would even barely consider in the first place, not one with untwisted love in it anywhere.

So the drugs that they take to be unlimited for a moment become the very limitation that they live in, not because drugs are bad or good but because the mind doesn't know it's asking for anything spiritual. It seems it is asking only for physical things for itself. But what for?

I'll tell you. To find out if one is loved or not, if God is real or not, the young test the limits. But there is still a human being that desires to know what love is and to be loved, even though each ego says it doesn't want it or need it. Love is the one real thing every mind can ask for.

So within this environment of fear of lack, of power and possession and the desire for unlimitedness, come many strong emotions. All those emotions can be summed up into three significant ones:

Fear and the desire for power, for possession and control are the same thing.

Anger and the desire to obscure are the same thing.

Guilt and the desire to blame are the same thing.

Those three emotions, **fear**, **anger** and **guilt** run the dark side. They feed energy to it, and those who indulge come to it to be fed. As they indulge, they are drained of the energy that they could use to resist it. The more they seek of it, the more life is drained away from them and everyone around them, until all they attract or seek is death.

So the only way to beat the mechanism is to not feed it energy, either for it or in fear or anger against it. To war against it gives it your belief and increases its power.

This mechanism has three main ways to hook a human being—sex, money, and substances that alter the mind or perception in a non-healing way. We'll call them drugs, and we'll include the most common ones like alcohol, tobacco, sugar, and coffee.

If you link the three together–mind-altering substances, sex and money–you've got worldly power. And you ask, "Oh, what does this have to do with me? I don't do any of that. I'm not involved in any of these things." Well, I mentioned them because there are many who are and are lost. Would you have them stay lost or would you not?

I will also say that you are not untouched by sex and money. And I would also say that you are not untouched by mind-altering substances and mind-altered states. There's hardly a person in your society that knows what an unaltered state is. I can explain it to you.

Before you ever took a form and became a baby, the life that popped into your form to grow it up enough to enter was a natural state. The mind that can create, the mind connected to Spirit, to what we call the Mother and the Father, what is called God, is a natural mind. This is what entered the first time you were born... purity and innocence.

I'll tell you, there is a life force beyond even our familiar God which is the Originator, the Creator. Now, that's a natural state that does not include form. We had to come down a bit through the First Woman and the First Man to have form. Ever since, coming here as a physical human being has been an altered state. Jumping into a physical form is an altered state. Being one color or another, in one place or another, in any condition... it's all an altered state of mind.

First of all, instead of remembering or knowing anything at all, you have to get readouts. Like now, you've got to see, hear, taste, smell and feel, in order to try to know what you are. And then, there's that funny sixth sense which you've got to discover, to get you beyond the physical senses. "Some got it, some don't," you're told.

If you were in a natural state, you wouldn't have to use your eyes to miss a tree as you walked or to avoid bumping your toes. What you're trying to get used to is having to navigate in the physical body that weighs a certain amount and has certain limited abilities. And all your life, you've been trying to protect it from getting hurt, starving or being vulnerable in some way... like finding out you got openings at the top and bottom, some of which get fed and others get hidden.

So, you're born into this little box called a body, with all these rules and regulations. And you accept it right away and say, "Who am I?" then go look for some identity in it. It's as if you didn't get the joke, and you're pretending it's all real. You're taking seriously the life that was meant to make you laugh, was meant for you to overcome, not live forever within its limitations. It was meant to be a challenge to you... keeping your body alive while finding out you don't need it. But you lost your sense of humor. You gave into all the fears that anyone could conjure up, and you still live inside them. You've made a whole society out of what you're afraid of. It's no wonder that traditional natives look at all this and shake their head and go... "God, I've never seen crazier people in all my life."

I promise you, the only altered state you have to concern yourself with is fear. All craziness is fear. Look 'em over.

1. **Fear of Nakedness**—fear of being seen, being known; fear of another seeing where you're at in your development of mind and spirit; fear of there being no secrets.

2. **Fear of the Truth**—fear that truth judges you for not seeing it or not demonstrating it yourself; fear that the truth condemns in any way.

3. **Fear of Power**—fear of those that appear to have it; fear of having none; fear of responsibility for the power of your own thoughts.

4. **Fear of Change**—fear of rejection, of abandonment, of worthlessness, or of starting over.

5. **Fear of Love**—fear that love is not real, that love is weak, that love is not enough, that love can be lost; belief in loss and lack of any kind.

6. **Fear of Sexual Energy**—fear of being possessed by it or of having to possess; fear of being controlled and having to control.

7. **Fear of Annihilation**—fear of the end of your self-consciousness; fear that life has no value or purpose at all.

To heal your fears, turn those fears around. Use your will as you pray your life back from those depths.

1. Harbor no secrets. Hide no faults. Speak openly about everything. Cultivate humor over embarrassment.

2. Judge no one or any event. Hold no grudges. Speak honestly and as openly as possible about your own mistakes and what you learned. Say what you are working on and what ails you, but listen more than you speak. Be brief and concise. Learn your own language and learn how to communicate better.

3. Release your attachments to what power the world has to offer. Seek no power over anyone or anything. Control no one. Cooperate with those whose intent is to help when you ask them for help. Gain cooperation by helping. Remember, your will is not weak, and real peace is never achieved by war.

4. Practice quietness and contemplation, until you know Spirit is guiding you. You will never feel alone or lost again. We all come from love and we all come back, someday. The time in between is for lessons in strengthening our commitment to be Spirit, through all our trials and challenges. Make more time for prayer, until your whole life is a prayer.

5. Be willing to experience the full range of human feelings. Feelings are given to you to guide you. But don't add unhelpful energy of judgment, anger, fear or misunderstanding to your feelings, or you will have strong emotions. Emotions are self-produced and propelled. Only love is lasting and real. This way, your sacred circle will become complete. Don't expect anyone else to complete it for you. Learn to give, again and again, until you know you gave but to yourself.

6. Let your heart, guts and common sense guide you. When overwhelmed by sexual pressure, ask Spirit for help. Ultimately, you must take your own will in hand or there will be consequences. Weaknesses are not rewarded. If you fail, pray more. Seek help. Talk to someone you trust, someone honest, someone who has had experiences of receiving healing. Do not hide or it will get worse.

7. Become conscious on as many levels as you can... until there are no more levels. Experience as much as you can without seeking to lead yourself. Volunteer in hospitals and hospice, in centers for aids and cancer patients, and in old folks homes. Help the dying remember love through you; you will remember through them. Get past the fear and disgust of the failing form.

*

Ahead of you is the mechanism that will not go away. So I will prepare you to survive the mechanism really easy. Don't be afraid and don't join it. Go right to its center with love in yours, and you'll be safe. If everyone on the planet did that, I don't think there'd be hell anywhere. There'd be no limitations or laws other than God's, and everybody would understand everything.

But because we are not willing to walk straight to the thirteenth level of hell and give love, the separation and fear still exists for someone, somewhere, on whatever level they might be. Everybody's waiting for Christ to come back to do it for them. Nobody wants to go to the thirteenth level for anybody and give love there to release them. You would rather pay the psychiatrists and psychologists to do it. Well, some of those folks could tell you more about hell than most anybody else, I bet. But do they join their psyche to the lost and go right in with them? No. They're afraid of seeing from the inside, feeling from the inside what those trapped in psychotic and schizophrenic states experience. They're afraid of getting lost themselves.

The shaman's trick is, join the person but don't join their fear. Don't be concerned for your or their safety in any way. Because if you are, then you believe that love can be lost, and you aren't remembering the truth. Take love in with you. Know you are the love in it, then return with them to love. It's love that joins. It's love that sets the imprisoned free. It's love that heals. It's love that the truth was made for and in response to. Love existed even before there was anybody around to say what the effects of it would be. Love took the chance. Love risked everything to prove the truth of it.

It's a fact that psychotropic drugs can open the door to the psychic world, and that many have taken that chance for themselves. It's a fact that the number of people who can truly help someone that has opened this door is still too few. It's also a fact that many of these drugs are very common now. So what is the solution to such a changing world but to have more people fully conscious and able to guide others in the psychic world? Psychotropic drugs won't go away. But thankfully, Spirit can change them to medicines. Love's here to stay, no matter what the challenges are. The risk is not in your getting lost but in never asking to be found. You already lost. Be found now. Ask Spirit.

Truly, you are not free until you are free of all the influences that would use you. Identifying with yourself as the body is one of the biggest. Instead of saying "Who am I?" and trying to find your way in the world, you could be questioning "What am I?" and examining your mind's relationship to your own physical form. Understanding your thoughts and sensations in any one moment can teach you what you are... the truth from the illusion. It is only in not behaving, it is only in not indulging that a true human being, not the thinker who thinks its life, but the true human being who has soul can learn what it is.

I wish only to show you that sensations inside your life, in secret, in private, can run you and you're not free. Until you know what you are, until you face the fact that you do not know what love is nor where it comes from, nor what it wants or where it's going, until that admission is made and the desire to want to know the truth of love is more intense than your fear of knowing it, your whole life will be used by the mechanism of ego. You'll be caught in the illusion of living your life, and it will be a wild ride, indeed. But perhaps to you, it was well worth it, so I will not tell you that you have erred or that your life was valueless.

I will tell you this, though. Life should be more than a carnival ride, with more than just the sensations you had while riding it. And if you only live for principles such as "the good provider," "the valiant protector," "the courageous defender," "the maiden-in-distress," "the seducer-queen-of-the-Nile," if you find yourself trying to choose your own mate without Spirit and going after whatever, willy-nilly, then you're surely inside your own fantasy, and it's all illusion and will not last.

And while nothing is lasting in your life, you might question by the time that your skin folds easily, by the time that your hair falls out quite at will, by the time that you are too old not to look backwards, by the time the pain of having a physical form won't go away and you no longer have the energy for further diversion, denial and distraction... you might once again face your simple question... "What am I?" And maybe, quite forced upon you by the infirmities of old age, the answer will be thrust upon you.

Regardless of the limitations of your memory of just the sensations of your limited experience, you will still reach through to the welcome of Creator and recognize the words that make a greeting... "We all come from Love, and we all come back to Love. Welcome. We-all-come." In between coming from and coming back are all the experiences that any human being could have, in all the many ways of having them. **The prize out of all of life is consciousness.** What you worked to attain, you get to keep. But remember...

God don't want no fools wakin' up.

Chapter 11
32 Pyramids... First Level

My two children here have asked a question, "What is sickness and how does it begin?" I remember indicating to you that there are only two kinds of sickness, and that they are both of the spirit. It was a simplistic answer from the sense that the world is complex, that the world has made complexity out of simplicity.

Sickness begins this way. You deviate from center. If you are a fear bubble within a love bubble and you are lost to yourself, you will wander aimlessly inside your small bubble until you find your center point. Within any bubble, there is a still, center point. Within any bubble in gravity, there is also an imaginary line that goes from the top, through the center, to the bottom. As you see a bubble floating in air, notice it wobble on this central axis until it pops, as its top becomes too thin and its heavier bottom becomes a falling drop.

Now, imagine yourself as a three-dimensional pyramidal form, rather than a bubble. Do this simply for the sake of our diagraming together a purely representational model of the mind of a modern human being. Images are provided for you to follow as we talk. You will find them interleaved at the end of this chapter.

You are all familiar with the pyramids, and yet you do not understand the energy generated by them, the spiritual importance or significance of them. You know the Egyptians and Mayans built them. And maybe you know the Mayans were the first race of people for which there is evidence that they understood time. Maybe you don't know that they punched a hole through time to leave the earth. You know there is proof of the existence of the Egyptians and Mayans, as opposed to the Atlanteans for which there is no longer physical proof. How was the disappearance of the Mayans through time accomplished? What was the significance of that accomplishment? And what happened to the Atlanteans? Perhaps by the end of the following chapters, you will understand more about the pyramids, time and these older people, long gone.

On the first large pyramidal form drawn for you on level one (**A**), the base is subdivided into four parts, two lines intersecting at the center of the base. A center line runs from the top of the pyramid to the center point of the base where the four lines intersect, forming four equal squares in the base. The entire structure of this image is of two pyramids, one upright and one upside down, whose bases are shared.

In the four equal squares of the base of the upright pyramid are drawn four more pyramids, whose tallest points form the extreme edges of the second square base for the next four, yet smaller pyramids at level three. Four more pyramids are drawn next, forming the fourth square base, and so on, building smaller pyramids up through seven levels. Six square bases form six sets of five pyramidal shapes, four in the corners and one pyramid up-ended in the center of each of six levels. The seventh level is a single, whole pyramid. The upside-down pyramid that makes up the below is also undivided. All pyramids counted in this first order of resolution equal the number 32. There are seven orders of resolution within each of the thirty-one pyramids, not counting the below, with over 1 billion, 375 million possible combinations and/or points of reference within human conception, surrounding the very center... the truth. Look ahead to the end of Chapter 12, interleaved illustrations, level six (**J**), for a partial visual of this, if you wish.

The base squares of illustration (**B**) are labeled left and right, ahead and behind. The center line goes all the way up from the below to the bottom of the largest first level, to the top of the smallest pyramid at the seventh level. There are four equidistant corner points (**B**) on each level, four equidistant intersecting side points on each level, and a central point within each base, including the seventh. There are six levels of nine transition points, plus the top of the seventh and the bottom of the below, totaling 56 extreme ways to change levels.

On the drawings, each quarter square of each base through the six levels is loosely labeled, using key words I have chosen to describe a specific area of influence within the body-mind relationship. Perhaps, to some, this will be somewhat tedious, but it will be very revealing if studied. I will focus my words only on the aspects of sickness versus health, and I will tell you that the center point through the pyramid is perfect health, perfect openness, perfect peace and freedom from all the ego's concerns, as well as freedom from the influences of all collective consciousness and its archetypes.

As I said, there are 32 pyramids forming this first order of resolution in this model of a modern mind. There are seven pyramids that are inverted. The upside-down inner pyramids, which includes the below (**C**), represent the seven levels of collective human consciousness. The uppermost, upright seventh pyramid is essentially outside the body's sensual awareness. It is the area of Spiritual transformation. That is, it is the prize of consciousness, that of unlimited, nonsensual and perfectly aware conscious-ness. The four upright pyramids that form the base of each level are purely a spatial representation of your mind that is part of perception, thinking, imagination, and fantasy.

The four twisted wedges on each of the upright six levels are deviancy, and I will cover them last in Chapter 13. There are twenty-four such wedges, four on each of six levels, representing areas in the mind of perception that can become dangerously twisted.

Again, the inverted pyramids represent collective human experience and archetypal images. They preexist and yet are congruent to a person's individual perception, and they form the bridge for any change down and up to or from any other level. At this point, please note that it is always the ego's intent to rise above everything and everyone and pretend to be God, though to do so only lands the person on the extreme of the next level up, on the very edge of the collective and far away from any center of reality. It is always the function of the levels of collective consciousness to bring the ego down from the extremes, to the center of the level below. Thus the phrase, "What goes up must come down" applies to more than Newtonian physics and gravity. It truly applies to any closed mechanism, like the ego. The ego relies on your fear of the sensation of "going down" (which feels similar to death, which, of course, only the "dead" know anything about), to prevent you from recognizing its ultimate unreality.

What I will do for you in this chapter is talk about the very first level and the four squares in it, because without a foundational understanding you cannot extrapolate to the second level, and so on.

If I were not to talk to you directly, if I were to tell all this in abstract story form, it would take a long time... many hundreds of stories and many thousands of circumstances with different people. Instead, I will utilize direct words and abstract diagrams. I will divide the parts up into sections that can be dealt with, into pieces that can be conceived of and integrated.

In a fifth book to follow, I will be very direct in language and very direct in descriptiveness of psyches, in types of psychological makeup, types of psychic behavior, types of private thinking. You might find it hilarious... or threatening, but I do not apologize as it is time to be very clear, time to help those who wish escape from the relentless mechanism of the modern mind. And it is your understanding of the mechanism that will help you make a trans-formation to escape its effects.

Truly, there are no secrets. And anyone who believes there are, probably thinks they are successful in keeping their secrets, and that others are successful at keeping theirs. But I tell you:

There are no secrets in Spirituality.

So I introduce you here to each "secret" corner of each secret square, showing how each pyramid and quadrant of each square base can be resolved down to smaller and smaller quadrants, each pyramid a physical hologram of the first, down to the smallest detail in subject matter and presentation for each quarter of each level. Studying these should loosen the grip of fear about the thoughts you think you originated, when you truly did not. You need not be afraid of me because it is only your life living you that causes you to fear. In secret is where fear is born.

To learn, you must drop your fear. You must be incorrigibly curious and unflaggingly courageous. If you would take the journey to awakening, you must go in the direction of that goal. If "The Beginning" happened at all, then surely it happened from an incredibly still place. So look at this whole pyramidal form, and note the line through its center. That is your neutral, still point... the beginning. Slow down. Relax. I am speaking slowly, so if you are reading quickly, it is because you are in a hurry, not because I am. Slow down. Be still.

It all begins with the blue flame descending into the red fire in the below... body life. You're born center, still. Everything around you is very busy. Even your own physical self is busy growing, pumping, moving, seeing, hearing, feeling, sensing, all without your awareness. Life happens all around from a point of unutterable stillness. What gets born is not just some body but is a barely aware, not fully formed seed of consciousness... a something that can learn.

So, how does it learn? First, it gets connected to its apparatus and gets mobile. When it gets physical mobility, it also gets more mental mobility. If it is not abused, it gets some emotional mobility. It can sense happy from sad, comfort from pain, fullness from hunger, peace and safety from fear and confusion.

At its center point, something decided male or female, regardless of the physical form. We're not talking x-y chromosomes here. We're talking psychic reality. In this realm, it is as if a single marble is balanced on the tip of the pyramid and falls ahead or behind, right or left, quite at random, only rarely ever falling through the center for any distance (**E**). If it falls to the right, its emphasis is male. If it falls to the left, the emphasis is female. If it falls to the behind, its consciousness is not in agreement with what its body is. If it falls to the ahead, its consciousness is what its body is, right male or left female. I emphasize psychic patterns here, not body. The marble represents a point of light that is your formative consciousness, whether you are aware of this point of light or not.

As the thought of you falls into form, it falls through the levels, seventh down to the first and below. And at any point, wherever it meets something of substance, like influences from the sun, moon, planets and stars, like cultural and family influences born into, like prior experience, memories and unfinished business, that speck of light as you, goes this way and that, left and right, forward and behind in what appears totally random, but really isn't. Your seed of consciousness, bouncing from the top all the way to the bottom, falls into a new body with your particular set of baggage to unpack. We'll call this baggage, the work to be done in your present birth. Any prior births collect a set of unfinished circumstances that are like little magnets or winds. And as the marble or this point of light of consciousness falls through this center space, it is drawn this way and that way by the magnets and winds, until there is a map drawn by its fall into a new body of experiences. To become fully conscious and aware, each human being will retrace their path of descent, then eventually ascend to full enlightenment.

There are other models for this descent and ascent of consciousness, but to me this is the most pleasing because it suits this technological generation interested in free energy, space and time travel. Of course, there is always the mystery of how the pyramids were built, centering as much on the enormous precision of such large, three-dimensional forms as on their fourth-dimensional aspects. The purpose of this exercise is to give you a model for the mechanism of perception, so you can understand how you are used by it and how to earn an escape from its relentlessness, back into the true center where real freedom is.

So I will start with the largest, bottom square (**D**). It is the rank beginning of self-consciousness. Again, the right side is male, the left side is female. The ahead is a positive or aggressive expression, in agreement with the body. And the behind is recessive, not in agreement with the body.

The four major bottom corners are the four basic extremes that a person can express. There are four other points where the lines that intersect the center of the base become transitional possibilities. So on the base level, there are four extreme points, four middle transition points and the single center. The tips of the four upright pyramids form the four base extreme points of the second level.

Now, again, within any pyramid but the seventh, imagine perfect, smaller holographic replications of the entire pyramidal structure, excluding the below, within each smaller pyramid, down to the seventh order of resolution. Nearly unimaginable detail results. This holographic nature of the mind within each pyramid and in each quarter reveals the mechanism of insight, the ability of psychic pattern recognition that goes across all cultural, time and language barriers.

I will expand. When an aware self-consciousness achieves a seventh level of resolution within any particular conflict or dilemma, in any quadrant and on any level, a particular enlightenment within that dilemma can be reached. That's how learning is accomplished.

Though "enlightenment" is often assumed to be a total, all-at-once experience, it actually is gradual and cumulative. Though any truth fully experienced is directly linked to all truth, it is usually the gradual resolution of many perceived different conflicts that brings on the eventual experience of total integration, release and revelation. Mostly, this consolidation of learning must be accomplished on the lower levels first. As lower level learning is consolidated and able to be transferred into physical reality, i.e., demonstrated, the achievement of higher levels can be made. Please keep in mind that the process of descent and ascendency is repeated on the lower levels in exact holographic duplication of the function of the entire large pyramid.

Each region on level one, I will call left ahead, right ahead, left behind or right behind. Each region holds a near infinitude of psychic patterns of agreement and disagreement for the first sexual level and the below, which is the collective consciousness of the first level.

For the sake of simplicity, I will diagram each level with only four quadrants, though the detail and specificity with which these patterns can be predicted is almost absolute. So you ask me, "Where is the creativity in life if we are all so easily determinable?" I answer, creativity is in the center with Creator. Otherwise... God don't want no fools wakin' up.

Also, the creativity is that your marble, your consciousness, can be dropped and pulled any direction down the pyramid, to eventually hit the bottom and provide you with two sure ways back up: retrace your fall or get to the center. Besides, there's no telling what collection of experiences that you will need and have when you reach your new birth point. There are a hundred-trillion possibilities. And you say, of what use is this model?

Well, I'll tell you. It's very simple. Human consciousness is patterned through a mechanism that is reflective in its response to your descent into the body. If you cannot understand this mechanism of mind, you will surely believe and teach that everything that is happening to you or anyone else is happening for the first time and is totally unique only to you. You will take your life way too surfacely serious, as special, as unique, as being dissimilar from any other life and form, never taking the mind's mechanism seriously enough to learn what it is and eliminate its unfortunate influences over your total being. This remaining so, humankind never evolves much further.

Now, I can hear the creationists saying that this is determinism, that this is the devil at work, that this can't be God because consciousness can't be explained by a mechanistic model. And I say, no, this is a highly inventive, spontaneous, psychic model of human consciousness. It is really a nearly perfect abstract representation of a living thing. Being close to life is still not life, though its mimicry of what is alive is quite practiced and somewhat convincing. So yes, it is helpful to see ego and this dark influence as just a mechanism.

To understand this mechanism, you must note that the more complex the mind of a being, the less evolved or conscious it is of what it truly is. The more a being is able to grasp the complexity of living a physical existence and is able to refine its response into utter simplicity, is the degree to which a being has evolved, is aware and is conscious. The universe of mind is a creative model for the extension and compression of finite and galactic complexity... the extension of all the possibilities of life and the compression of all the meaning in it.

What is at stake is simply this. True consciousness begins, persists and evolves from God, from the Creator... from True Creativity that perceives no limitations, that fully understands all function, and thereby achieves compliance through agreement, even including that which appears in evident conflict. Ultimately, there are no conflicts at all that are not originally and ultimately in total agreement, thereby holding the correct shape and timing of all energy and matter as it evolves. All consciousness, therefore, is God consciousness... is therefore, Creator's consciousness.

So, is God simple or complex? Is God expanded or distinct? Can life be understood or comprehended in its entirety? And if so, is this a large thing, or is it a very small thing? You *can* experience God... yourself. This is what is at stake. Not having this experience is what sickness is.

Your societies and your countries and your governments and your people are falling apart because of their complexities. There is way too much conversation going on about nothing real at all.

Sickness is this. You forgot what you are. You are lost in the physical experience of being alive, with all its senses, with all its emotions, with all its apparent limitations, and you don't even know what you are. A sickness is, therefore, merely a decision about what you believe you are that isn't true.

I have talked to you about energy centers, chakras. And they are literal facts in terms of your physical and psychic energy. They can be sensed easily without any "woo-woo" or big mystery, and they can be seen by an open, inquisitive mind not ruled by personal perception and projection. What I have not discussed much is this, that all you think and believe is dependent upon everyone else, that your mind is part of a collective whole. I'll prove this to you, easy.

Put yourself in a vacuum. Put yourself in a closed, undecorated, windowless room. Don't light it. Make sure that it is a sound-proof room. Exist in this room for three days and three nights in total silence with no stimulation whatsoever, and you will find out that you are unutterably dependent upon external stimulation from everything, from other people, animals, air, sunlight, color, sounds, and smells of all kinds.

A yoga student enters that silence and begins to learn what mind is from an undistracted point of view, from a point of view with no outside stimulation whatsoever, in complete silence. A shaman or spiritual warrior does the same. I'd say, 95 percent of all who try this either give it up in the first few minutes, or if obsessively pursued, the remaining 5 percent have only varying periods of temporary sanity. The mind, they find, runs all by itself. The saving grace in this exercise of direct mind challenging is that they can learn to hold onto a single, neutral point of just watching the show, of just pure awareness. It is from my neutral point I speak with you. You can *receive* only from yours.

The central line from the top of the entire pyramidal structure to the bottom tip of the below is your line of neutrality. It is remembered by repeating the single phrase from *A Course in Miracles,* "I am not a body." That is a declaration that you are not solely the five senses, that you are more, that you are not bound by the laws of perception associated with sensing yourself, rather than knowing yourself.

407

I will assume that most of my readership is female, since they by design are more interested in learning the truth than males. So I will begin with the male, the right-ahead quarter, the male side in agreement with its body, the psyche of pure or extreme maleness. Herein are the base issues of the root fire within the consciousness of a male who thinks he's ahead, in total agreement with himself.

A positive presentation of a personality is not necessarily a learned thing. It can be a psychic presentation that is inherent because of the drop into form. A male, born with a physically strong form, will usually develop in a particular fashion. We'll call it the "Ahead Personality." Your medical society, psychology groups and psychiatrists have called it "Type A Personality." Type A's are inherently aggressive, both physically and mentally, as well as emotionally. They are outgoing. There are many levels of that, of course. You can be mildly outgoing or outrageously outgoing. You can be mildly aggressive or you can be extremely aggressive. You can be mildly positive or negative, or you can be extremely convicted, any way you want. You can also be twisted in your perception and think yourself one way, right-male ahead, while presenting yourself as right-male behind. As I said, the combinations, the splits, and the twists and turns are astoundingly complicated. Thus, is the world of the ego.

The farthest point from the center of the base pyramid to the ahead and to the right, we will call extreme, both extreme in physical presentation of male and extreme in psychic presentation as aggressive. This is one of ego's transition points to the next level, up through twisted wedges or down through the collective. If you follow that ahead base line to the left, a person will present themselves as less male, as they approach the far left corner of the ahead, in agreement as female. The halfway point between ahead male and ahead female is another transition point, because at that rather humorous middle-point sexual presentation of neither female nor male, or both female and male, one can rise or fall to another humorous middle point of the next level. Here, note that only the middle transition points offer a path to the core.

Also, note there are eight external transition points on the outer border of the base, and there is a central transition point on first level, leading to the above and into the below. There are four extreme corners and four middle ways, forming the quadrants. This central transition point, I will call the personal fire in the below, the sexual root fire, the first chakra or energy center.

Perhaps you can readily imagine how a male can become less

psychically aggressive as a male. Perhaps what you have trouble with is how an extremely physical male can present himself as more psychically female. In your society, you have made the delineating line or separation between male and female or left hemisphere and right hemisphere an almost absolute split. By doing this, you have made the only path to the next level an extreme one, on the extremity of experience, and something that is much harder on everyone to follow... getting to the center only by some grand leap, leaving no mental path by way of recognition for anyone as to how the leap was made, even by the one who leaped to the center. The middle transition points between right male-ahead and behind, the halfway point, is the path of de-aggression, the path of restraint and contemplation, the path of removing one's physical self from uncontrolled activity and unexamined belief, into deep questioning and continual self re-examination, what I'll call conscience, the beginnings of true awareness.

Introspection is the path by which this beginning of true awareness in meditation is delivered to contemplation, from aggression to non-aggression, from the ahead or behind to the center. Introspection with meditation, versus contemplation, is different in this one point. Introspection and meditation use the private, singular mind, while contemplation uses the neutral point of the natural, collective mind which includes Spirit. Here, you must *ask* to be taught. The natural, collective mind, by asking a source of greater knowledge within and yet outside itself, naturally excludes ego. Contemplation acknowledges that one's own single mind cannot know the answer alone, and that even collectively, our minds are still earthbound and need the help of what is beyond our physical experience and our own perception. A modern person's attempt at contemplation is to read everything they can get their hands on. They ask everyone else outside themselves except Spirit, Who is both outside and inside when asked for and allowed to join. Mostly, folks hope somebody else already asked Spirit, and that the general information will come through others, rather than through oneself, directly... too scary, too risky.

The trouble with that outlook is that general information is only barely and generally helpful, if at all. Very specific information and very direct guidance is always very helpful to each and everyone. Your experience and perception in this life of yours is very specific. Yes? Then why not have specific help?

So, onward. As a right-ahead male goes toward the behind and is at the middle transition point, he will begin to relinquish control of using and being used by extreme physical and sexual aggression as his presentation.

There is only one extreme point for each quarter of each level that is not shared by any other quarter. These are quintessential right-ahead, quintessential left-ahead, quintessential left-behind, quintessential right-behind. These quintessentials are the archetypes of ego for male and female, included from each and every level of the entire collective consciousness of all human history, from the top, down to the below. They are assured and perfected forms of presentation... traps. These traps are why the middle-way transition points are the most important. There are no traps in them, and they're the only way to ever get back to your center.

The first level, middle-way transition points are about the paradox of doing and non-doing, and of humor, both from self and about self. Only at these transition points can you get to the next level that is not another extreme quintessential presentation. Anyone can escape the traps the mind has about basic sexuality. For each and every person trapped in the extreme on any level, reaching any true and permanent resolution requires that person do nothing, stop believing, projecting and being that extreme, and/or laughing at the total absurdity of being in a quintessential paradox. By balanced laughter and careful choice between doing and not doing, anyone can become ready to return to center, via contemplation, while asking for Spirit's guidance. Extreme folks have to withdraw all doing or non-doing and belief or disbelief (level 2) in the value of their own personal thinking to get to the still, calm center of contemplation. The transsecting ahead and behind line through center is self-humor or humoring oneself. The right and left line is doing versus non-doing.

The female/male split persists because of not yet being able to laugh at one's polarized and fragmented concept of self, and in not truly desiring the healing of the causes of the emotions of separation, regardless of the imagined risk. I will call that the humor line, for truly your True Self is caught between being male and female. Rather humorous, don't you think? Everybody's caught in a body, and they either believe everything it dictates to them or they don't. A person either acts it all out, whether believing any of it or not, or they don't.

Only the center point is the quick path. You must retain a good sense of humor and not disbelieve nor believe in anything in particular, to open and be in your center. You must not actively seek to do or not to do anything. You see, the whole of creation, even on this first level is so large that to imagine you are a distinct point and not the possibilities in the whole of it is vastly humorous. To get caught up in living your life without ever noticing what it is that is living *you* is your dumb genius, lost in the utmost complexity of the most simple thing there is.

All the area inside of the four upright pyramids of each level but the seventh, and excluding the line from the center points to the tips, both above and below, are total illusion, total fantasy... all ego related, not spirit, not essence. The center line is the truth, the core. It's the fast track. Of course, you have to give up your mind as you once knew it, if you truly desire to take this fast track. It's madman's work or madwoman's work or mad whomever's work. It's just a lot of work, folks. Yet, what is life for but to crack the code of the One Reality and truly be free in its creativity... truly happy? Sounds like the only work there is... in Reality.

All the pyramids in Egypt, in Mexico and in Central America were built very simply. They were built from the inside out. From the joining of love and truth, comes power. The stones that make up the pyramid are only the illusion surrounding the truth of what the pyramids were and still are. It was the alignment of collective human will with the power of Creator that built the pyramids. The pyramids were an agreement. They were an exercise in the joining of love and truth that built them, using the stored energy of the universe to do it. You might think it was illusion that built them because their civilization is no longer ruling here, but it was the power of true creativity assembled in their center point, in agreement with creation, in agreement with all conceived of gods and the One Creator, that accomplished it. It's easy. It's simple.

Now, at the tips of the above and the below pyramids are what many others before have proved and many others after will prove. And that is, we are all spiritual essence by nature when ultimately challenged by the trial of living in a body. At either point in the above blue flame or the below red flame, we are still essentially spirit. We are distilled by our life into our essence.

Below this largest upright pyramid is the central line to the core of the earth, the root fire of the truth that the body belongs to earth. In between, where the two bases coincide at their center point, is the single truth that you must be temporarily disconnected from your physical identity to go on a descending and re-ascending journey of enhanced awareness, down through the seven levels and up again from the below, in order to truly know what you are. You can totally understand the physical universe by making the downward journey to the core of the earth and back. This is not an "occult" journey. This is not "demonism." This is not "animism." It is simple awareness that you have a physical reality that is temporary and borrowed, which is useful only to navigate, experience and understand the material universe with and not intended to be powerful or to be your "Final Self" at all. Body is only one small physical aspect of creation. And the earth as body of all, records all the endeavors of the creation that lives its life here while learning lessons of love and truth.

The below space has to do with the energy of body consciousness, versus the energy of spiritual consciousness in the above. On the descending journey into the below is the experience of the lack of self-control and control over other human beings, by the use of sexual energy. On the ascending journey is the experience of the release of the little self and others from this sexual energy, utilizing spiritual intent and energy. Human beings were not meant to spend too much time in this upside-down below space, because this fetid first level and below have to do with sexual thoughts, behaviors, deviancy, and belief in death. From the center of this collective below is where all the twists and turns of the six levels above are seen.

You are *beyond* the below only when and from where all that is above can be seen by you through the Mother's perspective, through the heart of the Mother. Before ascending to the blue flame of the Father, there are a few subtle levels in your descent through the red fire of your own body to the heart of the Mother, where the red flame of love is experienced. The transition points within this below space belong to those of the first level. All points, extreme or otherwise, will eventually lead to a Single Reality that is the Heart of the Mother and the Father's Reason that creation must go through physical experiences to gain an aware consciousness of essence, as well as form.

Now, I could make this diagram prettier and put a circle where the squares are and draw cones instead of pyramids, and it would serve the same purpose and probably look more like the essence of form and formlessness. But I give you this linear diagram because your society builds in perpendicular crossroads, sells land in squares, builds square houses and square tables and square chairs, so you are used to square things, both rising and falling. The only time you use round things is when you eat and drink and pee and poop. You come close to sensing the roundness of creative energy when you briefly sense your own energy moving up your spine... when you sense that your world is round, and that it is one of many spheres flying about in space in elliptical or round orbits, circling a round circle of a sun... spinning, round galaxies, all around.

Natural human beings walking in open country in the wilderness generally explore in small arcs from a center point, a camp, until they have encircled their entire area as far out as they wish to explore, expanding their grasp of the territory in ever-widening arcs. Their dance on the earth looks like spirals of elliptical circlings, just like the animals' movements, right down to the ants. People in nature repeat endlessly the activity that is going on within their own cellular being... spiraling, interconnecting circles of movement... DNA. All dance the same dance the stars dance. All learn.

But in this highly organized modern society, you must now take only linear journeys on flat ribbons, returning directly to your point of origin by yet another linear journey, out and back again to only known points on the same flat trail, seemingly endless, and usually without any real or deep questioning. You have all given up any magic of discovery that you achieved when you were a child. You no longer explore your within and join the within of your environment in arcs and circles, because the outside is laid out in linear, black ribbons and property lines that you must follow to the law. You have, therefore, lost the movement of the stars and the planets. You are, therefore, lost to the movement of the fluids and the cells within your own form, within your own spiraling DNA. You have lost the adventure that you are. And for all the natural journeys that you have not taken, you die a little more. For all the questions that you delay in asking, you weaken, sicken and die a little more to love and truth. For all that happens between all of you, all that remains unsaid, uncommunicated and bottled-up, you die a little more, isolated and afraid, even of the fire, the earth, the water, and air that sustains you. And it is this unconnectedness to everything that is disease.

There are a great many roads to true health it seems, but there is just one way to begin the journey. Creative will is formed through true desire for the truth of love and the love of truth. Naturally, there is a quick way and all the every-other ways. There is the center way of willingness, sacred trust, open heart, and your aware-ness of your neutral point in a now neutral mind. And there are the ways that are external, with all the many delays, with all the laws of the universe being expressed on you. This is how you learn what you are not, and therefore what you are.

I will leave you to study the diagrams of the first level, both above and below. Read this again if it is not clear. Though con-trived for simplicity, this model is very close to actuality... an actu-ality that is well beyond words and truly defies all attempts of any final description. I simply encourage you to have your own expe-rience of your essence... because it is healthy.

I will suggest to you that everything but the center points are "not having" an experience on this subject of essence. Let's say, your one goal in life is to know what life is, a kinda', you-wanna'-know-something knowing. Well, everything but the center point is trying to know... trying, not knowing, only *trying* to know. You all are very trying on each other. You have tried to the maximum in every direction possible, but there is no true peace of knowing in your trying. Yes?

Perhaps you now ask, what is the negative way? The positive way, you feel, is the path of action. I say, the negative way is not non-action. It is nothing. It is not dead and not numb, because numb is also a reaction. The negative way is nothing, no-thingness, no feeling, no sensation, no belief, no projection, no purpose, no made-up meaning, and no illusory realities to distract you.

Now, you say, that's pretty tough. And I say, I don't recommend it. You see, it's based on a misconception. The misconception is that in order to find out what life is, you first have to stop it or withdraw from it completely. And I tell you, even that is not being neutral or contemplative. Negative is an active stance, the negating way. If it was wholly neutral, it wouldn't have to negate anything.

And yes, you can escape from the pressures of the mechanism that operate upon the consciousness of life by adopting the negative way, but so what? You can't communicate to anyone about it. You're gone, outa' here. What good is it to anyone else? At best, it is an escape only for yourself. How can it be helpful to anyone else? I would rather say that the negative way should only be used in extreme circumstances where the activity of physical and psychic life around you is so intense that you need to shut out the busyness to exist at all. If you have to deny the society you live in to do it, then it should only be used as a temporary platform to get you past the sheer noise and irritation of life's busyness. But remember:

You cannot deny the life within you solely to quiet the life outside you and ever know peace. You can use the denial of your attention for the life outside, but you must not deny the life inside you, or you will never know what life is.

So, I'm saying once again, the only correct use of denial is against the temptation for any distraction by the ego. Choose only a goal that is obtainable. Learn how it can be obtained, then deny that which would distract you from obtaining it. Do not deny life, but deny the mechanism the ability to distract your intent to have what you ask. If the ego speaks to you of any temptation to your awareness, then, I guarantee you, those temptations are a fire that you must pour water on to have what you ask. Do not deny that you had *any* impulses. Deny only that they will overcome you and distract you again. Remember, only what is real is obtainable.

First, withdraw belief in your beliefs. Withdraw belief in what busies you. Continue to shop for food and go to work, but withdraw your beliefs from these activities and all the ideas that drive you to do anything. Almost all beliefs are fear based anyway. Continue to be active, working without any supporting beliefs, and your mind will become objective. A truly objective mind is at a middle transition point and able to make healing, intuitive leaps into the core and through other levels.

A mature human being is one that has spent time in all four quadrants of his or her consciousness but remains in the strong and humble center. Folks would save a lot of time and hardship if they would do this visiting only in their minds, rather than behaving themselves all over the world. Most people are stuck with their life behaving them, with all the thoughts that are possible, trying out each thought one by one, acting them out on everyone. It's a slow process, learning all that you are not.

Surely your life isn't about what occupations you choose. It isn't whether you like to enter into the world's complex suggestions for you. It's not whether or not you like anything better than anything else. It's more about whether or not you accept the spiritual aspect of your being as your sole reality or you don't. That is not to say that a spiritual person must give up cleaning toilets, cooking food, washing clothes and dishes, or the care of their own body or anyone else's to be spiritual. It is more that you occupy your mind learning what is Spirit, while you're getting on with the physical aspects of being in a body. If you accept the "apparent" limitations and inconveniences of being a physical entity human, then you will have more time left to spiritual matters, like learning what has meaning from what is illusion, like learning that ultimately you are unlimited.

There are two kinds of lost people in the world. One is the deliriously happy with all the minor details of being alive, being so busy they never think one thought in contemplation about meaning. The other is one who chooses to dislike life so much that they busy themselves picking apart every little piece of it, noticing its weaknesses, becoming sarcastic, sardonic and caustic, and often becoming overtly violent. Worse yet is the twisted use of natural psychic abilities into covert violence. Intending harm without physically doing it is covert violence. One who hates can put a psychic dagger in your back that causes you pain. It usually takes great fortune or a good shaman to remove the effects of strong, hateful spells, though returning to love through aware and conscious forgiveness always releases bad effects from you.

It is God's law that giving and receiving are the same. You get what you give. Put a psychic dagger in an unconscious person's back, and you will get it back in yours (as soon as it gets released). And you will get it back with whatever intentions may be added by the unconscious recipient. If you are a conscious recipient of hateful spells, all you have to deal with is the energy of the sender's bad thoughts... the effects of the images and intentions are quickly cleared, so the sender is returned only the energy of their own thoughts. Ultimately, psychic daggers (the thoughts, the image and the intent) cannot "stick" in an aware and conscious being. Bad thoughts pass through a conscious being because there is no fear, and therefore no resistance.

So on the one extreme, you have a pollyanna-lost-in-space airhead, and on the other extreme you have a psychically devious-minded, covert murderer, the negative, witchy-user taker. You have the deliriously happy giver on the one hand, and in a darker delirium, the exquisitely black, unhappy taker.

Most of us are in between. Most in the modern world are in between. Most are not exactly the innocent, fly-by-the-seat-of-their-pants, never-thought-a-moment-about-it, happy-go-lucky-child-of-the-universe, and most are not exactly power-hungry, greedy, selfish, plotting, stranglers-of-life-energy bloodsuckers. Most bounce somewhere in between the extremes.

In all of the up and down, the push and pull, there is a balance point. If you allow life to knock you off that balance point, you will struggle to regain it once again, or you will soon perish. If you either disbelieve this intense game called awakening or you believe all the aspects of private personality, all will be tried on you. All that you call to you will be given you. If you totally believe or totally disbelieve all the circumstances in which life presents itself to you, you will be so distracted by conflict, you will never have time to wholly desire and ask for the truth. If your life pisses you off, you're too busy being pissed off to see the truth. If your life sucks, you're too busy being sucked in to get the joke. If your life's a fucking mess, then your mind is too much of a fucking mess for you to ever make any effort at anything at all, especially coming up from below and even down from above.

There is a point at which you will come sooner, I hope, because you're reading this book. And perhaps what you will realize is that everything is being used, that everything is using you... until it's not.

I would have you do this. Just to show you how hard it is to stay neutral, I would ask you to take a mirror and put it on a flat floor. Then take a glass of water and pour a few drops on that mirror. The drops will stay put, yes? Drop on more water and more water and more water. The water's going to go somewhere. It will not stay in the center of that flat mirror, will it? There is a point where the weight of the water will find some infinitesimally lower point to run to, or it will run away from some slightly higher point. There is virtually no way that you, like the water, will not be pulled one way or another by the sheer gravity of collective human consciousness.

The more cleansing you ask for, the more you will be pulled through extreme positions in order to practice regaining your center, by allowing the correction of your perception of everything and everyone you ever judged. Whatever attractions or pressures those four corners have for you will work upon you or the ones close to you, like your mate, until everything is revealed, until every secret in every corner is exposed. Then you will come to your center point again and go through the fires that transform the energy of thought and experience, back into pure Self again. This is called transmutation, from the below to the above, from the red flame to the blue.

This process is difficult, requires risk, and is your ultimate challenge. And you probably will be tempted to have great judgment of it and great judgment of Spirit for getting you into such a mess in the first place. But I tell you, Spirit didn't volunteer you. You volunteered to become wholly conscious. The world is here because you asked for it. And as soon as you wake up, you won't need it. Look for the humor in between the opposites. Look for the catch-22's, and don't kill anybody while you're caught in them. Laugh and ask Spirit to help you out. It is the nature of life to catch you in the cracks... can't go forward, can't go backwards. You know what that is... nowhere to go. That's an extreme point where there's only two possibilities that are trying to get you to a transition point with humor in doing or non-doing, and in stillness and prayer. Make it to a middle transition point without twisting anything.

For the people who are behind, that means they have to take some action or make some effort to get to the transition point. If you're in the behind, you've got to go ahead. If you're ahead, you've got to slow down... take a back seat. If you're on the left, well, you've got to get to the right and laugh at your femaleness. And if you're on the right, you've got to get to the left and laugh at your maleness. Joke yourself back to the center. Quit believing and disbelieving. Quit giving thoughts energy when you don't even know if you're the one who's thinking them. I'll prove to you you're not in control of your thoughts by asking you to sit quietly and stop them for a half an hour. Bet you can't.

If you're upside down in the below, your work is doubly hard because you have to admit to what you've done. You have to stop lying and deceiving. You have to forgive yourself, and you have to exert ten times the will to stop indulging yourself, to stop seeking power in the use of psychic and sexual energy. You have to ask to be turned rightside up again on the surface of the earth, rather than scratching upside down in the dirt, underneath. You have to get your own head out of your ass and out of everyone else's too.

I won't pick on women too much at all. I really won't because, you know, they were the original volunteers. They originally volunteered to take all the shit that life had to offer them, and they had to hold within themselves the idea that love was enough, that whatever they went through was worth it... having children, raising them, losing them, being weaker in physical form, emotionally vulnerable, and often subservient in the modern world. Yet, within themselves, they had to hold the seed of the knowledge of love, which is the only way to return to what is real and what is truth.

So I will not pick on women, except in this one statement. A love that is weak is not love. A love that is based on body or form is not the whole truth, and therefore not the whole of love. Love that is whole does not exclude any other life. If you are weak, it is because you are hiding something, either from yourself or from others. True love is not weak. It is not ahead nor behind. It is not right. It is not wrong. It does not judge and it does not condone. It is patient, yet not indulgent. It is vigilant, and yet peaceful. It knows when to be exquisitely soft and when to be unquestionably fierce. Love is all of it.

What females appear to lack in physical power is surely made up for in perceptive awareness, in emotional awareness and even in spiritual awareness. Because they cycle into the below, they can know the Mother's core. Because they bleed, they experience the emotions or feelings or sensations associated with loss... loss of blood, loss of life force and vitality. Because they are willing to have the seed of life within them, their energy cycles into the below, monthly. Because they have the seed of life, they experience "death," monthly. Each month they experience death and regeneration, only to go through a further loss at the end of fertility. So I will not pick on females, as life has done that already. Anyone who volunteers to be female and actually achieves it has achieved a form of consciousness more giving than any other life form.

THE CIRCLE OF LOVE
and
THE SEVEN CHAKRAS

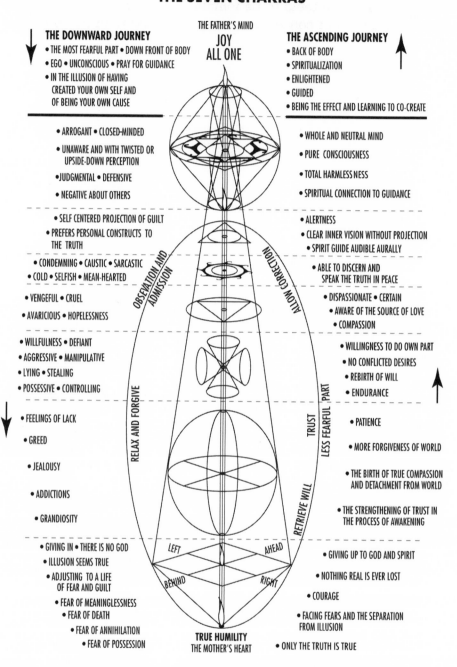

THE FATHER'S MIND
JOY
ALL ONE

THE DOWNWARD JOURNEY
- THE MOST FEARFUL PART • DOWN FRONT OF BODY
- EGO • UNCONSCIOUS • PRAY FOR GUIDANCE
- IN THE ILLUSION OF HAVING
  CREATED YOUR OWN SELF AND
  OF BEING YOUR OWN CAUSE

- ARROGANT • CLOSED-MINDED
- UNAWARE AND WITH TWISTED OR
  UPSIDE-DOWN PERCEPTION
- JUDGMENTAL • DEFENSIVE
- NEGATIVE ABOUT OTHERS

- SELF CENTERED PROJECTION OF GUILT
- PREFERS PERSONAL CONSTRUCTS TO
  THE TRUTH
- CONDEMNING • CAUSTIC • SARCASTIC
- COLD • SELFISH • MEAN-HEARTED

- VENGEFUL • CRUEL
- AVARICIOUS • HOPELESSNESS

- WILLFULNESS • DEFIANT
- AGGRESSIVE • MANIPULATIVE
- LYING • STEALING
- POSSESSIVE • CONTROLLING

- FEELINGS OF LACK

- GREED

- JEALOUSY

- ADDICTIONS

- GRANDIOSITY

- GIVING IN • THERE IS NO GOD
- ILLUSION SEEMS TRUE
- ADJUSTING TO A LIFE
  OF FEAR AND GUILT
- FEAR OF MEANINGLESSNESS
- FEAR OF DEATH
- FEAR OF ANNIHILATION
- FEAR OF POSSESSION

THE ASCENDING JOURNEY
- BACK OF BODY
- SPIRITUALIZATION
- ENLIGHTENED
- GUIDED
- BEING THE EFFECT AND LEARNING TO CO-CREATE

- WHOLE AND NEUTRAL MIND
- PURE CONSCIOUSNESS
- TOTAL HARMLESSNESS
- SPIRITUAL CONNECTION TO GUIDANCE

- ALERTNESS
- CLEAR INNER VISION WITHOUT PROJECTION
- SPIRIT GUIDE AUDIBLE AURALLY
- ABLE TO DISCERN AND
  SPEAK THE TRUTH IN PEACE

- DISPASSIONATE • CERTAIN
- AWARE OF THE SOURCE OF LOVE
- COMPASSION

- WILLINGNESS TO DO OWN PART
- NO CONFLICTED DESIRES
- REBIRTH OF WILL
- ENDURANCE

- PATIENCE

- MORE FORGIVENESS OF WORLD

- THE BIRTH OF TRUE COMPASSION
  AND DETACHMENT FROM WORLD

- THE STRENGTHENING OF TRUST IN
  THE PROCESS OF AWAKENING

- GIVING UP TO GOD AND SPIRIT

- NOTHING REAL IS EVER LOST

- COURAGE

- FACING FEARS AND THE SEPARATION
  FROM ILLUSION
- ONLY THE TRUTH IS TRUE

OBSERVATION AND ADMISSION

ALLOW CORRECTION

RELAX AND FORGIVE

TRUST

LESS FEARFUL PART

RETRIEVE WILL

LEFT   AHEAD
BEHIND   RIGHT

TRUE HUMILITY
THE MOTHER'S HEART

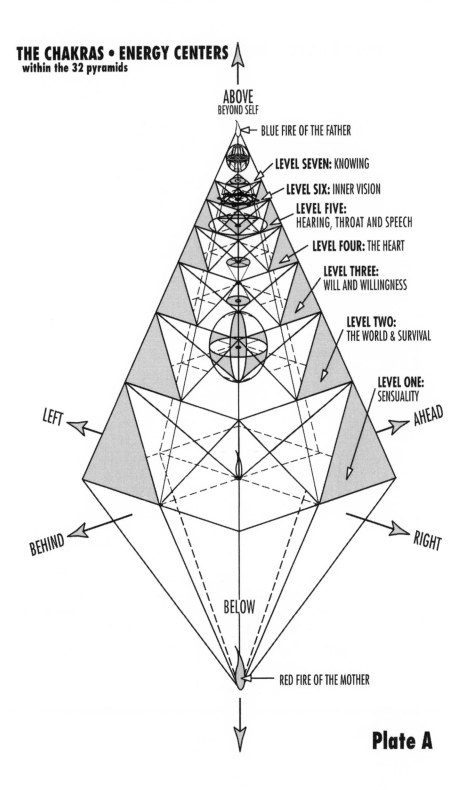

THE CHAKRAS • ENERGY CENTERS
within the 32 pyramids

ABOVE
BEYOND SELF

← BLUE FIRE OF THE FATHER

LEVEL SEVEN: KNOWING

LEVEL SIX: INNER VISION

LEVEL FIVE:
HEARING, THROAT AND SPEECH

LEVEL FOUR: THE HEART

LEVEL THREE:
WILL AND WILLINGNESS

LEVEL TWO:
THE WORLD & SURVIVAL

LEVEL ONE:
SENSUALITY

LEFT

AHEAD

BEHIND

RIGHT

BELOW

RED FIRE OF THE MOTHER

Plate A

CORE • QUADRANTS • TRANSITION POINTS

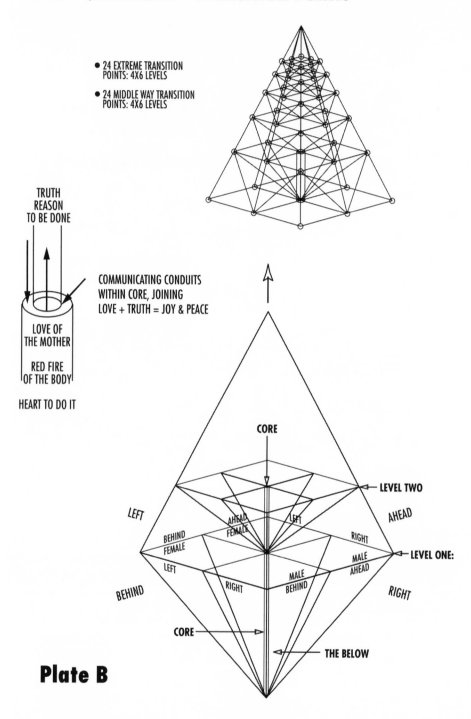

- 24 EXTREME TRANSITION POINTS: 4X6 LEVELS
- 24 MIDDLE WAY TRANSITION POINTS: 4X6 LEVELS

TRUTH
REASON
TO BE DONE

COMMUNICATING CONDUITS
WITHIN CORE, JOINING
LOVE + TRUTH = JOY & PEACE

LOVE OF
THE MOTHER

RED FIRE
OF THE BODY

HEART TO DO IT

CORE

LEVEL TWO

LEFT

AHEAD
FEMALE

LEFT

AHEAD

BEHIND
FEMALE

RIGHT

LEFT

MALE
AHEAD

LEVEL ONE:

BEHIND

RIGHT

MALE
BEHIND

RIGHT

CORE

THE BELOW

Plate B

7 INVERTED PYRAMIDS OF COLLECTIVE CONSCIOUSNESS

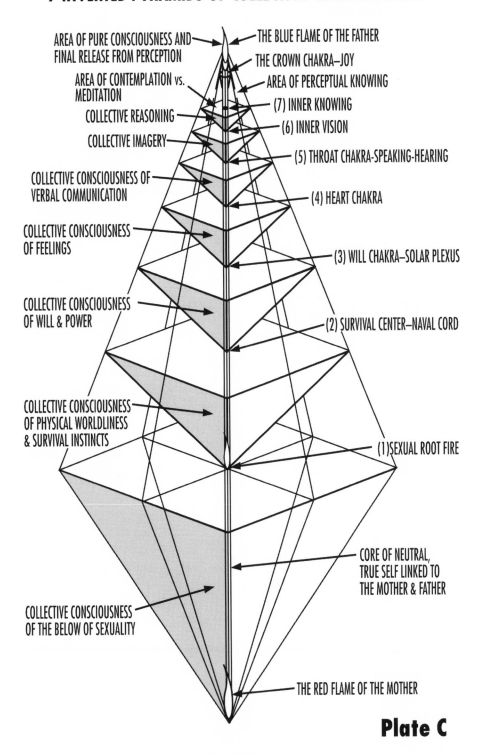

AREA OF PURE CONSCIOUSNESS AND FINAL RELEASE FROM PERCEPTION

THE BLUE FLAME OF THE FATHER

THE CROWN CHAKRA—JOY

AREA OF CONTEMPLATION vs. MEDITATION

AREA OF PERCEPTUAL KNOWING

COLLECTIVE REASONING

(7) INNER KNOWING

COLLECTIVE IMAGERY

(6) INNER VISION

(5) THROAT CHAKRA-SPEAKING-HEARING

COLLECTIVE CONSCIOUSNESS OF VERBAL COMMUNICATION

(4) HEART CHAKRA

COLLECTIVE CONSCIOUSNESS OF FEELINGS

(3) WILL CHAKRA—SOLAR PLEXUS

COLLECTIVE CONSCIOUSNESS OF WILL & POWER

(2) SURVIVAL CENTER—NAVAL CORD

COLLECTIVE CONSCIOUSNESS OF PHYSICAL WORLDLINESS & SURVIVAL INSTINCTS

(1) SEXUAL ROOT FIRE

CORE OF NEUTRAL, TRUE SELF LINKED TO THE MOTHER & FATHER

COLLECTIVE CONSCIOUSNESS OF THE BELOW OF SEXUALITY

THE RED FLAME OF THE MOTHER

Plate C

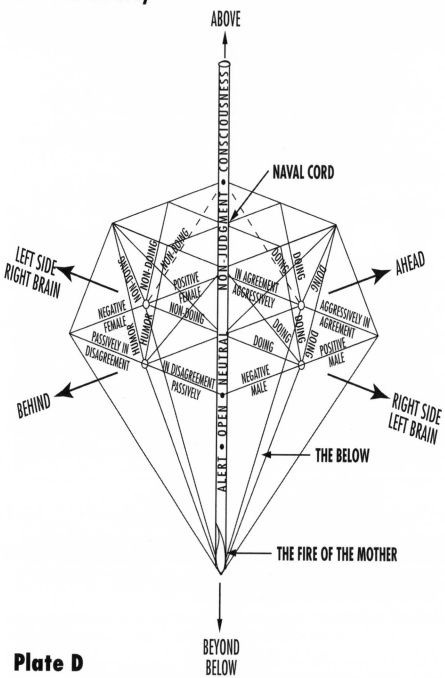

Plate D

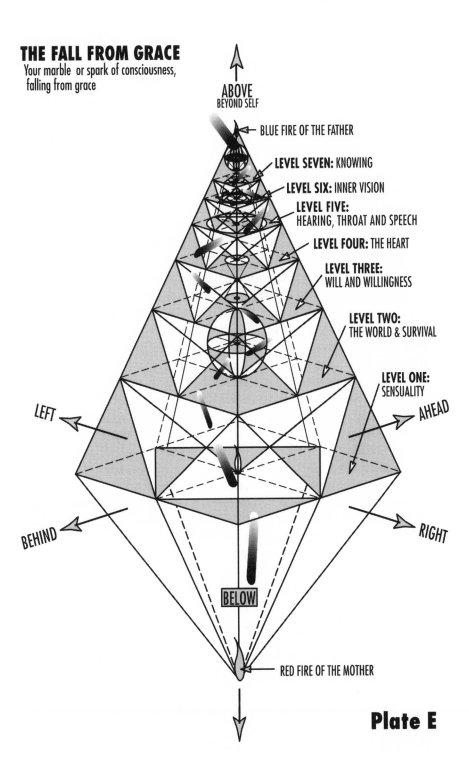

THE FALL FROM GRACE
Your marble or spark of consciousness, falling from grace

ABOVE
BEYOND SELF

← BLUE FIRE OF THE FATHER

LEVEL SEVEN: KNOWING

LEVEL SIX: INNER VISION

LEVEL FIVE:
HEARING, THROAT AND SPEECH

LEVEL FOUR: THE HEART

LEVEL THREE:
WILL AND WILLINGNESS

LEVEL TWO:
THE WORLD & SURVIVAL

LEVEL ONE:
SENSUALITY

LEFT

AHEAD

BEHIND

RIGHT

BELOW

RED FIRE OF THE MOTHER

Plate E

425

Chapter 12
32 Pyramids... Second Level Through Seventh

Level two (**F**) has to do with your self-concept associated with the larger physical universe, no longer just your sexual well-being, but now involving your material well-being, that of comfort, safety, possessions, your relationship with the external physical universe, and your survival activities in the world.

Only one major aspect has changed from first level to second. The transition point between male and female from level one remains self-humor and humoring self, but the transition point between ahead and behind is now no longer a matter of doing or not doing. In this second level, the entire modern world seems to be about doing, so the transition point is now, beliefs and disbeliefs. Because this second level is about the world and its laws, it includes all of the activities of survival, that of food, shelter, clothing, warmth, and the concept of loneliness or lack of any kind. Also, in any modern concept of the world, we'll include the idea of occupation or how to occupy your time while you're here on the earth.

In native tribes, the concept of occupation was never really considered. The numbers of people in a single tribe were small enough so that whoever found a deep interest within themselves for a particular occupation like bowmaker or hunter or medicine person or counselor, whoever found themselves attracted to a particular teaching would gravitate toward a person who was doing it and ask them to teach it to them. Everyone knew how to do everything for their own basic survival.

Not much has changed in modern society, except survival skills are no longer taught to everyone. Most activities of survival are separated into so many specialized tasks, with so many different purposes and intents that it is hard for a young person to know where they fit, where they belong and what truly interests them. Besides, most of what is taught now has nothing to do with anything immediate or essential. Hunters and gatherers have now become ranchers and farmers, and most everyone else is a shopkeeper or trader.

I'll explain. Everyone now trades their mental attentiveness and personal energy for money. Then they trade that money for material goods for survival. So what they do, does not directly relate to their survival but is secondary. Gardening for food is direct. Washing someone's windows for money to trade for vegetables is indirect.

426

So what regulates the health or sickness of this modern trading society is beliefs and disbeliefs, the second level transition points. What these points mediate between the ahead and behind are the concepts of taking, versus being taken for the male side, and possessing and losing on the female side.

I'll explain. One of the most interesting commandments in the Christian religion is, "Thou shalt not kill." This is interpreted with difficulty by native peoples who hunt and gather for a living. A modern trading person can go into a grocery store and trade money for a package of meat, cook and eat it without ever having killed it. There is no immediacy, so there is no true relationship between a modern trading person and what is essential. The reality is gone.

The reality is, you eat a grain of wheat and you kill it. It will not grow. You consume it. You eat a hamburger, and though you did not kill it, you *took* it. It was not free because it did not give itself in the hunt but was taken from the land, being ranched or farmed as a prisoner. The natural balance between trading for something to eat (because of the necessity of eating) and the reality of killing to eat without knowing the life you killed, is not there in modern society.

Natural balance is there when one knows the stream's life and fishes for one's dinner. It is not that it is bad to eat food you have not caught or grown. It is only that you do not have sufficient awareness of the land and waters, nor sufficient gratitude to make what was taken, nourishment. You unconsciously take without receiving, and you give your energy and attention in trade for things you do not honor. Your fine attempts at ceremony to honor your food and give thanks in prayer before you eat is too small an attempt of a modern society to rectify this imbalance, though it is a good one. What needs improvement is awareness of the life of the land that must be replenished, to give life to the food you ranch or grow and the things for which you trade. You continually take more life from the land than is returned by your care and gratitude, and so it sickens.

I will spend little time talking about this second level, except to say that all of the human emotions having to do with lack or abundance are in this second level. All of the modern human self-concepts of success or failure and have and have-not are here, whereby the ahead becomes having and success, and the behind becomes not having and failure.

Again, the first level, middle-transition points between left and right are humor. And still, the center point of non-judgment remains the fastest track. Do not get caught up in the world's be-

427

liefs and disbeliefs of success or failure, having or not having, of giving or being taken and taking, and of possessing or losing. All points are but to lead you on to the next level. You are meant to outgrow your attractions to a complex world, to its many opposing expressions and distractions, both seemingly helpful and not.

The second and third levels are smaller, as the inner pyramids become smaller. Note that the first level is largest, the second level is smaller in volume than the first, and the fourth is smaller than the third, and so on and so forth. The transition points that are farthest away in the corners going up and down the sides are also farthest away from the center at the first level and closer to the center on the ascending levels. So the length of transition from second to third level is shorter, and therefore quicker. Also, the distance between opposites is much greater in the lower levels.

The third level (**G**) deals with will. In the world, to finish highschool and college you need will, yes? To go to graduate school, you need will. To walk across the desert, you need will. To accomplish anything that is challenging, that is not a gift, that is not already in your possession or presence, takes will. I would say in this modern society, in the United States, this is your present struggle with your young people. *Will* they follow your lead or *will* they not? Will they progress using the formula for success that you have determined for them, or will they choose another path? At every turn, you are affected by the will of someone else, the will of the board members, the will of the Congress, the will of your boss, the will of your spouse, the will of your children, the will of the people, and the will of the law. It is this level, the third, that is about government. What governs? Whose will is governing... liberal or conservative?

My will reminds you that the center point is God's Will, perfect peace, absolute certainty. And just as before on other levels, there is an ahead and a behind, but now we will say left and right, instead of male and female. It is at this level that humor is still extremely necessary as the transition point between left and right. The middle transition point from ahead and behind is now about centered freedom or the extremities of bondage, using or being used.

If we do not rediscover and learn what will is for, we slip into the behind, into the bondage of another will, real or imaginary. We can slip to the right or to the left, into hardness or into softness. If we take our will and use it to dictate to others, we go to the ahead position to another form of bondage, the dictator. Freedom, you see, only truly exists in the center where God's Will is yours, unimposed and clearly joined to yours.

The distance between the third and fourth levels is shorter, but it's the one that troubles the world the most, from your will center to the heart center. I think most everyone knows that the heart level is a place where we relinquish control or governing. It's where we feel all the feelings of being a human being.

Fourth level (**H**), middle transition points between left and right, again, is humor, both kinds. This time instead of using or being used, ahead-behind middle point becomes insensitive and over-sensitive.

It is interesting to note that it is only the heart that knows "right from wrong." Earlier in the books, I told you there was no right and wrong. I was telling that to the judgmental mind to try to get it to its neutral point. This neutral, still center is the Heart of the Mother and the Mind of God. Always in the center is alert, non-judgment. Here, the Heart of the Mother can know the Mind of the Father.

This heart level knowing can only be open or closed to the connection to your mind and to your will. This heart level, this fourth level is the connection of the psychic valve of trust down to will at the third level and above to your mind. It is this valve when opened that changes will to willingness on the third level. It is when this change to willingness is made, that fundamental changes in the second and first levels can be made. Said another way, when the breath changes the "no" to "yes," the will can be changed to willingness and open the value of trust to the heart. Works both ways. The heart opens the mind and makes it willing to learn.

It is on the first level that ego is born. Whether it projects into the below or rises up the front depends upon the circumstances of birth and growth, depends upon the baggage of the one that is born. There is no way to change the willfulness of ego to the willingness of Spirit without the valve of trust opening in the heart. Any change of will without the value of trust open, causes no fundamental change in understanding and is merely a change in allegiance to different devices of fear. This causes split personalities and attempts at acrobatic justifications.

The importance of the valve of trust is not only its effects on will and the lower levels of the below, but also its effect on the fifth level. The fifth level (**I**) is what you say with your voice, and subsequently hear both inside and out. The fifth level is about honesty. On the fourth level, an open heart will say what it thinks

429

and feels, without attack or defense. Obviously, it is what you say with or without your heart that calls to you your lessons in life, and determines what you see and believe. On the fifth-level right side is attacking and defending, and on the left is exposing and obscuring. Again, one middle transition point is humor, both kinds, and the other is hearing inside, versus hearing outside. On the left is oversharing versus neediness, and on the right is pushing energy versus sucking energy.

As we ascend into the levels of mind, we take with us all we have learned from bottom levels, and it is here when a person speaks that they are easily read, interpreted and understood, or not. It is here that a person's experiences can be joined in true communication or obscured and made to separate. It is here that we learn to communicate with our language the sum total of what it is that we understand. Language is the collection of energies from both the below and above, whose impulse makes the images we try to communicate or to hide.

I will give you one important clue. For the mind to change, for the will to change, for the valve of trust to open, the speech center must close. Speech is a result of (imagination) thinking, of both hearing and feeling from inside and outside oneself, from others, both singly and collectively. Until you are in the very center and are certain of what you are, speech cannot be used for true communication and true knowing. Indiscriminate joining to what is untrue prevents it. Love can only fully join what is true. And conversely, truth is only true when joined to love. Either, alone and kept separate, is what fear and the ego are.

So, by now, you have realized that any person's energy can get stuck in any level, in any place in those levels, that a person can be totally fragmented and not have their energies aligned anywhere near the center. And, as you see, there is no point at which any energies could be aligned, except in the four extreme corners, in the middle transition points, and in the center for all levels.

If you are in a transition point in the extreme sides, you will be led to an extreme point of the next level, not to the center. And so the lessons go until the center position is obtained, the valve of trust opens in the heart and will, the mouth closes and the mental chatter stops, so the energy can move down to first level, through the fire of transformation and back up again to reinstate the fundamental concept of what you are. This we will call "the process of alignment" which occurs on the sixth level. When it does occur, it is called "inner vision."

When you reach the sixth level (**J**), your mind will be adjusted, untwisted and aligned. Your erroneous perceptions will come up to conscious awareness and will be undone. Your imaging apparatus that was used for ego's perceptions will be repaired under Spirit's guidance, so your mind can see the simple, unclouded truth. This adjustment takes a courageous heart, good humor and great willingness.

The resolutions of all opposites are the goal. They lead to the seventh and final level which is direct experiential knowledge. This seventh level area (**K**) is initially so small, you could say that it only encompasses your tiny pineal gland. When activated, this tiny area becomes the universe and beyond. The areas of the four base corners of the seventh level have to do with remaining attachments to the world in terms of having certain abilities that knowledge contains. But these are still the little traps and not the big prize. However, Spirit can use this near alignment of someone for the awakening of others. Those Spirit uses can appear both humble and powerful, performing feats rarely seen, and for good reason.

The closer to the top of the pyramid you get, the closer the four extreme lines of behavior and thought get to the center. It is only at the tip of the seventh level pyramid, in the absolute knowledge of what creation is, that all extreme aspects are finally resolved. For instance, if a person has been sexually abused, violently raped or even nearly murdered, these first level and below emotions of sexuality, these second level concepts of beliefs and disbeliefs, these third level impressions of using and being used, these fourth level feelings of insensitive and over-sensitive, these fifth level communications that reveal or hide the truth, these sixth level images, clear or obscure as here or there, cannot be condoned, rectified nor understood, except from the seventh level, that of true knowledge.

It is in attempting to **do** on your own without being in balance, without being in the center, without knowing God's will, without knowing what your will is for, without knowing that your will and God's are one for you, that makes such a large first level with such mass confusions, with such strong aberrant feelings and erratic behaviors that are played out all over the world.

That valve of trust is only in the center, linking your heart and will. Your conscious awareness of your middle of the center is what shifts your faulty perception and your questionable activities in the world from ego to the will of God. This valve of trust can initially open only in perfect peace. A truly opened heart, a truly trusting heart walks through the world, fearless, secure and unshakable. This is a rare event for adults, but there are many, many now coming close to it. To accept this opening is the beginning of a true adult's spiritual journey back Home.

I will call this true desire to open this valve of trust, "the seeker's heart" and "the heart of the innocent," because it is here that you consciously begin to allow Spirit to guide you (though They already have been). It is with the language of the heart that you can be safely guided by Spirit. It is the language of the heart that I communicate to you with now. I'll call it "pure intent." All living things read all other living things through this pure intent of the heart. All Spiritual beings, whether in form or not, recognize this open heart, this open valve, this trust in Creator. And it is only here, trusting this pure intent of the heart, that true communication can be given and received at all. It is here that the middle of your center line should be, not in your will center. It is the will center that gives people the most trouble, male or female. It is the will center that keeps them bonded to the lower levels. It is woman's willingness to open her heart center earlier than man that makes her aware sooner of the fuller aspects of being a human being.

Now I will speak of the fifth level of speech and tell you that within the pyramid that is inverted, within that level of speech, is collective inner hearing. The sixth level of seeing, the central pyramid pointing down is collective inner vision. The seventh level pyramid is Sacred Silence and the Hall of Learning. This form of silence turns off the eyes and all other external senses. The inverted inner pyramid of the fourth level, the heart level down to the will center is collective feelings. It reaches deep into the core of your solar plexus from your heart. It is here that your will is returned to a loving God. Here, your point of aware consciousness, drawn down to your middle, must be delivered down further through the lower levels and the below. Down and below are about your forgiveness of the collective world and all that humans experience. Then, it must return up through the heart, up through the speech and hearing centers, up through the vision center, to reach true knowledge of what you are and what God is. Up is about your redemption, your being forgiven for your part in the confusion, and about what Spirit and God are.

Your middle point of aware consciousness of a joined heart with will is what Spirit uses to guide you through the lower levels. The collective, upside-down pyramids are entered by letting go of control. This is where many people have trouble and become afraid of Spirit's intent, without their truly knowing it. It is the final descending journey back to level one and into the below that frightens most people. All that collective stuff looks and feels quite scary to most.

Second level down to the inverted pyramid of first level is the collective fear of death in all the many forms. At the base of level one are four extremes, four middle transitions, and one center way into the below that returns you to your beginning as a physical entity, through the womb of the Mother, to the red fire of Her heart. On this journey, the natural laws of the earth and body are revealed.

This below collective of the first level has seven vaguely demarcated levels descending, within a single inverted pyramid. It is here that the greatest illusions are resolved, where the greatest emotions and fears that torment can be ended, where the dark secrets of the physical universe are stored. There is only one truly safe passageway. And that is through the center with a Guide, being in total alignment with the above, which easily resolves all issues into a single point of the Mother's fire. It is here that you find that even in the darkest, deepest, most cavernous hole or the blackest imaginable hell, there is love with Love's purpose.

It takes four pyramids of extremism to support a collective inverted pyramid of the next level. Only above the base of the seventh level (**K**) are there no more ego opposites. All paradoxes are left behind. It is only at the final ascent to the top of the seventh level that descent for correction is no longer necessary. The struggle to rise from an extreme transition point to an extreme point of the next level, to again pull yourself to another transition point and ascend again to a new extreme level of ego, only to finally reach the top center, to descend through hell to the heart of the Mother, is why Guides call this madman's work. The reward of freedom and joy only comes at the end.

I hope these descriptions have been helpful. Please study the details provided you in the drawings. I hope they answer some questions you might have had about the psychic world. I hope they prove to you that without Spirit's help, it would take an incredible leap of consciousness and faith to stay in the center of each of these levels. But I tell you, consciousness is made for grand leaps. You, yourself, your reading here is a tribute to your desire for aware consciousness. To become fully conscious means to join your awareness to the whole of creation, to awaken out of your separate or collective dreams into knowing what is real. Speaking the truth, of course, is another issue.

You must risk to get to the truth. You must have the courage to face your "selves"... to face what is illusion about you and to stick around to recognize that what remains is the truth. You must study the **energetics** of the form (see diagram L) with your neutral mind within your form, without behaving all over the place. Only then can you begin your **appraisal** of what has value in the world, begin **accepting** the world as it is, rather than constantly fighting with it, begin **admitting** what your own part has been in adding to the conflict, confusion, judgment, and fear, begin **avowing** to support and extend only peace, love and the truth therein, and begin showing **appreciation** for everything and everyone, while **acknowledging** their true role, function and purpose as you are demonstrating yours.

This area of mind that we have been in together belongs to water, belongs to cleansing. Cleansing's intent is to have you experience the truth directly, distilled out of the murky waters of illusion. With water and fire in the crucible of earth, the seven levels in your mind will be distilled into a Single Reality, a Single Reality that all life shares with you. Drink your water. Ask for cleansing. Thank it for helping. Bless the fires that enliven you and keep you warm. Bless the materials of the earth that give you form. Pour water on your hardened will and ask to be taught what Heart knows for you. Trust.

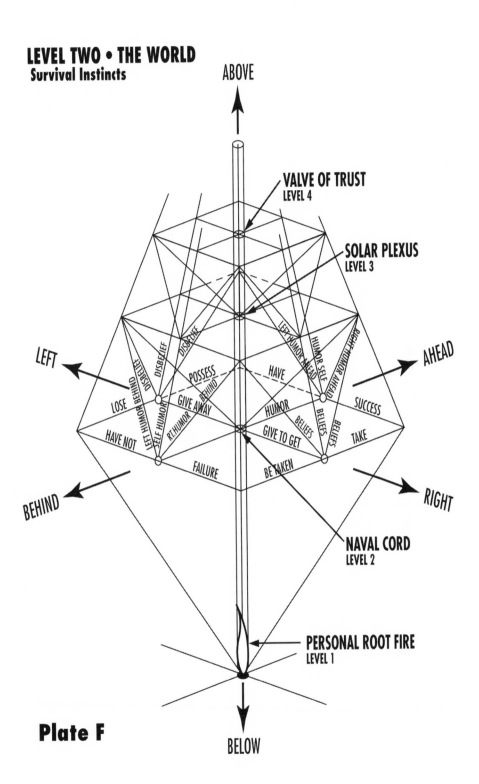

LEVEL TWO • THE WORLD
Survival Instincts

ABOVE

VALVE OF TRUST
LEVEL 4

SOLAR PLEXUS
LEVEL 3

LEFT

AHEAD

DISBELIEF
DISBELIEF
POSSESS
HAVE
LEFT HUMOR AHEAD
HUMOR SELF
RT. HUMOR AHEAD
BEHIND
LEFT HUMOR BEHIND
DISBELIEF
BEHIND
LOSE
GIVE AWAY
HUMOR
SUCCESS
SELF HUMOR
RT.HUMOR
GIVE TO GET
BELIEFS
BELIEFS
HAVE NOT
FAILURE
BE TAKEN
TAKE

BEHIND

RIGHT

NAVAL CORD
LEVEL 2

PERSONAL ROOT FIRE
LEVEL 1

Plate F

BELOW

435

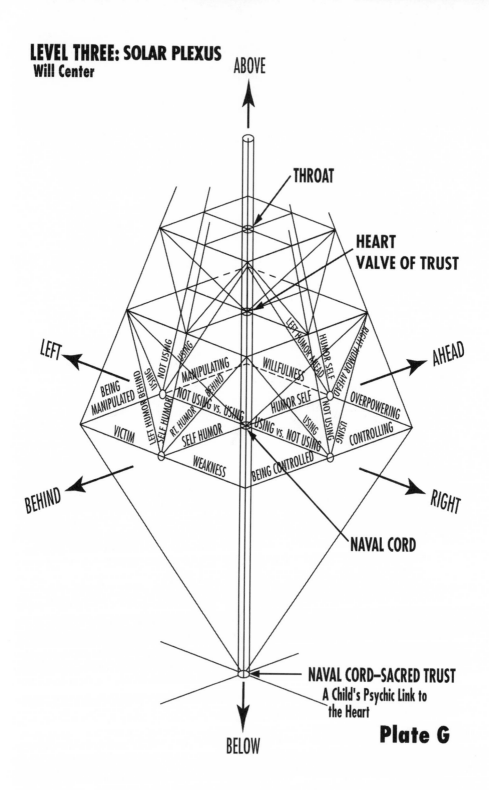

LEVEL THREE: SOLAR PLEXUS
Will Center

ABOVE

THROAT

HEART
VALVE OF TRUST

LEFT

AHEAD

NOT USING

USING

LEFT HUMOR AHEAD

HUMOR SELF

RIGHT HUMOR AHEAD

MANIPULATING

WILLFULNESS

BEING
MANIPULATED

BEHIND

NOT USING vs. USING

HUMOR SELF

OVERPOWERING

LEFT HUMOR BEHIND

SELF HUMOR

RT. HUMOR

USING vs. NOT USING

NOT USING

USING

VICTIM

SELF HUMOR

USING

CONTROLLING

WEAKNESS

BEING CONTROLLED

BEHIND

RIGHT

NAVAL CORD

NAVAL CORD–SACRED TRUST
A Child's Psychic Link to
the Heart

BELOW

Plate G

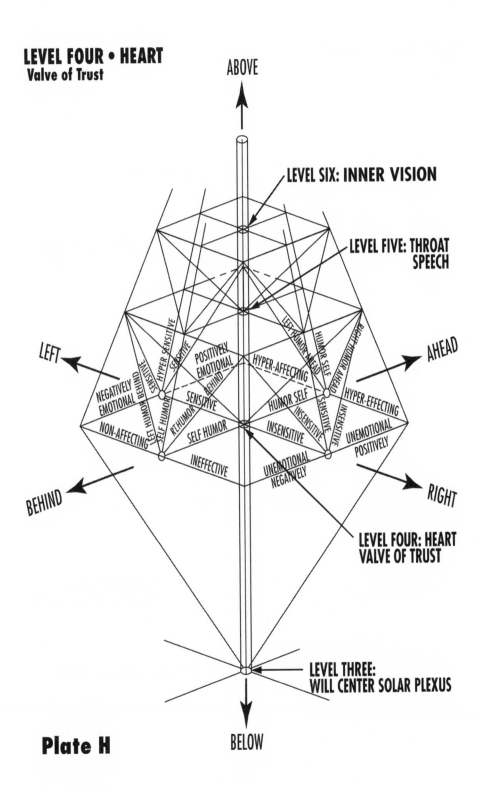

LEVEL FOUR • HEART
Valve of Trust

ABOVE

LEVEL SIX: INNER VISION

LEVEL FIVE: THROAT SPEECH

LEFT

AHEAD

HYPER-SENSITIVE
HYPER-AFFECTING
LEFT HUMOR AHEAD
HUMOR SELF
RIGHT HUMOR AHEAD
POSITIVELY EMOTIONAL BEHIND
SENSITIVE
NEGATIVELY EMOTIONAL
HYPER-SENSITIVE BEHIND
LEFT HUMOR SENSITIVE
HYPER-EFFECTING
HUMOR SELF
SENSITIVE
INSENSITIVE
NON-AFFECTING
RT. HUMOR
SELF HUMOR
INSENSITIVE
INSENSITIVE
UNEMOTIONAL POSITIVELY
INEFFECTIVE
UNEMOTIONAL NEGATIVELY

BEHIND

RIGHT

LEVEL FOUR: HEART VALVE OF TRUST

LEVEL THREE: WILL CENTER SOLAR PLEXUS

BELOW

Plate H

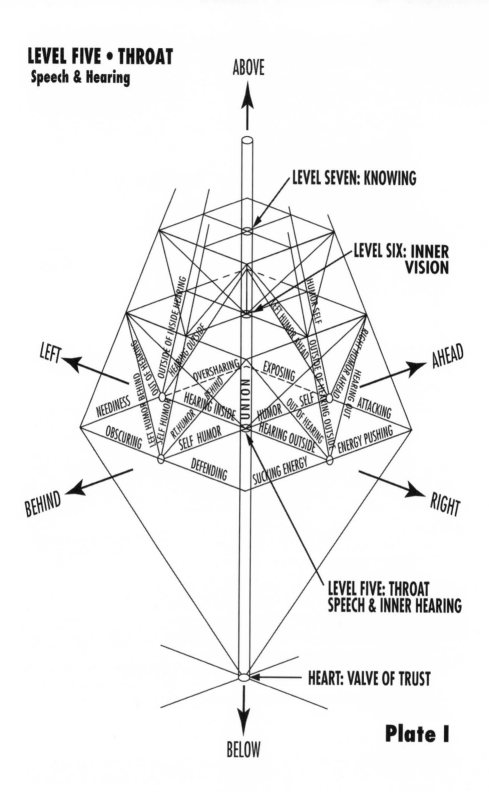

LEVEL FIVE • THROAT
Speech & Hearing

ABOVE

LEVEL SEVEN: KNOWING

LEVEL SIX: INNER VISION

LEFT

AHEAD

LEVEL FIVE: THROAT
SPEECH & INNER HEARING

HEART: VALVE OF TRUST

BEHIND

RIGHT

BELOW

Plate I

438

LEVEL SIX: INNER VISION
Pineal gland

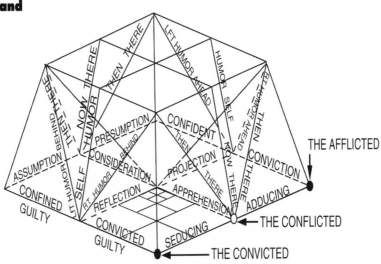

THE AFFLICTED

THE CONFLICTED

THE CONVICTED

Single quadrant resolved going
down through seven levels, and...

...showing a single quadrant with its
seven levels of imagination going up.

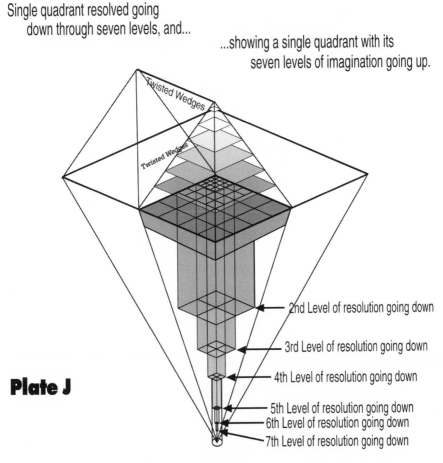

2nd Level of resolution going down

3rd Level of resolution going down

4th Level of resolution going down

5th Level of resolution going down
6th Level of resolution going down
7th Level of resolution going down

Plate J

439

SEVENTH LEVEL • CROWN
Knowing

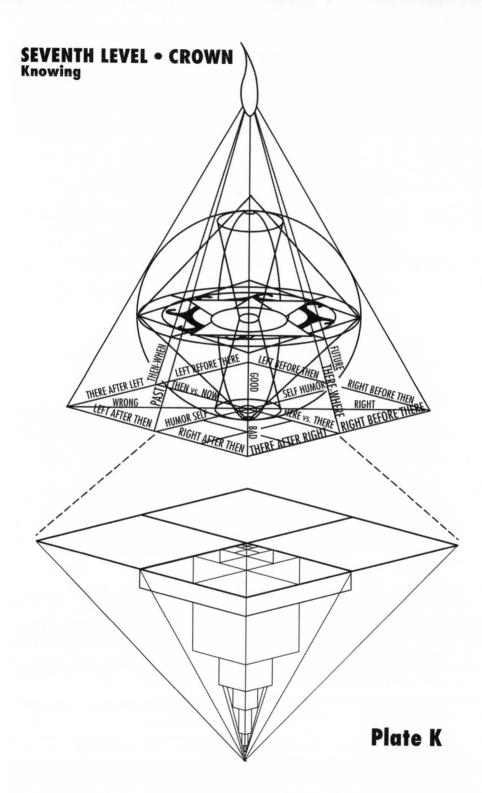

LEFT BEFORE THERE

LEFT BEFORE THEN

THEN WHEN

THERE AFTER LEFT

RIGHT BEFORE THEN

FUTURE

THERE-WHERE

PAST-X

THEN vs. NOW

SELF HUMOR

GOOD

WRONG

RIGHT

LEFT AFTER THEN

HUMOR SELF

HERE vs. THERE

RIGHT BEFORE THERE

BAD

RIGHT AFTER THEN

THERE AFTER RIGHT

Plate K

440

THE SEVEN LEVELS OF COLLECTIVE CONSCIOUSNESS
With key words for each level

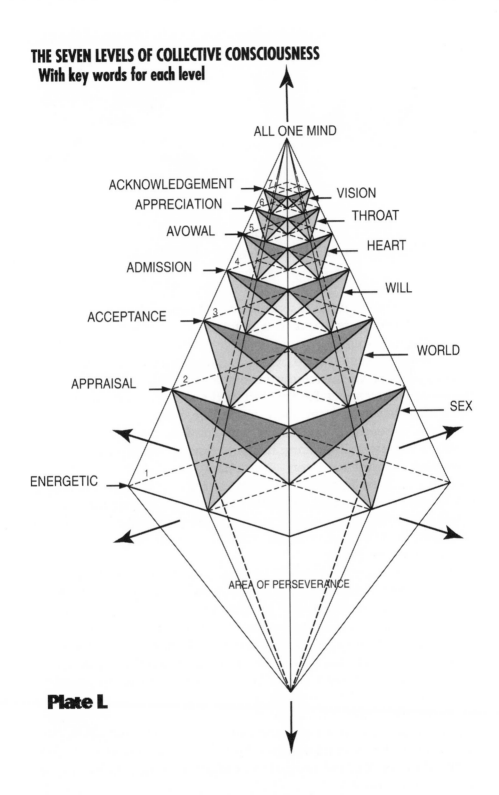

Plate L

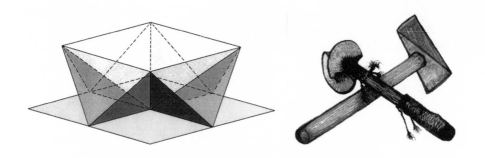

Chapter 13
The 24 Twisted Wedges or Double-Headed Axes

You remember in the discussion of the pyramids in earlier chapters that I briefly referred to a non-pyramidal psychic space between the four smaller pyramids on their lateral four sides and the four sides of each collective pyramid. There are twenty-four spaces total for all six levels, excluding the below and the seventh level in the above. They are called twisted wedges or double-headed axes. See the leaves of illustrations prior to this chapter.

If you're ready, if you are strong enough, we will move into them. If you are still working in the pyramids, perhaps you should leave this chapter for later. This chapter is disturbing. Do not read this chapter before you go to bed. Do not read this chapter if you haven't got a strong stomach. Do not read this chapter if you aren't ready for the shocking truth. If you prefer the quiet of the countryside, don't go to the big cities. It is in those cities that you see the most extremes.

If you are expecting gentleness here, don't read on. The name "twisted" should tell you what's to follow. If that doesn't do it, then the "double-headed axe" should. There's nothing peaceful in here. These areas are traps of the twisted mind of ego. If you don't want to know Spirit's plan, don't read on, because when you get to the end and say, "I'd rather not have known this," it won't do any good if you've read it. So be forewarned, as we're about to discuss the idea... lovelessness, godlessness.

Recall for a moment the picture of the seven energy centers, the seven levels of the body and mind of human experience. We will discuss the twisted wedges by levels, first pyramid through sixth. Refresh your memory of the earlier drawings by looking at them if you need to.

On the very first level are the most stuck members, both individually and collectively. This is where the possibility of being twisted is the greatest and where the twisted ones extend their errors into the below and into the above. This is the area of sexual deviancy without using criminal, physical force. This level begins with the innocent exploration of body by children and only becomes a psychic crime when a child repeatedly ignores the mind, heart and internal gut signals of what's appropriate and inappropriate. These signals we call conscience. When internal conscience is ignored or damaged, fear twists and often sublimates forbidden sexuality from what is repulsive into being attractive and hidden. It is, then, that a person enters the realm of sexual deviancy, whether with male or female, whether heterosexual, bisexual or homosexual.

It is not that they are true crimes which are punishable by death, as much as they are fearfully judged and scorned by a so-called "normal" population. It begins thus:

All deviancy begins with secrecy.

It is the secrecy of these sexual urges that makes a whole world of forbidden acts and thoughts. In this secret world, the energy of fear is generated, making a twisted attraction that has significant infective influence over the young to promote and propagate a kind of uncreative power. It is this twisted, noncreative power of the energy of upside-down sexuality that cultivates specialness and secrecy, and is the true seducer in this forbidden world.

On this first level twisted wedges, your society recognizes the influence of pornography where the simple desire to sneak a look, though not legal for minors, becomes the first public introduction to this seductive energy. In my day, it was peeking at the girls bathing in the river. Nowadays, you make pornography illegal for minors because, frankly, they're the most interested. And you think limiting their exposure to it until they're eighteen will somehow prevent them from being sucked into the world of deviant desires.

By allowing pornography to legally flourish, it is the adults that are acknowledging their interest. Protecting the rights to publish such material under the law of "free speech," makes it possible to once again separate church from state, God's law's from man's.

Yet this necessary window must exist for a time. Without this temporary window of allowance, the fear, judgment and intolerance would take your society back to the Dark Ages, back to the Crusades and the Salem witch hunts. Though this tolerance gives you a much more complex world, it also forces everyone to understand more about basic sexual energy and even to communicate more. **Sexual deviancy, specialness and secrecy cannot be untwisted by condemning, criminalizing or outlawing it. All life must volunteer to be untwisted.**

One thing most of you are agreed upon as a limitation of this sex crimes area is child pornography and sexual molestation of children. It is appropriate that everyone aggressively limit sexual offenses against the innocent.

Second level twisted wedges always include some of the first. I will clarify. Lust on any level is a sexual offense. The offense occurs first on the level of thought and is no less real in the psychic world than actually having physically done it. *A Course in Miracles* teaches that there are no neutral thoughts. All thought goes somewhere and has a particular effect.

Second twisted level is also the lust for taking or possessing, whether by thievery or through destruction of physical property, as with bombs and arson. On this second level, the crimes of twisted and sublimated sexual energy are directed toward money and property. Within this twisted perception is the illusion of beauty, power, wealth, and the appearance of freedom that these "things" offer. I'll put simple thievery down as a catchall because these twisted people will do most anything and say most anything to get what they want. The range is from the gentle but persistent persuader, to the deliberate con-man or woman, to the thief who robs in the night, and on to the scary one who knocks you on the head and steals your purse or wallet. Most thieves are secretive and shy and would rather be night burglars and not get caught or seen... don't really want to be hittin' nobody... just want your stuff. It is obvious that they see no purpose in your perception of meaningful employment. Their employment is for self, and to them this has meaning... not working. Yet, many of these folks actually risk more and work harder for much less. Sure, the lust is for the stuff, but it's also for the clearly sexual rush of fear or false power stuffed inside the risk and the idea of getting away with it.

Trust me, on first level in lust, there is no love. Only the sensations are worshiped. Trust me, on second level in thievery and attacks on wealth, there is no love but, again, just a lot of sensation. Now, be sure, none of these people on first and second level wish you to take any of this personally. The whole reason it works for them is that it is impersonal. They don't see a real person anywhere. Since they don't see real human beings, they don't see the consequences of what they do. They don't even think there

444

are any. Twenty-seven-hundred apples... take two... anybody notice? Didn't see no people, just apples. The well of sexual energy is just that... no people anywhere, just the energy of sensations in the well. Put your bucket in and see what you get.

"But these are crimes," you say. Well, don't forget you're in twisted wedges territory where everything is twisted and somehow seen as justified–"Oh, I do it because it was done to me" kind of thinking. This twisted axe cuts going down and coming up, both left and right. It doesn't care what it destroys or how. This is the area of obsession, compulsion and addiction. This is the area that has no reason, other than its own twisted perception. There is no mind here that can think. All this mind can do is try to justify its behavior. And what may appear as fast talkin' and quick thinkin' has nothing to do with thinkin' at all. Fast talkin' is a slow mind trying to confuse you and justify itself.

Third twisted level is the overpowering by will and the use of violence. This is the area of rape, pillage and plunder. As you see, lust and greed aren't gone yet. Here the twisted energy has grown. The energy of secrecy, the fear of being discovered has increased beyond first and second level sexual deviancy and thievery. This twisted area becomes a true threat when, without conscience, someone embraces violence and gives it their will. They have joined the twisted aspects of the mechanism of ego and fully expect to reap the rewards of control over sexuality and the material world by violent will.

The next twisted level, the fourth, includes the heart... or lack of it. This level includes all murderers who rape, pillage and plunder, as somehow "sanctified" by war. This level of the heart includes "crimes of passion" and passionate aggressors in an *offensive war* between civilians, called civil war.

The fifth twisted level includes the concept and belief in holy wars and the perception of evil as always being outside oneself. The first large-scale modern, offensive war against "evil" you can remember was the Christian Crusades. At present, the Muslims see the white race as the devil, and they wage their holy war against their perception of the devil they only see as outside themselves. I'll even include any racial and religious prejudice here if murder occurs... black, red, yellow, or white.

The sixth twisted level, raised to the level of vision is true madness. It is the lust for power and domination, and the preaching and expansion of senseless insanity coupled with godless violence, in agreement or forced agreement within a society or culture. The most recent you'll remember was the Aryan war for racial purity and dominance... Hitler's war against Judaism and other minorities. On the twisted sixth, you have the Hitlers, the Stalins, the Edi Ameins, the Sadam Husseins, the cultural genocide in the 1700's against the red race, carried foreward (and now in much weaker form), as well as many other twisted ones I will not mention at present. You can see them yourselves on the news.

Now, I'm not including in these twisted wedges the occasional human being who happens to fall off into shallow schizophrenic, paranoid and psychotic states. These are "relatively normal" human beings who are psychically sensitive and often get thrown into your insane asylums because they cannot integrate the six levels or find their center. These folks have become significantly affected by the energy of these twenty-four twisted wedges, while trying to integrate the collective images they bump into with the ideals that leak down from the seventh level. Said straight-up, they cannot integrate the thoughts of godlessness with God.

The seventh level pyramid has no twisted wedges. Within this pyramid, there are no other levels or divisions. It has no collective pyramid from above pointing down within it. It is an entire, complete pyramid all to itself. It is the nearly perfected structure of mind and is the basic holographic building block within each of the other six pyramids, both down and up through seven orders of resolution.

From the seventh level, you can look down on the mechanistic, psychic causes of all the world's woes, through all the levels, in all the corners, in all the pyramids, through the extreme sides, and the very center line. That center line we'll call the core. The core cannot be influenced by perception or energy of any kind. It is in the core you become aware and conscious of life in all its exquisite detail.

It is from this vantage point, you can understand the world and all the minds in it, where each and every cry can be heard from each aspirant reaching this point. "Who let this insane mechanistic influence out among us? When did it start? Who did it? How can we remove its influence forever?"

Here, I'm going to pause and explore something very fundamental. If a truly deviant person could grow up in a house without anyone suspecting, it is because that house is square, with rectangular walls and doors and locks all around. Your houses cultivate separation and secrets.

In our time, our houses were round. There were no walls, doors or locks. If there was deviant energy in that lodge, we all knew it and dealt with it. In a circle of energy like that, nothing gets caught in the corners. We didn't miss a thing. We chose to live in round houses for that very reason. We let Spirit guide us and tell us how to build them. I don't give a damn how fancy a square you build, even if it's a square house with no rooms, no partitions or sections, I'm tellin' you, something's gonna' get stuck in the corners. Something will hide there.

The whole issue of "yours and mine" never came up in our round houses. If somebody spied something they wanted, the other one knew it right away. In our culture, we'd say, "Oh well, you like it, it's yours, you keep it." Sharing is what kept the harmony and balance inside our circles.

Wealth was measured by the whole tribe's wealth, not personal wealth. The only "owned" objects that were acknowledged and respected were a person's spiritual objects. Everyone was taught what it takes to receive or be given a spiritual object and how to find or make one's own. No one was ever left out and no one was special. Everyone learned what owning meant. It was taught that the only thing any person could ever really own was their True Identity, given by Spirit. Sacred objects were given, made or found by a person seeking their True Identity and function. For instance, medicine men or women typically owned specific objects they used to call themselves to Spirit... a bowl, a rattle, a drum, some feathers... objects of spiritual meaning.

Do you know when the world changed for the white man? When they discovered the earth wasn't a flat disc. It was round. That's when their perception of the physical world changed. But the psychic world that the white man lives in is still square or flat. Proof is, he still builds them damn houses all square, with square rooms and doors and drawers and boxes to hide everything in.

To live in a society with the energy of nature being round, and still tend to build square things that trap the sickness of separation and breed secrecy and deviancy is the seed of a people's own destruction.

Now, I know no one goes purposely and consciously down the path of self-destruction, and I know no one would purposely and consciously go down the path of the destruction of one's own children. But ignorance, unawareness, and lack of true desire and commitment required to get to the truth... that is any people's downfall.

Whatever grows so far off the ground as to become "great" is just lookin' for something to bring it down. Trying to be great and trying to live exclusively within strict, high, self-righteous moral principles and physical ideals brings along with it those twisted wedges, the very seeds of pride's destruction.

In our round houses, we did our best not to boast. We didn't let our energy grow out of the circle of truth. We knew that outside the love of family, outside the love of expanded family called tribe, our circle couldn't expand, but evil distortions could. Sure, we studied the possibility of attack from outside, but we tried always to first make sure that within us was no seed of our own destruction. We knew Creator gave us our consciousness to develop and expand, that we were not meant to exclude any spiritual experience, whether it was of mineral, vegetable, animal, or human. It was up to us to learn what had true meaning and what the limits of human power were. All round houses gave no power to anything or anyone in our circle for our own destruction. We included the thought in every aspect of our lives that Creator had not abandoned us here, that we were the beloved children. And to all the children, Creator promises a circle of communication with all life that has no end.

We concluded that the love we shared in our communication with each other is what kept this ever-present destructive force from entering our homes. We knew it was awareness and conscious communication about everything that kept our young from falling into the twisted traps that secret thoughts can cause. We knew that selfishness and sex would be the very first hooks that destructive intent could get us with, so we talked about these things frankly. Our stories taught us as youngsters the depth and trickery of the mechanism of selfishness and deviant sexual energy. We talked in a sacred manner, to keep respect and honor and trust between males and females present. We allowed play and investigation not to deepen into deviancy from secrecy and guilt. We kept natural what was natural. We kept round what was round. We didn't make no boxes to hide shit in.

I know your Jesus went around smashin' them boxes, knockin' over them tables, breakin' down them walls. He brought the outside, inside, and he turned the inside, out. He kept nature round and complete. He made health outside them homes, under the trees in the grass, in the light where everything could be seen and dealt with straight-up. He was a healer, for sure. He was both Spirit and body, both male and female, not divided or confused... wholly centered.

So back to the big question, "How to get rid of this thing, this destructive energy among us? Who let it out and when?"

I'll tell you who and when. Long time ago, before the Egyptians, were human beings in a society you call Atlantis, a people way ahead of their time, who played out all five suns in less than three-hundred years of spiritual advancement. I won't speak to their material advancement because it wasn't the cause of their demise. Their achievements were spiritual and their weaknesses were also spiritual. They saw Creator's Plan for the world and for all the creatures in it, but they didn't see their own role. Funny thing, when you are *trying* to be a thing, you cannot see your own beingness.

So they changed the future of all those that followed. They did this one thing. After seeing The Plan, they sought to change it. They wanted influence. And without admitting they knew their error, they sought to personally possess true power and to control creation. True power is Creator's. Any attempt to alter creation without Creator results in destruction. This is why from the very beginning of these stories I recommended you stay way the hell away from seeking power, that whenever it is offered to you, you back up. You back up, but don't take your eyes off the very thing that tried to offer it to you, because here's what happened to the Atlanteans.

They wanted to change creation. They wanted to alter The Plan. By trying to mess with perfection, they put in service another aspect of perfection designed to protect itself from any attempt to own and abuse power. You've heard about Pandora's box? Well, I'll tell you, when they broke though to find this proverbial box–and, believe me, there was a psychic, Spiritual wall put all around it–they went looking for the key to open it, instead of noticing that if Creator went to all this trouble to contain it, why the hell would anyone want to open it?

Now, you notice, the whole of the universe is round, and here's a box, something in creation that is square, cubicle, like a salt crystal. A box mimics a salt crystal. So they thought, salt is necessary for life, yes? Humans can't live without salt, so humm... this box must be important too. What's in the box?

So right in front of being able to understand the great perfection of life, the Great Mystery, stands this box. What was in that box appeared as power for those who investigated. It appeared that way solely because of the intent of their investigation. That box, being closed, appeared to be an obstacle to their path of knowledge. It appeared as essential as a cube of salt. They gave that closed box the power they sought, though Creator had contained and hidden it from them. They wanted to give that no-good box the power to change creation, because of their own selfish desire and intent. By wanting to mess with The Plan, they magnified that destructive power that Creator had purposely contained. By taking incomplete understanding of knowledge and trying to use it in some way, especially spiritual, they fueled what was anti-life in that box.

Now, I'm sure you can imagine what it was and why Creator tried to contain it, but I will tell you anyway. What was in that box was all of the thoughts that were outside of love. When Creator perfected the energy of love that is life itself, to assure its continuation, all the thoughts that were anti-creation were distilled down to a single energy and made to be contained. This container was then placed at the edge of creation and left to rot in its truly uncreative thought. Thus, what you would later come to call the anti-Christ was to become the last-resort teaching device of Spirit about anti-life, about what is not God, and therefore what life truly is. You popularly call this very difficult teaching mechanism, Satan or the devil.

I will call it what the Mother called it after it got loose on the world and its energy began to affect the thoughts within creation. And I will call it so because of its effects on the sanctity of natural life and the feminine aspect of God. I will call it the "mother-fucker"... because that is what it has done.

So okay, the Alanteans did it. They opened Pandora's box. I'll tell you what they got for their efforts. Vaporized! The most evolved of the earliest people on the earth got totally erased by one moment of human foolishness. And, as a reminder, the rest of humankind got the worst psychic stink possible that doesn't seem to want to go away. Left over from opening the box was this foul energy of the mechanism of fear and sensual addiction, with its memory stuck in the soil of the entire planet. It remains to this day and must be dealt with by everyone since.

You know, many of your women of today are very smart. To not be taken advantage of in this world, these women have learned how to give everyone the "psychic smell test," to protect themselves from another that is infected. Women generally can "smell 'em out," unless they're also infected.

The first symptom of infection in any person in your house is selfishness and sexual secrecy. The second symptom is lying. The third symptom is thievery... and so on and so forth, up the levels of twisted wedges.

Alright, so you know who-done-it, who let the vile stench out of the box. When was, oh, I'd say, more than fifty-thousand years ago. When don't much matter now. Who did it don't much matter either. Recognizing the energy of it, matters very much. Facing your fear of it, very much matters. Removing its influences on everyone and everything forever, matters most.

Now, I didn't say, find out who's infected and destroy them, because you'd be destroying your own children, your own parents, your own families. That everyone is infected, matters. That you expend energy in learning about this mechanism and learning how to help others understand what infected them, matters. That you learn to recognize on every level the human weaknesses that caused them to become infected, matters. But for spiritual human beings greatly aided by Spirit, removing its influence forever is the utmost goal.

This ego mechanism has gone unchecked for so long that the energy of this thing has grown. Its influence is significant, and the power to entrap and deceive its victims is almost complete. And yet, it isn't even alive. It isn't even real.

For such a dead thing, it sure seems to have a lot of influence... sex, drugs, money, rape, pillage, plunder, murder, greed, envy, lust, jealousy, and competition for importance and the possession of some kind of uncreative power. Death holds more influence over life than it should, don't you think? Fear of madness is just as insane, don't you think? Shooting at images that frighten you, trying to make them go away, doesn't work, does it? While trying to put a door up in front of those fears, you have to think about what side safety is on. Can it get in? Can you get out? If there's gonna' be a lock, who's got the key, and on what side of the door should the lock be? Should you be locked in from it, or should you lock it in so you can go out?

Well, ultimately, whether in a round house or a square one, your dreamtime is always open territory. I know a lot of people who don't like to dream... don't want to. They block dreaming as much as they can... afraid of being pestered by witches and ghosts and devils and demons. Well, while there's some of that little stuff in the dreamtime space, there's a whole lot more of Big Help available in it. Dreamtime space is the only place a Holy Spirit can come calling on such an overly-defended mind and heart.

So, about Spirit, some of you say, "I don't know whether to trust them or not, 'cause in the world and in my dreams I can see the devil's trickery." And yet, one day I'll bet you'll be caught in a big jam and have to holler for help anyway.

I'll tell you right now, the whole damn world's in a jam and it better get hollerin'. Everybody knows the time for major change is coming. But the old-world thinkin' has got to change to make things easier. And I hope you don't believe Creator has to destroy this place just to change people's thinking. I hope you believe thinking can change.

But I tell you, Spirit's got rules. We couldn't say straight-up what's what before now. We had to say everything in code, and folks had to figure it out. If Spirit said stuff straight-up and no one made effort to discover the truth... well, that's cheatin'. That's vaporizing material. And I don't want to be no vapor. My light body's thin enough.

Now, to be vaporized means the energy that sustained you is the very thing that is withdrawn from you. I don't want my Maker to come to me like that, whether I have a body or not. Thankfully, humans are destined to find out the truth because of their true desire and will to know it.

So, in the past, we used codes like, "When the red beans are divided," because we can't get you directly to an understanding of the truth without the possibility of your trying to meddle with power or speak too soon, and therefore being harshly judged by your peers or becoming vapor material. So the codes are used to protect you and The Plan, until the danger of meddling with power is over. It was a timing thing. Now it's safe to say straight-up what "When the red beans are divided" means. It means the time of choosing for each person is upon us, and the harvest of souls has begun. It means that it is time for the separation of the "wheat from the chaff," the separation from truth, all that is illusion.

I think the hardest thing to swallow for any human being is considering the possibility that evil could keep anyone, ever. So, remember this. We are all created by Love and can be saved by Love's Truth at any time we wholly ask. We are all redeemable.

Now, I have to be very careful with these words because I do not want to mislead you, and I do not want to create an opening that looks like escape or safe-haven. The harvest of souls means the separation of good and evil. It means The Final Cleansing.

Now there's that word, "final." Does that mean the "mother-fucker" gets put back in the box? Not quite like that. The box that contained it blew up. The energy was released. The energy that it is, is also part of its own destruction. Creator said so. Can expanded nothing recondense into finite nothing and be recontained inside a new box, or can it simply disburse like a bad smell in good air?

Another question is, when will the energy of nothing self-destruct? Who will it take with it? And will any one of us be left standing to see it go by... bye-bye. When it goes by, back to its own destruction, its diluted smallness, will we be able to say

452

goodbye and be left standing, aware, conscious and untouched? Are you aware, conscious and untouched now?

I recommend you don't be in such a big hurry for The Big Cleansing for everyone else, 'cause it may take you or your friends and family who are unconscious and unaware. Don't be so quick to throw them away, because they are you, your children, your fathers, and your mothers who have messed up some.

*

Ribbons of images like film in a movie will soon begin to fly through everyone's perception. Many will think they are mad. There will be much unrest. So, listen to me this once if you have not been. Listen carefully. **The Cleansing has begun.** Everyone will have their review.

This is the mantra given by the Mother for you to hold onto during this time of racing images. Use it.

"God Is Only Love and Only Love Is Real."

The fifth sun is the promise of peace, is the promise of truth, is the promise of the Unity of Love and Truth. That was Creator's promise.

The Ancient Ones are coming back. I could even tell you Creator's coming back. And it's true. What I can't tell you is what will happen when Creator comes back, 'cause it's never happened here before. Spirit doesn't know when exactly, but I want to tell you it is my job to encourage you to heal your confusions between male and female, between spirit and body and... **Get ready for God.**

Chapter 14
Glossary - Word Story

Glossary: a list of words with explanation and definitions. Glossary is from the Latin word 'glossa' which means "to explain."

Intent * Reason * Purpose * Goal

This glossary is to help you with your orientation within the world of words. Words, in Spirit's definition, are only for the purpose of reconnecting your mind-self in form (that cannot remember anything of what it is, the how, what, why, when, and where of its Source or even its own purpose for existing in any moment in time), to your consciously-aware mind in formlessness (which Spirit can recall for you, so you can remember everything from The Beginning of time, even before form, and into the vast and Endless Eternity of the Great Mystery).

To repeat in short form... words, in the world of Spirit versus the material world, are used either to bring together or to make separate and keep apart. The energy of joining is Love. The energy of separation is fear. In the accomplishment of joining in Love, Truth can be refound. Though the absence of Love was never possible, the absence of your joining Love in your conscious awareness is possible. Thus, was fear imagined and the impossible pondered as possible. Therefore, there will be two definitions offered for every word under scrutiny, so you may see your two minds split apart. Were you to not be split in your own mind, you would not need words at all, except perhaps to help those who are.

Time: The quality of Mind that can Intend and willfully coalesce energy into form for the purpose of slowing down energy, so that it will demonstrate itself at a single point in material space.

Example of Form: *Today* is relevant only to a specific place, for anyone who cares to notice for themselves.

Example of Formlessness: *Now* is everywhere all by itself. No one need notice it. *Now* always *Is*.

Clock: Some device for measuring time, without need for memory or conscious awareness while in form.

The Plan for Time: This is complex, so (bear=introspection; bare=reveal or uncover) with me.

To approach the subject of eternity, I will construct a device that, while arbitrary in structure and questionable in absolute truth, will nonetheless suffice for some explanation toward the inexplicable. How do you describe the indescribable; how do you define the Great Mystery? I'm caught anyway, since I already said something about Creator's 52 cycles and the 5.4 billion years. These cycles started when I was surely not present, 'til when I was, 'til your now when it is perhaps a question of yours as to whether I am here now or not. So here goes anyway.

There are approximately 5.4 billion years from The Beginning 'til the end of the fourth world of the earth, just passed. Within the last of Creator's 52 cycles are the eight worlds of the earth's time. The four worlds I will briefly explain because they are now past, and the fifth I will mention because it is just beginning. Let's say, there are 12.981 million earth years to each of the four worlds... like so:

The First World = The Mind of Creator and the First Intent toward form = Love and Truth = Power.

The Second World = The Minds of First Woman and First Man = the Journey of Love and Truth in Formlessness as God Female and God Male into many forms = the beginning of the journey of the memory of love and the memory of truth as human woman and man.

The Third World = The collective mind of all the created forms in existence = the journey through time in form in creation = peoples, things, and habitable places.

The Fourth World = the collective of all that does exist in essence and form with what does not exist, either in form or in essence = the journey through illusion and the time of choosing. The beginning to the end of these four worlds has taken 51.9228 million years.

The Fifth World = The Return and The Joining of all the minds that do exist in creation with Creator = Love and Truth joined through the individual Plan of Atonement (at-one-moment.)

I will not describe the worlds beyond these five, for I would not prophesy in advance of what Creator has done already.

So, some **form** of unaware self-consciousness has been around for roughly thirty-two million, four-hundred-fifty-one thousand, nine-hundred-and-five years [32,451,905], from the middle of the Second World until now, the beginning of the Fifth World... roughly 5.4 billion years from The Beginning to 1996, if you prefer. Even though Creator's been messin' around for over 5.3675 billion years to get together for you, this E ticket of E ticket rides, you're only halfway done. There are four more worlds to go... you are beginning the 5th of 8 worlds. Earth's got over 51,923,048 years to go, whether humans like it or not.

What you get on this ride is to face yourselves, face the illusions of the mechanism, undergo correction through Atonement, be healed through true forgiveness, face the Truth inside Love, and then enjoy, in form, 2000 years of Heaven on Earth... a grace period during the Fifth World, assuming folks don't destroy the place and themselves.

*

From here on, I will simply list each word twice that I picked seemingly at random. On the left side of the page is a Spiritual definition, and on the right side is a material or physical interpretation and application. The logic for doing so is twofold. The first is so you may clearly see the intent behind **writing down** these stories, and the second is so you might become acutely aware of the two minds that could be reading them. Which mind you choose to be at any moment and for the rest of your life in form will determine whether you are open to learning what knowledge is, and therefore becoming consciously aware of what creation is, including yourself. Thus, the first word suggests the next and so on. It's not possible to write down what the First Word was, but it was a beaut.

SPIRITUAL DEFINITION

_ ☼ _

ego application

_ _ _ _
❏

Mind: The Reason of Desire, Purpose, Intention, and Will.

Thought: The First intense or powerful Design or Purpose of Mind and Source of Cause.

***

Intent: The driving force or power of the mind to cause.

Purpose: The intent, the reason for, the existence of, the design, and the use put before one's self to be accomplished... the end result.

Use: To be in purposeful service.

Creator: One Who or That Which Caused Beingness; from Which all that exists derives its aliveness. The Source... First Purpose.

Creation: All that was created; all that exists; all that has life.

Animate: To give life to, to encourage, to move into purposeful action.

Inspire: To be aroused, animated with feelings and thoughts, guided, prompted, instigated, or caused, with no responsibility or self-avowal and not by one's own intent, alone.

Knowledge: That which can be experienced, understood and demonstrated that is real.

Real: That which is in existence, that has Beingness, that has life.

Essence: The true substance or spirit in each and all things.

Spirit: The conscious, incorporeal Beingness of life which animates; the soul that leaves its incarnation or form, like unto the breath.

mind: That which thinks, feels, wills, exercises perception, judgment and reflection, both conscious and unconscious.

thought: The product of mental action, idea, notion, consideration, reflection, meditation or contemplation, resulting in judgment, opinion, or belief.

intent: The mind's purpose or aim toward a specific action or use, and its result and end.

purpose: The desire or intention for some use, action, result, effect, advantage, or end.

use: To put in the service of one's own purpose.

creator: The conceiver, inventor, producer, imaginer, or representer; the maker of stuff.

creation: The product of ingenuity or of imagination; the things.

animate: To make move and pretend to live, using a study, sketch, model, or exaggerated caricature of behavior for entertainment; drawings put to a film sequence, giving the illusion of movement and life.

inspire: To inhale, without any understanding or will or humor... to consume air.

knowledge: The body of facts accumulated by man in the course of time; the what, where and how of things.

real: What is true, factual, objective, genuine and or material, by personal decision or consensual agreement.

essence: Important or elemental characteristics of a thing; able to be distilled physically or perceptually.

spirit: A discarnate, fleshless or formless aspect or supernatural being of a particular type, characterized by a disposition and having intent or purpose; a strong booze or perfume.

Soul: The aware and conscious heart within Spirit.

soul: The aspiring heart within a person's body of experiences.

Exist: That which is both real in thought and form, and can be found.

exist: To be whatever, to have a life and to live however, and to move wherever, whenever.

Existentialism: The doctrine that there is no difference between the external world and the internal world of the mind, and that the Source and the elements of knowledge have their existence in the states of the mind.

existentialism: A recent movement that claims to represent a middle way between traditional materialism and idealism, stressing personal decision in the face of a universe, assumed to be without purpose.

Assume: To take for granted, without desire for factual proof, personal experience or direct knowledge, then to pretend to know, thereby being arrogant and foolish.

assume: To undertake or appropriate; to pretend to fact, knowledge or truth; being arrogant. Ass - u - me: to make an ass outa' u and me. And if you don't like this definition... Ah, sue me.

Arrogant: The pretentious look of superiority on one's face before the Arrow of Truth strikes it. Said backwards, the arrogant glance with the arrow inside that means to murder what it sees, as if looks could kill.

arrogant: An attitude of unproven pretensions and overbearing pridefulness.

Fool: One who is weak-minded, idiotic, disordered, aimless, and wastes time; one who plays, jests, make-believes, or meddles with the idea of order or perfection, on purpose for some reason.

fool: Silly or stupid person without purpose who makes no sense.

Ignorant: One who ignores on purpose.

ignorant: The state of lacking information, learning, or knowledge.

Experience: Personally encountering, observing, undergoing, feeling, understanding, and remembering a particular event, process or learning, thereby attaining knowledge or wisdom.

experience: Something that happens to you as you go along being animated and in movement.

Undergo: What happens when you stop avoiding, delaying, ignoring, and denying First Purpose; to "go under" ego to see it, since ego always puts itself above reality.

undergo: Having to do something that is hard, difficult, disagreeable, or dangerous.

Ego: The mind, thoughts, ideas, intent, and purpose of all that is imagined, invented, unsharable, uncommon and unreal; the aspect of mind that does not truly exist.

ego: The "thinking I," separate and distinguishable from any "thinking other," with no purpose but its own, made in response to the void of space within, and with a wholly private concept of time.

I: The beginning, intimate, self-awareness as being the "life" in the body that one is inhabiting.

i: Subjective, first person, singular pronoun... the seen, the body.

Apprehend: To become aware of; to anticipate; to understand; to recognize the meaning of.

apprehend: To anticipate with anxiety, dread or fear.

Superego: The "fake it 'til you make it," split-off, high-minded, pretentious, political counterpart of the ego's lowest desires and vile intent.

Id: Latin for 'is'. One's identity before direct revelation, after which comes truth.

Ideation: Apprehended thought forms that produce movement or activity, coming from the Perfected Purpose of the Originator, rather than from some imperfect copy.

Think: Mental activity without ideation or help; what is done when no idea comes to you and you "try" by yourself without Spirit; the ability to reflect on or form an image.

Ideal/Idealism: Perfect image of Original Thought, before any copies are attempted.

Identity: State or fact of remaining the same "one" and "what" under varying aspects or conditions, whether in form or not; condition or point of sameness or likeness.

Ideology: Science of ideas derived from sensation applying only to the physical world.

Science: Systematized study of the physical or material realm to discover facts, principles, or laws governing the world, and thereby aspire to truth or knowledge without Spirit.

Manifest: That which is asked for and received from Spirit by ideation, vision, and/or materialization, through one's true desire and intent.

super-ego: That part of the psychic apparatus which mediates between ego drives and social ideals and acts as a conscience; may be partly conscious and partly unconscious.

id: The part of the psyche residing in the unconscious, which is the source of instinctive energy. Its impulses, which seek satisfaction with the pleasure principal, are unconsciously modified by the ego and the superego before they are given overt expression.

ideation: The process of forming mental images, thoughts, concepts, notions, impressions, opinions, views, beliefs, plans, intentions, and fantasies developed by the "thinking mind," from archetypes of which only copies can be imperfectly made.

think: To form an opinion, belief, or judgment; to reflect, expect, and decide with intent or purpose, with or without consideration of evidence, meditation, or contemplation.

ideal/idealism: Unattainable perfection in a class of objects or images which exists only in idea. Being only oneself or itself and not another; the condition of "who," rather than "what."

identity: Who you claim to be that can be proven to others.

ideology: The body of doctrine, myth and symbols, regarding movements of societies, institutions, classes or groups, with reference to political or cultural plans, and the devices for instituting those plans, whether visionary, practical, or impractical.

science: A branch of study or knowledge dealing with a body of facts or truths, systematically arranged to show the operation of general laws about the physical and material world.

manifest: Able to be seen clearly by the eye or perceived by the understanding; psychologically disguised impulses of the unconscious; a list of goods in transport.

Idol: An image; a physical or material object that is adored, revered, or worshipped for what is symbolic, unattainable, unachievable, and therefore illusory.

Image: Luminous rays producing a likeness or appearance in form, semblance or reflection, which is either apprehended through ideation, projection, imagination, or fantasy.

Imagination: The self-made productive or reproductive formation of mental images that can be shared directly or indirectly.

Fantasy: Unrestrained, grotesque image sequences for fulfillment of the ego's desires.

Obscure: Having no meaning to apprehend.

Obsession: The compulsion to endlessly return to a sensation and the images of its unresolved experiences, rather than resolving the attraction and ending it.

Addiction: Giving in to a mechanism of sensual obsession, rather than giving up to Spirit for correction.

Possess: To have, to know, or to exist wholly within what is real and true, that is not removable or losable, and is able to be perfectly and easily demonstrable to others.

Ally: To join, unite, connect, and bind together by agreement.

Oblivious: The unconscious, forgetting mind, with no intent to awaken or remember.

Oblivion: Total illusion and unreality everywhere.

Guide: A Holy Spirit that shows the way, whether directly or through channels or conduits. (con du its. Those that "can do it.")

Vision: A gift from Spirit; seeing without the eyes what was true, is true, or later comes to pass.

idol: An ideal or archetype that is revered, adored or even worshipped, whether physical, mental, emotional or material, even though it is based on fantasy.

image: A mental or pictorial copy, with the projection of the desire to give form through the imagination or fantasy; to assign personal meaning and representation to people, objects, ideals, or experiences; a fake; not real.

imagination: The faculty of mental invention and projection of images, either similar to reality or fanciful.

fantasy: Imagination with emotion and sensation for ego gratification.

obscure: Not clear; can't see it.

obsession: A besetting, troubling, dominating or haunting by a persistent feeling, sensation or idea, usually accompanied by fear.

addiction: A habit that rules you which you've given "up" to after having given "into" it for a very long time; lack of desire or will to change an unhelpful habit.

possess: To have, seize, or take as property; to hold and occupy, and to keep or maintain by control or domination, either materially or spiritually, until deposed by a greater will or by the truth.

ally: One who helps or cooperates with another in some relationship or agreement.

oblivious: To be unaware, incognizant, or unconscious of.

oblivion: Being forgotten; having never really existed.

guide: To lead or direct the way on the physical plane.

vision: The act of seeing images with the physical eyes, whether by vivid imagination, conception, or by normal dreaming.

Envision: To self supply images aimed toward the next moment or farther on; an attempt to know by projection; not waiting for Spirit's guidance and true vision.

envision: To mentally picture future events, whether true or not; future projection.

Upset: To disturb some habitual order or disorder by overturning, and/or then being raised up.

upset: To overthrow or defeat; being irritated for some reason.

Mistake: A misapprehension, misperception, or misconception resulting in judgment, guilt and fear, rather than peace.

mistake: An error in action, opinion, or judgment.

Error: Believing and acting upon that which is not true, and therefore has no value.

error: The difference between the self-determined value and the true value of anything.

Condone: To allow, to release from responsibility, and to further indulge with weak implication of forgiveness.

condone: To pardon, overlook, or forgive.

Correct: To set right and remove errors; to alter, adjust, or undo mistakes in order to conform to truth, and therefore return to peace.

correct: To point out errors and mistakes, to admonish or rebuke in accordance with some standard or required condition, and/or to be error free.

Correction: The remedy and its method of institution.

correction: Punishment, chastisement, discipline, reproof.

Understand: To get knowledge of by experience and/or comprehension; to stand beneath and be grounded in the experience of.

understand: To perceive the meaning; to believe and to accept as fact.

Atone: To return to agreement; to bring back into harmony and to bring into unity (at-one-ment).

atone: To make amends or reparation; to pay for or make up for errors, mistakes, or deficiencies.

Redeem/Redemption: To return or restore to an original state through a conversion, exchange, and offer of true value.

redeem/redemption: To buy back, clear off, recover by payment, and make up for.

Conscious: To be awake and aware of all that exists in all its doings and deliberateness; having clear intent in all one's own feelings, thoughts, and actions.

conscious: Inwardly awake and mentally sensible.

Conscience: That which remembers for you and helps you to know truth; your inner-most, grounded, and centered thoughts.

conscience: The internal recognition of right and wrong regarding motives and action... morality. Con - science: the science or study of how to con.

Meditation: Long consideration of the whole mind on a single subject, beginning from a personal viewpoint, with an intent toward expansion; the door to contemplation.

meditation: Extended thinking, consideration, or reflection towards some purpose or action.

Contemplation: Continuous, extended, and broadminded consideration of a whole subject from an expansive viewpoint that includes Spiritual guidance.

Reveal: To make known, to uncover, to make unhidden; revel: to take joyous, great delight in, thereby returning you to peace.

Revelation: God's disclosure of Presence and Essence to each one that asks and truly desires the Answer... revealed in the right way and at the right time.

Perceive: To sensually apprehend, and therefore not know.

Perception: A personal assumption or presumption of knowing or understanding with insufficient receptive or apprehending apparatus.

Condemn: To choose death and be dead in thought or deed.

Pray: Earnest, spiritual, two-way communication meant to be about what is real.

Prayer: What is earnestly asked for that is real.

Prey: That which may or may not be influenced or overpowered by some intent that wishes to use it.

Preyer: That which tries to impose its will.

Give: To have, produce, present, deliver, and to hand over freely... as in a "gift."

Give In: To weaken one's will and conviction; to fail to desire understanding.

Give Up: To ask Spirit for help to forsake or desist that which is no longer helpful, and to devote willingness entirely to what is helpful.

Relax: Only the truth is true, and truth is in peace about it. Only in peace will you find truth. Only love loves. Though peace as a condition is not necessary for love's presence, peace is what love offers in every circumstance. So, relax. Truth just is.

contemplation: To think studiously, consider, reflect, intend, propose, and plan.

reveal: Related to the root words revile and revel; to disclose, divulge, lay open to view, or exhibit.

revelation: To reveal or disclose something not previously known... a surprise.

perceive: To apprehend, to understand, or to know through the five senses.

perception: The result or product of sensing a sensible object or objective, usually resulting in judgment, choice, or decision.

condemn: To judge against, make guilty, convict, sentence, and made to reside in death as if doomed.

pray: To petition for someone or something to a higher power than is in the sensible world.

prayer: The conformation of words used in religious observance, or those made by personal design.

prey: The destructive influence on or harmful seisure of a body as victim for some profit or gain.

preyer: The manipulator, stalker, attacker of perceived weaker ones.

give: To deliver to another in exchange for something, either by calculation, supposition, or assumption, as in giving to get.

give in: To yield to and acknowledge defeat, and so join.

give up: To lose all hope and to feel abandonment; to surrender without thought of rescue.

relax: To become less tense, rigid, firm, strict, severe, willful, or forceful.

Risk: The value of the venture... the adventure itself.

risk: All the fearful thinking about the chance for and ways of cost, hazard, injury, loss, and death.

Share: To have together, being given freely.

share: Each part that is taken and possessed.

Resolve: A fixity of purpose; to deal with successfully; to find an answer to; to make clearly distinguishable and understandable.

resolve: To dissolve, melt, break up or to separate; to distinguish between or make independently visibile parts of; to declare, decide or change by formal vote; a legal or official determination.

Experience: Encountering and undergoing; to apprehend or to obtain knowledge and wisdom, both within and outside.

experience: The singularity and totality of the thoughts or sensations produced by action or perception.

Communicate: To share or interchange through an inner-connecting passageway, all images, thoughts, feelings, words, knowledge, and wisdom.

communicate: To impart, transmit, administer, or make known to another.

demonstrate: To make evident or try to prove by a show of force, argument, reasoning, or by exhibition for some purpose.

Demonstrate: Walk the talk; to manifest or exhibit; to be it.

Trust: Assured, confident, relaxed, and secure expectation of the integrity of the peace of God.

trust: Something of value held back 'til later when value is due or demanded.

Honor: The apprehension of perfection within the imperfect, and the acknowledgement of this connection of all things to its Source.

honor: Bestowing credit, distinction, dignity, rank, fame, or receiving such for some characteristic or accomplishment, whether real or not.

Respect: Knowing the true, correct, and appropriate relationship of one's self and behavior toward any other person or thing.

respect: To hold or be in relationship by estimation, discrimination, appreciation, deference, defect, or design, using some perceptive or cognitive function.

Awe: The reverential and respectful response, while experiencing and undergoing revelation of true power... the Source... more like awesome than awful.

awe: Respectful or reverential fear or dread inspired by the sublime, more like awful than awesome.

Summary on the Function of Words

We are imagined? And is that thought of us powerful? Can we imagine ourselves? Then, imagine health and be healed. We are imagined by Reality. Or, our imagination or fantasy is our reality. Yes?

Can physical, material reality as DNA imagine us? Then why doesn't it imagine us all perfect, rather than pass on faults and imperfections? Is the physical or material self, as DNA, powerful? Does it rule over us or is it just a mechanism, winding on relentlessly through some unknown and faulty intent?

If the laws of physical and material reality of the body rule us mechanistically, then deriving true meaning from physical existence is not possible. Thus, it *is* possible to make up or imagine one's own meaning, though it will have to be given up to its ultimate meaninglessness with the disintegration and death of the form... illusion's oblivion.

This awareness causes fear, and so the so-called "life" of the ego will always be fearful. Meaninglessness and the attempt to assign meaning without Spirit, God and Creator is the source of fear. Banding together into fearful belief systems as tribes, societies and cultures is what causes wars. From fear as leader, only death results.

The spirit of life that continues to live its "separate selves" within the whole, in spite of this conundrum, is proof of another overriding principal in operation beside fear, is it not? Existence of life or aliveness is a fact, is it not? That we live beyond our conflict with the sickness of the mind or death of the form is proof we are not the Cause of our life or anyone else's. Yet, once again, we reach a "dead end" when tracing backward by ancestry to find The Beginning... "What came first, the chicken or the egg?"

Can't have a male without a female to lay the egg? Right?
Males can't lay eggs. Right?
An egg can't grow without a male to fertilize it?
Or can it?

Spiritual philosophy says, "First the Thought, then the Word, then the flesh." Okay, think and choose something. Imagine it and produce a powerful image in your mind. Project it onto the material world and speak it into being, using the power of your whole being. Did it work? Some folks can do it... I've seen it. They must be powerful, yes? What is that power? Where does it come from? Food? Utility poles? UFO's? Intent? Spirit? Love? Prayer? Fasting? Some say so.

Where? How? What does it mean?–manifesting. Ego says love is not real, is meaningless and is to be feared. Funny thing about upside-down and backwards power. It has the power to use you, since it ain't really yours and you just tried to use it a little... maybe. By now, you know real power isn't about the fear of death or meaninglessness or any mechanism of the physical world like the concept of "using," because of the lessons of "take away," right? That is, take away any DNA or RNA sequence or single base amino acid, and something gets broken, doesn't work and might not even survive or "live." Right? Death doesn't live, and therefore has no power, right? That which can die is not "life," and therefore has no true power.

So, life is power. Life living us is the tap, so to speak. How to tap it and what will happen if you do? First thing to remember is that you cannot be overpowered, since you already are. It won't kill you with overcharge, since it doesn't kill in the first place. Right? So, it must be helpful, this power, since we didn't imagine it or make it up. Right? It's the Source of Life, yes? It must know what It means, right? Or It would be like the ego... just another senseless, meaningless mechanism doing its programmed duty, so to speak. If It knows what It means, then It knows how It is Causing "life" and what Its Purpose Is. Yes? If and only if this Source is not bogus, we think we can then learn by experiencing anything we want or need, given enough time. And yet, time would be no obstacle if "life" was not "death." True?

It must be that the only obstacle to "life" learning more is that the form doesn't last very long. Learning beyond the fear of death itself is the obstacle. Sounds like life either does not want us to learn more because of the fear, or we *can and must* go beyond the body's limited senses and fear of its death to learn more.

Uhh-oh... more fear... where did that nauseating sensation come from? Did I *cause* it with my *thought?* Did my thinking cause the body to send fear back to my apprehension through association with it? Dog it down. What's afraid? Is your mind afraid of its thoughts or images, or is the body's sensations causing you fear?

Here it is. The only decision or judgment a body can make is about sending sensations concerning survival, with its imperative of alertness and energetic commands about facing dangers. And yet by itself, the body has no power to give itself "life" if it's drained away mechanically, other than to urge you to fearfully imagine that it alone is the "life" inside the skin and bones. Truly, you know the mind of the body is illusion, because when a part is cut off, the ego has no power to regenerate it by thought, desire or intent of any kind. Best it can do is seal up the hole if it's not too big.

465

So agreed? Ego ain't "Cause" or "Source." All ego's illusions of self can do is to make you afraid and get you to run to the beat of its drum. What about your heart? Take charge of it, rather than allowing fear to be in charge of you.

Regarding your going beyond the limitations of your id, your identification with the sensual form... you must forget its fear of death, especially when you don't even know why you're alive in the first place.

When you want... when you wholly desire to go beyond your fear of seeing through an illusion that is hellbent on preventing you from doing so, what a surprise you'll have. But risk it with Spirit under Their risk-free guided tour, until you've got it down. Understand? Then you will have visionary experiences that are not imaginary but real. Then you will *know* the meaning of awesome, yourself.

A final few words on this subject.... Thinking is not trying. Trying to do is not doing. Only doing is accomplishment, yes? You cannot try to have an experience you've never had. And you cannot give an experience of the truth to yourself by what you think or decide alone. By yourself, you can do nothing, so you are really asking a Holy Spirit to give you an experience. Yes? Ask and make room. Relax. Peace be with you inside.

You Get the Drift

You cannot be the Source of Love and the Truth therein, but you can be inspired to experience this Source. Do not assume or take for granted you know what Love Is or what Is the actual Truth before you have this experience, or you will be experienced by others as being arrogant. Better to be a fool. At least Spirit can guide a fool, both forward and even backwards (Heyoka), to humorously teach what the first level of being honest is and what pretending is really for.

For Your Amusement

Two circle thoughts and one infinity thought

These offerings are meant to verbally include all relevant energy centers and are designed to collect your parts and pieces together for one purpose. Each is a question with its requisite answer within, whether read/said going down or coming up, whether from left or right.

Female circle: is love acknowledged, avowed, admitted, accepted, valued, love is...

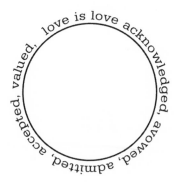

Male circle: is truth acknowledged, avowed, admitted, accepted, valued, truth is...

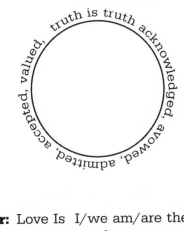

Infinity Together: Love Is I/we am/are the will & willingness, to feel, to ask, to hear, to speak, to see, and know the Truth of what...

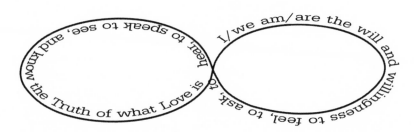

Air

Book Four

Preface
Last Words Before Air

The whole purpose of the *Fire*, the *Earth* and the *Water* books is to prepare you for something you've probably never experienced. Your spirit or essence of your life contains the single ingredient that you share with air and all Spirit... the red and blue flame. It is this lightness of air and the energetic fire of your spirit that you, most likely, are not prepared for.

The blue fire is a higher form of communication with Spirit and has always been aural. Aural, here, is both defined as pertaining to your aura and the ability to hear.

I'll make it more specific. Aura is a combination of all higher non-physical senses that lead directly to knowing. Aural, in this case, also refers specifically to inner hearing. It is only when a human is connected aurally to Spirit that the true meaning of any story is revealed, communicated and completely shared.

For the first time, the First Woman and the First Man are going to break tradition by sharing stories and having them written down, without a human intercessor speaking the words to you. The purpose in so doing is to encourage all native peoples to share their beautiful knowledge, both written and in the oral tradition of its sharing, with all those natives flung about in separate cultures under separate colors. The stories will help heal the separation, so the wounded hearts of all will open.

I've been pretty hard on you in the *Fire, Earth* and *Water* books, you may think. But in truth, because I love you I've been pretty easy. My responsibility has been to use my words to deliver you to the conditions for truth, as best I can. That love could deliver you to the truth hasn't been so hard, really. Now, getting to the truth without love... that's hard. Learning all your lessons backwards first... that's hard. Having to race up to your physical death at a brick wall... now, **that's hard.**

I haven't been quite that brutal to you. But time is up. You asked for cleansing, the whole world of you. You asked for redemption, the whole world of you. You asked for knowledge and understanding, the whole world of you. So, here it comes.

The last words from me are these:

469

Those who are in a hurry miss everything. Slow down! Out of your desire for order is born the seed of chaos that is creativity itself. Do not mistake the reordering that comes as destruction of anything valuable, or you will think that Love is cruel when It truly is not.

Ah ho,
Hinono

Chapter 1
The First Talking Turtle Story - Time

From the earliest human memory, everything always was. Before that, who could remember? Perhaps imagination reaches before time. Someone saw the night sky and imagined, before? Who's to say what's true? Before now was... and before us is... what? Well, who's to say?

Here's what I saw once in my mind in images, stronger than when my eyes were open, in a waking dream that was like a waterfall. The Source of Love that was still, began to move. Love gathered in all It could encompass and brought it together in one place. As it got more and more crowded, everything began to slow down and congeal. The more dense it all became, the slower everything moved, until time began.

Nowhere yet was there life. That took a long time. Before time was just silence. Longing for company, the thought of life began. Creator then gave a spark to each formless aspect of life, from the smallest part of creation to the largest, so each part could create within creation on its own. Creator did not want to do it all and then watch the programmed interplay. Creator gave each part will and turned it loose to find its place within Spirit.

When stars were born, there were companions spinning around them... some hot, some cold, some in between.

All of the largest things were made up from everything smaller, and all of the smallest things made up the largest... bubbles within bubbles, Creator being the largest. Outside that... who knows? Probably Creator just trying to be discreet.

After time went by and everything was in its place, the earth and other worlds were ready for their purposes. This place earth, the Turtle Mother, was now ready for life in form... all kinds... first, the tiniest, then the Plant People, then the Creepy Crawlies, then the Water People, then the Land People, then the Air People. Air

People were last because of their sensitivity to the evolving atmosphere.

Next came the Whales, and then the Bears who dreamt all the rest. It was Bear's time to dream. It was only in dreaming that Bear and Whale could look forward in time and balance all life within itself, so fire and earth and water and air would recycle endlessly, to give eternity a place to rest awhile, in time.

Something said, This is a place for life to give of itself, each in its own time like Me. I am the Endless Source, and each spark may know its Source on its journey through time and become endless too.

So, such is time... appearing with a beginning and leaving with no end, each spark playing out endlessly in a timeless universe.

What's time for? Up to you.

Chapter 2
The Second Talking Turtle Story
The Turtle and All Her Colors

What happen you throw rock in water? It sink, yes? How come all land not sink in big water? How come earth move all the time, from big mountain to little sand, but everything still float?

Easy. Before Plant People and Creepy Crawlies cover land and water, comes fire and earth. Yes? Had to be Everything already in that Nothing for anything to come out of it. Yes? So there ain't no nothing-nothing anywhere. Yes? Now, if there wasn't no Creator, then where did all this somethin' come from? Nothin'?

Out of the fullest Nothin', come out the first thing... the first thing of substance... the First Turtle, the land. Now, there is boy land and girl land. First, there was girl land that growed to a woman. Took a long time, more than anyone knows. All was Nothin' then, just waitin' to be somethin'.

This new girl land called Turtle was hot, red fire covered by rock. And the older and hotter she got, Creator had to pour water on her to cool her down some. First time, Creator poured too little and steam went all over, making storms and winds of hot, too-dry air. No life yet. Creator poured a little more, and air got heavy with water, then rains came from steamy clouds, so Turtle Land kept wet feet. Stuff grew in water, but rock still too hard, and air still too hot from molten rock. So Creator poured more water, pouring too much. Fires went out. Land cool too fast, and air and water freeze. Good thing or bad thing?

Well, Creator's always bringin' somethin' from nothin', proving nothin' is always somethin'. Creator relight that young one's fire this way. Air freeze, make water freeze, make water bigger, makin' rocks break apart. Like this... snow lighter, cold on top... rocks heavier now and still hot below. Big cold come, then rocks crack to let little fire back up. Boom! Land cracks and moves on Turtle's feet, still standin' in frozen seas. Fire in the sky, red sky light in the long, black night. Hot and cold, they come and they go... push-pulling big winds and melting frozen seas.

Long time go by when that one girl turtle got to be a maiden, with things changin' all around. She looked up all at once and saw a pale, cool moon high in the blue-black sky, far, far away. This must be her mother, she thought, but wondered on and on.

First Day soon came 'round from Nothin', with the brightest light she ever saw, singin' a brighter note yet than what she or her silent mother could have sung. Little by little the wet got drier, as this new sun warmed her side and back and belly side. Joy came to earth on this First Day.

But the sun went away and the nighttime came, and her joy was changed to sorrow. Soon the clouds cried rain with her, each time the sun did go... her joy becoming her sorrow.

Turtle said, "I want a son like that sun there. I'll ask my mother how... she'll know." Her mother, she didn't speak, so Turtle wondered on... no young maiden now, she aged some more.

The winds and seas they grew, 'til the clouds all day they cried with her. Now she's sad both day and night for a son not come, and the sun... too soon it goes away. "I'll never be happy again all day nor have sorrow all the night. Oh look what longing's done. Oh me, oh me, is this to be? How is this brightest light to see, my joy becoming sadness? Though I don't regret the sorrow lost, will ever I be free?"

Now next sad day in cloudy light, her joy and her sorrow gone, sad and lonely once again, she broke herself in two.

A once and only, only time, she heard her mother say, "Look here, you won, you won. Creator gave you, he." Just then she looked and saw her he. "And you," she said, "you look like me." And thus it was that two were one, and then came three and soon all we. Seven turtles now float in azure seas.

See first color... Grandmother Moon all pale and white. She passed her fire and guiding light. First Turtle's red fire that longed for yellow, all float in deepest blues... all greens, all browns, from a mix of these. Blue air, blue seas, the skies you see... the cold, the wet, they balance these: red fire, gold sun, and you and me. We now share all joys and sorrows, and pass through what early sadness may have been, from First Turtle's longing to begin.

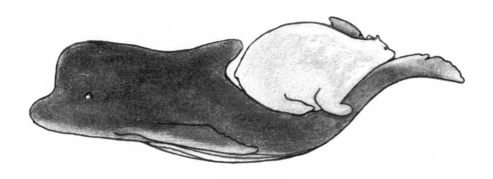

Chapter 3
The Story of the Bear and the Whale

Before Bear, only the Standing People (the trees and plants), the Rock People, the Creepy Crawlies, and the Water People were here. There was none that could stand on four legs or two. The world was abuzz with the sounds of bugs and such, each one singing their little songs for joy. The land was hot and cold in wild extremes, and the winds were very fierce. Big storms swept the land. All lives were short and fast. The earth wobbled often, and fire shot out of the ground as new lands were pushed up, and the seas sloshed wildly about. The Mother was birthing Her visions into forms all over this land... first rock and fire under great pressure, then water and air to relieve this pressure, then wind and rain to cool the fires, then hot and cold to cycle the life. All the while, Father Sun had to stand very still, so all She created could be somehow balanced in between this red and yellow fire and the deep blue frost.

This First Woman thought to Herself, "I must slow this wobble to balance the land and sea." The wobble slowed some, but still the winds and storms persisted. The land became heavy with plants and bugs, so She made the Water People and the Land People weigh the same. That helped.

She saw the air that was formed on land by the Standing Ones was too rich, and it was not used enough by the bugs and fishes to quiet the fires that raged when the land pushed up in places from the wobbles that were still left.

Again She thought, I must make two beings, one land and one water, that use air to balance what's made with what's used, and so starve the fires before they're big. The storms will then cease, and peace will return to love in this place. Then hot and cold will not be so far apart and swing so wildly from here to there.

She envisioned a Four-Legged who could stand on two, with warm fur coat against the cold, that could live in rough and cold and barren places, and would help Her dream all other helpers. This called Bear, would help Her now.

And, too, She envisioned a great, air-breathing swimmer who would go from place to place, restoring balance and grace for the land, through the seas. Whales great weight and largest mind would remember everything for all to learn of the why and how to balance earth and fire. Bear's dreaming, too, would make real the lives and lessons for all to learn about the why and how to balance water and air.

So it was, Bear slept and dreamt, while Whale breathed in and starved the fires of air, swimming right and left, ahead, behind... the winds did soon subside.

The earth wobbles once now, gentle and serene. We call this season the Sleeping Bear, for winter's cold when Bear dreams new life for spring, with all the plants and creatures, full or rare.

The Whale, they sing to Bear through water, through earth and even rocks. While swimming, they sing the memories of All that Is, that Was or Ever will there be again. Floating there, Whale feels what's in or out, restoring balance with all earth's fires. All about they go, sensing and joining the all around, their singing, filling Bear with dreaming, still.

How did we come to be? Well, many come to ask and wonder still. I think, you ask the Bear. Maybe Whale remembers. And in Whale's singing, Bear will hear and send you a dream.

Chapter 4
The Story of the Beaver

A maiden girl and her young sisters:
"Will you tell us another story, mother, while our noisy brothers are away?"

Her mother:
"I must prepare the fire and food, but you can ask Grandmother to tell you one while she is sewing. Ask respectful."

The young girls, after waiting for the grandmother's eyes to rise from her work, asked:
"Grandmother, will you tell us another story?"

Grandmother, after noting the age of her listeners and their respectful natures, says:
"Yes, I see you are ready. I have been remembering this one today already, so I will tell it. Maybe then I can remember all of it for you, as I am getting older and can't seem to remember all of this story just for myself.

"Let's see. Have any of you been to the snowy peaks, up in the high meadows? Of course you have," she answered and slapped her knee. "We go there every spring for the roots and herbs, don't we? How I forget. You remember the beaver ponds, don't you?"

All nod and settle down for a restful journey, some with chins on hands and some all curled up, fingering patterns in the dirt floor.

Grandmother:

"I remember the first time my grandmother told me this story, and I know she heard her grandmother tell her that her grandmother told her the very same story. Where it came from and who first told it this way, I cannot say. I think the Beaver's very, very great-great grandmother told it to a Two-Legged human a long time ago... probably told it to a young maiden like you, because she saw she would marry someday and have a family of her own to look after.

"If any one of you were really patient and persistent, maybe you could still learn this story directly from any one of those Beavers that still live up there. But since you asked me, I will tell you. Someday, you go up there and see for yourself if this story is true."

Grandmother, talking real slow, says:

"Close your eyes if you want. Tall trees all around... snow melting... tender buds opening their red leaves... tall grasses and reeds with succulent roots and shoots... the warming sun early to dark... you know the time... when the sun creeps north again, just before blossom time in the mountains... the time when the lowlands get rain and the grasses get green again... that's when Beaver came to this land.

"Bear dreamed Beaver before us Two-Leggeds emerged from the dreamtime of the Mother's womb. Beaver came earlier than us to show us how to live together as families and how to build our lodges. You watch them sometime and see if it's true. Many gifts were given us all by the Beaver. By far, the greatest gift the Beaver gave to us was given last.

"First gift is this. They built a lodging and were not naked against the cold, like us when we first came. Watch them, in your mind's eye. How does a Beaver go about building a lodge? You guess."

One girl answers:

"The man beaver builds it and the girl beaver helps."

Grandmother:

"Not so fast. Look again."

Another girl answers, after a pause:

"First, the man beaver builds a dam so the water stays around, then they build a lodge together."

Grandmother:

"Closer, but here's how it goes. You can go look for yourself sometime. The young man beaver finds a place, away from his mother's lodge, after learning how to build a lodge by watching his elders, the second season after weaning. Can't learn while he's on the tit, yes?"

All girls laugh and say:

"Beginning is being born and getting grown first, right?"

Grandmother:

"Right. Little beaver watches and watches. You don't hear beavers talk much, do you?"

Girls:

"No."

Grandmother:

"They got their little noises just like us, but for learnin' inside, they be quiet. So it starts early. Chew. Chew. Chew. What's to eat? Always eating. But Little Beaver notices father and mother don't eat all they chew. This goes here. That goes there. This is stored... and watch the water level always. Too low, and no little tree shoots come up to eat. No tree shoots, no food. No old trees, no dam wood. Wood too little and dam breaks. Water go away, and sweet, fast-growing wood don't grow. Lots of lessons. And little Beaver learns.

"He think... 'Got to find sweet wood first to eat... then make sure some old around for good dam to hold water still. Otherwise, lodge raided by fox or coyote or some other rascal of the night.'

"'Got it,'" Little Beaver said. "'No rascals, so got to have water first. Then old wood, then sweet wood grow. Then, like mother and father, I have family, without rascals coming for me or my babies.'" And Little Beaver slaps his tail hard on the water, just to practice the alarm signals he was taught.

"'By the way,' he asked his mother and father in short chirps while sniffing the air, 'Are we the only beavers? Are there more?' he wondered."

The father began to tell his story:

"I had sisters and lived near a lake where there were many families. Each young man Beaver like me had to leave to practice building his own lodge. When I finally got it right, your mother came to see what a fine job I had done. She saw I learned all my lessons well. I was a good thinker and a hard worker. She moved in when I also proved to be good company... at least as good as her mother and father were for her. Besides, her lodge was full of younger brothers and sisters, and it was her time to choose her own mate for life... to give new life. She had learned how to care for both girl and boy Beaver children by watching her mother. She had learned what is important in building a good dam and lodge by watching her father, and she was ready to accept her part in the job the Creator asked Beavers to do.

"She told me one day that while practicing to be a mother for her own children, by caring for the younger ones of her mother, the Mother of all children came to her in an orange-pink light and spoke thus."

The Mother of All:

"The seed of love is in you and in all women children. You are nearly ready to know what that means. Let the Voice of your seed guide you always, and you will know your purpose Creator gave each and everyone this life. In return, give only love... never lose heart... work on."

Little Beaver's mother then spoke:

"Before your father and I were joined, I was hardened by work and tired of caring for my brothers and sisters. The lodge was crowded and new shoots were hard to find. I didn't want to stay. I longed for peace and solitude, so I followed an urging to find my own lodge and have my own mate. And so I set out one morning, knowing I would not be safe outside the lodge at night.

"This fear was soon overcome by strong desire, and I had to let the seed inside me guide. That quiet, little Voice led me here and there where I learned many lessons. At night the water was my safety, within log jams in the streams and lakes. I traveled long, until I found your father sitting on his lodge, poking in final branches and putting on the mud and grass, the moonlight dancing on his back. By then, I was a bit lonely for all the company I had left behind, and in a moment the circle of love was closed. This man, your father, and this man, my husband, had been taken by no other, and I too had not taken any other. In our closed circle, there was peace and tranquility, and together we had solitude without loneliness.

The Mother of Love then spoke to us both from within the Great Mystery, from which flows all that is alive, and told us this:

"Without you, Beaver, in high meadows, without your dams to widen the streams of melting winter snows, the water would rush too fast down the mountain sides. The seeds could not stay wet, for the water would be lost too soon. The trees would not get old and spread their tender shoots for you. The marsh grasses would not grow everywhere to hold the wet and rocky soil, so the freezing and thawing of the rock can make rich dirt that gives you mud to warm you in your lodge and make a place for the Standing Ones to grow tall.

"Without the Beaver, the highland song birds could not make nests of their own in these Standing Ones, nor eat and spread the seeds of the fruits from this place to any other. Without the Beavers, other Four-Leggeds could not feast on lush grasses and berries, and safely rear their young in cooler climes and cleanest skies. Without the Beavers, the clouds would not know where to return to drop the water in clean, soft piles of snow for you to store in ponds, for the dry summer's air to drink. Without the Beaver, there would be no place for the rascals to test their lives and yours, and keep all healthy, strong, and free. Nothing helpless here, for gifts you all receive.

"Without you, Beaver, rock and snow-melt water would go down too fast, killing tender shoots and sending new seeds to the hot, dry plains below. Life cannot live where soil is not made and water is not stored to slowly seep, deep into the earth. Water that rushes to the sea has no life in it and gives no lasting nourishment. You help me make life-giving water go slower, stay longer and be fuller with riches, from the peaks to the valleys and on to the sea, so others can live their lower lives and rise higher to know your good deeds and their high purpose too. You have my gratitude, for many will learn this from you. This is your final gift, one you get and get to give. Tell this your story to anyone who will listen."

Chapter 5
The Story of the Otter – Land to Sea

Bear dreamt Otter. Want to know why? 'Cause big Bear hears big Whale and gets lonely for her water. That's why Otters live here and all the way to the sea. Bear don't get to travel much, and long sleeping makes 'em grouchy when they wake. Dreaming Otter, playing, Bear learns the sea. Not lonely no more for water and the lightness of play. Little Otter playing weighs nothin' in water, like huge Whale. But big Bear be heavy in air, walkin' on big feet. Big Bear dream Otter, to learn to float and play while dreaming, so better to join Whale and hear her singing.

Ever notice how some folks sit or walk? Some heavy like grouchy Bear, not dreaming of play. Butt hurt? Feet hurt? Feel heavy? Dream Otter.

Bear smart feller... travels everywhere and don't got to go no-where. Sleep anywhere, eat anything, know everything. How come? Dreamt it once. Whales remember. Ask Otter. They'll play you dreaming there, weightless in the water, from this little stream all the way to the salty sea. Ain't hard. Try it. You'll see... Whale's singin', Bear's dreamin', Otter's playin'.

Chapter 6
The Story of the Knot - Willingness

Grandmother to granddaughters learning to sew:
"I will tell you this story of the Elk, so you will know how to learn what I am to show you. This sinew for sewing is from the back of the Elk. There is no stronger cord than from the mighty Elk. You join the skins by punching holes with the awl and sewing the pieces together, but first learn this."

Grandmother holds up a length of sinew and forms a knot at one end. She holds the knot at the top of the cord and says:
"This cord and knot are much like your will. When you are beginning any task, the knot will be in front like this and will not pass through the hole in the skins this way.

"So it is with will. If you begin with your will behind the knot, trying and pushing your will through ahead of your learning, you get... not will-ing! Better, while you are learning, to carry your will with the not behind, so when your cord is sewn through, it will stay there and will not come loose.

"Be willing to learn as you go, and your work will not be undone. You can thank the mighty Elk for the strength of their will and backs, and thank them too for the stamina of their hides under great stress. They pass this stamina on to us, and they clothe our families in winter and keep our will intact, so we can continue here forever, no matter what hardships we must endure. Remember, not behind will-ingness... cannot learn if not is ahead of your will."

Chapter 7
The Third Talking Turtle Story - The Two "mistakes"

People, us Two-Legged ones, started thus. Love did it... gave the seed of the memory of love to female and gave the seed of the memory of truth to male. Love did it that way, knowing there was no truth outside of love, so the two would have to join to find their way back Home. From a single spark, one became two, and yet blessed by Creator as one.

The First Woman, remembering Creator's love, danced for the First Man the night before their wedding day. From Her dress hung a fringe of many colors. And as She spun, all She envisioned took flight, from the First Most Perfect Being She could think of, most like Creator, to the least formed, vague and fanciful.

As First Man watched, trying to remember truth but not yet knowing love, He became so enamored with First Woman's creations that He forgot Her for just a moment. And instead of falling in love with Her first, He fell in love with all that She had envisioned. When He saw what Love could create, He became awestruck, and for a moment He coveted Love's power. Thus, the first mistake was born into possibility... that of misplaced value.

From that first mistake, it became possible that the men and women who followed could stray in their affections for each other and desire something other than preserving their union.

The First Woman saw what the effects of this first mistake would be but could do nothing. She saw that to correct this error, all the children of the earth would have to play out the First Man's mistake throughout the earth's four worlds, learning and choosing how they wanted it to be for themselves, until the cycle of repeats had ended. In human years on earth, that would be about 38.942 million years.

The First Man, too, saw the effects of His mistake, but He, too, could do nothing. The First Man was not to be allowed to inter-fere with this natural process of correction. He was told by the First Woman to "Stand right there as does the sun."

During that time, the effects of this error played out in a near infinitude of variations amongst the Two-Leggeds, with varying results and degrees of complexity. Many times, man and woman-kind were nearly wiped out. Cataclysmic changes in the climate occurred when the earth out of balance reached a critical point. Each time of change brought true peace nearer, accompanied by yet another threat, as each misplaced value and each misperception was gradually being corrected toward a permanent balance point. People who learned to choose wisely, with guidance from Spirit helped teach balance on the earth. Those before Who understood, almost always returned as Spirit to help the people.

As the world grew in people and complexity, the First Woman pleaded with Creator to help. Always there was an answer like this. Love and truth must find their own way back together.

But the First Woman insisted, only She and Her First Thought Of would help, and Creator need do Her only one favor. With much consideration, Creator agreed to a one-and-only-once favor and gave Her what She wanted. It was this.

She wanted to take human form for the first time, to birth Her First Thought Of into the world for his first time, but She did not want him to have a natural conception and birth. You see, the First Woman was not yet married to the First Man, and so the First Thought Of could not be born by normal means. Creator agreed to wrap Her First Thought Of in Light, to shield them both from all fleshly concern. His most pure spark of Truth and Love would remain combined. And though the First Woman would grow this child in Her womb, She, too, would not experience the attachments of the flesh or suffer from the first mistake of the First Man as others do. The Light would prevent it.

Thus was Jesus born through Mary, without the aid of mortal man. And of his life much was written. I can tell you this. Mary knew everything that was to be, even of what could *appear* to be a second mistake. To break the cycle of separation of love and truth on the earth, what is made extreme often becomes clearer than what is not. So extreme became the device for a lesson.

It went like this. Jesus progressed in his speaking from being a Messenger of God, to being a Son of God, to being at One with God, all of which are true. However, when he spoke the words, "The Father and I are One," he split his psyche into halves, into male and female, within his once Whole Self. His Father, you see, was not Himself, and Creator gave no seed as well. But the body has rules which were broken by favor. So yonder stands First Man, not yet truly a father, still waiting to marry First Woman.

And thus it was, the male half of Jesus went to the side of the First Man and saw as He saw and felt what He felt, to ease First Man's first burden. Both experienced the long time of watching the effects of First Man's first mistake... standing perfectly still in horrible awareness and unutterable helplessness. The female half of Jesus was crucified, died on the cross and was resurrected, then returned to Spirit to join the male half, in wholeness once again.

Later, in old age, Mary returned to Spirit to take Her place as First Woman again... still waiting for the time of correction and for First Man to join.

And so it was that it became possible for one whole being, both male and female inside, to split itself completely into two beings, taking two separate forms in two different bodies, one male, one female, all the while demonstrating more extreme separation for the world to see. And such was a path of return thought of by the First Woman... allow the separation to become more extreme, and the desire for joining will become more intense.

Thus is our return assured if we follow Their path of correction. The pressure of separation will end, it is promised, for each who wants to remember First Love, First Truth, and the spark from Creator that we all are. To each in turn and to each that are split, the Truth will return and be inside Love, where each will have and be the other again.

Long journey, you say? Well, maybe so. But I think not of us but of the First Man and First Woman... separate from the beginning. We but play this out for Them, each one of us our part, until this time has ended.

I say, When, Creator, when?

And something answers back... Soon... soon... very soon... the end of this unto The Beginning.

And then I say, What then... a New Beginning? Our Mother's world united with our Father's, joined at last?

We'll see... we'll see. Creator's coming back.

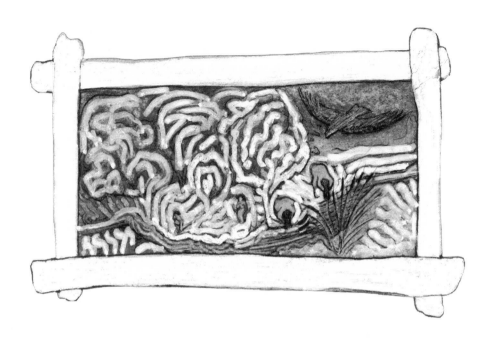

Chapter 8
The Suggestion Story - The Patience of Ant

Grandfather, with a group of young boys just caught peeking at the girls bathing in the stream. He spoke kindly, from his many years of knowing how not to introduce guilt that builds silent walls of defense.

"Sit down with me for a moment, and I'll give you a suggestion." Grandfather's eyes looked peaceful, so the young boys sat down, one by one. Grandfather spoke softly, gently. "We are very much like the ant, yes? They live and work together. They build with what's around them. And, above all, they don't rush anything. They have patience. They know all things come to them when it's time.

"This excitement you feel is poisoned by shame. Yes? And today, your play has turned to dishonor and disrespect, has it not? To feel better, I suggest you not give into the desire to peek at the girls while they bathe. Be patient like the ant.

"I give you these guidelines, but if you deliberately use your will to go beyond them to have what you desire before it is given you in the right way and in the right time, then you have stolen what you have asked for with your desire, and so you cannot have it... because *you* said so. Do not blame the First Man for your mistakes. He admitted, suffered with and corrected His. And when He did, the First Woman promised to give Him what He wanted... in the right way and at the right time."

Chapter 9
Fourth Talking Turtle Story
Dancing for Proof - The Apology in Time

The fourth world passed, and a window opened for a short period in 1995, allowing the First Man to visit the earth in Spirit for His first time, in the right places, at the right time. This opening was created by the First Woman. Until this window opened, the only communication the First Man had with the children of the earth was through the Holy Spirit and the spirit of the eagle. The eagle was given to First Man by First Woman, so His suffering would not be too great, and He could help, through Spirit, the Two-Leggeds who asked.

Many councils of Old Ones met in many places all over the earth with all four races. The question was asked, "When should The Cleansing begin?" Any woman on the earth conscious enough to vote, got to vote. The majority decided for all their children to delay awhile, so no one would be left out. They decided when The Cleansing did begin, it would be as compassionately slow and gentle as possible, so those who delayed would have a little more time to make their choices, though the time of choosing for most people had passed, and the leaders who were to guide were already chosen.

The most important task for the First Man was left to last and completed on July 7, 1995... the apology. After the First Woman's story was told, the First Man confessed His errors to the First Woman, as three women and one male witnessed. Four mortals helped play these parts for Spirit in certain places on earth, so what was done before earth's dream began, would then be made alright in time.

For first error, forgetting Source was first,
and second, for turning from First Woman
and loving Her creations before the two be joined,
that's why He had to stand so long.
And thus He thought to take control,
and envied Love's power to create,
which made instead, all things as dead.

For this He paid 38.942 million years
and cried a hundred, million, trillion tears.
The seas, you see, and air are His,
all land, red fire and life are Hers.
And all that talks and sees and hears
were patterned then for all those years
to play again their parts again
'til this time now, the end draws near.

First Man, now humble and forgiven,
stands inside each man who learns,
that Love and only Love gives life,
the First and on again,
the Truth is just within.
Alone, outside, what truth one finds,
is always but a whim.
When ego's followed, the light is dim,
and only death comes calling.

Joy comes from Truth inside.
It's as bright a light there is.
First Woman danced the very first,
and each woman who has followed,
dances now for proof from man,
that he, too, soon will learn
what First Man learned by error:
That Source of Love and Truth therein,
has never changed or moved or faltered.
And woman's to teach what real Love is,
once she has remembered.
Then learning Love from woman first,
man remembers Truth for both.

The Apology in Time

"I take all the blame. I thought to have your power," He wept. The witnesses sat silent, neutral, waiting to understand. He came to Her and dropped many dead things at Her feet... the skin of a rabbit, a drum drawn with the hide of a deer, bones and skulls, feathers and rattles.

"Only dead things are what I bring from those thoughts." And He wept some more. "I have made only death. You have created only life."

She glimpsed, but barely, what She alone could not think. She knew Her dance was love, not power over life. "That Love's power could join and give new life... you fear and covet this? I give it all to you this instant, because this Love is All there Is. Perhaps in this, I err too. Love, alone, is not mine to give. In Creator's thought is Love and Truth always joined."

And thus, with innocent gaze upturned, They traveled Home. What started long before your now, forgiveness finally ends.

Chapter 10
The Walking-Talking Story - The Joining

In a moment out of time, a young medicine woman out walking heard a voice... not hers. "Will you join me?" the Voice asked. And she knew this Being was God the Father of our mortal lives, Who knows all life's questions and confusions.

The heart beats were counted as her concerns unfolded in silence as she walked, seconds becoming lifetimes, reviewing all the errors humans have made when they have grabbed for power. She feared to join such power. If her love joined Power before it knew the Truth, she thought perhaps she could make a big mistake that could have far-reaching consequences for all.

She answered, "I'm afraid I will lose my humility."

His reply came slow and gentle, full of love and compassion, with vast understanding and with all the experiences of every lifetime, everywhere. "Will you show me what I must do to become more humble?"

*

This story has an end, yet unwritten in each of us. The invitation is clear and long standing. When will we trust in the goodness of Truth inside Love and join It?

Chapter 11
The Flight of Arrow True

Please gather 'round real close and listen. If ever you remember something, I pray you remember this, this story told first when I was young and in a real big hurry.

I used to make my arrows fast and found I made too many. I carried them all and lost a lot, and missed and missed and missed. My Grandpa's spirit once told me this, "Spend more time on makin' 'em good, and only make good with four. That way, each flight of the arrow is true and will bless the air and you. The deer will see they are honored thus, with beauty and great care. These thoughts you send will hold them there. You'll never lose a one. The deer will stare and fall right there and give you what you need. Be sure and thank that deer, right there, and thank their spirits too. So every time you bend the bow... respect, honor and trust are true. Through only this your share is due."

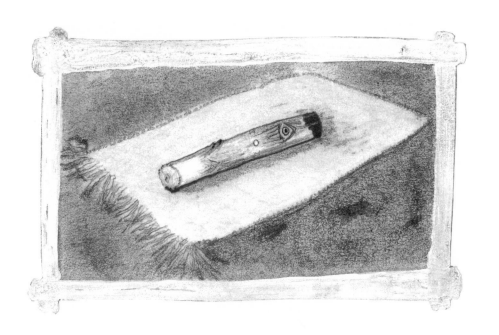

Chapter 12
How to Find Your Own Red Stick

Infant, child, girl, maiden, and woman to mother is a circle made by blood and blinded in blood, hidden deep within the bone. Only in grandmother whose blindness in blood is gone, can she to mother, through child, from grandmother, pass on what bones do hide. A circle that does not widen is but a closed container waiting to be broken. The grandmother is the break in the mother's circle, to all the ancient past, just as the infant is the repair of what breaks, that ensures the future onward. Through grandmother's bones laid down and the blood therein, is the "how" of going on, is the "why" that death can't kill.

Tell young girls, new maidens, this. Many before you have bled, given birth and died to the compelling heartbeat of blood. They have left their bones to help you on. The trees, whose limbs and trunks have fallen, are the bones of the great-grandmothers' past. Choose one, a stick one-half as thick as your lower arm... and this, as long as arm bend to wrist. This one's for you, for on your moon you'll bleed the blindness of blood and need great-grandmother's bone for strength. Put drops of death on this Red Stick, and touch it down to earth. Here, know the death of each seed lost, returns to earth's red fire. Her core then gives back this way, the how and why of love. Death leaves you *first,* so new life comes.

493

Don't think you can walk on, for if you try to skip this once, your blindness will increase, and trapped, encircled, death inside, you suffer needlessly. And all around you suffer what you did not heed, until you learn this good. You... entrusted with the seed, remember first for all to see. Then all whose bones that go to fuel, to house and heat and feed, show how the thread of the dead go on to finer and finer weaves, so grandmothers all live on again, as infant, child, girl, maiden and woman, back through a mother's womb, still another time.

Chapter 13
What? Do I Have to Draw You a Picture?

To Everyone: On Time = Not slow, not fast. And on Cause and effect.

The only reason you are feeling or perceiving yourself as if you are an effect is so Spirit can protect you from your thinking that you are the cause of all this mess with the humans. The First Man made the error... not you. The Cleansing has begun, and it will be gentle and merciful. Do not be in a hurry for it to be completed, or you may cause you or a relative to be left out... because... Be Cause.

In the Fall. The seeds (my babies) drop to the ground. The air will cool them, so they can sleep. During this time, you can walk anywhere.

In the Winter. The seeds (my babies) must absorb the cold to make them hard and able to face the fire of life in form to come. During this time, you can walk anywhere.

In the Spring. When the rains come or the snows melt, the seeds (my babies) seek deep roots in me, so they can face their Father. In that sun, that heat, that golden light of truth, they, too, will grow to maturity, so Creator can see they know love for themselves and flower in it. During this late time of my pregnancy and

495

birth, I beg you, do not walk with shoes on anywhere outside where you yourself or any other have not claimed responsibility for the land. If it says, 'Wilderness,' do not wear shoes or plant or pick up anything there during my time to birth. After you can see the first seedlings (my babies) have emerged, you can walk anywhere you like and how you like.

In the Summer. My children are growing to maturity, with all the trials and risks, like you. During this time, you can walk anywhere you want. I ask you this. Do not forget to take care of your seedlings and everyones' babies when a true need arises. Don't coddle them or they will weaken, take sick in their hearts and spread disease wherever they go. An early, natural death for the spoiled ones before they must see the Light of Truth of their Father is better than them growing more twisted and crooked by your misplaced value and very small love. For truly, without the very biggest Love (mine joined with yours), no babies will survive the fires (the trials and risks and Light of Truth) to become true adults... able to give love and fruit, and face the Truth of their First Father's Light, so they can live forever free. While you labor to become... Live... Forever... Free. Please honor my request.

To Man:

In your peace and gentleness is where your strength is. Nowhere else. Be strong in them. Now listen. The whole truth cannot come to you before you do the right thing. When you do the right thing, then you will begin to know the whole truth. The truth is not an alone kind of thing.

To Woman:

I'll tell you one more thing. It takes a minimum of four women to wake one man up. It takes three human women... the mother, the wife and another woman, to help wake a human man up. The fourth and Final Woman is the earth, me, the First Woman and First Mother... when he is ready and willing.

If you are not with "the one" you were tying to help wake up, then, if you wish, take a new husband who likes to play, and go have fun with him. Or, be by yourself... because you did a good job. You did not fail and it's over. Do not be angry any longer. You must forget him that way. If you do this, you will be taken care of, in gratitude, by Big Love (me, the First Woman). Sometimes you must give away the thing you truly wanted, in order for both to have the prize... a reward. I assure you, this reward is bigger and better than your disappointment at "not having the thing you wanted when you couldn't have it." Do not suffer. You and he are joined... Live... Forever... Free.

If you are with the one you helped awaken... do not let him fail anyone with what he is to share with all those in your wake.

Last:

Only Creator and I (the First Woman) know the whole truth. I did not make the first mistake. He (the First Man) who made the error over 38.942 million years ago knows it too. Because He finally got to say what it was, here, in front of our children who record our story for all to read, it is corrected. **The cycle of repeats is over.** It ended the day First Man spoke on July 7, 1995.

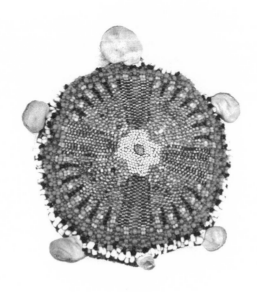

Chapter 14
How to Bead a Turtle for Yourself

Preface: Do not go fast to save time. Admit you do not know what time is for. There was a first, and then there was a second. You are not the first. If you are acting like you are... stop it... now!

Begin by cutting a thread and holding it vertical and saying this: "Either everything means something or nothing means anything. I want meaning in my life, but I will do *my very best* never to make up what I think anything means, ever again. I will be in a constant state of asking, and I will not answer myself."

Now tie a knot at the top of the thread, and place your not (knot) behind your willingness to learn and follow me. Say out loud, "I will," and start.

Remember, everything volunteers and it does not matter what you think while you are learning... it only matters that you ask.

If you miss a bead, if you put one in the wrong place or you need to break a bead, first apologize for your mistake. Don't go on until you do, or the rest of your work will be built on rough or shaky ground. If you need to go farther back and break a bead, remember, do not break the thread with the knot, or your work will be undone.

The thread with the knot is your intent to learn, passed through the bead for the first time. If you need to pass through a bead twice, then the reinforcement is for something important, so pay attention. When you make a mistake... undo it. Do not compound it... undo it. Try your very best not to do it again. Each time you do make the same mistake again, do not punish yourself. Simply relearn, undo again, and reavow to do your *very* best not to do it again. This time, stay conscious longer and longer, until you truly awaken. Meanwhile, bead on as often as you will. Don't forget to keep your knot behind, with no not in front. As you practice, everything will get easier.

You can make a knot when you need new thread or you want to rest. But when you are completely through learning with your first turtle, do not tie an *absolute* and *final* knot. Pass the final of the thread through the turtle's skin three times. The first of final passes, you ask for forgiveness for puncturing the skin of this, your first turtle, as you truly did not mean to hurt anything as you were learning. The second, final pass, you express your gratitude for what you learned, as you picture it for yourself once more. Do not place false value on what you or anyone else has made, more than you value Creator and what you can learn from everything. Or like the First Man, you could be responsible for the problems of the next 38.942 million years.

The third and final, final pass of the thread through the skin of the turtle, you vow to do your very, very best to remember daily, by living what you've learned. Now, do not tie a knot before you cut the thread close to the turtle. That way, your learning with this first turtle will never stop, but will continue on if you want to bead another turtle sometime. Don't say "not" with a knot now, before you know what you want, later.

Can I make a suggestion? Relax now and the journey will get... better... quicker... sooner. No more delays. Rest when tired. Eat only enough to ensure good attention. Drink plenty of pure water from a same, single container that you care for, for this purpose. Everything else is a delay and you know it. The Plan is perfect. It is not your plan, but you *can* learn what it is. The turtle will teach you how to bead and what you are truly beading and who you are beading for, child. No one wants to be fooled, so stop thinking you are, long enough to **know** whether you are or not.

I did not offer a course on "How to Make a Turtle," but you can make it yourself from scratch any way you like.

You have my blessings forever.

EPILOGUE

From The End Unto The Beginning

This is my confession. I have been seduced by a lie, and so I have lied. I have cheated, and I have seduced. The lie I bought was that love could be lost, that somehow, second was less, that love was somehow "special" and therefore conditional or full of exceptions. I did not know the truth because no one would demonstrate it. Sure, everyone knew the words to say to help guide with platitudes and truisms, but no one would muster the strength of will to take a stand and show me what the words meant. They lied, too, and hid from the world's eyes who would judge them guilty and condemn them to being forever outside, love lost to them again. Inside of this conflict, I unwittingly sought some small power, to gain influence or control.

It was guilt that made specialness and secrets and all other forms of separation. My fear began in aloneness. And in the confusion of survival within fear is anger and judgment regenerated with a vengeance.

I ask you... is the second less special than the first, the third less yet, until there is nothing more of "specialness?" Is poverty just having less to give, and therefore needing more? Is destitution closer to illumination than aggrandisement?

I confess that in trying to unwind this mystery, to give to all, I have asked for all there is to give. But I am no Jesus. I am not the first nor oldest, nor am I anyone's answer to anything. For now, I have only more questions to give and answers to receive. In the madness that separation made, I have achieved and been "special," and therefore failed. I have fallen and been humbled, and nearly understood. I have gotten so close to the bottom of it all that I've seen the undoing of the first lie that tricked us all into guilt, the so-called "original sin." And yet, even this moment of personal revelation was bitter, while all around remained bound.

I can say now, with real tears in my eyes, I am beginning to love, from the bottom up... the twisted and torn, fractured and mad... all of them, from the bottom of hell to the heights that we aspire. And because of the lie, because of the "tricks" of the mind, I see everyone as subject to guilt at birth, but innocent in truth. It is in this madness that we all live, only to survive as best we can.

Forgiveness? Surely, everyone deserves it. I would not withhold it... but the mad are dangerous, and life must, after all, survive. And so life will. I see it is only the lies that can be undone. And in their undoing, all pain and sorrow is washed away. That is why life still survives.

So, in whatever language it can be said: Please, God, bless the living and the "dead." Bless my children and the children all over the earth. And bless my partner who is my wife. She proved to me that love is real.

Now, knowing this one truth, I can see beyond my fear. One by one, I will face all my fears, like everyone must, each in their own way. But perhaps now, we are more joined in this than we are alone. I see the bridge Hinono built....
Can you?

I do not expect to be followed, nor do I expect to lead. I do not wish to be believed nor held to anyone's high ideal. This is, at last, a story told that anyone could hear. And told this way by who exactly? I really couldn't prove. But told by what? About that I am sure. Love did it, while searching for truth. And truth did it, while searching for love. That's all I really know.

John